AMERICA ASCENDANT

AMERICA ASCENDANT

From Theodore Roosevelt to FDR
in the Century of American Power,
1901–1945

SEAN DENNIS CASHMAN

NEW YORK UNIVERSITY PRESS
New York and London

NEW YORK UNIVERSITY PRESS
New York and London

New York University Press books are printed on acid-free paper,
and their binding materials are chosen for strength and durability.

Library of Congress Cataloging-in-Publication Data
Cashman, Sean Dennis.
America ascendant : from Theodore Roosevelt to FDR in the century
of American power, 1901–1945 / Sean Dennis Cashman.
p. cm.
Includes bibliographical references (p.   ) and index.
ISBN 0-8147-1566-4 (paperback : acid-free paper).—ISBN
0-8147-1565-6 (clothbound : acid-free paper)
1. United States—Politics and government—1901–1953.   2. United
States—Foreign relations—20th century.   I. Title.
E743.C277   1998
973.91—dc21   97-45320
                     CIP

Manufactured in the United States of America

10 9 8 7 6 5 4 3 2 1

Frontispiece: The aerial supremacy of the United States before and during World War II was a prime symbol and fact of ascendant America. The National Airport in Washington, D.C., (1941) was the first building to have a concave concourse, allowing landing strips to fan out from its central hub. Passengers await boarding calls for their pathway in the skies. (Office of War Information: Library of Congress)

About the cover of the paperback edition: Cathedrals of commerce turn midtown Manhattan into a city bristling with a thousand skyscraper turrets. This 1927 aerial photo of the Grand Central District, New York, shows (from upper left to upper right): Fifth Avenue from the New York Public Library (1911) and, behind it, Bryant Park (1884) to St. Patrick's Cathedral (1879) with its twin spires; and (from upper left diagonally to lower center): Forty-Second Street from Sixth Avenue to Grand Central Terminal (1889) and its attendant office-building complexes between Vanderbilt and Lexington avenues. (Library of Congress)

For Vincent D'Auria,

a generous mentor,
whose insights encouraged me to revisit
the history of America 1901–45
and to learn again as a student.

CONTENTS

PREFACE

AN ACCESSIBLE HISTORY of America from the Progressive movement at the turn of the twentieth century to the end of World War II in 1945, *America Ascendant* is a sequel to the third edition of *America in the Gilded Age: From the Death of Lincoln to the Rise of Theodore Roosevelt* (1993).

Since New York University Press brought out the first edition of the *Gilded Age* in 1984, I have written (and NYU has published) four twentieth-century histories. Because some readers who enjoyed them asked for a compilation, Niko Pfund, director and editor-in-chief, and I considered how to condense those four books into a single volume, incorporating new scholarly findings and ideas while retaining the original narrative history and cultural emphases. Thus, *America Ascendant* is part compilation, part new.

In considering the format for *America Ascendant*, Niko Pfund and I debated the different merits of having chronological chapters on politics complemented by some thematic chapters on social and cultural history or a straightforward sequence of more integrated chapters. We were helped by answers given by historians who kindly took the time to respond to questions I posed to them at a meeting of the Organization of American Historians at Louisville, Kentucky. The questions covered such subjects as the nature and time frames of different historical periods; the sorts of subjects usefully covered in integrated chapters and those usefully covered in separate thematic chapters; and the uses of bibliographies, primary sources, and illustrations. From this meeting and elsewhere, it seemed that, as the twentieth century neared its close, there was a shift in preference among professors and teachers toward integrated, narrative history rather than thematic treatment of such subjects as gender, race, and class, and industry, technology, and the arts.

In addition, current historical interpretation considers the years of the Cold War from 1945 to 1991 as a distinct historical period. This has sharpened our acknowledgment of the first half of the twentieth century as a clearly defined period wherein the United States and the USSR created two distinct modern societies, the earth was plunged into two world wars, and the United States emerged at the zenith of global power in 1945.

As to details of how *America Ascendant* has been drawn from the four earlier books: chapters 1, 2, 3, 4, 5, and 6 are from *America in the Age of the Titans: The Progressive Era and World War I* (1988); chapters 7, 8, 9, 10, 11, 12, and parts of 13 are from *America in the Twenties and Thirties: The Olympian Age of Franklin Delano Roosevelt* (1989); parts of chapter 13 and chapters 14, 15, and 16 are from *America, Roosevelt, and World War II* (1989); and parts of chapters 4, 6, 7, 11, 12, 13, and 14 are from chapters 1 and 2 of *African-*

Americans and the Quest for Civil Rights, 1900–1990 (1991), which, themselves, first appeared in *America in the Twenties and Thirties* as chapter 8. However, some sections of the current volume are new, inspired by histories published between 1987 and August 1997, when this book went into production. Some historians took advantage of the collapse of the USSR in 1991 and the opening of Soviet archives to explore Communism afresh. The various fiftieth anniversaries of events of World War II in 1989–95 stimulated more books on the Grand Alliance, the Holocaust, and the atomic bomb. I incorporated some new findings on these subjects and also rewrote chapters on technology and the arts.

The opportunity to reconsider material first written over ten years ago and to add new cultural and social interpretations later was a privilege enhanced by work in various academic and editorial posts: as professor at New York and Adelphi Universities, as editor for the Youth Commission on Urban Poverty at the Ford Foundation, as theater and music reviewer and commentator for the *New Haven Register*, as a writer for the *Encyclopedia of New York City* for Yale University Press, and as administrator for the New England Music Academy.

As with the previous books, I acknowledge research contributions by friends that are now published for a second time: Iain Halliday, Daniel Couzens, Chris Hasson, Chris Harries, and Stephen Harrison. J. A. Thompson of Cambridge and Princeton Universities, who criticized the material on Progressivism, gave me the benefit of his scholarly advice; and Daniel Cornford of the Emma Goldman papers offered advice on labor. Stephen Harrison also read and criticized the last three chapters.

This is a work of synthesis. All historians have their favorites among influential secondary sources. In my case, chapters 1, 3, and 6 of *America Ascendant* owe much to Mark Sullivan, whose history of America from the 1890s to the 1920s, collectively entitled *Our Times*, provides invaluable anecdotal information and, in volume 5 on America and World War I, an underrated interpretation. I also appreciate Arthur S. Link's monumental scholarship on Woodrow Wilson; Daniel Snowman and William E. Leuchtenburg's insights on the 1920s; John Kenneth Galbraith's classic interpretation of the Wall Street crash of 1929—indispensable for the writing of chapter 8; Alan Brinkley's, James MacGregor Burns's, and Ralph F. de Bedts's informative writings on the New Deal; the different insights of Stephen Ambrose, Gaddis Smith, Walter LaFeber, and Gar Alperovitz on World War II; William Manchester's anecdotal accounts of the 1930s and 1940s; historian John Major's introduction to the contemporary world, which proved invaluable for chapters 1, 4, 5, and 16; Gerald Mast's definitive history of the movies; and Paul Goldberger's writings about skyscrapers. I have drawn information and interpretations from these authors and also from others listed in the bibliography, notably Wyn Craig Wade on the Ku Klux Klan, Harvey Klehr on American Communism, James Goodman on the Scottsboro boys, and Laurence Bergreen on Al Capone and his era. In addition I referred to recent books on fascism, Bolshevism, the USSR, and Japan under Emperor Hirohito.

Many chapter titles and subheadings are quotations or wordplays on quotations from famous lines in novels, poems, films, or songs. Some provide straightforward commentary; others are ironic. For example, the title to chapter 14, "Kissing Hitler? Round Up the Usual Suspects," juxtaposes the cynical instruction of the amiable corrupt police chief (Claude Rains) in *Casablanca* to his men to cover the murderous tracks of hero Rick (Humphrey Bogart) with Tony Curtis's off-screen comments about his love scenes with Marilyn Monroe in *Some Like It Hot*. Of course, very few people would admit to having kissed both Adolf Hitler and Marilyn Monroe, although several princes of appeasement did kiss one part of Hitler (figuratively speaking). Perhaps they and some later statesmen would actually have kissed Monroe, if (like the Kennedy brothers) they could have done so.

Compared to the extensive bibliographies contained in the four earlier books, the one included here is short. It concentrates on general accounts that have stood the test of time, a few contemporary sources from the period 1901–45, scholarly texts published in the 1990s, and other sources referred to directly in the text. The bibliography, arranged by chapter, lists books under the first chapter in which they are principally used. Statistics provided in *America Ascendant* on population, immigration, agricultural and industrial production, and election returns are usually taken from the U.S. Bureau of the Census, *Historical Statistics of the United States*, 2 vols. (Washington, D.C., 1975). A useful abridged version of the bicentennial edition is Ben J. Wattenberg, ed., *The Statistical History of the United States from Colonial Times to the Present* (New York, 1976).

In *America Ascendant* I have mainly used the modern English transliteration of Chinese names, such as Cixi (Tz'u-hsi), Guangzhou Bay (Kwangchow Bay), etc. Director Pfund and the academic reader of the manuscript, however, preferred that Chiang Kai-shek remain in his original English transliteration (rather than the later form of Jiang Jeshi) since they considered him in this particular context as a character in American history.

I thank director Niko Pfund, managing editor Despina Papazoglou Gimbel, her assistant, Andrew Katz, associate editor Jennifer Hammer, and designer Elyse Strongin of NYU Press for their care and thoroughness with this project. In particular, I appreciate director Pfund's willingness to consider different ways of rewriting and editing the manuscript. Thanks are due to Colin Jones, previously director of NYU Press and now president of Routledge, for his long-term support of my series of histories. As was the case with the earlier books, Mary Ison, Maja Keach, and Jerry Kearns of the Library of Congress, Washington, D.C., helped select illustrations.

I am particularly indebted to patrons who provided invaluable support by way of material resources and financial help through the final years of a very long project: Mike Katz, president, and Jerry Mastrangelo, vice president, of World Gym Fitness Centers of Hamden and Branford, Connecticut; and architect Donald Baerman and his wife, Basha. In each and every case, their confidence not only sustained me through *America Ascendant* but also provided me with different perspectives from my own. A history book written in an architect's office and a gymnasium? Well, there have been far less auspicious writers' studios. Moreover, the author had no excuse for not working out.

Without the expert intervention of the Manchester Royal Eye Hospital in 1977, I should never have been able to embark on the series of histories for NYU Press in 1982. Twenty-one years and several operations later, I should not have been able to complete this book but for the courageous and skilled surgery of Andrew Tullo and Susan Ormond in 1998. If it really is true (as the phrase from World War II has it) that we do the impossible immediately but that the miraculous takes a little longer, then what Manchester Royal Eye Hospital achieved over time was miraculous: they, literally, saved my eyesight not once but twice. Of course, waiting for, and recovering from, operations in both eyes is not the most appropriate circumstance for completing crucial proofreading, devising an index, and undertaking final scrutiny of a long book with many illustrations. I thank Nick Mirra who discovered and corrected many errors in the page proofs. His differences with the original copyeditor over presentation were instructive and amusing.

My long association with NYU Press and even longer experience with the Manchester Royal Eye Hospital underlined what we all know instinctively: how precious a commodity is human vision and how special are the people who can use it with perception.

AMERICAN STUDIO, 87 NASSAU ST., N.Y.

APR 17 1916

CHAPTER 1

A Hot Time in the Old Town Tonight

Theodore Roosevelt and the Progressives

A L T H O U G H it begins as a mountain cascade, the Hudson River is too small and too crammed with boulders to carry even a canoe out of Lake Tear-of-the-Clouds, whence it rises. Above the lake stood Vice President Theodore Roosevelt, his spirits dampened by autumnal mists over the Adirondack Mountains. They seemed like mists of political anonymity stifling his political career. But while there, he learned on September 13, 1901, that President William McKinley, grievously wounded by an assassin but not killed outright, was now close to death. When McKinley died the next day, Roosevelt became president.

Theodore Roosevelt was to become a symbol of the American national character, with its confidence in material and democratic progress; its audacity and enterprise in world affairs; and its flair for experiment, invention, and publicity. His personality and abilities were attuned to the forces that would make the twentieth century the American century.

Although the assassin's bullet that made TR president was an accident, there was nothing accidental about the fact that he was next in the line of succession. A grandson of Cornelius Van Schaanck Roosevelt, a real estate investor of Anglo-Dutch descent and a founder of Chemical Bank, Theodore Roosevelt was born on October 27, 1858, and graduated from Harvard in 1880. Roosevelt's rising political career in New York City led to his being appointed assistant secretary of the navy in McKinley's first administration (1897–1901), where he helped prepare for war with Spain. When the United States did go to war with

---

FACING PAGE:

The Flatiron Building, New York, by Daniel H. Burnham and Company (1903). In what architectural historian Paul Goldberger calls "a time of intense, almost delirious growth," the Flatiron Building dominated the junction of Broadway and Fifth Avenue that determined its particular shape. Compromiser Burnham, however, softened its distinctive profile with historicist ornament. (Photo of 1916; Library of Congress)

Spain to free Cuba in 1898, Roosevelt, together with professional soldier Leonard Wood, organized the first U.S. volunteer cavalry—"the Rough Riders." As Colonel Roosevelt, he led a successful charge in Cuba up San Juan Hill, according to legend. The song "A Hot Time in the Old Town Tonight" became associated with TR and the famous charge.

The short war of 1898 with Spain left the United States in control of the defunct Spanish empire in the Pacific (the United States acquired the Philippines and Guam at this time) and the Caribbean (it also acquired Puerto Rico and gained a protectorate over Cuba). These acquisitions established the United States as an imperial power with overseas possessions.

On his return to the States, the increasingly popular Theodore Roosevelt was elected Republican governor of New York. There he alarmed the old guard of party bosses with reforms that threatened their control. Partly against his will, TR allowed himself to be nominated as McKinley's running mate in the election of 1900. McKinley received 7,218,491 votes to Democratic candidate William Jennings Bryan's 6,356,734, a majority of 51.7 percent. McKinley carried 28 states to Bryan's 17 and, with them, 292 votes in the electoral college to Bryan's 155, thereby setting a seal on a Republican ascendancy. But in September 1901, with McKinley dead, Theodore Roosevelt was president of this new, mass society of the United States, different from any before it.

America was truly ascendant. The United States already had the incipient capacity for global domination. The most obvious feature of the mass society was its steadily rising population. Immigration on an unprecedented scale, an increase in the birth rate, and a decline in the death rate all had a profound impact on the population. In 1900 the population of the continental United States and its overseas possessions was 76,094,000; by 1910 it had swelled to 92,407,000. There were forty-five states, and three territories would soon be admitted to the union as states: Oklahoma (1907) and Arizona and New Mexico (1912).

The foremost use the United States made of its rising population was to increase its industrial might. America led the world's industry with exports no other country could match. The value of American exports rose from $1.49 million in 1900 to $2.3 billion in 1914. Imports increased from $929 million in 1900 to $2 billion in 1914. At the turn of the century, the primary leaders in American industrial growth were the automobile, electric power, and chemical industries. These industries stimulated production in related industries and affected the structure of industry across America, just as they reshaped social patterns and lifestyles. Whereas in the early twentieth century food and textiles accounted for 47 percent of total manufacturing production, by 1945 they accounted for only 19 percent. However, industries related to the automobile, electric power, and chemical industries grew. Thus, in 1900–1945 metal products rose from 10 to 41 percent of manufacturing production while chemicals rose from 5 to 13 percent.

There were two manufacturing belts across the nation along a path of cities: the first, down the Atlantic from Maine to Virginia; the second, west of the Allegheny Mountains and north of the Ohio River from Pittsburgh and Buffalo in the east to St. Louis and Milwaukee in the west. A complementary agricultural revolution hastened the Industrial Revolution. The increase in production per farm allowed a transfer of labor from agriculture to industry without reducing the country's food supply. The profits derived from agriculture could be used for buying manufactured goods, thereby further stimulating industry and manufacturing. In 1900 7.89 million people were employed in industry, manufacturing, and construction; another 4.89 million people were employed in trade and transportation.

Factories were growing in size, and the nature of their operations was increasing the distance between workers and bosses. By 1900 over a thousand factories had workforces of more than 500 people. Thus, the meatpacking firm Swift and Company expanded from its single plant with 1,600 workers in 1886 to seven packinghouses, employing 23,000 people, in 1903. Superb industrial organization allowed large industries to achieve economies of scale in production, distribution, and marketing. Already many important industries were dominated by a few large corporations that often controlled the source of raw materials and certainly did their own purchasing, production, and distribution.

The South, however, with a colonial economy, fell behind the general economic boom. The North extracted farm produce, raw materials, and semifinished goods from the South and, moreover, secured them at bargain rates. The great northern companies of the Mellons, the Morgans, and the Rockefellers took control of the South's mines, railroads, and corporations. The majority of products left the farms, forests, and mines of the South as raw or semifinished materials to be manufactured further in northern factories.

It seemed everything came easily to American industrialists in the halcyon years of Theodore Roosevelt. And TR's enthusiasm for his nation was infectious. TR was a man of considerable physical presence. Since his early years had been marred by asthma, he had built up his body. Even his speeches were punctuated by expressive physical jerks. He had a high brow to set off his pugnacious features, and a dazzling smile. From his first days in the presidency, there spread across the country the legend of a new, vital man in the White House with an enormous capacity for work and a forthright, energizing approach. Author Richard Washburn Child concluded, "You go into Roosevelt's presence, you feel his eyes upon you, you listen to him, and you go home and wring the personality out of your clothes."

TR was going to need all his energy and stamina. For, despite its economic ascendancy, the American republic faced two pressing domestic challenges: the emergence of new politics engaging the great mass of people, and the increasing complexity of industrial society. The first came from mass politics, itself a product of the rapidly expanding population and suffrage for all white male citizens.

Mass politics put pressure on the existing political system for better representation and reform. The second challenge came from expanding industry, manufacturing, and the sector of service.

America's phenomenal industrial development and the rise of big business had been nourished by the conventional economic wisdom: laissez-faire. Laissez-faire declared that a nation could best develop its economic potential if its entrepreneurs were left to manage business, industry, and commerce as they saw fit. Government interference should be minimal, lest it frustrate economic development. Industry called for laissez-faire when it thought the federal government might regulate its affairs. But it wanted government intervention to achieve subsidies or to levy a protectionist tariff to eliminate cheap foreign goods.

Whether as strategy or philosophy, however, laissez-faire had proved unequal to the considerable social turmoil resulting from the Industrial Revolution. Traditional cherished notions of equality of economic opportunity and free competition seemed a mockery to small businessmen in an era of large enterprises in industry and manufacturing. Moreover, laissez-faire had not brought prosperity to the whole community. The economies of all the advanced countries, not only the United States, seemed to be caught in alternating and vicious cycles of booms and slumps. During depressions millions faced unemployment.

The benefits went to a minority. In its report of 1916 the Industrial Commission divided the distribution of wealth in the United States between a rich 2 percent of the population, who owned 60 percent of the wealth; a middle class of 33 percent of the people, who owned 35 percent of the wealth; and a poor group of 65 percent of the population, who owned 5 percent of the wealth. In short, two million people owned 20 percent more of the national wealth than the remaining 90 million. Thus the commission emphasized the gross injustice of the unequal distribution of wealth. At the top of the scale, forty-four families had annual incomes of $1 million or more. Those were families "whose members perform little or no useful service but whose aggregate incomes totalling at the very least" $50 million per year, were "equivalent to the earnings of 100,000 wage earners at the average rate of $500."

In the context of this imbalance, the most troublesome individual questions were those surrounding the "trusts," the giant corporations consolidating industrial production and distribution in the hands of a few capitalists. A merger boom was reshaping corporate capitalism decisively. Whereas between 1887 and 1897 there were only eighty-six industrial combinations, with a total of less than $1.5 billion, in the period 1897–1902, combinations with a total capital of $6.32 billion swallowed 2,653 independent companies in mining and manufacturing. The single most famous combination was financier J. P. Morgan's consolidation of various iron and steel enterprises into the United States Steel Corporation on March 3, 1901. As a result of the general wave of mergers and consolidations across business and industry, a single firm came to account for 60 percent of production in fifty different industries. For example, Du Pont came to control

85 percent of chemicals, and General Electric (another merger made possible by Morgan) came to control 85 percent of electric power.

The trusts challenged the basic assumptions of American liberalism. Their overwhelming economic weight allowed them to crush the separate interests of their suppliers, employees, competitors, and customers. Now what would the U.S. government—state and federal, executive, legislative, and judicial—do about such problems of modern mass society? Benefiting both from his superior social background and from his intellectual gifts, Theodore Roosevelt developed a wide-ranging political outlook from what might otherwise have remained a closed, conservative base. He defended the dominant social order while understanding the claims of the disaffected.

As president (1901–9), Theodore Roosevelt had three prior goals: to make himself the preeminent leader in his party, to transform the office of president into the most important section of the federal government, and to make the federal government the most decisive influence in national affairs. TR maintained that he would be president of the United States and not just of any one section. He refused to abide by precedents associated with the spoils system. "If I cannot find Republicans, I am going to appoint Democrats." Thus he gave the pivotal spoils position of the collectorship of the port of New York to an independent Republican; ignored the Republican machine in certain states; and restored to civil service rules and protection fifteen hundred positions in the War Department that his predecessor, McKinley, had removed in an executive order of 1899. Also, to Roosevelt the bulk of government was not legislation but administration. In all, Roosevelt sent 421 messages and 40 vetoes to Congress—a record at that time.

Roosevelt made the animated and tenacious style of his presidency clear to all by the way he intervened in a long coal strike of May to October 1902, bringing together labor leaders and management. The strike of 147,000 anthracite coal miners, led by John Mitchell, had threatened consumers with a serious coal shortage. Roosevelt's insistence that the rights of the public be respected forced operators, led by truculent George F. Baer, and miners into an agreement to settle the dispute by arbitration.

In November 1902 TR went on a bear hunt in Mississippi but refused to shoot a small bear brought into camp for him to destroy. Thereupon, Clifford K. Berryman of the *Washington Post* drew a cartoon showing Teddy "Drawing the Line in Mississippi," the caption itself implying all sorts of things about party politics, race relations, industrial disputes, and not going too far. For reasons both symbolic and whimsical, the public interpreted the bear story as disclosing the bare necessities of Roosevelt's politics. Toy makers took advantage of the notion of the Berryman cartoon and created new bear toys for children of all ages that superseded the traditional woolly lambs.

Roosevelt himself realized he had a singular advantage: to use the expanded mass media of the press and promote the office of president as a platform, an organ of propaganda for defining great national problems and proposing practicable solutions to them. He called it a "bully pulpit." The press spread Roosevelt's fame because everything he did was good copy. One editor, who was critical of Roosevelt, admitted that Roosevelt had a way of "slapping the public on the head with a bright idea." Roosevelt knew that everything emanating from the White House was potentially news, and he capitalized on the fact. His incessant activity was a godsend to cartoonists, who never lacked a subject while this most impetuous and masterful of politicians, with his facile gift for pointed phrases, was in office. He had only to say "Speak softly—but carry a big stick," or "the spear that knows no brother," or "square deal" to invite a series of melodramatic cartoons of himself as fearless opponent of the dragon trusts. TR's gleaming, protruding teeth and thick spectacles could be accentuated to convey a wide range of facial expressions.

In 1902 Roosevelt elevated another articulate spokesman for the new liberal sensibility to a position of great influence when he appointed Oliver Wendell Holmes to the Supreme Court. Holmes, a lawyer and a Harvard professor, had served as an associate justice of the Massachusetts Supreme Court from 1883 to 1899; he served on the U.S. Supreme Court from 1902 to 1932, where he rendered around thirteen hundred opinions. He was popularly known as "the great dissenter" because his liberal opinions were initially at sharp variance with the court's conservative majority.

It was the Supreme Court, however—specifically in the case of *Champion v. Ames,* decided by a majority of 5 votes to 4 on February 23, 1903—that gave TR the confidence to exploit presidential powers to their utmost. The Court sustained a federal law banning the shipment of lottery tickets in interstate commerce and thereby recognized a federal police power. Just as states might regulate intrastate matters in order to protect the health, morals, and welfare of their citizens, so might Congress use its authority to regulate interstate commerce for the same purposes. The lottery case of 1903 thus cleared the way for increased federal police power, especially in industry.

Theodore Roosevelt turned the sights of government toward modest social reform to redress political, social, and economic problems that had already provoked an agrarian revolt in the 1890s. In this respect he acted as a spokesman for the Progressive movement.

Progressive Winds across the 42nd Parallel

Theodore Roosevelt's presidency signaled the opening of the Progressive Era of 1901–17. Progress, whether in inventions, industry, or democratic government, is the key to modern America. Progressive reformers tried to bring rational order to politics, industry, and cities.

There were three sorts of Progressives: those who promoted reforms in government and business on the grounds of efficiency—such as business modernizers and efficiency experts, including Alexander Cassatt of the Pennsylvania Railroad;

those who supported humanitarian policies in government and whom we might call liberals, such as Edward A. Filene of the Boston department store; and prairie radicals, heirs to the Populists—the agrarian agitators of the 1890s—such as politician George W. Norris of Nebraska. The Progressives were urbane, middle-class people. They included the most articulate, literate, and expert members of the new or burgeoning professional classes. A rapidly industrializing society was creating its own large professional middle classes with new skills, expanded knowledge and discipline, and greater expectation of their future roles. Between 1870 and 1910 the number of middle-class, salaried employees rose from 750,000 to 5.6 million. Most of these professional groups—doctors, lawyers, university professors, teachers, journalists, and architects—undertook their formative organizations in 1895–1905, creating professional associations in industrial cities.

The professionalization of the middle class helped create organized, effective political lobbies. Social workers, members of women's clubs, teachers, and lawyers supported doctors in their campaigns for improved standards of public health. Lawyers drafted the specialist bills based on the doctors' informed analysis of what was required. The Progressives' leaders were usually white Anglo-Saxon Protestants from affluent backgrounds and with a college education.

Some local men of property and prestige deeply resented their relative loss of status in a society increasingly dominated by big business. Those disaffected included not only professional men but also small industrialists who resented large corporations. Small-town lawyers found themselves unheeded by large corporations requiring younger counsel with specific skills to interpret the new problems of management as firms merged. Clergymen found themselves beginning to be disregarded by an increasingly secular society. But people in such professions as architecture, journalism, and university teaching were rising in status as society came to depend more on their expertise. These groups were even more reform-minded than those who suffered a loss in status.

Progressives wanted to limit the power of big business, to make the political system more representative, and to extend the role of government to protect the public interest and to ameliorate poverty and social distress. Progressive social reforms included the abolition of child labor; regulation of hours and conditions of work for men, women, and children; minimum wage laws (especially for women); compulsory insurance against unemployment, accidents, sickness, and old age; codes of standards in housing; and reforms in education. The Progressives proposed to meet the costs of their proposals and, at the same time, to redress the unequal distribution of wealth by imposing direct taxes on high incomes and sizable inheritances.

The Progressives cut their teeth on reforms in the cities, where the nation's problems seemed most glaring. The cities were the nerve center and the storm center of U.S. civilization. For modern society was increasingly an urban society. Of the total U.S. population in 1900, 39.7 percent lived in urban centers and 19 percent lived in cities of over five hundred thousand inhabitants. Although cities offered special opportunities for work and leisure, it was in the city that the economic repercussions and social dislocations of industrialization were most strongly felt. The worst consequence of precipitate urban growth included low wages, bad housing and sanitation, general squalor, and high levels of mortality. Immigrants congregated in slum housing of ethnic ghettos and were exploited in poorly paid and often dangerous jobs. As late as 1900, cities such as Baltimore and New Orleans had no sewers, and two-thirds of Chicago's streets were mud. Among city evils was the proliferation of vicious gangs in service to corrupt politicos and businessmen. One was the Italian Five Points Gang, led by former prize-fighter Paul Kelly (Paolo Antonini Vaccarelli) from headquarters on Great Jones Street, New York. The gang had ties with the Democratic Party and was also a training ground for criminals Johnny Torrio, Lucky Luciano, and Al Capone.

In city after city Progressives extended the scope of utility regulations. They began to limit the profits and duration of franchises for street lighting, gas, electricity, intracity transport, and refuse disposal. The sort of one-sided contracts exacted by construction companies for laying pipes that had been excused when the demand for fresh water, piped gas, and sewage disposal was urgent, were now scrutinized anew by Progressives intent on maximum efficiency, minimum profit, and optimum fairness.

Social Gospel ministers advocated progressive social reforms to redress poverty in the cities. They used arguments drawn from the New Testament and from the second writer of the book of Isaiah. The Social Gospel movement was strongest among Congregationalists, Episcopalians, and Unitarians—denominations that appealed to urban, middle-class liberals. Social Gospel ministers occupied influential positions in urban pulpits, seminaries, the religious press, and interdenominational movements such as the Federal Council of Churches. At its first meeting in 1908 the Federal Council of Churches adopted a manifesto, "The Church and Modern Industry," proposing welfare legislation and the strengthening of labor unions.

Progressives believed that one solution to the problems of civic government in a mass society would be to reform the city's formal system of government. There were usually a large number of elected officials with little executive authority. Progressives wanted to replace them with appointed commissioners who would have strong municipal control over vested interests, such as those of transit magnate Charles Tyson Yerkes of Chicago. The impetus for this reform came from people in business and the professions who wanted efficiency.

FACING PAGE:

Below the soaring new buildings, street and market were one and the same at the turn of the century on such thoroughfares as Hester Street, a social center of Jewish immigrant communities from central and eastern Europe on New York's Lower East Side and an arena for progressive reformers to study. (Photo of 1900, by Detroit Publishing Company; Library of Congress)

In 1900 a hurricane and a tidal wave overwhelmed both the city of Galveston, Texas, and the city's council government. Local property owners appealed to the state capital for emergency government by commission. The Texas state legislature responded by appointing five commissioners to take over the management of Galveston. The experiment was so successful that the commissioner system was made elective in 1903. By 1913 more than four hundred other cities had followed suit. Another flood, this time in Dayton, Ohio, in 1913, led to a variation on municipal government by commission: the appointment of a professional city manager. By 1919 more than 130 cities had adopted the city-manager plan.

In city after city progressive and reform candidates found they could get themselves elected mayor, despite the opposition of previously entrenched political machines. Samuel Milton ("Golden Rule") Jones carried Toledo (1897–1904); Tom Lofton Johnson won Cleveland (1899–1909); Seth Low was elected in New York (1901–3); and James D. Phelan took San Francisco (1897–1902).

Following their successes in cities, Progressives turned their attention to state government. First they fielded charismatic leaders; then they proposed major reforms. Once again, the same mix of factors yielded progressive success and failure in state government as it had in the cities. Often, important progressive governors began their careers as leaders of intraparty factions. They were interested in power rather than in implementing a specific program, but a program was sometimes forced on them by certain sections of their middle-class followers. This could lead them away from progressive reforms. Albert Cummins of Iowa (1902–8) created his first coalition from Republicans opposed to prohibition of alcohol. The supporters of Hoke Smith of Georgia (1907–10, 1911) obliged him to propose racist restrictions upon African Americans. In office, progressive governors faced the unenviable task of having to pilot legislative programs, direct administration, and hold somewhat diffuse coalitions together, all at once. The most skillful, such as Robert La Follette of Wisconsin (1901–6) and Hiram W. Johnson of California (1911–17), did so by getting progressive reformers to concentrate on persuading state legislators to pass certain measures.

Teddy the Trustbuster

Theodore Roosevelt was a major force behind Progressivism, yet his commitment was a direct consequence of the new mood. Roosevelt's genius was not for crusades but for poses. He could show that he was a committed Progressive while doing no more than going down the middle of the road.

Few presidents have been so learned. TR's grasp of history, literature, biology, and military and naval strategy reflected his unique mind with its highly developed curiosity, analytical skills, and zest for knowledge. Though neither profound nor systematic, he drew on those qualities in others, inviting novelists and poets, inventors and explorers, as well as men of business, labor, and empire, to the White House. Through an astute mix of humor and graciousness, TR's sec-

"The President's Dream of a Successful Hunt." When Theodore Roosevelt went on a bear hunt in Mississippi in November 1902 but refused to shoot a defenseless small bear, Clifford Berryman provided the *Washington Post* with a cartoon showing TR "Drawing the Line in Mississippi." Thereafter, the teddy bear became indelibly associated with Roosevelt. In this cartoon Berryman extends the symbol to show TR's own political distinction between good trusts, subservient to government, and bad trusts, rampaging all over it, until Roosevelt sets his foot upon them. (Pen-and-ink drawing, no date; Library of Congress)

ond wife, Edith Kermit Carow Roosevelt, put a brake on TR's recklessness. She redecorated the dowdy presidential dwelling while he changed its official title to the White House. But Roosevelt's significance as a reform president was not so much what he achieved as what he made possible. By his speeches, giving the impression that he was about to tackle society's problems personally, Roosevelt provided the Progressive movement with new momentum.

Roosevelt was also much aided by his trusted advisers and most senior civil servants. During these years, the federal government acquired the services and skills of a wide range of professionally trained experts in the fields of architecture, education, and public health. They included Dr. Harvey Wiley, chief chemist in the Department of Agriculture, whose specialized knowledge was most useful in the drafting of the Pure Food and Drug Act; and forester Gifford Pinchot and geologist W. J. McGee, who helped plan conservation projects based on fire control and sustained-yield forestry. Roosevelt gave considerable responsibility to those cabinet members he trusted, notably Secretaries of War Elihu Root (1899–1904), who continued the reform of the army he had begun under McKinley, and William Howard Taft (1904–8); Secretary of the Interior James R. Garfield (1907–9); and Attorney General William H. Moody (1904–6).

What the public knew about the trusts in particular came from their own experiences with public utility corporations and railroad companies and hearsay about the nearest giant corporation. What they knew about trusts in general was provided by the literature of exposure, beginning with Henry Demarest Lloyd's seminal work on Standard Oil, *Wealth against Commonwealth* (1894). In 1899 and 1900 28 books and 150 articles critical of the trusts were published. In 1893 pioneer editor Samuel S. McClure created *McClure's*, a magazine retailing for only fifteen cents. It employed scholars to make clear to ordinary readers the way their lives were being shaped by the maneuvers of the great corporations. Starting in 1902 with Ida M. Tarbell's "History of the Standard Oil Company," McClure went on to employ Lincoln Steffens, who contributed "Enemies of the Republic" and "Shame of the Cities." When Steffens discerned an overarching fraternity of interests connecting industry, banks, and politicians, he called it "the System." To novelist Frank Norris, it was "the Octopus."

Investigative journalists wanted the federal government to regulate economic activity and municipal governments to reform themselves in the interest of efficient, caring, and accountable government. Yet, it was difficult for the federal government to intervene and regulate affairs that the Constitution seemed to reserve to the states. This included the individual state economies. The Supreme Court usually supported states' rights.

The federal government had attempted federal regulation of commerce across the nation with the Interstate Commerce Act of 1887, establishing a regulatory commission to oversee all commerce that moved across state lines. Its subsequent attempt to ban monopolies in restraint of trade, by way of the Sherman Antitrust Act of 1890, failed, partly because of adverse decisions by the Supreme Court that used the Fourteenth Amendment—originally intended to protect African

American citizens—as a basis for guarding property rights. There was a difference between the letter of the law and the rules. The letter of the law must capture its spirit. The rules were the cogs by which the law operated. The rules were often determined by the civil service and by court decisions in cases that set precedents—not by the legislators who passed the original legislation. The failure of the Sherman Act was to a certain extent due to the government's tacit admission in the depression of 1893–97 that successful monopolies could alleviate the depression. It was primarily because business was above the law.

Moreover, those who wanted increased federal control of, and intervention in, business were divided about the ends they preferred and the means they might use to achieve them. One school of thought was that business monopoly was either essential in certain commodities (such as oil or electricity) or in certain fields (such as transportation and communication) or irreversible. This school argued for government recognition of this position, with federal intervention only to curb blatant abuses. Another option was for the federal government to enforce the antitrust laws, to disband the huge monopolies, and thereby to stimulate small businesses. People who identified with the Democrats' support of states' rights favored this option.

People preferred to think that Roosevelt was a trust buster. In scores of drawings by W. H. Walker, an innocent child representing the "common people" was rescued by Roosevelt from the villain "Trusts." In his first message to Congress on December 3, 1901, TR proposed supervision and control rather than outright prohibition of monopoly. Satirist Finley Peter Dunne captured the ambiguity of Roosevelt's fork-tongued philosophy in the words of his Irish-American saloon-keeper, Mr. Dooley (first created for the *Times* and *Collier's* in 1893): "Th' trusts, he says, are heejous monsthers built up be th' enlightened intherprise iv th' men that have done so much to advance progress in our beloved country, he says. On wan hand, I wud stamp thim undher fut; on th' other hand, not so fast." Not so fast indeed. The Republican Party owed much to vested interests within it. For all his sharp words, Roosevelt knew he was, in essence, their front man.

Prompted by Roosevelt, Congress passed three acts in 1903 to control big business more closely. The Expediting Act gave preference to federal suits brought under the Interstate Commerce Act and the Sherman Antitrust Act. The Elkins Antirebate Act tried to clarify the law on the notorious railroad practices of rebates and drawbacks. And the third act established the Department of Commerce and Labor with a subsidiary Bureau of Corporations, created to make "diligent investigations into the organization, conduct, and management of corporations."

In 1904, when Roosevelt knew that he had secured his position within the Republican Party, he moved proceedings forward against a trust: the Northern Securities Company, created by omnipotent financier J. P. Morgan. Morgan did this partly to resolve a struggle for control of the Northern Pacific Railroad between Edward H. Harriman of the Union Pacific Railroad on one side and

James J. Hill of the Great Northern (Morgan's ally), on the other. It was mainly to consolidate profit and power. Morgan tried to forestall any attempt at regulation by TR's administration. He visited Roosevelt and declared, "If we have done anything wrong, send your man to my man and they can fix it up." News of Roosevelt's determination depressed prices on stock markets everywhere. The Detroit *Free Press* satirized the gloom: "Wall Street is paralyzed at the thought that a president of the United States would sink so low as to try and enforce the law."

The political tool that Roosevelt used against the Northern Securities Company was the Sherman Antitrust Act of 1890. In the case of *Northern Securities Company v. United States*, decided by 5 votes to 4 on March 14, 1904, the Supreme Court dissolved the holding company. Stimulated and encouraged, Roosevelt embarked on forty-four antitrust prosecutions against such huge corporations as the chemical giant E. I. Du Pont Company, American Tobacco, and Standard Oil. Roosevelt's antitrust prosecutions exposed a raw nerve among corporation executives. Just as they were confused by their inability to make their corporations truly cohesive, an aggressive president rubbed the harsh salt of public odium in their sores.

Recognizing just how formidable was their charismatic opponent, the most sagacious corporation executives began to reconsider their strategy. They started to accept federal reform in order to strengthen their companies. However, different businesses adopted different strategies. Small businesses, organized in the National Association of Manufacturers, favored enforcement of the Sherman Antitrust Act. But when Roosevelt established a Bureau of Corporations in 1903 within the new Department of Commerce, the larger trusts reacted differently. Standard Oil expanded its legal department and tried to hide proof of its system of illegal railroad rebates. Companies dominated by the House of Morgan, such as U.S. Steel and International Harvester, obtained so-called gentlemen's agreements with the Roosevelt administration. By these agreements they would give information to the Bureau of Corporations in exchange for a tacit understanding that their trade secrets would remain secret and they would be immune from prosecution for past violations. Morgan executive George W. Perkins judged that large corporations would seem more legitimate if they accepted a measure of public accountability.

Roosevelt was a skilled political opportunist. In 1904, when he feared that Wall Street was pumping $5 million into the Democratic campaign to elect the ultraconservative Alton B. Parker to the presidency, he abandoned his much-touted principles and allowed his campaign manager to tap the trusts. Roosevelt's position with Republican regulars was never more secure. Yet Roosevelt knew he still had a reputation as a power-hungry autocrat with no respect for constitutional niceties. "It is not well that a strong executive should be a perpetual executive," he said.

Money came flowing in from all areas of business. Edward H. Harriman, president of the Southern Pacific Railroad, personally contributed $50,000;

financier J. P. Morgan supplied another $150,000. TR's campaign slogan (and platform) was "the Square Deal," based on his antitrust actions, his intervention in the anthracite coal strike, and his conservation policies. On the eve of the campaign, Roosevelt defied Democratic charges by making a royal payoff to a particular bloc of Republican voters, Union veterans, when he unilaterally increased their pensions.

In the actual election on November 9, 1904, Roosevelt received 7,628,461 votes (57.4 percent), Parker, 5,084,223 votes (37.6 percent), and Eugene V. Debs, the Socialist, 402,283 votes (3.0 percent). Roosevelt took 336 votes in the electoral college to Parker's 140. He had gained the highest percentage of the popular vote to that time. Roosevelt was genuinely surprised by the magnitude of his victory. Thus moved, he immediately announced his previously (but privately) contemplated decision not to run again in 1908. His decision turned out to be a colossal political blunder.

Following his election victory, Roosevelt embarked on a series of reforms to provide stricter regulation of railroad rates. Railroad magnate and steel executive Henry Clay Frick complained, "We bought the son of a bitch and he didn't stay bought."

Moderate political progressives, however, were more concerned with modifying and reshaping, rather than with restructuring the economy. The bitterly debated Hepburn and Mann-Elkins Acts of 1906 brought regularity and efficiency to the railroads by breathing life into the Interstate Commerce Commission (ICC), created in 1887, confirming powers that had been nullified by the courts during the 1890s. The two new acts combined to empower the ICC to effect reasonable rates. They extended its jurisdiction to cover express and sleeping-car services; separated railroad management from other enterprises, such as mining; forbade unfair rebates and passes to favored clients; and abolished the dubious distinction between long and short hauls—a discredited argument for price differentials. When it came to railroad reform, what the Progressives wanted was regularity of procedure rather than absolute justice.

Everyone recognized that without Roosevelt's driving force, the controversial Hepburn bill would not have been passed at all. Public interest in the measure abated only once, diverted by the calamitous news of the San Francisco earthquake of 5:13 A.M. on April 18, 1906. The earthquake killed hundreds as they slept and injured thousands. Fire engulfed the city, started by gas from broken mains, exposed electric wires, and overturned stoves. The fire raged for three days. To prevent its spread, soldiers dynamited half a mile of proud mansions in San Francisco's most exclusive residential district. The earthquake rendered two hundred thousand people homeless. This disaster of epic proportions prompted reconsideration of the responsibilities of government and debates on the viability of building cities above the San Andreas Fault in California. Congress appropriated $2.5 million for relief and the reconstruction of San Francisco.

The more it was fed, the more the public appetite for exposure of corporate misdeeds increased. Certain journalists saw how to take purely commercial advantage by publishing sensational stories without the conscientious scholarship supplied by such authors as Ida Tarbell and Lincoln Steffens. Stock market operator Thomas W. Lawson of Boston revealed the shady secrets of his dealings with captains of industry as "Frenzied Finance" for *Everybody's*, mixing facts with fantastic exaggeration. Within a year the circulation of *Everybody's* rose from 150,00 to 750,000.

At a Gridiron dinner on March 17, 1906, Theodore Roosevelt took as a theme for his speech a passage from *Pilgrim's Progress* by John Bunyan concerning "the Man with the Muckrake, the man who could look no way but downward with his muckrake in his hand; who was offered a celestial crown for his muckrake but who could neither look up nor regard the crown he was offered but continued to take to himself the filth of the floor." The conservative press now applied the term *muckraker* to all investigative journalists.

Among TR's most crucial appointments in his second administration was that of able lawyer Henry L. Stimson, who became district attorney for the Southern Judicial District of New York, centered in Manhattan. Stimson's lazy predecessor had brought to trial only 27 of 610 active cases against giant corporations. Stimson brought firebrand lawyer Felix Frankfurter into his staff. Together, they persuaded TR to appoint an extra federal judge, Charles M. Hough. Within three years Hough had exacted fines of over $500,000 from two corporations for violations of the Elkins Act. Almost $3 million was recovered from other corporations that had withheld it from the federal government. Eight officers of three corporations were imprisoned or fined for infractions of the antitrust laws.

Although Roosevelt and his lawyers secured twenty-five indictments under the Sherman Act, and his successor, William Howard Taft, obtained another forty-three, the actual results of trust-busting were disappointing to more radical Progressives.

There were several strategies to reshape business practices. Businessmen sought expansion, stabilization, and rationalization. They realized that moderate federal regulation would undermine socialist appeals for an alternative, more dangerous form of reorganization. They accepted progressive reforms, knowing that they could bend them to their will. Accordingly, business would be regulated (but also licensed) by impartial federal regulation; labor would be represented (and also held in check) by responsible unions; and social problems would be met by various calculated reforms. Such was the philosophy of the National Civic Federation. It drew together the different talents of such people as corporate executives Elbert H. Gary and George W. Perkins, labor leaders Samuel Gompers and John Mitchell, and civic official Seth Low.

Another motive of corporate executives for welcoming federal regulation was to anticipate numerous state laws that would probably be more varied and therefore harder and more inconvenient for them. Whatever the source of agitation, the trusts were likely to be subject to increasingly greater public pressure and thus more radical legislation—as had been the experience of the railroads. This became clear in the campaign to protect the nation's health from vested interests. There were several interrelated concerns: the need to outlaw dangerous preservative practices in preparing food, the need to control dangerous practices in making medicines and patent medicines, and the need to improve standards of packing food, especially meat.

Dr. Harvey Wiley of the Department of Agriculture had long agitated for the protection of consumers from dangerous foods and adulterants. In 1906 matters came to a head when western Progressive Upton Sinclair published *The Jungle*, a powerful novel of an immigrant worker in the Chicago stockyards. *The Jungle* became a bestseller and was translated into seventeen languages. Sinclair's principal intention was to fire public interest in the need for better protection and higher wages for stockyard workers. However, middle-class readers, revolted by his descriptions, were more interested in the consumer.

Sinclair built his narrative to a climax, leading to a hard punch in the guts of his readers' consciences as he described the workmen and the dangers they encountered. Men in the pickle rooms who scraped their fingers on the trucks might have their finger joints eaten by the acid. Butchers and trimmers lost their thumbs, slashed away by knives. These were the workers as victims; for those "who worked in tank rooms full of steam, . . . in some of which there were open vats near the level of the floor, their peculiar trouble was that they fell into the vats; and when they were fished out, there was never enough of them left to be worth exhibiting—sometimes they would be overlooked for days, till all but the bones of them had gone out to the world as Durham's Pure Leaf Lard!"

The Jungle fueled public dissatisfaction with mass-produced food, especially meat. The momentum in favor of some form of a pure food act and a meat inspection act was now immense. It was sustained by middle-class awareness of the dangers from adulterated foods and politicians' belated realization that they must deal with public anger. The American Medical Association (AMA) told the Republican leader, Senator Nelson W. Aldrich, in no uncertain terms that its 135,000 member physicians in two thousand counties would urge their patients to lobby the Senate if the Senate did not pass the pure food bill. Despite its ties to vested food interests, the Senate passed the bill on February 21, 1906, by 63 votes to 4.

There was still considerable opposition in the House, however. The matter was brought to a successful conclusion in the furor over the crusade for meat inspection. Theodore Roosevelt ordered Secretary of Agriculture James Wilson to ascertain the facts. Roosevelt and Wilson's investigating commission included two settlement workers, James Bronson Reynolds and Charles P. Neill (who was also a labor commissioner). Their report emphasized the unhygienic conditions in which meat was prepared.

Roosevelt used the report to persuade Congress to pass an amendment to the agriculture appropriation bill, sponsored by Senator Albert Jeremiah Beveridge of Indiana. It proposed to extend government inspection to all processes in preparing meat. The Senate passed it, after three days, on May 23, 1906. Meat-packers realized that it was to the advantage of the larger and better food manufacturers to have dangerous or dishonest practices eliminated among their competitors. Thus the packers saw how the meat inspection amendment might save their businesses. It would provide a federal stamp on their products as a sort of certificate of character to restore public confidence and their lost trade. Thus they advocated limited reform. Nevertheless, the large packers, known collectively as the beef trust, objected to the dating of meat and having to pay for inspection. Yet, they could fulfill federal regulations more easily than could smaller meat-packers, who prudently decided to concentrate on intrastate sales, not touched upon by the bill.

Roosevelt was ready to settle for what was possible politically and practicable to operate. But he was not willing to abandon the principle of meat inspection. By threatening the meat industry with further exposure, he blackmailed Nelson Aldrich and his cohorts into giving him their support. Thus, they revised the Wadsworth meat inspection amendment, which provided for expanding federal inspection of meats for interstate commerce, to accord with Roosevelt's views. The House passed the Wadsworth amendment (without a roll call) and so did the Senate. The president signed it on June 30. (During this same period, the House was also discussing the pure food bill, which it passed on June 23, 1906, by 240 votes to 17.) Thus the Meat Inspection Act set new standards—and enduring ones. The method of inspection was known as "sniff and poke" after the cursory mode of analysis used by Agriculture Department inspectors. It awaited refinement for ninety years. In July 1996, after various scares involving contaminated meat and poultry that killed up to four thousand people each year and as a result of negotiations with the meat and poultry industry, President Bill Clinton (1993–) proposed more exacting rules and scientific analysis for meat products—Hazard Analysis Critical Control Point (HACCP)—to take effect in 1997.

As with progressive campaigns for major reforms in the area of food and drugs, the agrarian campaign for the prohibition of alcohol served to unite middle-class Progressives from various professions, notably medicine and sociology, and to link them to the progressive tradition of agrarian dissent and rejection of the new values of the cities.

A prohibition wave began after the Civil War with the spread of scientific information on the physiological effects of alcohol. Scientists showed that alcohol depressed the heart and made alcoholics prone to illnesses such as arteriosclerosis, gastritis, cirrhosis of the liver, and tuberculosis. The two most effective prohibition organizations were the Women's Christian Temperance Union (WCTU), founded in 1874, and the American Anti-Saloon League (ASL), given definitive form in 1895. The ASL concentrated on one object only—closing the saloon—and thus appealed to a wide catchment area, including those who, although they detested the saloon and such social evils as prostitution and the boss politics that it maintained, were themselves advocates of temperance, rather than prohibition.

Among those evils associated with prostitution was the coke peddler, the drug pusher of "Heaven Dust" who preyed on impressionable youngsters in the back-rooms of red-light bars. Many different sorts of people used cocaine, morphine, and opium. Cocaine was a popular tonic taken in wine, sniffed in powder form, and sprayed into the nostrils. Doctors prescribed morphine to ease pain. Patent medicines included small portions of cocaine and heroin. Clients could order both drugs from state mail-order houses. Progressives learned from doctors that they were deadly, habit-forming drugs. The Pure Food and Drug Act of 1906 banned indiscriminate availability. Early attempts to control the use of cocaine proved more successful than efforts to control opium and its derivative, heroin. In New York State Assemblyman Alfred E. Smith sponsored a law that made cocaine obtainable only through a physician. This was the beginning of the attempt at control that would culminate in the Harrison Act of 1914 and lead to a decline in cocaine use until the 1930s.

Among Theodore Roosevelt's lasting achievements was his support of modern spelling of the English language—another instance of progressive desire for reason, order, and efficiency. The American Philological Association had first proposed abrupt breaks with traditional English spelling in 1876. The changes included such amputations as *through* to *thru* and *axe* to *ax*. Francis A. March in the *History of Spelling Reform* (1893) noted that the word *could* was "a markt exampl of unpardonabl spelling; the 'l' is a blunder, the 'ou' has the wrong sound." It would be better to reform the spelling to *cud, cood, kud,* or *kood*. There were at least twenty different ways of spelling the sound *sh*, as in *sh*ip, *psh*aw, o*c*ean, par*t*ial, man*s*ion, and so on. A cardinal idea of the reformed-spelling movement was that reformed spelling would be more economical, thereby saving costs in printing. Steel-tycoon-turned-philanthropist Andrew Carnegie provided the Spelling Reform Association with at first ten thousand dollars and later twenty-five thousand dollars a year to promote its reform campaign.

On August 27, 1906, Theodore Roosevelt, roused by various considerations, ordered the public printer to modify and simplify the spelling of three hundred words in government publications. Unnecessary *u*'s were to be omitted from such words as *honor, labor, color,* and *rumor*. With their final letters eliminated, *programme* would become *program* and *catalogue, catalog*. The French influence was to be expunged from words ending in *re*. The final letters would be reversed, creating *center* and *theater*. Similarly, *cheques* would become *checks, comptrollers* would become *controllers*, and *judgement* would become *judgment*. Vowels in *subpoena, phoenix,* and *mediaeval* would be eliminated, making *subpena, phenix,* and *medieval*. In some words, *s* was to be superseded by *z*, making *idolize, legalize,* and *compromize*. The soft *c* became *s* in *license* and *defense*.

Among the newspapers that enjoyed a field day of pretended outrage, the *New York Times* of November 24, 1907, quoted Woodrow Wilson, president of Princeton, describing a British cartoon he had seen about TR's crusade to reform spelling. The cartoon showed Roosevelt using a small hatchet to nick a tree representing the English language. Bystander Uncle Sam sighed, "Ah well, boys will be boys!" Whereas Wilson thought "it hit the nail on the head," it was, in fact, TR who eventually had his way—despite howls of anguish from Wilson and other literati. It was they who could not see the forest for the trees. Roosevelt did.

TR's supreme domestic accomplishment was his sponsorship of conservation measures to save forests, minerals, and other natural resources from wasteful exploitation. Previously, business had assumed that there were enough natural resources for all. This shortsighted presumption partly explains the excessive exploitation of natural resources by business with the connivance of the federal government. The federal policy of granting millions of acres to railroads and other enterprises that could freely use the oil, lumber, and metal on their lands was, it seemed, supported by the tradition of pioneer individualism. Although there was indeed plenty, the best prizes went to the strongest and most unscrupulous, and the supply was not limitless.

Theodore Roosevelt, under the guidance of conservationist Gifford Pinchot, was largely responsible for reversing conventional acceptance of this traditional exploitative point of view. After graduating from Yale, Pinchot had spent time in Germany and Switzerland studying forestation. In 1896 he organized the National Forest Commission. Later, he became head of the Bureau of Forestry in the Department of Agriculture. Even hardened industrialist entrepreneurs, such as railroad magnate James J. Hill, realized that exploitation would, in time, imperil America's supply of minerals and wood. Influenced by Pinchot, TR made conservation a subject of his first message to Congress, declaring that "the forest and water problems are, perhaps, the most vital internal problems of the United States" and that "the whole future of the nation is directly at stake."

In 1902 Congress passed the Newlands Reclamation Act, sponsored by Francis G. Newlands, Democratic senator from Nevada. Roosevelt endorsed the act and gained much credit for it. The act's purpose was twofold: reclamation and irrigation of farming land in the Great Plains. By the terms of the Newlands Act, the federal government accepted responsibility for the entire irrigation program. Money from the sale of western lands (sold in lots of 160 acres or less and paid for within ten years) went into a revolving fund that was applied to conservation projects. By 1915 the federal government had invested some $80 million in twenty-five separate projects, the largest being the Roosevelt Dam on the Salt River in Arizona. Meanwhile, Roosevelt was expanding the government reserves set up under the Forest Reserve Act of 1891. In 1907 western congressmen succeeded in getting some 68 million acres of coal lands (all known coal deposits in the nation) included in these reserves. In total, Roosevelt's administration added about 125 million acres to the national forests.

Western congressmen also prepared the way for a new government policy on electric power by reserving some 2,565 water-power sites, including Muscle Shoals on the Tennessee River. In the 1930s it was to become a New Deal showpiece in the Tennessee Valley Authority. In 1907 Theodore Roosevelt appointed the Inland Waterways Commission to prepare "a comprehensive plan for the improvement and control" of river systems. In 1908 it reported that future plans for navigation should take into account such things as water purification, power development, flood control, and land reclamation. In 1909 Congress created the National Waterways Commission for that work.

Roosevelt used his authority to set aside forests from exploitation. When his opponents forced on him a rider to an agricultural appropriation bill, making future withdrawals the responsibility of Congress, rather than the president, Roosevelt had Pinchot and his team survey the public domain in six northwestern states. Their findings allowed him to recognize and withdraw sixteen million acres of forest land before he signed the bill transferring the authority to Congress.

Despite his successes hitherto, Roosevelt's fortunes began to change. He had already lost his leverage with Congress in the midterm elections of November 1906, when the Democrats gained enough seats to make it difficult for him to hold a majority for his program. His problems were compounded by the panic of 1907, which was precipitated by wild speculations on the New York Stock Exchange. In the fall of 1907 banks outside New York (interior banks) wanted to withdraw the funds they had deposited in New York banks in order to have sufficient resources to finance farmers who wanted to harvest more crops. The total amount due to the national banks and other banks was considerable—$410 million.

Because they were investing the money for their own purposes, New York banks could not meet their obligations to the interior banks. Accordingly, on October 31, 1907, New York banks suspended payments. They telegraphed their correspondents across the country that they could no longer honor drafts for money. In fact, they still had $224 million in their vaults. The crisis was exacerbated by gross individual acts of exploitation. Trust company executives and speculators Charles W. Morse and Augustus Heine were trying to corner the copper market. Their failure to do so led to a run on the companies with whom they had been associated, including the Knickerbocker Trust Company, which was forced to close on October 23, 1907.

Earlier, in a speech at Provincetown, Massachusetts, on August 20, 1907, TR had declared that a swift and savage depression was partly caused by "ruthless and determined men." They were hiding "behind the breastworks of corporate organization" and retaliating at the "determination of the government to punish certain malefactors of great wealth." Their strategy was to bring about "as much financial stress as they can" to discredit the government and try to get it to change its policies.

Despite the supposed hostility between Roosevelt's administration and corporate executives, the way government and Wall Street responded to this desperate situation exposed the trusting relationship between them. Leading financier J. P. Morgan conferred with entrepreneurs and industrialists such as Henry Clay Frick, Edward H. Harriman, and others to save the situation by importing about $100 million in gold from Europe. John D. Rockefeller provided another $10 million in government bonds. Then Secretary of the Treasury

George B. Cortelyou announced the government's willingness to deposit $150 million of federal money in banks. This was to restore public confidence that they could redeem notes in gold or securities.

It seemed likely that an independent steel company, Tennessee Coal and Iron, might fail and thereby disturb some of the Wall Street firms investing in it. Accordingly, Morgan agreed to a rescue attempt by which U.S. Steel would buy Tennessee Coal and Iron and thus put its immense financial power behind the company. Morgan did this only after securing a tacit promise from Roosevelt, through his intermediaries, Elbert Gary, president of U.S. Steel, and Henry Clay Frick, that the federal government would not use antitrust legislation against the merger. Once the crisis was averted, it was all too easy for critics to charge that U.S. Steel had exploited a general panic to acquire a valuable company at a rock-bottom price.

Widespread unemployment accompanied the panic of 1907 and continued into 1908, with the effect of depressing wages for those still at work. In New York the daily breadlines of indigent poor seeking free coffee and rolls from the Bowery Mission were two thousand more than usual. The panic aggravated existing pressures for financial reform and stimulated many citizens to reconsider their ideas on finance. What if the catastrophe should continue beyond 1908, or disappear, simply to recur? Sensitive to public opinion, Congress established a commission to formulate proposals to revise banking practices.

A sure sign that progressive political philosophy and humanitarian sentiment was making headway even among entrenched groups came with the Supreme Court's decision in the case of *Muller v. Oregon*. It made Boston lawyer Louis D. Brandeis famous on account of the "Brandeis brief," an unorthodox and innovative means of argument for a lawyer to use. Brandeis succeeded in arguing that Oregon's law of 1903, setting a maximum of ten hours for women working in laundries, was valid. Rather than simply relying on the traditional legal argument of precedent, Brandeis amassed statistical, historical, sociological, and economic data to support his case. On February 24, 1908, the Court agreed unanimously that longer hours might impair the childbearing of women workers. Thus, the justices accepted the state's limitation of ten hours as a health measure, properly within the state's police power. Thereafter, Brandeis became one of the chief spokesmen for the philosophy of regulated competition and of unhampered enterprise and economic freedom for small businessmen.

By adroit use of patronage at the Republican National Convention in Chicago in 1908, Theodore Roosevelt ensured the nomination of his preferred successor as president, Ohio-born and Yale-educated Cabinet member William Howard Taft. Taft had been a success as one of the first shuttle diplomats. Between 1900 and 1908 he traveled over one hundred thousand miles as Philippine commissioner (1901–4) and as secretary of war (1904–8) and on assignments to Manila, Rome, Panama, and Cuba. Although he was obese, weighing around 350 pounds, Taft carried his flesh majestically on a huge, wide frame. "He looks," said Arthur Brisbane, "like an American bison, a gentle, kindly one." During the campaign of 1908 TR advised the corpulent Taft: "Photographs on horseback, yes; tennis, no; and golf is fatal." Taft continued to play the upper-class game of golf, however—and to be photographed at it—oblivious to the impression of affectation on ordinary people. TR also advised Taft against riding. With Taft's obesity, it was "dangerous for him and cruelty to the horse."

The Democrats nominated their shopworn, former standard bearer, William Jennings Bryan, thereby inviting him to lose a presidential election for a third time. A native of Illinois, Bryan had risen from a political base in Nebraska to national preeminence on account of his spellbinding oratory. Congressman from 1891 to 1895, Bryan was still a pivotal figure among Democratic politicians in the early twentieth century. His historical reputation rests on his three unsuccessful electoral bids for the presidency in 1896, 1900, and 1908. Yet his contemporary renown was based on his continuous campaigning in primaries, his numerous appearances on the Chautauqua lecture circuit, and his pronouncements on all subjects in a way that made him good press copy. His well-routined speeches mixed nostalgia for the never-never land of rural America, suspicion about industrialism, and outrage at the manipulation of capital and government by corporation executives.

In the campaign of 1908 Roosevelt was far and away the most expert tactician in either party, although he often became impatient with his slow pupil. In the election Taft received 7,675,320 votes (51.6 percent) and 321 votes in the electoral college, whereas Bryan received 6,412,294 votes (43.1 percent) and 162 electoral votes. Socialist candidate Eugene V. Debs took 420,793 votes (2.8 percent), and the prohibition candidate, Eugene W. Chaffin, had 253,840 votes (1.7 percent).

On March 4, 1909, for the last time, the journey of president and president-elect from White House to Capitol was made in a horse-drawn carriage. Breaking with custom, Roosevelt did not ride back to the White House with Taft after the ceremony. Instead, to the left of the new president rode Mrs. Helen Herron Taft, who cared not a whit for various protests at her usurpation. This was the most glorious day of her life.

Hamlet without the Prince—Taft in Quicksand

"When I hear some one say 'Mr. President,'" confided William Howard Taft to White House aide Archie Butt, "I look around expecting to see Roosevelt." Taft's chief fault was that he differed from Roosevelt; his chief misfortune was that he followed Roosevelt as president.

The initial warmth between Roosevelt and Taft was dispelled by chills of lasting coldness. Having agreed to retain four members of Roosevelt's Cabinet, including Secretary of the Interior James R. Garfield, Taft went back on his word and appointed an entirely new team. Taft's wife, Helen, and his half-brother and financial sponsor, Charles, were deeply jealous of Roosevelt for his role as architect of Taft's political fortunes. Critics praised Taft's kindliness, candor, and integrity but attacked him for his obsession with the Constitution. They thought he was primarily an interpreter of laws, rather than an administrator, that he should have been a judge rather than a president. This was true. Almost all the positions Taft held until he was elected president were appointive offices. He could not survive the hurly-burly of politics in which TR thrived.

As president (1909–13), Taft's achievements were far from negligible. He exercised his executive powers more than Theodore Roosevelt had in conservation, antitrust suits, and the application of railroad laws. His most singular achievement was in persuading Congress to pass the Sixteenth Amendment, on July 12, 1909, empowering Congress to levy a general income tax. It was duly ratified

FACING PAGE:

The Progressive generation: five portraits

Upper Left: George W. Norris of Nebraska, first as congressman (1903–13) and later as senator (1913–43), was the very embodiment of the progressive spirit among prairie Republicans. He led the House revolt of Insurgents against Speaker Joe Cannon in 1910; fought continuously for federal water-power regulation and public ownership of hydroelectric plants; and saw his efforts come to fruition in the Tennessee Valley Authority, created in 1933. (Photo by G. V. Buck, 1908; Library of Congress)

Upper Right: Robert Marion ("Battling Bob") La Follette, Republican maverick who, as congressman (1885–91), governor of Wisconsin (1901–6), and senator (1906–25), challenged entrenched interests and created his own personal machine for a long political career. He failed to secure a progressive presidential nomination in 1912 but ran as progressive candidate in 1924, when he polled 13 percent of the popular vote. (Library of Congress)

Center: Ida Minerva Tarbell, an articulate progressive investigative journalist noted for her well-argued indictment of the way John D. Rockefeller had achieved the Standard Oil monopoly. A champion of several feminist causes, she nevertheless opposed woman suffrage because she believed the achievement of a fictional social equality through the vote would enable industrialists to elude legislation protecting women and children in factories. (John Rylands University Library of Manchester)

Lower Left: One of the most charismatic men in labor history, Socialist leader Eugene V. Debs inspired great affection among the radicals who followed him and great fear among conservatives. His legendary career included his valiant but thwarted role in the Pullman Strike of 1894; founding the Socialist Party of America in 1901; and running as its presidential candidate several times, receiving 6 percent of the popular vote in 1912 — the election that proved to be the high-water mark of socialism in the United States. (SPA election publicity photo, 1904; Library of Congress)

Lower Right: William D. ("Big Bill") Haywood, assertive leader in the Industrial Workers of the World, or Wobblies, the most controversial of all American labor movements. Haywood's unconventional methods—including intimidation, violence, and murder—and his uncompromising stands frequently set him at odds with radical allies as well as opponents. At the height of the Great Red Scare, he fled to Moscow, where he died and was buried. This photo of 1907 by Myers, Boise, Idaho, when Haywood was at the height of his notoriety, minimizes his desperado appearance. (Library of Congress)

EUGENE V. DEBS

and went into effect on February 3, 1913—just before Taft left office. This reform was profound: perhaps the reform of the Progressive Era with the widest-reaching and longest-lasting repercussions. It laid the groundwork for supporting the expense of future progressive political and social reforms. Taft also recommended, and Congress enacted, a 2 percent tax on the net income of corporations.

By executive order, Taft placed eight thousand assistant postmasters under the civil service, thereby weakening the discredited system of patronage in the postal system. Also on Taft's recommendation, Congress established a postal saving system allowing individuals to deposit up to five hundred dollars at 2 percent interest. It was during the Taft administration that the parcel post was instituted on January 1, 1913, to carry up to eleven pounds by fourth-class mail at, initially, five cents for the first pound and one cent for each additional pound. Taft also signed a bill creating a bureau of mines with authority to recommend safety improvements in mining. Moreover, Taft had more suits brought against the trusts than had Theodore Roosevelt. The fact that he received less credit than TR suggests more about the way he and his policies were perceived than about the policies themselves. The Progressive movement had developed beyond the ability of the federal government to co-opt it simply by adopting some of its features. Furthermore, Taft lacked Roosevelt's true geniality and his easy ability to dominate others.

To make things more difficult, Taft found his presidency engulfed by Progressivism at flood tide. A group of committed midwestern Progressives in Congress, the Insurgents, posed a threat to Taft's authority. The terms *Progressive* and *Insurgent* were almost synonymous, but *Insurgent* was preferred at this time. There were thirty Insurgents in the House and fourteen in the Senate. Representatives of state and local Progressivism who began arriving in Washington during Roosevelt's second term, they were determined to see their reform ideas put into effect and to unite middle-class Americans in a crusade against the social injustice and economic inefficiency wreaked by monopoly capital. Senators Jonathan Dolliver of Iowa (1900–1910) and Albert Beveridge of Indiana (1899–1911) were joined by newcomers Senators Robert La Follette of Wisconsin (1906–25), Joseph G. Bristow of Kansas (1909–15), and Albert Cummins of Iowa (1908–26) in identifying themselves with reform—even to the extent of defying Republican Party whips. The Insurgents also favored better coordinated policies on such subjects as conservation, child labor, and labor legislation. In the House they included Victor Murdock of Kansas (1903–15), George W. Norris of Nebraska (1903–13), and Charles A. Lindbergh (1907–17), father of the aviator. The Insurgents disturbed the existing, convenient political framework of the solid Democratic South, a mainly Republican North, and competition between the parties elsewhere.

In the states they included New York Senator Franklin Delano Roosevelt, fifth cousin of Theodore Roosevelt, who led twenty-one Democratic Insurgents in Albany. *New York Times* reporter W. A. Warn wrote on January 22, 1911,

"With his handsome face and supple strength, he could make a fortune on the stage and set the matinee girl's heart throbbing. . . . behind that highly polished exterior, [his] quiet force and determination . . . are sending cold shivers down the spine of Tammany's striped mascot."

Progressives wanted to extend democracy, to retain the advantages of the representative system—notably its compactness, experience, and legal knowledge—and to eliminate its disadvantages, especially both haste and delay, complexity, corruption, and errors. They wanted to make government truly responsive and accountable by a package of democratic measures: the initiative, the referendum, the recall of judges, the accurate registration of voters, the direct election of senators, proportional representation, direct primaries, and secret and simple ballots.

The general principle of the referendum was for state and local ordinances to be scrutinized by the electors. If, within thirty days of the passing of a city ordinance (or ninety days in the case of a state law), 5 or 10 percent of the voters signed a petition asking that the ordinance or law be submitted to the entire electorate at the next election (or at a special election if 15 or 20 percent of voters so petitioned), and if a majority of those voting favored the measure, it became law. If a majority were against it, it was vetoed by the people. The exceptions to this practice were measures governing immediate public health, peace, or safety.

In the case of the initiative, the public took the initiative in requesting a certain law, again by use of a petition signed by 5 or 10 percent. If 15 or 20 percent so petitioned, then the measure had to be submitted to the electorate at the next election.

Primary elections were the means by which voters who were registered with either party chose that party's candidates for election. The first primary election was held in Minneapolis in September 1900. The previous month a state convention in Madison, Wisconsin, declared for direct primaries.

Recall was the means by which the people could oblige officials whom a petition, signed by a certain proportion of the electors, had deemed to have failed them, to submit themselves to a special election before their term of office had expired. Recall was first applied in some cities in 1903, adopted by the state of Oregon in 1908, and used in ten other states by 1914.

Machine politicians favored direct legislation and primary elections. These reforms would give greater political power to their organizations—the sort of cohesive organizations that could turn out voters in large numbers. Ironically, as democracy was being extended, public participation in elections fell markedly. As people were more likely to vote independent of party, landslide victories became a periodic feature of elections.

There were two astonishing limitations on the extension of democracy. First, women had the vote in only a handful of states, and the woman suffrage campaign took over fifty years before the Nineteenth Amendment gave them the vote in 1920. Second, whereas the so-called solid South supplied well over 80 percent of all the Democratic votes for president in the electoral college, the South was the region where voter participation was lowest. On average, only 37 percent of those in the South eligible to vote did so. The only citizens allowed to vote there were white men. African Americans were systematically disfranchised by a battery of undemocratic practices—poll taxes, grandfather clauses, literacy tests, all-white primaries, and overt exclusion by state constitutions. These restrictive practices were subversive of true democracy. Nevertheless, they were sustained by racist court decisions.

The Progressives' tendency to elitist solutions also led them to urge proposals that would curtail, rather than extend, the part played by the people in government. Thus, some advocated a so-called short ballot, to reduce the number of elected officials. This was on the grounds that the long ballot was democratically specious. They argued that voters could not be expected to make informed judgments on the merits of minor office holders and, in practice, tended to endorse an entire party ticket. Instead, Progressives would have simply turned over the authority to run a whole administration to a few senior executives from whom they expected professional expertise.

In Congress the Insurgents, who were ranged against the stand-pat policies of William Howard Taft and his cohorts, enjoyed complaining about their self-imposed exile from power. In the Senate the prime object of their criticisms was Republican majority leader Senator Nelson W. Aldrich of Rhode Island (1881–1911). Senate rules then allowed the leader of the majority to determine the composition of committees and use this power to extract and distribute campaign contributions. Aldrich was a tall, imposing man with luminous eyes, an authoritative manner, and an easy temperament. But the assertive Aldrich now had to endure a series of challenges to his authority from the Insurgents. The most crucial involved a proposed constitutional amendment for the direct election of senators.

The system of having U.S. senators elected by state assemblies was a bone of contention between Insurgents and conservatives. In the past this system had led to some senators being nominated by state bosses. Thus, they represented certain economic interests rather than the people. During the 1890s the Senate was known as the millionaires' club. Senator James McMillan (1889–1902) represented shipping and lumber rather than Michigan; Joseph Foraker (1897–1909) served Standard Oil rather than Ohio. Progressives targeted this form of indirect democracy for reform. By 1912 twenty-nine states were experimenting with various ways of electing senators directly. They usually did so through primaries. They put the names of the winning candidates at the primary on the ballot at the general election and pledged the candidates or the state legislature to elect the senatorial candidate who received the most votes.

Nelson Aldrich opposed the direct election of senators. He had William E. Borah of Idaho, then a newcomer to the Senate, appointed to the Committee on the Judiciary. Aldrich knew Borah was an outstanding lawyer in his state who had represented great corporations. However, Aldrich mistook Borah's allegiance. Borah cast the deciding vote, approving the Seventeenth Amendment.

Conservatives in Congress now accepted the proposed Seventeenth Amendment. They knew that opposition would result in their own defeat at the next election. Urban legislators wanted to counter the system of apportionment of seats—a system that failed to give appropriate weight to expanding urban communities. The rural areas were mainly Republican and the large cities were mainly Democratic. Thus, urban Democratic legislators favored reapportionment—basing electoral districts on accurate reevaluation of where people lived rather than on some geographic approximation—to increase the influence of their constituents.

When the Seventeenth Amendment was reported out of committee to the Senate, it moved through passage in both houses (by May 13, 1912) and ratification by the states (on April 8, 1913). The Seventeenth Amendment declared, "The Senate of the United States shall be composed of two Senators from each State, elected by the people thereof, for six years and each Senator shall have one vote." Those qualified to vote would be those qualified for "the most numerous branch of the State legislature." When vacancies occurred in a Senate seat, the executive of the state had to issue a writ of election to fill the vacancy. However, the state legislature could empower the executive to make temporary appointments to the Senate until the election.

The tariff was a cause of continuous political vexation. In the days before the general income tax, it was a basic source of governmental revenue. Moreover, a high tariff could be used to stimulate U.S. manufacturing since higher prices on foreign products meant that American goods would be cheaper to buy. Consumers resented high tariffs, however, when industry and manufacturing were enjoying high profits. Moreover, a high tariff also served to insulate manufacturing from economic realities and encourage the consolidation of companies into monopolies. TR knew that the tariff was political dynamite. He had postponed resolute action, prompting cartoonists to portray him as an irresolute Hamlet, a prince who knew something was rotten in the state but who could not make up his mind what to do about it.

Taft called Congress into a special session for March 13, 1909, with the intention of enacting a lower tariff. This was exactly what the Insurgents wanted, given their belief that the trusts could be thwarted by regulated exposure to foreign competition. Buttressed by Taft's words, the Insurgents began a spectacular fight for reduction throughout the long, hot Washington summer. They divided the various schedules (the tariff rates for different products and the underlying formulas) among them, assigning cotton to Jonathan Dolliver of Iowa, sugar to Joseph Bristow of Kansas, and so on. Aldrich and the conservative majority, who favored a protectionist tariff—the Payne-Aldrich Tariff—were not prepared for this strategy. Aldrich was frequently so embarrassed by Dolliver's well-researched assaults that he left the Senate chamber, silenced and red in the face. Exhausted, Aldrich announced that he would retire in March 1911. However, the Payne-Aldrich Tariff passed Congress comfortably.

The strain of having to stand on his own two feet had already made Taft irascible. He was warned that unless he vetoed the tariff, he would antagonize the West, which would then saddle him with a Democratic Congress in the midterm elections of 1910 and defeat him in his reelection campaign in 1912. Nevertheless, he signed the bill on August 5, 1909, leaving Jonathan Dolliver to damn him with a caustic indictment: "President Taft is an amiable man, completely surrounded by men who know exactly what they want." The act provided for a tariff commission that would bring tariff control under systematic, rather than purely political, control.

In the House the Insurgents directed their grievances at the speaker, Joseph Gurney ("Uncle Joe") Cannon. A man of mixed Quaker and Huguenot ancestry, Cannon was perhaps the most politically sophisticated and deceitful person in public life. He considered that, of all proposals for change, half were harmful and the other half useless. Cannon's great power was based on the existing rules of the House that allowed him to appoint a majority (all Republican members) of the all-important Committee on Rules and of various other committees that he expected to retard or advance bills at committee stage, according to his wishes. Congressman George W. Norris of Nebraska presented a motion to have the Committee on Rules elected by the House, instead of being appointed by Cannon. After twenty-nine hours of continuous debate, the House passed it on March 17, 1910, by 191 votes to 156. Norris became a congressional hero.

Taft was embroiled in another controversy when he replaced Roosevelt's secretary of the interior, James R. Garfield, with Richard Ballinger, a man who wanted to distribute public natural resources to private interests for development. Yet, Taft had retained Gifford Pinchot, another Roosevelt man, as chief of the forestry service in the Department of Agriculture. It was inevitable that the two would clash. Pinchot accused Ballinger of secretly planning to turn over valuable coal lands in Alaska to a Morgan-Guggenheim syndicate.

Taft publicly exonerated Ballinger and dismissed Pinchot for insubordination. A congressional investigative committee decided in favor of Ballinger, but Progressives considered Pinchot a defender of national interests against vested interests. Six months later, Ballinger resigned, his usefulness impaired by the evaporation of his credit. Taft staunchly maintained, however, that Ballinger was the victim of defamation, prompting the *New York Evening Post* to comment, "Mr. Taft consents to Mr. Ballinger's resignation in a blaze of indignant relief."

Theodore Roosevelt had been abroad for a year, hunting big game in Africa and lecturing in Europe. When he disembarked in New York on June 16, 1910, he met with a ticker-tape parade of unprecedented size, the zenith of his love affair with the American public. Roosevelt tried to organize the state convention in New York. Now TR tried to appease the old guard, for example, by praising tariffs, campaigning in Massachusetts for Henry Cabot Lodge and in Ohio for

Warren Harding, Republican gubernatorial candidate. Nevertheless, Roosevelt knew that Taft was firmly against him.

Rebuffed, the ex-president set out on a great tour of the West. Roosevelt was preparing a platform. He chose the dedication ceremonies of abolitionist John Brown's battlefield at Ossawatomie, Kansas, on August 31, 1910, to announce the New Nationalism. The old nationalism had been used since the Civil War "by sinister and special interests" toward their own ends. Roosevelt proposed a "New Nationalism" that would bring special interests under government control and put them to work toward an ideal of social welfare and justice. Roosevelt's proposed reforms included a federal trade commission to regulate business and industry and a tariff commission that would ensure benefits of protection for consumers. Roosevelt the warrior had become a priest.

The Ossawatomie speech caused a sensation. To conservatives, the New Nationalism was heresy. The *World* called it "an outburst of Marxian madness." Yet, Roosevelt had already spelled out much of the New Nationalism in three messages to Congress in 1907 and 1908. Roosevelt made his speech after reading *The Promise of American Life* (1909) by Herbert Croly, a progressive journalist from New York, wherein he redefined the national interest in the light of Roosevelt's earlier speeches.

By spring 1910 Taft had joined the old guard of the Republican Party in a generously funded campaign to eradicate insurgency. The old guard wanted to secure the defeat of progressive Republicans in the forthcoming primary elections in the Midwest. But state after state—Indiana, Wisconsin, Minnesota, the Dakotas, Kansas—renominated progressive candidates. The election results of 1910 were a debacle for the Republicans. The Democrats took the House by 228 seats to 162, a majority of 66. They carried the governorships in twenty-six states, including Ohio (Taft's state) and New York (Roosevelt's state). They also succeeded in electing Woodrow Wilson, president of Princeton University, as governor of New Jersey.

As governor, Wilson found himself the focus of numerous political eyes across the nation. He applied his preferred prime ministerial model to state government, preparing a legislative program and then working through the party caucus to ensure discipline. He succeeded with a primary law, a corrupt-practices statute, workmen's compensation, a public service commission to regulate transportation, and another to oversee public utility companies. Then Wilson successfully opposed Democratic boss Jim Smith's bid for the U.S. Senate, backing William Jennings Bryan's reform candidate, James E. Mantine, instead.

In Congress, having captured the House, the Democrats were in the advantageous position of having a majority in one chamber without being responsible for the government as a whole. They exploited their position to embarrass Taft. They did this partly by introducing so-called popgun tariff bills, aimed at unpopular schedules in the Payne-Aldrich Tariff; and partly by prolonging the embarrassing investigation of Secretary of the Interior Richard Ballinger.

The numerous Republican reverses were not simply a consequence of the feud between Taft and Roosevelt. They were an expression of the changing fortunes of the Progressive movement across the country. Progressivism was declining in certain localities, because reformers had achieved their aims or reached a practical compromise with business or local government, and because that achievement had dulled the urge to reform. Progressives had also aroused resentment among people whose lives they were trying to improve. Millions of city folk did not care about city budgets or actually wanted their children to work instead of going to school. Progressive arrogance exasperated them.

Hence, Progressives deepened the division between middle- and working-class people. As a result, certain local bosses survived the onslaught of progressive crusades. Now it was Progressives who were on the defensive, as bosses appropriated, modified, and implemented their ideas. In certain states the old guard rallied and helped defeat progressive leaders who had become unpopular. This was the fate of Albert Beveridge of Indiana, who failed to be elected as governor in 1911 and in 1914 failed to be reelected to the Senate.

Taft tried to counter the adverse publicity stirred by Roosevelt's presence by starting a series of antitrust suits, twenty-two bills in equity and forty-five indictments in all, against corporations for having violated the Sherman Act. The crusade against the trusts came to a climax with the 1911 ruling of the Supreme Court to dissolve Standard Oil.

In September 1901 federal prosecutor Frank B. Kellogg had brought a suit to dissolve the parent Standard Oil company, Standard Oil of New Jersey. Kellogg amassed detailed evidence of the way Standard Oil had created its monopoly, the most hated of all the trusts. He disclosed its exorbitant profits—said to be almost $1 billion over the brief period of twenty-five years. John D. Rockefeller, the reviled founder of Standard Oil, gave evidence. At sixty-nine he looked older, a shrunken man with hollow cheeks, wearing a white wig. To his own lawyers he affected a benign manner, describing the way he had created his empire in affectionate terms. When cross-examined about the dark deeds of his past, his mind was as opaque as an oyster shell.

Rockefeller's considerable skills as an actor did not distract the justices of the Supreme Court. Chief Justice Edward Douglass White read out his opinion—all twenty thousand words—describing how "the very genius for commercial development and organization" that had created Standard Oil in the 1870s had also created a monopoly to "drive others from the field and exclude them from their right to trade." On May 15, 1911, the Supreme Court ruled 8 to 1 that Standard Oil must divest itself of all its subsidiaries within six months.

This was not so harsh a ruling as it first seemed. The dissolution was to be achieved by apportioning shares in the various constituent concerns pro rata to the stockholders of the holding company. Although the Supreme Court returned each of Rockefeller's thirty-eight companies to the state where it operated, the companies were still owned by Rockefeller and his associates. By far the largest of these companies was Standard Oil of New Jersey, which had served as the holding company for the rest.

Furthermore, the Supreme Court introduced a new concept in its decision of 1911, the rule of reason. Previously, the court had held that any combination that restrained trade, whether "reasonable" or "unreasonable," was a violation of the Sherman Antitrust Act. But in the Standard Oil decision the majority opinion declared that only unreasonable combinations and undue restraints of trade were illegal under the Sherman Act. Using the rule of reason, the trusts could justify their existence as the natural growth of a single business.

Taft also tried to correct his mistakes over the Payne-Aldrich Tariff by supporting a progressive bilateral tariff with Canada. His attempt ended in a rout. The treaty, signed on January 7, 1911, proposed to place more than one hundred articles on the free list and to reduce the tariff on four hundred others. Both houses passed the treaty. Taft openly acknowledged the support of press magnate William Randolph Hearst. He expressed his "high appreciation of the energetic work of the seven Hearst papers and of your staff for their earnest and useful effort to spread the gospel of reciprocity." This statement inflamed hostile opinion in the United States, Canada, and Britain. It was widely known that Hearst favored the outright annexation of Canada. Taft's well-intentioned statement swelled fears in Canada that reciprocity might be the first step toward absorption. After all, the United States had only recently acquired the Philippines and Puerto Rico. James Beauchamp ("Champ") Clark, Democratic speaker of the House, exacerbated the controversy by talking about the U.S. flag "floating over every square inch of the British possessions of North America." The Canadian prime minister, Sir Wilfred Laurier, had the Canadian parliament dissolved. He went to the country in an election that was widely interpreted as a referendum on reciprocity. So great was the fear of annexation in Canada that the Canadian electorate repudiated reciprocity, to Taft's evident embarrassment.

1912: Roosevelt or Bust

If exercising presidential power had both fulfilled and restrained Theodore Roosevelt, relinquishing it unleashed his white-hot anger and diminished him. The final precipitating event in the deteriorating relations between Roosevelt and Taft occurred in October 1911 when Taft's administration brought its antitrust suit against U.S. Steel. The pivotal charge was U.S. Steel's 1906 acquisition of the Tennessee Coal and Iron Company, which Theodore Roosevelt had approved. When TR read that Attorney General George W. Wickersham was going to pursue this issue, he was outraged at press innuendoes that, as president, he had been duped. He also felt betrayed by Taft, who had, after all, endorsed his action at the time.

In 1911 TR's fury against Taft reached all parts of the country. His supporters ranged from former Rough Riders such as Frank Knox of Michigan, social workers such as Jane Addams of Chicago, conservationists such as Gifford Pinchot of Pennsylvania, and impetuous reformers such as Everett Colby of New Jersey to such unlikely businessmen converts as Bill Flinn of Pittsburgh and Insurgents such as Albert J. Beveridge of Indiana. Editor William Allen White compressed press comment into the slogan "Roosevelt or bust."

Robert La Follette had already organized a National Progressive Republican League to provide him with a clear path to the Republican presidential nomination. But Roosevelt's reentry into national politics undermined La Follette's faltering authority. Seven Republican governors urged Roosevelt to enter the race against Taft. Roosevelt used their letters as the basis for a joint request actually drafted by himself and calling on him to stand for the Republican nomination. At Columbus, Ohio, on February 22, 1912, he spoke of his proposed personal platform, a "Charter of Democracy."

Many Republicans did not mind Roosevelt's progressive politics. Their affection for the Republican Party was such, however, that they could not bear to see an incumbent president denied renomination or the unwritten rule against a third term broken. Hardened Republican professionals included prominent old-time bosses such as Boies Penrose of Pennsylvania, William Barnes, Jr., of New York, and Murray Crane of Massachusetts, who would rather see the Republican Party torn apart than let Roosevelt have the nomination. *Life* was sarcastic, claiming, "The popular demand for Colonel Roosevelt is steadily increasing; but, however great the demand may become, it can never be as great as the supply."

The Insurgents, led by the interested Robert La Follette, had been advocating the use of direct primaries to supersede conventions as the means of selecting and instructing delegates to national party conventions. Oregon had adopted presidential primaries in 1910. In 1911 the states of California, Nebraska, New Jersey, North Dakota, and Wyoming did so. Campaigns for direct primaries elsewhere met with little interest until Roosevelt announced his candidacy. His ardent supporters realized that only by this reform could they furnish their darling with the requisite number of delegates to offset boss control of the Republican National Convention. As a result of the campaign, Illinois, Maryland, Massachusetts, Pennsylvania, Ohio, and South Dakota held meetings of their state legislatures and adopted presidential primary elections in 1912.

Although Roosevelt was the overwhelming first choice among Republican voters across the country, he stood no chance of winning the Republican presidential nomination. When the Republican National Convention met in Chicago in June, Taft used patronage to shut his erstwhile patron out of the contest. The hardened old guard chose Taft, the certain loser, over Roosevelt, the acclaimed winner. Their choice sprang from their antiquated ideology and their calculations regarding proven political allegiances among the electorate. No single element weighed more in their repudiation of Roosevelt than his criticisms of the courts, because they expected the courts to maintain the interests of private property and unrestrained business enterprise.

However, Roosevelt's arrival in Chicago on June 14 sparked mob demonstrations. To a reporter who asked after his health, Roosevelt replied, "I'm feeling like a bull moose." This imaginative answer was carried on the front pages of ten thousand newspapers the next day, giving the name "Bull Moose party" to TR's personal following. While the Republican National Convention was still going on in Chicago, he agreed to the formation of a Progressive Party as a vehicle for his bid for the presidency. Frank Munsey, a newspaper magnate, and George W. Perkins of U.S. Steel promised to help finance the venture.

Thus the Progressive Party came into being in Chicago on August 6, 1912. The leaders were professional men and women. Out of 260 leaders present at the inaugural convention, there were 95 businessmen, 75 lawyers, 36 editors, 19 college professors, 7 authors, 6 professional social workers, and a scattering of others in various professions. The Progressive Party opened national headquarters on Forty-Second Street, New York, whence Frances Kellor directed its research, education, and legislative efforts. Roosevelt's younger backers included Alfred M. Landon, Felix Frankfurter, Henry A. Wallace, Walter Lippmann, and Dean Acheson.

Since conservatives would not be voting Progressive in any case, the Progressives made no attempt to propitiate them. The Progressive platform was the most radical platform of any major party hitherto. It recommended effective legislation to prevent industrial accidents, occupational diseases, overwork, and unemployment; to establish minimum standards of health and safety in industry; to institute federal control of interstate commerce and taxation to maintain those standards; to prohibit child labor; to provide a "living wage" for workers throughout industry; to establish an eight-hour day for women and children; to set minimum wages for women and to prohibit night work for women; to institute one day's rest in seven for wage earners; and to limit shifts to eight hours in plants operating twenty-four hours continuously.

By comparison with the charismatic Roosevelt, the more ascetic Democratic presidential candidate Woodrow Wilson's political philosophy was rooted in temperament, nurture, and high-minded righteousness. Woodrow Wilson was born on December 28, 1856, in the Shenandoah Valley of Virginia, the son of a Presbyterian preacher. He was raised in Confederate Georgia and later, during Reconstruction, in South Carolina. Whereas Theodore Roosevelt had suffered from asthma as a child, Woodrow Wilson may have had a debilitating handicap long unrecognized. He did not learn to read until he was nine and never read quickly. Edwin Weinstein speculates (1981) that Wilson may have suffered from dyslexia, caused by a congenital brain defect. Yet Wilson applied himself and succeeded academically. He graduated from Princeton in 1879 and became a professor of political economy at various universities.

As president of Princeton University (1902–10), Wilson revitalized Princeton's curriculum and its teaching. Yet, his stellar career as an educational leader floundered after 1907 over two failures. First, alumni protest obliged Princeton trustees to rescind their initial approval of the so-called quad plan that would have made Princeton more like Oxford and Cambridge with the tutorial system. Second, in 1910 Wilson lost a battle over the location of a new facility for graduate students. Wilson's political ambition was so strong, however, that he campaigned for governor on a program of reforms that Progressives of both parties had been calling for. In 1911 Wilson subdued party bosses when he persuaded a reluctant legislature to accept practically his entire reform program: a direct primary system, legislation against corrupt practices, workmen's compensation, and strict control of railroads and public utilities.

As a Democratic presidential hopeful, Wilson faced resentment from southern Democrats who looked on him as an outsider; from reclaimed Populists, such as Thomas Watson of Georgia, who distrusted Wilson's dismissive attitude toward William Jennings Bryan; and from party professionals. Thus, Speaker Champ Clark, who was, after all, the Democratic Party's highest-ranking officeholder, had the advantage of secure party loyalties and entrenched credentials as well as the support of William Jennings Bryan. In most primaries and conventions outside the South, Clark outpolled Wilson and earned the support of press tycoon William Randolph Hearst. When the Democratic National Convention met, Clark was one hundred votes ahead of Wilson. As timing, stamina, and irony would have it, the Democrats' progressive candidate owed his nomination to the party's antiquated two-thirds rule. Wilson's manager, William McCombs, prevailed on Wilson to stay his ground and make a pact with another hopeful, Oscar Wilder Underwood of Alabama. Wilson also required the pivotal support of William Jennings Bryan. He won his victory after forty-seven ballots cast over four days.

While Theodore Roosevelt preached regulation of monopoly, Wilson's program, the New Freedom, proposed regulation of competition to destroy monopoly. In Wilson's view, freedom to compete had to be maintained at all costs. The middle classes had to be protected from the rule of labor on the one hand and the control of capitalist monopoly on the other.

Since both Roosevelt and Wilson were progressive candidates and agreed on what problems faced the country, the distinction between their solutions was less important than the contest of personalities. In retrospect, public opinion has alighted on the definition provided years later by William Allen White in his *Woodrow Wilson* (1924): "Between the New Nationalism and the New Freedom was that fantastic imaginary gulf that always has existed between tweedle-dum and tweedle-dee."

The results of the election of 1912 showed that Roosevelt failed to attract progressive Democrats to his Progressive Party. This fact alone ensured his defeat. Wilson polled 6,296,547 popular votes (41.9 percent), Roosevelt 4,118,571 (27.4 percent), and Taft 3,486,720 (23.2 percent). The multiple division of the popular vote meant that Wilson's victory in the electoral college was of landslide proportions. He gained 435 electoral votes against Roosevelt's 88 and Taft's derisory 8. People responded to Roosevelt's character, but he could not generate a new political mechanism. In the congressional elections the Progressives captured nine seats in the House and one in the Senate. They won only about 250 local offices and one governorship. The two-party system was rooted in deep political habits and extensive organization at local, state, and national levels. It was too resilient to be overthrown even by as charismatic a leader as the once invincible Theodore Roosevelt. Bust it was.

CHAPTER 2

Virtue Is Its Own Reward

Woodrow Wilson and the New Freedom

THIS IS HOW Woodrow Wilson, in his last scholarly lectures—given at Columbia University in 1907 and published as *Constitutional Government in the United States* in 1908—remarked on how the president could become a strong party leader and the national spokesman who could appeal to people over the heads of Congress:

> The president is the political leader of the nation, or has it in his choice to be. The nation as a whole has chosen him, and is conscious that it has no other political spokesman. . . . Let him once win the admiration and confidence of the country, and no other single force can withstand him, no combination of forces will easily overpower him. . . . If he rightly interpret the national thought and boldly insist upon it, he is irresistible.

As president (1913–21) Wilson intended to become a leader who could master multitudes, teach them to keep faith with the past, and implement progressive policies that would conserve as well as reform.

People differed greatly in their response to the kind of political personality that Theodore Roosevelt had shown in the first decade of the twentieth century and the kind that Woodrow Wilson would show in the second, but no one doubted their forcefulness or the fact that they shaped American society and politics decisively. The theme that links TR's and Wilson's presidencies is their interest in the location and application of political and economic power, the relationship between great private enterprises and groups, and the expanding power of the federal government. TR and Wilson set their mark on American government as the first progressive presidents, even as they helped mobilize the human and material resources of the United States for the pivotal role it would play in world affairs. Whereas in 1901–9 TR set the sights of government toward a modicum of social reforms to redress the conditions that had produced the agrarian revolt and labor protests of the 1890s, in 1913–21 Wilson brought the program of progressive political reform to a peak of achievement.

William Orpen's study of President Woodrow Wilson did full justice to Wilson's penetrating gaze, tight-lipped tension, and general hauteur. (Library of Congress)

Wilson's views on effective presidential leadership had been radicalized, first by the emergence of the United States as a world-class power and second by the way Theodore Roosevelt had revived the presidency. In *Congressional Government* (1885), Wilson criticized the diffusion of political power not only between the various branches of government but also within them, particularly in Congress, declaring that the committee system made congressmen less accountable to their constituents.

Wilson was a spellbinding speaker, especially gifted in communicating high ideals and touching men's spirits. Nevertheless, he sometimes said things he did not really mean, and his meaning was sometimes abstruse. During extemporaneous speeches his oratory took flight and became a virtuoso solo, something to be felt rather than understood. Moreover, as prolific Wilson scholar Arthur Link explains (1954), "There was always the temptation to idealize unpleasant situations and necessities, and this in turn led Wilson to romanticize objectives and to refuse to confront hard realities."

Calvinists such as Woodrow Wilson may bear tidings of great joy, but Wilson gave most people the impression that he was at best reserved, distant, and cold and at worst, self-righteous and vain. Many people disliked his habit of polishing his spectacles while they were talking to him. Editor William Allen White said his handshake was like a "ten-cent pickled mackerel in brown paper." Behind the scenes Wilson was far from a prude. He enjoyed vaudeville and courted his second wife, Edith Bolling Galt, with the song "Oh, You Beautiful Doll." Although he was hardly lascivious, his love of female company beyond his first wife, Ellen Axson Wilson, and their three daughters, had led him, during his period in New Jersey, into at least one love affair. This was with the persistent Mrs. Peck, who cost him dearly later. When he was president, Mrs. Peck exercised a subtle form of blackmail upon him with periodic requests for financial aid. Wilson had other problems, besides—a long history of illnesses, including a mild stroke when he was thirty-nine and chronic bowel complaints. None of these experiences taught him much about charity. The most cynical interpretation of Wilson as politician was that he was a trimmer, far less progressive than those he led. He was successful in getting enabling legislation enacted when his general understanding of just when to compromise was at its best. But he was least successful when his passion for morality made him intolerant—as was the case with Mexico.

His publications not only showed Wilson's admiration for such statesmen as George Washington, Abraham Lincoln, and the English prime minister William E. Gladstone, who believed in an orderly, organic growth of political institutions, but also his concern about the concentrated economic power of the great corporations and the inefficiency of Congress. From William Jennings Bryan Wilson had inherited a Democratic Party with a strong reformist wing. He developed its reform traditions by appealing to what became a coalition of less advantaged groups that eventually sought to improve their interests through what later generations might call a welfare state.

His secretary, Joe Tumulty, had grown up in urban, machine politics. Tumulty believed in lubricating administrative and political machines. He fed Wilson information by clipping items from the newspapers and by summarizing press coverage in general. Still, Wilson's habitual solitariness prevented him from seeing different points of view. Yet this had an advantage: it gave him appropriate detachment. As to his personal life, Wilson continued along his restrained, middle-class existence. He wrote out his speeches in his own shorthand, and he typed his letters on his own typewriter.

In 1913 the greater part of opinion in both parties wanted tariff, tax, and currency reform; a program to regulate banks, railroads, public utilities, and manufacturing industry; and various forms of protection for artisans, farmers, women, and children. Wilson's task was straightforward: to synthesize reform ideas, arrive at a consensus, and lead Congress to see reforms enacted. Instead of relying on a coalition of reform-minded congressmen as Theodore Roosevelt had done, Wilson decided to govern through his party. Wilson also wanted to broaden the base of the Democratic Party, discipline it, and strengthen it for the future. In order to counterbalance the weight of southern Democrats who chaired important committees in Congress and who had reservations about his policies, Wilson decided to deploy presidential patronage as effectively as possible. He did so through his postmaster general, Albert S. Burleson. He also believed that his own spirited leadership and natural eloquence could convince the Democratic Party to accept his program.

The disruption of the Republicans in the period 1910–16 allowed the Democrats large majorities in the House and workable majorities in the Senate. They were also strengthened by support from insurgent Republicans. The 114 novices among the 294 Democratic congressmen in 1913 were eager to pass reforms and also anxious to please Wilson. Their future careers depended upon the success of the Wilson administration and the continuation of party patronage. Even southern conservatives believed it was better to support reform than risk opprobrium nationwide. Moreover, they were genuinely proud to have a native son as president. Thus, few congressmen dared challenge Wilson.

The closest of Wilson's advisers was the shrewd and ubiquitous Col. Edward M. House, who, through his attentiveness and his refusal to accept a Cabinet position, came close to sharing presidential influence. When Wilson went on vacation to Bermuda before his inauguration, it was House who drew up plans for the new Cabinet, which necessarily reflected the interests within the Democratic Party. William Jennings Bryan secured the prestigious position of secretary of state (1913–15), despite Wilson's distrust of his supposedly radical policies. The inclusion of the Bureau of Labor in the Cabinet marked a culmination of the struggle that had begun as early as 1865. It had been partially fulfilled in 1903 when Theodore Roosevelt created the Department of Commerce and Labor. William Bauchop Wilson, a former secretary-treasurer of the United Mineworkers and a congressman for Pennsylvania, was appointed (1913–21) in recognition of his efforts to establish the bureau.

The New Freedom

Wilson became one of the most controversial of all presidents. First, he was a spectacularly successful legislative and party leader in 1913–14. His feat in those years was repeated later only by Democrats Franklin Roosevelt in 1933–36 and Lyndon Johnson in 1964–65. Second, Wilson led a coalition that promoted the interests of certain economic sections and occupational groups at the expense of certain others. Third, his presidency was marred by a core of divisiveness. With respect to the trusts, both Roosevelt and William Howard Taft had appealed to Republican Party unity and thereby moved the Republicans to stricter regulation of big business. Their achievements were moderate and practical. But TR and Taft's approach, while avoiding open division, led to big business's reconsolidating itself.

The great quartet of New Freedom legislation, achieved in nineteen months from April 1913 to October 1914, consisted of the Underwood-Simmons Tariff; the Federal Reserve Act; the Clayton Antitrust Act; and its partner, the Federal Trade Commission Act. By making a priority of such fundamental legislation, Wilson brought his best skills into play.

Indeed, Wilson's very first action in office was spectacular. On the day of his inauguration he summoned a special session of Congress. Then, on April 8, 1913, breaking a tradition in effect since President Thomas Jefferson (1801–9), he appeared in person before a joint meeting of the House and the Senate to deliver a short message, in which he expressed his determination to reduce the tariff that had protected U.S. industry from foreign competition since the Civil War.

On April 22, 1913, Oscar Wilder Underwood of Alabama, chairman of the House Ways and Means Committee, presented a tariff first drafted two years earlier when Congress had passed three Democratic tariff bills that Taft then vetoed. The Underwood-Simmons bill reduced the average so-called ad valorem rate from the (approximately) 40 percent of the Payne-Aldrich Tariff of 1909 to an average of about 29 percent. Several important products were put on the free list, including wool and sugar. Where it could be shown that U.S. products dominated the world market, the bill proposed that rates should be either abolished or drastically reduced. Agricultural machinery and most consumer goods went on the free list, as did products such as iron and steel manufactured by the trusts.

To recover revenue that would be lost because of the new tariff, Congressman Cordell Hull of Tennessee drafted a section for the bill that provided for a graduated income tax under the terms of the Sixteenth Amendment (passed on July 12, 1909, and ratified on February 13, 1913). It authorized Congress to impose taxes on incomes from any source and without apportionment to the states. The income tax provided by the Underwood-Simmons Tariff was modest. It levied a tax of 1 percent on incomes over $3,000, or $4,000 for married couples, and a surtax of 1 percent on incomes of $20,000, increasing gradually to 6 percent on incomes over $500,000. Later, on January 24, 1916, the Supreme Court affirmed the constitutionality of the income tax law by 7 votes to 2 in the case of *Brush-aber v. Union Pacific Railroad Co.*

The Underwood-Simmons bill had a stormy passage through Congress. Lobbyists for manufacturers did their utmost to have it rescinded. Wilson called their bluff and made a public statement on May 26, 1913, denouncing "so invidious a lobby" as the vested interests in Congress. Thus, Wilson succeeded where his predecessors had failed in 1896 and 1909.

An investigating committee showed that many senators stood to lose money on investments in such businesses as sheep farming and sugar production if the tariff were passed. The effect of this exposure was to crush any Democratic resistance to the bill, leaving only two determined senators from Louisiana to vote against it. On October 3, 1913, Wilson signed it into law. However, the outbreak of World War I in 1914 led to a disruption of trade that was just as eliminative as a prohibitive tariff.

Banking and currency reform were high on the list of provisional legislation in 1913. The national system of banking was inefficient in catering to the needs of a large industrial nation. Many banks were not under national control at all. So-called national banks were, in fact, interstate banks with substantial assets. They operated as independent units under federal supervision. Their ability to issue notes was related to their holding government bonds. The system did not allow for the expansion of credit when this was required, nor did it meet the seasonal needs of farmers.

The short-lived but intense bankers' panic of 1907 had led to the establishment of an interim system that provided for more mobile reserves and a more elastic money supply. Moreover, the Aldrich-Vreeland Act established the National Monetary Commission, headed by Senator Nelson W. Aldrich. In 1911 and 1912 it investigated possible options and advised Congress of its recommendations. The separate investigations of 1912 for the House, led by Arsene Pujo, disclosed the existence of a small group of financiers sometimes known as the Money Trust. These financiers controlled banks and trust companies, insurance companies, express companies, and industrial and public utility companies worth, collectively, $23 billion. The Money Trust was supposed to be so powerful that it decided where and when to construct railroad lines and whether to stimulate national prosperity or recession.

In place of Nelson Aldrich's plan of reform, which was a Wall Street banker's dream, radical Progressives would settle for nothing less than full governmental control of the banking system. On June 11, 1913, lawyer and presidential adviser Louis Brandeis convinced Wilson that Secretary of State Bryan and other Democrats were right—that only the federal government should issue currency and control the banking system.

The outcome was the most important single act of Wilson's administration, the Federal Reserve Act of 1913. It drew from the varied protests of a wider spectrum of opinion than did any other single piece of legislation: the antifederalists opposed to economic privilege; the enemies of the Bank of the United

States in the years of President Andrew Jackson (1829–37); and, in the 1890s, the Populists, who excoriated the eastern voices of Wall Street. It also responded to the interests of those who wanted subtreasury plans to achieve regional fiscal autonomy and a flexible currency, the greenbackers and free silverites, the farm and labor leaders who had protested on behalf of the huddled masses, and isolated farmers who thought they had been dispossessed by industry.

The Federal Reserve Act—also known as the Owens-Glass Act—established the Federal Reserve System (FRS) with twelve private regional Federal Reserve Banks supervised and controlled by the Federal Reserve Board (FRB) in Washington, D.C. The Federal Reserve Board comprised six men (of whom two must have banking experience) appointed by the president; the secretary of the treasury and the controller of the currency were to be included. Each reserve bank was to be controlled by a board of nine directors, six to be elected by the banks and three to be elected by the FRB. Of the six directors selected by the banks, three must be selected to represent the general public interest of the reserve district by the stockholding banks. The Federal Reserve Board had power to remove these three directors if they did not fairly represent the general public interest.

The act provided for the creation of a flexible currency, allowing the Federal Reserve Board, through its member banks, to issue currency equal in amount to collateral (such as notes, drafts, or bills of exchange arising out of commercial transactions) deposited in the banks. It established a permanent reserve fund of 35 percent to provide for prompt redemption. The regional banks would have, initially, $105 million in capital and $531 million in deposits. Thus, each legal-tender note was to bear a letter of the alphabet signifying its original reserve bank: A for Boston, B for New York, and so on to K for Dallas and L for San Francisco.

After explosive debates, the Federal Reserve Act passed the House on September 18, 1913, by 287 votes to 85. A similar struggle took place in the Senate. When Senator Elihu Root of New York denounced the bill as a sure cause of inflation, its proponents reviewed the measure and tightened the reserve requirement. The Senate passed the bill on December 19 by 54 votes to 34, and Wilson signed it into law on December 22, 1913. He had won by leading rather than driving.

The act compelled national banks to join the system. It encouraged state banks and trust companies to do so. Within its first year, the system came to represent nearly half the nation's banking resources, and by the 1920s, four-fifths. The act's sponsors intended it as a reform on the grounds of greater efficiency rather than as social restructuring. The Federal Reserve Act made the capitalist economy of the industrialized United States run more smoothly by providing an elastic currency that could survive economic crises across the nation.

The Federal Reserve Act earned almost universal praise, as much for Wilson's leadership as for the final result. Wilson's artfulness was greater than his achievement. The FRB had much control, but the regional banks, notably the richest of these, the Federal Reserve Bank of New York, exercised great independence and had far more influence over interest rates. Officers of regional banks were to be elected by member banks in those regions. Thus, Wall Street came to dominate the Federal Reserve Bank of New York. On its first day of business, November 16, 1914, the Federal Reserve Bank of New York took $99.61 million in deposits from 479 commercial banks.

Progressive Pressures Continue

Woodrow Wilson's administration still faced a serious challenge from diverse progressive groups. By 1913 calls for economic and social justice were as strong as they had ever been, with campaigns for regulation of industry, federal child-labor legislation, and government aid to labor, farmers, tenant farmers, and the unemployed. Organized groups dedicated to reform causes included the American Association for Labor Legislation, the National Consumers' League, the National Child Labor Committee, the National Association for the Advancement of Colored People (NAACP), and organized social workers. Organized labor was another reform cause—despite the reluctance of unions to be associated with either middle-class or professional students of labor problems. Farm organizations, such as the National Farmers' Union and the Non-Partisan League, demanded a program of government intervention on behalf of farmers, especially the establishment of a governmental system of long-term rural credit.

The question of the day was whether or not Woodrow Wilson and the New Freedom were sufficiently flexible to satisfy these various progressive groups. Progressives were perplexed by Wilson's lack of commitment to the egalitarian ideals of the New Freedom. Their confusion was compounded when Wilson began his moves toward regulation of the trusts.

In his address to Congress on January 20, 1914, Wilson spoke of breaking up interlocking directorates, of defining, forbidding, and punishing "hurtful restraints of trade," and of creating a commission to inform and advise business. The emphasis was to be on legal prohibition rather than on federal supervision. Under the influence of lawyer Louis Brandeis, Wilson initially maintained his opposition to the ideas proposed by Theodore Roosevelt in 1912. Once the legislative debate was under way, however, Wilson began to shift emphasis. His insistence on prohibition waned, and his interest in a strong commission to administer antitrust rules and prevent unfair competition waxed. Congress responded with two acts, the Clayton Act and the Federal Trade Commission Act.

The Clayton bill, discussed by Congress in 1914, was designed both to modify and to intensify the terms of the Sherman Antitrust Act of 1890. It was in accord with the vague principles of the New Freedom campaign of 1912. It sought to establish fair competition by providing precise definitions of restraint of trade and clarification of the rule of reason. But it was a long way from the desires of labor leaders, such as Samuel Gompers of the American Federation of Labor (AFL). When Gompers read the text of the Clayton bill, he told the press angrily, "Without further delay, the citizens of the United States must decide whether they wish to outlaw organized labor." Wilson and congressional leaders offered labor a compromise amendment that provided for trials by jury in case of criminal contempt, limited the issue of injunctions in labor disputes, and declared that neither labor unions nor farm organizations should be declared in restraint of trade when they sought legitimate objectives by lawful means. The House passed the bill on June 5, 1914. When it came to the Senate on August 5, it was practically unrecognizable, compared to the original proposal.

The Clayton bill was left adrift in the Senate. The Senate weakened virtually every one of its strong provisions. Conservatives modified the prohibition against mergers because they wanted it to apply only to those cases in which mergers would tend to decrease competition. The Supreme Court further weakened the act by its successive decisions.

The Federal Trade Commission Act outlawed unfair trade practices in general terms and gave the commission plenary authority to oversee business activity and issue cause-and-desist notices. The Federal Trade Commission would be entirely dependent on its members for its character. Morgan executive George Perkins, the National Civic Federation, and others who had been among the advocates of the rejected Hepburn amendments of 1908 to the original Sherman Antitrust Act supported the establishment of the Federal Trade Commission (FTC) in 1914. Wilson deeply disappointed Brandeis and other Progressives by appointing a board that was sympathetic to the needs and wishes of big business, as the FTC proved to be.

In 1913 and 1914 Wilson stood high with his colleagues, his party, his opponents, and the people. In fact, he was praised for collegial relations. At a press conference on November 3, 1913, he modestly claimed: "I haven't had a tariff program; I haven't had a currency program. I have conferred with these men who handle these things and have asked the questions, and then have gotten back what they sent to me—the best of our common counsel." Radical John Reed said in an unpublished article: "I never met a man who gave such an impression of quietness inside." For Wilson had an inner core, "a principle, a religion, a something upon which his whole life rests. Roosevelt never had it. Nor Taft. Wilson's power emanates from it. Roosevelt's sprang from an abounding vitality." Thus, Reed's impression of Wilson's White House office was of a "powerful organization, as if no moment were wasted—as if an immense amount of work were being done."

Nevertheless, the weakening of the administration's antitrust program was only the most marked in a gradual series of moves toward outright conservatism. One reason for this shift was the insidious worldwide depression in 1913 that followed hard on the tightening of credit in Europe because of the Balkan wars and the fear of a major European war. In 1914 Wilson began to welcome such men as financier J. P. Morgan, Jr., and automobile manufacturer Henry Ford to the White House, where he listened to their advice. Also in 1914, Attorney General Thomas Watt Gregory started to use a new method in dealing with alleged combinations in restraint of trade. He invited any large corporation that had doubts about the legality of its structure to come and talk it over amicably with members of the Department of Justice. Many corporations did so, including AT&T. In effect, the president of the United States was saying to business leaders, "Send your man to my man and they can fix it up."

Corporations were strengthened by the economic boom that resulted from U.S. economic support of the Allies in World War I and U.S. military intervention in 1917. The *Abstract of the Census of Manufacturing* found that by 1919 corporations accounted for 31.5 percent of the total of business organizations, but they employed 86 percent of all wage earners and produced goods worth 87.7 percent of the total value of manufacturing.

The Harrison Act of 1914, sponsored by Congressman Francis Burton Harrison from New York, tried to protect the public from fraudulent patent medicines. It was also the first comprehensive federal law against the trade in narcotics, with enforcement entrusted to the Internal Revenue Service. Progressive reformers met the increasing use of heroin in major cities, notably New York, with drug treatment programs, the most famous of which was at Towns Hospital, New York. But the method of treatment there was controversial because it entailed powerful doses of drugs, purging the patient's body and thereby detoxifying it to end drug craving. In New York expert Ernest Bishop gave heroin addicts regular doses of opium. But according to public opinion, drugs should not be administered to patients indefinitely. The controversy came to a climax in 1919 when the Supreme Court prohibited treatment based on indefinite drug maintenance.

The ever widening progressive crusade against drugs and alcohol gained further momentum with the Anti-Saloon League's persuasive arguments before state legislatures to ban bars. Thus, by 1914 very different state laws against alcohol had succeeded in drying out 70 percent of the United States, in which lived 30 percent of its population.

As might have been expected, in the midterm elections of 1914, the Democrat majority in the House fell from 73 to 25. Most of the losses were in the Northeast and the Midwest. In the West Democrats retained most of their House seats and gained two new governorships.

In the second phase of Wilson's domestic program, beginning in the first nine months of 1915, there were seven major pieces of legislation, including a tariff commission, a shipping board for the merchant marine, the prohibition of child labor in interstate commerce, workmen's compensation for work under government contracts, an eight-hour day for interstate railroad workers, increased income taxes, and an inheritance tax on the wealthy.

Yet, Wilson drew fire from advanced Progressives in both parties who wanted a stronger program of federal support for farmers, industrial workers, women, children, and the huddled masses in general. As far as they could tell, Wilson had achieved little in the war against the trusts or by way of humanitarian measures for the working class. In the summer of 1914, Wilson rebuffed farmers who wanted government-backed, long-term credit. Not until 1916, when political circumstances left him no choice, did he lend his support to farm credit with the Federal Farm Loan Act and the Federal Farm Loan Board.

The Federal Farm Loan Act of 1916 provided farmers with long-term credit facilities, similar to those made available to industry and commerce by the Federal Reserve Act. The act divided the country into twelve farm districts and established the Federal Farm Loan Board, consisting of the secretary of the treasury and four other members. Each district had a Farm Loan Bank, capitalized at $750,000, in which cooperative farm loan associations were members. Farmers belonging to these associations could secure long-term loans of between five and forty years on farm mortgage security at interest rates between 5 and 6 percent, rather lower than those of commercial banks. To assist farmers in financing their crops, the Bonded Warehouse Act of 1916 authorized licensed and bonded warehouses to issue warehouse receipts negotiable as delivery orders or as collateral for loans against specified agricultural commodities, including grain, cotton, tobacco, and wool.

Wilson supported the Furuseth seaman's bill to improve safety and conditions of work for merchant sailors, enacted on March 4, 1915. This act, also known as La Follette's Seaman's Act after its sponsor, was one of the great measures of social justice to come out of the Progressive Era. The proposal that resulted in the act had gained support in 1912 when the British ocean liner *Titanic* hit an iceberg on its maiden voyage on April 15 and sank, with the loss of many lives. Of over 2,000 on board, only 705 passengers and crew members were saved. The spectacular crisis dramatized the tragic dangers at sea for sailors as well as passengers.

Andrew Furuseth, president of the Seamen's Union, had campaigned for his bill for twenty years. He saw it come close to defeat at the last minute when Wilson withdrew his support. Wilson disliked the fact that the bill did not accord with the less exacting terms of a convention drawn up by the International Conference on Safety at Sea in November 1913. Thus, to Wilson, to enact the Furuseth bill would mean abrogating the convention. Wilson relented when Robert La Follette guaranteed that Congress would allow time for the negotiation of new international treaties and after Secretary of State William Jennings Bryan had shifted his allegiance to Furuseth following a moving plea from the old sailor.

The act was designed to improve the living and working conditions for seamen and to attract more people to the sea. It applied to crews of vessels registered in the United States and to foreign ships while they were in American ports. It regulated hours of work at sea and in port; it also regulated payment of wages, fixed minimum amounts of food, and set certain standards of quality. It required that at least 75 percent of the persons employed in each ship's department must be able to understand the language spoken by the officers.

As Woodrow Wilson became immersed in World War I, he did not seem to appreciate the extent to which he had disillusioned Progressives across the nation. In November 1914 he wrote that the legislation of the New Freedom had already righted fundamental wrongs and that the future would be "a time of healing because [it would be] a time of just dealing." Moreover, he assessed—rightly—that both country and government needed time to get used to the earlier, dramatic reforms. The implication of his remarks, however, was that Progressivism had achieved its goals and was now obsolescent. Most Progressives would have disagreed. In the newly formed progressive journal, the *New Republic*, editor Herbert Croly said, "He deceives himself with these phrases, but he should not be allowed to deceive popular progressive opinion."

Despite some loosening of his progressive ties, Wilson paid tribute to the progressive tradition by appointing Louis Brandeis to the Supreme Court. He did so in part to amend an earlier mistake: the nomination of his undistinguished attorney general, James C. McReynolds, to the Court. McReynolds remained on the Court for twenty-three years as a reactionary jurist disliked among his colleagues for his divisive presence. Since Wilson—like others—soon regretted McReynolds, he named Louis Brandeis to atone for his mistake. Brandeis was confirmed in the Senate by 42 votes to 22 on June 1, 1916, after a bitter battle in which Brandeis's Progressivism and his Judaism were held up to vicious censure. Fifty-five Bostonians, including the president of Harvard, protested the nomination on the grounds that Brandeis lacked the necessary judicial temperament.

After the outbreak of World War I, reforms were more piecemeal, accommodating the interests of labor, commercial farmers, and small businessmen—the last converts to Progressivism. On September 1, 1916, Wilson signed a law on child labor. The Adamson Act of December 1916 provided for an eight-hour workday on interstate railroads, with no reduction in wages, and for a commission appointed by the president to observe the operation of the new workday. It was introduced to avert a threatened railroad strike with all the economic disruption that would have entailed. On this occasion Congress had no qualms about proposing federal intervention in the free workings of the economy in order to prevent a damaging strike.

Roosevelt and Woodrow Wilson contributed to the American presidency by dramatizing the role and the office, by broadening and deepening people's political education and perception, and by governing through party leadership. TR seized new opportunities for publicity through the mass media, to which he owed much for his fame and his charisma. Woodrow Wilson was more controlled than Roosevelt and personified a less exuberant exercise of power. But he pursued his more conventional politics with resourceful single-mindedness. Woodrow Wilson considered it the duty of political leaders to educate the public. He cooperated with his party organization to draft and defend legislation.

The third "Progressive" president, Franklin Delano Roosevelt (1933–45), wrote to Wilson's biographer, Ray Stannard Baker, on March 20, 1935: "Theodore Roosevelt lacked Woodrow Wilson's appeal to the fundamentals and failed to stir, as Wilson did, the only profound moral and social convictions. Wilson, on the other hand, failed where Theodore Roosevelt succeeded in stirring people to enthusiasm over specific individual acts." Whatever Wilson's shortcomings as a Progressive according to his critics, the Wilson era was, in the words of Arthur Link, "the time when the American people through their leaders found the first, though incomplete and imperfect answers to the question of how to bring a dynamic, growing, and competitive economy under effective social control."

CHAPTER 3

RPM

The Flowing Rhythm of Modern America

A S T H E American wheels of progress moved cars, planes, and energy, they transformed society across the world. American inventions and industry were literally revolutionary.

When we speak of the modern world as a global community, we acknowledge not only the effects of imperialism, mass migration, and economic ties between nations geographically far apart, but also the influence of advances in communication and transportation. Telephone and radio, and later television, satellite links, and computers, made communication instantaneous. In transportation, automobiles and airplanes reduced distance and almost eliminated it as an impediment for politics, trade, socializing, and—it must be admitted—war.

Americans had a special facility for inventions and for adapting others' inventions to their own purposes. To Thomas Alva Edison we ascribe the electric light, the phonograph, motion pictures, improved telegraphs, and more than a thousand other inventions; to Alexander Graham Bell, the telephone; to Orville and Wilbur Wright, the airplane; and to Henry Ford, the mass-produced automobile. But it was the managerial skill of Edison and Bell, as much as their scientific abilities, that led to the transformation of society.

Bell invented the telephone in 1876. In 1880 various telephone companies were reorganized as the American Bell Telephone Company; then in 1885 another reorganization formed the American Telephone and Telegraph Company (AT&T), a merger partly financed by investment banker J. P. Morgan. Consumers quickly grasped the use of the telephone for business communication and for socialization. Whereas in 1910 there was one telephone for every 14.5 people, in 1920 there was one for every 8.5 people. AT&T and its telephone were the first harbingers of the profound communications revolution that would extend to the phonograph (1877), motion pictures (1896), wireless telegraphy (1896 but notably from 1920 on), television (1927 but notably from 1945 on), and computers (1945).

Edison invented the electric light in 1879. This was the crucial breakthrough in electrical power. In 1892 Edison's electric company merged with its great rival,

Thompson-Houston. The House of Morgan and other bankers also capitalized the deal at $50 million to create General Electric (GE). Although Edison was the most prolific inventor in history, he was not a lone pioneer but the titular and professional head of a research team and factory that produced pioneer inventions. The same was true of Henry Ford and automobiles.

The automobile revolution that manufacturer Henry Ford spearheaded was the cutting edge in a social revolution that made Americans more independent because more mobile than ever before. In the early pioneering stage of automobile production (1893–1903), inventors Charles E. and J. Frank Duryea had built the first gasoline-powered car, the Duryea, in Springfield, Massachusetts, on September 21, 1893. And, after a few false starts, Ransom E. Olds began to make complex, high-quality, expensive automobiles, notably in Lansing in 1901, where he made the Oldsmobile. Instead of making each part himself, Olds bought parts in quantity from various suppliers and concentrated on the assembly of vehicles. At this time there was no standardization of engine, transmission tools, or process, but the public showed itself increasingly interested in the automobile and its possibilities for transportation and social life.

This was the context in which Henry Ford of Dearborn, Michigan, formed the Ford Motor Company in June 1903. Ford realized that what would sell in huge quantities was not the sort of elaborate, expensive automobiles that most engineers and drivers liked, but instead something light and reliable, simple and cheap, that would appeal to a mass market. In 1907 Ford made his famous dramatic statement:

> I will build a motor car for the great multitude. It will be large enough for the family but small enough for the individual to run and care for. It will be constructed of the best materials, by the best men to be hired, after the simplest designs that modern engineering can devise. But it will be so low in price that no man making a good salary will be unable to own one—and enjoy with his family the blessing of hours of pleasure in God's great open spaces.

Henry Ford's statement was breathtaking as a farsighted and accurate prediction of a new social order. So, Ford built a cheap car—the Model T—within

FACING PAGE:

The Wheels-within-Wheels of capital and labor.
Above: Henry Ford and his first car. Automobile manufacturer Henry Ford transformed society by a combination of technical prowess in the new field of automobiles, self-interested paternalist management, astute marketing, and assertive determination. (Library of Congress)
Below: In *The Bank*, actor-director Charlie Chaplin demonstrated his ability to jolt audiences with bathos at the beginning of his films. He strolls into a bank, turns the vault safe with immaculate precision, and opens it to remove a mop and pail, thereby disclosing the difference between capital and labor. Chaplin was the preeminent cinema artist of the silent era; his comedies mixed social comment, lyricism, and ingenious clowning. (Museum of Modern Art Film Stills Archive)

GENTLEMEM
OUR
COUNTRY

HENRY FORD. AND HIS FIRST CAR.

the reach of almost everyone. The Model T projected a new lifestyle for the masses, implying a new kind of egalitarianism. It did so not in the name of political justice or social needs but in economic consumption.

To ensure the success of the Model T, Ford found ways to build it cheaply. He created a giant plant extending over sixty-five acres in Highland Park. He tried to cut back on dividends to stockholders in order to plow profits back into production. The whole process entailed a huge financial commitment because of the range and number of specialist tools required. The axis of mass production in Ford's factory was an assembly line, a conveyor belt running the entire length of a long nave along which hundreds of workmen performed specific, specialized tasks while the slow-moving conveyor belt carried the chassis to and from each workman. Coming in from the sides were feeder belts carrying such parts as carburetors, motor blocks, bolts and screws, windshields, batteries, gasoline tanks, and wheels. The idea of continuous movement depended on two principles: bringing the work to the worker and keeping the work waist high so that no one would have to stoop continuously to perform delicate tasks. It took almost seven years to perfect the system, standardizing processes and products and integrating supply industries. Successive refinements made it possible to reduce the time it took to produce a car. In 1920 a Model T ran off the production line once every minute; in 1925, once every ten seconds.

Ford produced the Model T for almost twenty years, from 1908 to 1927, never changing the basic design model, or even the body color—black. The Model T was sometimes known as the Tin Lizzie but more often as a "flivver"— so called because it shook the liver. Sales of Ford's Model T cars climbed steadily from twelve thousand cars in 1909 to nearly eight hundred thousand in 1917. By 1918 Ford had 50 percent of the U.S. market. Although Ford solved many problems of production, he created new ones. The assembly line created a new sort of workforce, one in which the old distinction between highly skilled and manual labor was becoming extinct since the largest number of employees performed repetitive tasks as assemblers. The degree of mechanization reduced workers to cogs in giant wheels; men were quickly trained, easily dispensed with, and frequently dissatisfied by the monotony of their work.

Although Henry Ford allowed only minor variations to his assembly line, his continuous reductions in price compensated for public weariness with the traditional design. The Model T cost $950 in 1909 and $290 in 1926. By improving production efficiency, Ford could increase output and thus sell automobiles at ever lower prices, thereby initiating successive cycles of greater production and lower costs. Advised that customers wanted a choice of body colors, he remarked, "They can have any color they want, so [long as] it's black." As a result of Ford's strategy, car ownership came within the reach, if not the grasp, of millions of Americans.

Ford's career showed how far the idea of business success had become keenly identified with the business of being American; it was the embodiment of America in an era of the continuing Industrial Revolution, made possible by the spirit of free enterprise and the product of loyalty to thrift, hard work, and self-reliance. Yet Ford was an uncharismatic eccentric whose personal life was marked by inconsistency: he was a cheating husband and an especially cruel father to his only son, Edsel. In his professional life he was arbitrary, jealous, and crack-brained.

Nevertheless, Ford's cars and those of his competitors took over the world. In 1909 auto manufacturers sold 4,192 passenger cars for a total of $4.89 million; in 1920 they sold 1.9 million cars for $1.8 billion. The impact was profound. It was not simply that the motor car took people and goods from one place to another. It transformed transport, eliminating the need for draught horses, their maintenance, their manure that stank up the city streets, and the clattering noise of their shoes on the street. The automobile made possible the development of the modern city beyond walking distance to a metropolis with a greater geographic size and endless suburbs. Cars also altered the streets and the buildings beside them. In place of a focal town center where offices and shops converged, they encouraged a series of centers within ever spreading towns whither people commuted by car or bus and linked by streets that turned into strips—series of single- or few-story buildings for diners, groceries, real estate sales, garages, and gas stations.

The value of the automobile industry, compared to the value of other industries, rose from 150th place in 1900 to first place in 1925, when it also accounted for 6 percent of the total value of American manufacturing. Furthermore, automobile production had three profound consequences in manufacturing: the further introduction of mass-assembly production; a greater emphasis on marketing, as distinct from sales; and executive management with flexible, centralized control. The auto industry also encouraged innovations in tributary industries. Because cars ideally required lighter metals, the steel industry developed various alloys. The need for more durable tires encouraged the rubber industry to make better-wearing materials. Detroit, in common with other cities concentrated on automobile production, grew dramatically. The motor capital grew by 126 percent during the decade 1910–20, a rate second only to that of Akron, the tire capital, at 173 percent.

The automobile led to the construction of major roads and highways. The extent of surface roads in America was 161,000 miles in 1905, increasing to 521,000 miles in 1925 and 1.52 million miles in 1945. At first, it was local authorities who built roads. Massachusetts had established a highway commission in 1893. By 1913 all the states had adopted similar legislation to that of Massachusetts. To pay for improved roads and to maintain a check on drivers, New York State established a car registration fee in 1904. In 1919 Oregon introduced a novel tax on gasoline. To provide better coordination between the states for interstate travel, Congress passed the Federal Aid Road Act of 1916, which provided federal aid for roads as national policy administered by the Bureau of Public Roads within the Department of Agriculture. The first appropriation was $5 million, based on an estimate of $10,000 of federal aid per mile of road construction, obliging the states to shoulder all maintenance costs after the roads had been built.

The Federal Aid Highway Act of 1921 reflected the opinion of lobby groups such as the Good Roads Movement, that all major centers of population should be linked by a truly federal road system. The new act required the federal government to distinguish between state and local highways, designating state highways eligible for federal funds but limited to 7 percent of the total road mileage in the state. The system was further divided between interstate roads that could not exceed three-sevenths of total mileage and the remainder, designated as intercounty roads. Federal aid was limited to 50 percent of the total estimated cost of construction.

The automobile also fueled the production of petroleum. Between 1900 and 1920 the petroleum industry grew rapidly in an already existing region of oil fields across a narrow strip 160 miles long, running from southwest to northeast in western Pennsylvania and New York. The strip included twenty thousand wells, pipelines, and refineries. And just as new markets for oil were being created, great sources of additional supply were discovered in California, Oklahoma, Texas, and the Lima field that ran across northeast Indiana and northwest Ohio, Kansas, and Illinois. In 1907 the new state of Oklahoma was the leading oil producer of all the states. By 1913 it produced a quarter of the nation's oil. By 1919 the United States, at 577 million barrels, was supplying two-thirds of all estimated world oil production. By the 1920s oil and gases refined from crude petroleum had over two hundred commercial uses, not only as lubricant, illuminant, and gasoline but also in paint, asphalt, and medicine. Oil was sixth among the country's industries, worth $2 billion in 1925.

The most widely applied form of energy at this stage of the Industrial Revolution was not oil but electricity, still a new form of physical energy, greater than the sum of all previous forms of energy. Mastery of electricity made it possible to apply energy in precise quantities, wherever it was needed—something impossible in the old days of steampower and waterpower. Electricity could provide light for a house, run a streetcar, work a sewing machine, and illuminate a skyscraper. Moreover, electric light could be transmitted for hundreds of miles, allowing manufacturers to choose the best sites for raw material, labor, and transportation, rather than having to remain close to supplies of coal, water, or oil.

By 1903 three electrical companies were operating more than one thousand central power stations that lit 1.25 million electric lights. The energy of electric power in manufacturing rose from 1.7 million horsepower in 1909 to 3.8 million horsepower in 1914. In 1914 energy produced by electric current accounted for 17.3 percent of all installed primary power in manufacturing. In the period 1914–19 installed primary power more than doubled, reaching 9.34 million horsepower, and this accounted for 31.6 percent of the total horsepower of manufacturing industries. In 1900–1920 public utility corporations adopted alternating current, requiring larger and more efficient generators driven by steam turbines or hydroelectric power. Increasingly, hydroelectric power established itself as the principal power source, with steam power used as an auxiliary source.

The Newlands Reclamation Act of 1902, as amended in 1906, included a clause allowing for a lease of surplus power from dams for irrigation. Power could be leased for up to ten years, and preference was given to municipal authorities over private companies. The Federal Water Power Act of 1920 limited licenses to hydroelectric power to fifty years and thus allowed for their eventual repossession by the federal government.

Journalist Mark Sullivan expressed the boundless optimism of Americans at the turn of the century excited by industrial progress. They favored a new interpretation of wealth and argued its more even distribution throughout society. Although Sullivan was writing about automobiles, he might have been expressing the concept that energy equaled wealth, as applied to new inventions from airplanes to movies and new means of power from electricity to oil.

> The new wealth was not in the form of things, it was in the form of energy, of power of action; it was atoms in motion. Since the new kind of wealth was essentially motion, it did not lend itself to amassing or withholding; it could come into being only through use, and the use of it necessarily enriched the user. The entrepreneurs of the new forms of wealth, the industrial leaders identified with it, could make profit for themselves only insofar as they conferred upon the average man the power inherent in electricity and in the internal combustion engine; they could only enrich themselves by persuading the average man to use the new forms of energy.

This interpretation of energy as wealth gained additional meaning in the Progressive Era. It took flight with the Wright brothers. Powered flight was a singular American achievement, just as the telephone, the phonograph, the incandescent light bulb, and the motion picture of Edison and Bell were quintessential American achievements. Without the perception and determination of Orville and Wilbur Wright, the airplane would never have come into existence. The development of powered airplanes in the period 1903–8 was also made possible by the convergence of a number of different lines of experimentation and innovation: the discovery and tapping of a fuel (petroleum), and finding ways of converting it to energy, and the development of lightweight aluminum, precision energy, and electrical power.

Flight pioneers Orville and Wilbur Wright were close brothers, sons of an affluent bishop of the United Brethren Church. They both left high school at age seventeen. Neither went to college. As to financial and technical support for their endeavor, the Wrights had only a bicycle shop, a small manufacturing and repair business, and the casual interest of a few friends. But they wanted to invent a powered airplane. The Wrights concentrated on gliding, rather than on powered planes, because they grew impatient at the waste of mounting delicate machinery on wings no one knew how to manage, and then seeing the whole fabric destroyed by clumsiness, miscalculation, or hostile elements.

As significant as the Wrights' invention of the plane was their mastering the physical act of flying. Without the practical experience of flying a plane, it would not have been possible for the Wrights and their successors to design and build ever more sophisticated planes. The practice of flight depended on natural laws and principles of physics to which man and his plane had to conform. The Wrights—like Edison, Bell, and Ford—applied cautious business methods to invention. All five approached their objective via an ordered system. They planned their route all the way from the first inkling of an idea to a finished invention with a minimum of waste. Thus, the Wright brothers avoided all pitfalls of previous aeronautic design, such as those of ill-fated aviation pioneer Samuel Langley. Wilbur understood from watching buzzards how a successful airplane would have to fly on three axes in order to incline from side to side, to ascend and descend, and to steer to left and right. Flight control was of prime importance. To achieve it, Wilbur devised gliders that could twist and adjust their wings—something like buzzards. In achieving three-axis control, Wilbur made a major contribution to aerodynamics and practical flight.

For their glider experiments, the Wrights chose Kitty Hawk in North Carolina, a region of rolling sand dunes. Having worked on major innovations in aircraft construction and having assembled scientific data, the brothers began to build a powered airplane with a total weight of 750 pounds and a 170-pound, twelve-horsepower gasoline engine. This, *Flyer 1*, subsequently known as the *Kitty Hawk*, was an entirely new biplane with a wingspan of 40 feet, 4 inches and a wing area of 510 square feet. The pilot lay prone on the lower wing beside the engine. The Wrights' first successful flight occurred when Orville flew the plane on December 17, 1903, at 10:35 A.M. He achieved a successful takeoff in wind of 20–22 miles per hour, flew for twelve seconds, attained a height of 120 feet, and landed successfully. Almost no one knew that man had flown a powered airplane.

The Wrights flew forty-nine flights in different planes between 1903 and 1905, ranging from 11 miles to 24.5 miles at an average speed of 38 miles per hour. They stopped all trials between October 16, 1905, and May 6, 1908, when they returned to Kitty Hawk with the much improved *Flyer III* and a posse of journalists assembled to witness the miracle of flight. Reporter Byron R. Newton's dispatch to the *New York Herald* of May 14, 1908, concluded: "With the ease and swiftness of a huge eagle, the Wright brothers' aeroplane made a flight of three miles at ten o'clock this morning. . . . There is no longer any ground for questioning the performance of the men and their wonderful machine."

In 1908 the Wrights began production of planes for the army under license. Other gifted inventors seized the initiative and continued to develop airplanes, including Alexander Graham Bell, who founded the Aerial Experiment Association (AEA) in October 1907. Bell's interest ensured wide publicity. But it was AEA cofounder, inventor Glenn Curtiss, a dour machinist from Hammondsport, New York, skilled in making and racing bicycles and motorcycles, who now emerged as the foremost airplane inventor. It was Curtiss's system, the aileron, rather than the Wrights' wing warping, that became the practical standard for the future. Curtiss also developed the first successful seaplane, *Flying Fish*.

Planes could open up the interior of North America with far greater flexibility than steamboats and railroads. The first regular air service in the United States began in Florida in 1914 when pilot Tony Janus established the St. Petersburg-Tampa Airboat Line with one tiny seaplane that carried one passenger at a time across Tampa Bay. On May 15, 1918, the first regular airmail service was inaugurated when two army pilots flew a Curtiss Jenny from Washington, D.C., to New York. In 1919 Eddie Hubbard began flying airmail from Seattle to Vancouver across the Canadian frontier in a single-engine seaplane. His first passenger, Bill Boeing, was the man who built the plane.

Not all inventions were as spectacular as airplane and automobile. But some lesser inventions transformed all societies and helped American manufacturing to penetrate the world. Mass society needed food in ever larger quantities that was easy to prepare—in fact, mass produced. In 1874 I. Solomon of Baltimore introduced pressure cooking for preserving food to be canned. The invention of the drop press by Allen Taylor (also in 1874) improved the sealing of cans, as did the flow machine (1876). From 1900 on, the open sanitary can eliminated faulty canning. In 1914 55 million cans of vegetables were sold around the world. *Collier's Weekly* of September 25, 1915, had an advertisement for Van Camp's Pork and Beans that offered to save the housewife "100 hours yearly"; Campbell's Soups wanted her "to get some fun out of life," now that it was not necessary for her to let the "three-meal-a-day problem tie you down to constant drudgery." Between 1890 and 1917 the chilling and transportation of frozen foods expanded greatly. Kelvinator Corporation and the Frigidaire Corporation began the production of small-scale refrigerators for family homes in the decade 1910–20. By 1927 more than 2 million refrigerators were in use.

Mass society also moved to new standards of personal hygiene. In 1903 King Camp Gillette, inventor of the safety razor, produced 51 razors and 168 blades. This revolution became a flood. In 1904 Gillette's factory manufactured 90,000 razors and 12.4 million blades. In the decade beginning with 1910, he had factories in Britain, France, Germany, and Canada. Thus, men no longer had to scrape facial fuzz with dangerous strop razors; instead, they could use a reliable method of shaving that transformed standards of hygiene and taste.

In 1907 immigrant industrial chemist Leo H. Baekeland transformed phenol and formaldehyde into Bakelite, a moldable black or brown plastic that could substitute for celluloid, as well as for rubber and shellac in electrical insulators, pens, and buttons. A later generation of inventors in the 1930s recognized its possibilities for sculptured use on cars and planes to give them a streamlined look. However, as plastic aged, it became brittle. Ironically, although designers at the turn of the century thought that plastic would turn America's towns into an environment of startling artificial beauty, by the second half of the century, the very word *plastic* conjured up everything critics thought wrong with American culture and the nation's soul.

Since many inventions changed indoors more than outdoors, they revolutionized the lives of women more than men. Besides canned food, these included vacuum cleaners and new kitchen cookers. *Cosmopolitan* of June 1915 had an advertisement for a manufacturer of vacuum cleaners, promising "Push the Button—and Enjoy the Springtime!" The drift of advertisements was that by buying such products as Wizard Polish and Minute Tapioca, women would have more time to enjoy themselves at leisure outside the family home. A woman in *Ladies Home Journal* for April 1918 told her friend, "I don't have to hurry nowadays. I have a Florence Automatic Oil Stove in my kitchen." The mighty pull of advertising began in earnest, getting prospective customers to buy, getting present consumers to buy again, and enticing them all with arguments on three lines: sexual attraction, retaining their children's love, and asserting feelings of social superiority.

What the public school was to education, the department store was to manufacturing and commerce: a warehouse of American values as well as American goods. Taking advantage of the new speed and reliability of transportation for mass-market distribution, entrepreneurs such as Marshall Field in Chicago and John Wanamaker in Philadelphia expanded their range of merchandise from dry goods to jewelry, china and glassware, furniture and foodstuffs, and toys and clothing. Many German Jews, such as Adam Gimbel, entered the business and became experts in marketing, using fixed low prices without bartering, money-back guarantees, and enticing window displays to lure and retain customers. Among this new generation were Isidor and Nathan Strauss, who bought the New York–based firm R. H. Macy in 1888, moved it from Fourteenth Street to Thirty-Fourth Street and Broadway, and expanded it successively until it was the largest department store in the world.

There were mass-produced objects, both elegant and utilitarian; the ready processing of immediately available food; and the expanding city's function as a market for mass consumption; but perhaps no big-city pleasures appealed to a wider selection of people than the automat, the harbinger of fast food and fantasy in a cafe. The Horn and Hardart Company of Philadelphia opened the first automat in New York at 1557 Broadway in Times Square on July 2, 1912. The automat became an American recreational mainstay and a cultural icon through midcentury. English child immigrant (and later actress) Claire Bloom first sampled the Horn and Hardart Automat on West Fifty-Seventh Street in Manhattan opposite Steinway Hall in the 1940s when automats were at the height of their popularity. Her words (1996) ring true for the previous decades:

> The walls of the vast eating area were lined with metal containers bearing glass windows, in which rested every imaginable food available; delicious and delectable pies, both sweet and savory, Salisbury steak with gravy, macaroni and cheese, Boston "pork and beans" baked in their own earthenware crock, frothy lemon meringue pies, and glistening iced angel food or coconut layer cakes. Single portions could be freed from their glass prisons by inserting nickels into the slots; the win-

dows would fly open, leaving the hungry customer—in this instance me—to simply remove her chosen plate of food, ready to plunge in.

Cathedrals of Commerce

Before any goods could be bought, mass production—whether of cars, plastic, or anything else—depended on scientific management, a phrase made popular by lawyer Louis D. Brandeis of Boston in 1910. Scientific management was synonymous with the name of Philadelphia engineer Frederick A. W. Taylor. Taylor was among the first to use methodical analysis to help management review the work process. He devised schemes to eliminate the possibility of workers' producing less than their maximum attainable rate. Taylor based his system on four principles: research, standardization, control, and cooperation. He recommended wider use and standardization of machine tools and increased managerial control of the routing of materials and scheduling of machines. Few managements adopted Taylorism in its entirety, but many drew freely from Taylor's ideas.

Superb industrial organization allowed large industries to achieve economies of scale in production, distribution, and marketing. Already, many important industries were dominated by a few large corporations that often controlled the source of raw materials and certainly did their own purchasing, production, and distribution. Big business used large numbers of workers. To operate, maintain, and rebuild large factories, it attracted larger investment from more people. Big business used complex technology. Many factories now had far higher costs than before and were thus reliant on regular levels of operation to achieve low costs per unit of output. Thereafter, ownership and management separated. Because it was necessary to raise large sums of money to fund a company, ownership was dispersed among a large number of investors. Firms were run by a new tier of salaried managers, professionals who usually had little or no ownership of the business. Big business abandoned narrow specialization, expanding its range of functions to achieve vertical integration. Big business was characterized by an elaborate managerial structure to coordinate different, interrelated activities.

The makers of complex machines began to create extensive marketing organizations almost from the beginning and soon became global enterprises. In 1917 the total number of leading companies in electrical machinery, transportation, equipment, and machinery was fifty-eight. This was a quarter of all manufacturing firms in the United States with assets of more than $20 million. The leaders in machinery making included Singer Manufacturing, Remington Typewriter, Burroughs Adding Machine, Deere and Company, Moline Plow, Babcock and Wilcox, Otis Elevator, Mergenthaler Linotype, and Westinghouse Electric.

Modern business enterprise reflected an organizational response to changes in new processes of production and means of distribution. Thus, the perfection of high-volume processes in such industries as oil and chemicals, rubber and glass, metals and machinery, and food led to an enormous volume of production.

Changes in communication increased demand. Changes in transportation revolutionized distribution. Manufacturers now integrated mass production with mass distribution. The result was a whole series of giant industrial enterprises little affected by public policy or shaped by individual entrepreneurial talents or, even, capital markets.

The promoters of these enterprises were, however, obsessed with image. The great commercial enterprises were eager to invest in impressive buildings, ever taller skyscrapers, as potent symbols of their might. Skyscrapers combined new technologies in buildings at the service of corporate needs—functional, decorative, and rudimentary marketing of prestige. They represented a new American civilization of business ambition and human determination to excel as they turned America's major cities into manmade vertical canyons. It was as if, says *New York Times* architecture critic Paul Goldberger in a review (1996), that the entrepreneurs ordered their architects: "Make it show the world we are in charge, that we have arrived," much as soaring Gothic cathedrals were statements of arrogance and power in medieval Europe.

In the 1880s progressive architects, enthusiastic about the invention of the elevator, had started experimenting with buildings beyond ten stories. Ever higher buildings created new problems—greater loads and thicker masonry walls. Although more substantive foundations and iron piers could support heavier loads, there was a price: far less interior space, especially at ground level—the most valuable retail floor. Architects and builders experimented with structural iron and steel to reduce the size of walls and piers. Hence, it was the new technology of engineering, based on improved processes of steel and the construction of bridges, that made skyscrapers possible. Skyscrapers were not built by placing one stone on top of one another but by erecting a great steel frame with an outer sheath of brick or stone, glass and wood. Before air conditioning, a skyscraper had to become a tower in order to provide offices access to air. Ironically, as they were developing the cultural phenomenon of modern skyscrapers, architects had precious little idea exactly how to build them.

The most distinguished among the first generation of skyscraper architects was Louis Sullivan, who believed that a building should express a total cultural purpose. Buildings were not just physical enclosures. They were there to convey their own emotional presence as people inhabited or simply moved through or by them. The seminal Chicago partnership of Sullivan with engineer Dankmar Adler from 1883 to 1895 was a perfect complement of mind and method. Adler ensured that their buildings were well constructed with respect to acoustics, struc-

FACING PAGE:

The Woolworth Building, New York, by Cass Gilbert (1913). By an adroit mix of modern engineering and Gothic ornament, Gilbert adorned his capacious commercial building with an impression of delicacy. The lower building to the left is the Municipal Building, now demolished. (Photo by Irving Underhill; Library of Congress)

Woolworth Bldg. from Municipal Bldg. 61830
Copyright 1922 by Irving Underhill
N.Y.C.

tural engineering, and spatial plan. Sullivan ensured that they had a clear aesthetic identity. Sullivan's Schlesinger & Mayer Department Store of 1901–4 (later known as the Carson, Pirie, Scott & Company Building) exploited the possibilities of new steel frames to the fullest with a layered grid pattern that allowed a continuous flow of horizontal space through its large windows and also revealed the beams, columns, piers, and spandrels that supported the structure. Here was the origin of the glass-curtain wall that became a central feature of modern architecture.

Between 1900 and 1917 New York took the lead in skyscraper construction. In comparison with idealist Louis Sullivan, the more commercially successful architect-businessman Daniel H. Burnham was a born compromiser. Burnham understood the significance of the great merger movement. He also knew that if he were to cash in on the trend to gigantic commercial organizations, he would have to cover the aggressive new technology with pretentious historicist facades. His triangular Flatiron Building (1903) in New York was a striking achievement more on account of its remarkable shape, dictated by its site at the junction of Broadway and Fifth Avenue, than for its ornate covering of French Renaissance ornament. Viewed from the north, it looked like a powerful ocean liner.

Other successful compromisers included Charles Follen McKim, William Rutherford Mead, and Stanford White, who championed historicist architecture as taught at the Ecole des Beaux Arts in Paris. The school's policy, shaped in the reign of Louis XIV, aimed to produce French art as a standardized high-quality product that combined beauty, clear planning, and pragmatism. When the firm of McKim, Mead, and White won a commission to design New York's Municipal Building (1913), they tried to create a skyscraper that would be a classicizing civic monument, but the result had the stylistic hallmarks of a wedding cake. Prolific and extravagant, Stanford White was known as a master of effects, an impresario of architecture, as skilled in interior decoration as he was as a designer of buildings.

Architects Napoleon Le Brun and sons mixed old and new in the Metropolitan Life Tower in New York, constructed in 1909, producing a replica of the Campanile of St. Mark's in Venice. They achieved a handsome skyscraper, rising narrow and free with a clock face three stories high, a welcoming symbol of the benign face of capitalism.

Architect Cass Gilbert's Woolworth Building of 1913, rising to 792 feet, enjoyed the title of tallest building in the world for seventeen years. Its soaring mix of modern engineering and Gothic ornament inspired the epithet "Cathedral of Commerce" that delighted its chain-store owner F. W. Woolworth and which he used as the title for a brochure of 1917 about the building. Reverend S. Parker Cadman wrote, "Just as religion monopolized art and architecture during the medieval epoch, so commerce has engrossed the United States since 1865." The *New York Times* reporter contrasted the nickels and dimes of the customers who had, in effect, paid for the design, and the rags-to-riches success of Woolworth himself. Cass Gilbert realized that medieval Gothic architecture could be successfully molded to very tall modern buildings because it emphasized the skeletal structure within the outer stone sheath.

The new cathedrals of commerce would have been no more than individual curiosities if they had not had encouraged successful imitations at the vernacular level. Moreover, certain architects continued to believe in masonry buildings covered with Renaissance detailing. One such was Hungarian immigrant Emery Roth of Stein, Cohen, and Roth in New York. Roth's first major commission was the Belleclaire, an apartment building with a round corner tower, decorated with ornamental arches, built on Broadway at Seventy-Seventh Street in 1903. From 1903 to the 1930s Roth and his company filled New York City with a hundred such apartment buildings, including the San Remo and the Beresford on Central Park West. They combined details from various periods of Italian architecture with the new, overall massing of twentieth-century skyscrapers.

Offices in tall buildings depended on new means of communication and illumination—typewriter, telephone, elevator, and electric light—all invented in the 1870s. The interior space of such buildings created for architects and designers as many problems as the exteriors, partly because of the buildings' many functions and partly to avoid any sense of claustrophobia.

America's most famous twentieth-century architect, Frank Lloyd Wright, was determined to rid his buildings of any sense of confinement within a closed box. When he designed his first major commission, the Larkin Building of 1903–4, in Buffalo, New York, he realized that the four supporting towers did not need to stand at the corners of any four-sided building. By moving the towers and using twice as many, he could open the corners of the box, thereby allowing air, light, and people to circulate throughout the building. At the same time, he used the towers to provide such services as ventilation, plumbing, and conduits for electrical wiring. From the start, people recognized the Larkin building as a creative way of organizing space. Those who worked there enjoyed its sense of spatial freedom, although, ironically, it was also the first hermetically sealed, air-conditioned building in the world. The newly positioned towers supported the walls and floors on a cantilever principle that Wright liked to demonstrate by a tray balanced on the upturned fingers of a waiter. The fingers are the cantilevers that take the load as they are spread and balance it, while the arm acts as the central support. Not only was the cantilever system economical in its use of materials, but it was also flexible and capable of bearing shifting loads. The most spectacular proof of Wright's conviction came when Wright's cantilevered Imperial Hotel (1916–22) in Tokyo, Japan, survived an elsewhere devastating earthquake of 1923 without damage.

While skyscrapers gave their inhabitants opportunities to enjoy air and sky, they darkened the streets for the huddled masses below. The congestion of New York at ground level was legendary. From that crowding there supposedly followed ideas, energy, and power. But even at the turn of the century, it was a far from comfortable environment. In response to public and corporate concern about the massive bulk of the Equitable Building at 120 Broadway, planner John M. Carrere drew up a scheme to restrict tall buildings in New York within the limits of a plane that passed at an angle of twenty degrees from the vertical on the opposite sidewalk. Hence, the city's zoning laws provided the twenty-degree envelope within which a building could rise, encouraging architects and their sponsors toward so-called setback skyscrapers that allowed sunlight to reach the streets below. However, when New York first turned the proposal into a zoning law in 1916, it did so less to protect the public interest in access to air and sky than to safeguard the owners of commercial buildings who feared the consequence if every city block was developed on the lines of the Equitable. For then every building would be in shadow, and they would all fall in value. The zoning law also regulated the number of occupants permitted in any one building. Other cities adopted the principles of Carrere's plan.

The New York zoning laws inspired architects to create ever higher towers within the letter of the law, partly to achieve greater plasticity of form. The New York Telephone Company or Barclay-Vesey Building (1922–26) by Ralph Walker was one such. The site was in the shape of a parallelogram, thus inducing Walker to introduce, through successive designs, a twist between the base of the building and the Gothic, art-nouveau tower, supported by the raised, surrounding setbacks.

Not only were skyscrapers impressive for those who watched them rise from the ground, but the vistas they opened up from on high also changed people's perceptions as well as their vantage points. As skyscrapers rose ever higher, and people looked down from above, they saw the world laid flat like a pattern with the ground plan of the modern city turned into a map and yet containing the movement of people, carriages, and automobiles. This ground plan provided the space in which the most progressive American art would unfold.

Despite its success as a technological achievement and an advertisement, to its critics the skyscraper represented the dominance of the machine over man, an urban environment in which the community spirit had declined. Novelist Henry James, returning to America from Europe after an absence of twenty years, was disturbed by profound changes in the urban scene. He described his arrival in *The American Scene* (1907), explaining how shocked he was by the skyline, through which "monsters of greed" had transformed Manhattan into "a huge, jagged city." It was—as expressed in the title of a popular song—"The City Where Nobody Cares."

Other songs of the period, such as "Give My Regards to Broadway" (George Cohan, 1904) and "Shine on Harvest Moon" (Nora Bayres and Jack Norworth, 1908), suggested that the city was more attractive, and these songs had both more immediate and more lasting appeal. Such songs reflect the fact that growing numbers of Americans were living and working in major cities. By 1920, when the total U.S. population was 106.46 million, the city had surpassed the countryside with 54.15 million people living in urban areas and 51.55 million living in rural areas. It was already apparent in 1910 that big-city life was attracting ever more people since 8.5 million lived in cities with a population above 1 million, 3.01 million lived in cities of above 500,000, and 12 million lived in cities between 50,000 and 500,000.

Despite America's astonishing prowess in tall buildings, it was only established cities, such as New York and Chicago, that boasted skyscrapers, and then only in the downtown areas. The new cities, such as Los Angeles, were ever expanding, wide geographical areas characterized by low density of settlement. In fact, the new city of Los Angeles provided the model spatial plan of a typical twentieth-century city—a city dominated by the automobile. By 1920 Los Angeles was the tenth largest city in the nation with a population of 577,000. A warm climate and the presence of oil made the city attractive to investors, residents, and light manufacturers, turning Los Angeles into a capital of fruit and vegetables, motion picture production (and, beginning in the 1940s, aircraft, aerospace, and war research industries). Oil revenues contributed to the cost of constructing an ocean port at Long Beach and rail connections to the East and the rest of the Southwest. The new transportation infrastructure made Los Angeles a preferred site for warehouses and branch plants of such national corporations as Ford and Goodyear.

The single-family house was attractive to Angelenos—and to others across America—because of skillful real estate marketing; because of encouragement from the profitable construction, transportation, and utilities industries; and because of the craze for automobiles and the freedom of individual movement they made possible. The creation of endless suburbia depended on extensive provision of water and other public utilities—as well as on cars and roads on which to drive them. Speculators also built a complex of interurban streetcars with lines extending twenty, thirty, thirty-five miles from the city center. People in cities were well aware that they were cutting themselves off from their rural roots. And among them, socially conscious Progressives were concerned about the standard of city life. But the popular songs that sold well—such as "Give My Regards to Broadway" and "Shine on Harvest Moon"—sold well in part because they eased the shock. They also represented something else: metropolitan show business.

The Custom of the Country

During the twentieth century American popular culture became highly commercialized, with commodities mass produced by a multinational entertainment industry. It existed through a complex web of live performance in theaters, concert halls, and auditoriums; sheet music; performances recorded on disk and film; performances on radio (starting in 1920) and television (1936–39 and after 1945); and a complex network of distribution. The beginnings of this development can be traced back to the early twentieth century when a stream of new music styles and the new invention of the phonograph altered popular music.

Music publishing was dominated by companies based in New York, first located on Twenty-Eighth Street between Sixth Avenue and Broadway. This was Tin Pan Alley, where companies like Thomas B. Harms, Inc., Willis Woodward, and Isidore Widmark typified a profitable business of writing and publishing songs on the basis of extensive market research. Songwriters were salaried employees rather than freelance artists. Market research was carried out by song pluggers, who played drafts of songs to audiences in theaters, department stores, and sheet music shops. Tin Pan Alley itself changed its location to West Forty-Second Street (1903–8), then to West Forty-Fifth Street (1911–19), then to near Forty-Ninth Street in the 1920s. By that time its omnibus name "Tin Pan Alley" was synonymous with popular music.

FACING PAGE:

Art and Entertainment, high and low, when the American Renaissance was in full flower

Upper left: Elie Nadelman, *Dancing Figure* (1916–18), gold leaf on bronze, 29½" × 12" × 11½". Polish expatriate sculptor Elie Nadelman fled to New York in 1914, where his refined works, reducing the human form to a series of elegant curves, won him the patronage of Helena Rubinstein. (Collection of Whitney Museum of American Art)

Upper right: By his Wild West show, Buffalo Bill Cody transformed the rough-hewn cattle herder of the 1870s from his shaggy, unkempt reputation into the cowboy of legend, recreating the taming of the West in the form of a traveling circus that enthralled eastern America and western Europe up to World War I and defined the myth of the western for the twentieth century. (Publicity photo; John Rylands University Library of Manchester)

Lower right: The Midway, the section of the Buffalo Exposition (1901) that provided entertainment, refreshment, and relief, played its part in the official cult of white supremacy with an outsize white head inviting visitors to enter a dreamland of minstrel shows and fantastic voyages. (Photo by C. D. Arnold; Library of Congress)

Lower left: Henry James by John Singer Sargent (1913). It was inevitable that Sargent, the most famous American portrait painter of the day and a master of the surface glamor and inherent superiority of Edwardian society, should meet and paint Henry James, the novelist who captured the shifting quicksand of expatriate society and the paradoxes underneath. (National Portrait Gallery, London)

In 1900 the music business was primarily a matter of selling sheet music to a piano-playing public. Publishers used the nationwide circuit of vaudeville halls to publicize their latest songs. The combined forces of music talent and market research for Tin Pan Alley produced a succession of bestselling songs that became firmly fixed in the emerging popular culture: for example, "My Gal Sal" (Paul Dresser, brother of novelist Theodore Dreiser, 1905), "By the Light of the Silvery Moon" (Gus Edwards, 1909), and "When Irish Eyes Are Smiling" (Ernest R. Ball, 1912). The typical Tin Pan Alley song had simple melodies and consisted of verses and a repeated chorus. These features defined the basic form of popular songs for the twentieth century. Lyrics referred to the city not as the city where nobody cares but as a warm, lively place, or they recalled memories of a country childhood with affection.

Even while Tin Pan Alley ruled popular taste, however, ragtime was transforming popular music. In their ragtime pieces, or "rags," African American composers drew on the precise rhythms and classical harmonies of European marches, the syncopated rhythms of African American dances such as the cakewalk, and the zest of early African American music as played on the banjo and by itinerant brass bands. The interest and excitement of ragtime derived from the contrast between the syncopated, "ragged" rhythm of the right hand playing off the beat and the symmetrical march rhythms of the left hand. Ragtime could be heard in black cabarets, first on midtown Manhattan's West Side and later in Harlem at Leroy's, Barron's, and elsewhere, from the scintillating fingertips of pianist Eubie Blake, Willie ("the Lion") Smith, and Jelly Roll Morton. The leading composer was classically trained African American composer Scott Joplin, "king of ragtime writers," who wrote the first popular ragtime tune, "Maple Leaf Rag," in 1899. And it was sheet music sales of ragtime that made the first huge commercial profits for the music industry: Joplin's "Maple Leaf Rag" sold more than 1 million copies.

Ragtime was not universally popular. Older folk disapproved of it as a pernicious influence on young people; whites disapproved because it was black music; blacks disapproved because it was associated with cabarets and brothels and because they considered the lyrics no better than racial slurs. Hence, ragtime was banned from school concerts. Yet the spreading popularity of ragtime allowed African American composers to penetrate Tin Pan Alley, including Shelton Brooks with "Some of These Days" (1910), a typical song of the new sensibility that treated rejection in love to raunchy complaisance. Vaudeville adapted itself to the new crazes. In a career that began with Ziegfeld's Follies in Hartford, Connecticut, in 1909 Russian-Jewish immigrant chanteuse Sophie Tucker acquired "Some of These Days" and turned it into a signature song that she belted out in sundry places with seasoned abandon. Thereafter, she relished her reputation as "the last of the red-hot mamas" in a career of sixty-two years that included burlesque and nightclubs as well as vaudeville.

Ragtime also entered mainstream culture. In 1911 Russian-American composer Irving Berlin contributed music and lyrics for *Alexander's Ragtime Band*, a show that incorporated ragtime within its revue framework. In the following decade ragtime encouraged new dances, including the turkey trot, the fox trot, and the tango, all of which became the rage for the middle classes, especially when led by James Reese Europe for dancers Vernon and Irene Castle. The widespread appeal of new dances prompted the building of special dance floors at restaurants, now known as lobster palaces.

Yet, ragtime declined as public enthusiasm for the phonograph broadened the arena of popular music. In 1900 there were 100 companies in America making pianos. In 1920 phonograph companies pressed over 100 million records or disks. In 1920 the old cylinder system was replaced by the grooved disk, and Columbia and the Victor Talking Machine Company mass produced record players. As recorded on phonograph disk, music became both a consumer item and a manufactured product. It was no longer necessary to be able to play the piano in order to have an evening of home entertainment. Alongside the phonograph revolution, a second, more potent musical infusion from the African American community, jazz, succeeded and displaced ragtime.

The term *jazz* first appeared in print around 1915, but it had been previously used in the early 1900s to mean sexual intercourse. *Jass* was also Elizabethan slang, meaning to perform anything with enthusiasm or gusto. It later became the basis for the expression "to jazz it up." The term *jaser* may have been imported from West Africa, where it was derived from *jaiza*, referring to the rumbling of distant drums. Whatever its origins, the first recorded jazz music was by the Original Dixieland Jazz Band in 1917. In its earliest stages, jazz mixed many styles—West African rhythms, European church and dance music and marches, and American spirituals and ragtime. However, jazz was always played with a pronounced beat or emotional pulse. Another major influence, blues, had developed after the Civil War from spirituals and work songs but with lyrics that were personal rather than religious. Not only did the blues have a distinctive twelve-measure progression, but they also used so-called blue notes—the lowered 3rd, 5th, and 7th degrees of a key—sung with emotional intensity. The tragicomic flavor of many blues lyrics combined bitterness with irony as in singer Bessie Smith's "Outside of That" with the words, "He blackened my eyes / I couldn't see / Then he pawned the things / He gave to me."

The commercial success of jazz propelled dynamic black artists into the white entertainment industry. The band leader who exercised the most decisive influence on the future direction of jazz did so more as an impresario than as a musician—Fletcher ("Smack") Henderson. Other leading African American talents included cornet and trumpet player Louis ("Satchmo") Armstrong, saxophonist Coleman Hawkins, and arranger and sax player Don Redman, all of whom became leading jazz artists in the 1920s. They were also specialists in New Orleans jazz, so called because many of the artists migrated from the Storyville section of New Orleans that the authorities closed down in 1917. Jazz was drawn into the mainstream of American popular music just as the demand for gramophone records necessitated an expanded supply of popular and diverse music.

Whereas staid English music critic Ernest Newman called jazz "musical insanity," a product of "breathlessness and boredom," American band leader Paul Whiteman termed it "the folk music of the machine age." It was precisely that— and much more. Jazz, like ascending in skyscrapers, was a new sensation. Its form was different from that of any classical or popular music hitherto, giving greater freedom of expression and making higher demands on its interpreters, for a central characteristic of jazz was improvisation. This improvisation was not entirely spontaneous but rather reworked by leading instrumentalists from their repertoires to produce an original synthesis. Combined with the new technology and the new marketing of music in sheet music, phonograph disks, and soon radio and movies, jazz penetrated every house. It introduced African American artists into mainstream popular entertainment and suffused cities with its insinuating musical cadences, potent sexual allure, and primitive expressions of pain and joy.

The phonograph not only popularized the strains of jazz but also changed the fortunes of classical music, especially vocal music. The most popular classical interpretive artist in the Progressive Era was Neapolitan tenor Enrico Caruso, world renowned but indelibly associated with the Metropolitan Opera in New York, after he made his debut on the opening night of the 1903 season as the Duke in Verdi's *Rigoletto*. His tenor voice was unusual for its lyricism, strength, and suppleness and for the warmth of its lower register. Not only was Caruso the Met's most famous artist, but he also exercised a decisive influence on the fortunes of phonographic disks, their comparatively short length in the 78 rpm format being admirably suited to display his most charming features. His recording of "Vesti la giubba" from Leoncavallo's *Pagliacci* was the first to sell a million copies, and his vocal bloom, style, and élan set the standard for all tenors who followed him.

As to pictures without words, in 1910 there were at least five thousand nickelodeon theaters in the United States, special theaters where pianists accompanied movies with improvised music. The invention of motion pictures was a classic instance of the simultaneity of invention. To Americans the crucial breakthrough was Thomas Alva Edison's Kinetoscope in 1893; to Europeans, the Cinématographe of the Lumière brothers. But it was American movies that conquered the world. Edison took the credit for inventing motion pictures overall, whereas others invented the key parts. In 1889 his assistant, William Dickson, built the kinetophonograph, a projector that flashed pictures on a screen in synchronization with a phonographic disk. George Eastman invented the sprocketed celluloid film. Edison cameraman Edwin S. Porter used camera, action, and shots to move freely between different locations by so-called elliptical editing to emphasize fluid movement, psychological focus, and energy, notably in *The Great Train Robbery* (1903). But Edison himself remained the pivotal player. He opened the first indoor film studio at 41 East Twenty-First Street, New York, in 1901. As with so many other inventions, financial backers understood that Edison's name would assure public confidence.

Edison and these backers realized that making films was insufficient without owning exhibition as well as production. Without exhibition, it would be impossible to maximize profits and control markets. Accordingly, in 1896 Edison and his financiers acquired the rights to the Vitascope and thereafter teamed up with, bought out, or blocked competitors. Between 1909 and 1917 Edison led a vicious monopoly, the Motion Picture Patents Company. Within a few months, two dissatisfied members, Carl Laemmle in New York and William Swanson in Chicago, broke free, urged the growth of independent producers, and initiated a war against the trust.

Various other entrepreneurs besides Edison also recognized that producing, exhibiting, and distributing films must be a truly integrated process. Russian-Jewish immigrant Louis B. Mayer of Boston lost his scrap metal business in the recession of 1907 and started working in the Hub, a nickelodeon on Dover Street. He studied the crude features and noted what formulas pleased the mainly immigrant public. Thereby he learned to anticipate public taste before opening his own nickelodeon, the Gem, in Haverhill, Massachusetts. Among Mayer's various ventures was the Jesse Lasky Feature Film Company, a partnership that included Samuel Goldfish (later Goldwyn) and playwright Cecil Blount DeMille as well as Mayer and Lasky. In 1913 Cecil B. DeMille, now a director, made *The Squaw Man* in a barn on what was to become Hollywood Boulevard. Southern California soon became the base of film production by the independents for a variety of reasons. It had powerful scenic attractions of desert, mountains, and ocean and an even and reliable supply of sunshine. It was far removed from the trust's wrecking crews in New York and close to the Mexican border and escape. By 1915 producers Carl Laemmle, William Fox, Samuel Goldfish, and Adolph Zukor had given definitive form to film programs with a major feature film supported by one or two short films and the promotion of leading players as stars. The creators of Hollywood knew they had to develop powerful theater chains and all-encompassing distribution networks, nationwide and internationally. As part of the process, Carl Laemmle invented the star system, luring Florence Lawrence ("The Biograph Girl") and then Mary Pickford to his independent motion picture company, known as Universal from 1906 on.

Three directors transformed movies: Mack Sennett, Charlie Chaplin, and David Wark Griffith.

Impresario Mack Sennett, off-screen police chief of the Keystone Cops, turned human beings into imperfect mechanical toys at odds with their surroundings. Inspired by the technical wizardry of camera and film, Sennett drew the maximum comic possibilities from falling buildings, colliding automobiles, and close-flung custard pies, partly through comic invention, precise timing, and slow shooting but fast projection.

Whether as mimic or writer, director or producer, Charlie Chaplin exerted a long-lasting influence over cinema. Having invented and perfected his silent-screen Little Tramp, a nimble clown with bowler hat and twirling cane who turned slapstick into something endearing and deft, Chaplin moved into social satire with picturesque exaggeration in such two-reelers as *Easy Street, The Cure,* and *The Immigrant* (all 1917). In the 1920s he broadened the canvas and softened the comment in full-length masterpieces: *The Gold Rush* (1925), *The Circus* (1928), and *City Lights* (1930). Whether courting, married, or divorced, Chaplin had few peers in the other function of film stars, as a newspaper subject for gossip and innuendo about his sex life.

David Wark Griffith created the first masterpiece of the American cinema for Reliance-Majestic, the Civil War epic *The Birth of a Nation* (1915). "History written in lightning" was how Woodrow Wilson described *The Birth of a Nation.* It stunned viewers with its advanced cinematic techniques, notably the complex editing of long shots and close-ups to achieve frenetic climaxes. People admired the historical pageant, appreciated D. W. Griffith's craft, and found themselves moved by intimate moments and scandalized by Griffith's romanticization of the infamous Ku Klux Klan and his denigration of African Americans. The outsize commercial success of *Birth of a Nation* provided distributor Louis B. Mayer with a profit of six hundred thousand dollars, the financial base of his future operations. However, the commercial failure of Griffith's equally dazzling technical triumph, *Intolerance* (1916), a multithreaded religioso protest piece, put Griffith in debt. He resurfaced with less ambitious but more evocative films for United Artists, such as *Broken Blossoms* (1919) and *Way Down East* (1920). His themes were social disruption and reunification, the destructive forces of sexual license, religious hypocrisies, and social violence.

As to the showcases, movie theaters expanded to become outsize, opulent auditoriums with comfortable, padded chairs. The first movie palace was the Regent Theater (1913, seating 1,800) on 116th Street, New York. Designed by Thomas W. Lamb after the Doge's Palace in Venice, it was managed by Samuel L. ("Roxy") Rothafel, who subsequently acquired a chain of New York cinemas. In New York Lamb also designed the Strand (1914, seating 3,000), the Rivoli (1917, seating 2,000), and the Capitol (1919, seating 5,000). For their movie palaces, architects appropriated and mixed the styles of Baroque Spain, ancient Egypt, and Bourbon France. Inside such hallowed portals of illusion, Roxy Rothafel added live symphony orchestras, variety acts, and ballets to the screening of movies.

Movies were not just a new form of entertainment that would take its place alongside theater and vaudeville. Movies were a mass entertainment. They also had profound consequences for fashion, moral values, and feeding people's subconscious desires. Furthermore, they were a means of education, not simply because they could disseminate news, propaganda, and history through storytelling, but also because of the way they presented American society to itself and the world—energetic, fun-loving, immaculate, spacious. All the way from New York to San Francisco people saw and copied for themselves glamorous standards of modern appearance by way of stars' clothes, hairstyles, and slimness. The movie producers' marketing of artists like exotic perfumes led to the promotion of Theodosia Goodman of Chicago as Theda Bara, the first "vamp"—short for *vampire*—in *A Fool There Was* (1915). Supposedly an Arabian siren descended from the seven Cleopatras of ancient Egypt, Bara fed off men's desires.

Extraordinary though it seems, the panda bear eye makeup of Theda Bara that later generations were to find so amusing forecast the significance of the face on the screen for the millions of viewers enthralled by Hollywood films. When John Gregory Dunne, screenwriter for *Up Close and Personal* (1996), a film starring Robert Redford and Michelle Pfeiffer, exasperated by seven years of writing, rewriting, and delays, asked producer Scott Rudin what the picture was really all about, Rudin's reply hit the nail on the head: "It's about two movie stars." Columnist Larry Gelbart, reviewing Dunne's account of his travails, *Monster: Living Off the Big Screen* (1997), interpreted the movie star phenomenon in a sly parody of the book of Genesis:

> In the beginning was the word. However, that applied merely to all of Creation. The first line in the Hollywood bible states: in the beginning was the Face. The face of the star. From [Mary] Pickford to Pfeiffer, from [Buster] Keaton to [Tom] Cruise, it has been the stars, that select group of former mortals, who are responsible for drawing the masses into the movie houses. Their faces and physiques, and not for one moment any of the words they say. The stars are blessed, according to Robert Towne, with having "features that are ruthlessly efficient," with being able to convey a staggering amount of information without ever opening their mouths.

The combination of new technology producing new textiles, new demands for what was practical and convenient, and the allure of cinema changed fashions, in particular women's fashions, dramatically in the years from 1910 to 1920. The decade 1900–1910 had been famous for elaborate fashions, with affluent women forcing their figures into tight steel corsets to give them tiny waists and ample figures above and below, aided by frills, padding, and trailing skirts. They crowned the whole effect with long, luxurious hairstyles. The ideal of feminine beauty was still the Gibson girl with billowy figure and billowing hair, as idealized in artist Charles Dana Gibson's drawings of his wife.

In the decade 1910–20 fashion changed irreversibly. Mass production led not only to uniformity and simplicity in clothes but also (and paradoxically) to greater variety by way of textures, styles, and colors and to more types of clothes for different occasions—professional, formal, and casual. It dawned on the clothing industry, the "rag trade," that women grew up to wear certain dress sizes, seven of which would fit half the women in the entire country. With the advent of synthetic fabrics and mass-produced tailoring, the whole concept of fashion and style in dress changed. The lines of clothes became longer and more svelte. Moreover, advertising photographs promoted slimness rather than curvature. Because drawings and photographs were essentially two-dimensional, what was important was not so much that clothes looked good on the human figure in the round as that they did so on line drawings and photographs in print. Horizontal and vertical lines were more important than depth. Not only the drawings but also the models who displayed the clothes had to look good in photographs on the page. Accordingly, they needed to be as slim and elongated and as two-dimensional as possible.

Changes in dress were both the symptom and the emblem of more dramatic changes in lifestyle made possible by the growth of cities and their ambience, so different from the country. Telephones and cars, jazz and movies, cities and fashions—they not only had a profound influence on lifestyles in general but also on moral values in particular.

As technological advances and economic progress began to narrow, superficially, the gulf between the classes, middle-class and lower-class women felt free to do some of the same things as women in the upper classes. Traditional morality was already dissolving in the Progressive Era as families became smaller and communities became larger. The developing cities encouraged freedom from the supervision of the church, the home, and small communities, allowing individuals more opportunities to choose their social behavior. By the second decade of the century, social commentators saw that the automobile, in particular, was changing dating and allowing more sex outside marriage. The telephone permitted a new and regular intimacy between people separated by distance. Factories and offices offered a much wider assortment of partners for friendship, love, and sex.

Greater freedom and opportunities tended to erode confidence between generations and establish a prefigurative bourgeois culture in which it was the young people who led their elders. Thus, Dorothy Dix observed for the *Boston American* of August 1914 that there had been

> so many changes in the conditions of life and point of view in the last twenty years that the parent of today is absolutely unfitted to decide the problems of life for the young man and woman of today. This is particularly the case with women because the whole economic and social position of women has been revolutionized since mother was a girl.

One of the biggest sensations of the expanding mass media was the fatal attraction of architect Stanford White for Evelyn Nesbit. Already stricken with renal disease, the formerly prosperous White was dwindling into calamitous debt when he was shot and killed on the roof garden of his own Madison Square Garden in New York (the second Garden, designed in Moorish style in 1880), on June 25, 1906. His murderer was Harry Thaw, unbalanced husband of twenty-two-year-old showgirl Evelyn Nesbit. Evelyn was "the girl on the red velvet swing" with whom White was having an affair. White's murder was only one of many crimes that the new mass media would describe as the crime of the century. However, the culprit, Thaw, eluded the full penalty of the law. At Thaw's second trial, the jury accepted his defense of insanity. Then (as later), a prurient American public and a pliant jury would prefer an outrageous defense fabrication to the hard evidence of a hapless corpse. After seven years' imprisonment, Thaw was released; he then divorced his wife.

In *The Architect of Desire* (1996), White's great-granddaughter, Suzannah Lessard, sets out to justify her punning title, concluding that Stanford's "obsession with beauty existed in an interrupted continuum with his destructive qualities, driving him to rip apart palazzi and plunder vulnerable young girls." Paradoxically, the publicity surrounding the trials of Harry Thaw led to White's transformation from a heartless hedonist into a charismatic romantic.

Possibly in keeping with the implied sexuality of authoress Elinor Glyn's novels, William M. Reddy, editor of the *St. Louis Mirror*, coined the phrase "sex o' clock" in 1913. Already in that decade such writers as H. W. Boynton in "Ideas, Sex and the Novel" for *Dial* (1916), Robert W. Chambers in *The Restless Sea* (1918), and Arthur Pollock in "Are We Immoral?" for *Forum* (1914) thought that society and literature were liberating themselves from Victorian values and enjoying a new moral freedom.

In *Years of Discretion: A Play of Cupid at Fifty* by Frederic Hatton and Fanny Lock Hatton, staged by David Belasco in New York and Chicago in 1912, the widowed heroine of forty-eight declares, "I intend to look under forty—lots under. I have never attracted men but I know I can" and "I mean to have a wonderful time. To have all sorts and kinds of experience. I intend to love and be loved, to lie and cheat."

It was the same for people from lower classes in the towns. The *Chicago Herald and Examiner* of March 10–17, 1920, ran a series of extracts from the diary of Ruth Vail Randall, a woman dissatisfied with her husband and with routine work in a department store because there was no romance in either of them. She took a series of lovers, and fearing that the last would eventually leave her, she killed him and herself on March 6, 1920. Because Ruth Randall and her husband, Norman, lived in a neighborhood with a continuously shifting population, they could live anonymously and choose their own moral values. Ruth Randall did not want children and had an abortion. She chafed at the traditional womanly role of submission expected by her husband. "Why cannot a woman do all a man does?" she complained. She drank, flirted, and had sex freely with other men. Automobiles and telephones facilitated her promiscuity. But her various lovers disappointed her as much as her husband by their lack of companionship and tenderness. She thought often of suicide and in her disillusion noted, "I am miserable. I have the utmost contempt for myself. But the lake is near and soon it will be warm. Oh God, to rest in your arms. To rest—and to have peace."

The most singular and noble woman's story and one of the most remarkable achievements for the century of expanded communication was that of Helen Keller, who had already met adversity with tenacity. Illness had made her blind and deaf in early childhood. Partially sighted tutor Anne Sullivan taught her the means of communication, including speech. From recognizing the sign for one thing—water—Keller learned that everything had a sign. She mastered those signs, graduated from Radcliffe College, and published *The Story of My Life* (1903).

In the Room Where the Women Come and Go/ Talking of Michelangelo

As new technology was providing people with new ways of seeing the world, it was inevitable that this change would be reflected in the subjects and styles of art and literature. In serious literature and art there was a high road with the searching novels of Henry James and Edith Wharton and the paintings and sculptures of the American Renaissance, conceived and executed in a grand tradition; a second, harsher road of abrupt realism with the environment overwhelming the inhabitants in the novels of Theodore Dreiser and the painters of the Eight; and a third road of experimental approaches in art and poetry that took its cue from the new European mode of cubism.

On the high road, novelist Henry James, "the Master," captured the shifting quicksands of expatriate society and the paradoxes underlying the surface in his masterpieces *The Wings of the Dove* (1902), *The Ambassadors* (1903), and *The Golden Bowl* (1904). James's acute faculty of self-criticism was so well developed as to make every element in his writing a conscious intellectual movement in the overall orchestration of characters, plot, and subtext. His friend Edith Wharton, another expatriate, proved herself in *The House of Mirth* (1901) a superb writer of the exterior who transcended superficiality, in comparison with the extraordinary James, who was a writer of the interior without being claustrophobic. Wharton continued her acute moral investigations with *Ethan Frome* (1911), *The Reef* (1912), *The Custom of the Country* (1913), and *The Age of Innocence* (1920), wherein the done thing reigns. Originally completed in 1903 but first published commercially in 1918, *The Education of Henry Adams* was a demure autobiography by a scion of a major political family written in the third person. Academics admired it for its dry comment on things Bostonian, its whimsical humor, its detached way of presenting a subject, and its tender portraits.

Physiologist, psychologist, and philosopher William James, Henry James's older brother, believed that will was the dominant factor in human expression. "We feel sorry because we cry, angry because we strike, afraid because we tremble," observed William James in *Principles of Psychology* (1890). An object sets up a reaction in us and our emotion is our feeling of this reaction. James's most famous expression of the primacy of the will was in his *Pragmatism* (1907). *In The Will to Believe* (1897) he argued that, faced with a choice of options, we should select the one we believe would work best in practice.

Creative literature bridged rural generations in the best work of novelist Willa Cather, a writer slow and meticulous in her style and her use of myth and symbol. She found her own voice with the publication of *Alexander's Bridge* (1912).

Darwin D. Martin House, Buffalo, New York, by Frank Lloyd Wright (1904). This Prairie House was famous for Wright's emphasis on horizontal planes in keeping with the surrounding landscape, his versatile use of interior space, and his general sense of harmony and proportion. In 1967 the State University of New York at Buffalo acquired the house for the president's residence. (Photographed by Jack E. Boucher for the Historic American Buildings Survey in May 1965; Library of Congress)

She drew from her earlier life amid immigrant farmers of Nebraska for *My Antonia* (1918) and *One of Ours* (1922).

William and Henry James, Edith Wharton and Willa Cather all believed that the individual was part of society. He was in society. Moreover, they instinctively understood what Viennese psychiatrist Sigmund Freud spelled out. In *The Interpretation of Dreams* (1900) and *The Psychopathology of Everyday Life* (1901) Freud explained the importance of the subconscious as a motivating factor in human behavior and our dreams—the only element of our subconscious that we come into direct and knowing contact with. Through his analyses of his patients' dreams and neuroses, Freud discovered a conflict between human instinct and the rules of society. The inner individual said, "I want." Society, with its broader responsibilities, said, "But you can't." The Old World came to signify tradition. Americans rebelled against its parental dictates while envying its cultural sophistication.

Freud's theories were titillating in the extreme to those who saw his psychology as a means of escape from the inhibiting legacies of previous decades: sexual repression, patriotism, fundamentalist religion, and political idealism. In fact, Freud was not an advocate of permissive behavior but a conservative, moralistic rationalist. He disliked America: it was too brash and vulgar in comparison with the claustrophobic refinement of his native Vienna. A visit to the United States to lecture at Clark University in Worcester, Massachusetts, in 1909 confirmed him in his opinion.

Philosopher and professor John Dewey, who taught, successively, at the University of Michigan, University of Chicago, and Columbia University, also pondered the social responsibilities of the individual in society. He helped form the New York Teachers Union (1916) and the New School for Social Research (1919) but was best known as a prolific author who continued to write books until his death at age ninety-three. Dewey exerted great influence as the leading education reformer of his time partly because his pragmatic philosophy and liberal leanings had a special appeal to Americans. In *Studies in Logical Theory* (1903) Dewey argued that thinking was just as much a function of the human body as walking and served as a means of adjustment and survival. Thinking came into play to surmount obstacles when instinct and habit broke down. In his *Reconstruction in Philosophy* (1902) Dewey proposed to replace this traditional contemplative or spectator view of knowledge with "creative intelligence." Evolution implied continuous change. Hence, any ideas must be tentative: any idea we consider fixed and immutable retards our advance.

In fact, the belief that everything was finite and could be measured and that problems were susceptible to rational solutions was now being challenged by new theories across the Western world. Not only psychologist Freud but also Parisian philosopher Henri Bergson emphasized that men were irrational and that they often responded to forces not only beyond their control but also beyond their understanding. Others were exploding accepted truths about the physical world. English physicists J. J. (Sir Joseph John) Thomson and Ernest Rutherford showed that the atom, hitherto considered the ultimate unit of matter, was a complex structure of interrelated particles. By the theory of relativity, German physicist Albert Einstein disrupted the mechanistic cosmology that had dominated physics for three centuries.

The cumulative impact of these discoveries was even greater than the considerable sum of the parts. For a time, educated Progressives could maintain their cherished notions of inevitable progress and their belief that human and material relationships were determined by immutable natural laws. Their convictions were confirmed by positive discoveries in such fields as health, industry, and agriculture. Nevertheless, the cumulative effect of new ideas as they were popularized was momentous as increasing numbers of educated people began to understand their disturbing implications. Progressives could no longer put their faith in a general philosophy, such as positivism, that did not correspond to the world that scientists were still investigating.

The impact on literature and art was stupendous.

After the First International Copyright Act of 1891, which eliminated the competition of cheap reprints based on material from foreign sources, new publishers such as Frank Nelson Doubleday (in partnership with Samuel McClure starting in 1897, with Walter Hines Page from 1900 on, and with George Doran from 1927 on) began to promote new writers of fiction and nonfiction through aggressive salesmanship, including the commissioning of articles, advance payments, and promotion campaigns.

Taking advantage of such developments and choosing the middle road of realism, a combination of passionate imagery and brute determination led resourceful writer Theodore Dreiser to create an epic literature in which the environment played a leading role alongside his famous protagonists Carrie and Hurstwood in *Sister Carrie* (1900), and Clyde Griffiths in *An American Tragedy* (1925). For these novels and his "Trilogy of Desire" (1912–14, 1947), Dreiser found his inspiration in the varied fortunes of his own large German-American family and the impact of industrialization and urbanization on the human spirit. In Dreiser's novels humankind is at the mercy of the materialistic world he has created: the environment determines his behavior. The individual is not so much in society as submerged by it. The profligate and libertine Carrie rises to become a glamorous figure in society while her mentor, Hurstwood, falls into the abyss of modern life. Men and women try to project a desired public image to attract wealth without earning it, and thus they remain unfulfilled.

Novelist and polemicist Upton Sinclair graduated from juvenile pulp fiction and wrote more than a hundred serious books, many promoting socialism, in a style that missed evocative language but rewarded readers with surveys containing a great quantity of information in an age that placed a premium on the display of factual knowledge. Naturalistic short story writer O. Henry (pseudonym of William Sidney Porter) developed a startling new technique well suited to periodicals and also to newspapers such as the *New York World* that needed stories to fit around their main art form, enticing advertising copy. O. Henry's novel contribution in stories for the *World* and collections *Cabbages and Kings* (1904) and *The Four Million* (1906) was the surprise or twist ending to pull the rug from under his characters' feet and remove the wool from their eyes. En route to editorship of the *Transatlantic Review* (1924) and publication of works by Ernest Hemingway and James Joyce, elusive English novelist Ford Madox Ford's ability to make up his life as he lived it spilled over into his creative works with their obsession with betrayal, all the way to his masterpiece *The Good Soldier* (1916).

More aggressive than realists were courageous authors who experimented with new methods, forms, and opinions. From 1912 on, volumes of poetry began to flood out and sometimes even to compete with the novel as a marketable commodity in works by Vachel Lindsay, Amy Lowell, Edgar Lee Masters, Carl Sandburg, Ezra Pound, and Edna St. Vincent Millay.

In 1911, at the age of twenty-three, St. Louis-born and Harvard-educated

T. S. Eliot had completed *The Love Song of Alfred J. Prufrock*, a precocious poem with vivid images, flexible tone, and expressive rhythms. Whereas the title suggests a pun about a prude in a frock, the poem itself investigates the staleness of modern hell, which it defines as the pretentiousness of women visitors to an art gallery, the triviality of a life measured in coffee spoons, and the fragmentary experiences of incoherent people. Eliot's early poems are set in the adolescent keys of unresolved self-doubt, self-absorbed hypersensitivity, and defensive posturing. Critics later interpreted Eliot's adolescent terrors as a psychological complement to the gathering storm of World War I.

Ezra Pound recognized T. S. Eliot's *The Waste Land*, written in 1915 after a devastating mental illness, as a masterpiece of the modern movement. No other poem in the English language provokes such extremes of feeling in readers. As edited by Pound and published in 1922, it reads as a random series of symbolic images, but it is subtly controlled by continuing narrative and an inconstant narrator, Tiresias. Its use of crosscutting is akin to that of the movies of D. W. Griffith, and it has one of Griffith's themes: time—living through it, seeing its healing properties, and watching it make things disappear.

If T. S. Eliot was the invisible poet, then his editor, Ezra Pound, was the elusive poet, a scholar who remained suspicious of English literature, avoided iambic pentameter, and hammered out his own hard surfaces in his imagist phase of 1912–14. Work as a translator taught Pound that, in translation, language was concerned with transmitting information and experience as clearly as possible and thus became neutral. Although Americans had inherited the English language, they had not inherited the tradition and experience that that language was forged to convey. Pound was instrumental in the formation of the liberating theory of imagism that grew out of his obsession with Japanese *haiku* or pictographic poetry. Imagism was the ultimate in literary economy. It entailed using no superfluous word—no adjective, adverb, verb, or conjugation—that did not reveal something crucial to the reader. "In a Station at the Metro" from the collection *Lustra* (1915) provides a singular instance: "The apparition of these faces in the crowd; / Petals on a wet, black bough." Pound's explanation was: "In a poem of this sort one is trying to record the precise instant when a thing outward and objective transforms itself, or darts into a thing inward and subjective."

Ezra Pound left the United States for Europe in 1908 and lived mainly in Rapallo, Italy, where he composed the *Cantos*. He did not return until 1946 under tragic circumstances. As European editor (1912–19) of the little magazine *Poetry*, Pound was responsible for the publication of important works by new authors T. S. Eliot and Robert Frost. As English editor of the *Little Review* (1917–19), he placed James Joyce's *Ulysses* with one of its first publishers. Pound is remembered for *Hugh Selwyn Mauberley* (1920) and his monumental *Cantos* (1925–68). Modeled on the poems of Homer and Dante, transformed by echoes of Robert Browning and Walt Whitman, *Cantos* constitutes a striking compendium of poetic technique. Pound and Eliot left personas such as Mauberley and

Tiresias to face the superficiality and aridity of urban society. Pound and Eliot also illuminated the path of American expatriate writers in Europe, whom Pound himself called the "American Risorgimento."

Whether affectionate toward Europe or immersed in the American urban scene, American writers at the turn of the twentieth century and beyond helped define themes that would haunt twentieth-century literature and, indeed, art: the fragmentation of society and the increasing alienation of the individual from society and from himself or herself.

Maverick composer Charles Ives, the son of a Connecticut music teacher, bandleader, and acoustician who experimented with the sound of quarter notes, studied music at Yale under academic composer Horatio Parker but chose insurance as his professional career. Ives was an American composer rooted in the soil and texture of New England life. His compositions are of daring, modernist complexity, not only mixing quotations from popular tunes, revival hymns, barn dances, and European classics but also employing polytonal harmonies, dissonance, and polymetric constructions. In the second movement of his *Three Places in New England* (1903–14), the music conveys an impression of two bands approaching and then passing one another as each plays its own melody in its own key, tempo, and rhythm. The *Second String Quartet* (1907, 1911–13), quoting Beethoven, Brahms, and Tchaikovsky, was conceived as a conversation between four men that turns into a political argument that is finally resolved.

In art, as in literature, there was a grand, a realistic, and an innovative approach.

In its richest flowering in 1901–17, the American Renaissance boasted many fine artists and two giants. Painters, sculptors, and decorators of the American Renaissance drew on the techniques, inspiration, and humanity of the Italian Renaissance of 1420–1580 in support of an effervescent and proud nationalism, glorifying American material progress and imperialism. The art of the American Renaissance was fiercely nationalistic, appropriating the images, symbols, and techniques of previous civilizations to create a magnificent pageant in which the United States was the culmination for an age that believed in progress. For example, the directors of the Pan American Exposition in Buffalo in 1901 had the buildings designed in the style of the Spanish Renaissance—not in white but in a myriad of colors—to celebrate the American Revolution, the contribution of the railroads to the settlement of the West, and the superiority of white people over Indians, Hispanics, and Asians.

Architects of the American Renaissance such as Daniel Burnham and the firm of McKim, Mead, and White borrowed from the vocabulary of classical buildings of Greece and Rome as had such earlier American architects as Thomas Jefferson. However, Jefferson was supposedly drawn to the buildings of antiquity for their democratic associations, whereas McKim, Mead, and White and their contemporaries were enticed by their imperial allusions. The American Renaissance movement fielded a City Beautiful Movement that, under the leadership of Senator James McMillan of Michigan, turned the city of Washington's sights back to French landscape planner Pierre Charles L'Enfant's late-eighteenth-century plan for the capital. New public buildings were placed on the major axes of L'Enfant's original design. Most impressive of these was the Lincoln Memorial (1913–22), a white marble, neo-Greek temple crowned by a monumental marble statue of Lincoln by Daniel Chester French.

Under the Public Buildings Act of 1913, the Public Buildings Commission was instructed to devise standards for public buildings. In 1926 it was awarded $50 million to construct public buildings, notably the monumental buildings of the Federal Triangle in Washington, D.C. By such means the American republic appropriated to itself the grandeur that was Rome on the scale of the line accredited to (but never uttered by) architect Daniel Burnham: "Make no little plans: they have no power to stir men's blood." One such classical building that survived on account of proven standards that mixed a majestic facade with functional interior spaces was the main building of the New York Public Library (1911) at the corner of Fifth Avenue and Forty-Second Street, designed by John Carrere and Thomas Hastings from a sketch by the first director, John Billings.

However, the mammoth project that united the advanced technology of the machine age with the American Renaissance was Pennsylvania Station, New York. Railroad president Alexander J. Cassatt drew together the material resources of several railroads to create a massive terminus to deliver commuters from Long Island and travelers from points north and south on the mainland to a giant terminus on Manhattan between Seventh and Eighth Avenues and Thirty-First and Thirty-Third Streets. Cassatt's outstanding team included American engineer Alfred Noble, who headed the hazardous construction of four tunnels under the East River; British tunneling engineer Charles M. Jacobs in charge of the twin tubes that would carry the railroad under the Hudson River; and electrical engineer George Gibbs. To architect Charles Follen McKim fell the glory of the terminal building, completed in 1910. Its facade along Seventh Avenue was a colonnade inspired by Giovanni Bernini's Tuscan colonnade surrounding the Piazza of St. Peter's in Rome and built with pink Milford marble from Massachusetts. McKim patterned the waiting room inside after the *tepidarium* of the Baths of Caracalla in Rome. Station, tunnels, tracks, and electrification had cost $160 million altogether by the time the entire project was completed in 1917— about $2 billion in 1990s terms.

Sculptor Paul Wayland Bartlett specialized in public statues of American heroes from the period before the Civil War, such as *Lafayette on Horseback* (1899–1908), exhibited in the Louvre as a gift of the American people to the French people in acknowledgment of Bartholdi's Statue of Liberty. Once again, murals became a major art form. Murals by John La Farge, Gari Melchers, and H. Siddons Mowbray adorned state capitols, churches, libraries, and expositions. Mural subjects ranged from the biblical to the allegorical, to the contribution of arts, science, and technology in the new world of scientific achievement.

Of all Renaissance artists, John Singer Sargent was the supreme American portrait painter of the period, despite the fact that he was "born in Italy, educated in France . . . looks like a German, speaks like an Englishman, and paints like a Spaniard." Sargent excelled in formal portraits of English aristocracy, conveying the imperial hauteur of the Edwardian men and the charm and self-confidence of the women who knew they were in charge of social custom and fashion. His *Acheson Sisters* (1902) was not only a variation on the Three Graces but also a homage to eighteenth-century artist Sir Joshua Reynolds. Sargent's complementary giant among American sculptors was Augustus Saint-Gaudens. Saint-Gaudens borrowed liberally and effectively from Greek sculptures of antiquity, but he gave his subjects a tender personality, as if their heroic qualities were veiled by sadness.

Theodore Roosevelt recognized the possibilities of the American Renaissance in service to the rising imperial state as well as the special talents of sculptor Saint-Gaudens. In 1904 and 1905 Roosevelt ordered the Treasury to have American coins redesigned. He commissioned Saint-Gaudens to undertake the work and thereby give the country "the most beautiful coinage since Hellenic Greece."

Among the artists rooted in the realist tradition, Robert Henri (originally Robert Henry Cozad), teacher at the New School of Art in New York, insisted that his students subordinate their skill to their emotional response to a scene in order to capture art for life's sake, based on personal experience and feeling. When the National Academy of Design rejected paintings by a number of his friends and associates in 1907, he withdrew his own entry and had the Macbeth Galleries in New York sponsor an exhibition of the rejected painters at 450 Fifth Avenue from February 3–15, 1908, and thereafter in nine other cities. Named the Eight by sympathetic critic James Gibbons Huneker, the painters faced hostile epithets such as "the revolutionary black gang" and "the apostles of ugliness." This group of stylistically diverse painters comprised the urban realists Robert Henri, John Sloan, George Luks, William Glackens, and Everett Shinn; the impressionist Ernest Lawson; the postimpressionist Maurice Prendergast; and the romantic symbolist Arthur Davies.

Of the Eight, John Sloan was preeminent in his ability to capture the city for modern art. Trained as a newspaper illustrator for the Sunday editions of the *Philadelphia Press*, Sloan painted with an intensity that showed his affection for city life, portraying its brooding tall buildings in broad masses of dark and light akin to a poster, appropriate for someone committed to socialism.

As the age of electricity superseded the age of steam, art responded to accelerated changes in society and celebrated the new by turning its machines into symbols of the new technological age. The new mode in art was cubism, promoted in Paris by Pablo Picasso and Georges Braque. Hitherto, the pivot of naturalistic art in the Western world was single-point perspective to convey depth, based on the fact that objects seem smaller the farther away they are from the viewer. In *Les Desmoiselles d'Avignon* (1907), Pablo Picasso's mix of African and Iberian art finally broke through the conventional Western art form of representation. Here, decisively, was an art of the century, for cubism generated every major movement in modern art.

Among those who appreciated Cézanne and Picasso was American expatriate art collector Leo Stein who, with his sister, Gertrude, started buying paintings from Ambroise Vollard's Paris gallery. Gertrude adapted Picasso's simultaneity and shattering of single-point perspective (in his easel art) to her prose to create a cubist literature. Her most ambitious project was *The Making of Americans*, published in 1925 but written almost twenty years earlier. This was her attempt to write a history of America by reporting in infinite detail the history of the Hersland family. Whereas brother Leo earned a reputation as the most daring and discerning of early-twentieth-century art collectors, sister Gertrude earned a reputation as the best known literary figure whom people did not read—an icon who symbolized modernism from the center of her Parisian salon surrounded by a galaxy of expatriates. She was well aware of her reputation as a difficult writer for readers. As she observed in a story in *Three Lives* (1909): "Nobody knows what I am trying to do but I do and I know when I succeed."

Modernism crossed the Atlantic with art patron and photographer Alfred Stieglitz, who gave European moderns, including Matisse, Rodin, Cézanne, and Picasso, their first exhibitions in the New World at 291, a small gallery named after its approximate location on Fifth Avenue, Manhattan. But it was the infamous Armory Show of February 17 to March 15, 1913, that introduced modern art to an incredulous American public. This was the International Exhibition of Modern Art held at the Sixty-Ninth Regiment Armory at Lexington Avenue and Twenty-Fifth Street, New York, organized by the Association of American Painters and Sculptors (AAPS), led by Walt Kuhn and Arthur Davies. The Armory exhibition extended to sixteen hundred works, including paintings by three hundred American artists. About a third of the paintings were by foreign artists. These scandalous painters from Europe who could not even reproduce the human form naturalistically stole the show. To the critics, cubism was "insurgency in art," "Ellis Island Art," and "bedlam in art."

The Armory Show's most reviled painting was Marcel Duchamp's *Nude Descending a Staircase, no 2.* In *Everybody's*, Julian Street called the painting "an explosion in a shingle factory." Cartoonist J. F. Griswold provided a satirical version for the *Evening Sun*: "The Rude Descending a Staircase (Rush Hour at the Subway)." These hostile remarks contained unintentional tribute, for they implicitly recognized that cubism captured things in motion by extrapolating splinters of movement and freezing them in time. Although public reaction to the show was overwhelmingly antagonistic, as it traveled to other cities, it had everyone talking about modern art. Cubism destroyed the illusions of perspective and presented the world from a myriad of angles akin to the fractional world emerging with the machine. Once again, the technique was comparable to crosscutting in the movies.

Among the American moderns who exhibited paintings at the Armory Show were John Marin, Max Weber, Marsden Hartley, Arthur Dove, Stanton Mac-Donald Wright, and Georgia O'Keefe. MacDonald Wright predicted the end of naturalistic painting and the beginning of a disembodied art of color and light.

John Marin married traditional watercolor techniques to airy and distorted land-scapes. Kuhn, Davies, and their associates were past masters at promotion, pro-ducing 50,000 pamphlets and a series of 57 half-tone postcards of exhibits—the first example of a practice later followed by every gallery in the world, turning the art world into the art business. Ironically, as critic Malcolm Bradbury sug-gests (1996), "If modernism was indeed chiefly a European movement, sprung from the cultures and contradictions of European life, it became, largely thanks to Americans, an international school with a deeply trans-Atlantic flavor."

As for twenty-five-year-old iconoclast Marcel Duchamp, he responded to his outsize *succès de scandale* at the Armory Show by laying down his palette. De-riding painting as a "retinal" art that appealed to the eye rather than the mind, he said there were more important tasks than cultivating beauty. Within the next ten years, turning to different art forms, Duchamp completed his most important pieces. They include the famously cracked *Large Glass* and the works we know as his "ready-mades," common objects like a bottle rack and a snow shovel that he decided to exhibit as art. When he drew a mustache on a picture of Leonardo Da Vinci's *Mona Lisa*, Duchamp proved that he could spin art from adolescent insolence—raising the forbidden subject of Leonardo's homosexual orientation.

Not all artists before World War I were optimistic about the machine. Some saw it as threatening, dehumanizing. The idea that man's inventions could rise against him was a myth of the Industrial Revolution. From 1914 on, the new machinery was turned upon humanity itself. The war accelerated the shifts of sensibility in art and literature that had already jolted progressive confidence at the turn of the century.

CHAPTER 4

No Gods, No Masters

"A M E R I C A   I S God's crucible, the great Melting Pot where all the races of Europe are melting and reforming!"

Such was the provocative outcry by the hero, David Quixano, in the first act of *The Melting Pot* (1908), a play by Israel Zangwill, an English Jew. It was an influential statement about assimilation.

"We the people," begins the preamble to the Constitution of the United States. The people included not only politicos, plutocrats, and inventors but also new immigrants, women, organized labor, and African Americans, all of whom made their presence felt in U.S. society in the first two decades of the American century—despite the ways in which the law discriminated against them. New immigrants, labor, African Americans, and women of all classes were among America's most precious human resources. They made possible its immense material progress. Through their struggles for recognition, in different ways and with varying degrees of success, labor, African Americans, and women brought certain fundamental political and humanitarian issues to the fore.

Would women gain the vote, and could African Americans regain it? Would new immigrants become assimilated, acculturated, and free? Would labor win the right to form unions? Would exploited workers ever share in the prosperity of the bosses? How far were these groups protected by the Constitution? The labor, socialist, feminist, and precursor civil rights movements were not united or even complementary left-wing movements. Their various threads snarled and tangled with one another. Organized labor opposed alliances with political parties and proposed immigration restriction. Some Progressives opposed woman suffrage.

Once again, the overwhelming new factor operating politics and society was the population explosion, creating a new, mass society in which immigration played a decisive role.

In the period 1890–1917 almost 18 million people entered the United States. And in the years 1905–14 American immigration reached its zenith. More than a million immigrants entered the United States in six separate years: 1905, 1906, 1907, 1910, 1913, and 1914. The year 1907 marked the absolute peak of immigration in U.S. history in any one year with 1,285,349 immigrants. Mass

Left: A family of Italian immigrants on board the ferry from Ellis Island to New York;
Above: An Albanian woman with distinctive dress and headdress. (Both photos of 1905; John Rylands University Library of Manchester)

We the People:
The very presence of new immigrants from southern and central Europe challenged ordinary social assumptions of Euro-Americans

migration from Europe was one of the great events of history, made possible by new, improved steamboats. From 1896 on, new immigrants—people from central and southeast Europe—outnumbered the old immigrants—people from northwest Europe. Like their predecessors, most of the new immigrants came to the United States seeking economic opportunity. Many were refugees from agrarian mismanagement. Some—Russian Jews—were fleeing persecution.

The new immigrants dramatically altered the politics, economy, and culture of American society while they, themselves, were also changed by the society around them. They increased the population, swelling the cities and the number of industrial workers and widening the market for manufactured goods and services. They required additional churches, schools, and hospitals. As they increased the electorate, their presence aided the movement for more accountable government.

In 1910 immigrants accounted for 14.5 percent of the total population (not much more than the 1860 percentage, 13.2). Immigrants were increasingly concentrated in the industrial Northeast. Four states contained almost half the foreign-born population: New York, Massachusetts, Pennsylvania, and Illinois. Germans (still the largest number of first-generation immigrants) settled in the Midwest, New York, Pennsylvania, and New Jersey. Scandinavians concentrated in the Midwest and Washington State. The Irish settled in New England and the mid-Atlantic states as well as in California and Illinois, states that also received the greatest number of Italians. Immigrants from Russia and Austria-Hungary settled in New York, Pennsylvania, New Jersey, Massachusetts, and Illinois. Poles settled in northern industrial cities from New York to Illinois, as did Greeks. The flood of European immigration stopped short of the South, leaving that region further isolated in its differences from the rest of the country.

Whatever their rising numbers, immigrants did not threaten to overwhelm the native-born population. They never accounted for more than a seventh of the total. Some male immigrants were birds of passage—swallows—so called because they moved across the Atlantic in both directions. In the end only 67 percent of all immigrants settled permanently in the United States.

Cities in which immigrants congregated became clusters of ghettos. In 1910 78.6 percent of new immigrants lived in towns or cities. Roughly 75 percent of the population of New York, Boston, Chicago, Detroit, and Cleveland was composed of first- and second-generation immigrants. San Francisco was noted for its immigrant communities, especially Chinese and Japanese. In 1916 the mother tongue of 72 percent of its population was a language other than English. The two immigrant groups most likely to settle and cluster in cities—the Irish and the Russians—represented both the old and the new immigration, with over five-sixths of each group in urban communities.

In 1914 1.4 million Jews lived in New York—more than the city's entire population in 1870. Soon the Lower East Side had the largest Jewish community in the world, crammed into an area little larger than a square mile, eastward from the Bowery almost to the East River and southward from Fourteenth Street to Brooklyn Bridge. Chicago was divided among Germans (north of the Loop), Poles (northwest), Italians and Jews (west), Bohemians and Lithuanians (southwest), and Irish (south). Immigrant groups that took over particular districts were as much regional as national in character: New York's Italian districts comprised Neapolitans and Calabrians (Mulberry Bend), Genoese (Baxter Street), Sicilians (Elizabeth Street), and Tyrolese (West Sixty-Ninth Street).

From the perspective of the leaders of immigrants, labor, and women, cities provided a social forum for debate. Proximity and congestion supplied formidable political persuasion through press, social clubs, mass meetings, and churches.

Yet the concept of the melting pot that Israel Zangwill proposed in his play

Left: Bandit's Roost, by progressive photojournalist and writer Jacob Riis, records the menace that accompanied the squalor in the dark courts of New York's Lower East Side. (Library of Congress)

Right: Meanwhile, the supposedly wild West was being softened with bourgeois comforts, as this Kansas farmhouse parlor with a piano suggests. (Photo of 1900; Library of Congress)

of 1908 was flattering to native-born Americans because it suggested that the United States was a haven for refugees who would learn democracy and thereby become Americans—culturally better than Europeans. In the last act of the play David Quixano declares, "A fig for your feuds and vendettas! Germans and Frenchmen, Irishmen and Englishmen, Jews and Russians—into the crucible with you all! God is making the American!" But Zangwill's play offended immigrants who were trying to preserve their ethnic identity while becoming acculturated to American society because it implied that losing the first was the price they had to pay for gaining the second. Orthodox Jews disliked it because it proposed intermarriage as a means of assimilation. In fact, assimilation was far from smooth for immigrants. The whole process was a series of conflicts. American society competed with traditional elements of immigrant families or ethnic institutions.

The phenomenon of Jewish-American literature was outstanding, beginning with Abraham Cahan's *Yekl! A Tale of the New York Ghetto* (1896) and coming to a climax with Cahan's masterpiece, *The Rise of David Levinsky* (1917), a classic distillation of the Jewish immigrant experience. The story is about the search for individual economic success within the context of assimilation. Russian immigrant David Levinsky compromises his enthusiasm for scholarship in exchange for material success. He becomes a clothing manufacturer, employs cheap labor to maximize profits, evades union regulations, and opposes socialism. Levinsky laments how the process of becoming Americanized has undermined his religious practices. "The very clothes I wore and the very food I ate had a fatal effect on my religious habits."

Yet the pull of the old country remained strong for many immigrants. Foreign-language newspapers abounded. In 1920 there were 1,052 foreign-language papers, including 276 in German, 118 in Spanish or Portuguese, 111 in various Scandinavian languages, 98 in Italian, and 70 in Polish.

The Roman Catholic church was the principal church of immigrants. In 1900 there were seventy dioceses and ten thousand churches. Yet Catholicism not only united new immigrants and old; it also divided them. It restricted the new immigrants' attempts to create autonomous religious groups because their desire was in conflict with the church's own need to impose centralized authority. German, Polish, and French-Canadian Catholics resented Irish-American domination of the church. Old immigrants distrusted some new immigrants' religious practices—such as carrying a statue of a revered patron saint through the streets. Protestants regarded these ceremonies as no better than pagan rites. To prevent a schism, the Vatican tacitly conceded to immigrants' demands for national (or ethnic) parishes. At this time it was converts who supplied intellectual leadership in the Roman Catholic church. They were better prepared educationally than the working-class immigrants who constituted the rank and file, and they came from, and understood, the surrounding non-Catholic culture.

Immigrants wanted to achieve a satisfactory position in the U.S. economy. They did not simply want to abandon traditional cultural values. To Italians and Greeks, family ties were more important than education and success at work. Although compulsory public school education opened a door to material success, it also led children down a corridor of assimilation away from their parents. The public school was a warehouse of American culture. Each school day opened with a communal salute to the American flag, a patriotic exercise intended to stimulate common loyalty. So, too, did lessons on national heroes such as George Washington. By learning to read and write in English and by the way they were taught arithmetic, children were also being taught to strive for material rewards. Adults who attended night schools learned not only English but also civic government so that they could qualify for citizenship.

If they could afford it, Catholics from whatever ethnic group showed a marked interest in real estate, and their choice linked them to a parish. God's holy work was rooted in particular times and places. This was, as John T. McGreevy suggests (1996), an "incarnational" outlook that regarded material things as holy. In fact, urban Catholic identity was wrapped up in the life of the church at the center of the parish.

Not everyone welcomed the great tide of immigration. Immigrants faced outright hostility from three vociferous groups that spurred effective nativist agitation against them: labor unions, which regarded unskilled immigrants as a threat to organized labor; social reformers, who believed the influx of immigrants exacerbated the problems of the cities; and Protestant conservatives, who dreaded the supposed threat to Nordic supremacy. New immigrants were open to criticism for what they were not. They were Catholic, Jewish, and Greek Orthodox, rather than Protestant. Religious and ethnic minorities had played no more than insignificant parts in winning American political liberties. A persistent charge against immigrants was that they were radicals and some were terrorists.

Russian-born Emma Goldman from Lithuania became both legend and parody of such international anarchists. In 1885 she left Kaunas, Lithuania, and immigrated to the United States. For a time she worked in a clothing factory in Rochester, New York, where she attended meetings of German socialists. She moved to New York in 1889, where she became involved with Alexander Berkman, would-be assassin of steel tycoon Henry Clay Frick in 1892. Berkman was arrested for the botched assassination and sentenced to twenty-two years in prison. In 1893 Goldman herself was imprisoned for inciting a riot in New York. Goldman and Berkman were, of course, anarchists rather than socialists. Following the ideas of the French social theorist Pierre Joseph Proudhon, they believed that the state should be abolished and that free agreements between individuals should supersede laws based on coercion and the protection of property, which operated in the interests of a ruling elite. After Berkman's early release in 1906, the two continued with anarchist activities until they were arrested in 1919 during the height of the Great Red Scare of 1917–21 on the grounds of obstructing the military draft; they were deported to Russia.

Nativists could point to the indisputable fact that every radical movement had a large immigrant following. The great majority of immigrants, however, were true conservatives who not only resented European ideas on revolution but also opposed domestic proposals for social reform. Yet these new immigrants were supposed to be radical, rather than conservative. The Irish, dominant among Catholic clergy, were quite likely to criticize Italian Catholics saying that, by their special rituals, they delayed WASP acceptance of other Catholics. German-American Jews had comparable complaints about Russian-American Jews.

The Russo-Japanese War of 1904–5 provoked renewed fears of a Yellow Peril on the West Coast and led to demands for Japanese exclusion. In the first so-called gentlemen's agreement of August 1906, Japan agreed to impose limits on emigration by refusing to issue passports. After the San Francisco earthquake of 1906, the school board ordered Chinese, Japanese, and Korean children to attend a separate school, ostensibly to prevent overcrowding. President Theodore Roosevelt intervened, and the board rescinded its order on March 13, 1907. This did not propitiate racist opinion. The federal government moved toward a definite gentlemen's agreement in a series of notes of 1907–8. But the agreement allowed Japanese residents in the United States to send for their wives.

Thousands did so. A series of state laws limited the right of the Japanese first to own (1913) and then to lease (1920) farmlands.

Senator William Paul Dillingham of Vermont led a joint committee of both houses of Congress on immigration (1907–10), which published a lengthy report (1911) in forty-one volumes. Its tenor was that new immigrants were less fit physically, intellectually, and culturally than earlier settlers. Bills proposing literacy tests passed both houses of Congress three times between 1897 and 1915. They were prevented from becoming law only by the successive vetoes of Presidents Cleveland, Taft, and Wilson.

The case of Leo Frank demonstrates how economic tensions fueled nativism. Frank, the son of Russian Jews, came to Atlanta to run a pencil factory owned by his father. In 1914 he was found guilty, on flimsy evidence, of murdering Mary Phagan, a factory employee. He was vilified by the press for exploiting southern workers. When the governor of Georgia commuted his death sentence to lifetime imprisonment, some people organized a boycott of Jewish-owned stores. A virulent mob stormed the jail and lynched the hapless prisoner.

Woodrow Wilson argued that the Burnett immigration bill was selective rather than restrictive and would constitute a fundamental reversal of historical policy without being based on any popular mandate to do so. The literacy test was "not a test of character, of quality, or of personal fitness," and these were the only precepts on which selection could be justified. However, in January 1917 Congress reenacted the Burnett general immigration bill. This time the forces of restriction won the battle. In February both the Senate and the House overrode Wilson's veto.

The act of 1917 required all immigrants over sixteen to read "not less than 30 nor more than 80 words in ordinary use" in English or another language or dialect. However, the act waived the literacy test for immigrants fleeing religious persecution, and its terms did not prevent otherwise eligible citizens from joining members of their immediate family already settled in the United States. The act codified previous legislation, doubled the head tax to eight dollars, and added to the lists of excluded persons alcoholics, vagrants, and persons of psychopathic inferiority. It also defined the southwest Pacific as a barred zone, thereby excluding almost all Asian immigrants not covered by the Chinese Exclusion Act of 1882 and the gentlemen's agreement with Japan of 1907–8.

Work Like Hell and Be Happy

It was primarily the Industrial Revolution with its splendid promise of economic opportunity that attracted immigrants, old and new. Without such massive immigration, the United States could not have developed industrially at anything like the rate it did. More significantly, the new immigrants' willingness to take on manual work enabled earlier groups to assume more skilled work or to enter the professions. The Dillingham Commission discovered that immigrants accounted for 57.9 percent of employees in twenty-one industries.

Cotton Mill Workers in the Olympia Cotton Mill, Columbia, South Carolina, *ca.* 1900. Although the symmetry of the machines and the artistry of the photographer have turned this routine scene into a well-balanced shot, nothing can obscure the fact that four of these workers are exploited children. (National Museum of History and Technology)

In 1910, when 1,041,570 immigrants entered the United States, their skills ranged across the spectrum of agriculture and industry. They included 288,745 farm laborers, 216,909 construction and other laborers, 121,847 craftsmen, and 260,002 people with no fixed occupation. Another 96,658 worked in private households. There were also 14,731 managers, 12,218 clerical workers, 11,793 farmers, 9,689 professional workers, and 8,977 service workers.

Who worked where and why often depended on all sorts of social and economic factors. It was largely Italian labor that built the New York subway systems and major bridges. In Florida Italian immigrants rolled cigars; in California they cultivated vines. In New York the rag trade employed almost 50 percent of the Jewish men and boys living in the city. The clothing industry was attractive to Russian Jews because it was an avenue to commerce. Pay was by piecework, and thus earnings were related to individual effort. Workers could amass capital and invest in their own businesses. In fact, it was those immigrants who had developed skills as merchants or artisans in Europe who adapted themselves most easily to American towns. Sixty-six percent of all Jewish men and boys who immigrated to the United States in the period 1899–1914 were skilled, compared with an average of only 20 percent for all male immigrants in the same period.

Industrial expansion afforded an especially large number of economic opportunities for lower grades of workers as new mechanical inventions allowed novices to operate automatic equipment. Mechanical cutters ate through coal faces with a speed no skilled miner could match. Whereas before 1890, most miners in the bituminous coalfields of Pennsylvania were native Americans or immigrants from Britain, Ireland, or Germany, after that they were Poles, Italians, and Slovaks.

Statistics for America's heterogeneous labor force reveal something of the changing economic nature of society, turning from agriculture to industry and manufacturing, and from industry and manufacturing to service. Thus, in 1910, of the total labor force of 37.48 million people age ten and over, the greatest single occupation was agriculture, accounting for 11.77 million people. But industry overall accounted for comparable numbers, with 8.33 million in manufacturing, 1.94 million in construction, and 1.06 million in mining. In addition, there were 1.85 million in railway work, which mixed industry and service. In the sector of service, there were 5.32 million in trade, 2.09 million in domestic work, 595,000 in teaching, 150,000 in seafaring, and 68,000 in fishing. Unemployment was at 5.9 percent of the labor force.

Provocative expressionist artist William Gropper drew a series of pointed cartoons against the capitalist order. For the *Liberator* of 1922 he had a tailor, entrapped in a sewing machine of utmost efficiency, endure a caption "Work Like Hell and Be Happy." Indeed, working in America's industries was grueling, dangerous, and poorly paid. In 1910 only 8 percent of workers had regular schedules of 48 hours a week or less; almost 70 percent labored for more than 54 hours a week. In 1914 the average number of hours of work per week for all workers was 55.2. Long hours and intensive labor practices combined to produce one of the highest accident rates in the industrial world. A national survey of industrial accidents in 1913 found that twenty-five thousand people had been killed and seven hundred thousand seriously injured at work. In one Pittsburgh steel mill, nearly 25 percent of recent immigrant employees were injured or killed each year between 1907 and 191—3,723 in all. The relentless drive for efficiency, increased production, and profits almost always took precedence over considerations of safety and health.

The most infamous industrial accident of the Progressive Era was the Triangle

Shirtwaist fire in New York's notorious garment industry. On March 25, 1911, at 4:30 P.M., a fire swept through the Triangle Shirtwaist Company on the top three stories of the Asch Building on the corner of Washington and Greene Streets. The employers had locked the doors to keep the 500 women employees at work, thereby sealing off the escape route on the ninth floor. Thus, within fifteen minutes, 146 women either burned to death or died jumping from windows with their dresses on fire. When the firefighters arrived, their ladders could only reach the sixth floor. They could not get the water pumps near the building because the pavement was carpeted with the bodies of victims who had jumped to their deaths. Their safety nets broke when workers jumped together in threes and fours.

The owners of the company were charged with manslaughter; although they were acquitted, they were ordered to pay $75 to each of the twenty-three families of victims who had sued them. The Triangle fire was one of the most vivid lessons to American labor that it would need to organize itself better—if only to protect workers. New York City established the Bureau of Fire Investigation under Robert F. Wagner, which awarded the fire department additional powers to improve factory safety.

Industrial safety was only one problem. The final report by the Commission on Industrial Relations of 1916 listed four principal causes of industrial unrest: the unjust distribution of wealth and income; unemployment; workers' being denied justice in the creation, adjudication, and administration of law; and workers' being denied a right to form effective labor unions.

In 1910 the average yearly wage was $517. The highest paid occupations among wage earners were those of railroad engineers and conductors, glassblowers, and certain steel and construction workers, who might expect to earn between $1,500 and $2,000 per annum. This would provide a modest standard of living for a family of moderate size, including high school education for the children and an insurance policy, but it was not enough to see the family through misfortune. Moreover, such a worker would have to be well above average in physical strength and endurance, as well as having served a long apprenticeship and possibly would have played his part in a strenuous battle for better wages. But the Commission on Industrial Relations discovered that one-third of men working in factories and mines earned less than $10 a week; between two-thirds and three-quarters earned less than $15 a week; only a tenth earned more than $20 a week.

Of the total labor force of 37.29 million in 1910, 29.85 million were male and 7.44 million were female. In the ensuing decade, however, as the workforce expanded, the proportion of working women remained about the same, at around one-fifth of the total. In 1920, when the labor force was 42.20 million, 33.57 million were male and 8.63 million were female.

Working women were supplementing the meager earnings of their men. By their presence and the way they were exploited, they threatened the existing basis of the wage scale. Between two-thirds and three-quarters of women workers in factories, stores, and laundries earned wages of less than six dollars a week. The commission's report of 1916 was eloquent as to what $6 would buy. It was the price of three tickets to the theater, or a week's supply of gasoline for an automobile, or the cost of a dinner for two, or a pair of shoes or three pairs of gloves: "To the girl it means that every penny must be counted, every normal desire stifled, and each basic necessity of life barely satisfied by the sacrifice of some other necessity," reported the commission. "If more food must be had than is given with 15-cent dinners, it must be bought with what should go for clothes. . . . If the breaking point has come, and she must have some amusement, where can it come from? Surely, not out of $6 a week."

The commission was especially concerned about the exploitation of children: 20 percent of children in the largest cities were undernourished, and poor children were dying at three times the rate of middle-class children: "It is certain that at least one third and possibly one half of the families of wage earners employed in manufacturing and mining earn in the course of the year less than enough to support them in anything like a comfortable and decent condition."

Set against the hardship of labor was the affluence and might of the plutocracy. The commission found that wealth in the United States was distributed among a rich 2 percent of the population, who owned 60 percent of the wealth; a middle class of 33 percent of the people, who owned 35 percent of the wealth; and a poor 65 percent of the population, who owned 5 percent of the wealth. In short, 2 million people owned 20 percent more of the national wealth than the remaining 90 million. The commission emphasized the gross injustice of the unequal distribution of wealth:

> Massed in millions at the other end of the social scale are fortunes of a size never before dreamed of whose very owners do not know the extent nor, without the aid of an intelligent clerk, even the sources of their incomes. Incapable of being spent in any legitimate manner, these fortunes are burdens, which can only be squandered, hoarded, put into so-called "benefactions" which, for the most part, constitute a menace to the State, or put back into the industrial machine to pile up ever increasing mountains of gold.

Yet the commission concluded that, with a reasonably equitable division of wealth, the entire population should occupy "the position of comfort and security which we characterize as middle class." The commission proposed that Congress should redress inequalities by introducing a federal inheritance tax. The revenue raised should be used to extend education, develop social sciences, undertake construction of roads, and provide reforestation. But labor had to seek relief elsewhere.

The AFL, the IWW, and the SPA

The working class was dominated by European immigration, enticed by the world of socialist politics, and yet sustained by an intense working-class consciousness fostered by exclusion and nurtured by relative powerlessness. Radicals found it extraordinarily difficult to raise working-class consciousness among a labor force fractured by conflicting cultures of impoverished immigrants, unskilled native-born workers, and skilled, native-born workers. The three most important workers' organizations were the American Federation of Labor (AFL); the Industrial Workers of the World (IWW); and the Socialist Party of America (SPA).

The first leaders of the American Federation of Labor, founded in 1881 and 1886, intended it to build class consciousness and the economic power of workers by organizing them by occupation. Under the long, conservative leadership (1886–1924) of Samuel Gompers, the AFL pursued policies designed to win short-term economic gains for a membership that, at the turn of the century, represented less than 5 percent of wage workers. Gompers believed in negotiation and conciliation in labor disputes and in resort to strikes only after other methods had failed. His primary concern was the status of skilled labor, and he consistently opposed alliances between labor and political parties. In an industry with a simple production process, such as cigar making, a craft union might represent almost all employees. But in industries such as automobile production, which employed a mix of skilled, semiskilled, and unskilled workers, the system of craft unions was meaningless. Important industrial unions in the AFL included the United Mine Workers (UMW) of 1890 and the International Ladies' Garment Workers' Union (ILGWU) of 1910. The AFL believed immigrant labor was undesirable and unorganizable. For that reason it became a leading advocate of immigration restriction on both economic and nativist grounds.

A small number of businessmen were ready to work with labor. In 1901 employers founded the National Civic Federation (NCF) with Republican Party power broker Marcus Hanna of Ohio as president. Small employers felt differently. In Dayton, Ohio, in 1900 employers formed a citywide association against so-called restrictive trade union practices. By opposition to the closed shop and through blacklisting union members, they routed organized labor from Dayton. Employers initiated the Dayton plan in Chicago, Indianapolis, Louisville, and other cities in the Midwest. By 1903 anti-union employers had taken control of the National Association of Manufacturers (NAM), an organization formed in 1895 to encourage exports. In the first decade of the new century, it spent money on election campaigns to defeat candidates friendly to labor; it established agencies that recruited strikebreakers, detective firms, and company spies, nationwide.

Business moves against unions came to a climax with the case of *Lowe v. Lawler*, the Danbury Hatters' Case. The Supreme Court ruled unanimously on February 3, 1908, that a union attempting to organize workers in a factory in one state by a secondary boycott of stores in other states selling that factory's products was in violation of the Sherman Antitrust Act of 1890 because it was a combination in restraint of trade. The normally conciliatory Samuel Gompers was now outraged. Referring drily to the rush of anti-union injunctions, he said, "Yes, there is no hesitancy on the part of our courts to grant us certain rights—

for instance, the rights to be maimed or killed without any responsibility to the employer; the right to be discharged for belonging to a union; the right to work as long hours for as low pay as the employer can impose."

Some workers sought more extreme remedies than those advocated by the AFL.

In January 1905, Western Federation of Miners (WFM) leader William D. ("Big Bill") Haywood, together with a small band of labor radicals and Socialists, including Socialist leader Eugene Debs, converged on Brand's Hall, Chicago, to form the most adventurous radical organization in U.S. labor history, the Industrial Workers of the World (IWW)—the Wobblies. The IWW drew support not only from the WFM but also from the Western Labor Union and the American Labor Union. The Wobblies' goal was anarcho-syndicalism—the principle that labor organizations could regulate both economy and society without any need for formal state institutions. By organizing the mass of workers who were excluded from the AFL, the Wobblies aimed to engage the employers in an unrelenting class war, culminating in a general strike to force the issue of redistributing power and wealth.

For the first five years, the Wobblies' plans were no more than rhetoric. But there were disturbing signs to suggest that IWW activities would soon generate notoriety. When miner Harry Orchard was charged with the murder of former governor Frank Steunenberg in Caldwell, Idaho, on December 30, 1905, he confessed that he had murdered not only Steunenberg but also various other people over the previous ten years. He said he had done so at the behest of IWW leader William Haywood. Labor lawyer Clarence Darrow defended Big Bill Haywood at a trial for conspiracy to murder in 1907. The jury acquitted Haywood because in Idaho no one could be convicted on the unsupported evidence of an accomplice. But across the nation, people were not convinced.

Their suspicion that such union leaders were no better than anarchists hardened into deep conviction as a result of the McNamara case of 1910–11. Union organizers and brothers John J. and James B. McNamara were found guilty of having caused an explosion that wrecked the plant of the *Los Angeles Times*. Nineteen people had died and another thirty were injured in the blast. Defending lawyer Clarence Darrow's flair for publicity brought him to the verge of bankruptcy after the McNamara trial when he was indicted for conspiring to bribe jurors. At his own trial, the jury could not agree and the indictment was dropped.

The Wobblies found it difficult to build strong organizations, especially in the South and the West, where they recruited lumber and agricultural workers in the face of stiff opposition from employers, trade unions, and vigilante groups. IWW activists encouraged intermittent strikes, slowdowns, sabotage—all militant tactics suited to the spontaneous revolt of unskilled workers. However, they could never coordinate their tactics into an overall strategy. The transient nature of the IWW's main constituency hampered its attempts to establish a stable, grassroots infrastructure prior to strikes and prevented consolidation of achievements after strike victories.

For the workers' most disruptive tool against industrial bosses was still the strike. Strikes erupted either when the level of unemployment fell off sufficiently to encourage dissatisfied workers to think they had a chance of success or when their standard of living fell precipitously. Strikes took more dangerous forms when they became mass strikes, such as the one at the Pressed Steel Car Company in McKees Rocks, Pennsylvania, organized by the IWW in 1909. It initiated a new period of industrial unrest.

In New York in 1909 a militant group of women clothing workers promoted the Uprising of the 20,000. Enlisting the support of the International Ladies' Garment Workers' Union (ILGWU), women shirtwaist workers battled police on picket lines and obliged clothing companies to accept collective bargaining under the famous Protocol of Peace. The old guard United Garment Workers were fainthearted about militant strikes. In 1914 Sidney Hillman, a dynamic young Jewish-Russian cutter who was descended from rabbis, moved to New York. His experiences in the failed Russian revolution of 1905 had deepened his commitment to socialism. He led rebel workers in founding the Amalgamated Clothing Workers of America, a militant union that challenged the nativism and timidity of the old AFL union with socialist principles, thereby earning the enmity of Samuel Gompers and the support of Progressives Louis Brandeis and Florence Kelley.

In Massachusetts a state law reducing the maximum work week for women and children from fifty-six to fifty-four hours resulted in the most furious industrial conflict of the Progressive Era. Employers in Lawrence's textile industry complied with the new law, but they also cut wages accordingly. A group of young Polish women protested their lower wages on January 11, 1912. Their walkout led to a major strike that polarized opinion across the entire town. The town of Lawrence was ruled by the giant American Woolen Company. Nearly 35,000 people worked in various textile mills, infamous for their poor wages and wretched conditions. When 23,000 workers, encouraged by IWW leaders and Italian anarchists, struck for three months, the employees fought police and state militia, held their own, and won significant wage increases.

In the main, however, strikes were ephemeral. If workers wanted to revolutionize their position, they had to look beyond conservative or terrorist labor organizations.

In 1901 railway leader Eugene Debs formed the Socialist Party of America (SPA). Although based in part on the principles of German revolutionary Karl Marx's *Das Kapital* (published in three volumes in 1867, 1887, and 1895), which cast the proletariat as heroes against the manipulative capitalists of the bourgeoisie, Debs's socialism was not nearly as doctrinaire as that of such predecessor organizations as Daniel De Leon's dogmatic Socialist Labor Party (SLP). Debs and his followers wanted to reform society—not to overthrow it—on the basis of common humanity, providing a more efficient as well as a more egalitarian system.

Debs's brand of socialism flourished in the period 1901–12, only to decline in the domestic crises of World War I. Starting with 10,000 members in 1901, the party grew steadily, achieving 120,000 members by 1912. That year it also held 1,200 public offices in 340 municipalities. In 1912 Socialists published 300 periodicals of all kinds, and the major journal, *The Appeal to Reason*, had a circulation of 760,000. Debs won 900,672 popular votes (6 percent) in the presidential election. In 1914 radical immigrants in New York's Lower East Side elected Socialist labor lawyer Meyer Landon to Congress. But the party's principal strength was limited to a few groups: the tenant farmers of the southern plains, particularly Oklahoma, the German trade unionists in Milwaukee, the eastern European Jews in New York's rag trade, lumbermen in the West, and metal miners and migrant laborers in the IWW. In 1911 Socialist strength was strongest in small cities and towns. By 1917 it had increased its hold in larger cities of the industrialized East and Midwest. But after 1912 the organization began to crumble.

The first city to elect a Socialist mayor (George R. Lunn) and the most influential in municipal socialism was Milwaukee. Like the Progressives, Socialists came to power in the cities on account of voters' dissatisfaction with the major parties. Once in office, Socialists proved cautious, fearing to alienate business and the public by introducing reforms that would involve higher taxation. They concentrated on trying to win elections, to stay in power, and to work for reform within the existing framework. Thus, they favored economical, efficient government, especially in regard to the city's credit rating. Socialism was most successful in winning power when it was progressive, as so-called gas-and-water socialism. When working-class Socialists joined forces with middle-class professional workers in reform campaigns, they differed over programs to institute city-manager or commission forms of government because these reforms weakened neighborhood control of municipal politics, which was one of their specialties. There were other differences. Victor L. Berger wanted piecemeal municipal ownership of public utilities; Eugene Debs wanted more fundamental control. Middle-class Socialists were motivated by the Social Gospel; blue-collar members wanted to use the party as a means of attaining material, social, municipal, and political gains.

Restless middle-class folk flocked to Greenwich Village, New York. Their journal was the *Masses*. Under radical journalist John Reed's prompting and Max Eastman's editorship, the *Masses* promoted various experiments and became especially noted for its irreverent cartoons of Art Young and Robert Minor and drawings of blue-collar life by artists John Sloan and Robert Henri. Sloan illustrated heart-wrenching stories about the poor and drew topical cartoons that exposed selfish business interests. He sometimes disagreed with fellow artist Art Young, who was always willing to conform to the requirements of propaganda to make a Socialist point. "If we put an ash-can in a drawing," observed Young, then the artists were contributing to the realization of a revolution. Young's telling phrase gave a collective title to five painters who constituted the Ash Can School (Sloan, Henri, William Glackens, George Luks, and Everett Shinn).

Yet socialism failed to take hold in the United States. This was partly because the working class was disparate ethnically, dispersed geographically, and fragmented occupationally. It was partly because of general American dislike of intellectual and foreign ideologies and partly on account of overwhelming acculturation of immigrants to American society through schools and social emphasis on material success.

Once again, there was the classic example provided by Henry Ford. Ford—and other manufacturers after him—recognized that they must employ workers not at minimal wages but at higher wages so that they could become maximum consumers of new energy and new products. Ford and others came to think of labor as potential consumers: workers must be enriched so that they can consume more.

By 1914 Ford had been manufacturing more cars than anyone else in the world for almost ten years, but he was almost unknown as a person. To the public at large, his name was the name of a product, not of a man. Then on January 5, 1914, Henry Ford made a highly dramatic announcement. As a means of sharing his profits with his thirteen thousand employees, Ford said that he would pay a minimum wage of $5 for an eight-hour day. In the press that news completely overshadowed all other national and international news, including the news of civil war in Mexico. The *New York Times* suspended disbelief, exclaiming that "the lowest paid employees, the sweepers, who in New York City may claim from $1.00 to $1.50 a day, are now to receive $5 in Ford's plant." It was, said the *New York Herald*, "an epoch in the world's industrial history." However, Ford attached certain social conditions to his minimum wage: he required wholesome workers who would abstain from alcohol and tobacco. The little-known manufacturer became the subject of intense press scrutiny. In seven days alone the New York press printed fifty-two columns about him. The public learned that Ford lived modestly, enjoyed skating, disliked Wall Street, raised pheasants, which he fed on custard, and placed no special value on college education.

Whatever Ford's underlying motive for paying $5 a day to men he could have employed for $2, his own explanation that it was "a plain act of social justice" was considered disingenuous. But Ford's decision expressed what his company needed. If it were to continue to grow, it must have a wider constituency of consumers than the limited few who could buy a car in 1914. New consumers could be created among blue-collar workers only if they had additional wages allowing them to play the new part allotted to them.

But there was a tactical factor in the dwindling appeal of socialism as well. Where Socialists made successful political inroads in Europe, it was always by means of effective local organizations. In Europe socialist parties had been built around the caucus, and the Socialists devised a system of branches with open membership, closely tied to party headquarters. Thus the party became the indispensable means of getting out the vote. In the United States, however, local politics had the long tradition of the town meeting, which had led in recent times to the Populists' and the Progressives' assumption of local political control. The Socialists came too late to the political fray to achieve supreme power in the United States by extending direct democracy, although they would continue to exert their influence. More radical Socialists posed more subterranean threats as the century unfolded.

Rising African American writer W. E. B. Du Bois believed that socialism provided the optimum solution to reverse racial discrimination, the main problem facing African American citizens. He reasoned that in a truly socialist society racial prejudice would disappear. In his article "Socialism and the Negro Problem" for the *New Review* of February 1, 1913, Du Bois asserted, "The Negro problem . . . is the great test of the American Socialist." It was a test that many Socialists failed to pass. The founding convention of the SPA acknowledged the "peculiar position" of African Americans in the working class but failed to declare opposition to lynching or segregation, and the entire subject was omitted from later conventions. This was not a subject that would go away.

Two Souls, Two Thoughts, Two Unreconciled Strivings

In the twentieth century, when a primary theme of art was the relationship of the individual to society, the shifting fortunes of African Americans proved a fertile subject for artistic protest. As African Americans moved from slavery and incarceration to freedom and citizenship, they were especially privileged to articulate the problems of other men and women in society.

Five weeks into his presidency, on October 18, 1901, Theodore Roosevelt invited African American spokesman Booker T. Washington to the White House. Roosevelt was committed to trying to reconcile the South to the Republican Party. His invitation was intended as a symbolic gesture to African Americans and was widely interpreted as such. There was terrible logic in the subsequent outrage of racist southerners when the story broke. The *New Orleans Times-Democrat* thought Roosevelt's action mischievous: "When Mr. Roosevelt sits down to dinner with a negro, he declares that the negro is the social equal of the White Man."

Of the total U.S. population of 76.09 million in 1900, 8.83 million were African Americans—about 11.5 percent of the whole. Over 85 percent of them lived in the South—the eleven states of the old Confederacy and five others: Oklahoma and Kentucky to the west, and Delaware, Maryland, West Virginia, and the District of Columbia to the north. Of the total population of 24.52 million of this "Census South," 7.92 million were African Americans. Thus, whereas the ratio of African Americans to whites across the country as a whole was approximately one in nine, in the South it was one in three. In two states, Mississippi and South Carolina, African Americans predominated.

The regular intimacy of contact between Euro-Americans and African Americans in the South under the dark shadow of slavery was superseded in the late nineteenth and early twentieth centuries by a caste system that resulted in an

Noted African American polemicist W. E. B. Du Bois, photographed by C. M. Battey in 1918. After taking three degrees at Harvard, he became professor of history at Atlanta University and devoted himself to race relations, on which he adopted a militant position. In 1910 he became director of publicity and research for the NAACP, a post he held for twenty-four years, during which he organized the Pan-African Congress (1919), before returning to Atlanta University as head of the department of sociology (1933–44). (Library of Congress)

inexorable gulf. In 1903 analyst Charles W. Chestnutt commented that "the rights of the Negroes are at a lower ebb than at any time during the thirty-five years of their freedom, and the race prejudice more intense and uncompromising." Although African Americans were the largest of America's ethnic minorities, they were segregated in schooling, housing, and places of public accommodation, such as parks, theaters, hospitals, schools, libraries, courts, and even cemeteries.

This ironclad segregation began when poor white farmers came to power. Moreover, a new generation of African Americans had grown up who had never known slavery. None of the states passed a single comprehensive Jim Crow segregation law. Instead, they proceeded piecemeal over a period of thirty to sixty years. Thus, South Carolina segregated the races in successive stages, beginning with trains (1898) and moving to streetcars (1905), train depots and restaurants (1906), textile plants (1915 and 1916), circuses (1917), pool halls (1924), and beaches and recreation centers (1934). Georgia began with railroads and prisons (1891) and moved to sleeping cars (1899) and finally pool halls (1925), but refused to segregate places of public accommodation until 1954.

The Supreme Court upheld social segregation. Its most notorious decision came in *Plessy v. Ferguson* on May 18, 1896. Louisiana state law required "separate but equal" accommodations for African American and white passengers on public carriers and provided a penalty for passengers sitting in the wrong railroad car. Homer Plessy was an octoroon who usually passed for white. However, when he sat in a railroad car for whites, he was arrested. He argued that the state law of Louisiana violated the Fourteenth and Fifteenth Amendments. The Supreme Court ruled otherwise. Eight justices approved the doctrine of separate but equal.

In the South white planters manipulated the operation of the law and persuaded federal and state agencies to ensure their control over land policy, labor recruitment, and finance. In the case of *Hodge v. United States* (1906) the Supreme Court ruled that the Thirteenth Amendment had made African Americans citizens and not wards of the nation. Therefore, they must fend for themselves in the states and not rely on federal protective policy. Later, William Pickens, a field secretary for the National Association for the Advancement of Colored People, said the Court's decision rendered the Thirteenth Amendment inoperative in Arkansas, Louisiana, and Mississippi, which he dubbed "the Congo of America."

The South reacted against the natural tide of resentment by African Americans to its restrictive policies with more repression. Mississippi was the first state to effectively disfranchise African American citizens by a constitutional convention in 1890. It was followed by South Carolina (in 1895), Louisiana (1898), North Carolina (by an amendment in 1900), Virginia (1901 and 1902), Georgia (by amendment in 1908), and the new state of Oklahoma (1910). Four more states, Tennessee, Florida, Arkansas, and Texas, achieved the same ends without changing their constitutions. The various constitutions introduced poll taxes, literacy tests, grandfather clauses, and other specious devices to disqualify African Americans. These devices were nothing if not effective. In the South as a whole, African American participation fell by 62 percent between 1890 and 1900.

African American leaders found it almost impossible to develop consciousness among African Americans on a scale to combat the considerable forces of white racism arrayed against them, notably the adverse political climate, the indifference of the Supreme Court, and white intimidation. Their political vote was silenced. There was no African American congressman for twenty-seven years, between 1901, when George H. White of North Carolina left Congress, and 1928, when Oscar De Priest was elected for Chicago.

Yet the African American community had a few vigorous leaders who wanted equal rights for African Americans. But because they were trapped half in and half out of American society, their struggle alternated between a desire for assimilation with white society and a desire to assert African American independence from it. Preeminent leader Booker T. Washington believed that the optimum strategy for the rural masses of African Americans was to concentrate as much as possible on economic independence by thrift and the acquisition of property. With this in mind, he created three major institutions for African Americans: the Normal and Industrial Institute for Negroes, a college in rural Alabama devoted primarily to agricultural and technical education; the Tuskegee Machine, a lobby of African American intellectuals, politicos, and educators and white philanthropists who supported Washington's political and economic aims; and the National Negro Business League, committed to establishing a system of African American entrepreneurs within the existing framework of white capitalism. For the time being, they were to disregard disfranchisement and social segregation.

By contrast, W. E. B. Du Bois described the dilemma of African Americans in *The Souls of Black Folk* (1903): "One feels his twoness, an American, a Negro, two souls, two thoughts, two unreconciled strivings in one dark body." With this book Du Bois tore down what he called "The Awful Veil"—the conspiracy of silence to cover the harsh truths of racism and poverty. In so doing he solidified protest.

Du Bois had already predicted the future. In a six-part series for the *New York Times* of November 17 to December 15, 1901, he foretold the impact of industrialization on African Americans and on race relations: "Into the large cities will pour in increasing numbers the competent and the incompetent, the industrious and the lazy, the law abiding and the criminal. Moreover, the conditions under which these new immigrants are now received are of such a nature that very frequently the good are made bad and the bad are made criminal."

This new leader, William Edward Burghardt Du Bois, was born in Great Barrington, Massachusetts, graduated from Fisk and Harvard Universities, and attended the University of Berlin. After returning to the United States in 1894, he taught at Wilberforce University in Ohio and at Pennsylvania University before becoming professor of sociology at Atlanta University. In *The Souls of Black*

Folk Du Bois voiced two objections to Booker T. Washington's achievements. First, that Washington had become spokesman for African Americans not on account of black support but by white approval. Second, that by subordinating African American economic interests to white *laissez-faire* (which was, of course, not laissez-faire at all but stringent control) and restricting hopes of African American improvement through education and acquiring property, he was discouraging African Americans from higher aspirations that could make them great. What Du Bois and his supporters saw as a result of Washington's accommodation were three tragedies: the disfranchisement of African Americans; legal sanctions to ensure civil inferiority; and the steady withdrawal of economic support from institutions of higher education for African Americans. As the *New York Times* reviewer of Du Bois's book—who was more sympathetic to Washington than to Du Bois—conceded, "These movements are not, to be sure, direct results of Washington's teachings but his propaganda has, without a shadow of a doubt, helped their speedier accomplishment."

What Du Bois proposed in *The Souls of Black Folk* was for African Americans to withdraw the palm branch and to stand firmly upon civil rights guaranteed by the Thirteenth, Fourteenth, and Fifteenth Amendments: "We feel in conscience bound to ask three things: 1, The right to vote; 2, Civic equality; 3, The education of youth according to ability." Du Bois was especially insistent on higher education for African Americans. Du Bois invited like-minded activists to a national conference at Fort Erie in July 1905 that established the Niagara Movement, an elite cadre of about four hundred professional people. However, it failed to attract funds and to find a distinctive national voice.

Some African American activists began to agitate for desegregation on trains. They reckoned that railroads would realize it was more expensive to have segregated seating and would thus yield, if only for the sake of economy. In 1904 the Maryland Suffrage League began campaigning against the new Jim Crow law there and financed a successful lawsuit against segregated travel in 1905. In 1909 the National Negro Conference denounced segregation and the oppression of African Americans. Streetcar companies either ended segregation or went out of business, such as the streetcar company in Richmond, Virginia. However, the wave of protests was short-lived.

It was becoming obvious to increasing numbers of African Americans and sympathetic whites that a strategy of accommodation was futile in the face of racist hostility. Presidents Roosevelt and Taft had to hold together a diverse coalition of Republicans that included a section of gross racial bigots, the lily-whites, who wanted to establish an all-white Republican Party in the South. To appease this faction, both presidents limited the number of federal appointments of African Americans.

Even those who argued that nurture, rather than nature, determined human behavior, were reluctant to challenge popular stereotypes. Intellectual John R. Commons expressed the dominant reformist view in 1907. He claimed that African Americans had opportunities "not only on equal terms, but actually on terms of preference over whites." Their failure to rise "is recognized even by their partisans as something that was inevitable in the nature of the race at that stage of its development." Southern legislatures starved African American schools of adequate funds, thereby making it impossible for them to approach anywhere near the standards of white schools. In 1910 the eleven southern states spent an average of $9.45 on each white pupil but only $2.90 on each African American pupil.

Arguments about genetic inferiority were confounded when boxer Jack Johnson, an African American stevedore from Texas, won the world heavyweight boxing title from Canadian Tommy Burns in Sidney, Australia, on December 26, 1908. Johnson's victory aroused consternation throughout the white community, which set out to discover the great white hope who could defeat the black colossus who moved and struck with the grace of a panther. The search took seven years; mediocre fighter Jess Willard won the heavyweight title from Johnson in Havana, Cuba, in 1915.

Given the prevailing atmosphere of hysteria stoked by institutional racism and the pseudoscientific jargon of prejudiced scientists, African Americans became helpless victims of race riots by malicious whites, such as one in Atlanta, Georgia, in 1906, in which ten African Americans were killed. In 1908 after a white woman claimed she had been raped, whites invaded the African American section of Springfield, Illinois, lynched two African Americans, and flogged several others. Although the white assailants escaped prosecution, the North was influenced by an article denouncing the outrage, "Race War in the North," written by a southern socialist, William English Walling. Together with settlement workers Mary White Ovington and Dr. Henry Moskowitz, Walling persuaded Oswald Garrison Villard, editor of the *New York Evening Post*, to call a conference in 1909, the centenary of the birth of Abraham Lincoln.

Accordingly, at a meeting in New York on May 31 and June 1, 1909, African American and white radicals led by Moskowitz, Ovington, and Walling proposed a new national organization to protect African American rights: the National Association for the Advancement of Colored People (NAACP), with its declared goal of "equal rights and opportunities for all." The NAACP was an elite organization, committed to legal protest against injustice. Under its first president, Moorfield Storey, the NAACP formed several hundred branches. In 1919 the association had 88,448 members distributed among 300 branches, of which 155 were in the South. Under the editorship of Du Bois, its journal, the *Crisis*, attained a circulation of 100,000. Du Bois's column, "As the Crow Flies," attacked white racism. The NAACP's base was in the North, but its principal officers were natives of the South—William Pickens, Robert W. Bagnall, Walter White, and James Weldon Johnson. Johnson, a graduate of Atlanta University, was a distinguished novelist and poet who had served the State Department in Nicaragua and Venezuela. As NAACP secretary (1920–30), he expanded the association's activities.

The NAACP's most distinctive strategy was litigation to challenge racist laws.

For example, in 1917 the NAACP challenged a statute of Louisville, Kentucky, requiring "the use of separate blocks for residence, places of abode, and places of assembly by white and colored people, respectively." Moorfield Storey took the case to the Supreme Court when it was peopled by arch conservatives. Nonetheless, in the case of *Buchanan v. Warley*, the Court unanimously decided on November 5, 1917, that "all citizens of the United States shall have the same right in every state and territory, as is enjoyed by white citizens thereof, to inherit, purchase, lease, sell, hold and convey real and personal property." The *Buchanan* decision resulted in a spate of private restrictive covenants, however, under which residents agreed to sell or rent their property to individuals of one race only. The Court subsequently upheld this pernicious practice in *Corrigan v. Buckley* (1926), maintaining that civil rights were not protected against discrimination by individuals.

Another sequence of NAACP cases tested the constitutionality of disfranchisement. In 1910 Oklahoma introduced its own grandfather clause to prevent African Americans from voting. The NAACP prosecuted two of its election officials for carrying out the new state law. When the officials were found guilty of violating the Fifteenth Amendment by a district court, they appealed to the Supreme Court. In the case of *Guinn v. United States* (1915), the Court unanimously declared that the grandfather clause was "an unconstitutional evasion of the 15th Amendment guarantee that states would not deny citizens the right to vote because of their race." On the same day the Court ruled by 7 votes to 1 in the case of *United States v. Mosley* that it "upheld congressional power to relegate elections tainted with fraud and corruption." Oklahoma reacted quickly, however, passing a new election law that provided permanent registration for those entitled to vote according to the unconstitutional law and allowing African Americans only twelve days to register or be disqualified from voting for life.

The second oldest surviving civil rights organization, the Urban League, was founded in New York in 1911. It was primarily a social welfare organization, assisting migrants in finding work and accommodations and trying to relieve the worst excesses of African American urban poverty. It, too, had a journal, *Opportunity*, founded in 1923.

African Americans were making economic progress. The African American community, like the white, was stronger economically than ever. In 1913 African Americans owned 550,000 houses, worked 937 farms, ran 40,000 businesses, and attended 40,000 African American churches. There were 35,000 African American teachers, and 1.7 million African American students attended public schools.

Despite such indications of economic and social progress, President Woodrow Wilson's administration proved the most racist since the Civil War, with southern Democrats dominant in Congress, the White House, and the Supreme Court. Shortly after Wilson's inauguration, Oswald Garrison Villard called on the new president and presented him with an NAACP plan for the appointment of a

National Race Commission to study the problem of race relations across the nation. Wilson seemed "wholly sympathetic" to the suggestion. Villard then left for a visit to Europe, confident that the commission would soon be appointed. On his return, however, Wilson refused to grant him a second interview and wrote explaining that the political situation was far too delicate for any such action.

Inasmuch as he had views on the subject, and spurred on by his first wife, Ellen Axson Wilson, Wilson acquiesced in renewed segregation. His postmaster general, Albert S. Burleson, introduced the subject at an early cabinet meeting, suggesting separation to reduce friction between white and African American railway clerks. In spring 1913 the Bureau of the Census, the Post Office Department, and the Bureau of Printing and Engraving began to segregate workers in offices, shops, restrooms, and restaurants and cafes and to do so as unobtrusively as possible. Employees who objected were discharged. In the South, post office and treasury officials were given free rein to downgrade or even to discharge African American employees. The result of the Wilson policies was that only eight African Americans working for the federal government in Washington retained their appointments. In Georgia a collector for the Internal Revenue Service announced, "There are no government positions for negroes in the South. A negro's place is in the cornfield."

Activist William Moore Trotter led a delegation of African Americans to the White House to protest Wilson's segregation policies. Their meeting with the president was stormy. Wilson later regretted his harsh words: "When the negro delegate threatened me, I was damn fool enough to lose my temper and to point them to the door," he told Secretary of the Navy Josephus Daniels. "I lost my temper and played the fool."

Wilson's racist policies had a momentous effect on public attitudes because of the contemporary exodus of African Americans from the South to the North. For the second and third decades of the century were also years of the Great Migration. The immediate reason for the exodus was the industrial requirements of World War I. Whites were being drawn increasingly into the armed services and the newly created war industries. However, the war prevented European immigrants from coming to the United States and taking their place as laborers. Thus, in 1915 agents for northern employers began recruiting African American labor from the South. But at least four times as many African Americans went north on word of mouth than did so at the prompting of labor agents. The exodus was mainly spontaneous and largely unorganized. The collective motive was bad treatment in the South. The Great Migration was facilitated by railroad transportation and continued after the war was over. In sum, the South lost 323,000 African Americans between 1910 and 1919 and 615,000 in the 1920s— about 8.2 percent of its African American population.

At the outset, white attitudes toward the migration in both North and South were ambivalent. As time went on, they became alarmist: northerners resented another ethnic disruption following in the wake of the new immigration: southerners did not want to lose their ready supply of cheap labor. Some southern communities passed laws to prevent African Americans from leaving. This happened in Montgomery, Savannah, Greenville, and elsewhere.

Political Feminists and Social Feminists

Of all groups seeking political and social reform, women were the most successful in the Progressive Era. Not all, but many women wanted the vote, wanted easier divorce, and wanted control over conception. Their successes in attaining two of these ends and the right to the third were not simply a matter of overwhelming numbers that put inexorable pressure on the status quo. Of the population of 92.40 million in 1910, 47.55 million were male and 44.85 million were female. The various reforms of the loose coalition of the women's movement constituted a slow-burning fuse that resulted in an explosion of social and economic changes.

The campaign for woman suffrage—political feminism—not only argued for giving women votes and extending democracy on the grounds of civil rights, but it also claimed that this extension of the franchise would introduce both the superior ethics of women into politics and their skills as housekeepers into government.

The first important figures in the movement for woman suffrage were Susan Brownell Anthony and Elizabeth Cady Stanton. An indefatigable speaker to audiences, both welcoming and hostile, Anthony formed the National American Woman Suffrage Association (NAWSA) in 1889, which she served as president (1892–1900). Its goal was a constitutional amendment to grant women the vote. After meeting Anthony in 1851, superb orator and journalist Stanton decided to join her, and they became a remarkable team. Stanton became the first president of the National Women Suffrage Association (1869), the precursor of NAWSA, which she also served as president. A third campaigner was Carrie Chapman Catt, who succeeded Anthony as president of the NAWSA, serving two terms (1900–4 and 1915–20), and led NAWSA to the climax of its crusades to get the Nineteenth Amendment passed and ratified. Although Catt condemned urban political machines, she adopted their tactics to summon her own party and organize them for election drives throughout New York City.

The franchise had been first extended to women in western states, led by Wyoming (1893), Colorado (1893), Utah (1896), and Idaho (1896). These were all sparsely populated states that were trying to attract settlers. In such areas women proposed and men supported woman suffrage as a conservative device to ensure the dominance of white Anglo-Saxon Protestants in politics. By 1912 five more states had adopted woman suffrage—California, Arizona, Washington, Oregon, and Kansas. Another twenty-two states had woman suffrage on certain subjects.

New York City proved a fertile ground for the movement, because it had a greater mixture of classes and social groups than elsewhere and because poverty

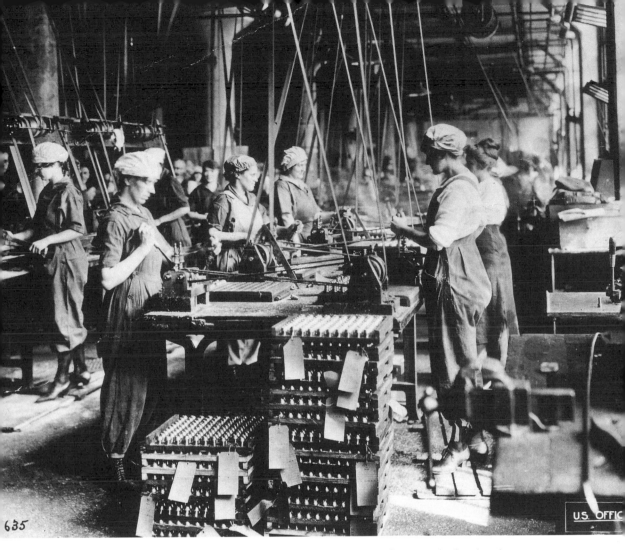

635

The dreary routine of manufacturing for women workers slotting fuses on the head end of fuse bodies in the Gray and Davis ordnance plant in Cambridge, Massachusetts, during World War I. (Library of Congress)

and its attendant problems provoked more militant activism there. In 1907 Harriet Stanton Blatch founded the Equality League of Self-Supporting Women, aimed at recruiting wage-earning women to the suffrage movement and using more aggressive tactics, including mass parades down Fifth Avenue. English suffragette Emmeline Pankhurst spoke in Carnegie Hall.

About 1910 suffragist leaders decided to forgo the piecemeal campaign to win suffrage state by state and to concentrate upon promoting a constitutional amendment. Led by Alice Paul, suffragists adopted the sort of tactics also being used by English suffragettes—picketing government buildings (notably the White House); chaining themselves to railings; and, once in jail, going on hunger strikes to bring shame on the authorities.

Women working for an improved quality of life for women, whether by an extension of the franchise or the introduction of social reforms, recognized that they could achieve their aims only by creating organizations to rally support, educate the public, and lobby politicians. Half of the important women's organizations were established in the 1890s, but many professional women's groups were founded during the first twenty years of the twentieth century, including the National Organization of Public Health Services (1912), the International Association of Policewomen (1915), the Medical Women's National Association (1915), the Federation of Teachers (1916), the National Association of Deans of Women (1916), and the National Federation of Business and Professional Women's Clubs (1919).

These new women's groups were encouraged by urbanization, industrialization, and increased opportunities in higher education. Another factor was the increased leisure time of middle-class wives, allowing them to be introduced, through lectures, to such subjects as national prohibition of alcohol, political corruption, and international affairs. Many clubs were active forces for change and helped establish such community services as kindergartens, playgrounds, public laundries, public baths, parks, and libraries. In New York it was the Women's Municipal League that decided in 1906 to investigate the reception procedures for immigrants at Ellis Island in an attempt to protect newcomers from harassment and fraud.

Another index of the changing position of women was the admission of women to all levels of education, including higher, professional, and technical education; they were organizing themselves for a wider variety of careers. Yet, despite the growth of activities open to women, almost all of them fell within the traditional pattern of women's activities, such as domestic work and child rearing. This reflected the old idea of separate spheres for men and women.

In *Everyone Was Brave* (1969) historian William O'Neill describes women whose primary concern was to serve others and society and calls them "social feminists," in comparison with those (political and economic) feminists whose main aim was to widen opportunities for individual women workers, irrespective of the ends to which new opportunities might be put. This second class of feminists rejected "the social feminist compromise that enlarged women's sphere of action while channelling their energies" in directions acceptable to society run by men. "Social feminists wanted the vote on the perfectly reasonable ground that it would advance their reforms. Ardent suffragists wanted it for its own sake." The growth of social feminism imposed a crucial limitation on the women's movement. "The chief feature of social feminism was that it created roles for women that militated against their full emancipation." Yet, by comparison with the suffragists, who, after fifty years, had little to show for all their hard work, social feminists could point to positive achievements in the fields of education, careers, and social work. Ironically, social feminists, by their very activities outside the family, actually undermined the movement for political and social equality. They were simply increasing a range of opportunities for women that were extensions of women's activities in the home.

The movement for woman suffrage attracted support from men and women whom we might think of as conservative and opposition from those we prefer to think of as liberals.

The most concentrated opposition to woman suffrage came from the South in states favorable to prohibition of alcohol and most intent on denying their citizens access to liquor. In the end only ten states refused to ratify the Nineteenth Amendment, nine in the South, and Delaware on the border between North and South. All these states, however, ratified the Eighteenth (national prohibition) Amendment. The Democratic Party, dominated by its southern section, refused to support woman suffrage by constitutional amendment as late as 1915. What the South feared was that the entire issue of suffrage would be reopened. The South had recently disfranchised African American men by subterfuges such as grandfather clauses, poll taxes, and literacy tests. Such devices were subversive of the Constitution but technically unassailable as long as the North accepted the racist arguments of the South. If woman suffrage were adopted, argued racists, then African American women, as well as white, would be legally entitled to vote. The sort of systematic violence and coercion that had been used to intimidate African American men could not so easily be applied to African American women without attracting unfavorable publicity and adverse political consequences. Moreover, southern politicians from states producing textiles feared that if women gained the vote, then middle-class women would work to reduce, and possibly eliminate, the child labor upon which much southern industry relied.

Another crucial factor in the fifty-year campaign for woman suffrage was growing awareness of just how radical a proposal it was. On the surface it seemed that little would change socially. However, more was expected of woman suffrage by those in favor and those opposed. Radicals such as Charlotte Perkins Gilman thought that, empowered by suffrage, middle-class women would have a chance to influence politics directly influencing women. They were proved correct. Woman suffrage appeared radical because it could not be accommodated in the traditional idea of separate spheres: the aim was to demolish the walls between them.

Not only men but also women worked against the suffrage of women in various groups of "Antis," especially in those states where the suffrage movement was strongest (Illinois, Indiana, Iowa, Massachusetts, New Jersey, New York, Ohio, and Pennsylvania). Moreover, women prominent in public life took part in the campaign against woman suffrage, notably investigative journalist Ida Minerva Tarbell, economist Annie Nathan Meyer, and prison reformer Kate Barnard. Their reason was a fear that woman suffrage would disrupt the family. Underlying their arguments lay the traditional assumption that the differences between men and women extended beyond biology into the suitability of one sex for a social and political role and the suitability of the other for a social role only. Ann Watkins declared in 1912, "You cannot dodge the fact women have work in the world that men cannot do. Neither man nor woman is superior to [or] inferior to the other. The two are just different, positive and negative, two great manifestations of a still greater force." Moreover, they feared that woman suffrage would undermine protective legislation for women and children. Once woman suffrage became law, the just (and long-fought-for) arguments for special protective legislation for women in industrial work would be eroded on the grounds that equality at the ballot box had eliminated any need for women to receive any special consideration. Unfortunately, this proved to be an accurate prediction.

The suffrage movement was part of that broader trend of feminism, the freeing of women from all sorts of taboos. In society, women suffered various legal disadvantages, as litigants, as property owners, and as heirs to property. In marriage, the law gave husbands many rights that made their wives less equal, and customs gave the husbands other privileges, notably absolute sexual rights. This was still a period when convention assumed that marriage was the price men paid for sex and sex was the price women paid for marriage.

One part of this trend, and another index of changing social expectations of women in the Progressive Era, was the increase in divorce. The divorce rate rose. In 1900 there was one divorce in every twelve marriages. In 1909 the ratio was one to ten; in 1916, one to nine. In *A History of Matrimonial Institutions* (1904) social scientist George F. Howard explained the rising tide of divorce in the context of industrialization and urbanization. Not only was the old patriarchal family being dissolved, but new forms of marriages with higher spirituality were coming into being as the single individual, rather than the family, became the functional unit of society.

Two-thirds of all divorces were granted to women. Critics of easy divorce began to question women's traditional role as guardians of family stability and morality. They feared that the swelling tide of divorce would undermine this role and then society itself. In a symposium on divorce, "Are Women to Blame?" the *North American Review's* women panelists accused American women of responsibility for the soaring divorce rate, charging them with being spoiled and jealous of men. Margaret Deland, a champion of unmarried mothers in Boston, believed that civilization "rests upon the permanence of marriage." Easier divorce would undo civilization: "If we let the flame of our idealism be quenched in the darkness of the senses, our civilization must go upon the rocks." Women should tolerate men's adulteries for the sake of social harmony.

Those who favored easier divorce laws were mainly sociologists, liberal clergymen, and feminists. Some American liberals felt that conventional marriage was repressive, that it discriminated against women, and that easier divorce offered opportunities for marriage reform. A widely known argument was that women needed to be protected from their husbands' excessive sexual demands. Feminist playwright Jesse Lynch Williams asked in 1914 if a woman "allowing herself to be owned body and soul by a man she loathes [is] doing right?" Not only did their husbands' sexual rights make victims of many wives, but they also exaggerated the significance of sex and denied women the right to develop fully because they placed too high a premium on nubility and desirability.

Public opinion began to change. Organizations opposed to divorce, such as the New England Divorce Reform League (1881–1913) and the Committee on the Family of the Federal Council of Churches (1911–19), failed. The press, once staunchly opposed to divorce, began to shift emphasis and adopted the critical stance of such progressive journals as the *North American Review, The Outlook,* and *The World's Work.* The *World's Work* published "The True View of Increasing Divorce" in 1910. It found that the rate of divorce had not reached epidemic proportions and that divorces could not be excessively restricted.

One of the most controversial aspects of social feminism was contraception. Fearing that spreading information on contraception would encourage greater sexual license, both federal and state governments enacted sumptuary legislation. Moreover, contraception was a taboo subject for a society that needed to reproduce in order to maintain a high labor force. The most widely publicized cases involved Margaret Sanger. Yet Sanger's great will to create a widely based movement for birth control and the skill with which she promoted it probably affected a wider social spectrum of women than any other movement of social reform in the twentieth century.

Trained as a nurse, Margaret Sanger campaigned for birth control to free women in the home rather than the workplace. Her experience of life in New York's Lower East Side taught her that working-class women were chained to enforced motherhood and poverty. Their only alternative was a "five-dollar abortionist." In her memoir, *My Fight for Birth Control* (1931), Margaret Sanger described her conversion:

> As I stood at the window and looked out, the miseries and problems of that sleeping city arose before me in a clear vision like a panorama: crowded homes, too many children; babies dying in infancy; mothers overworked; baby nurseries; children neglected and hungry; mothers half sick most of their lives; women made into drudges; children working in cellars; children aged six and seven pushed into the labor market to earn a living; another baby on the way; still another; yet another; a baby born dead—great relief; an older child dies—sorrow, but nevertheless, relief—insurance helps; a mother's death—children scattered into institutions; the father desperate, drunken. . . . Within five years four children are born. The mother, racked and worn, decides this can't go on, and attempts to interrupt the next pregnancy. The siren of the ambulance, death of the mother, orphan children, poverty, misery, slums, child labor, unhappiness, ignorance, destitution . . . I watched the lights go out, I saw the darkness gradually give way to the first shimmer of dawn, and then a colorful sky heralded the rise of the sun. I knew a new day had come for me and a new world as well. I could now see clearly the various social strata of our life; all its mass problems seemed to be centered around uncontrolled breeding.

In March 1914 Margaret Sanger published the first issue of the *Woman Rebel,* in which she tried to make working-class women think for themselves and not simply accept the general dictates of their husbands. Its slogan was "No Gods, No Masters." Margaret Sanger's demand for public information on birth control was one step in the revolt against paternalism. She declared that "suffragists, feminists, and all women's organizations will never make progress until they recognize the fact that women cannot be on an equal footing with men until they have full and complete control of their reproductive functions."

The paper was an immediate success. Sanger decided to use some of the money from subscriptions to publish a pamphlet, *Family Limitation*, that would provide information on contraception. Before *Family Limitation* was in print, she was indicted by the federal government for violation of the mails because she used them to distribute an "obscene" article in the *Woman Rebel*. Rather than to face trial and a possible jail sentence of forty-five years, she left for Europe in fall 1914. In the end the federal government chose not to prosecute her and thereby publicize her cause.

By the time Sanger returned to New York in 1916, a group of liberal women had created the National Birth Control League with the aim of getting laws on birth control revised. Their leader, Mary Ware Dennett, tried to recruit members from the subscription lists at the *Women Rebel* but failed to gain enough members. Arrested for publication and renewed distribution of the *Family Limitation*, Sanger nevertheless set off on a nationwide tour to elicit support and funds for her plan to establish birth control clinics. In Portland, Oregon, she was again arrested for distributing *Family Limitation*. The publicity was such that her name and the idea of professional control were spread by newspapers across the country.

Sanger opened her first birth control clinic in the United States in the Brownsville section of Brooklyn on October 16, 1916. For a fee of only ten cents, she explained to Italian and Jewish immigrant women how to use birth control devices and helped about five hundred women to get a diaphragm fitted. After ten days she was arrested. When she was being whisked away to trial, a mother ran after the police wagon, crying out, "Come back and save me!"

Sanger challenged police interpretation of the law, claiming that the specific code, section 1142, was unconstitutional because it compelled women to run risks of death in childbirth. Thus, it did not promote the health and welfare of the community. After she had spent thirty days in Queens County Penitentiary, the judge who reviewed her case ruled that doctors could prescribe contraception but also that birth control was a matter for the legislatures, not the courts.

Although the feminist and socialist movements trod separate paths, Sanger found allies in one political group—the Wobblies: "Only the boys of the IWW seemed to grasp the economic significance of this great social question." The IWW provided her with the names of labor organizers. They also offered her assistance to pass her information on family limitation to workers and their wives.

Meanwhile, the movement for woman suffrage came to a climax. During the period 1910–20 the publicity associated with middle-class women who defied the law, got arrested, endured prison, resisted force feeding, and then did everything all over again began to convince thousands of hitherto apathetic women that woman suffrage was a cause worth fighting for. In 1915 four eastern states held referenda on woman suffrage. Although the motions were defeated, they came close to being carried, with a 46 percent vote in Pennsylvania, a 42 percent vote in New York and New Jersey, and a 35 percent vote in Massachusetts. Membership in NAWSA climbed close to 2 million with a gross income of $750,000.

At first, President Woodrow Wilson refused to support woman suffrage. Years earlier, the mother of a Princeton graduate student had suggested to Wilson that he make the college coeducational in order "to remove the false glamour with which the two sexes see one another."

"My dear Madam," said Wilson, "that is the very thing we want to preserve at all costs."

Wilson was overtaken by events he himself had helped set in motion. He came out in favor of woman suffrage in 1915 and proposed it as a campaign issue in 1916. The decisive factor in the campaign for woman suffrage and women's general emancipation, however, was not the political support of a president or Congress. It was the tragedy of World War I. The war came at a time when political success was within the reach of suffragists. For one thing, women took the place of workingmen drafted into the services. They became telegraph messengers, elevator operators, and streetcar conductors. They also worked as full operatives in munitions factories and railroad works. Their numbers expanded within professions traditional to women, such as nurses, stenographers, and clerks. Industry hired forty thousand more women than before. Full employment increased the average real income of blue-collar women by 20 percent. Men could no longer deny them the vote. A Joint Resolution submitting the Women's Suffrage Amendment to the states had been passed by the House but rejected by the Senate in 1917; on June 4, 1919, the Senate, by a vote of 56 to 25, adopted it, and it was ratified by August 18, 1920. By now almost all leading politicians—including Woodrow Wilson—supported the amendment. Whatever their private thoughts, they knew the amendment was about to pass and that resisting it would injure their careers. Besides, they wanted the votes it would produce.

The Nineteenth Amendment simply announced that "The right of citizens of the United States to vote shall not be denied or abridged by the United States or by any State on the grounds of sex." The initial results of women's franchise were disappointing for the feminists. In the elections of 1920 and 1924, for the only times in American history, less than half the electorate turned out to vote. Women were enfranchised only a few weeks before the election of 1920 and perhaps needed time to get used to exercising their rights. However, the proportion of women who voted did not equal that of men until 1956—thirty-six years after women gained the vote.

More disturbing from the feminists' point of view was that, although the suffrage movement had become central to the whole feminist cause, woman suffrage had almost no discernible effect upon the position of women. This was ironic because advocates of woman suffrage had predicted that it would lead to social reform, even to a reduction in vice and crime. Thus, within three years after the Nineteenth Amendment had been ratified, radical feminist Alice Paul proposed a new amendment, the Equal Rights Amendment (ERA), providing that "equality of right under the law shall not be denied or abridged by the United States or by a State on account of sex." However, the majority of suffragists considered the ERA a betrayal of all they had fought for because it would nullify existing special protective laws for women. "The cry Equality, Equality, where Nature has created inequality," declared Florence Kelley of the National Consumers' League, "is as stupid and as deadly as the cry Peace, Peace, where there is no Peace."

As to contraception, after World War I laws against spreading contraceptive information remained on the statute books but were more honored in the breach than the observance. Margaret Sanger's organization, the American Birth Control League, developed into a middle-class reform movement and gained support from doctors, and the number of birth control clinics multiplied. Sanger maintained that effective birth control would produce "more children from the fit, less from the unfit." In time, it won over many from the middle class and the medical profession and became a part of the new majority.

CHAPTER 5

Making Waves in World Affairs

WHICH WOULD COME FIRST—the war or the revolution? This question troubled leaders of the great nations at the turn of the century.

Ascendant America rose to globalism amid the decline of western Europe and havoc in the Far East in 1900–1945—crisis years devastated by wars and disfigured by revolutions on left and right. The British and French empires in Africa and Asia faced plangent appeals for freedom from their subject peoples. Germany slid into barbarism when it fell into the control of Adolf Hitler and the Nazis (1933–45). Japan entered its dark valley of military dictatorship at home and aggression overseas (1926–45). Communist Russia (1917–91) endured colossal tyranny under Joseph Stalin's dictatorship (1927–53). Irreconcilable antagonisms between the great powers culminated in the destruction and genocide of World War I (1914–18) and World War II (1939–45). European domination of the globe dwindled and was superseded by the new superpowers, the United States and the Soviet Union, in the bitter years of the Cold War (1945–91).

What was a world power? In the twentieth century a world power had to have complementary attributes: extensive territories, a large population, and massive industrial resources. In 1900 Britain and the United States met these qualifications. Russia did not.

Britain dominated world affairs in 1900 because its domestic industrial base and overseas mercantile empire penetrated the globe through trade, finance, and political control. The British Empire covered 16 percent of the surface of the earth; its population accounted for a quarter of the earth's population. But Britain could not forge its disparate, overseas dependencies into a political unit as cohesive as the United States. The United States was the fifth largest nation in area and the fourth largest in population. Not only did it lead the world in the industrial production of coal, steel, and oil, but it had also acquired a strategically valuable empire in the Caribbean and the Pacific. Russia was an embryonic world power—a huge continental empire in Europe and Asia, comprising peoples of many cultures and having the world's third largest population. Geoffrey Hosking emphasizes (1997) how weakly developed was the Russian sense of national identity because for Russian leaders imperialism was more important than nationhood. Moreover, Russia was economically and industrially backward. Its autocratic government was bureaucratic and brutal toward political dissenters and Jews—many of whom immigrated to the United States.

One of the clear signs that the twentieth century would be the American century was the continuing overseas expansion of the United States. This was less a matter of acquiring colonies than of expanding trade and penetrating the economies of other nations. American manufacturers were seeking markets abroad, and American financiers were beginning to invest capital overseas. "Our industries have expanded to such a point that they will burst their jackets if they cannot find a free outlet to the markets of the world," Woodrow Wilson told the Democratic National Convention of 1912. "Our domestic markets no longer suffice. We need foreign markets."

Literally dozens of U.S. companies were establishing themselves around the world, notably Coca-Cola, Quaker Oats, and AT&T. In chemicals, they included Du Pont and Standard Oil of New Jersey; in machinery, General Electric, American Gramophone, Mergenthaler Lino Type, and National Cash Register. Sensing the opportunity for international sales, pioneering automobile manufacturer Henry Ford opened his first factory in Canada in 1909 and his first British factory in 1911. By March 1913 the Ford Motor Company had branches in fourteen cities abroad.

Companies expanding overseas followed a similar pattern. First, they created an extensive foreign marketing organization through branch offices. Second, they built factories abroad, partly to elude American and foreign tariffs, partly to avoid high costs of transportation, and partly to take advantage of low costs of labor in foreign countries. Having achieved integrated production and marketing overseas, they bought raw or partly finished materials locally because they cost less. Thus, in chewing gum, American Chicle had three million acres of land in Mexico where it produced its material. It also operated factories in Britain and Canada. After 1900 the domestic and foreign demand for meat was so great that the great American meatpacking firms no longer had sufficient supplies to meet it. Leading meat-packers Armour and Swift obtained packing plants in Argentina, Brazil, and Uruguay to process meat for Europe.

As a result of such developments, the United States was acquiring a vested interest in the political and economic stability of Europe, Asia, and Latin America—if only to protect American business and its general economy. The upshot was that the politics, economics, and societies of other countries were profoundly affected. For example, in 1908 80 percent of Mexico's railroads and almost 50 percent of its total wealth were owned by U.S. citizens. In times of crisis the investors sought protection of their investment from the federal government. Now, instead of avoiding entangling alliances, the United States needed diplomatic partners. Furthermore, advances in communication and transportation were drawing the world more closely together. Advances in shipbuilding—especially of submarines—were dissolving the strategic value of the Atlantic Ocean. Thus, another pressing reason for expanded U.S. foreign policy was the

"GOOD OFFICES"

Above: The military possibilities of aircraft over land and sea were already being recognized before World War I. This photograph of January 18, 1911, shows the reconnaissance plane *Ely* just after it took off from the USS *Pennsylvania.* (Library of Congress)

Left: Theodore Roosevelt used his considerable diplomatic skill to achieve the Treaty of Portsmouth, New Hampshire, at the end of the Russo-Japanese War. This cartoon by W. A. Rogers for *Harper's Weekly* of June 24, 1905, shows the modestly clad American and uncharacteristically retiring president holding apart the two resplendently attired rival emperors. (Library of Congress)

pressure of power politics as the major powers jostled for imperial, commercial, and strategic supremacy.

The rivalry of the great powers developed from two major yet contradictory processes. First, the new technology of steamships, railways, and telegraphs encouraged the development of a truly cosmopolitan network of commerce, an international division of labor based on economic complements of food, raw materials, and manufactured products. It was financed primarily through a system of credit and insurance centered in London. By 1913 the volume of world trade was twenty-five times greater per capita than it had been in 1800. This first development brought people of different countries closer together.

The second process, however, divided people. It amounted to increased rivalries and tensions among the great powers as shown by their scramble for colonies, military alliances, arms races, and jingoism, all rooted in the propaganda of hatred. New technology aggravated this process. A firepower revolution of high-explosive shells, quick-firing artillery, machine guns, mines, and torpedoes was about to render battlefields more deadly. The first trend encouraged international cooperation; the second led to violence and destruction.

At the turn of the century there were fewer than 50 countries recognized as independent, sovereign states across the world. In 1996, the centennial year of the modern Olympic Games, the organizing committee invited 197 independent, sovereign nations to present teams to the competition. This quadrupling of nations followed the disruption of empires that controlled a third of the globe in 1900.

The Western Hemisphere, where formal colonies were few, was under the hegemony of the United States. Eastern Europe was held by four imperial monarchies: Germany, Austria-Hungary, Russia, and Turkey—although the bulk of the Turkish empire was in the Middle East. Africa was almost completely colonized, primarily by France in the northwest and the western bulge, and by Britain with a chain of colonies from north to south. Only Liberia, Ethiopia, and Morocco stood outside the colonial system. They did so on the sufferance of the mighty European powers.

Russia had expanded across Asia from the Black Sea to the Pacific Ocean. Elsewhere in Asia, Britain had colonized India, Burma, and Malaya and had footholds in China and the East Indies; France occupied Indochina; the Dutch held the Netherlands East Indies (NEI); and the United States was in the Philippines and Hawaii.

Among the leading powers, Germany and Japan desperately wanted to become world-class powers and planned to do so by further colonization. The history of international relations from 1890 to 1945 centers around their unsuccessful bid. Germany, by its defeats of Austria (1866) and France (1870), had not only achieved unification in the Second Reich (1870–1918) but had also become the greatest power on the continent of Europe and the one with the most efficient army. Like the United States, Germany had achieved lightning industrial growth, especially in steel, electricity, and chemicals. But although the German empire in the continent of Africa and the Pacific islands was large, its economic value was negligible. Japan was the most industrial nation in Asia, but its overall territory and population were only slightly larger than the British Isles.

Nevertheless, Germany and Japan, confident of their outsize military potential and urged on by an aggressive military elite, wanted to reach the front rank. Given their deficiencies in territory and limitations in human resources, they knew they could become great powers only by seizing territory for expansion. The only areas open to them were, for Germany, eastern Europe and for Japan, southeast Asia. Austria-Hungary and Turkey became part of Germany's economic orbit. The proposed Berlin-Baghdad Railway was to be the axis of a new economic community. Japan focused on defenseless China, which had survived encroaching European imperialism, notwithstanding the loss of certain territories. China offered Japan the tempting prospects of territory for settlement and a mass market for trade.

Such was the context of America's rise to globalism.

Pacific Overtures, the Rising Sun, and the Sleeping Giant

After the Spanish-American-Cuban War of 1898, by which the United States acquired the Philippines, Guam, and Wake Island in the Pacific and, in the Caribbean, Puerto Rico and the right to intervention in Cuba, U.S. statesmen soon learned that it was easier to acquire a colonial empire than to govern it. The United States had also annexed the Pacific archipelago of Hawaii. But territorial imperialism was to prove a headache, a heartache, and a disappointment.

The Treaty of Paris, granting the Philippines to the Unites States, was followed by a Filipino uprising, led by Emilio Aguinaldo, that lasted two years and in which more people died than in the war of 1898. The American public recoiled from the terrible cost in human life of subduing the Filipino rebellion. The U.S. military government of the Philippines was replaced on March 4, 1901, by a civil commission of four members. William Howard Taft, then a circuit judge, headed the commission to establish a civil government. Ironically, commercial and naval opinion now held that the Philippines were of no value for developing trade with Asia.

In Cuba, Gen. Leonard Wood, as temporary governor-general, devised the future form of the island's relations with the United States. The Platt amendment to an army appropriation bill of March 2, 1901, allowed the president to end the occupation of Cuba after the Cuban government agreed to five conditions: never to make a treaty that would impair its independence; never to contract a debt it could not repay; to consent to American rights of intervention to preserve Cuba's independence and stabilize the government; to execute a sanitary program; and to allow the United States a naval base on the island. Thus, Cuba remained an American protectorate. By a treaty of March 22, 1903, the United States obtained the right to intervention to preserve Cuban independence and governmental stability.

The agreement was put to the test on September 28, 1906, when President Tomas Estrada Palma resigned in the face of a rebellion and the Cuban congress could not decide on a successor. The island was soon plunged into chaos. President Theodore Roosevelt dispatched Secretary of War William Howard Taft to Havana and then carried out his advice to assume temporary control. The second military occupation of Cuba ended on January 28, 1909, with the inauguration of President Jose Miguel Gomez.

As to Puerto Rico, the other Caribbean acquisition of 1898, the Foraker Act of April 12, 1900, provided for a small amount of self-rule, allowing the islanders to elect a lower house and giving the president the right to appoint the governor, the heads of the executive departments, and members of the upper house. In a series of test cases, the Supreme Court decided on May 27, 1901, that the Philippines and Puerto Rico were territories appurtenant to, but not part of, the United States. Thus, their peoples were subjects, not citizens. The United States could therefore both acquire the islands and erect a tariff wall against their crops of sugar and tobacco. On March 2, 1917, the Foraker Act was revised by the (second) Jones Act, which granted citizenship to Puerto Ricans and allowed them to elect both chambers of the Assembly.

Problems of imports and tariffs punctuated the course of the Philippines' progress toward independence. On July 1, 1902, Congress passed the Civil Government, or First Organic, Act for the Philippines. First, it made Filipinos citizens of the Philippine Islands. Second, it established an executive branch of government, comprising a five-man commission, headed by a governor-general to be appointed by the president of the United States, with the consent of the Senate. It provided for a legislature of two chambers to be established after two years, the lower house to be elected by the Christian tribes and the upper house simply to consist of the commission. William Howard Taft was the first governor-general. His sympathetic nature and proven honesty supposedly did much to win the Filipinos to U.S. rule. However, Taft, with well-intentioned but undisguised racist candor, described the Filipino as "the little brown brother." His remark drew a riposte from U.S. soldiers who hated their task: "He may be a brother of Big Bill Taft/But he ain't no brother of mine." The occupation bred new legends of ugly Americans.

To further the cause of Philippine independence, a later governor-general, Francis Burton Harrison, agreed with Filipino leaders Sergio Osmenia and Manuel Quezon to transfer as much power as possible to Filipino leaders and thus convince Congress that the islands were worthy of, and ready for, full independence. By 1913 four of the nine commissioners, 71 percent of civil servants, 92 percent of teachers, and all governors of the Christian provinces were Filipinos. President Woodrow Wilson agreed in principle with Harrison, but the Republicans, who controlled Congress, did not. The compromise between Wilson, Harrison, and Congress took the form of a Second Organic Act for the Philippines, the (first) Jones Act, passed on June 29, 1916. While reserving sovereignty to the United States, the Jones Act created an elected senate in the Philippine legislature to supersede the commission, eased suffrage requirements, and allowed the governor-general, with the consent of the Philippine senate, to appoint heads of most executive departments.

Their troubles in the Philippines quelled Americans' initial enthusiasm for expansion when they realized that, unlike settlement of the Great American Desert, imperialism overseas did not simply mean driving away the native inhabitants and acquiring more free land. It meant administering established communities.

Such considerations led American statesmen to turn increasingly to China, the sleeping giant of world affairs. China extended 4.5 million square miles and had a population of over 400 million. It was, however, an underdeveloped country with vast, untapped resources and a social and economic infrastructure that could be bent to the will of an imperial power—without hateful physical occupation. The other great powers—Britain, France, Germany, Japan, and Russia—had already obtained major concessions from the sleeping giant in trading rights, leaseholds, ports, or strategically placed territory. The dowager empress, Cixi, exclaimed of China's predators, "The various powers cast upon us looks of tiger-like voracity, hustling each other in their endeavors to be the first to seize upon . . . our territories."

Among these powers, Russia and Japan were the leading contenders in the projected dismemberment of China. Tensions arose between Russia and Japan over Manchuria, a state north of the Great Wall, comprising the provinces of Heilongjiang, Liaoning, Rehe, and Jehol. Manchuria provided the most direct route from the west to Vladivostock. The Russians extracted a Chinese concession to build, maintain, and guard a railway across it, the Chinese Eastern Railway, linked with their Trans-Siberian Railway, begun in 1891. They also wanted to build a second railway to the ice-free ports Dalian (Dairen) and Lushun (Port Arthur) across the Liaodong Peninsula. Manchuria was attractive to Japan because it had resources of coal and iron ore.

Japan was apprehensive about Russian penetration of Korea, a country of southeast Asia from which it had already exacted special privileges and over which it had fought China in the First Korean War in September 1894. When Japan was victorious, it ensured that the Treaty of Shimonoseki of April 17, 1895, awarded it valuable prizes: Formosa (Taiwan), the Douglas Islands, Lushun, the Liaodong Peninsula, and Chinese recognition of Korean independence. China's defeat by Japan was a clear signal that China could not defend itself against modern armies and navies.

France, Russia, and Germany were disturbed by Japan's dramatic success in upsetting the balance of power in Asia. Thus, they put pressure on Japan to forgo one concession—the Liaodong Peninsula, including the harbor and fortress of Lushun. These were the keys to northern China. Japan's capitulation to pressure lived on in Japanese historical legend as the Triple Intervention. The Japanese could certainly accuse the West of hypocrisy. Within five years, Germany had taken Tsingtan, France had secured Kwangchow Bay, Britain had secured the lease of Weihai and Hong Kong, and Russia had taken control of the Liao-dong Peninsula and Lushun. But the event that most outraged Japan was the Russian acquisition of the very territory it had yielded in 1895.

In this disturbed situation the strategy of Secretary of State John Hay (1898–1905) was to try to get all the major powers to agree to peaceful and equitable economic penetration of China in a so-called Open Door Policy, announced in a series of unilateral notes—the First Open Door Notes of September 6, 1899, to March 20, 1900; and the Second Open Door Notes of July 3, 1900. In between came the Boxer uprising of June 13, 1900, a terrifying demonstration in which foreign legations in Beijing were attacked by staunch Chinese nationalists who killed 231 foreigners.

The First and Second Open Door Notes represented an American attempt to persuade China to accept the United States as moderator in its relations with other powers. John Hay hoped that China would identify its economic interests with the United States. However, the Open Door was also a symbol that the American advocates of expanded markets, commerce, and shipping were gaining ground at the expense of those who wanted outright colonization. But the Open Door depended on accommodation among the nations. For a war over China was outside America's interests and beyond its military capacity.

Russia used the Boxer Rebellion as a pretext to occupy Manchuria and would not leave. Theodore Roosevelt was furious—but powerless to act. After due consideration about this unwelcome development, Japan signed an alliance with Britain on January 30, 1902 (renewed in 1905 and 1911). Britain gained a counterweight to Russia in the Far East; Japan gained tacit British acceptance of its interests in Korea. Then Japan took action. First it broke off diplomatic relations with Russia on February 6, 1904. It engaged Russian vessels off Seoul on February 8, before formally declaring war on February 10. The London *Times* commented, "The Japanese Navy has opened the war by an act of daring which is destined to take a place of honor in naval annals."

The American public also thought that "Gallant Little Japan" was standing up to the ferocious Russian bear. This was certainly Roosevelt's view. Nevertheless, he knew that a decisive Japanese victory might prejudice the development of American interests in China and eventually lead to a war in Asia between the United States and Japan. Thus, he offered to mediate to end the damaging Russo-Japanese war. Although Japan had scored a series of military and naval victories, both sides were ready for peace by 1905. Japan had overextended itself financially: it could not afford to lengthen its lines of transportation and communication any farther. Russia had been defeated on land and at sea, and its defeat was all the more galling because it was at the hands of an Asian power.

In addition, the ruling dynasty of the Romanovs faced acute political problems at home—nothing less than a confrontation between the autocratic government of Czar Nicholas II and industrial workers, peasants, and the armed forces. Czarism was an archaic system of government, out of touch with contemporary needs. The impending storm against it would revolutionize the world. In 1905 in the

Plumed Eagles Ready to Fall

Left: Kaiser Wilhelm II of Germany (*left*) at naval maneuvers with Winston Churchill of Britain (*right*), then first lord of the Admiralty (1911–15). Churchill began the process of modernizing the British navy for war with Germany. Having stumbled into World War I, the insecure but arrogant kaiser (who reigned 1888–1918) found himself overwhelmed by events he could not control. His military failures cost him the throne. Controversial member of parliament and statesman, Churchill belonged, at different times, to both the Liberal Party and the Conservative Party, serving them both in various cabinet positions, including chancellor of the exchequer (1924–29). He survived years in the political wilderness in the 1930s until his eloquence as an orator and credibility as a consistent opponent of appeasement of Adolf Hitler led to his return to government, notably as prime minister (1940–45; 1951–55); he was the savior of his country. (Library of Congress)

Right: Nicholas II, czar of Russia (reigned 1894–1917) (*left*), and George V, king-emperor of Britain (reigned 1910–36) (*right*), cousins with marked physical similarity emphasized by haircut, beard, and regal-military costume. Nicholas II's inability to adapt the archaic system of czarism to Russia's twentieth-century needs and his mismanagement of World War I was a contributory cause of the Russian Revolution that felled him. George V's astute realization that he must reign as a constitutional monarch and his diplomatic skills behind the scenes eased Britain's troubled passage from a quasi-autocratic to a more democratic form of government. After his abdication, Nicholas II discovered to his cost that water was thicker than blood. George V ensured that the Russian imperial family with an unpopular German-born czarina would not find refuge in England. (Library of Congress)

capital, Saint Petersburg, workers coordinated strikes through councils, or Soviets. The strength of agitation forced Nicholas II to issue the October Manifesto, promising a representative government—reforms that were later withdrawn. From exile in Switzerland, the revolutionary leader Vladimir Ilyich Lenin had already divided the Social Democratic Party in 1903. The Bolsheviks (*bolshevik* means "majority") believed in the violent assumption of power by a small, highly organized elite that would use all available means, notably control of transportation, communication, and the army, as instruments to impose a dictatorship in the name of the working classes. The Mensheviks (*menshevik*, "minority") argued for a parliamentary approach to Marxism. The reverberations of the moderate Russian revolution of 1905 were soon felt in subsequent revolutions in Persia (1906), Turkey (1908), China (1911 and 1912), and in the encouragement it gave to nationalist movements in India and Indochina.

Meanwhile, Theodore Roosevelt arbitrated a peace between imperial Russia and imperial Japan. In the Treaty of Portsmouth, New Hampshire, of September 5, 1905, Russia agreed to transfer to Japan the lease of the Liaodong Peninsula, including Lushun and Dalian, and the branch of the Chinese Eastern Railway below Changchun (soon renamed the South Manchuria Railroad), as well as the northern half of Sakhalin; Russia also agreed to recognize Japan's "paramount political, military, and economic interest in Korea." Both countries agreed to evacuate Manchuria (apart from land leased to them) within eighteen months. However, American planners were disturbed by their recent, wartime realization that Japan could take enemy strongholds on hostile shores. Japan had demonstrated that a non-European state could master the sophisticated technology of modern warfare and use it to reverse the tide of the Euro-American deluge of Asia.

Moreover, American planners reckoned that Japan could also seize both the Philippines and Guam with small chance of their being recaptured. Roosevelt was particularly apprehensive that Japan might have designs on the Philippines. Accordingly, he had Taft, under cover of a visit to Manila, visit Tokyo in secret, where he concluded the Taft-Katsura secret agreement of July 27, 1905. The United States now gave its approval to Japan's penetration of Korea, in exchange for an assurance that Japan would not interfere in the Philippines. Later, the two countries reached the Root-Takahira agreement of November 30, 1908, which consolidated American-Japanese friendship. Not only did Japan guarantee not to attack the Philippines, but it also supported the Open Door in China. Thus, Roosevelt acquiesced in Japanese domination of Korea (which could not be defended) and recognized the special position of Japan in Manchuria (which betrayed the spirit of the Open Door). Among Japan's subsequent thanks for TR's good offices was a gift of cherry trees to adorn Washington, D.C.

Russia and Japan subsequently reconciled and signed a secret convention on July 30, 1907, dividing Manchuria into Russian and Japanese spheres of influence. And in Korea, Japan had consolidated its position to such an extent that it could dispose of the king. On August 22, 1910, Japan annexed the country that it was to rule for thirty-five years.

In 1911 revolution overthrew the Manchu Qing Dynasty in China. At first, the imperial government quelled the republican Wuchang Uprising on October 11, 1911. But after fifteen provinces declared their secession, on December 12 provincial delegates proclaimed a republic with Sun Yat-sen as provisional president. In February 1912 revolutionaries compelled the boy-emperor, Pu Yi, to abdicate. Sun himself stepped aside to allow Yuan Shikai to become president. The United States was the first power to recognize the new republican government in China. However, President Woodrow Wilson and Secretary of State William Jennings Bryan (1913–15) canceled President William Howard Taft's earlier project for American bankers to loan China money. They thought it would undermine Chinese independence. Yuan's failure to retain authority in China, whether as president or as self-proclaimed emperor in 1915, led to years of ineffective central control. China fell under the rule of warlords and was open to renewed penetration by Japan.

Speak Softly, but Carry a Big Stick

Theodore Roosevelt was the first U.S. president to act consciously as the leader of a great power. Moreover, he was indefatigable as an evangelist for international cooperation. Woodrow Wilson also advocated international involvement and world leadership. In so doing, he raised overwhelming support from the Democratic Party, leading the party in foreign policy in a direction they would not have taken without him. Yet it was TR who came to be regarded as a supreme diplomat who negotiated peaceful resolution to dangerous disputes. His aphorism, "Speak softly, but carry a big stick," showed due respect for civilized priorities. It was the availability of power, rather than its use, that made for effective diplomacy. TR claimed he was not really an imperialist. He said, "I have as much desire to annex more islands as a boa-constrictor has to swallow a porcupine wrong end to." By his support for a permanent Court of International Justice, his attempt at compulsory arbitration between the New World and the Old, his voluminous correspondence with European kings and statesmen, and his visit to the Panama Canal in November 1906—the first visit abroad by an incumbent president—TR set precedents for the future.

When Kaiser Wilhelm II of Germany tried to test the new Anglo-French understanding, or Entente Cordiale, of April 8, 1904, by suggesting an international conference on the subject of Morocco's future, Roosevelt could not resist the temptation to get involved. The crisis illustrated the ill feelings of the great European powers as they aligned themselves in rival blocs of Alliance (Germany, Austria-Hungary, and Italy) and Entente (France, Russia, and Britain). Roosevelt's instructions at the Algeciras Conference on January 16, 1906, to Henry White, his envoy, clearly indicate that he considered Germany a threat to peace. He ordered White to support Britain and France. France wanted unrestricted control of most of Morocco, with Spain occupying a smaller zone. American support for France ensured that it could establish a protectorate over

Morocco a few years later. The General Act of Algeciras was signed on April 7, 1906, and the Senate approved it on December 12, 1906, although the debates were notable for a barrage of criticism.

The principal means of transportation overseas was sea power. Roosevelt was convinced the United States had to build a larger navy, appropriate for its new territorial responsibilities. Roosevelt insisted on building ten battleships and four armored cruisers by 1905. In 1907 he secured additional appropriations for building more battleships to compete with Japan. As he repeatedly claimed, it was only by strength that the United States could safeguard its interests: "The American people must either build and maintain an adequate navy or else make up their minds definitely to accept a secondary position in international affairs, not merely in political, but in commercial matters. It has been well said that there is no surer way of courting national disaster than to be 'opulent, aggressive, and unarmed.' " Roosevelt capped his achievements when he dispatched a U.S. fleet of sixteen battleships and twelve thousand men on a tour of the world, from December 16, 1907, to February 22, 1909—to demonstrate its augmented size and potential.

One of the most spectacular coups in Roosevelt's entire career in pursuit of these aims was his single-minded achievement in the creation of the Panama Canal. The sinking of the American ship *Maine* in Havana harbor in 1898 had brought to a head public support for an isthmian canal. During the war with Spain, the United States needed to mobilize its ships and concentrate a fleet in the Gulf of Mexico, but it was not possible to do so immediately. One indispensable battleship, the *Oregon*, was on the wrong side of the continent in the Pacific Ocean off San Francisco. It took seventy-four days for the *Oregon* to make its way down the Pacific Coast, around Cape Horn, and up the Atlantic. That delayed mission brought forward American determination to cut an isthmian canal.

From inception to completion and thereafter, the history of the Panama Canal was a paradigm of U.S. twentieth-century overseas intervention, encompassing adventure and vision, bending nature to man's will—this time by a well-executed feat of civil engineering, penetration of Latin America in service of the naval strategy and economic security of the United States, and humanitarian concern.

In March 1899 Congress created an Isthmian Canal Commission to inspect routes and draw up plans for construction. It persuaded Britain to abandon its rights to a canal under the Clayton-Bulwer Treaty of 1850 and to accept the Hay-Pauncefote Treaty of November 18, 1901, transferring the projected canal to sole U.S. control. The arrangement suited both parties. Britain wanted to withdraw its fleet to concentrate it in the North Atlantic against the rapidly expanding German navy.

There were still many hurdles for the great enterprise. A political map of the isthmus with its several small republics was rather like the neck of a giraffe with its special markings. Moreover, the region was unstable. There had been fifty-seven revolutions in these Central American countries in as many years. Theodore Roosevelt was to play a decisive role in the next one. After some disagreement over the rival claims of Colombia and Nicaragua as to the optimum canal route, Congress finally chose Colombia in the Hay-Herran Treaty of January 22, 1903. According to the treaty, the New Panama Canal Company was to sell its property to the United States; Colombia was to grant the United States sole right to cut, operate, and maintain the canal for a hundred years in exchange for these rights; and the United States would pay Colombia $10 million immediately, and from 1912 onward, an annual rental of $250,000.

However, Secretary of State John Hay antagonized the Colombian Senate, which defeated the treaty on August 12, 1903. The Colombians' most substantive complaint was that the down payment to Colombia was only a quarter of the amount paid to the Panama Canal Company. Roosevelt reacted to the Colombians' request for a higher fee with unbridled fury, calling them the "contemptible creatures in Bogotá" and "foolish and homicidal corruptionists." TR considered seizing the isthmus.

There was no need. A successful revolution in the province of Panama, organized by engineer Philippe Bunau Varilla, led to the secession of Panama from Colombia and, hence, to U.S. negotiations with a new republic. The success of the Panamanian revolution of November 3, 1903, depended on the cooperation of U.S. forces. Roosevelt had ordered a U.S. ship, the *Nashville*, to the isthmus "to prevent landing of any force, either government or insurgent, at any point within fifty miles of Panama." Three days after the revolution, the United States recognized the new Republic of Panama. Roosevelt's action was so hasty as to invite accusations of collusion. Panama was more than willing to exploit its greatest asset, the canal route.

The new canal treaty with Panama of November 18, 1903, improved on the original terms with Colombia. It granted the United States permanent control of a strip of land five miles wide (instead of three) on each side of the proposed canal and of four minute islands in the Bay of Panama. Within this zone the United States could cut, operate, maintain, and defend a canal. The compensation to Panama was a down payment of $10 million, to be followed by an annual rental of $250,000 to begin in 1912, later brought forward to 1908. Moreover, the United States had to guarantee and maintain the independence of the Republic of Panama. Thus, Panama became a U.S. protectorate.

Despite widespread suspicion about Roosevelt's part in the revolution, the call for party unity among Republicans was compelling, especially in an election year. The Senate approved the treaty on February 23, 1904, by 66 votes to 14. Roosevelt's usurpation of the national rights of Colombia for the sake of U.S. interest provoked protests about Yankee imperialism throughout Latin America. Roosevelt himself referred to Northeast mugwump critics of his Panama dealings as "a small body of shrill eunuchs." However, the comment of Secretary of State Elihu Root (1905–9) on Roosevelt's self-justification before the cabinet was that he had acted like a man accused of seduction but found guilty of rape. In effect, Roosevelt had invented a new state in order to serve U.S. interests.

The actual cutting of the Panama Canal was a great feat of engineering that owed much to technical skill, medical knowledge, and individual heroism. In May 1904 Congress established a commission of seven men (five engineers, one naval officer, and one army officer) to organize construction. The forty-mile stretch of the Canal Zone was a damp, tropical jungle. It was intensely hot, swarming with mosquitoes, and a natural home of typhus, dysentery, and yellow fever. Unless these diseases could be controlled, the Americans would never have a real chance of completing the canal. Roosevelt was persuaded by a delegation representing the American Medical Association and other medical groups to appoint an eighth, subordinate commissioner in charge of sanitation. This was Col. William Crawford Gorgas, who had exterminated yellow fever in Havana, Cuba, in 1902.

Unfortunately, the rest of the commission took no notice of army pathologist and bacteriologist Dr. Walter Reed's accurate but revolutionary theory about the stegomyia mosquito transmitting yellow fever or Gorgas's proposed precautions, until the outbreak of an epidemic in November 1904. Their incompetence and the spreading of the disease led to wholesale desertion by construction workers and ships' crews. Roosevelt dismissed the canal commission. He retained Gorgas, however, in order that he could now employ the same progressive methods against yellow fever in Panama as he had done earlier in Havana. Gorgas did so, and by September 1905 he had exterminated yellow fever in Panama.

Roosevelt then became discouraged by the painfully slow progress of canal construction. There were numerous delays because of emergencies that a cumbersome commission of seven men, restricted by procedure, could not resolve. Roosevelt decided to form a new commission of army and navy officers under the chairmanship of Lt. Col. George W. Goethals and now including Gorgas. Gorgas tried to eliminate malaria, propagated by the anopheles mosquito. He had stagnant waters drained and vegetation cut within a two-hundred-yard radius of human habitation. He encouraged people to keep lizards and spiders that preyed on mosquitoes. Month by month between 1906 and 1913, the proportion of canal workers suffering from malaria fell from 40 percent to 10 percent. However, malaria was not eliminated. Gorgas attributed this to the fact that Goethals, the new chairman, entrusted the sanitation work to laymen without specialist knowledge, Nevertheless, as a result of Gorgas's work, the death rate was only 6 per 1,000 per annum in the canal zone, compared with 14.1 per 1,000 per annum in the United States. It was Gorgas who made possible the Panama Canal, which formally opened to commercial ships on August 15, 1914.

There remained the diplomatic problem of reconciling, first, Panama and Colombia and, second, Colombia, with the United States. Despite continuous efforts by a series of statesmen, the U.S. Senate did not endorse the tool for this, the Treaty of Bogotá of April 6, 1914, until April 20, 1921. In the final version the United States granted Colombia compensation of $25 million and certain rights to the Canal Zone but refrained from making an apology. In return, Colombia recognized Panama. There was also a dispute about tolls. President William

Howard Taft proposed to give American ships passing through the canal a rebate, until diplomatic pressure from European nations persuaded both him and Congress otherwise.

For almost a century the Panama Canal remained a symbol of U.S. dominance of the Western Hemisphere—popular with Americans, suspect in Latin America. In 1977, despite widespread U.S. opposition, President Jimmy Carter (1977–81) signed two treaties with Panamanian president Omar Torrijos Herrera, transferring the Panama Canal and the Canal Zone back to Panama by December 31, 1999.

Just as ships were the principal means of travel and trade, so the new prime means of communication overseas was radio—the transmission and reception of communication signals made up of electromagnetic waves—which was in the early twentieth century intimately related to sea power. The climax of decades of experimenting to achieve wireless communication came when Italian Guglielmo Marconi sent signals across the Atlantic in 1902.

The early development of radio depended on classic great-power politics; competition between rival economic cartels and rival nation states, and human interest in using the new tool to overcome distance and to improve safety at sea. Radio also proved to be another means of communication that would move the earth toward a global community. Like the telephone before it, radio brought people closer together and made separation by distance more acceptable through an aural illusion of intimacy.

The federal government, alert to the military, naval, and commercial possibilities of wireless telegraphy, encouraged rival American companies, notably the De Forest Wireless Telegraph Company of 1902–7. A second generation of radio technology began in the next decade with the invention of a valve to transform an alternating current, such as a radio wave, into direct current; a vacuum tube to make high-frequency signals audible; a charged grid (or audion), to amplify the sound; the improvement of the detection (rather than sound projection) of radio signals with the crystal radio set and the cat's whisker; and the development of syntonic tuning. However, the dominant industrial force in the growth of radio alone was the firm British Marconi. In 1915 Marconi began negotiations with General Electric to gain exclusive use of the most powerful transmitter of the day, the Alexandron Alternator.

As to safety, the wireless industry devoted itself primarily to maritime shipping. In 1909 the crews of eighteen ships owed their lives to radio distress calls. Marconi still led the field. Its commercial strength was such that at one time it could order its shore stations to communicate only with ships that rented Marconi receivers.

Farsighted specialists, disturbed by the anarchy caused by selfish monopolies and governments, at an international conference in Berlin in 1903 called for international regulation of radio. At a second conference in 1906 they made a whole series of wide-ranging decisions, which included the introduction of SOS as the global distress signal. Congress refused to support the 1906 agreements because many congressmen feared that they would make American radio subject to foreign control. However, the first Radio Act of 1910 incorporated many of the 1906 agreements, principally that ocean-going ships carrying more than fifty passengers and steaming between ports that were two hundred or more miles apart had to carry radio equipment with a range of at least one hundred miles.

The loss of the *Titanic* when it struck a great iceberg off the Newfoundland coast in 1912 highlighted serious shortcomings in wireless legislation. That major shipping disaster provides another instance of capitalism outstripping its ability to protect its customers and its servants. J. Bruce Ismay, managing director of the White Star Line, oversaw construction of the *Titanic*, and he wanted it to outdo any luxury liner before it. The great vessel comprised 46,000 tons of steel and stood eleven stories high. On its fatal maiden voyage, the passenger list included millionaires John Jacob Astor and Isidor and Ida Strauss. Not content with luxury, managing director Ismay obliged Captain Edward J. Smith, "the Millionaire's Captain," to set new speed records.

Wireless operator Harold Bride stayed bravely at his post as the ship sank, trying to contact other ships with the new distress signal SOS. But not managing director Ismay, who surreptitiously boarded one of the lifeboats while the crew remained behind. He turned his back in grief as the ship went down. The 705 survivors were picked up by the *Carpathia* and saved, thanks to radio. But the ship that answered the signal came from fifty-eight miles away; a much nearer ship failed to give assistance simply because its only radio operator had fallen asleep.

Another international conference spurred the United States to amend its act of 1910. The amendment stipulated that any ship with fifty or more passengers traveling over whatever distance between ports had to have radio, a secondary power supply, two or more operators, and direct communications between the operator and the bridge.

Dollar Diplomacy? Latin America and the Caribbean

With the removal of Spain from the Western Hemisphere and the partial withdrawal of Britain from the Caribbean, Presidents Roosevelt, Taft, and Wilson determined to preserve stability in a region essential to its own security. One pressing problem was intervention by European powers in Latin America.

When first Britain and Germany and later Italy mounted a blockade of Venezuela in 1902 to force the government to repay its debts, Theodore Roosevelt did nothing. After all, he had written to the German ambassador, Speck von Sternberg, on July 12, 1901, "If any South American state misbehaves toward any European country, let the European country spank it." When all parties to the dispute agreed to settle according to arbitration, the crisis dissolved.

The Roosevelt Corollary of 1904 to the Monroe Doctrine was shaped by the Venezuelan debt crisis. Roosevelt realized that the American public disliked European powers' sending troops to Latin American countries to collect debts. But on February 22, 1904, the Hague Court ruled that European powers had the right to use force to collect bad debts. Roosevelt's preferred solution was for the United States to collect and distribute revenues from unstable Caribbean republics. In his message of December 6, 1904, he emphasized that the United States had no intention of acquiring new territory in the Western Hemisphere. What it wanted was the stability of neighbor states. The United States would "exercise an international police power to redress chronic wrongdoing." Here it was— this crucial expression, "international police power"—that would resound through so much twentieth-century diplomacy. What it meant was an army.

In 1905 Roosevelt undertook to settle controversies about the $40 million debts of the impoverished Dominican Republic. He established a special financial agency that deprived European holders of defaulted Dominican bonds of any excuse for action by their government in violation of the Monroe Doctrine. He also declared that some $20 million in claims was unjustifiable. The special financial agency reorganized the U.S. Customs Service. This yielded enough revenue for the government to repay foreign debts and cover its expenses in so doing.

Roosevelt's exuberant expressions suggested a somewhat guilty conscience. His policies sowed a legacy of distrust in Latin America, especially through the Panamanian affair and the Roosevelt Corollary. It remains a fact, however, that TR intervened less in Latin America than either President Taft or President Wilson. Moreover, TR's moves to establish the protectorate of Santo Domingo (1902) and to restore order in Cuba (1906) showed a nice regard for the opinion of Latin American nations.

Whereas Theodore Roosevelt had never been much interested in trade and investment and paid little attention to those who were, both President William Howard Taft and his secretary of state, Philander C. Knox (1909–13), identified American foreign policy more closely with the interests of the business community. Knox was a somewhat lazy, irascible, and condescending secretary, whose abrupt style antagonized sensitive Latin American diplomats. Yet Knox wanted to extend Roosevelt's policies for Latin American debts by creating special debt funds in the United States in order to provide no excuse for European military intervention. He negotiated the Knox-Castrillo Convention of June 16, 1911, with Nicaragua, by which Nicaragua agreed to refund its debts. However, the Senate refused to approve the treaty. In the meantime, the Taft administration, expecting Senate approval, had encouraged New York bankers to make a loan to the government in Nicaragua. After the Nicaraguan government of Adolfo Diaz fell to revolution on July 29, 1912, Taft ordered twenty-four hundred sailors and marines to occupy the country on September 19 in order to save the bankers from loss. Taft's critics accused him of indulging in "dollar diplomacy." Investment abroad, they said, was exploitative of backward nations.

Woodrow Wilson was more committed than any previous American statesman to intervention abroad in pursuit of moral principles. In a speech on Latin American relations at Mobile, Alabama, on October 27, 1913, he declared that it was the duty of the United States to demonstrate that its professions of friendship were based on the ethics and principles of honor.

> We must show ourselves friends by comprehending their interest whether it squares with our own interest or not. It is a perilous thing to determine the foreign policy of a nation in terms of material interest. It is not only unfair to those with whom you are dealing, but it is degrading as regards your own actions. . . . We dare not turn from the principle that morality and not expediency is the thing that must guide us and that we will never condone iniquity because it is most convenient to do so.

Thus, as was the case with his domestic policies, by his words and deeds in foreign affairs, Wilson raised the sort of formidable (and still unresolved) questions that British Liberal prime minister W. E. Gladstone had raised before him: How far can the rights of minorities—including national ones—be reconciled with democracy, in which the will of the majority rules? This question in particular troubled the secession states of the Austro-Hungarian and Ottoman empires all the way through the twentieth century. Should foreign policy be inspired by moral principle, or do you deal with people like Pancho Villa, Kaiser Wilhelm II (and, after them, Adolf Hitler and Joseph Stalin) as duly accredited players, treating foreign affairs and diplomacy as a giant game of chess? As a later secretary of state, Henry Kissinger (1973–77), suggested (1994), "For three generations critics have savaged Wilson's analysis and conclusions; and yet, in all this time, Wilson's principles have remained the bedrock of American foreign-policy thinking."

Nevertheless, in practice, the foreign policy of Woodrow Wilson and Secretary of State William Jennings Bryan (1913–15) differed very little from that of Roosevelt and Taft. Before World War I, Wilson had a harmonious relationship with William Jennings Bryan. They had meetings for regular consultation. As to policy, Wilson might try to justify his intervention in the Caribbean or Latin America according to moral principles. The consequence was much the same as before—an extension of America's economic and political power. The greatest controversy about Woodrow Wilson's hemispheric policy was his refusal to recognize governments he regarded as morally tainted. Wilson condemned revolution in Cuba, Ecuador, Haiti, and the Dominican Republic by withholding recognition on the grounds of unconstitutionality: "I am going to teach the South American republics to elect good men," he boasted. Congress gave tacit approval to his policy. But Wilson's morality capsized after the Mexican revolution.

On May 25, 1911, a Mexican revolution led by idealist Francisco Madero toppled the corrupt dictatorship of Porfirio Díaz but fueled political instability and terrorist violence. A second revolution of February 18, 1913, led to the overthrow and murder of Madero, his brother, Gustavo, and the vice president, Pino Suarez, and established Victoriano Huerta as president. Huerta sought U.S. recognition. Wilson, who sympathized with moralist Madero, would not recognize Huerta's government because he thought recognition would be interpreted as approval of the violence by which Huerta had come to power. Thus, in a State Department announcement of November 24, 1915, Wilson withheld recognition. Wilson hoped that his new policy would undermine Huerta, persuade him to hold free elections, and thereby establish a constitutional government. Indeed, Wilson's opposition helped render the position of the new president untenable and led to the establishment of a third new government under Venustiano Carranza. But this was only after another complicating incident.

Wilson chose the mistaken arrest of eight U.S. sailors from the *Dolphin* at Tampico on April 9, 1914, to justify U.S. intervention. Their commanding officer, Rear Adm. Henry T. Mayo, insisted on the sailors' release, a full apology, and a formal salute to the U.S. flag from Mexico. Huerta refused. On April 20, 1914, Wilson ordered a blockade of the Mexican coast. In addition, U.S. sailors and marines, acting on Wilson's orders, captured the port of Vera Cruz with a loss of four dead and twenty wounded. Mexican casualties were in the hundreds. Wilson's final decision to use sixty-seven hundred troops to capture Vera Cruz was made when he learned from Mayo that a German ship with war supplies— which could be used by Mexico against the United States—was about to enter the harbor. A nasty incident was defused by an order of mediation from the ABC powers (Argentina, Brazil, Chile). The crisis was resolved at a conference at Niagara Falls, which began May 20. Besieged by the constitutionalists, Huerta abdicated on July 15. On August 20, 1914, Carranza entered Mexico City in triumph.

Even the new Carranza government in Mexico incurred Wilson's displeasure. Carranza was challenged by one of his former generals, Francisco ("Pancho") Villa, who began a civil insurrection against him on September 13, 1914. Americans read all about it. Socialist John Reed, who was roving correspondent for the *Masses*, rode with Pancho Villa's army against Huerta's troops. His articles, later collected in the book *Insurgent Mexico*, made him an overnight hero of the American left because of their direct, passionate style. Mexican historian Enrique Krauze tells (1997) how Hollywood scouts found Pancho Villa so charismatic that they supplied him with uniforms and food in exchange for filming his battles. Actor (later director) Raoul Walsh, who played Villa in the fictional footage, recalled that the scouts asked Villa to schedule big shootups at sunrise so that the cameramen had optimal lighting.

Between January and April 1915 another Mexican commander, Alvaro Obregon, led the Carranzistas to victory against Pancho Villa, who was driven ever northward with his army. Wilson recognized Carranza on October 19, 1915. The next day Wilson imposed an embargo on the export of arms that would discriminate against Pancho Villa. Villa retaliated by trying to divide Wilson and Carranza. On March 9, 1916, Villa led a band of 1,500 Mexican revolutionaries across the border and into New Mexico. They attacked the town of Columbus and an adjacent camp of the Thirteenth U.S. Cavalry, killing nine civilians and eight soldiers. The cavalry pursued the bandits fifteen miles into Mexico and killed 120 of them.

The outrage was a climax to years of trouble on the border. Wilson reported to the Senate that over the previous three years, seventy-six Americans had been killed in Mexico and another thirty-six had been killed by Mexicans on U.S. soil. Wilson hoped that Carranza would be able to subdue these vicious bandit gangs, but he was not able to. In response to public outrage, Wilson agreed to a punitive expedition of six thousand under the command of Brig. Gen. John J. ("Black Jack") Pershing. Its task was to invade Mexico on March 15, 1916, capture Pancho Villa, and bring him back to stand trial in the United States.

Pershing's force was inadequate for such a guerilla campaign. Villa divided his forces into small groups, who hid in the wooded ravines away from Pershing's slow-moving army. Carranza complained about the abuse of Mexico's sovereignty. On June 16 his general in the north, Jacinto Trevino, ordered Pershing to advance no farther. On June 21 Mexican and U.S. troops clashed near Carrizal. Twelve Americans were killed and twenty-three captured. On June 28 Carranza, now in a conciliatory move, had them released. He assured Wilson he would do everything he could to prevent future raids on U.S. soil. Pershing withdrew his forces. Faced with the imminent prospect of intervention in World War I, Wilson decided to cut his losses with Mexico. Acting on the advice of Secretary of State Robert Lansing (1915–20), he recognized the Carranza government on March 13, 1917.

Despite U.S. problems with Mexico, the supremacy of the United States in the Western Hemisphere was total and assured. U.S. forces intervened in trouble spots in defense of American property and lives. The usual reason given was to maintain law and order.

On July 27, 1915, a revolution in Haiti, led by Dr. Rosalvo Bobo, succeeded in overthrowing President Vilbrun Guillaume Sam, who was hounded from his refuge in the French legation. He was tortured, killed, and mutilated on July 28, 1915. From the harbor of Port-au-Prince, Rear Adm. William B. Caperton of the USS *Washington* sent a force to restore order. On September 16 he signed a treaty with the new president, Sudre Dartiguenave, providing for American supervision of the island's finances. By withholding funds for public services, Caperton obliged the Haitian senate to ratify the treaty. American occupation of Haiti continued until August 1934, and U.S. military staff supervised construction of roads and sanitation programs but remained unpopular.

The United States continued to acquire territories and rights. On February 18, 1916, the Senate confirmed a treaty with Nicaragua by which the United States, for $3 million, acquired two naval bases and the rights to build a canal across Nicaragua. On August 4, 1916, Secretary of State Robert Lansing and the Danish minister, Constantin Brun, signed a treaty for the purchase of the Danish West Indies by the United States for $25 million. On September 7 the Senate agreed to the treaty, and the United States took possession of the Danish West Indies on March 31, 1917.

Most Americans believed there was natural harmony between nations who must naturally be committed to peace. Surely no nation could profit from war?

How ironic. This belief was widespread in a nation that had achieved independence in a revolutionary war, acquired sizable territory through punitive wars, preserved national unity through a bitter civil war, and established an empire through a controversial overseas war.

To counteract the misguided optimism of many that great wars were monsters of the past, President Roosevelt, Taft, and Wilson tried to persuade the Senate of the need for treaties creating diplomatic machinery for the peaceful resolution of disputes. Yet even the United States steadily refused to make any commitments that might reduce its freedom of action. The Second Hague Conference of June 15, 1907, was attended by forty-four nations. Before it adjourned on October 18, it had adopted twenty-one understandings in all. Satirical bar owner Mr. Dooley, invented by Peter Finley Dunne, described them as decisions about "how future wars shud be conducted in th' best intherests iv peace."

From a mix of commercial and disinterested motives, the United States actively sought to promote greater cooperation both among Latin American republics and between them and the United States. Elihu Root made a goodwill tour of seven Latin American countries in 1906, and Philander Knox visited ten Caribbean islands in 1912. Their emphasis on American goodwill was complemented by a series of conferences held in Mexico City (1901–2), Rio de Janeiro (1906), and Buenos Aires (1910). In 1914 Wilson and his adviser Edward House devised a Pan American pact based on four points dealing with territorial integrity, boundary disputes, arbitration, and an arms embargo.

In 1913 and 1914 William Jennings Bryan concluded thirty bilateral treaties for the advancement of peace. Signatories agreed to submit disputes to a permanent commission that would have a year to investigate the facts; during that year neither side would begin hostilities. This was the original "cooling-off period." Only ten commissions met, and none ever investigated a dispute.

Then came the war, and with it, the revolution.

CHAPTER 6

Tell That to the Marines!

America and World War I

T H E W A R in which the virtuous Woodrow Wilson intervened as a test of his statesmanship destroyed both him and his statecraft.

The United States went to war with Germany in 1917 over unrestricted submarine warfare because President Woodrow Wilson's foreign and military policies, formulated according to his high-minded morality, left him no option. Growing economic trade with the Allies, Britain and France; sympathy for their cause; and deepening conviction that the defeat of Germany was in the national interest—these factors drove Wilson to reverse his initial policy about neutral rights and declare war on the kaiser.

World War I (1914–18) was initially fought between the Central Powers of Germany and Austria-Hungary and the Entente powers, or Allies, which included France, Russia, and the United Kingdom. The momentous storm had been gathering for a generation. Tensions were heightened by crises in the Balkan states and provinces that had once belonged to the Turkish empire. In the early years of the century, aggressive diplomats in Vienna and Berlin enflamed matters. In addition, Britain abandoned Turkey. Russia, humiliated by Japan in Asia, renewed its interest in Slavic nationalism. In 1908, when Austria annexed the Balkan states of Bosnia and Herzegovina, Russia and Serbia held back from war because Germany backed Austria.

When a second crisis erupted in the summer of 1914, they were determined not to repeat the experience of 1908. The occasion was the assassination by Gavril Princip, a Bosnian student, of Franz Ferdinand, heir to the Austrian throne, on June 28, 1914, in Sarajevo. The Austrians, suspecting that the Serbian government had connived in the murder, issued Serbia an ultimatum. After receiving an evasive reply, they declared war. Russia mobilized its troops in support of Serbia. Germany countered by declaring war on Russia. This led to war with France in accordance with German military planning for a campaign on two fronts. Within three weeks of the assassination, half of Europe was at war.

The Great War extended to twenty-seven countries across four continents. It brought revolution to four great powers and widespread social dislocation to the others. In economic terms, this was a civil war of the Western world. However, the tragedy promoted America's ascendancy to global preeminence. The United States was safe from invasion. It emerged fortified from the war, partly because American war matériel supplied the Allies, partly because America's expanded agriculture fed much of the world, partly because its military intervention was decisive in the Allies' victory in 1918, and partly because its outsize loans supported the Allied war effort throughout—thereby transferring the financial capital of the world from London to New York.

Woodrow Wilson's proclamation of neutrality of August 10, 1914, told the American people: "We must be impartial in thought as well as action. The United States must be neutral in fact as well as in name." Thus, Americans must on no account enlist in the army of a belligerent or any armed vessel to be used in the war. For their part, belligerent nations must respect America's neutrality and not allow their ships to make war in U.S. waters or use U.S. ports as part of their naval strategy.

Behind the scenes, Wilson thought and spoke differently. When Brand Whitlock, U.S. minister to Belgium, told Wilson, "In my heart there is no such thing as neutrality: I am heart and soul for the Allies," Wilson agreed. "So am I," he said. Nevertheless, Wilson knew that a policy of open partiality would divide Americans at home. Besides, the United States had a moral duty to remain out of the conflict so that it could then exercise its full weight in the interests of peace at an opportune moment.

The essence of German strategy in 1914 was first to make a swift attack on France before it mobilized and then to concentrate huge forces on Russia. Since the Franco-German frontier was heavily fortified, Germany could achieve a quick decisive victory only by marching its troops through Belgium. To do so would violate a treaty of 1839 guaranteeing Belgium's territorial integrity. This was the action that brought Britain into the war.

Despite major losses among its overseas colonies in Africa and the Pacific, only a few short weeks after its invasion of northern France, Germany dominated Europe. Now it possessed rich industrial resources in Belgium and France and occupied territory in Russia twice the area of the Second Reich. However, there was to be military stalemate for the first three years of the war. When France won the battle of the Marne on September 6, 1914, it found it could not exploit its victory. In their retreat from the Marne, the weary Germans stumbled on a tactical discovery that shaped the course of the war: men in trenches with machine guns could resist all but the most overwhelming odds. The Germans dug themselves in: so did the British and the French. By November 1914 a line of trenches stretched across western Europe, extending from Switzerland to the English Channel. Siege warfare replaced conventional battles.

The first attempt at trench warfare was the first battle of Ypres of October 12 to November 11, 1914. Every day new forces replaced those at the front line until both sides were exhausted. The only way for either side to advance was to order thousands upon thousands of young men to certain death when they as-

In 1917 silent screen star Douglas Fairbanks (Sr.) invites assembled Americans to buy war bonds and support U.S. intervention in World War I on the side of Britain and France. He stands in front of what is now known as Federal Hall National Memorial in Lower Manhattan (1842), astride the monumental (1883) statue of George Washington, who had warned against such entangling alliances. (John Rylands University Library of Manchester)

cended the trenches and went over the top. In July 1915 Herbert H. Kitchener (conqueror of Sudan and now England's secretary of war) and Douglas Haig (commander in chief) tried to break the German line in a tremendous joint assault with the French at the Somme. This was intended as a knockout blow. The Germans replied with their machine guns. The prolonged slaughter lasted until November. Britain lost 420,000 men, France 194,000, and Germany 465,000. Thus, for the loss of 600,000 men, the Allies gained nothing better than a sea of mud.

As Belgian cities and their inhabitants fell victim to German aggression, the attitude of the American public turned toward sympathy for Belgium and criticism of Germany. Edward S. Martin, editor of *Life*, observed in the issue of January 7, 1915, "Belgium is a martyr to civilization, sister to all who love liberty or law; assailed, polluted, trampled in the mire, heel-marked in her breast, tattered, homeless." Belgium soon found its food supplies exhausted and its supply routes cut off. American millionaire-engineer Herbert Hoover organized a team of volunteers into a special Commission for Relief in Belgium with a fleet of thirty-five ships. It moved supplies of food valued at $5 million per month from the United States, Canada, and Argentina across the Atlantic and distributed them in Belgium.

In Europe, dismayed by the stalemate of trench warfare, Britain, France, and Russia committed themselves to the outright destruction of Germany as a great power. They realized that they would require material aid from the United States. To secure that aid they needed effective propaganda to get the Americans on their side. Thus, fifty-three British authors, acting as "press agents," pitted their wits against twenty-two heads of German universities. Britain had cut the only German cable to the United States, thereby reducing German contact to the still imperfect new invention of radio and the haphazard mail delivery that Britain intercepted. Accordingly, the news the United States received about the war was colored by its route from London and Paris. Most significant, the English language united American and British culture through a complex web of sentiment and literature that eclipsed all things German.

At home the press reached a zenith of influence during the war. Newspapers were the only source of news. Their circulation rose with every calamity. Allied propaganda alleged that Germans had mutilated Belgian women and babies and had crucified Canadian soldiers by sticking bayonets through their hands and feet. It was said that the German quest for efficiency was so grotesque that they scavenged battlefields for corpses, then bundled them into bales and had them shipped back to Germany to be treated chemically and made into lubricating oil, fertilizer, and soap. In World War II similar inventions became reality, though they suspended belief: in World War I they were gruesome fiction.

As the war continued, it drew in idealistic young American men who enlisted as ambulance drivers for the Entente powers. The most famous were emerging writers of stature, including journalist Ernest Hemingway, architecture student John Dos Passos, and poet e. e. cummings. As writers of the "lost generation," they would distill their battle-scarred experiences into powerful novels of heroes rendered impotent by the hypocrisy of statesmen and the blunders of generals in this most terrible of wars. World War I obliterated faith in technology as a benevolent machine. Not only were people's cherished images of progress shattered by the fierce instruments of war, but so also were their words. Language was broken by the terrors of trench warfare, the hypocrisies of government propaganda, and the new terrible age of industrialized, mass death. The war changed words in literature and images in art forever.

Foremost among the hypocrisies of propaganda were the specious words to cover the motives of statesmen. A cartoon in *Life* hinted that a major reason for the United States not intervening directly in the war was the immense profits it accrued by manufacturing products for the Allies while it was technically neutral. The Allies bought vast quantities of munitions. Britain controlled the seas. Its ships could move unhindered across the Atlantic until German submarines took action. Germany was also entitled to buy munitions, but unlike Britain, it could not carry them home. German merchant shipping was almost completely paralyzed while, initially, British shipping carried on unperturbed.

As a belligerent, Britain was not interested in protecting neutral rights and began to violate them. It declared contraband thirty-two raw materials that could be used by Germany, including copper, rubber, gasoline, and also food. It seized ship after ship carrying them from the United States to other neutral countries. Moreover, Britain drew up a blacklist of some eighty U.S. companies that it suspected of trading with Germany—something they were entitled to do. Next, it prevented those companies from trading with neutral countries. Although the claims and counterclaims of Britain and Germany confused Americans, there remained a fundamental distinction between their naval tactics. Britain seized ships: Germany sank them and their American passengers.

Disputes between the United States and Germany arose when Germany declared on February 16, 1915, that the very nature of its submarines made it impossible to disembark passengers and crew before sinking ships or to seize neutral vessels carrying contraband and take them to port. Wilson warned Germany that the United States would hold it to "a strict accountability" if its submarines destroyed U.S. ships and American lives. But he was cautious as well. "Our whole duty for the present, at any rate, is summed up in this motto: 'America First.' Let us think of America before we think of Europe in order that America may be fit to be Europe's friend when the day of tested friendship comes," he said in a speech in New York on April 20, 1915.

The sinking of the *Lusitania* off the Irish coast by the submarine *Untersboot* 20 on May 7, 1915, with the loss of 128 American lives among 1,198 people who were drowned, put Wilson's policy of neutrality to its first major test. The United States required Germany to repudiate the submarine attack. Germany curtly refused on the grounds that the *Lusitania* had been carrying contraband cargo. Wilson dispatched a second note so stern that Secretary of State William Jennings Bryan resigned in protest. Yet, the *Nation* summed up the general sense of outrage against Germany across the United States in its issue of May 13, 1915, when it wrote that, by the sinking of the *Lusitania*, Germany had "affronted the moral sense of the world and sacrificed her standing among the nations."

In place of Bryan, Wilson appointed Robert Lansing, formerly counselor of the State Department, as secretary of state (1915–20). Wilson did not think Lansing big enough for the job; he chose him out of convenience. However, whatever Wilson's subsequent misgivings about Lansing's loyalty, it would have been too embarrassing for Wilson to fire Lansing. Moreover, Wilson was drawing more into himself.

What the Allies most wanted was U.S. intervention. Various factors combined to draw the United States closer to war on the side of Britain and France. U.S. trade with Germany and Austria had dwindled. The United States was providing the Allies with vital economic aid, food, and munitions. Between 1914 and 1916 the total value of exports to the Allies rose from $824.86 million to $3.2 billion. The sale of American munitions to the Allies increased from $40 million in 1914 to $1.29 billion in 1916. This increase in foreign trade rescued the United States from a recession. Within a year, the fabric of American life was so interwoven with the economy of the Allies that the United States now had a stake in Allied victory.

The Allies could not continue to pay the United States indefinitely without some system of credits or loans. On October 15, 1915, Britain and France secured a loan of $500 million from bankers led by the House of Morgan. Wilson tacitly approved the loan at the urging of Secretary of State Robert Lansing and Secretary of the Treasury William Gibbs McAdoo (1913–18). By the time the United States formally entered the war in 1917, it had loaned $2 billion to the Allies, as compared with $27 million to the Central Powers.

However, commercial support was a different matter from armed intervention. Despite the *Lusitania*, progressive journalist Walter Lippmann told a British socialist, Alfred Zimmern, in a letter of June 7, 1915, "The feeling against war in this country is a great deal deeper than you would imagine by reading editorials." This was partly on account of repugnance to war, partly because of a fear that the loyalty of German-Americans would be strained by a war with Germany, and partly because of "general international irresponsibility and shallowness of feeling." In 1915 only Americans on the Atlantic seaboard would have supported outright intervention in the war. In the West and the Midwest, news of the *Lusitania* caused a temporary sensation but it did not move public opinion.

In the United States the war stirred different loyalties among Irish, Italian, Polish, Russian, Hungarian, and German ethnic groups, who began to take sides in foreign-language newspapers. Claims and counterclaims by some groups about what was happening in Europe gave rise to the term "hyphenated Americans." This led to doubts among Americans as to whether they really existed at all. Was the United States really a nation or just an international rooming house?

In Congress opponents of U.S. intervention found common cause in the Gore-

McLemore Resolution of February 22, 1916, warning U.S. citizens that they must not travel on the vessels of belligerents. In practice, this would have meant British ships since there were no German merchant ships on the seas. The speaker, Champ Clark, warned Wilson that the action would pass Congress by a majority of two to one. This was the last thing Wilson wanted. He wrote an open letter against it to Senator William Stone of Missouri, chairman of the Senate Committee on Foreign Relations. As a result, the House decided by 275 votes to 135 to table the resolution.

Submarine warfare continued to take a terrible toll on Allied ships. On March 24, 1916, a French ship, the *Sussex*, was sunk in the English Channel. Several Americans were seriously injured. This time the American protest of April 18, 1916, amounted to an ultimatum. Unless Germany discontinued submarine warfare against ships carrying passengers and freight, the United States would break off diplomatic relations with Germany. On May 4, 1916, Germany undertook not to sink merchant ships without warning and without saving human lives. This undertaking is sometimes known as the *Sussex* pledge. For nine months, from May 4, 1916, to January 31, 1917, Germany sank no ships in violation of the American code.

Making the Mold

Wilson and his supporters began to promote preparedness and to campaign for a better army and navy. In 1914 there were only 92,710 men authorized for the regular army. Nearly half of them were abroad. In December 1915 Wilson advised Congress to raise the standing army to 141,843 with a reserve of 40,000 volunteers to be trained for two months a year for three years. The National Defense Act increased the regular army. It integrated the national guard into the National Defense System, and it created an officers' reserve corps. The Naval Appropriation Act authorized the construction of new cruisers and battleships. The Shipping Board appropriated $50 million to buy and construct merchant ships.

As always, Wilson understood that the public cared more about feeling than argument. His well-paced, dexterous speeches made precisely the impression that he intended. If he wanted to be reelected in 1916, he had to speak *for* preparedness but *against* intervention. Wilson's nomination at the Democratic National Convention in St. Louis was a foregone conclusion. The phrase, "He kept us out of war," was forced on him by campaign manager Joseph Tumulty and convention chairman Governor Martin Glynn of New York. The slogan was interpreted as a pledge: elect me and you will be kept out of war.

At their convention in Chicago, the Republicans nominated Charles Evans Hughes, a former progressive Republican governor of New York and present associate justice of the Supreme Court. Not only was Hughes a candidate of proven ability, but he was also noncontroversial, having taken no part in the

Republican schism of 1912. From the sidelines, Roosevelt called Hughes "the bearded iceberg." Democrats accused Hughes of appealing to the hyphenated votes of Irish- and German-Americans, those ethnic groups opposed to Britain whose size was such that they might determine the outcome of the election.

In order to make doubly sure of progressive support, Wilson began to cultivate the editors of the main progressive journal, the *New Republic*, funded by the wealthy Straight family and edited by Herbert Croly, Walter Weyl, and Walter Lippmann. Lippmann was not taken in. He declared, "What we're electing is a war president—not the man who kept us out of war." Nevertheless, Wilson was much impressed with the *New Republic*'s scheme of April 1916 for an international union of liberal peoples united in collective action against aggressor states. This was the embryo of the League of Nations.

The outcome of the presidential election was in doubt for several days. First returns from the eastern states suggested Hughes had won. However, the next day it became clear that Wilson was taking normally Republican states west of the Mississippi, as well as the South. It was "the winning of the West by Woodrow Wilson," observed Edward House. According to later tallies, Wilson received 9,127,695 votes (49.4 percent of the total) and Hughes had 8,533,507 (46.2 percent). Thus Wilson had thirty states and 277 votes in the electoral college, and Hughes had the remainder and 254 votes in the electoral college. So great was Wilson's appeal that former Bull Moose Progressives voted for him. So did Socialists John Reed and Max Eastman.

Wilson decided to instigate peace negotiations through Edward House. House was in Europe in June 1915 and again in December 1915 and January 1916, whence he dispatched pro-Allied messages according to his own firmly held convictions. Accordingly, on December 18, 1916, Wilson appealed to the belligerents for an end to hostilities. House misled Britain by depicting Wilson's mediation proposal as a pretext for getting the United States to enter the war; he misled Wilson by saying that the British wanted mediation whereas they wanted U.S. aid. When widower Wilson became involved with widow Edith Bolling Galt, she became his confidante on international affairs and lessened his reliance on House. Wilson showed her confidential political and diplomatic papers because he believed a display of power would prove a reliable aphrodisiac.

However, more was at stake. Negotiations for peace broke on an inescapable fact. What was compromise for one side was defeat for the other. Coming to terms without victory would have been an open admission of failure by European leaders—that countless sons at the front had died in vain. The Allies had taken their nations to war after they had demonstrated that their national interest was in peril: they had to continue the fight by convincing their peoples that the war entailed something far greater than the national interest. To entice Wilson, the Allies were ready to present themselves as champions of self-determination for Italians, Slavs, and Turks. Thus, the Allies changed their original war aims to a commitment to revise the maps of Central Europe and the Middle East.

Although the Turks had been dislodged from the Balkan states by 1914, they

still held the Middle East. Britain, France, and Russia wanted to establish themselves there. Not only was the Middle East strategically important because it
bridged three continents, but it also held the promise of oil reserves that would
fuel automobiles. In March and April 1915 the Entente powers agreed in a series
of secret notes that Russia should take Constantinople and the Straits. In 1916
the Allies went further and agreed to partitions of Syria (to France), Mesopo-
tamia (to Britain), and Armenia and Kurdistan (to Russia). Thus would the oil
of the Middle East fall into British hands. What the Allies first wanted from the
Arabs, however, was support against the Turks. Having reached contradictory
territorial agreements with two rival Arab princes, Britain also saw that it could
use Jewish occupation of part of Palestine to create a buffer state between British
Egypt and French Syria and thus keep the French out of the Suez Canal. On
November 8, 1917, the Balfour Declaration promised Palestine as "a national
home" for the Jews. In part the British were responding to a movement we might
call political Zionism, dating from the first Zionist congress in Basel, Switzerland,
in 1897, which had called for the recreation of a Jewish nation-state after
thousands of years of the Diaspora. However, twentieth-century Palestine was
mainly inhabited by Arabs.

In addition, by the notorious secret treaty of London of April 26, 1915, Italy,
hitherto neutral, agreed to make war against Austria-Hungary in exchange for
the promise of non-Italian land in the Tyrol and Dalmatia.

Woodrow Wilson held very different views from the Allies about imperialism
and the national self-determination of nations. He suggested guidelines for a
future peace in his "peace without victory" speech delivered to the Senate on
January 22, 1917. The new world order should be based neither on military
peace nor entangling alliances, but rather on the democratic principles of self-
government, freedom of the seas, and limitation of armaments—all principles
that Wilson ascribed to the United States. Wilson also committed himself to the
principle of collective security through an international agency in which the
United States would play a pivotal role: "In every discussion that must end this
war, it is taken for granted that the peace must be followed by some definite
concert of power which will make it impossible that any such catastrophe should
ever overwhelm us again. It is inconceivable that the people of the United States
should play no part in this great enterprise."

Meanwhile, the German policy of unrestricted submarine warfare was spectacularly successful. In February 1917 Germany sank 536,000 tons of shipping;
in March 603,000 tons; in April 1.25 million tons. U.S. naval headquarters advised Walter Hines Page on June 25, 1917, that "ships are being sunk faster
than they can be replaced by the building facilities of the world. This means
simply that the enemy is winning the war. There is no mystery about that. The
submarines are rapidly cutting the Allies' lines of communication. When they are
cut or sufficiently interfered with, we must accept the enemy's terms." The rate
of sinking was more than twice the rate of ship construction. In 1917 German
submarines destroyed 6.61 million tons of shipping altogether. The total naval

construction in Allied and neutral countries throughout the world was only 2.70 million tons.

The American public demanded a positive response from Wilson in defense of American rights. Wilson reacted on February 4, 1917, by breaking off diplomatic relations with Germany. On February 20 Wilson asked Congress for authorization to arm merchant ships and for an appropriation of $100 million to do so. The House passed the enabling legislation to arm merchant ships by 403 votes to 13. In the Senate eleven senators, led by Robert La Follette, opposed the measure and thereby delayed it until the end of the session in March, after which it would lapse. On March 3 a majority of seventy-five senators, anxious to see the bill pass, published a protest denouncing the recalcitrant eleven. Supported by Attorney General Thomas Watt Gregory, Wilson took the law into his own hands. Using a piracy statute of 1819, he announced on March 9 that merchant ships were being armed.

On February 24 the State Department rallied public opinion behind Wilson by publishing the so-called Zimmermann telegram, which the British had intercepted. This was a note from the German foreign minister in Berlin to the German minister in Mexico, proposing a German-Mexican alliance that might also include Japan, should the United States go to war against Germany. In return for its support, Germany promised Mexico the recovery of Texas, New Mexico, and Arizona—territories ceded by Mexico after the war of 1848.

Other events played a part in America's conversion to intervention. They helped determine the ideological conflict between the United States and Russia that spanned the twentieth century. In Russia the disaster of war provoked widespread unrest in the army and among the people. This aggravated the grievances of conservatives and reformers alike against the czar and encouraged more disruptive agitation by the revolutionary intelligentsia. The first major climax came with the enforced abdication of Nicholas II on March 15, 1917, and the advent of a republican government, eventually led by social revolutionary Alexander Kerensky. This constitutional revolution seemed to transform the war into a clear conflict between democracy and autocracy, with the Entente powers representing parliamentary democracy and the Central Powers, military autocracy. But the revolution continued to roll. In Petrograd (formerly St. Petersburg) workers and deserting soldiers formed a council, or Soviet, modeled on that of 1905, to dictate industrial action.

Confident of the progress of democracy and that right must triumph, the idealistic Wilson decided that he must take the United States into the war, both to protect its rights at sea and to ensure that his grand design could be realized. However, he needed a *casus belli*. On March 12, 1917, a German submarine sank the unarmed American ship *Algonquin*. On March 18, German submarines sank three other ships. Wilson faced the difficult task of appearing before a somewhat reluctant Congress and persuading it to declare war on Germany on April 2, 1917. This required the most emotive speech of his career. In order to anticipate ethnic divisions in the United States, he concentrated on distinguishing between the German government and the German people. One he equated with "Prussian autocracy" and "autocratic governments backed by organized force which is controlled wholly by their will, not by the will of their people." The other aroused feelings of "sympathy and friendship." At the same time, he gave concrete assurance that the United States sought "no indemnities," and "no material compensation," and had "no selfish ends to serve." He crowned his speech with a masterstroke. Declaring the path America must follow, he proclaimed, "God helping her, she can do no other." This was a paraphrase of Martin Luther's famous declaration, "Ich kann nicht anders" at the start of the Protestant Reformation. In Wilson's rhetoric, therefore, America's intervention was in the spirit of a religious crusade, to restore freedom to the German people. The priest had become a warrior. On April 4 the Senate approved the war resolution by 82 votes to 6 and the House did so on April 6 by 373 votes to 50. It was Good Friday.

Theodore Roosevelt wanted to lead an army division. In an interview of April 10, 1917, he asked Wilson to allow him to do so. Although the meeting passed off agreeably enough, on May 19, 1917, Wilson refused TR's request. Wilson knew that Roosevelt was aging and in ill health. He would not bestow military command that would brighten Roosevelt's political prospects as the next Republican presidential nominee.

The irony of American intervention in World War I was not lost on any maker of public policy nor on those who profited by it. After years of attempting to control big business, those Progressives who led America were putting big business back into the saddle. Many Progressives favored intervention, genuinely believing that the war was a crusade for international liberty and justice. They included Charles A. Beard, Albert J. Beveridge, John Dewey, Felix Frankfurter, Harold L. Ickes, and Stanley King. In their editorials for the *New Republic*, Walter Lippmann and Herbert Croly showed faith in Wilson's ideals, declaring that "the liberal peoples of the world are united in a common cause." Staunch Progressives from the West and the Midwest remained resolutely opposed to intervention. They included Senators Robert La Follette of Wisconsin and George W. Norris of Nebraska, whose isolationism was deep rooted. Congressional opponents of intervention assailed Wilson and the interventionists for maneuvering the United States into a false position that made military intervention inevitable, the better to benefit bankers and manufacturers. They argued that U.S. involvement in a European war would result in needless sacrifice of young American lives.

Some historians conclude that outright opposition to the war was simmering underneath a facade of patriotic conformity. For example, the Socialists opposed American intervention on the grounds that the war was a struggle of competing capitalist orders. On April 7, 1917, the SPA adopted a resolution, "We brand the declaration of war by our government as a crime against the people of the United States." The Socialists advocated "continuous, active, and public opposition to the war, through demonstrations, mass petitions, and all other means within our power." In August 1917 Oklahoma had a Green Corn Rebellion of protest against the war from farmers, Native Americans, and African Americans, who burned bridges and cut pipelines in protest.

Before the war the peace movement had been educational and legalistic. By 1917, when the more established peace societies, such as the Carnegie Endowment, were accepting intervention, some Progressives were founding new peace organizations. The war was a threat to their values, their concept of a world in which problems could be solved. The new pacifists included Socialists, social workers, social-gospel clergymen, and feminists, as well as people with religious scruples about fighting. Several new societies—the Women's Peace Party, the American Fellowship of Reconciliation, the American Union against Militarism, and the People's Council of America for Peace and Democracy—were expressions of this phenomenon.

African American leaders felt ambivalent about American intervention. W. E. B. Du Bois initially opposed the war effort. However, as of June 1918, Du Bois began to support it on the assumption that an Allied victory would somehow yield to African Americans the right to vote, work, and live without continuous harassment. Other activists disagreed. These included A. Philip Randolph and Chandler Owens, editors of the *Messenger*, a journal they had founded in 1915 as part of a strategy to recruit African American hotel workers into a labor union. Randolph, from Crescent City, Florida, emerged as one of the great civil rights leaders of the century. He traversed the country making speeches against the war: "Lynching, Jim Crow, segregation, and discrimination in the armed forces and out, disfranchisement of millions of black souls in the South—all these things make your cry of making the world safe for democracy a sham, a mockery, a rape of decency, and travesty of common justice." After an antiwar meeting in Cleveland in 1918, Randolph was arrested and jailed for several days.

The millions of African American migrants who moved to the North to work in war-related industries were condemned to a life in squalid tenement ghettos. They faced resentment from white workers who feared for their own livelihood. In 1917 there were race riots in towns and on army bases. In July 1917 a savage race riot in St. Louis killed between forty and two hundred African Americans and drove almost six thousand from their homes.

But, despite voices of protest from Socialists, pacifists, and minorities, on the whole the public was now ready to persuade itself that here was a war different from imperial wars of the past: a war to make the world safe for democracy and a war to end all wars. Many Progressives transferred their confidence in the ideal of political and social progress within the United States to the international scene.

The Metal Cools

World War I exerted a decisive influence on the course of democracy as the crises of mass society, total mobilization, and increased militarism snarled and tangled.

The outcome of modern warfare depended largely on the logistics of supply. To win a total war, the whole of society, not just its army or navy, had to be turned into a cohesive, efficient machine. Every major belligerent mobilized industry, economy, and people. The United States certainly did so. Woodrow Wilson himself retained control of the American war effort, which essentially amounted to providing the Allies with matériel in abundant and continuous supplies. To coordinate its supplies, the federal government regulated communication and transportation—telephones, telegraphs, railroads—and some basic industries, such as coal mines. The United States moved closer to a planned economy. "It is not an army that we must shape and train for war," said Wilson, "it is a machine." World War I was the event that brought the federal government's hesitant control of industry, business, and agriculture together.

But democracy was under siege from the mentality engendered by the war in which winning was of paramount importance. The governments of all leading participants, including the United States, imposed more stringent controls of their citizens than they had in the past—including restriction of speech.

Wilson accepted military conscription as a terrible necessity. He had already approved draft legislation secretly devised by Secretary of War Newton D. Baker (1916–21) on lines suggested by Generals Leonard Wood, Hugh Scott, and Tasker Bliss and Judge Advocate Enoch M. Crowder. They proposed a procedure that they estimated would be least offensive to the public. It would actually look like volunteering—even, in Baker's words, like men "going to the polls to vote." The very term "selective service" was invented to overcome Americans' deep resentment of conscription. Thus, men of draft age would register in their local precinct, and local civilians (sheriffs and governors, rather than army officers) would choose those to be selected for military service. To create the necessary machinery would take at least two months. Even before Congress passed the Draft Act, Baker, Crowder, and their official, Maj. Hugh S. Johnson, had the Government Printing Office print more than 10 million blank draft forms. In Congress the debate over conscription divided the parties, opponents saying it would "Prussianize America" and "destroy democracy at home."

Nevertheless, Congress passed the draft bill and Wilson signed it into law on May 18, 1917. It required all men between twenty-one and thirty to register with a draft board on June 5, 1917. Subsequently, the age group was widened to from eighteen to forty-five. The penalty for evasion was one year's imprisonment. Those exempt from service were federal, state, and local government officials, aliens, felons, ministers, and munitions workers. Those selected for actual service were chosen by means of a token lottery drawn in the Senate Office Building on July 20, 1917. Secretary of War Baker drew a capsule from a board. It was number 258. Every man assigned the number of 258 in each of the 4,500 local boards across the nation was obliged to take a medical examination as the next stage in the process. Only 70 percent were found medically fit to serve. The three successive drafts altogether drew 23,908,576 men in the United States and another 325,445 in the territories. This was 44 percent of the adult male pop-

Left: Patriotic sheet music portrays American troops going "over the top" of the trenches to attack German soldiers rather like jaunty sailors fearlessly riding the crest of a wave. The reality of trench warfare with muddy slime, mass slaughter, and the psychological horror of shell shock with its enduring posttraumatic hysteria, was far less salutary. During the war Allied governments kept the truth from their public. (Library of Congress)
Right: Organized for the national prohibition of alcohol and the outlawing of the saloon, the Anti-Saloon League, through its giant press in Westerville, Ohio, distributed thousands of pamphlets and posters warning people of the evils of demon drink, such as this cartoon of the alcoholic youth unfit to fight in the war to end all wars. (Library of Congress)

ulation. The cost was $30 million. Only 6,373,414 men actually went into service. The draft set a precedent beyond enforced military service. It signaled a new form of government activity—an immense, carefully orchestrated publicity campaign—supported by secret and elaborate preparations to nullify any opposition and make the public receptive to government plans.

In 1917 there was a boom in weddings among men who thought marriage would provide a shelter from the draft. Draft boards also granted exemption to 56,830 members of religious sects opposed to military service, such as the Quakers, the Brethren, the Mennonites, and others. More troublesome to the board was a class of conscientious objectors moved by ethical scruples. An executive order of March 20, 1918, recognized this category of objectors—about 3,900 in all—and arranged for them to engage in noncombative service, provided they could satisfy a board of inquiry regarding their sincerity.

To train and discipline the draftees within three months, the federal government created sixteen army camps under canvas in the South and another sixteen cantonments in the North, each with a capacity for 40,000 to 50,000 men. All camps provided a sixteen-week period of preliminary training for forty hours a week. Here was the staple of folk legend. In "Oh! How I Hate to Get Up in the Morning," songwriter Irving Berlin, who was a sergeant at Camp Upton, New York, delighted draftees because his song emphasized that the army bugle blew at 5:45 A.M., turning reveille into "I can't get 'em up / I can't get 'em up."

The federal government looked to wars of the future as well as the present. On July 14, 1917, the House voted appropriations of $640 million for the creation of an air fleet, and on October 4 the War Department announced that it had awarded contracts for building twenty thousand airplanes.

The war to make the world safe for democracy was not intended to free society from racism. The armed services were completely segregated. In April 1917 the army had four African American regiments of enlisted men. Col. William Hayward of the 369th Regiment was told that his unit could not accompany the so-called Rainbow Division to France because "black was not one of the colors of the rainbow." All told, about 42,000 of a total of 380,000 African American troops were assigned to combat duty. The others were placed in labor and stevedore battalions. Some were not even given military training. In the navy African Americans were employed only as mess boys.

In July 1917 Wilson appointed Gen. John J. Pershing commander of the American Expeditionary Force (AEF). In all, 2,086,000 men served in the European theaters. Their contribution was decisive. Like other combatants, U.S. troops experienced shell shock, battle fatigue, tuberculosis, poison gas, and the cold, wet, and filth of the trenches. More than 50,000 Americans died in France, compared with 3 million British, French, and Russian soldiers in all theaters.

The scourge of venereal disease infected about one man in every five in the AEF. For a time the military authorities pretended the problem did not exist, despite rudimentary medical control of official French brothels. In the end the Allies agreed that free treatment of venereal disease was an essential way of protecting society. Military experiences of venereal disease abroad helped stimulate a concerted, but small-scale, preventive campaign at home. In 1918 the Chamberlain-Kahn Act appropriated $4 million for the establishment of a Division of Venereal Diseases in the United States Public Health Service.

Although Woodrow Wilson took personal charge of the federal government, he isolated himself, staying close in his private rooms and seeing few people. Wilson disliked assertiveness in others. He liked the qualities of sensitivity, delicacy, insight, and intuition, and he expected these of his closest associates. He found them in three trusted executives: Secretary of War Baker; investment banker Bernard Baruch, now chairman of the War Industries Board; and George Creel, chairman of the Committee of Public Information.

Bernard Baruch's task at the War Industries Board (WIB) was to coordinate the different components of American industry for war as surely as Henry Ford did for motor cars in his automobile factories. Baruch carefully selected an elite of professional men and businessmen who had risen on account of their imagination, forcefulness, and flexibility. They included Charles M. Schwab of U.S. Steel, Alexander Legge of International Harvester, Robert S. Lovett of Union Pacific, and Samuel M. Vauclain of Baldwin Locomotive Works. Baruch organized the WIB in eleven sections to administer such things as finished-product facilities, price fixing, and particular products—steel, chemicals, textiles, explosives, and building materials. The WIB had the power to regulate what industry produced and for whom. When it discovered that eight thousand tons of steel per annum were used for corsets, it discontinued the manufacturing of girdles: the steel could be put to more fundamental use.

Moreover, the WIB assisted industrialists in converting factories to wartime production of such things as masks and belts for the army medical corps. Shirtwaist factories turned to signal flags, radiator factories to guns, automobile factories to airplane parts, and piano factories to airplane wings. Building materials became so scarce that those who wanted to construct houses or barns had to get a certificate of necessity from neighborhood committees. The conservation division of the WIB set itself the task of eliminating waste by persuading manufacturers to standardize their products. Thus, 232 different kinds of buggy wheels were reduced to 4, and 287 styles and sizes of auto tires were reduced to 9. Shoe colors were reduced to three—black, white, and tan. To spare more leather for soldiers' boots, shoemakers reduced the height of shoes. These changes had profound and lasting impacts on fashion. Never again would women's dresses skirt the ground.

Under the stimulus of war, U.S. industry expanded greatly, notably in steel, coke, aluminum, and electric power. As to greater steel production, the total number of steel ingots and castings rose from 23.1 million long tons in 1914 to 45.06 million long tons in 1917. Enlarged demands for munitions placed a premium on the construction of by-product coking ovens to provide coal tar for explosives. By 1919 by-product coke amounted to 56.9 percent of the total of 44.2 million tons. Because the war increased the demand for special alloys, electric-furnace production expanded greatly, rising from 27,000 long tons of aluminum in 1914 to 511,693 in 1918. Industry and manufacturing required additional electric power. In the period 1914–19 installed primary electric power more than doubled, reaching 9.34 million horsepower. This accounted for 31.6 percent of the total horsepower of manufacturing industries.

The problem of domestic transportation for military supplies and personnel and for goods forced Wilson and the federal government to temporary nationalization of the railroads—precisely the sort of federal intervention Progressives had resisted earlier. As Europe required ever greater supplies, U.S. railroads carried more military supplies and food to the Atlantic coast. By 1916 the rail tonmileage was 30 percent higher than in 1915. In 1917 it was another 43 percent higher.

The Army Appropriation Act, passed on August 29, 1916, had a provision to create a Council of National Defense "for the coordination of industries and resources for the national security and welfare." It agreed that the American Railroad Association, now comprising eighteen railroad managers, should establish a special committee on military transportation, led by Daniel Willard, president of the Baltimore and Ohio Railroad. Their principal problem was the shortage of railroad cars to cope with expanded demand. By March 1917 the railroads had 145,000 fewer cars than they needed, and by November they were short 158,000 cars. To compound their problems, as many as 3,400 locomotives already ordered had been delayed in production because of priority given to engines for Europe.

Threatened with railroad paralysis caused by lack of locomotives, freight cars, and fuel, as well as escalating costs, Wilson took control of the railroads by proclamation on December 28, 1917. Wilson appointed his son-in-law and secretary of the treasury, William Gibbs McAdoo, director general of railroads. Wilson upheld the property rights of railroad owners in a subsequent Railroad Control Act of March 21, 1918. It declared that the companies would receive adequate compensation based on average annual earnings in 1914–17.

McAdoo was an administrator of proven eloquence. He concentrated on three things—rates, wages, and equipment. He divided the entire railroad network into three regions (eastern, southern, and western), placed stringent standards controls over freight to ensure that it always went by the fastest route, and ordered the building of 1,930 locomotives and 100,000 cars at a cost of $380 million. By his decisions McAdoo discouraged nonessential passenger traffic; eliminated unprofitable or duplicate passenger services; rationalized timetables; and, to save food, reduced dining facilities. Thus, McAdoo abolished 67 million passenger-train miles in 1918—thereby reducing the passenger-train service of 1917 by one-tenth. Railroads made further economies by taking Pullman cars off trains. Despite such economies, American railroads had 8 percent more passenger traffic in 1918 than in 1917. At the same time, freight rates rose by 28 percent.

The whole wartime arrangement was most costly. Total operating expenses for the twenty-six months of federal control from January 1, 1918, to March 1, 1920, cost over $900 million, plus another $200 million subsequently paid to the railroad companies as compensation for their claims that rolling stock had not been adequately maintained.

In 1917 and 1918 the government increased the number of shipyard workers from 50,000 to 350,000 and built 341 shipyards with a total of 1,284 launching ways. In 1918, July 4 was celebrated by launching 95 ships. In that year, 533 ships with a total of 3,030,406 tons were completed. Hog Island in the Delaware

River was transformed into the biggest shipyard in the world, 846 acres with 250 buildings and 80 miles of railroad tracks, employing 34,049 workers.

The asset of new ships, important in itself, would have been wasted without major revisions in Allied strategy. Rear Adm. William S. Sims argued against traditional British tactics in submarine warfare, trying to patrol large areas of the Atlantic and failing to provide ships with adequate cover. Sims persuaded British prime minister David Lloyd George to institute a system of convoys—fleets of merchant ships protected by destroyers. The first convoy left Gibraltar on May 10, 1917. Before convoys started, a quarter of all ships were lost; after the system was introduced, fewer than 1 percent of ships were lost from all causes. The number of ships requiring convoy was about 140 each week. As a result of these measures, German submarine warfare became far less effective. Between February and July 1917 German submarines sank 640,000 tons of shipping per month; between August 1917 and January 1918, it was an average of 300,000 tons; and from February 1918 to the Armistice it was 200,000 tons per month.

Machines

Europe needed grain as well as arms. Herbert Hoover was the obvious candidate for food administrator. This entailed management of crops so as to feed not only the newly expanded army and the civilian population but also the Allies' armies and their civilians abroad. Hoover's task was nothing less than to make food go three times as far as in peacetime, whether by increased production, increased saving, or better distribution. Hoover had an uncanny ability to absorb specialist knowledge about sources and distribution and to manipulate the supply to meet the needs of three hundred million people across the world. As a result of Hoover's herculean efforts, the amount of bread produced rose from 3.32 million metric tons before the war to 10.56 million metric tons in 1918–19. The amount of meats and fats rose from 645,000 metric tons before the war to 2.36 million metric tons in 1918–19.

In order to get the best balance of food supplies between the United States and Europe, Hoover knew he had to modify the dietary habits of 120 million Americans and, in particular, their tendency to waste food. Although he had the power to take away the business licenses of any manufacturers and dealers whose business was worth one hundred thousand dollars per annum, if they indulged in war profiteering, he preferred to make violators give a contribution to the Red Cross in lieu of a fine. On January 26, 1918, Hoover published a weekly timetable of voluntary denial: wheatless Mondays and Wednesdays, meatless Tuesdays, and porkless Thursdays and Saturdays. On May 26 he set a weekly ration of two pounds of meat per person. There were also heatless days, when fuel administrator Harry A. Garfield decided to have towns reduce their consumption of electric power. Daylight saving time was introduced.

What was necessary for food was also necessary for drink. U.S. intervention in the war was the decisive factor in the introduction of national prohibition of alcohol by the Eighteenth Amendment, passed in 1917, ratified in 1918, and put into effect in 1920. To its admirers it was a fulfillment of the best traditions of urban reforms, a means of cleansing cities and their inhabitants of social and political ills. To its numerous critics it was a gross and crude mistake, a parody of reform, a joker in the mixed pack of Progressivism. As Charles Merz, *New Republic* journalist and pioneer historian of the wet cause in *The Dry Decade* (1930), explains, "The war did three things for prohibition. It centralized authority in Washington; it stressed the importance of saving food; and it outlawed all things German."

The prohibition movement gained momentum with the wartime rationing of foodstuffs at the expense of brewing and distilling. Drys (proponents of prohibition) argued that, while the United States was assenting to voluntary rationing to provide Europe with grain, it was subversive of the war effort to liquidate crops and turn them into alcohol. They advised the administration to keep alcohol away from army camps and shipyards. Secretary of the Navy Josephus Daniels was a confirmed dry and, as early as April 5, 1914, had forbidden the use of alcohol in the navy. Herbert Hoover persuaded Woodrow Wilson (by a proclamation of December 8, 1917) to reduce the alcoholic content of beer by weight to 2.75 percent. He also limited the amount of food that could be used in brewing to 70 percent of what it had been in 1916. The Agricultural Appropriations Act of 1917 banned the use of foods in beer, wine, and spirits. Wartime prohibition thus passed Congress to take effect on July 1, 1919—unless the armed forces had been demobilized by then.

The final resort of the drys was the Eighteenth Amendment. In the course of the debates in Congress, the wets (opponents of prohibition) tried to buy time. Thirty-six of the forty-eight states would have to ratify the measure before it became part of the Constitution. The wets counted on controlling thirteen state legislatures. The two sides compromised at seven years for ratification in exchange for another wet proposal: that after ratification the liquor trade should have a year to wind up its affairs. The amendment passed the Senate by 65 votes to 20 in August 1917 and the House by 282 to 128 in December.

The Eighteenth Amendment banned the "manufacture, sale or transportation of intoxicating liquors" in the United States and empowered Congress and the states "to enforce this article by appropriate legislation." It did not prohibit buying and drinking alcohol, nor did it explicitly proscribe possession of alcohol or its domestic manufacture. The Anti-Saloon League and its allies were past masters at lobbying state legislatures. After the amendment passed Congress, lobbyists who claimed support from millions of voters presented the case for ratification to the state legislatures. Forty-six states ratified the amendment. Again and again, prohibitionists used a basic appeal put forward in the Senate by William Kenyon of Iowa: "If liquor is a bad thing for the boys in the trenches, why is it a good thing for those at home? When they are willing to die for us, should we not be willing to go dry for them?"

The American people would cooperate in the war effort if they knew what was expected of them. On August 29, 1916, Congress established an official Council of National Defense, consisting of six cabinet officers, the secretaries of war, navy, interior, agriculture, commerce, and labor, and an advisory committee of civilians. The advisory commission included business leaders who were familiar with nationwide companies: Walter S. Gifford of AT&T, Julius Rosenwald of Sears Roebuck, and Daniel Willard of the Baltimore and Ohio Railroad. The commission established 184,000 local councils across the country to execute its provisions and report back on the needs of particular communities.

On the eve of the war declaration, Wilson had pondered whether the United States could participate in World War I without becoming brutalized. He confided his doubts to Frank Cobb, editor of the *New York World*, who recalled their conversation:

> "Once lead this people into war," he said, "and they'll forget there ever was such a thing as tolerance. To fight you must be brutal and ruthless, and the spirit of ruthless brutality will enter into the very fibre of our national life, infecting Congress, the courts, the policeman on the beat, the man in the street." . . . He said a nation couldn't put its strength into a war and keep its head level: it had never been done.

On June 15, 1917, Congress passed the first Espionage Act, which forbade obstruction of the draft and insubordination in the services, providing penalties of up to twenty years in prison and a fine of ten thousand dollars. On May 16, 1918, the Sedition Act forbade writing or printing any "disloyal, profane, scurrilous or abusive language intended to cause contempt, scorn, contumely or disrepute as regards the form of government of the United States, or the Constitution or the flag." It warned against obstruction in the sale of war bonds, inciting insubordination in the services, and attempts to discourage recruiting. The Trading-with-the-Enemy Act of October 1917 allowed the government to censor the foreign-language press.

Thus, domestic support for American involvement in the "war to make the world safe for democracy" was based on a paradox. To set Europe free, the United States had to be restricted. Freedom of speech and radical dissent were suppressed as much as possible. Wilson's fear came true. Methods of suppression received the tacit approbation of the public and enthusiastic execution by people in authority. Socialist John Reed said in fall 1917 that the United States had "acquiesced in a regime of judicial tyranny, bureaucratic suppression, and industrial barbarism."

The newly created Committee on Public Information (CPI) began as a simple clearinghouse for everyday information about government. Chairman George Creel developed it into something far more formidable and sinister. As he became ever more confident, Creel increased the scope of CPI activities, creating a Division of Pictorial Publicity under artist Charles Dana Gibson that drew on the myriad talents of painters, illustrators, cartoonists, and sculptors. Among those artists who designed war posters were Howard Chandler Christy ("Win the

War—Buy a Bond"), Edward Hopper ("Smash the Hun"), and James Montgomery Flagg ("Tell That to the Marines!").

Clergymen made hatred of all things German fashionable, describing the kaiser as the "beast of Berlin" or the "werewolf of Potsdam." Ardent prohibitionist Billy Sunday spoke for many when he told the House, "No nation so infamous, vile, greedy, sensuous, bloodthirsty ever disgraced the pages of history." All manner of people and things German were subject to censure. The mayor of East Orange, New Jersey, prevented violinist Fritz Kreisler from playing in concert. Sauerkraut was renamed liberty cabbage.

George Creel organized a motion picture division to boost public morale. During movie intermissions he had special orators speak on a subject of current interest or propaganda. These speakers numbered seventy-five thousand altogether and were known as Four-Minute Men. They exhorted the public to buy bonds, to support the draft, and to help conserve food. Altogether, they made 7.55 million speeches in movie houses, schools, churches, synagogues, and camps to an aggregate audience of 314.54 million people. The most widely known was a French priest, Capt. Paul Perigard, a hero of Verdun.

Elsewhere, Creel's impetuous behavior was to stir up future trouble for Wilson in Congress. Creel ridiculed congressmen critical of Wilson in a way that increased tensions between Republicans and Democrats. He never lost an opportunity to hold Senators Hiram Johnson of California and James Reed of Missouri up to contempt. However, he reserved his most deadly salvo for Senator Henry Cabot Lodge, crediting him with ignorance, rather than dishonesty. "The Lodge mind [is] like the soil of New England—highly cultivated, but naturally sterile. An exceedingly dull man and a very vain one—deadly combination—his vanity fosters his ignorance by persistent refusal to confess it."

Suppression of protest against the war provided a convenient cover for the suppression of radicals with whom critics of the war were identified. Labor agitation could be crushed not because it was radical but because it was, supposedly, unpatriotic. Max Eastman, editor of the *Masses*, told an audience in July 1917, "You can't even collect your thoughts without getting arrested for unlawful assemblage. They give you ninety days for quoting the Declaration of Independence, six months for quoting the Bible, and pretty soon someone is going to get a life sentence for quoting Woodrow Wilson in the wrong connection."

Under the new laws, 1,532 people were arrested for disloyal statements, 65 for threatening the president, and 10 for sabotage. Here was the real beginning of the Great Red Scare. William Haywood and 94 other members of the IWW were tried and sentenced to prison, as was Socialist leader Eugene V. Debs, who was brought to trial for a speech in Canton, Ohio, in which he had declared, "The master class has always declared the war, and the subject class has always fought the battles. The master class has had all to gain and nothing to lose, while the subject class has had nothing to gain and all to lose—especially their lives." The court found Debs guilty and sentenced him to ten years' imprisonment.

The *Masses'* long record of hostility brought it into direct conflict with Woodrow Wilson's administration, and the entire editorial board was charged with conspiracy to obstruct the draft. Yet George W. Anderson, a federal judge from Boston, later declared that 90 percent of the pro-German plots were fictitious.

The mobilization of all sectors of society required organization on an unprecedented scale. The cost was colossal. How was the money raised?

Two-thirds of the cost of the war was financed by loans, the other third by taxation. At the outset there was not enough money in the Treasury to finance the war. Accordingly, on April 24, 1917, Congress authorized the Treasury to borrow $5 billion in bonds. Secretary of the Treasury William Gibbs McAdoo decided to raise the money through banks and by Liberty Bonds sold across the nation, many in small denominations so that all classes of society could take part. The first Liberty Bond drive exceeded $3 billion—50 percent more than was required. By the end of the war the government had raised $21 billion altogether by the sale of bonds. War Savings Stamps were promoted by the slogan "Lick the stamps and lick the Kaiser."

To raise additional revenue, the government applied the principle of progressive taxation to all existing taxation. Income tax was raised from 1 percent on everything over the first $3,000 to 2 percent on everything over $10,000. In 1916 surtaxes were 1 percent on incomes over $20,000 and 13 percent on incomes over $2 million. Thereafter, a surtax of 1 percent was imposed on incomes over $5,000 and 50 percent on incomes over $2 million. The public was scandalized by the great profits made by firms manufacturing and selling war matériel. In response to public disquiet, the Revenue Act of 1917 taxed such profits at rates ranging from 20 percent to 60 percent. Progressives led by Robert La Follette wanted to increase these rates. Corporation income was taxed at 6 percent. There were also taxes on excess profits. The sum total of these various measures was as follows: The amount raised by taxes increased from $788 million in 1916 to over $5 billion in 1919. The federal deficit was $153 million in 1917, $9 billion in 1918, and $13 billion in 1919.

The war accelerated economic changes within the United States. As a result of wartime inflation, the purchasing power of the dollar fell from 100 cents to 45. A new poor, dislocated from its previous social position, confronted a new rich. Those who lived on fixed incomes, such as the return from bonds, mortgages, and rents, and who had previously been affluent, now shared a new poverty with those living on fixed salaries, such as teachers and government officials. Between 1916 and 1919 salaried workers lost 22 percent of their purchasing power. The new rich, those who profited from inflation, were people with investments in land or shares in corporations and industry and artisans, whose wages had also risen. The war created 42,000 new millionaires, and the number of people earning between $30,000 and $40,000 tripled. With their lapse from social position because of their fall in fortune, the former rich were no longer the guardians of morals and the arbiters of taste. Reduction in their real income was a contributory cause of intellectuals' alienation from society. The moral license of the Jazz Age of the 1920s began with the shifting economic fortunes of classes in the war.

The Fourteen Points versus the Communist Manifesto

The omens for an Allied victory were not good in 1917. Britain was being starved of food by submarines that were also destroying its ships. The French army launched an assault on the western front, but it failed; this led to mutinies in the army. Russian armies were disintegrating with mutinies and desertions. In the fall Austria and Germany launched a major offensive against Italy.

At this crucial time, the Bolshevik Revolution, led by Vladimir Lenin and Leon Trotsky, felled the constitutional Kerensky regime in Russia. The Bolsheviks' coup of November 6, 1917, met with only feeble resistance. The Bolsheviks seized transportation and communication and soon reestablished the ancient city of Moscow as the capital. The sagacious Lenin had persuaded his followers to abandon their belief in incremental progress toward communism through a succession of political and economic stages—feudalism, bourgeois capitalism, and socialism. Instead, the Communists decided to maximize the chaos of the czar's war and, once they had seized power, to move Russian society from feudalism to communism without any intermediate stages. Therefore, Lenin exploited the grievances of the peasants and promised them what they wanted—an end to the war, and economic and social justice. The underlying principle was that it was the proletariat who had created industrial society; their needs and their will should prevail through a dictatorship. Kerensky was driven into exile, first in western Europe, and from 1940 on, in the United States, where he lectured at universities in New York for the last three decades of his life.

The vast Eurasian empire of the czars would become the nucleus of the Soviet Union or Union of Soviet Socialist Republics (USSR), created from, at first, four states in 1922 and propelled by an ideological force, Marxism, which the Soviets claimed was driven by historical law. Yet the Bolshevik regime was much shaped by the autocratic institutions it inherited from the czars, including the secret police and the system of exile in Siberia. Moreover, the Communists believed the Russian Revolution of 1917 was only the first in a whole series of revolutions in industrialized countries.

American socialist John Reed fell victim to the siren call of revolution. Indicted under the Espionage Act for his opposition to the war, Reed visited Russia in fall 1917. He was not merely a witness to the revolution but also a participant. He addressed the Third Congress of Soviets and went on patrols with the Red Guards. His *Ten Days that Shook the World* (1919) was a vivid account of the Bolsheviks' seizure of power and a testament to Reed's own conversion from socialism to communism.

As committed Marxists, the Bolsheviks wanted to show that the war for democracy was really a capitalist contest for spoils. They did so by opening up the

The official composite portrait of the *Signing of the Treaty of Versailles* in the French palace's famous Hall of Mirrors by Sir William Orpen. The German envoys cower before the triumphal trio of Woodrow Wilson of the United States, Georges Clemenceau of France, and David Lloyd George of Britain. (Imperial War Museum, London)

imperial archives and publishing documents, thereby revealing various secret treaties—deals, really—between Britain, France, czarist Russia, and Italy. These secret deals were at odds with Allied propaganda about the war being a war for democracy. Thus the Bolsheviks hoped to turn the Allied peoples against their governments. The revelations were a calamity for Woodrow Wilson, as if to ridicule his rhetoric, his intentions, and his integrity. Although Wilson tried to forestall publication of the secret treaties in America, pacifist Oswald Garrison Villard printed the texts in the *New York Evening Post*.

Democratic capitalism stood in stark opposition to the tumult of communistic revolution as World War I revealed all-encompassing U.S. military and economic power to the world. This was because U.S. military intervention came at the most opportune moment from the Allies' point of view, because of America's outsize loans to the Allies and because the United States was about to exercise a profound impact on the peace settlement. The new situation was ironic. Since the United States was now an outsize creditor nation, with $7 billion invested or loaned abroad and only $3.3 billion of foreign capital in the United States, Woodrow Wilson could insist on the implementation of ideas just as revolutionary as those of Lenin. Wilson wanted to set U.S. participation in the war on a sure moral footing; to correct what he considered territorial injustices across Europe; to reestablish a concert of nations to prevent future wars; and to put a philosophical stamp on America's part in the peacemaking.

George Creel set himself the task of giving Wilson's various speeches about the postwar world truly universal circulation. A Foreign Mail Press Bureau, directed by Ernest Poole, dispatched printed material every week. Wilson's speeches were translated and transmitted across the world. Consequently, two decades before the cult of personality became a device of propaganda associated with European dictators, there was a Creel phenomenon, the cult of Wilson. The cult of Wilson spread across Europe to Russia. In the East it spread as far as China, where Creel claimed an edition of Wilson's speeches had become a bestseller, and in the West to the Peruvian Andes. Creel's agent in Russia, Edgar G. Sisson, persuaded Creel and Wilson that, if the president's messages were to be truly effective in Germany and Russia, they must be condensed and distributed to ordinary people in the form of a succinct and itemized list. Accordingly, with the help of Col. Edward House, Wilson restated his war aims and peace terms in the Fourteen Points.

What Wilson needed first were the facts and an informed secretariat to give substance to his utopian blueprint. While journalist Walter Lippmann was working in the War Department as an aide to Secretary Newton D. Baker, he and Wilson aide Col. Edward House conceived the idea of a research body to gather political, cultural, and geographical information about Europe and its colonies that the administration would use at the end of the war. The organization, known as the Inquiry, was headed by Sidney E. Mezes with Lippmann as executive secretary. In December 1917 Mezes, Lippmann, and others tried to coordinate the specific interests of the movements of national liberation across

Europe with the provisions of the secret treaties, providing House with a special document, "The War Aims and Peace Terms They Suggest," on December 22, 1917. In their final version, the Fourteen Points were the work of Wilson, House, Lippmann, and Mezes.

Wilson devised the first five and the last point to cover general principles: open diplomacy, freedom of the seas, lower tariffs, disarmament, the rights of colonial peoples, and the League of Nations. These points aroused widespread enthusiasm. The remaining territorial points were of crucial interest to the belligerents. Point Six recommended that revolutionary Russia be allowed to continue its own political development without outside interference. Point Seven recommended the evacuation and restoration of Belgium. Point Eight wanted the restoration of Alsace-Lorraine to France. Point Nine disposed of Italy's exaggerated claims to the Austrian Tyrol, Trieste, and the Dalmatian coast, recommending that Italian frontiers should be fixed "along clearly recognizable lines."

Point Ten called for internal (or federal) autonomy for nationalist groups within the Austro-Hungarian Empire. On Point Eleven, about the Balkans, Wilson revised the specific recommendations of the Inquiry about Serbia and Bulgaria. Wilson merely wanted Serbia to have access to the sea with frontiers based on national, economic, and historic rights. Point Twelve proposed the security of Turkey and guaranteed autonomy to its subject peoples. As to Point Thirteen, about Poland, the Inquiry wanted a revived Polish state attached to a democratic Russia or Austria-Hungary. However, Wilson insisted on an independent Poland to include territories inhabited by "indisputably Polish populations" but with access to the sea through lands that were predominantly German.

Wilson announced the Fourteen Points in a speech to Congress on January 8, 1918. Wilson was not surprised by the ominous silence of the Allied governments to his momentous speech. He wanted to excite their peoples to put pressure on governments to end the war.

Thus, here it was: the incipient, century-long conflict between the United States and Communist Russia, two philosophies, two economies. On one side, all-penetrating democratic capitalism and the Fourteen Points. On the other, all-pervasive socialism through the dictatorship of the proletariat, the legacies of Marx and Engels's *Communist Manifesto* (1848), put into practice by the Bolsheviks in a way that would have surprised the authors. U.S. and Russian leaders began to think that they were engaged in competition for the future of the human race.

Intent on wide social reform within Russia, the Bolsheviks made a separate peace when they treated with Germany in the peace of Brest-Litovsk on March 3, 1918. Germany demanded (and the Bolsheviks agreed to) a punitive peace, claiming the Baltic provinces (Latvia, Lithuania, and Estonia), Poland, Byelorussia, the wheatlands of the Ukraine, and the oil fields of the Caucasus. Russia lost a third of its population, a third of its agricultural land, four-fifths of its coal mines, and half of its industry.

A clear signal that the Bolsheviks would impose a yet more callous regime than that of their antique predecessors came with the brutal murder of the imperial family itself on June 17, 1918, in the Siberian mining town of Ekaterinburg. The Bolshevik regime was not secure. Russia was in a state of civil war begun by White Russians, and the Bolshevik regime was further endangered by the invasion of several European countries. As long as the czar's family could be used as pawns in negotiations with foreign powers, they might live. With the possibility of their rescue by the Whites, Lenin disposed of them. When the assassins fired their weapons at the imperial family in the infamous "House of Special Purpose," the bullets ricocheted off the jewels hidden in the corsets of the czarina and the grand duchesses. Then, the assassins bayoneted their victims and bludgeoned them to death with their rifle butts. All but two of the bodies were buried in a common grave in the nearby forest—the site and remains not identified irrefutably until 1991, nor officially recognized until 1998. The murders were prophetic of the chilling incompetence of the Communist state and remained the subject of widespread speculation.

Germany seemed to be on the point of winning the war in Europe in 1918, only to have defeat snatched from the jaws of victory. After the treaty with Russia, Germany transferred troops to the western front, from which it launched a great offensive on March 21, 1918. First the British and then the French were driven back with appalling loss of life. In this crisis Georges Clemenceau, the French prime minister, proved himself of indomitable will. He persuaded the Americans and the British to accept a unified command of their forces under Gen. Ferdinand Foch. The arrival of about 750,000 U.S. troops that spring provided the Allies with enough extra forces to mount a counteroffensive on the highway from Château-Thierry to Soissons on July 18. Halted, the Germans suffered a shock to morale. Each day brought more U.S. troops to the front and victory for the Allies closer. A second British offensive on August 9 breached the Hindenburg line, where the Germans had been entrenched since 1914. The Allies were now able to make use of armored tractors—tanks—to puncture the German lines.

Despite these advances, the war might have continued on the western front had not the Central Powers begun to crumble in the east. Turkey was eliminated by Allenby at the battle of Megiddo on September 19. Bulgaria signed an armistice on September 29. The Allies could now break into Central Europe. German commander Ludendorff persuaded a reluctant German government to seek an armistice and thereby to consolidate his shattered forces.

In the United States in October 1918 Wilson made an unnecessary appeal to the American electorate. He wanted them to use the midterm congressional elections to cast a vote of confidence on his foreign policy. Republicans across the country, who had supported the administration loyally in the war, interpreted Wilson's request as ingratitude. On November 5 the electorate returned a Republican majority to Congress, 240 to 190 in the House and 49 to 47 in the Senate. By 1918 Republican foes William Howard Taft, Elihu Root, and Boies

Penrose were turning to Theodore Roosevelt for leadership. It seemed he would be the Republicans' presidential nominee in 1920.

Yet, whatever the Republicans would have preferred, Wilson was still at the helm. And since the Allies had not defined their war aims, they had only themselves to blame that Wilson decided for them with the Fourteen Points. The Allies jibed at two of the Fourteen Points in particular. They wanted to reserve complete freedom of interpretation about freedom of the seas (Point Two). They insisted on reparations from Germany for damage to their civilian populations as well as the restoration of French territory (Point Seven).

Journalist Walter Lippmann had joined Col. Edward House's staff in Paris at the time House was explaining Woodrow Wilson's Fourteen Points to the Allies in order to get them accepted. This required a close definition of the meaning of the Points, which House sought from Lippmann and from Frank Cobb, editor of the New York *World*, on October 25. House demanded the qualifications within twenty-four hours. Lippmann prepared memoranda on thirteen of the points; Cobb provided a memorandum on the last point. Lippmann tried to reconcile the Fourteen Points not only with the secret discussions of the Allies before and during the war but also with the secret discussions taking place at the end. In order to justify these discussions in view of Point One, which called for "open covenants, openly arrived at," Lippmann provided a sophistical distinction. Confidential negotiations were permissible so long as their final outcome was made public. It was not so easy to reconcile the difficulties with some of the other points. Wilson postponed resolution in the hope that the League of Nations would do something about them once it was in session.

The Allies grudgingly accepted the Fourteen Points on November 4, 1918. The Ottoman government signed an armistice with Britain on October 30; the Austro-Hungarian high command did so with Italy on November 3. By his stand on democratic principles, Wilson contributed to the fall of the kaiser, who fled to Holland and abdicated on November 9, 1918. A German delegation then signed an armistice with the Allied forces on November 11. Under the terms of the armistice, Germany had to evacuate Alsace-Lorraine, Belgium, Luxembourg, and northeast France and forsake the Treaty of Brest-Litovsk; its troops had to abandon territory west of the Rhine.

The financial cost of World War I to all sides was put at $337.94 billion by Professor E. L. Bogert of the department of economics of the University of Illinois in a postwar investigation undertaken for the Carnegie Endowment for International Peace. Direct costs were $186 billion and indirect costs $151 billion. The total loss of life was 9,998,771—more than twice the estimated loss in all other wars from Napoleon onward. The price might, in the future, said the report, include "the very breakdown of modern economic society."

As if to parody the cruel deaths in the trenches, an epidemic of influenza followed the war. In the United States it appeared first in Boston, Philadelphia, and New York, with deaths rising slowly until the fall of 1918 when there were, on average, 175 deaths a day. By October thirty-six states were affected. Almost a quarter of the population fell ill. Of every 1,000 sick, 19 died. The total number of deaths in the United States was between 400,000 and 500,000, most of them persons between the ages of twenty and forty. The young and the old escaped. The highest death rate was in Baltimore, where the weather was too cold for burial services. As a result a plague from the accumulated corpses was a real possibility. In early 1919 the pandemic vanished like a symbol of an old society passing away.

As to passing symbols, the great Theodore Roosevelt died on January 6, 1919, in Oyster Bay, New York. Among the mourners at his funeral two days later were ever-faithful Gen. Leonard Wood and estranged former ally William Howard Taft.

American and European society got a glimpse of technological possibilities for the future when, on June 15, 1919, English pilot Capt. John Alcock and American navigator Lt. Arthur W. Browne arrived at Clifden, Ireland, after flying 1,960 miles from St. John's, Newfoundland, in sixteen hours and twelve minutes. They won a prize of fifty thousand dollars offered by the *Daily Mail* of London for the first nonstop transatlantic flight. Alcock and Brown's achievement should have caused a sensation across the world. However, mankind was not as yet ready to acknowledge the achievement. The miracle of flight was upstaged by earthbound politics in Paris.

Rust

The Peace Conference at Paris first opened on January 12, 1919, with delegates from twenty-seven countries. The chief task of negotiations was undertaken by a Council of Ten and, in turn, a Council of Four: David Lloyd George of the United Kingdom; Georges Clemenceau of France: Vittorio Orlando of Italy; and Woodrow Wilson.

The peace settlements of 1919 were the first of three times in the twentieth century when the map of the world was redrawn, in this instance, creating or acknowledging new countries out of the ruins of the German, Austrian, Ottoman, and Russian empires. The second time was at the end of World War II in 1945 and the third after the collapse of the Soviet Union in 1991.

In 1919 Wilson went to Paris at the head of the American delegation against advice and precedent. He was accompanied by Secretary of State Robert Lansing; Col. Edward House; the permanent military representative on the Supreme War Council, Gen. Tasker Bliss; and a retired diplomat, Henry White. The only Republican, White, was of no significance in his own party. Although the Senate would have to consent to the treaty, Wilson had not asked it to endorse the Fourteen Points. The exclusion of leading senators affronted principal Republicans and stored up trouble for the future.

Wilson's arrival in Paris was a tumultuous public success but dangerous. He had raised expectations among Europeans that all had won and all must have prizes. Adulation turned Wilson's head, with disastrous effects on his political skills. The hero of 1919 was to leave office in 1921, his health broken, his party crushed, and his great dream in fragments.

Wilson made world peace by collective security the cornerstone of his peacemaking. The term "collective security" itself was not coined until 1932; the principle was imperfectly understood in 1919 and throughout the 1920s. Wilson's ideals shaped public perception as to what was desirable in the concert of nations. Wilson's cardinal weakness was his moral intensity that would not brook criticism or opposition. The Fourteen Points were too simplistic for the ethnic, religious, territorial, and political complexities of Europe, and the spirit behind them was tarnished by four years of bitter hostilities.

Those who hated Germany forced their leaders into extreme positions. Georges Clemenceau, the French premier, had won a vote of confidence of four-fifths of the French chamber of deputies. "He had one interest, France," writes historian William E. Leuchtenburg (1958), "and one concern, that Germany must never march again."

In the Treaty of Versailles with Germany, Clemenceau secured the reduction of the German army to a maximum of one hundred thousand men without heavy artillery and without an air force. Ironically, because it was to be a force of men on long service, it turned out to be capable of providing the nucleus for a rapidly trained conscripted army. To compensate France for wartime devastation to its own industry, the mining reserves of the Saar valley were placed under international control. After fifteen years the people there could decide on their future affiliation—whether to France or Germany—by a plebiscite. As a safety precaution, the right bank of the Rhine was to be demilitarized. The left bank and its bridgeheads of Cologne, Coblenz, and Mainz on the right were to endure an army of occupation for fifteen years that Germany would have to support and maintain.

Germany was forced to pay an immediate indemnity to the Allies of $5 billion and to agree to pay further reparations of an unspecified amount to be decided later. Moreover, in its war-guilt clause, the Treaty of Versailles pronounced Germany the sole cause of the war. Wilson could hardly repudiate the war-guilt clause since his own wartime rhetoric had done so much to incriminate the kaiser and the German military aristocracy. Rather than assent to the treaty, the German cabinet of Philipp Schneidmann resigned on June 23, 1919. A German national assembly adopted a new constitution at Weimar on August 11, 1919.

The conference also concluded peace treaties with the other defeated powers—each treaty named after a Parisian suburb: with Austria at St. Germain on September 10, 1919; with Bulgaria at Neuilly on November 27, 1919; with Hungary at Trianon on June 4, 1920; and with Turkey at Sèvres on August 10, 1920. The United States negotiated in all but the Treaty of Sèvres. However, only the Treaty of Versailles was submitted to the Senate.

When the Austro-Hungarian empire broke into pieces in October 1918, the core states of Austria and Hungary declined into rumps. The task of drawing frontiers of the so-called succession states was left to experts of the various foreign offices. In some cases, the principle of self-determination could not be applied evenly to two or three different ethnic groups living in the same territory.

Czechoslovakia, a country in Central Europe formed out of northern provinces of the Austro-Hungarian empire, united Czechs from Moravia-Bohemia and Germans from the Sudetenland in the west with Slovaks in the east. Because of its central location and natural mountain borders, possession of this country would give its ruler control of Central Europe. Yugoslavia, a country in southeast Europe bordering the Adriatic Sea, was founded in 1919 as, first, a kingdom of Serbs, Croats, and Slovenes from former provinces of the Austro-Hungarian and Ottoman empires (Moldavia, Slovenia, Croatia, and Bosnia and Herzegovina). It also comprised the previously independent Serbia and Montenegro and parts of Macedonia appropriated from Bulgaria.

In November 1918 nationalist Poles had used the chaos at the close of World War I to revive Poland, the country of north central Europe that had been partitioned in the 1790s. The Paris conferees acknowledged Poland, according to the Wilsonian principle of self-determination of nations. However, contrary to the self-determination of nations, Germans were placed under Polish rule in Silesia, and a corridor giving Poland access to the sea at Danzig (later Gdansk) separated East Prussia from the rest of Germany. Lloyd George insisted that Danzig become a free city under the so-called Polish Customs Union.

Outside Europe, however, things were very different, and 1919 proved to be the zenith of European imperialism in Africa and Asia. Of the German colonies in Africa and the Pacific, Cameroon and Togo went to Britain and France; Ruanda-Urundi went to Belgium; German East Africa went to Britain; Southwest Africa went to South Africa. Pacific territories were divided among Japan, Australia, and New Zealand. To cover these acquisitions with a specious gloss, the chief of the South African Legation, Gen. Jan Christian Smuts, devised the term *mandates*. The sophistry was that the foreclosing powers held their new colonies in trust to the League of Nations until they were ready for full independence.

In the Middle East Britain and France secured the trophies on which they had fixed their sights. From the old Ottoman Empire, the Hashemite Kingdom and the imamate of Yemen achieved sovereignty, but the rest was divided between Britain and France. France obtained Syria and Lebanon, and Britain obtained Palestine, Iraq, and Transjordan. Wilson disapproved of the secret wartime agreements about Turkish territories. However, since the United States had never declared war on Turkey, he could hardly justify interfering. Because these acquisitions were in flagrant violation of the principle of self-determination of nations, the Allies used sophistry to confuse what they were doing.

China once again became a victim, this time of Japan, the Asian power bent on world-class status. During the course of the war, Japan had taken full advantage of Germany's concentration of its forces in Europe to seize the German base of Tsingtan on November 7, 1914. Instead of simply concentrating on its footholds in Shandong, southern Manchuria, and Inner Mongolia, the Japanese foreign minister, Kato Takaahira, devised a series of Twenty-One Demands, which were presented to nationalist leader Yuan Shikai on January 18, 1915. Not only did they cover the transfer to Japan of Shandong and various territorial and railroad rights in Manchuria, but they also insisted that China should employ Japanese political, military, and financial advisers and that China should purchase half of its war matériel from Japan. Japan obliged China to sign two treaties: the first conceding the transfer to Japan of Germany's interests in Shandong, the second giving Japan privileges in southern Manchuria and the eastern part of Inner Mongolia. In 1919 the Paris conferees granted Japan formal entitlement to Shandong.

Wilson found his reputation undermined by the way that the Paris settlement clearly violated the Fourteen Points. The treaties were not open covenants, openly arrived at, but bargains negotiated behind closed doors. Given such flouting of the principle of the self-determination of nations as resulted from turning over the Austrian Tyrol to Italy, putting Germans under Polish control in Silesia, and placing Chinese under Japanese control in Shandong, it was not difficult for Wilson's enemies in the United States to arouse opposition to the Democrats from German-Americans and other American ethnic groups.

All that Wilson could hope for was that the inequities of the settlements would be reconsidered by the League of Nations. But Wilson's greatest diplomatic coup proved his most costly political mistake when the Paris Conference decided, on January 25, 1919, to make the League Covenant an integral part of the Treaty of Versailles. Repudiating objections by more than a third of the U.S. Senate to the constitution of the League until after the peace was signed, Wilson said in New York on March 4, 1919, that there were "so many threads of the treaty tied to the covenant that you cannot dissect the covenant from the treaty without destroying the whole, vital structure."

The Covenant of the League of Nations, first drafted by the British, gave every member an equal vote in the Assembly. The United States, Britain, France, Italy, Japan, and four other countries elected for a limited period would comprise the Council, an executive body. League members were pledged to "respect and preserve as against external aggression the territorial integrity and existing political independence of all members." Members agreed to submit all disputes to arbitration and to refrain from hostilities until after a "cooling-off period" of three months after the arbiters investigating disputes had made their decisions. If the League Council so recommended, the Assembly would impose military, naval, and economic sanctions on nations breaking the Covenant. It was the Council that had jurisdiction over the former colonies of Germany and Turkey as mandates and over conditions of labor, traffic in women and children, arms and munitions, and health.

The conference broke up. "I think I did as well as might be expected," Lloyd George observed wryly of fellow conferees Wilson and Clemenceau, "seated as

I was between Jesus Christ and Napoleon Bonaparte." As far as Clemenceau was concerned, although Wilson talked like Jesus Christ, he acted like Lloyd George—he spoke like a puritan but acted like a businessman.

There remained the problem of Communist Russia—inchoate but with immense potential. Although the Paris settlement permitted the survival of Russia as a great power, the Allies did not want to see Communism triumphant. Alarmed by uprisings that left Communists briefly in control of Berlin, Munich, and Budapest, Britain and France sent troops to seize Russia's ports and aid the counterrevolutionary White insurgents. Wilson was persuaded by diplomat William C. Bullitt to see what could be obtained from Lenin. Bullitt returned from a diplomatic mission to Moscow with a promise that Russia would pay its war debts and offer concessions to the West in exchange for recognition of the Bolshevik government. However, by now the Allies had persuaded Wilson to withhold recognition. Although in the aftermath of war Russia surrendered Finland, Latvia, Lithuania, Estonia, Poland, and part of the Caucasus, it held the Ukraine, Byelorussia, Georgia, Armenia, and Central Asia. In effect, the Allies used the succession states to isolate Bolshevik Russia, turning them into buffer states.

When Woodrow Wilson called Congress into special session in June 1919 to debate the Treaty of Versailles, he encountered ugly resistance. Because they had won the midterm elections, the Republicans had been able to place Wilson's most bitter critic, Henry Cabot Lodge of Massachusetts, in the chair of the Foreign Relations Committee. The prospect for the treaty was bleak. Lodge led a group of Republicans jealous of the president's prerogative in foreign affairs, determined on complete American independence from Europe, and anxious to resist the Democrats' intention of fighting the 1920 elections as the party that had led the United States through a victorious war to a conclusive peace.

In 1919, despite widespread criticisms, the majority of Americans were ready to accept U.S. membership in the League. Their support is evident in the accounts and opinions published in newspapers, especially of polls, and resolutions passed by thirty-two state legislatures, labor unions, women's groups, farm organizations, and professional societies. When Congress convened in May 1919, among the four different schools of thought two groups of senators were especially opposed to the treaty as it stood. Those who would accept the treaty only with major amendments were the so-called Strong Reservationists: twenty-one Republicans and four Democrats. Led by Henry Cabot Lodge, they included Warren Gamaliel Harding of Ohio, later president. Then there were the die-hard Irreconcilables, consisting of fourteen Republicans and two Democrats, including Republicans William E. Borah of Idaho, Philander C. Knox of Pennsylvania (secretary of state under Taft), Frank B. Brandegee of Connecticut, and Hiram W. Johnson of California; Democrat James A. Reed of Missouri; and Robert La Follette of Wisconsin. They had formidable oratorical skills.

The treaty went for examination to the Senate Foreign Relations Committee. When diplomat William C. Bullitt appeared before the committee, he revealed the bitter truth of the political maneuvers behind the scenes at Paris. He recalled

Robert Lansing's private remarks that the treaty was a disaster and the League useless. When Bullitt had finished his testimony, Wilson looked as unscrupulous as Lloyd George but not nearly so accomplished.

Wilson was unable to counter the personal and political resistance to his proposals. Yet he was unwilling to accept more than mild amendments to his grand design. He embarked on a speaking tour of the United States on September 4, 1919. This fateful tour was a forlorn attempt to appeal to the conscience of ordinary Americans across the country. The Irreconcilables followed him wherever he spoke. They countered with ridicule his conviction, "I can predict with absolute certainty that within another generation there will be another world war if the nations do not concert the method by which to prevent it."

Wilson had little remaining strength to continue the struggle. On September 25, 1919, he collapsed with a stroke at Pueblo, Colorado, and returned to Washington. One day in early October, he was found half conscious on the bathroom floor, having suffered a second stroke. Thereafter, he was too ill even to be shaved. He was broken forever; he never again filled the office of president even adequately. His wife, Edith, and his doctor kept all visitors from him except Joseph Tumulty, who had to avoid exciting him. George Creel recalled later, "At sight of me he gestured pathetically, a tragic sweep of the hand that took in the whole of his helpless wasted body, and great tears filled his eyes."

In the face of repeated assertions from Edith Wilson and Joe Tumulty that Wilson was not disabled, the Senate dispatched a so-called smelling committee, led by Senator Albert B. Fall of New Mexico, to ascertain the facts for themselves. On a second occasion, Wilson exerted maximum effort to appear cogent and in control for half an hour before them. Cut off from his allies and friends by his illness, Wilson nevertheless insisted on controlling a battle he could not even fight. To meet Wilson's arguments, Lodge and the Senate Foreign Relations Committee had, by November 6, 1919, reduced their numerous early criticisms to fourteen reservations. The most significant concerned article 10 of the Covenant of the League of Nations—by which the signatories agreed to respect and preserve the territorial integrity and political independence of all members of the League. The United States, they argued, could accept no such obligation without the specific assent of Congress for each and every instance. Two other reservations would have given the United States exclusive authority over the tariff and immigration. By themselves, the Irreconcilables did not have enough votes to block consent to the treaty. On November 19, 1919, the Senate rejected the Treaty of Versailles twice: first, with Lodge's reservations (which Wilson wanted his supporters to suppress); second, without the Lodge reservations (which the Irreconcilables resisted). To both sides it was a case of all or nothing.

Although the Senate Democrats, led by Gilbert Hitchcock, were willing to pay the Republican price for ratification and compromise, Wilson was not. Yet a majority of Republicans and Democrats in the Senate still supported U.S. membership in the League. They blamed both Wilson and Lodge for their obduracy. When the next session opened in January 1920, attempts were made to compromise. However, Wilson dismissed Secretary of State Robert Lansing in a bitter rage on February 7, 1920, after he learned that Lansing had been calling cabinet meetings without him. At a final vote on the League on March 19, 1920, there was a substantial majority in favor of ratification of the treaty with reservations but seven votes less than the necessary two-thirds. The 35 votes against the 49 in favor included twenty-three of Wilson's loyal followers agreeing with twelve Irreconcilables in accordance with Wilson's wishes. As Senator Frank Brandegee put it to Lodge, "We can always depend on Mr. Wilson. He never has failed us."

Wilson had set a noble ideal for all humanity, but he compromised it by his arrogant insistence that he himself knew the truth, the whole truth, and nothing but the truth. Moreover, the United States was not ready for the obligations of the League of Nations.

Under the Wheels

Events at home began to displace foreign affairs. The social harmony of wartime America came to an end in 1919 with unprecedented inflation, labor disputes, race riots, and the climax of the Great Red Scare. Government and corporations finally purged the labor movement of its most radical activists. The Wobblies were smashed, the Socialists defeated, and the newly formed Communist parties scattered into competing factions. Underlying a profound public unease at the end of the war lay fears of Bolshevik conspiracy.

First came the scare of inflation and the demands of labor. According to some estimates, the cost of living rose by 51.7 percent in the period 1917–20. Labor shortages provided workers with an opportunity to attack managerial efforts to undermine their control in the workplace. Although the number of workers organized in unions doubled from about 2.5 million in 1916 to about 5 million in 1920, the disputes erupting in industry involved much more than simply the right to form a union; workers were asking a range of questions about managerial prerogatives, work rules, pay systems, and the operation of industries. They brought the various struggles closer together than at any other time in U.S. history.

Second, the United States now had to contend with Communism on its own ground. American radicals founded two Communist parties in 1919. The Communist Party of America, led by Charles Ruthenberg, claimed twenty-four thousand members. The Communist Labor Party, led by John Reed and Benjamin Gitlow, had perhaps ten thousand members. Both parties proposed the violent overthrow of the state. Carl Paivio wrote in his newspaper, *Class Struggle*, that "a rioting mob is the one and only possible means for organizing a fight . . . in these last open and decisive blood-battles between the capitalists and the working classes. . . . To hell with the teachings of peaceful revolution. The bloody seizure of power by the working classes is the only possible way." Paivio found himself under arrest.

In Russia Lenin had taken steps to foment worldwide revolution through the Communist International—the Comintern. The Comintern established headquarters in Moscow and then formed Communist parties in foreign countries, sometimes by enticing players from existing socialist groups. Beginning in 1922 the USSR funded the Comintern with equipment and resources, usually in the form of gold, silver, and jewels appropriated from the czars. It was, for instance, the Comintern that sent Vietnamese Ho Chi Minh, whom the Allies had rebuffed in Paris, as a Communist agent to Guangzhou in southern China in 1924.

In the United States the end of the war unleashed a virulent wave of nativism that shattered America's radical groups and completed the liquidation of radical leaders begun in 1917. On February 4, 1919, the Senate, stirred by a declaration from Senator William King of Utah that the Bolsheviks were indeed working to overthrow capitalistic governments, appointed a committee to investigate Bolshevik activities in the United States. On February 11 the Department of Justice had fifty-three Communists deported at Ellis Island. On March 10 the Supreme Court sustained the wartime conviction of Eugene V. Debs for violating the Espionage Act in his speech of June 16, 1918, and confirmed his sentence of ten years' imprisonment. Debs replied that the judges were "begowned, bewhiskered, bepowdered old fossils, who have never decided anything." On March 12, 1919, Debs, in a farewell speech at Cleveland, added insult to injury when he referred to Lenin and Trotsky as the "foremost statesmen of the age."

Third, American working-class militancy reached previously unknown heights. In 1919 over 4 million workers, representing 22 percent of the work force, took part in strikes and lockouts across the country. Workers demanded increased wages, shorter hours, union recognition, and rights of collective bargaining. The long series of strikes and lockouts began with a strike by harbor workers in New York on January 9, 1919, and continued with a strike of 35,000 dress and shirtwaist makers who wanted a 15 percent wage increase and a forty-four-hour week. On March 12 4,500 employees of the Public Service Railway Company, which ran through 141 towns and cities in New Jersey, walked out, thereby forcing the company to close down its services. On August 7 New England railroad shopmen walked out, causing the cancelation of 102 passenger trains.

The most radical mass strike involving AFL unions took place in Seattle. On January 21, 1919, 35,000 shipyard workers stopped work in protest over an unfair wage rate and appealed to the Seattle Central Labor Council to call a general strike. Local unions created a general strike committee to run the strike and to continue to provide the city with such essential services as garbage collection and hospital laundry. The General Strike Committee, under heavy pressure from the international officials of the various AFL unions, finally voted to call off the strike on February 11, 1919.

The most damaging dispute of all was the steel strike, beginning on September 22, after U.S. Steel, led by Judge Elbert H. Gary, refused to accept the formation of a new union of steel workers organized by the radical wing of the AFL. On the first day, union leaders claimed that 279,000 out of 350,000 workers had quit. The companies said that no more than 20 percent were on strike. The key organizer was syndicalist William Z. Foster from Philadelphia—a former street fighter, hobo, and union leader. Strike solidarity varied from place to place. Most workers in Chicago, led by Foster, stayed out; most workers in Pittsburgh continued to work. The strike was punctuated by violent clashes. Five men were killed at New Castle, Pennsylvania. The strike widened. When the Bethlehem Steel Company rejected union demands, a further strike was called and more workers came out, turning the steel strike into the biggest strike the country had yet seen.

The brutal conflict finally ended in defeat for the strikers, who gave in on January 8, 1920. A report by the Interchurch Commission concluded: "The United States Steel Corporation was too big to be beaten by 300,000 working men. . . . It spread [over] too much of the earth—still retaining absolute central control—to be defeated by widely scattered workers of many minds, many fears, varying states of pocketbook and under comparatively improvised leadership." When the steel strike failed, leader Foster moved to Communism.

Fourth came terrorism, the bitter climax of the Great Red Scare.

On April 30, 1919, what was alleged to be a nationwide plot to assassinate various public officials on May Day was thwarted by the discovery of sixteen packets containing bombs in the New York General Post Office. Another thirty-four bombs, intended for celebrities such as Justice Oliver Wendell Holmes, Secretary of Labor William B. Wilson, and Attorney General A. Mitchell Palmer, were also seized. Some bombs exploded and injured people. Four hundred soldiers, sailors, and marines raided the office of the New York *Call*, a socialist magazine, on May 1, beat up several journalists, and damaged the plant. Conservatives believed random bomb attacks were a prelude to a Communist uprising. One climax of terrorist activities came on June 2, 1919, when Attorney General Palmer's Washington home on R Street was badly damaged by a bomb thrown by an unknown man, who was killed in the explosion.

When 1,117 men of the Boston police went on strike on September 9, 1919, to protest their commissioner's refusal to allow them to join the AFL, they turned a volatile atmosphere into a hysterical one. Of all wage earners, the police had the most cause for complaint. Their salaries had risen little during the war, especially when compared with inflation. The police decided to form unions in the belief that they could thereby improve their lot. The Democratic mayor, Andrew Peters, called out the Boston companies of state troops to maintain order and put a stop to widespread looting. Governor Calvin Coolidge of Massachusetts issued an edict on September 11, calling on citizens to uphold law and order. The next day new men, many of them war veterans, were appointed in place of the striking police. At this point Samuel Gompers of the AFL pleaded that the defeated strikers be allowed to return to their jobs, only to receive in reply Coolidge's famous telegram, "There is no right to strike against the public safety by anybody, any time, any where." Coolidge became a national hero.

Fifth, came the backlash. The public found its savior from the Great Red Scare in Attorney General Palmer, a man of exaggerated presidential ambition. Declaring that it had discovered a revolutionary plot, the Department of Justice began a systematic nationwide raid on Reds and arrested more than two hundred people in New York. Legend has it that Palmer's kangaroo courts served more than five thousand arrest warrants and deportation orders in thirty-three cities across the country.

In the Southwest, the Great Red Scare struck directly at the remnants of grass-roots socialism that had survived the war. Kansas and Oklahoma legislators joined Arkansas in passing so-called red-flag laws to prohibit any display of radical sympathy. In Washington State among the lumberjacks were several IWW activists who wanted the lumberjacks to be paid in federal money, rather than in company scrip. Against them were ranged the combined forces of the Employers Association and their tool, the Loyal Legion of Loggers and Lumbermen, a mix of veterans and workers. They raided IWW meeting places to beat up and lynch the organizers. In Centralia on Armistice Day 1919 they captured Wesley Everest, who was shielding an IWW secretary, Britt Smith. They mutilated Everest, castrated him with a razor, and hanged him from a bridge.

The public had become so intolerant that it even accepted the expulsion of duly elected legislators. On November 10, 1919, the House of Representatives voted by 309 to 1 to unseat Socialist Congressman Victor L. Berger of Milwaukee. On January 7, 1920, the New York State Legislature refused to admit five Socialists elected from New York City.

Big Bill Haywood was also imprisoned for his supposedly subversive activities during the Great Red Scare. During a period out on bail, he fled the country and went to live in Moscow. His health already broken, he died within two days. He was cremated and his ashes were interred at the foot of the Kremlin walls. John Reed was once again indicted for sedition. In 1920 he, too, fled the United States and returned to Russia. There, in October, he died of typhus; and his remains were also interred in the Kremlin walls. He was thirty-two.

The flame of the early romance of communism flickered and guttered. Lenin and Trotsky cemented the Russian Revolution with brute force. Communist revolutions failed elsewhere. The two American Communist parties merged in 1921 under Charles Ruthenberg as the Communist Party of the United States of America (CPUSA). The CPUSA went underground, partly to protect resident aliens from deportation, partly because they expected an imminent Bolshevik triumph in America.

American Communism had its charlatans. Foremost were father and son Julius and Armand Hammer. Physician Julius, a Russian-born Marxist, was among the founders of the Communist Party but he retained an ineradicable urge to make money the capitalist way. In 1920 Julius went to prison for manslaughter for causing the death of a woman who had had an abortion at his clinic. In fact, it was his son, Armand, then in his last year of medical school, who had performed the abortion that went wrong. Julius then dispatched son Armand to Russia to look after his company, Allied Drug and Chemical. Armand allowed the secret police, the Cheka, to infiltrate Allied Drug and Chemical and took $75,000 to be distributed to underground Communists in the United States. In 1921 he met Lenin. In the words of biographer Geoffrey Wheatstone (1996), Hammer became "Lenin's chosen first capitalist." Thereafter, Hammer was in and out of Russia, "using his family's company to help finance Soviet espionage in America."

The sixth postwar episode of intolerance came with the scourge of race riots. African Americans suffered more than radicals in the notorious Red Summer, notably in Washington, D.C., and Chicago. The worst riot of all was in Philips County, Arkansas, in October. To protect themselves against abuse from exploitative landlords, African American tenant farmers formed a union, the Progressive Farmers and Household Union of America. They threatened to withhold their cotton crop and charge landlords with peonage. Their stand aroused whites in Arkansas, Tennessee, and Mississippi, who came down in droves with arms to quell a supposed insurrection. At least five whites and twenty-five African Americans were killed. Governor Charles H. Brough used federal troops to round up African American dissidents and confine them in a stockade. U. S. Bratton, former postmaster of Little Rock, told an African American newspaper that he could find "no basis for the belief that a massacre was planned by the Negroes and, in point of fact, it was the Negroes who were massacred."

Sixty-five African Americans were tried for rebellion. Twelve were sentenced to death and fifty-four were given prison sentences ranging from one to eleven years. Of those sentenced to death, the state supreme court released six in 1923 on the grounds of irregularities in the trial. The Supreme Court allowed the other six a retrial. It ruled, in the case of *Moore v. Dempsey* on February 29, 1923, by 6 votes to 2, that mob hysteria and inadequate counsel had prevented them from receiving a fair trial.

White southerners blamed the African American press. In August 1919 Congressman James F. Byrnes of South Carolina called on the Department of Justice to prosecute the editors of the *Crisis*, the Chicago *Messenger*, and other African American papers under the terms of the Espionage Act. However, the editor of the Oklahoma City *Black Dispatch* of October 10, 1919, denied that radical policies were mixed with the African American quest for civil rights: "It does not take an IWW to clinch the arguments that the majority of Negroes in the United States cannot vote. . . . It does not take a Bolshevist to inform us that . . . a separate status as citizens is designed for the black man."

The end to the great crusade was signaled in other ways. On February 28, 1920, Wilson signed the Esch-Cummins Railroad bill into law. The act returned the railroads to private control from March 1 onward. The various clauses of the act were based on the idea of genuine cooperation between the railroads under the supervision of the ICC, with a guaranteed net income in each rate-making group equal to 5.5 percent on the value of roads within the group. It allowed consolidation of railroad lines and created a Railroad Labor Board to settle railroad disputes. Existing rates, wages, and government rents would continue until September 1, 1920. The roads were to be allowed ten years to refund their indebtedness to the federal government. This was ironic. For Wilson understood the drift of the revolution in industry and transportation. He observed privately in 1919, "It seems certain commodities will have to become the property of the state—the coal, the water powers, and, probably, the railroads."

The world war was over. Or was it?

CHAPTER 7

Tales of the Jazz Age

IN MAY 1927 one man was on top of the world.

The solo flight of Charles A. Lindbergh, Jr., across the Atlantic Ocean from Roosevelt Field, Long Island, to Paris on May 20 and 21, 1927, in *The Spirit of St. Louis* demonstrated not only the potential of airplanes as a means of rapid transportation but also how advanced was American technical prowess. Although Lindbergh liked to give an impression of casualness, prompting the *Times* of London to call him "the flying fool," Lucky Lindy's numerous achievements in his Ryan-model NYP-1 plane depended on meticulous preparation and care. When he returned from Paris to New York, the city brought down a storm of ticker-tape to celebrate an achievement that all Americans could take pride in. Lindy's achievement set the seal on America's cultural and technical ascendancy in the 1920s—the Jazz Age, the Aspirin Age, the Age of Miracles and Ballyhoo.

On May 14, 1920, Republican presidential hopeful Senator Warren Gamaliel Harding of Ohio interpreted America's needs: "America's present need is not heroics but healing; not nostrums but normalcy; not revolution but restoration; not agitation but adjustment; not surgery but serenity; not the dramatic, but the dispassionate; not experiment but equipoise; not submergence in internationality but sustainment in triumphant nationality."

Whatever Harding would have preferred, the American norm was not relaxed stability but social mobility, economic development, and cultural experiment. Yet Harding's important speech suggested a basic political truth—that a society with deep problems was not likely to try to resolve them. The remedy might prejudice the comfortable lot of its privileged members. Novelist F. Scott Fitzgerald observed, "It was characteristic of the Jazz Age that it had no interest in politics at all." He might have been referring explicitly to the presidential elections of 1920 and 1924 when less than half of the electorate went to the polls, prompting the *Philadelphia Inquirer* to run the headline "Apathy of Voters Dismays Leaders" on a story about the 1920 election. But Fitzgerald's comment ran deeper—to public unwillingness to address politics that had to do with social ills. Society prized novelty in entertainment, fashion, and invention. But it disparaged criticism and radical dissent.

Nothing illustrated this better than the extraordinary Sacco-Vanzetti case of 1920–27.

Police arrested cobbler Nicola Sacco and fish peddler Bartolomeo Vanzetti, Italian immigrants and anarchists, for the theft of a sixteen-thousand-dollar payroll of the Slater and Morrill shoe factory in South Braintree, twelve miles south of Boston, on April 15, 1920, and for the murder of the paymaster, Frederick A. Parmenter, and his guard, Alessandro Berardelli. At the trial of Sacco and Vanzetti, District Attorney Frederick A. Katzmann concentrated on ballistic evidence. He also exploited the defendants' poor English and their anarchist beliefs to play upon the most base emotions of a biased jury and a malicious judge, Webster Thayer. On July 14, 1921, the jury convicted Sacco and Vanzetti. Judge Thayer sentenced them to death. The case was now a public sensation, touching on such sensitive issues as the new immigration, anarchism, and terrorist conspiracies.

Blue-collar workers Aldino Felicani and Gardner Jackson organized the Sacco-Vanzetti Defense Committee, which, over the years, raised thousands of dollars and distributed two hundred thousand pieces of literature. When a convicted murderer, Celestino F. Medeiros (or Madeiros), confessed to the South Braintree murders, the *Boston Herald*, previously hostile to Sacco and Vanzetti, reversed its position. Editorial writer F. Lauriston Bullard wanted Madeiros's confession tested in court: "The criterion here is not what a judge thinks about it but what a jury thinks about it."

There was no new trial. When he appeared before Judge Thayer for the last time, Bartolomeo Vanzetti, educated and radicalized by his experience, made a moving plea that exposed the chasm between entrenched WASPS and the strange new immigrants of the cities: "I am suffering because I am a radical and, indeed, I am a radical; I have suffered because I am Italian, and, indeed, I am Italian; I have suffered more for my family than myself."

Sacco and Vanzetti and Madeiros were electrocuted on August 22, 1927. Their funeral procession in Boston on August 28 degenerated into a riot among mourners, fifty thousand spectators, and police. Mass grief did not atone for the shame felt by artists, radicals, and intellectuals. Novelist John Dos Passos declared that, from the moment of their execution, the United States was two nations and Sacco and Vanzetti were victims in a struggle for supremacy between the elite establishment and the masses.

The supremacy of the old guard was never in doubt. Back in 1920 presidential aspirant Warren Gamaliel Harding was the tool of an ambitious corporation lawyer, Harry Daugherty. Daugherty reckoned that here was a good-looking candidate who would fulfill a popular concept of a president. Harding had worked as editor of the *Marion Star*, then served as lieutenant governor of Ohio, before becoming a senator. After the autocratic style of Woodrow Wilson, congressmen yearned for an amenable president. In the dark recesses of the original smoke-filled room of the Blackstone Hotel in Chicago, fifteen men of the old guard decided to nominate the available man for president at the Republican National Convention. The only spontaneous event in the Chicago convention was when Wallace McCamant, delegate from Oregon, climbed on his chair to

nominate Governor Calvin Coolidge of Massachusetts, popular hero of the Boston police strike, for vice president. Delegates nominated Coolidge with tumultuous applause.

Meeting in San Francisco, the Democrats nominated Governor James M. Cox of Ohio, who had championed progressive legislation, notably in workers' compensation. His running mate was Assistant Secretary of the Navy Franklin Delano Roosevelt. While Harding and Daugherty conducted their campaign from Harding's front porch in Ohio, Cox campaigned in eighteen states west of the Mississippi, from which he garnered not one electoral vote. Cox could not believe the country's indifference to the League of Nations. Harding received 16,143,407 popular votes (60.4 percent) to Cox's 9,130,328 (34.2 percent). Socialist Eugene V. Debs (fighting the election from inside prison) received 919,799 votes (3.4 percent). Harding carried 37 states and 404 votes in the electoral college to Cox's 11 states and 127 votes. Politicians interpreted the result as a repudiation of Wilsonian policies abroad.

This was ironic. For, throughout the 1920s, the United States was consolidating its position as the world's preeminent commercial power. According to the Department of Commerce, in 1930 America accounted for almost 16 percent of the world's exports and 12 percent of imports. Its industrial track record was greater still. By the end of the 1920s the value of American industrial production was 46 percent of the world total. As for national income, according to *The United States in the World Economy* (1943), the total for the United States in 1929 was the same as the sum total for twenty-three other leading nations, including Britain, France, Germany, Canada, and Japan. In finance, World War I had reversed America's prewar position. Whereas in 1914 the United States was a debtor nation with net obligations of $3.7 billion, in 1919 it was a creditor nation owed $12.5 billion by other countries. Of this, $10 billion was in war debts. Moreover, what was owed American companies in the private sector had almost doubled, while what they owed others had been almost cut in half. By 1929 foreign loans and direct investment had increased private net assets to over $8 billion.

Contemporary commentators described the 1920s as a decade of affluence,

FACING PAGE:

Above: Charles A. Lindbergh, Jr., the attractive, gangling pioneer aviator, beside his *Spirit of St. Louis.* Lindbergh's solo transatlantic flight of May 1927 not only demonstrated the endurance of America's pioneer tradition and its superb technical prowess but also revived flagging public interest in aviation as the new means of opening up the world. (John Rylands University Library, Manchester)

Below: Model-T cars en masse from a Ford factory. The cheap, black, and ugly Model-T, based on the principle of interchangeable parts, opened a horizon of mobility for all but the poorest classes, allowing them the luxury of reliable personal transport and opportunities for daily commuting from suburbs to city centers, as well as all manner of rural recreation. (John Rylands University Library, Manchester)

with increased consumer spending on such durable items as automobiles and domestic appliances, for example, vacuum cleaners and refrigerators. Aggregate statistics on production, income, and consumption are indeed impressive. The real Gross National Product (GNP) rose by 39 percent between 1919 and 1929, and real per capita GNP rose by 20 percent, while personal disposable income rose by 30 percent. Appliances flooded the market and general personal consumption increased. Whereas between 1909 and 1918 the annual sale of durables to consumers was, on average, $4.29 billion, between 1919 and 1929 it was, on average, $7.06 billion—an increase of 65 percent.

The revolution in consumption was most apparent in the home. Between 1920 and 1930 the percentage of households with inside flush toilets rose from 20 to 51. There were equally significant changes, but on a smaller scale, in the percentage of homes with vacuum cleaners, rising from 9 to 30; of washing machines, from 8 to 24 percent; and of mechanized refrigerators, from 1 to 8 percent.

Some of the advances were spectacular. As a result of technological changes, the capacity of electric generating stations rose from 23 million horsepower to 43 million between 1922 and 1930. These changes included a better design of machinery, which reduced the cost of generating power; improvements in the means of transmission of power over long distances; and interconnection between separate stations to make the distribution of power more even between localities. Thus, whereas in 1920, 35 percent of the population lived in homes lit by electricity, by 1930, 68 percent did so.

However, the idea that widespread consumption in the 1920s suggested widespread prosperity was challenged even at the time. In 1916 philanthropist Robert Somers Brookings founded the Brookings Institution in Washington to undertake economic and public-policy research. The Brookings Institution's study *America's Capacity to Consume* (1934) emphasized the poverty of most Americans. The 1920s were golden only for a privileged few. The top 1 percent of the population earned almost 15 percent of all earned income. The Brookings Institution report also showed that consumption was unequal. In 1929 the highest 24 percent of all spending units made 50 percent of all purchases; the highest 20 percent made 50 percent of all expenditures on housing; and the highest 20 percent made 36 percent of all purchases of food and 50 percent of all expenditures on education, health, and recreation.

Wage increases were relatively small for most workers. The distribution of income became yet more unequal. Certain industries and some regions failed. Sick industries included farming, coal mining, textiles, railroads, shipping and shipbuilding, and shoe and leather production. The most prosperous regions were the Northeast and the middle Atlantic and Pacific coasts. The least prosperous were the agricultural states of the South and the Northwest. Few realized how ominous were America's economic trouble spots. The expanded mass media concentrated on pleasures.

The Happiness of Pursuit

Of all the new inventions that shaped the United States in the 1920s, the automobile led the way as harbinger of the new society. In 1920 American auto manufacturers produced 1,905,500 cars; in 1930 they produced 2,787,400. There were, altogether, 7.5 million automobiles on America's roads in 1920. In 1930 there were 26.5 million—one car for every five Americans. The rise in the number of miles traveled was equally dramatic—from 55,027 miles per vehicle in 1921 to 206,320 miles per vehicle in 1930.

People came to regard cars less as a convenience than as a necessity, as part and parcel of the happiness of pursuit and upward mobility—the glamorous mirage conjured up by advertising. When Sinclair Lewis satirized the small-town world of a middle-aged realtor in his novel *Babbitt* (1922), he observed, "To George F. Babbitt, as to most prosperous citizens of Zenith, his motor-car was poetry and tragedy, love and heroism. The office was his pirate ship but the car his perilous excursion ashore." The wife of an unemployed worker in Robert and Helen Lynd's sociological study, *Middletown* (1929), said, "I'll never cut on gas! I'd go without a meal before I'd cut down on using the car." In fact, less than half of the blue-collar families owned automobiles. But owning an auto was not a sign of affluence when people could buy a used car outright or with five dollars down and monthly installments of five dollars.

Immediately after World War I, Henry Ford dominated automobile manufacture nationally and internationally. In 1920 one car in two throughout the world was a Ford Tin Lizzie. But in the course of the 1920s, two other giant auto companies, General Motors (GM) and the Chrysler Corporation, rose to take their place along with Ford as the big three automobile manufacturers. Chrysler was new; GM was as old as Ford. The new giants scored over the inflexible Ford on account of innovative management, marketing, and design.

William Durant first formed General Motors in 1908 from a combine of other companies, including Oldsmobile and Chrysler. From 1915 on, Chrysler enjoyed the huge financial resources of the Du Ponts—a wealthy American family of French descent with a fortune based in textiles, chemicals, and explosives. While Ford remained in the groove of his earlier manufacturing strategy, GM took advantage of new methods. Hence, under successive GM presidents Pierre Du Pont and Alfred P. Sloan, Jr., division managers controlled their own production, marketing, purchasing, and engineering; a new general office with executives and specialists controlled planning and coordination along clear lines. GM also led the way in improved automobile mechanics and design. Charles Kettering, general manager of GM's research laboratories, directed research on improving diesel engines and the development of a nontoxic and noninflammable refrigerant. Moreover, GM designers recognized the need for improved body styling, especially after the introduction of closed cars, which steadily increased their share of the market from 10 percent in 1919 to 85 percent in 1927. Innovative designer

Harley Earle created a wide range of styles within the same basic design by subtle changes in body, color, and attachments.

The second new giant was the Chrysler Corporation, formed by Walter P. Chrysler in 1925 out of the faltering Maxwell Motor Company. He acquired the Dodge Brothers Manufacturing Company in 1928 and produced the Plymouth, a successful model that allowed Chrysler to compete as one of the big three car manufacturers.

The motor vehicle facilitated the growth of suburbia, and the specific needs of the motor vehicle began to change the look of urban America. Driving changed the social culture of the nation, necessitating the construction of roads and the creation of highway codes, traffic lights, garages, and parking meters.

The preferred solution to traffic problems was a specially designed environment—superhighways to cater to automobiles, buses, and trucks traveling resolutely at a maximum speed consistent with safety and with minimum interruptions. These highways were entities separate from homes, businesses, pedestrians, and cross traffic. The highway accommodated two or more lanes of traffic in each direction but without a central strip to separate left and right. The freeway was distinguished by multiple traffic lanes and a central median strip. The parkway's most distinctive features were its limited access and its being placed in a carefully designed landscape. The leading parkway designer was Gilmore D. Clarke. The first automotive parkway was the Bronx River Parkway, constructed in 1919–23 from the North Bronx to White Plains in Westchester County. It set the pattern for future parkways, with an initial road of four lanes, two in each direction, occasionally separating to enfold hillocks and copses but following the undulating meander of the Bronx River.

As city traffic jams occurred increasingly in the 1920s, citizen protest prompted the organization of local safety councils and encouraged cities to enact ordinances limiting speeds and parking and to erect traffic lights to control movement. In 1922 New York introduced the first manually operated traffic lights, which were soon developed into an automatic system by Philadelphia and Cleveland. Boston first introduced the parking charge, but not until 1932 did the parking meter make its debut in Oklahoma City. The first shopping center with an adjoining parking lot opened in Kansas City in 1924, and in 1929 the first parking garage was in use in Detroit.

The car's influence was everywhere, and nowhere more than in its creation of new sorts of cities. In 1920 for the first time the number of people living in towns—communities of 2,500 or more—exceeded the number living in the country: 51.4 percent in towns, compared with 48.6 percent in the country. Sixty-eight cities contained 100,000 or more inhabitants. In 1930 there were ninety-six such cities, and their total population accounted for 44.6 percent of the whole nation. America's large cities offered their inhabitants a variety of work and recreation way beyond the scope of the rural areas or small towns.

Skyscrapers became the most prepossessing emblem of the new cities as well as America's most distinctive contribution to modernist architecture. The essential components of modernism in architecture were the use of new materials and techniques to create a contemporary interior environment and a modern facade. Modernist architects used not only steel, glass, and brick but also concrete, aluminum, and formica in buildings that extolled the power of corporate America.

In 1922 the *Chicago Tribune*, to find a design for its proposed new building, launched a competition that captured wide public interest. It attracted 281 entries from around the world. What the *Tribune* wanted was a downtown building that could impress on the city of Chicago all the wealth and power of WGN, an acronym for World's Greatest Newspaper and also the call letters of its radio station. In his winning design, architect Raymond Hood tried to create a monumental landmark that would also suggest the exultant enterprise of the newspaper. He devised a towering skyscraper but disguised its load-bearing steel frame with Gothic tracery and superfluous flying buttresses. Old and new together—this was how the *Tribune* saw itself: the weight of tradition balanced by business needs—another cathedral of commerce.

Raymond Hood was the most inventive architect of New York skyscrapers; between 1922 and his death in 1934, he produced a series of dazzling towers. The American Radiator building (1924) had a sheath of black brick outside its steel-framed setbacks, with a golden Gothic tower; the *Daily News* building (1929–31) played with assertive vertical strips; the McGraw-Hill edifice (1930–31) alternated dark green horizontal slabs with light green vertical panels and windows. The skyscraper with the most inventive profile, however, was the Chrysler building on the corner of Forty-Second Street and Lexington Avenue, conceived primarily as advertisement for the mighty car corporation. William Van Allen transformed the original design of site developer William Reynolds, eliminating the proposed glass dome, increasing the height to 1,050 feet and seventy-seven stories, and crowning it with a Krupp KA2 crest of stainless steel with triangular windows lit at night to enhance the effect.

The pace of industry, the craze for cars, and huge buildings soared: there was no end to the beckoning social horizon of urban life—provided you had the funds. With such a plethora of household inventions, the spurt of the latest technology, the rise of assertive new buildings, and the provocative use of daring fashions, it is not surprising that American culture in the 1920s was prefigurative, with adults learning from the younger generation of adolescent girls, creative writers of the lost generation, and students.

Society paid greater attention than ever to youth partly out of respect for the thousands of young men lost in World War I. It was in some measure out of deference to the thought that society should nurture individuals while they are young. It was also because the automobile could be handled dexterously by young people. Social changes gave youth economic, moral, and intellectual independence.

The proportion of high school graduates among all seventeen-year-olds increased from 16.3 percent in 1920 to 27.5 percent in 1929. Middle-class children completed school at age seventeen. In 1926 one out of every eight young Americans between eighteen and twenty-one was in college. This was four or five times the number in other developed countries. Graduate schools made higher demands of students in medicine, law, and engineering.

Women had the vote. Had the new woman emerged fully clothed into society?

The mountains of paperwork generated by modern corporations created a need for clerical workers, a need filled by women secretaries. The so-called feminization of the clerical labor force drew nearly 2.25 million women to work in offices by the end of the 1920s. Correspondingly, between 1920 and 1930 the proportion of women who worked in domestic service fell from about a third of all women wage earners to a quarter. But even with as many as 4 million wage earners in the workforce in 1930, it was difficult for them to pry open the doors of organized labor. They were already largely excluded from the male-dominated internationals; a proposal by the Women's Trade Union League to organize separate federal locals for women was also rejected by the AFL. As a result, only 250,000 women belonged to unions at the end of the decade, and half of them were in the garment industry. Moreover, the progressive principle of protecting women and children workers was rejected by the courts. In the case of *Adkins v. Children's Hospital*, decided by 5 votes to 3 on April 9, 1923, the Supreme Court invalidated an act of Congress setting a minimum wage for women and children in the District of Columbia. The majority found that the law was a price-fixing measure in violation of freedom of contract, which was protected by the Fifth Amendment. This decision proved correct all those who had forecast that woman suffrage would undo protective legislation.

The emergence of the new woman was symbolized in many people's minds by the flapper. The term *flapper* was first used in England. Pundit H. L. Mencken introduced it to the United States in 1915. A girl who flapped had not yet attained full maturity, and her flapper dresses were intended to transform juvenile, angular figures into an aesthetic ideal. Her hairstyle was a Ponjola bob, first worn in the United States by dancer Irene Castle during the war. Her dresses were short, tight, and plain with a low waist; her stockings were silk or rayon, flesh-colored, and could be rolled below the knee or taken off in hot weather. This was not a boyish figure. The whole effect carried the eye from body to arms and legs to emphasize their lines. The effect was ultrafeminine in its provocative use of makeup and display of leg.

Flapper styles were not restricted to adolescent girls. The Sears Roebuck catalog deliberately aimed at women in middle America and drew on the fashions of New York society and *Vogue* magazine, offering modish dresses at moderate prices. Novelist F. Scott Fitzgerald noted that the flapper was passé by 1923 when other age groups began to copy her style. Such simple clothes as the flappers wore could be produced for almost any figure, saving the time and cost of fitting and alterations, and were manufactured in great quantities.

Tried and True, Chicago Style

There was a revolution in the world of communications as the expanding mass media of newspapers and magazines began to shape popular culture toward an increasingly urban point of view. The first tabloid newspaper was the *New York Daily News*, which went to press in 1919. Its success encouraged a new form of journalism, copied in New York by Bernarr Macfadden's *Evening Graphic* and William Randolph Hearst's *Daily Mirror* and in Chicago by the *Daily Illustrated Times*. The *Daily News*, run by Joseph Patterson, eventually had the largest circulation of any American paper. It carried more photographs and cartoons than news and comment, and more advertisements than either. Its copy concentrated on gossip rather than news, on what one critic called "more sex than sense." In Chicago, under the editorship of Patterson's cousin, Robert McCormick, the *Tribune* became an immensely profitable and extremely influential newspaper, bulging with sensational reporting, advice columns, comic strips, and brazen advertising.

The tabloids came to specialize in crime stories, divorce reports, national disasters, sports, strip cartoons, and personal columns offering advice. All these subjects provided plenty of opportunity for titillation. What was missing was serious news on politics, economics, and social issues and critical reviews of the arts. News reporters became masters of innuendo. Their doyen was Walter Winchell, whose gossip column "On Broadway" for the *Daily Mirror* was syndicated across the United States and in eleven foreign countries. The tabloids encouraged "keyhole journalism," intimate details or conjecture about the personal lives of show-business stars and the outrageous figures of cafe society, as well as the unsavory secrets of the demimonde. The city of Chicago abounded in scandalous murder stories that the booming press trivialized as entertainment.

In 1924 the tabloid press sensationalized the case of child murderers Nathan Leopold, Jr., and Richard Loeb and exploited the fact that they were both wealthy, Jewish, and homosexual. Their trial proved the most difficult case of veteran defense lawyer Clarence Darrow's career. The youths were graduate students at the University of Chicago. Leopold's father, Nathan Leopold, Sr., was a millionaire many times over. Albert Loeb was vice president of Sears Roebuck and Company. The youths had planned to commit the perfect murder and get away with it. Their victim was thirteen-year-old Bobby Franks, son of real estate millionaire Jacob Franks. They kidnapped the boy, murdered him with a hammer, and disfigured the corpse with acid. Traced, cornered, and arrested, Leopold and Loeb broke down and confessed. Darrow saved them from the electric chair by adroit use of an Illinois statute whereby, if a defendant pleaded guilty, the judge had to hear evidence in mitigation before passing sentence. Darrow produced four psychiatrists to testify to the condition of Leopold and Loeb. He portrayed the sorry-looking murderers as victims of parental neglect and emotional dependence on one another—as maladjusted boys who wanted to be gods.

Judge Laverly, who had worked with Clarence Darrow for the corrupt Democratic machine of mobster Michael ("Hinky Dink") Kenna in Chicago years before, sent Leopold and Loeb to prison for ninety-nine years.

Whereas Darrow, the controversial defense lawyer, could take deserved credit for saving Leopold and Loeb from execution, it was the press that saved Chicago murderesses Belva and Beulah—Belva Gaertner and Beulah Annan—from conviction in 1924. Both married women had killed their sex partners. However, *Chicago Tribune* apprentice reporter Maurine Watkins sensed murder-as-entertainment within their stories. Watkins capitalized on the fact that her readers would prefer the murderesses' outrageous falsehoods to the evidence of their victims' corpses. Watkins's ingenious transformation of the women from coldly vengeful killers to tabloid saints of the demimonde satisfied credulous public appetite for diversion, celebrity, and exoneration.

On March 11, 1924, when Cook County policemen discovered the body of Walter Law slumped over the steering wheel of the car of Belva Gaertner, a married cabaret singer with a long history of infidelity, she denied responsibility for the shooting. Confronted with the fact that the gun was hers, she replied: "I don't know. I was drunk." Reporter Maurine Watkins dutifully recorded Belva's later, disingenuous observation, "I liked him and he loved me—but no woman can love a man enough to kill him. They aren't worth it because there are always plenty more." Watkins opened her account of an interview with Belva with: "No sweetheart in the world is worth killing—especially when you've had a flock of them—and the world knows it."

On April 3, 1924, police arrested the second deadly woman for killing her lover. Beneath a headline, "Woman Plays Jazz as Victim Dies," Watkins wrote: "Mrs. Beulah Annan, a comely young wife, played a foxtrot record named 'Hula Lou' . . . then telephoned her husband and reported that she had killed a man who 'tried to make love' to her." Watkins's stories of the "prettiest murderess" covered Beulah's hiring of prominent defense attorney W. W. O'Brien and her metamorphosis into pliant penitent. When Beulah announced that she was preg-

FACING PAGE:

The New Woman enfranchised by her bob, her short skirt, her auto, and the vote
Top: 1924 advertisement for the Ponjola bobbed hair, introduced in World War I, which first astounded a society used to luxurious skeins of women's hair. (Library of Congress)
Left: A flapper alights from her car. Suzette Dewey, daughter of Assistant Secretary of the Treasury Charles Dewey, photographed in full flight in December 1927. (French Collection; Library of Congress)
Right: Following ratification of the Nineteenth Amendment, competing skin-clad Republican and Democratic Adams woo a winsome Eve in the Political Garden of Eden. All they want is her vote in the forthcoming November 1920 election. However, it was not until 1956 that American women voted in the same proportion as men. (Cartoon from the *Dallas Morning News* of August 29, 1920; Library of Congress)

THE TWO ADAMS: "IT WAS MY RIB, EVE"

nant, Watkins manipulated this twist on May 9 with her headline "Beulah Annan Awaits Stork, Murder Trial." When the jury reached its verdict in the Annan trial, Watkins captured the festive spirit in the courtroom. Quoting the prosecutor's request that the jury decide "whether you want to let another pretty woman go out and say, 'I got away with it,' " Watkins concluded, "And they did." Ten days later, another jury acquitted Belva Gaertner.

Maurine Watkins took an editorial position in New York, enrolled at the new Yale School of Drama, and turned her Chicago articles into a comedy named *Chicago*. When the play opened on Broadway in 1926, *New York Times* critic Brooks Atkinson opined: "*Chicago* is not a melodrama but a satirical comedy on the administration of justice through the fetid channels of newspaper publicity—of photographers, 'sob sisters,' feature stunts, standardized prevarication and generalized vulgarity."

Another provocative dramatist was Mae West, whose witty wordplay bulged with double meanings. She wrote about interracial relationships, prostitution, homosexuality, and drag queens. In 1926 New York's acting mayor, Joseph V. McKee, had her play, *Sex*, raided for indecency, thereby prompting a much publicized obscenity trial. The court fined West five hundred dollars and sentenced her to ten days imprisonment on Welfare (later Roosevelt) Island. At the end of her prison sojourn, she posed for press photos and gave the warden a check for one thousand dollars for the prison library. "Censorship *made* me," she claimed later. On stage and screen her most famous character, Diamond Lil (also known as Lady Lou), danced the line between what was sexually provocative and what was socially permissible with much-quoted witticisms and a widely imitated throwaway delivery. As West said, "My fight has been against depression, repression, and suppression."

Babble On, Babylon

In 1922 ten magazines each claimed a paid circulation of over 2.5 million and another twelve claimed a circulation of over 1 million. The majority were pulp magazines, so called because they were printed on cheap wood-pulp paper and devoted mainly to lowbrow detective, western, or movie fiction. Compared with magazines of the early 1900s, magazines of the 1920s carried far fewer serious articles and devoted more space to sports, fashion, and leisure. The most notable of the new magazines was *Time*, founded in March 1923 by Henry Luce and Briton Hadden. Its mission was to explain the news, which at first it summarized from two sources, the *New York Times* and Walter Lippmann's editorials in the *New York World*. It appealed to middle-class folk in towns and cities across the nation, for whom it adopted a pose of omniscience.

While the Luce magazine became an office primer for diplomatic and industrial strategists of the American century, the *Reader's Digest* became their showroom salesman. The *Reader's Digest*, published by DeWitt and Lila Wallace from Pleasantville, New York, starting in 1922, filled a genuine need in a society of gradually rising standards of mass education: summarize the news, condense received wisdom, make ideas accessible, and provide role models. In the early years Wallace condensed articles by others that he read in the New York Public Library, typed them up, and hand-delivered them to a mail train for the printers. To educate a mass readership, he wanted the *Reader's Digest* to cover everything "except despair and defeat." By 1936 the *Reader's Digest* was reaching 1.8 million readers, whom it told what to think. Meanwhile, Emily Post in the first edition of *Etiquette in Society and Business, in Politics and at Home* (1922) told the newly educated masses how to behave.

Wits seeking sophistication laced with humor turned the pages of the *New Yorker*, a weekly magazine launched in February 1925 by Harold Ross and Jane Grant (of the *New York Times*) from an office on West Forty-Third Street. Its features included "Talk of the Town," a weekly cocktail of reporting and banter, celebrity profiles, discursive articles, and listings of cultural events. Its wits included drama critic Alexander Woollcott and humorists Robert Benchley and Dorothy Parker. They were all irreverent sages of the Algonquin Round Table in the Algonquin Hotel on Forty-Fourth Street nearby and used every caustic literary trick to encourage the *New Yorker*'s reputation as a chic institution.

But it was radio, rather than newspapers or magazines, that became the principal medium for carrying news and entertainment and political and sports events into people's homes. This was as profound a revolution in communication as automobiles had been in transportation.

Modern radio broadcasting began in the United States on July 1, 1920. General Electric, its subsidiary Radio Corporation of America (RCA), and AT&T agreed to a patent pool. RCA would sell radio receivers produced by General Electric that incorporated the latest in radio technology—the Armstrong patent for a supersensitive receiver owned by Westinghouse. AT&T would use radio telephone equipment for its telephone business and produce transmitters. Hitherto, radio had been used selectively to carry messages to ships at sea. Now it became a prime means of mass communication of news and entertainment.

On November 2, 1920, station KDKA began broadcasting from Pittsburgh, with its announcements of the Harding-Cox presidential election returns. The overnight success of KDKA raised questions of funding for long-term ventures. Stations had to acquire corporate support if they were to transcend their earlier, amateur status, transmitting broadcasts with primitive equipment from hotel rooms. In December 1922 RCA created WDY in Roselle Park, New Jersey, and General Electric opened WGY in Schenectady, New York; KOAS in Denver, Colorado; and KGO in Oakland, California. The patent pool dominated broadcasting. In February 1923, of 376 stations listed by the Department of Commerce, 222 were owned by General Electric, RCA, AT&T, or Westinghouse.

As radio developed, the two primary characteristics of American broadcasting were toll advertising and network affiliation. WEAF, an AT&T station, became the first to broadcast commercials—for a condominium in Jackson Heights, New York—on August 28, 1922. At first, local radio stations were sidelines to their sponsor companies, usually newspapers. Newspapers, such as the *Detroit News* with station WJA, owned 69 stations, educational institutions owned 72, and department stores owned 29.

The economic impact of radio was colossal. Whereas in 1920 shops sold one radio set for every five hundred households, in 1926 they sold one radio for every six households. By 1926 manufacturers were fitting radio sets with controls for volume, tuning, and the on-off switch by one knob within mahogany cases. As people were becoming addicted to radio, the stations sold them—the audience—to manufacturers as prospective consumers of the manufacturers' products in order to pay for the programs with advertising revenue. Since competition was intense between radio stations for airwaves, the quality of reception deteriorated. The confusion was sometimes so great that one government official likened radio reception to "a peanut roaster with assorted whistles." The Radio Act of 1927 established the Federal Radio Commission (FRC) to oversee radio.

As to programs, in 1925 over 70 percent of the airtime of major stations in New York, Kansas City, and Chicago was devoted to live music, of which 35 percent was dance music. In 1922 Secretary of Commerce Herbert Hoover used his authority to prohibit the broadcasting of music on disks because he thought that radio stations that did so were cheating their listeners by giving them nothing more than they could enjoy at home without radio. Meanwhile, radio was opening up new possibilities. It furthered what we might term the populist tradition, encouraging grassroots debate.

Among those who benefited was a young Roman Catholic priest from Canada, Father Charles E. Coughlin. He borrowed seventy-nine thousand dollars from the archdiocese of Detroit to build the brown-shingled church of St. Therese, the Little Flower of Jesus, seating six hundred people. Coughlin persuaded Leo Fitzpatrick, manager of the local radio station, WJR, to let him broadcast his appeals on the air. From his first broadcast on October 17, 1926, he was an immediate success. By 1930 Coughlin was able to mount regular Sunday evening broadcasts, "The Golden Hour of the Little Flower," for seventeen CBS stations. Beginning in 1930 Coughlin made his broadcasts political. He entranced millions of listeners espousing the cause of the underdog so that, by 1933, a national poll voted him "the most useful citizen of the United States."

Television was potentially an even more powerful influence than radio. Its genesis provides another classic instance of the simultaneity of invention with claims and counterclaims made by the Americans, the British, and the Russians as to who was first in the field. In 1927 the British Broadcasting Corporation transmitted its first television program, and that same year Herbert Hoover sat before a camera and microphone in Washington, D.C., and was heard and seen in New York City. But the true advent of television was to be delayed by depression and war.

In the meantime it was radio that carried sports into people's homes, and sports helped a nation divided by race, class, and ethnicity to recognize that it had a common identity. Sports represented an escape for blue- and white-collar

Dempsey and Firpo by George Bellows (1924), 51" × 63¼". Boxing contests allowed spectators to sublimate ethnic loyalties in enthusiasm for the skill and prowess of a new generation of champions. Assigned to cover the September 3, 1923, fight between Jack Dempsey and Luis Firpo of Argentina for the *New York Evening Journal*, Bellows chose the famous episode in the first round when Firpo knocked Dempsey through the ropes into Bellows's own lap. Dempsey climbed back into the ring and in the second round knocked out Firpo. For the painting, Bellows modestly moved himself to the extreme left. (Geoffrey Clements Photography; Collection of Whitney Museum of American Art, New York)

workers, by celebrating physical skill, endurance, and courage. Most important as devices to maintain social equilibrium were spectator team sports. The players expended their emotional energies in physical competition; the spectators sublimated theirs in adulation of a favorite star. Footballer Harold E. ("Red") Grange of Illinois enjoyed a meteoric but ephemeral career. According to the *New York Times* of October 19, 1924, sixty-seven thousand people watched him and the University of Illinois team beat Michigan in the Illinois Memorial Stadium. Of all sports stars, the most idealized was baseball batter George Herman ("Babe") Ruth, first of the Boston Sox and later, from 1920 to 1934, of the New York Yankees. For the Yankees Babe Ruth hit 659 of his 714 home runs, and he maintained his superiority as a hitter over other players for several decades.

And what Babe Ruth was to baseball, Bobby Jones was to golf and Big Bill Tilden was to tennis. In fact, Jones and Tilden were much more. By their mesmerizing artistry as well as their professional skill, they made hitherto elite sports interesting to the masses. This was especially true of Tilden in his contests with William M. Johnston, notably in the Nationals in Germantown in 1922. To their adoring fans, rivals Tilden and Johnston were "Big Bill" and "Little Bill," the David and Goliath of sports.

Former journalist William Tatum ("Big Bill") Tilden II of Philadelphia won his first U.S. Championship in 1920 when he was twenty-seven, and throughout the 1920s he was ranked number one tennis champion, winning the National Singles Championship six years in a row (1920–25) and again in 1929 and the Clay Court Championship in singles seven times (1918 and 1922–27). Such was Tilden's renown that in 1921 promoters built a new stadium at Forest Hills, New York, to accommodate the huge crowds that Big Bill could draw to tennis. In 1926 promoter C. C. Pyle organized a professional tour and thereby created professional tennis. By the 1930s Tilden was his principal star. The mercurial Tilden was an elusive sports hero, but he lived for tennis, continuously reworked his repertoire of strokes, and wrote about the game more eloquently than any other player.

The financial incentive for stars, promoters, and managers, as well as newspaper reporters, to invest in major sports fixtures was unprecedented. The public's capacity for vicarious satisfaction reached a peak in attendance at the two heavyweight boxing matches between Jack Dempsey and Gene Tunney in Philadelphia on September 23, 1926, and in Chicago on September 22, 1927. Dempsey and Tunney represented different Americas. William Harrison ("Jack") Dempsey was a young tough from the Colorado mines, whose vicious fighting style, stemming from a well of lower-class discontent, had earned him the title "The Manassa Mauler." James Joseph ("Gene") Tunney from New York owed his success to his poise, restraint, and technical skill. Tunney, the fighting marine, was a mix of hero and manager who won both his bouts against Dempsey, the unreclaimed outlaw. Tunney won the first match, on September 23, 1926, by decision after ten rounds. For that first Dempsey-Tunney match, 120,000 people paid almost $2 million. The result of the rematch in Chicago on September 22, 1927, was controversial. In the seventh round, Dempsey knocked Tunney to the canvas, but he delayed retiring to a neutral corner. The referee did not begin the count until Dempsey did so. Tunney got back on his feet on the count of nine. Tunney completed the ten-round fight and won by decision. For that second match, 145,000 people paid $2.5 million, of which Tunney received $990,000. The Chicago amphitheater, Soldiers' Field, was so enormous that two-thirds of the audience on the periphery did not know who had won. Almost 50 million listening on radio to commentator Graham McNamee did. Eleven radio listeners died of excitement during the bout.

Whether in nightclubs, on disks, or on radio, the unmistakable sound of the 1920s was jazz music in all its forms. The combination of jazz, phonograph, and radio gave African American artists the advantage of potent invisibility, providing them with a well-defined aural space within which they could devise new styles of performance; they also achieved fame, fortune, and the opportunity for immortal art as jazz brought African American artists to the fore of the entertainment spectrum.

When cornet player Louis ("Satchel Mouth," later "Satchmo") Armstrong joined the popular Fletcher Henderson Orchestra in New York in 1924, he soon became a star performer. His manager, Joe Glaser, persuaded him to make a career in the big bands and to introduce more conventionally commercial material into his repertoire. He moved from cornet to trumpet and was the first soloist to improvise new melodies within the harmonic framework of a song. Hitherto, improvisation had been confined to embellishments around an existing melody. The extraordinary range of Armstrong's trumpet playing, coupled with a golden tone and superb confidence, served as a model for all who followed him. His recordings with the Hot Five and Hot Seven bands in the period 1926–28 were his most influential of all, renowned for superb technique and innovative solos. His sound was large, expressive, and vital, with a rare ability to phrase around the beat. Biographer Laurence Bergreen shows (1997) that Armstrong had outsize appetites: he cheated enthusiastically on all four of his wives; he smoked marijuana almost every day; he ended many concerts by playing 250 high C's. For, as to work, Satchmo was a disciplinarian. He told a reporter a year before his death in 1971: "I didn't wish for anything I couldn't get and I got pretty near everything I wanted because I worked for it."

Saxophonist Coleman Hawkins, by his art, raised the status of the saxophone from a novelty to a serious musical instrument. The saxophone, invented by Belgian Louis Saxe around 1840, was the only reed instrument made of brass, serving as string band and woodwind. It was heart, soul, and spirit of the jazz orchestra. Coleman Hawkins's tenor sax sound was large and husky but warmed by an expressive vibrato. His specialty was extracting all possible notes implied in a given set of chord changes. This was something known as vertical improvising because of the vertical notation of chords on the musical staff. His recording "One Hour" with the Mound City Blowers in 1929 established a new mood for jazz ballads, being more romantic than the shriller sounds of the mid-1920s.

Bessie Smith, originally from Chattanooga, Tennessee, was acclaimed "Empress of the Blues." By 1923, when she was working with Clarence Williams, a pianist who was also a representative for Columbia Records, Smith had already had considerable experience singing in Atlanta, Birmingham, and Memphis. Her phrasing was sophisticated yet she was able to convey deep emotion directly. Bessie Smith's first record, "Down in the Dumps," sold 780,000 within six months and became a continuous bestseller, as did most of her records until her last, "Downhearted Blues," in 1933.

The most commercially successful exponent of scored jazz in the 1920s was rotund white band leader Paul Whiteman. Having heard composer George Gershwin's short modern opera, first called *Blue Monday* (1922) and later *135th Street*, Whiteman commissioned him to write the first-ever formal composition based on jazz elements. Whiteman's "semiclassical" orchestra gave *Rhapsody in Blue* a sensational premiere with Gershwin himself as soloist at the piano on February 10, 1924, at Aeolian Hall in New York.

Jazz also permeated popular music. Vaudevillian Helen Kane inserted the words "boop-a-doop" here and there in "I Wanna Be Loved by You" and "Button Up Your Overcoat" (both 1928) to achieve what Sigmund Spaeth called "sillysyllabic singing." And if the actual words of "Makin' Whoopee" (1928) were cynical ditties about divorce and alimony, the music itself expressed the careless abandon of frenetic urban social life. The title phrase, "makin' whoopee," passed into everyday speech to describe anyone who threw caution to the winds, such as a husband cutting loose from marital reins or a sucker spending freely in a nightclub. As people's knowledge of songs came to depend less on human memory than on phonograph and radio, the most people could recall was a line of the chorus or a phrase of the melody.

Among popular social crazes were the new dances, notably the Charleston and the Black Bottom. Both were innovative African American dances, the furthest imaginable distance from the stately waltzes and polkas of white bourgeois society. Their most assiduous promoter was white dancing instructor Arthur Murray of East Harlem. He dispatched his mail-order dance instruction kits from Atlanta, Georgia, but he used a New York address in order to maintain a cosmopolitan image, eventually opening a dance studio in Manhattan. His astute marketing, like that of Bible-thumping evangelists and nativist organizations, was aimed at socially insecure people with such advertisements as "How I Became Popular Overnight."

The world of classical music accommodated two native-born American singers of incandescent ability. Rosa Ponselle, an Italian-American dramatic soprano born in Meriden, Connecticut, made her Met debut as Leonora in Giuseppe Verdi's *La Forza del Destino* opposite Enrico Caruso in 1918, thereafter playing twenty roles in nineteen seasons. Her signature role was Norma, Vincenzo Bellini's Druid priestess torn between duty and love, in which her velvet sheen and dramatic fire were heard to best advantage. The brilliance of her voice was never truly captured on phonograph disks, but this did not lessen her enormous popularity until a disappointing appearance as Carmen brought her singing career to an end in 1937 and 1938 as she suffered mental illness, endured electric-shock therapy, and went into premature retirement.

Good-looking Lawrence Tibbett, a native of Bakersfield, California, dominated Met performances of Verdi operas, notably *Rigoletto* and *Simon Boccanegra*. Tibbett's performance as the pathologically jealous Ford in *Falstaff* so electrified the Met audience in February 1925 that he received an unprecedented ovation of seventeen minutes and earned a place on the front page of the *New York Times* the next day.

Of all new American cultural influences, the most insidious was the cinema, in which Hollywood dominated the countries of Europe as much as it did the United States. For millions around the world, Hollywood was American civilization. Whereas radio offered words without pictures, movies offered pictures without words—until Al Jolson spoke and sang in *The Jazz Singer* (1927). In 1927 there were seventeen thousand movie theaters in the United States, and in many places the movie theater was the most impressive new building. The "cathedral of the motion picture" reached its apogee of opulence with the Roxy theater (1927–61) of Samuel Rothafel on Fiftieth Street and Broadway, New York. Designed by W. W. Ahlschlager at a cost of twelve million dollars, it seated six thousand people, whom it chilled with an advanced refrigeration system and nursed in its own infirmary.

The cinema could bring Broadway to a weekly audience of ninety-five million, inculcating them with a cheerful myth of the Roaring Twenties. Unique mime and director Charlie Chaplin and his fellow United Artists, swashbuckling hero Douglas Fairbanks and Mary Pickford, America's sweetheart, influenced styles profoundly. Buster Keaton was known as the Great Stone Face on account of his deadpan expression in the face of comic disasters. He acquired such stoicism as the child star of a vaudeville act in which his father pushed physical clowning into the realm of child abuse. Keaton was the most inventive of silent comedians, turning the very scenery around him into an integral part of his dangerous, surrealist stunts, all the way to his masterpiece, *The General* (1925). Harold Lloyd personified the eager city slicker with optimistic eyeglasses and a three-piece suit. His stunts were as hair-raising as they were funny, including the celebrated scene in *Safety Last* (1923) where he dangles from a clock way above a Los Angeles street. A courageous man, Harold Lloyd injured his right hand badly in an explosion in *Haunted Spooks* (1920) and thereafter wore a special glove to conceal the loss of several fingers while continuing to exercise his athletic prowess and courage.

In 1923 *Time* coined the name *movie moguls*, first as *cinemoguls*. Some were Irish-Americans, such as Eddie Mannix at MGM and Winfield Sheehan at Fox; some were Greeks such as the Skouras brothers, also at Fox. The majority, however, were Jewish, first- and second-generation immigrants from Russia and Poland. In 1924 Marcus Loew, owner of a chain of cinemas, created Metro-Goldwyn-Mayer (MGM) by drawing together two unsuccessful picture companies (Metro and Goldwyn) and some of their executives. Loew also acquired another theater owner, the tyrannical Louis B. Mayer, and Mayer's boy-wonder assistant Irving Thalberg. Mayer was instrumental in founding the Academy of Motion Picture Arts and Sciences in 1927. The moguls aimed the academy at the unions, but people soon identified it with Hollywood's annual, self-congratulating award ceremonies, the Oscars. Mayer's associate, Marcus

Loew, achieved vertical integration: MGM shot its pictures in Goldwyn's studio and distributed them across his own chain of cinemas. The movie moguls reasoned that if their films were to appeal to the widest possible audience, they had to be accessible to a mass audience, specifically blue-collar workers and their families.

Thomas Ince was the first American director to understand the shift from artistic innovation in the early years of Hollywood to industrial production in the early 1920s; he reveled in his elevation to producer of several films at once. He expected individual directors to make a finished product from a blueprint that specified exact dialogue and shooting and production schedules. Directors planned production to ensure that the entire process of filming was cost effective, assembling cast, crew, and equipment for the shortest possible time.

One of film's great attractions was its ability to capture sensuality and eroticism. Whether as Arabian sheik or Latin lover, Rudolph Valentino seduced on-screen heroines with profligate sensuality. His kissing of their upturned palms titillated millions of women in moviehouses. This uncanny ability of movies to show passion onscreen and arouse viewers to pleasure or protest proved a liability. Elinor Glyn maintained that the pronoun "it" really stood for sex appeal and declared that discovery Clara Bow had it in *It* (1927). Vivacious Clara Bow rose from beauty queen to sex symbol, but her career, tarnished by sex scandals and drug abuse, took a final dive when talking pictures exaggerated her abrasive accent. She slid into melancholy obscurity punctuated by a series of nervous breakdowns. Director Cecil B. DeMille, a shrewd storyteller known for his biblical and historical epics, such as *The Ten Commandments* (1923 with Richard Dix), took credit for shaping the feature film. His meretricious extravaganzas mixed pretentious moralizing and lubricious suggestiveness.

However, society was hypocritical in its attitude toward sex. Self-appointed guardians of public morality, including the Federal Motion Picture Council in America and the WCTU, mobilized their constituencies against moral license on screen. In the early 1920s a series of scandals ranged from extramarital affairs and drug use to murder and rape by Hollywood directors and stars, including Wallace Reid and William Desmond Tanner (or Taylor). The most widely publicized scandal drew a tight noose on the career of Roscoe ("Fatty") Arbuckle. In September 1922 the mysterious death of call girl Virginia Rappe at a party given by Fatty Arbuckle at the St. Francis Hotel, San Francisco, led to Arbuckle's trial for involuntary manslaughter. He was acquitted at a second trial but not before innuendoes that his great weight had ruptured Virginia Rappe's gall bladder and caused her death ended Arbuckle's career before the cameras.

The threat of federal censorship prompted the movie moguls to appoint their own censor. They chose Will Hays, postmaster general, who, as a WASP, was presumed to represent more closely the "typical" audience. Hays became president of the Motion Picture Producers and Distributors of America (MPPDA), commonly known as the Hays Office. He was not content to provide a front of Puritan decency so that Hollywood could enjoy Babylonian license in the bedroom. Chicago publisher Martin Quigley and Jesuit Daniel A. Lord of St. Louis University drew up a code of guidelines that the MPPDA accepted in 1930. In 1934 they made it compulsory when Catholic journalist Joseph I. Breen took charge. Any member of the MPPDA who released a film without Breen's approval risked a fine of twenty-five thousand dollars. The code's preamble stipulated, "No picture shall be produced which will lower the moral standards of those who see it. Hence, the sympathy of the audience shall never be thrown to the side of crime, wrong-doing, evil, or sin." The way Hollywood observed the code was both superficial and hypocritical.

The explosion of the mass media—press, motion pictures, radio—stimulated society socially, culturally, and economically. Movies and the press set standards of fashion and taste, but they also tended to generate passivity in their mass audience, reducing all people to the same level of intelligence, cultural awareness, and emotional immaturity. Did Americans have the power to control the mass media? Or did it control them?

Youth and Charm Invade My Arms

The "lost generation" dominated creative writing, producing a new school of letters that made its special contribution with the assertive, twentieth-century theme of individual alienation—the self apart from society. The very epithet "lost generation" suggests alienation, disillusionment, and cynicism with tradition, religion, and even literature itself. According to critic Malcolm Cowley (1934), the lost generation was lost because its training had prepared it for a different world from the one that existed after the war, and the war had prepared it for nothing. In a period of violent change, war novelists, led by Ernest Hemingway and John Dos Passos, expressed the feelings of millions disabused of their former beliefs.

A gap yawned between those who had fought in World War I and their civilian elders who had not. Not only had their elders first blundered into the war, but then they had also lost a generation of young men in the slaughter of the trenches and, finally, had lost the peace. All that remained intact was the machine—the machine of government propaganda—as well as the weapons of industrialized warfare. According to poet Ezra Pound, young men had died "for an old bitch gone in the teeth, / For a botched civilization."

The author who best found the words of disillusionment was Ernest Hemingway with *The Sun Also Rises* (1925) and *A Farewell to Arms* (1929). Hemingway supposedly based his *Farewell* characters on his own experience as an ambulance driver for the American Red Cross on the Italian front and his wartime affair with nurse Agnes von Kurowsky. The most noted weapon in Hemingway's stylistic armory was his ability to compress meaning and emotion, giving his work authority and thrust. Every page of clear prose seemed to pass judgment on any excesses in previous writing. In *The Sun Also Rises*, Hemingway's masterstroke was his icon of the impotent hero, the soldier who went to war to prove his manhood but instead had it destroyed by the war. Instead of finding the Old World more civilized than the New, the lost generation found Europe, in critic Malcolm Bradbury's words (1996), "a shattered place of disorder, conflict, decadence, and sexual permissiveness."

Novelist and short story writer F. Scott Fitzgerald was a key player among the lost generation, highly regarded for the stylistic grace, emotional impact, and penetrating psychological characterizations in his best works. Fitzgerald caught the external glitter and internal anguish of the smart young men whose beautiful world was about to disintegrate. *The Great Gatsby* (1925) remains a powerful evocation of all that was rotten in the American dream in general and the dream decade of the 1920s in particular. The decay of the characters' souls is more tragic than the casual violence that snuffs out Jay Gatsby's life.

After his wrongful imprisonment in a French concentration camp in World War I, poet e. e. cummings wrote *The Enormous Room* (1922), a prison journal full of comic invention and insight. In his poems, cummings dismantled the components of poetry and reassembled them: punctuation became a series of arbitrary signals sometimes even used as words. He changed the function of nouns, pronouns, adverbs, and adjectives. Poet William Carlos Williams always wrote in a mode based on the rhythms of the speaking voice, with idiomatic language, colloquialisms, and an intense interest in language and locale as subject and setting.

The year 1922 was seminal in literature with the publication of T. S. Eliot's poem *The Waste Land* (1922), which set the pattern and established the mood

FACING PAGE:

Tales from the Jazz Age: The Damned and the Survivor
Above: Novelist and short story writer F. Scott Fitzgerald, a key player among the lost generation, noted for the stylistic grace, emotional impact, and penetrating psychological characterization in his best works. In the 1930s, when the public mood shifted, it was no longer ready to tolerate the perceptions of an increasingly alcoholic writer tormented by the mental problems of a deranged wife. (John Rylands University Library of Manchester)
Below Left: Vibrant Bessie Smith, "empress of the blues," whose soul-searching powers of communication melted musical hearts—but not well enough to prevent her bleeding to death after a road accident when an automobile refused to take her to a nearby hospital for whites only. (Photo by Carl Van Vechten, 1936; Library of Congress)
Below Right: Louis ("Satchmo") Armstrong was not only a powerful jazz trumpet player, renowned for his golden tone, but also the first soloist to improvise new melodies within the harmonic framework of a song. The first singer to record scat singing and the first jazz artist to introduce mainstream material into the jazz repertoire, Satchmo retained his popularity for forty years because of his effervescent manner and the astute marketing by manager Joe Glaser. (Joe Glaser photograph; Library of Congress)

for the subject of disintegration in twentieth-century literature, and Walter Lippmann's *Public Opinion*, a penetrating political analysis of the way we think politically by means of outdated assumptions and stereotypes. Also in 1922 Sinclair Lewis explored the bourgeois world of a small-town, small-time, and middle-aged business real estate agent in his novel *Babbitt*. Lewis's affectionate parody of popular slogans of health, progress, and optimism was uncannily prophetic of the fads of the decade and of consumerism and conformism long afterward. Later, in *Arrowsmith* (1925), Lewis turned his acid-bitten censure on medicine, in an account of the losing fight by two men for whom scientific truth is religion, Max Gottlieb, an unworldly German bacteriologist, and Martin Arrowsmith, his idealistic American disciple.

Sociologists Robert and Helen Lynd unraveled the fabric of Muncie, Indiana, and presented the results as *Middletown* (1929). Whereas the expatriates of the lost generation represented an elite who were comfortable traveling abroad, writers who described the immigrant experience focused on characters in the United States itself. Henry Roth showed tensions between different ethnic groups— Italian-Americans and Jewish-Americans—and between two generations of American Jews.

Theodore Dreiser achieved singular success with *An American Tragedy* (1925), recounting antihero Clyde Griffiths's crime and punishment in such detail that the first edition ran to 840 pages. Having made humble coworker Roberta Alden pregnant, Clyde believes he has the prospect of wealth through marriage to well-heeled Sondra Finchley. Clyde is a callow young man who is impaled on the hook of his obsession with the affluence that Sondra represents. If he abandons Roberta, she will expose their relationship and he will lose Sondra. Suppose he goes on a boating trip with Roberta and the canoe tips over? Dreiser recounts with consummate skill, first how Clyde becomes bloodguilty step by easy step, and then the whys and wherefores of society's retribution.

Novelist William Faulkner of Mississippi began to describe and analyze the distinct culture, atmosphere, and psychology of the South in writing of daring structural and stylistic complexity. In the first of his masterpieces, *The Sound and the Fury* (1929), Faulkner elaborates on typical southern stereotypes, such as promiscuous girl, idiot child, unbalanced student, and sharp-witted cad—all scions of a dissolute southern family.

A most unlikely bestseller was *Coming of Age in Samoa* (1927), in which Columbia University anthropologist Margaret Mead implicitly contrasted the storm and stress of Western adolescence with the peaceful awakening to sexuality that occurred in the South Seas. Her masterstroke was to focus on the adolescent girl in a period when American folklore had made an icon of the flapper. Mead titillated her public with sexual innuendo and transformed the discipline of anthropology into a popular subject. Former sportswriter and columnist Ring Lardner achieved fame with short stories that established him as a sardonic humorist. He wrote *How to Write Short Stories (with Samples)* (1924) and *The Love Nest and Other Stories* (1926).

Boulevard comedy prospered on Broadway, "the great white way"—the name of New York's theater district around Times Square as well as the name of its seventeen-mile diagonal thoroughfare. With various collaborators, critic and playwright George Kaufman supplied gentle satires of metropolitan life, such as (with Edna Ferber) *The Royal Family* (1927) and *Dinner at Eight* (1932) and (with Morrie Ryskind) *The Coconuts* (1925) and *Animal Crackers* (1928). Kaufman found his ideal partner in Moss Hart for *Once in a Lifetime* (1930). In *June Moon* (1929) Kaufman's collaborator was Ring Lardner. They poured sentiment as lethal as cyanide into their spoof on Tin Pan Alley, based on Lardner's own short story *Some Like 'Em Cold*. Guileless and clueless would-be lyricist Fred Stevens assures his girl, "I got no use for a man who don't respect a woman's hood." Later he courts her with "I don't believe God ever meant for a woman to endure a life of druggery."

Serious playwright Eugene O'Neill peered into his own psyche with obsessive tenacity and therewith made explicit the subconscious needs and desires of his characters in intense psychological treatments of insanity, alcoholism, and sexual passion. O'Neill's work owed much to the teachings of Viennese psychologist Sigmund Freud. In an experimental drama, *The Emperor Jones* (1921), O'Neill expressed the psychological torment of his leading character, an African American Pullman porter who has managed to become dictator of a declining black state. Jones suffers from "little formless fears" that are in fact his subconscious but that appear to him to be physical presences in the jungle around him. *Desire under the Elms* (1925) presented a variation on the Oedipus complex. *The Great God Brown* (1926) was a bitter examination of the personality masks that people use. *Mourning Becomes Electra* (1931) had a rare psychological intensity in a play indebted to Aeschylus, transposing Greek tragedy to the Mannon family of New England in the era of the Civil War. The hypnotic power of O'Neill's language and his combination of emotional themes and experimental forms revolutionized serious American theater.

Sigmund Freud's discoveries not only proved indispensable to serious artists in their investigations into the mysteries of life, but they were also titillating to those who saw Freudian psychology as a means of escape from the inhibiting legacies of previous decades: sexual repression, patriotism, fundamentalist religion, and political idealism. The popularity of psychoanalysis affected an entire range of social consciousness. Once analysts started to emphasize the self, as an alternative to society, as an explanation of human behavior, they were insisting on a self apart from society. Frederick Hoffmann writes (1962) that the literature of the 1920s has "many examples of the mind turning in upon itself, examining, explaining and excusing itself in psychological terms. Interest in self took the place, and argued the futility of, a sense of social responsibility."

Starting in 1928, when he moved from Detroit to New York to teach "applied Christianity" at Union Theological Seminary, radical Protestant theologian Reinhold Niebuhr produced a stream of effectively argued invective against immoral, materialist man and even-more-immoral society. Niebuhr explained social tensions as the outcome of man's perverse avoidance of God's will. God demands man's intense engagement in history. Man's contribution acquires meaning only through God's transcendent purposes.

The 1920s also yielded a wealth of artistic and literary talent among African Americans in Harlem, New York, who also expressed the conflict of values in society and the self apart from society. Harlem was originally settled by whites, many of them German Jews. Between 1900 and 1930, three hundred thousand West Indians immigrated to the United States, and half of them settled in New

York City. They accounted for a quarter of the black population of Harlem and contributed to the Harlem Renaissance. In fact, only one leading artist—Countee Cullen—grew up in Harlem. The Harlem Renaissance was at its peak from 1925 to 1930. It did not represent a particular style or ethos, but rather offered African Americans the chance to become part of a vibrant cultural community, stimulated by various resources: Episcopal and Baptist churches, newspapers, and white publishers who turned African American writing into a vogue, as well as increasing consciousness of forerunners such as W. E. B. Du Bois and James Weldon Johnson.

In fact, Johnson was the pivotal figure. He followed his *Fifty Years and Other Poems* (1917) with a collection of others' work, two books of Negro spirituals, a book of African American sermons in verse, and an indictment of discrimination against African American Gold-Star mothers. Johnson capped his considerable achievement with the reissue of his 1912 *Autobiography of an Ex-Colored Man* (1927) and with two works that told the story of the Harlem Renaissance, *Black Manhattan* (1930) and *Along the Way* (1933).

The most cosmopolitan and prolific writer, Langston Hughes, was also the most wide-ranging and rebellious in content and form. He described himself as the first African American literary sharecropper and created a body of work that drew on traditions established by Walt Whitman and Vachel Lindsay. He crowned his achievements with a novel, *Not without Laughter* (1930), a collection of short stories, *The Ways of White Folks* (1934), and his autobiography, *The Big Sea* (1940). Claude McKay's *Home to Harlem* (1928) is beaten through with the rhythm of jazz and pervaded by optimism: "The sky was a grand blue benediction, and beneath it, the wonderful air of New York tasted like fine dry champagne." Yet McKay explores the dark underside of city life, as in the overwrought scene in which Ray sniffs happy dust in desperation. Other leading writers of the Harlem Renaissance included Jean Toomer and Nella Larsen. The leading sculptor was Augusta Savage.

The Harlem Renaissance also confirmed the special gifts of African American performing artists, notably the multitalented actor and singer Paul Robeson. The writer-producer team of F. E. Miller, Aubrey Lyle, Eubie Blake, and Noble Sissle established a vogue for revues by African Americans, thereby turning Josephine Baker and Florence Mills into incandescent stars.

The American art world in the 1920s was dominated by the same themes of conflict between old and new and the isolation of the individual. John Marin led modernist painters in expressing the vitality of New York City. Edward Hopper fused the styles of French impressionism and American realism. By subtle distortions of scale and distinct contrasts of light and shade, he explored the themes of loneliness and isolation in cities and their offices and in movie theaters, diners and automats. Hopper painted men and women whose relationships had deteriorated, capturing the irritation of closeness and the ache of impending separation. Charles Demuth and Charles Sheeler successfully combined realist and abstract forms to treat the American scene in a modernist style, transforming commonplace subjects into monumental icons. Alexander Calder used biomorphic shapes, kinetic art, surrealism, and constructivism. He eventually astonished Europe with his wire toys and circus figures and his invention of the mobile, a hanging sculpture whose parts moved of their own accord.

Among private sponsors who encouraged artists and art appreciation, Lillie P. Bliss, Mrs. Cornelius Sullivan, and Abby Aldrich Rockefeller founded the Museum of Modern Art (MoMA) in New York in 1929 (originally in the Heckscher Building on Fifth Avenue) as a permanent museum for the best modern works of art produced since the 1880s and to encourage and develop public appreciation of all the visual arts, including film. Then in 1930, Gertrude Vanderbilt Whitney, sculptor and art collector, founded the Whitney Museum of American Art, at first located in her Greenwich Village studio.

Whatever their subjects, journalists also moved readers to appreciate the subtle rhythms of capitalist society. H. L. Mencken believed that American culture had become stultified on account of its adherence to Puritan morality; he expressed his iconoclasm in his coeditorship (with George Nathan) of the magazines *The Smart Set* (1914–23) and *American Mercury* (1924–33), whence he spread his pungent, impressionistic remarks far and wide. Mencken was totally indifferent about whether he gave offense or not. It was said that he put his genius into his works and his far more modest talents into his life.

Yet more profound about the shifts in society, columnist Walter Lippmann in his *Men of Destiny* (1927) explained how five controversies of the 1920s above all others engaged people's interests and concentrated their emotions. They were those concerning immigration, national prohibition, the Ku Klux Klan, fundamentalism, and Catholicism.

> Prohibition, the Ku Klux Klan, fundamentalism, and xenophobia are an extreme and authentic expression of the politics, the social outlook, and the religion of the older American civilization making its last stand against what looks to it like an alien invasion. The alien invasion is, in fact, the new America produced by the growth and prosperity of America.
>
> The evil which old-fashioned preachers ascribe to the Pope, to Babylon, to atheists, and to the devil, is simply the new urban civilization, with its irresistible economic and scientific and mass power. The Pope, the devil, jazz, the bootleggers, are a mythology which expresses symbolically the impact of a vast and dreaded social change. The change is real enough.

Best Cellars

National prohibition became the most widely discussed subject in American society. What, when, and how people drank were questions affording limitless speculation. Drys believed that poor people now drank less; that there was a decline in absenteeism from, and inefficiency at, work; that people spent more money on food, clothing, and shelter; and that everyone shared in the prosperity of society.

The Anti-Saloon League had proved itself a superb lobby organization to achieve the new prohibition laws. But it could not persuade the American people to observe them. What it had was a facade of power that it used insidiously in politics. It was divided into two factions. One, led by its charismatic, megalomaniac counsel, Wayne Wheeler, wanted ever stricter prohibition-enforcement laws and control over prohibition appointments. The second faction, led by Ernest Cherrington, wanted to leave enforcement to the government and concentrate on educating the public through its giant press, the American Issue Company, in Westerville, Ohio.

The Eighteenth Amendment took effect on January 16, 1920. Wayne Wheeler had devised the National Prohibition Act of October 27, 1919, named after its congressional sponsor, Andrew Volstead of Minnesota. It was the Volstead Act that proscribed beer and wine as well as spirits on the grounds that an intoxicating beverage was one with 0.5 percent of alcohol. At the outset of national prohibition, the amount of liquor people drank decreased from a peak of 1.69 gallons per head in 1911–14 to 0.97 gallons per head in 1920–21. Only in the later years from 1927 to 1930 did the amount rise again to 1.4 gallons. But the most enduring legend associated with prohibition, and the one that has captured public imagination, is that of abuse of law and order. Prohibition afforded innumerable opportunities for tax-free free enterprise to soak up excess capital with the implicit connivance of government. It provided literally millions of people with additional employment all the way from criminal bootleggers and speakeasy operators to law-abiding taxi drivers and nightclub entertainers, and including law-enforcement officers. All benefited from the high-and-dry spree that lubricated urban society.

The principal ways of obtaining alcohol were by smuggling, bootlegging, home brewing, and moonshining. From 1923 onward they were used ever more widely.

Smuggling provided the surest way of getting high quality liquor into the United States. The total frontier was 18,700 miles, made up of 12,000 miles of coast, 3,700 miles of land borders, and 3,000 miles of lake and river front. An individual could buy beer in Canada for five dollars a case and sell it in Plattsburgh, New York, for ten dollars, or for as much as twenty-five dollars in New York City. Thus, a smuggler with a carload of twenty-five cases could make five hundred dollars on a run from Canada to New York, less traveling costs. Larry Fay built up (and lost) a nightclub business on his early profits from running a fleet of taxis from New York to Montreal and back. Smugglers smuggled alcohol into the United States from Canada, Mexico, and the West Indies and from ships outside the three miles of territorial waters around the coast, the so-called Rum Row. Unctuous bootlegger Arnold Rothstein tried to organize a national syndicate of crime based on cooperation among different gangs. He instituted a capital buying office to procure alcohol from Canada, the West Indies, and even the United Kingdom. In 1922 the syndicate, sometimes known as the Big Seven, enjoyed a monopoly of liquor traffic on the North Atlantic coast from Boston

In the early 1920s downtown Chicago was dominated by a medley of skyscrapers, turning the city into a series of vertical, manmade canyons. The *Chicago Tribune* building (*left*), by Raymond Hood and John Mead Howells (1925), was a Gothic creation crowned by a circle of buttresses, whereas the tower of the white Wrigley building (right), by Graham, Anderson, Probst, and White (1921), was inspired by the Giralda (Moorish tower) of the cathedral in Seville, Spain. (Library of Congress)

to Baltimore. The syndicate depended on cooperation among different ethnic groups—Italian, Irish, and Jewish.

Brewers, who had the capital, the product, and the expertise, began to co-operate with gangsters, who distributed the products and protected them from the law. Unlike wine and spirits, beer was a bulky commodity. It could not be manufactured or transported in secret, and it was profitable only when sold in large quantities. Beer peddlers required considerable resources: a fleet of trucks, weapons and ammunition, hit men to ward off competitors, and funds to bribe police and authorities. Only large and brutal gangs could supply what was required. And it was the gangs who took the fall when the law penetrated and broke the organization.

In Chicago brewer Joseph Stenson and his three brothers collaborated with gangsters Terry Druggan, Frankie Lake, and Johnny Torrio (originally of New York's Five Points Gang) in the operation of five breweries. From 1925 on, Torrio's successor, Al ("Scarface") Capone, another graduate of the Five Points Gang, became the most flamboyant and most notorious gangster on account of his brutal control of gangland territories and municipal politics in Chicago, especially during the corrupt mayoralties of William ("Big Bill") Thompson.

Capone and his mixed South Side Gang of Italians, Jews, and Poles fought a war for control in Chicago against Jewish and Irish gangs from the North Side who regarded the city as their preserve. Their most famous victim was rival Irish-American mobster and florist Dion O'Bannion. These were days of outrageous public demonstrations of grief for fallen mobsters when there would be as many cars to carry the floral tributes as to ferry the mourners. At the funeral of Dion O'Bannion, ten thousand people gathered at the cemetery gate while another ten thousand marched in a mile-long procession with three bands and a police escort.

The Department of Justice estimated that Al Capone's South Side Gang took in some $105 million in 1927 when Capone was twenty-eight years old. He was able to demonstrate his authority by kicking his own handpicked mayor, Joseph Klenha, down the steps of the town hall of Cicero, Illinois, while a policeman on his beat simply looked on. Yet biographer Laurence Bergreen emphasizes (1994) how Capone "consolidated his power not by plotting murders but by running an organization, taking care to stay well behind the front lines and benefitting from the mayhem taking place all around him." Capone's mix of prestige and notoriety eclipsed that of other mobsters because of his political flair and his compulsion to be seen in public.

Speakeasies were illegal bars—the name first used to describe an unlicensed saloon in 1889; they were located in a basement, a back room, or an upstairs apartment. Speakeasies introduced women other than prostitutes to bars. They led to uneasy alliances between the proprietors and the gangsters who protected them from the police. In general, they sold raw liquor at high prices and were commonly scenes of fights, unlicensed behavior, and raids. Police commissioner Grover Whalen estimated that there were thirty-two thousand speakeasies in New York—twice the number of legal saloons before prohibition. The greatest concentration in New York was on Fifty-Second Street between Fifth and Sixth Avenues. The single most famous speakeasy was Jack and Charles's 21, which had a chute to dispose of the evidence in case of a police raid. Across the nation, speakeasies led to the firm establishment of nightclubs, which survived the repeal of prohibition.

Speakeasy clients delighted in a new mixed drink, the cocktail—a concoction of wine or spirits and fruit juice or soda. In fact, there were more than three hundred varieties of cocktail before prohibition, including the mint julep and the scotch highball. A cocktail mix also masked the foul taste of converted, industrial alcohol.

To enforce the new laws, the federal government established the Prohibition Unit (from March 3, 1927 on, the Prohibition Bureau). The unit had none of the prerequisites for making a success of its job: good salaries to make graft superfluous, continuity of personnel, and cooperation from state governments and from the general public. Deprived of excise laws during prohibition, the federal government had less revenue to spend on enforcing the antiliquor laws. Throughout the 1920s Congress awarded the unit an average of $8.8 million per year. The total number of agents in the unit at any one time varied between 1,500 and 2,300 men, and the entire staff was never more than 4,500. In the first eleven years there were 17,972 appointments, 11,982 resignations, and 1,608 dismissals for various corrupt practices.

The number of prohibition cases was far more than the judicial system could accommodate. In 1920 federal courts tried 5,095 prohibition cases out of a total of 34,230 criminal cases altogether. In 1929 alone, federal courts tried 79,298 prohibition cases. The failure of courts to maintain prohibition discredited the law. The Jones Act of 1929 made violations a felony, providing penalties of a $10,000 fine or five years' imprisonment, or both, for a first offense. However, the national average fine was $130 and the average prison sentence was 140 days. In some parts of the country, judges, prosecutors, and juries were so hostile to prohibition that true enforcement was impossible. No one claimed that Congress took a sincere interest in prohibition enforcement. Assistant Attorney General Mabel Walker Willebrandt published an exposure of Congress in her *Inside of Prohibition* (1929). Congressmen advocated prohibition in their speeches, but they persistently violated the Volstead Act. A waiter once dropped a bottle of whiskey in the Capitol restaurant, yet an agent who applied for a warrant to search the building was refused.

Historian Edward Behr (1996) places responsibility for the thievery encouraged by national prohibition directly on the Anti-Saloon League general counsel, the megalomaniac Wayne Wheeler. Wheeler hated "the Irish, the continentals with their beer and wine, and the guzzling wet Democrats in the North and East." Accordingly, until his death in 1928, Wheeler worked assiduously to deliver the votes that maintained dry laws even if they could not dry out the country.

Tried and True: Knights of the Klan

Walter Lippmann's second controversial subject was the revival of the Ku Klux Klan—a potent expression of primitive fear. The second Klan, the "Invisible Empire, Knights of the Ku Klux Klan," lasted from 1915 to 1944. It was as secret, violent, and subversive as the original Klan of the Reconstruction period. In addition it was ultrapatriotic, nativistic, and moralistic.

William J. Simmons of Alabama, a Methodist circuit preacher, had launched the second Klan on Stone Mountain, near Atlanta, Georgia, on October 26, 1915. Two disciples, Edward Henry Clarke and Elizabeth ("Bessie") Tyler, appreciated the commercial opportunities in a secret organization collecting high initiation fees. In July 1921 Clarke sent 214 organizers, or kleagles, across the country to recruit initiates, converting 90,000 people. The revived Klan's catchment area was not simply the South but, more particularly, the Southwest (especially Texas), the Midwest (especially Indiana, Ohio, and Oklahoma), and the Far West (especially Oregon and California). The elaborate rituals and secret signs of the Invisible Empire appealed to a rural populace roused against foreigners by wartime propaganda. In 1923 total Klan income was $3 million, and business boomed for southern manufacturers involved with the Klan, such as the Gate City Manufacturing Company, manufacturer of Klan regalia.

In the 1920s the Klan became openly racist, representing itself as a defender of white against black, Gentile against Jew, and Protestant against Catholic. Edward Clarke proposed sterilizing African Americans. Simmons declared that never in history had a mongrel civilization survived. His goal was "one-hundred-percent Americans." Differences in ethnicity, rather than theology, explained the Klan's heated opposition to Catholics. Catholicism was a symbol of cultural differences between the new immigration and the old. Simmons warned the Junior Order of United American Mechanics in Atlanta on April 30, 1922, that, far from being a melting pot, America was "a garbage can! . . . When the hordes of aliens walk back to the ballot box and their votes outnumber yours, then, that alien horde has got you by the throat." The Klan afforded recreation and fraternity to the little hick adrift in the hustle and bustle of the industrial city. Its rituals compensated him for any sense of personal defeat as it dubbed him a knight of the invisible empire.

However, Klan leaders could no more redress the grievances of their members than they could undo the Industrial Revolution. Instead, they indulged in political bribery and the intimidation, torture, and murder of Catholics, liberals, and African Americans. Discontented former klansmen exposed the Klan's atrocities to the New York press, which syndicated their tales across the country. The *New York World* ran a series of well-documented, alarmist, and sensational articles from September 6 to 26, 1921, laying bare the Klan's history and its aims. By publicizing the Klan, the press unintentionally encouraged membership drives in the North and the East. The Klan continued on a foul path of murder and mayhem. In the course of the 1920s the Klan assaulted well over a thousand victims in Texas and Oklahoma and scores in other states. Most notorious were the ghoulish Mer Rouge murders of liberals Watt Daniels and Tom Richards in Morehouse Parish, Louisiana, on August 24, 1922.

The Klan had considerable political power. In 1922, 1923, and 1924, it helped elect governors in Oregon, Georgia, Maine, Ohio, Colorado, and Louisiana, congressmen in several states, and local officials throughout the country. Warren Harding disgraced the presidency and the White House by being inducted into the Klan there. In Indiana David C. ("Steve") Stephenson built up the Klan as a mass organization and a political machine. For his coronation as Grand Dragon before a crowd of one hundred thousand in Melfalfa Park in Kokomo, on July 4, 1923, he descended from the skies by airplane.

The second Klan provides another indication that the reaction against modern times and the threat of the growing power of the cities was strongest in the South. Pundit H. L. Mencken's contempt for the South knew no bounds. He characterized it as "the bunghole of the United States, a cesspool of Baptists, a miasma of Methodism, snake-charmers, phoney real-estate operators, and syphilitic evangelists." For the *Southern Oligarchy* of 1924 William Henry Skaggs produced a vitriolic catalog of evils: political corruption, illiteracy, peonage, racism, lynching, and landlords' exploitation of tenants. In *Darker Phases of the South*, also of 1924, Columbia professor Frank Tannenbaum denounced the white peonage of cotton. Its exploitation accounted for soil erosion, poor race relations, poverty, ignorance, and peonage.

Southern society not only accepted the political shenanigans of the Klan but also tolerated the barbarism of lynching. Many African Americans were victims of lynch law, especially in the South, where the trees of small towns bore strange fruit about once in every generation. The common charge was that African American victims of white lynch laws had tried to rape white women. Between 1918 and 1927, according to NAACP officer Walter F. White in his *Rope and Faggot* (1929), 456 people were victims of lynch mobs. Of this number, 416 were African American. Forty-two of the victims were burned alive, and eight were beaten to death or dismembered.

The act of lynching was an event for white men, women, and children to attend to relieve the boredom of small-town life—a modern auto-da-fé. They wanted entertainment. Prolonging the torture of hapless victims and taking bizarre photographs of the cruel scene gave them sadistic pleasure. A contributory factor in the epidemic of lynching was the depressed provincialism of isolated southern communities. A county given to lynching was characterized by poverty and decadence with incomes well below average and three-quarters of its population likely to belong to Southern Methodist and Baptist churches. Historian David M. Oshinsky finds (1996) that "Mississippi led the nation in every imaginable kind of mob atrocity: most lynchings, most multiple lynchings, most lynchings of women, most lynchings without an arrest, most lynchings of a victim in police custody, and most public support for the process itself."

The principal African American organization, the NAACP, assumed that if it publicized lynchings, mass public indignation would demand reform. Thus, it organized meetings, lobbied public officials, and stimulated press investigation. In 1921 the NAACP established an office in Washington. Its aim was to lobby Congress in support of Congressman L. C. Dyer of St. Louis, who had introduced an antilynching bill in 1919. The Dyer bill proposed to eliminate lynching by making counties in which the offense occurred responsible. If they failed to protect citizens or prisoners from mob rule, then the county would be fined.

Although the Dyer bill failed in Congress because of a southern filibuster in the Senate, the publicity it earned helped reduce the extent of the evil. Southern papers asserted that southern courts could handle the problem and punish aggressors without needing a federal law to show them how. According to the *Negro Year Book* (1932), whereas the total number of lynchings was 83 in 1919, it fell to 11 in 1928.

Black Is Beautiful

While southern racists continued to rejoice in the subjugation of African Americans, new voices of protest asserted a measure of defiant black pride. Of the total American population of 105.71 million in 1920, 10,951,000 were African Americans—about 10.5 percent of the whole. Eighty-five percent of them still lived in the South, many in conditions of sleepy peonage and most of them still deprived of the franchise. But the voice of human rights could not be quieted forever.

Jamaican immigrant Marcus Garvey was inspired by Booker T. Washington's autobiography, *Up from Slavery*, to organize the Universal Negro Improvement and Conservation Association in Kingston, Jamaica, in 1914. In 1916 he opened a branch of the United Negro Improvement Association (UNIA) in Harlem, initially among West Indian immigrants (who made up a quarter of the population of Harlem). Garvey was a commanding and charismatic speaker. He promoted the slogans "Africa for Africans at home and abroad" and "Up, you mighty race, you can accomplish what you will."

The UNIA aimed to establish a universal cofraternity of African Americans, civilize tribes in Africa, encourage race pride, and develop a "conscientious Christianity"—Garvey himself was a devout Catholic. The organization reached its peak of membership in 1921 with, perhaps, between 1 million and 4 million supporters. In fact, the UNIA was the first truly mass movement of African Americans, a predecessor of later organizations advocating black power and black pride. The Garvey movement opened up a fissure, however, that would eventually become a chasm between two African American schools of thought. Both wanted political, economic, and social improvement for African Americans, but one advocated integration and the other separatism. Prominent NAACP editor W. E. B. Du Bois recommended integration, and Garvey advocated separatism. Yet Garvey's followers were also discriminating, as George M. Fredrickson suggests (1995), picking and choosing among Garvey's different ideas.

The UNIA established the Black Star Steamship Line with three vessels to carry migrants across the Atlantic. It also petitioned the League of Nations to transfer the former German colonies in Southwest Africa and German East Africa, held as mandates by South Africa and Britain, respectively, to Garvey's control.

Then it all fell apart. The Liberian government withdrew its colonization agreement. Integrationist James W. H. Eason, a Philadelphia minister and prominent member of the UNIA, quarreled violently with Garvey, withdrew from the UNIA, and set up a rival organization, the Universal Negro Alliance. Eason was due to testify against Garvey over various irregularities in Black Star finances, but he was shot at a speaking engagement in New Orleans in 1923. Eason died before he could identify his assailants, and they were released. Then Garvey found himself arrested on a charge of using the federal mails to defraud the public, convicted, and imprisoned in Atlanta. In December 1927 he was deported to Jamaica; he died in obscurity in London in 1940. Premature reports of his death had already circulated, and he had the misfortune to die reading his own obituaries.

Garvey's contribution to black consciousness was that he convinced millions of African Americans that it was white racism and not failings or inadequacy on their part that was responsible for African American poverty and sense of powerlessness. James Weldon Johnson of the NAACP commented that Garvey had collected more money "than any other Negro organization had ever dreamed of." In a prophetic statement, the *Amsterdam News* of November 30, 1927, declared that "Marcus Garvey made black people proud of their race. In a world where black is despised, he taught them black is beautiful."

A second African American association, one working for improved race relations in the 1920s, was the Commission on Interracial Cooperation (CIC). It was founded in Atlanta on April 9, 1919, by a group of African Americans and whites who were disturbed by the race riots of 1919. They gave priority to the special social needs of African American soldiers and their families in the process of demobilization. By 1920 there were five hundred interracial commissions, and by 1923 there were about eight hundred. Will W. Alexander, a former Methodist minister and YMCA worker from Nashville, became leader of the CIC. His strategy was to get African Americans and whites to cooperate with one another by sharing common tasks of welfare. The CIC was supported by the NAACP, the African American press, the Methodist church, and governors in seven states. It persuaded Governor Hugh M. Dorsey of Georgia to publish an account on April 22, 1921, of 135 atrocities against African Americans in the previous two years.

Tried and True: Scopes, Bryan, and Darrow

The third controversy Walter Lippmann discerned was fundamentalism. The conflict between old and new, countryside and town, extended to religion and reached another climax with the Scopes trial of 1925. The trial centered on the conflict between modernism and Charles Darwin's theory of evolution on the one hand and religious fundamentalism—the literal interpretation of the Bible—on the other. Darwin's *Origin of Species* (1859) had been a threat to narrow-minded theologians from the time it was first published. If people rejected the book of Genesis as an explanation of the origins of life, how could the Bible retain its authority as a guide to human behavior? In 1910 the first of ten pamphlets entitled *The Fundamentals* asserted the literal truth of the Bible and declared that Darwinism could have no contact with Christianity.

The South was the fortress of Protestant America. In the Southeast 61.4 percent of adults were church members in 1926 as compared with 54.3 percent in the nation as a whole. Three-quarters of these church members were either Methodists or Baptists. In 1918 Dr. William Bell Ripley, pastor of the First Baptist Church of Minneapolis, founded the World's Christian Fundamental Association (WCFA) to propagate the fundamentalist cause. The most persistent fundamentalist was J. Frank Norris, a Baptist minister of Fort Worth, Texas. Through a magazine, *The Searchlight*, he exposed teachers of suspect views and indicted various Methodist colleges for false teaching. As a result of his activities, six college professors had to resign their posts.

In Dayton, Tennessee, George W. Rappelyea, a manager of iron and coal mines, persuaded John W. Scopes, a young biology teacher, to provide the American Civil Liberties Union (ACLU) with a case to test the state's Butler Act, which forbade the teaching of evolution in public schools. All Scopes had to do was to teach evolution and get arrested. The case became a sensation, partly because both sides sought maximum publicity by getting celebrities to take part. William Jennings Bryan, now a front man for Florida realtors, was on the prosecution team. "We cannot afford to have a system of education that destroys the religious faith of our children," he declared. "There are about 5,000 scientists in the United States and probably half of them are atheists. Are we going to allow them to run our schools? We are not." Walter Lippmann cynically observed, "The campaign in certain localities to forbid the teaching of 'Darwinism' is an attempt to stem the tide of the metropolitan spirit, to erect a spiritual tariff against an alien rationalism which threatens to dissolve the mores of the village civilization."

Clarence Darrow led the defense team. He argued that the Butler Act was unconstitutional because it violated freedom of religion by making the Bible the test of truth. Further, he declared that it was unreasonable, given modern knowledge of evolution. The implication of his argument was that truth was inimical to any closed order because it threatened basic assumptions. Although Judge Raulston restricted the number of scientists and theologians that Darrow wanted to call, the trial educated the public in North and South. Darrow cross-examined Bryan and tripped him into compromising the book of Genesis with evolution:

"Do you think the earth was made in six days?"

"Not six days of twenty-four hours."

Having made the old man look ridiculous, Bryan invited the judge to instruct the jury to find John Scopes guilty, which they did on July 21, 1925. Five days later, the teetotal glutton Bryan died in his sleep of apoplexy.

The Tennessee supreme court heard the appeal in Nashville. No doubt sensitive to the way the state of Tennessee had made itself absurd across the world, the court decided to bring the affair to closure. In its decision of January 14,

The Scopes ("Monkey") Trial of 1925 in which biology teacher John Scopes was convicted of teaching evolution in contradiction to the state laws of Tennessee that required all teaching about Creation to conform literally to the myths of Genesis. Scopes was defended by Clarence Darrow ("attorney for the damned"), standing in front of the table, whose eloquent arguments educated America about the merits of Charles Darwin's theory of natural selection. John Scopes is seated immediately behind Darrow. (Library of Congress)

1927, the court upheld the Butler Act but reversed the original judgment on the technical issue of the fine of one hundred dollars. The victory of fundamentalism led to its defeat. News of the Scopes trial spread information about evolution across the United States. Tennessee repealed the Butler Act in 1967.

However, right through the 1920s, the malign powers of ignorance and intolerance were still at work outside the respectable temple of religious observance.

CHAPTER 8

Nine Mocking Years with the Golden Calf

"NINE MOCKING YEARS with the golden calf and three long years of the scourge!" was how Franklin Delano Roosevelt described the 1920s and early 1930s. "Nine crazy years at the ticker and three long years in the breadlines! Nine mad years of mirage and three long years of despair!" The pattern was clear: complacency, crash, consequences.

Although World War I had apparently strengthened American industry, the nation's economic structure was now seriously warped. The war had expanded and speeded up industrial capacity, first to supply Europe, and later to supply the United States. In 1920 American exports had reached $3.25 billion, an increase of 4 percent over 1919 and of 333 percent over 1913. The cost of imports was about $5.75 billion, an increase of 35 percent over 1919 and almost 300 percent over 1913. However, America's capacity to produce was way beyond its capacity to consume during peacetime or to export abroad once other nations had resumed their normal production. In the 1920s few discerned these bad omens that would shatter the economy in 1929.

Social and commercial, political and economic—during the 1920s America was in the midst of a whole series of momentous transitions: "No longer rural, but not yet dominated by either industry or the white-collar professions; no longer overwhelmingly Anglo-Saxon or Protestant but not yet resigned to becoming a genuinely pluralistic society," argues radio producer Daniel Snowman (1968). One result was conflict between the new urban civilization and traditional rural values. At stake was social, political, and religious intolerance. The darker side, revealed dramatically in the Sacco-Vanzetti case of 1920–27, the resurgence of the Ku Klux Klan, and the intransigence of fundamentalism, surfaced with alarming frequency as if to show that society could not accommodate its tensions: "These manifestations took two major forms: intolerant extremism and anti-social self-indulgence."

Immigration was the lightning rod for the profound social tensions of the age. Forty years of continuous immigration on a massive scale had made the United States the most heterogeneous nation ever. In 1920 the population comprised 105,710,620 people in the continental United States and 12,279,997 in its overseas possessions. Of this population, 53.5 percent were children of white native parents, 7.0 percent of mixed native and foreign parentage, 15.5 percent of for-

Arshile Gorky, *The Artist and His Mother* (1926–29), oil 60" × 50". Armenian artist Gorky, whose original name was Vosdanig Manoog Adoian, immigrated to the United States in 1920. In the 1930s he became friendly with abstract artists Stuart Davis and Willem de Kooning. He set himself the task of translating European modernism into American modes by retracing in his own works the European artistic revolution from impressionism to cubism and surrealism. In this painting, he acknowledges the influence of Pablo Picasso. (Collection of Whitney Museum of American Art, New York; gift of Julien Levy for Maro and Natasha Gorky in memory of their father)

eign parents, 10.5 African Americans, and 13.5 percent first-generation Americans.

Nativism was stoked by eugenics, a term coined in 1883 by Charles Darwin's cousin, Sir Francis Galton. His American disciple, Charles Davenport, defined eugenics as the science of "the improvement of the human race by better breeding." American eugenicists conducted research into the inheritance of various physical, mental, and personality traits. Eugenicists developed close ties with the newly emerging profession of psychometrics—the psychological theory of mental measurement that constructed standardized IQ tests. Prominent psychometrists included Lewis Terman and Robert Yerkes, the Harvard psychologist who designed Army IQ tests during World War I. They believed that mental functions were innate or genetically determined. In 1910 Davenport established the Eugenics Record Office (ERO), which served as a repository and center for eugenics research until 1940.

Eugenics was made popular outside universities by books such as *Mankind at the Crossroads* (1914) by E. G. Conklin, *The Passing of the Great Race* (1916) by Madison Grant, *The Rising Tide of Color against White World Supremacy* (1920) by Lothrop Stoddard, and *The Fruit of the Family Tree* (1924) by Alfred E. Wiggam. The American Eugenics Society, founded in 1923, grew to twelve hundred members in twenty-nine states by the end of the decade. In 1928 the American Genetics Association claimed that there were 376 college courses devoted to eugenics. Americans also embraced eugenics as a political argument for halting the new immigration on the grounds that the new immigrants were defective in some way—"the dregs of humanity," inassimilable, or mentally retarded as determined by Henry Goddard's tests at Ellis Island and other reception centers.

Moreover, by February 1921 Ellis Island, the immigration reception area in New York, was jammed by the number of immigrants. In New York already 40 percent of the population was foreign born. There was, moreover, a shift in immigration with women and children joining their husbands: two-thirds of Italian and Slavic immigrants were now female. Congress approved an emergency restriction act that passed the House within hours without a roll call. The Senate adopted it shortly afterward by 78 votes to 1. President Warren Harding signed this interim Emergency Quota Act on May 19, 1921.

The act declared that no more than 357,000 immigrants could be admitted to the United States in any one year. That figure represented about a third of the assumed totals of immigrants in the years before World War I. The framers of the act intended to base the new restricted immigration on a mix of old and new immigrants according to quotas. Each quota was to represent 3 percent of the immigrants from any particular country in the United States in 1910. But Congress discovered that its assigned quotas were at variance with its proposed aggregate ceilings. In 1924 the total number of immigrants entering the country was 700,000.

The quotas of 1921 applied only to Europe, the Near East, Africa, Australia, and New Zealand. There were no restrictions on immigrants from countries within the western hemisphere. The act restricted Asian immigrants to one hundred per year. It specified, moreover, that "no alien ineligible for citizenship shall be admitted to the United States." Despite Secretary of State Charles Evans Hughes's warning that this was a pointed insult to Japan, now supersensitive, and with whom the United States was seeking naval limitation, Congress, alert to anti-Japanese sentiment on the West Coast, insisted on retaining the restriction. In 1923 the Supreme Court decided in *Ozawa v. The United States* that people of Japanese birth were ineligible for naturalization.

Because immigration restriction had to seem fair, Albert Johnson, head of the House Committee on Immigration and Naturalization, held a series of hearings preparatory to introducing a bill that would limit the new immigration even more drastically. Accordingly, Johnson appointed Harry H. Laughlin of the Eugenics Records Office as "expert eugenics witness." In 1922 Laughlin cited IQ data, army test results, and family-pedigree analyses of institutionalized persons to demonstrate the defective biological nature of the new immigrants. In 1924 Laughlin presented data showing that prisons and mental asylums housed a disproportionate number of new immigrants. Another expert witness, Herbert Spencer Jennings of Johns Hopkins University, found that Laughlin had grossly overstated his case. But Jennings was given only five minutes to testify on the last day of the hearings.

The act of 1924, the National Origins Act, reduced the maximum number of immigrants to 164,000 by pushing the base year for the quota proportions back to 1890 and cutting the annual quota for each nationality to 2 percent. Congress chose 1890 as the new base year because that was the last census year before the number of new immigrants exceeded the old. During debates congressmen openly reviled the new immigrants of the great cities. "On the one side," claimed Congressman Jasper Napoleon Tilcher of Kansas, "is beer, bolshevism, unassimilating settlements, and, perhaps, many flags—on the other side is constitutional government; one flag, stars and stripes."

The 1924 act stipulated that beginning in 1927, administrators were to compute national quotas from the number of foreign born in the United States whose origin by birth or ancestry they could attribute to a specific national area. The act assigned this invidious task to the secretaries of state, commerce, and labor. In effect, the act held immigration from 1925 to 1931 to an annual average of 300,000. However, contrary to the intention of its sponsors, the new act seemed to encourage immigration of people of Spanish and Indian origin from Mexico and Puerto Rico, and of French origin from Canada. Not only conservatives but also many Progressives, liberals, and labor leaders welcomed the act because they believed that the problems of American society could be solved only if its composition remained stable. Although Congress relaxed quotas and ceilings somewhat over the years, it did not overturn the underlying principles until the Immigration Act of 1965.

The act of 1924 took full effect in 1929, establishing a total limit of 153,714 people, excluding the western hemisphere and Asia. It allowed Britain an annual quota of 65,361 immigrants but restricted Italy to 5,803, Poland to 6,524, and Russia to 2,784 immigrants. Ironically, people of color from the West Indies were unaffected by the restrictive legislation since they came from these colonial island possessions of Britain and therefore fell within its generous quota. The State Department instructed U.S. consuls abroad to refuse visas to prospective immigrants who did not have fifty dollars in cash. The problems associated with immigrants and the fears they provoked were but a loose and troublesome thread in the tapestry of social life that conservatives thought was unraveling. Because the act also insisted that immigrants had to present visas from the country of origin, immigrants now arrived with their names correctly spelled.

In contrast with its treatment of immigrants, in 1924 the federal government conferred U.S. citizenship upon all Native Americans. According to the Bureau of the Census, there were 125,000 Native Americans in the United States in 1920. This was a period when people were likely to minimize their Native American ancestry; thus, the number of people with Indian blood was probably higher. Secretary of the Interior Hubert Work commissioned an independent report on Indians, *The Problem of Indian Administration*, usually known as the Meriam report. It disclosed the failure of the Dawes Severalty Act of 1887 that had aimed to turn nomadic Indians into farmers of minimal lands, and the desperate conditions of Indians in terms of poverty, health, and education. Sensitive to sympathetic shifts in anthropology, the Meriam report suggested that Indian culture should be allowed to follow its own path. Nevertheless, it assumed that the federal government must encourage Native Americans to adjust to white society, using knowledge from the social sciences to this end.

The Available Men

In electing Warren Harding as president in 1920, the American people may have gained a president who looked like a leader, but they did not gain a president

FACING PAGE:

In the 1920s, three Republican administrations attempted to show that they represented business as usual — meaning prudent investment — but as the skeins of finance unraveled, their presentation took on a different meaning from the one they intended:
Above: One of several paintings of Calvin Coolidge in the lonely farm in Vermont, taking the oath of office from his father, a notary public, in the small hours of August 2, 1923. The charm of the imagined lamplit scene appealed to those who yearned for a more idyllic past, but it was at variance with the hard-nosed realities of business interests in politics that dominated the 1920s. (Library of Congress)
Below: "She Had So Many Children, She Didn't Know What to Do." A cartoon of the federal government overwhelmed by social problems in the 1920s, ranging from national prohibition of alcohol and gangsterism to sexual permissiveness and its critics, and including fundamentalism and racism. The resulting conflicts in society took such forms as intolerant extremism and antisocial self-indulgence. (Library of Congress)

"SHE HAD SO MANY CHILDREN, SHE DIDN'T KNOW WHAT TO DO!"

who led. As president (1921–23), Warren Harding proved an amiable simpleton, manipulated by sinister forces. Whereas George Washington could not tell a lie, Warren Harding could not tell a liar. He took into office the so-called Ohio gang, led by Harry Daugherty, who became attorney general. From the Senate, Harding chose Harry S. New as postmaster general, the devious Albert B. Fall as secretary of the interior, and later, John S. Weeks as secretary of war. Harding made the unscrupulous Col. Charles R. Forbes head of the Veterans Bureau.

Halfway through his Cabinet selection, Harding raised its stature, appointing Charles Evans Hughes secretary of state (1921–25), Herbert Hoover secretary of commerce (1921–28), Henry C. Wallace secretary of agriculture (1921–24), and Andrew W. Mellon secretary of the treasury (1921–32). Mellon, who owed his fortune to aluminum and steel, reluctantly resigned directorships in sixty corporations to ensure his confirmation. It was later said of Mellon that three presidents served under him.

Warren Harding could move from individual acts of kindness, such as ordering the release of the aging Socialist leader Eugene Debs from prison in 1921, to generous acts of political skill, such as persuading the steel magnates in 1922 and 1923 to reduce the twelve-hour shift to eight hours. But he was inadequate to the major tasks. A Republican regular if ever there was in following established practice, Harding repeatedly announced his commitment to economy in government. The Budget and Accountancy Act of June 20, 1921, provided for the establishment of the Budget Bureau in the Treasury with powers to revise the estimates of various departments and make each truly accountable.

Business urged the Republicans to lower taxes, raise the tariff, and provide federal subsidies without imposing restrictions on business practices. Business also argued that burdensome taxes on wealth inhibited creative investment by the rich. According to this argument, if government continued to cream off the cat's share of profits, then business would not take the risks necessary for industrial and commercial expansion. Thus, in the Revenue Act of November 23, 1921, Congress removed the wartime excess profits tax and revised the maximum surtax to 50 percent. To assuage the less affluent, Congress raised the tax threshold for heads of families with an annual income of $5,000 or less from $2,000 to $2,500 and also raised the exemption for each dependent from $200 to $400. It set the tax on net profits of corporations at 12.5 percent, instead of 10 percent. The federal government collected about $4 billion in annual revenue and spent just $3 billion. It used the surplus to liquidate the national debt, which fell from $24 billion in 1920 to $10 billion in 1930.

Both industry and agriculture demanded a protective tariff against cheap produce from abroad. Congress supplied the Fordney-McCumber Tariff of September 21, 1922. The vote was along party lines, and it passed only after acrimonious debate in which the Senate proposed 2,082 amendments to the original House bill. The underlying principle was to give U.S. producers the advantage in the U.S. market. It was especially aimed at such products of Germany and Japan as silk and rayon, china, cutlery, and toys. In one respect the Fordney-

McCumber Tariff represented an improvement on its predecessors since it provided for a more efficient administration of tariff regulations, based on systematic classification of products. Moreover, the president, on the advice of the commission, could raise or lower duties by up to 50 percent on specific items in order to achieve parity between American and foreign costs. However, of thirty-seven changes under Harding and his successor, Calvin Coolidge, thirty-two were upward. The five exceptions were picayune—on millfeeds, bobwhite quail, paintbrush handles, cresyllic acid, and phenol.

Harding's administration became most notorious for its graft and corruption.

At the Veterans Bureau Charles Forbes diverted $36 million intended for the medical care of injured veterans and hospital construction to fraudulent contractors and to himself. Learning of his misdeeds and knowing the scandal would break, Harding and Daugherty arranged that Forbes should first go abroad and then resign. The Senate started an investigation. While Forbes was away, his legal assistant, Charles F. Cramer, shot himself dead in his bathroom.

It became an open secret that the surest way to advance sinister interests was to bend the ear of the unscrupulous attorney general through his protégé, Jess Smith. Daugherty and Smith sold bootleg liquor impounded by the prohibition authorities and held in a house at 1625 K Street. William J. Burns ran the Department of Justice for Daugherty as a private protection racket. His agent, Gaston B. Means, took $7 million altogether from bootleggers who bought pardons. The money was left in a goldfish bowl before being turned over to the Department of Justice. The gullible and greedy Smith could not stand the strain of prolonged public gaze, and he, too, committed suicide by shooting himself.

Warren Harding was worried by mounting evidence of misconduct by the Ohio gang. He threw himself with abandon into his hobbies of golf during the day and poker with his cronies at night. His health was not up to the arduous tour to the West and Alaska he undertook in June 1923. For years he had indulged in food, drink, and finally worry. He died in the presidential suite of the Palace Hotel in San Francisco on August 2. Vice President Calvin Coolidge was staying at his family's farmhouse in Plymouth, Vermont, when he was awakened at 2:00 A.M. with the news. Coolidge's father, a notary public, administered the oath of office to his son in the sitting room. Coolidge's tart recollection of his private thoughts are at odds with the charming legend of the candle-lit scene:

"What was your first thought when you heard that Harding was dead?" portrait painter Charles Hopkins asked Coolidge later.

"I thought I could swing it."

Among those who rode in Harding's funeral procession was the stricken Woodrow Wilson, who had, against custom, continued to live in Washington after he left the White House. Wilson conducted himself with considerable dignity, however, a broken reclusive man but not one who caused trouble for his successor. Wilson endured his political repudiation with far more serenity than his family expected from him. He told Margaret, his eldest daughter, that when the American people did join the League—as they surely would—they would do so because they realized that this was the right course of action: "Perhaps God knew better than I did, after all." Wilson died on February 3, 1924, only a few days after Lenin, the other world spokesman for a (very different) world order.

The biggest scandal of the Harding administration now broke.

Senator John B. Kendrick of Wyoming discovered that Secretary of the Interior Albert B. Fall was leasing certain oil lands (usually known as Teapot Dome because of the shape of one hill) that were supposed to supply the navy, to a private corporation, Mammoth Oil Company, owned by Harry F. Sinclair. Under pressure from the Senate, the Department of the Interior admitted that not only had Fall leased Teapot Dome to Sinclair's company but that he was also going to lease the Elk Hill reserve in California to the Pan-American Petroleum and Transportation Company, headed by Edward L. Doheny. They explained that wells on adjoining lands were drawing oil from these reserves. Thus, government reserves would be exhausted within a few years, anyway. However, Senator Robert La Follette of Wisconsin was not satisfied with this disingenuous explanation. He persuaded the Committee on Public Safety to instigate a formal investigation. The chair of the special committee, Senator Thomas J. Walsh of Montana, was an Irish-American Catholic with a penetrating mind and inexhaustible energy. At the public hearings, beginning on October 25, 1923, the weight of technical evidence was that the leasing of oil reserves to anticipate drainage at the ends was unjustified. The oil supply was intended for the navy. It had been irregular of Secretary of the Navy Edwin Denby to allow Secretary of the Interior Albert B. Fall to issue leases to commercial companies. The hapless Denby could not endure the situation and he resigned.

Walsh's investigations lasted over eighteen months and attracted attention from various people who wanted to settle old scores against Fall. Walsh learned that Fall had moved from penury to opulence within two years. Edward Doheny of Pan-American Petroleum had loaned Fall $100,000 to improve his ranch. Fall stood condemned. He had taken $100,000 from someone to whom, in his official capacity, he was about to grant a valuable lease. Then he had lied about the money.

President Calvin Coolidge (1923–29) chose Owen J. Roberts, a Republican lawyer from Philadelphia, and Attlee W. Pomerone, a former Democratic senator from Ohio, as special counsels to prosecute the case. The various trials of Fall, Sinclair, and Doheny on several charges of conspiracy and fraud resulted in the surprising acquittal of Doheny for fraud (December 16, 1926), and of Fall and Sinclair (April 21, 1928). However, Fall was convicted of accepting a bribe (October 25, 1929), sentenced to a year's imprisonment, and fined $100,000. Thus was Fall the first cabinet officer to go to jail. Paradoxically, Doheny was acquitted in March 1930 on a charge of bribing Fall. Harry F. Sinclair refused to give the Walsh committee straight answers. The Senate cited him for contempt.

He was tried and convicted in the criminal courts and sentenced to a fine of $1,000 and three months in jail.

The Teapot Dome scandal shook confidence in public officials. To remedy the damage, Coolidge and the new attorney general, Harlan Fiske Stone, tried to improve the watchdog of public activities, the Bureau of Investigations, originally an investigative branch of the Department of Justice, established in July 1908. In 1928 Stone had it reorganized under a new director, J. Edgar Hoover. This was the agency that adopted the title of the Federal Bureau of Investigation (FBI) in July 1935. It was the task of the bureau to investigate crimes and undertake domestic intelligence activities. In 1930 it began to collate and publicize public crime reports from various police forces.

J. Edgar Hoover had one of the most extraordinary careers ever in public office, serving as director of the FBI from 1924 until his death in 1972. A native of Washington, D.C., Hoover had already worked in the Justice Department for seven years, notably as a special agent in the Enemy Public Aliens Bureau. His special gifts had been most apparent during the Great Red Scare, when he became special assistant to Attorney General A. Mitchell Palmer. It was Hoover who masterminded the kangaroo courts and the deportations of radicals and subversives, real or imagined. He continued his obsessive anti-Communist crusade throughout his directorship. Long considered above reproach, Hoover's posthumous reputation was tarnished by revelations of his jealous smear campaigns against successful FBI agents in the 1930s and vindictive investigation of radicals in the 1960s as well as the discovery of bizarre secrets of his sex life. A closet homosexual, he was an occasional and furtive cross dresser.

The test of the reformed federal government came with the presidential election of 1924. Incumbent president and Republican nominee Calvin Coolidge wooed business. But the election was most remarkable for the disunity and chaos of the Democrats and the revival of a Progressive party.

The Democratic National Convention met on June 24, 1924, in the sweltering heat of the auditorium of Madison Square Garden, New York. When Alabama delegate Forney Johnson rose to nominate Senator Oscar W. Underwood of Alabama, he also asked the convention to take a stand against secret un-American organizations such as the Ku Klux Klan. Underwood's stand brought a dangerous and divisive issue into the open. For the Klan, determined to help William Gibbs McAdoo win the nomination, had participated in some state Democratic conventions and had seen to it that perhaps eighty delegates from Arkansas and Texas were sympathetic to the Klan, if they were not actual knights. The *New York World* estimated that about three hundred delegates were klansmen. As the controversy continued, it became ever more heated, dividing delegates in northern states from those in the South. When it transpired that a majority of delegates did not want to condemn the Klan, the matter went to a special committee that opted for a compromise resolution proposed by William Jennings Bryan, representing Florida. In the end the Klan secured a majority of

$543\frac{3}{20}$ votes in favor of Bryan's compromise plank to $542\frac{7}{20}$ against. The Democratic party would not condemn the Klan.

The decision was a disaster for the Democrats. It embittered the convention and prevented the nomination of any leading contender—McAdoo, Al Smith of New York, or Underwood. Instead, the convention, after 103 ballots cast over seventeen riotous days, nominated a compromise candidate, John W. Davis, a Wall Street lawyer originally from West Virginia. The convention, broadcast by radio nationwide, divided Democrats across the country on a scale unknown since the Civil War and unsurpassed until 1968.

The Republicans' indifference to reform and the Democrats' incapacity led to a progressive revival under Senator Robert M. La Follette of Wisconsin. The Progressives organized themselves into three different political groups. The American Labor Party of 1919 was based on trade unions. The Committee of Forty-Eight, composed of old Bull Moose Progressives, was led by J. A. H. Hopkins, a New Jersey insurance broker, who favored a farmer-labor party in 1920. Most significant was the Conference for Progressive Political Action (CPPA), based on railroad brotherhoods and formed in Chicago in 1922. The CPPA's proposed reforms included the abolition of the electoral college; the introduction of direct primaries for all elective offices, including the presidency; the rapid convening of new Congresses; and the exclusion from government of special-privilege interests. Progressives included Senator George W. Norris, tireless champion of public rights against the interests of monopolies, especially utility empires; Senators Edwin F. Ladd and Lynn W. Frazier of North Dakota; Burton K. Wheeler of Montana; Magnus Johnson and Henrik Shipstead of Minnesota; and Smith W. Brookhart of Iowa.

The CPPA, sensing advantages to be gained from problems within the Republican and Democratic Parties, held a national convention in July 1924 that was attended by six hundred delegates from labor unions, farmers' organizations, and the Socialists. Robert La Follette insisted that, instead of forming a distinct third party and thus jeopardizing the position of many sympathetic Progressives in Congress who held seats as nominal Republicans and Democrats, they should concentrate on the presidential contest, nominating La Follette himself, with Democratic Senator Burton K. Wheeler of Montana as his running mate. The Progressive plank declared that the great issue was "the control of government and industry by private monopoly" that had "crushed competition" and "stifled private initiative and independent enterprise" for the sake of extortionate profits. However, Progressives did not want to accept the Socialist remedy of government ownership of industry. They advocated the right of labor to collective bargaining, urged an end to the use of injunctions in labor disputes, proposed a constitutional amendment to restrict the use of judicial veto, and advocated ten-year terms for federal judges.

In the election Coolidge received 15,718,211 popular votes, exceeding the combined total of Davis's 8,385,283 and La Follette's 4,831,289. Thus, Coolidge had 54.0 percent of the popular vote, Davis had 28.8 percent, and La Follette had 16.6 percent. Coolidge had 35 states, giving him 382 votes in the electoral college, and Davis, with 12 states, had 136 votes. La Follette carried only his home state, Wisconsin. The Coolidge landslide gave the Republicans control of Congress. In the House there were 247 Republicans to 183 Democrats, 2 Farmer-Laborites, and 2 Socialists; in the Senate there were 56 Republicans to 39 Democrats and 1 Farmer-Laborite.

La Follette's unsuccessful campaign scared bosses in both parties. He came second in eleven states (California, Idaho, Iowa, Minnesota, Montana, Nevada, the Dakotas, Oregon, Washington, and Wyoming). He took enough votes in thirteen others to rob Coolidge of outright majorities. Those dissatisfied with the Republicans were as likely to vote for La Follette, who was liberal, as for Davis, who was not. Leading Democrats concluded that if their party was to win again, they would have to field liberal candidates with liberal programs. La Follette died of a heart attack on June 18, 1925. He was succeeded in the Senate by his son, Robert, Jr.

As to the Klan, although it remained a potent political force, it was riven by feuds that culminated in a series of bizarre court cases, most notoriously in Indiana, where kingmaker David C. ("Steve") Stephenson of Indiana was found guilty of the death of Madge Oberholtzer. Madge, state superintendent of public instruction, had refused Stephenson's sexual advances, had been kidnapped by him, and had committed suicide by taking poison. This was not the end of the Klan's troubles. When new leader Hiram Evans, a Dallas dentist, sued former klansmen in western Pennsylvania for damages of one hundred thousand dollars in 1927, David Stephenson, now in prison for the manslaughter of Madge Oberholtzer, released his files to expose Evans's own malpractices. The Stephenson files showed widespread corruption by politicians who had agreed to promote Klan policies in exchange for votes and campaign contributions. Governor Ed Jackson of Indiana explained that a Klan check he had received for twenty-five hundred dollars was not a fee for services rendered. Instead, he claimed it was a payment for a horse that had since choked to death on a carob. In the end, twenty leading Republicans went to prison, but not Governor Jackson, who was saved from jail by a legal technicality.

Elected president in his own right, Calvin Coolidge remained a Puritan in Babylon. Aloof and austere, some said of Coolidge that he spoke so little that, each time he did open his mouth, a moth flew out. There were numerous anecdotes about his mordant wit.

"What is your hobby?"

"Holding office."

To the society woman who said to him at dinner, "I made a bet I could get more than two words out of you," he said, curtly, "You lose."

The greatest governmental ally of business at the courts of Harding and Coolidge was Secretary of Commerce Herbert Hoover, a constructive critic of business practices. He had the Bureau of Standards and the Bureau of Foreign and Domestic Commerce undertake research into ways of eliminating waste. He encouraged the formation of trade associations along the lines of the National Association of Manufacturers (NAM) of 1865. The NAM funded agencies that distributed information on process, production, credit, insurance, and relations between employers and employees. It published this information for the benefit of member corporations and individual stockholders. It also funded political lobbies to advance or retard particular legislation and to restrain government from using its right to regulate business.

For instance, it was the duty of the Federal Power Commission of 1920 to supervise the manufacture and distribution of electric power, with authority to grant licenses for the construction of new plants, to regulate rates of currents across state borders, and to require uniform systems of accounting. Because the commission initially comprised the secretaries of war, agriculture, and the interior, it soon assumed a conservative complexion.

In the course of the 1920s technological improvements and interconnections between different companies allowed great expansion of electric power facilities. But the changes were expensive and only the strongest companies could afford them. The route to strength was amalgamation. In 1926 there were one thousand mergers in public utilities. Public utility magnates acquired municipal plants. By 1930 ten so-called groups of systems controlled three-quarters of the nation's electric power. They sold power to industry at lower prices than those they charged domestic consumers. They did this to discourage industry from investing in its own plants. However, they also lowered the price charged to domestic consumers.

Senator George W. Norris of Nebraska, exasperated by the way Presidents Harding and Coolidge, by conservative appointments, had helped destroy the new federal system of regulatory commissions, wrote a scathing attack that the *Nation* published on September 16, 1925. In heavy sarcasm, Norris denounced Republican policies:

> It is an indirect but positive repeal of congressional enactments, which no administration, however powerful, would dare to bring about by any direct means. It is the nullification of federal law by a process of boring from within. If trusts, combinations, and big business are to run the government, why not permit them to do it directly, rather than through this expensive machinery, which was honestly established for the protection of the people of the country against monopoly and control?

To some critics, the bending of government will toward business interests was far more damaging to democracy than the outright political corruption of the Harding administration. Such covert alliances between big business and the federal government would provoke caustic criticisms all the way from the third administration of Franklin Delano Roosevelt (1941–45) onward, reaching special concern in the administrations of Richard Nixon (1969–74), Ronald Reagan (1981–89), and Bill Clinton (1993–   ).

1928: When They Vote, It's Counted, When They Drink, It Ain't

The bitterly fought presidential election of 1928 drew together the divisive themes that had haunted the two nations of the 1920s. The wet, Democratic, and Catholic governor of New York, Al Smith, stood against the dry, Republican, and Quaker secretary of commerce, Herbert Hoover. The campaign was the climax of the conflict between rural America with its allegiance to proven values and urban America with its masses committed to modernism and social experiments. It also represented the climax of fifty years of debate about prohibition in which the determining factors were nativist pride, religious prejudice, and political bigotry.

Al Smith was the son of poor Irish Catholics and had started to work in the Fulton Street Fish Market in New York when he was twelve. He rose in the Democratic Party as a loyal Tammany man who was also a progressive reformer and served four times as governor of New York between 1919 and 1929. People claimed that Smith's success was proof of his "Americanism," the philosophy that merit determined success in a pluralistic society. There was open public debate about the suitability of a Catholic for the presidency and whether Smith would break the unwritten law that no Catholic could ever become president. In 1926 Catholics accounted for 15.97 percent of the population. Of the remaining 84.03 percent, 27.36 belonged to Protestant churches and only 3.50 percent attended Jewish synagogues; 53.17 percent had no religious affiliation. These statistics, however, belied the religious intolerance of the age.

At the Democratic National Convention in Houston, Texas, in 1928, responsible southerners reckoned that after the fiasco of 1924 it was better to risk the handicaps of Smith's Catholicism and his wetness than to alienate four million Catholics in New York, Illinois, New Jersey, and Massachusetts. As the Democratic Party's first ever Catholic nominee, Smith compounded his problems by taking advice from a golfing cabinet of rich industrialists such as General Motors executive John J. Raskob, whom he made his campaign manager. Smith and Raskob hoped to convince the electorate that the Democrats had the support of big business. Raskob, however, alienated the rank and file of the party by his own assertive Catholicism and his wetness.

After his nomination as Republican candidate, Herbert Hoover promised a federal commission to investigate prohibition, which he referred to as "a great social and economic experiment, noble in motive and far-reaching in purpose." His words, reduced by others to "noble experiment," proved offensive to diehard wets and drys. But Hoover's proposal served to undermine Smith's appeal to all wets: they could now vote for Hoover on the assumption that he would first investigate and then change the law. The underlying issues of the campaign were partly obscured under a decent veil of loyalty to the supposed reform of prohibition. As poet lariat, the cowboy satirist Will Rogers observed, "If you think this country ain't dry, you just watch 'em vote; and if you think this country ain't wet, you just watch them drink. You see, when they vote, it's counted, when they drink, it ain't."

Al Smith's main strategy was a whistle-stop tour of the country. He faced harassment in the South, the West, and the Midwest by the Ku Klux Klan. In 1928 it was still a vibrant force. The Klan received covert support from various Protestant churches, led by the unscrupulous and venal Methodist bishop James A. Cannon, Jr., now the leading spokesman of the Anti-Saloon League. Democratic Party regular Cannon diverted moneys to campaign against the party nominee and also into his own pocket. He went on extensive campaign tours, deliberately inciting religious and ethnic hatred:

> Governor Smith wants the Italians, the Sicilians, the Poles, and the Russian Jews. That kind has given us a stomach ache. We have been unable to assimilate such people in our national life, so we shut the door to them. But Smith says, "Give me that kind of people." He wants the kind of dirty people you find today on the sidewalks of New York.

There was a heavy turnout at the polls, with 67.5 percent of voters casting their ballots. Smith won the largest popular vote of any Democrat to that time—15,016,169 (40.7 percent). Hoover took 21,391, 993 (58.2 percent). He had 444 votes in the electoral college to Smith's 87. Six southern states went Republican (Florida, Kentucky, North Carolina, Tennessee, Texas, and Virginia). But normally industrial Massachusetts and Rhode Island went Democrat—as they had done in 1912. Although Smith lost Pennsylvania, Illinois, and Wisconsin, he narrowed the Republican lead there. Senator Thaddeus H. Caraway of Arkansas observed that the election proved that most Americans wanted prohibition, but whether it was for themselves or their neighbors, he could not say.

Never again would the Democrats count on the Solid South. Instead, they would search out new catchment areas. Smith, moreover, inaugurated a trend that was to make the Democrats the future majority party. In the twelve most populous cities, the Democrats had a majority of 38,000 in 1928, whereas the Republican majority had been 1,252,000 there in 1924. Thus, Smith cleared the path for Franklin D. Roosevelt's victory in 1932. More women voted than in 1920 and 1924, and Catholic women gave their votes to Smith. As for Congress, the Republicans took 267 seats in the House, against 163 for the Democrats and 1 for the Farmer-Laborites. They now had 56 seats in the Senate against 39 for the Democrats and 1 for the Farmer-Laborites. The Republicans won 30 gubernatorial contests and the Democrats 18. Having claimed responsibility for the boom of the 1920s, both Republicans and drys had to take the blame for the Wall Street crash of 1929 and the depression of the 1930s.

The defeat of Al Smith was the last victory for the second Ku Klux Klan. The *Washington Post* of July 6, 1929, estimated that there were only 82,000 Klansmen left. On November 3, 1930, it reported that the figure was 35,000. This decomposition was partly due to public disgust at Klan atrocities and feuds, but more than that it occurred because the initial causes of Klan enrollment—postwar xenophobia and inner-city frustration—had been dissipated by the siren calls of the cities, eroding rural prejudice.

Political life had turned Al Smith's head. No longer a protagonist for the workingman, Smith coveted an ostentatious lifestyle. Thus, John J. Raskob gave Al Smith a consolation prize that proved his best memorial: presidency of the Empire State Building. Raskob conceived the idea for the Empire State Building in early 1929. By August he had raised the money, selected architects Shreve, Lamb, and Harmon and contractors Starret Brothers and Eken, and found the site on the corner of Fifth Avenue and Thirty-Fourth Street—occupied by the magnificent Waldorf-Astoria Hotel, only thirty-two years old. The Waldorf was demolished.

Potential tenants of the new edifice were promised that the Empire State would be open in May 1931—and it was. Raskob, Smith, and Company decided that the Empire State Building should look like a pencil. Otherwise, they would fill in the space allowed by the 1916 zoning law and create a typical setback skyscraper of the 1920s. Hence, the Empire State's five-story base gave way to a skillful piece of massing of 102 stories crowned by a rounded tower, 1,250 feet above street level. The facade mixed granite and limestone with nickel and aluminum. It was soon recognized as an architectural masterpiece, dominating the cityscape and yet blending with it. It became the symbol of corporate America, U.S. technological prowess, and the city of New York. By then, everything had tumbled on the sidewalks below.

The Brittle Glass of Welfare Capitalism

In the Jazz Age American prosperity stood on brittle glass. Despite the Republican party's insistence that the 1920s was a decade of progress and prosperity, in simple economic terms society was digging its own grave, its citizens the victims of an inadequate economic mechanism. In 1929 the mirror cracked when the economy was shattered by the Wall Street crash. The crisis for the old order had been brewing for many years. The climax lasted for three months—September, October, and November of 1929. The consequences continued for many a year afterward as the Great Depression spread its shade over the land.

On the surface all seemed well with the American economy. Between 1925 and 1929 the number of factories increased from 183,877 to 206,663. The value of their production for the domestic market rose from $34 billion to $37.78 billion. The Federal Reserve index of industrial production rose from 67 in 1921 to 100 in 1925 and then to 126 in June 1929. However, there were cracks in the economic plates just below the surface. In the early 1920s economic growth was greatest in construction and the automobile industry. Starting in 1925, both were in decline. Automobile production continued to grow in the late 1920s but at a slower rate than previously. This, in turn, reduced the production of steel, rubber, glass, and other tributary industries. By 1929 all of these industries were overextended. Since there was no new industry to supersede the auto industry as the pivot of the industrial economy, it was inevitable that a serious recession would ensue.

In the bituminous coal industry, the boom of World War I was followed by a crisis in overproduction with domestic markets becoming glutted. Too many mines producing too much coal set a context in which miners struck in 1919 and 1922. The new president of the United Mine Workers (UMW), John Llewellyn Lewis, was forced to accept a settlement that preserved existing wage rates but gave no protection for jobs. In the 1920s the continuous surplus of labor meant that a typical miner was working between 142 and 220 days a year and often bringing home less than $2 a day, instead of the expected $7.50 union minimum. Miners and their families lived on diets of beans, euphemistically nicknamed "miners' strawberries," gravy, and bread. Between 1920 and 1927 the number of miners working in the industry fell from over 700,000 to approximately 575,000.

Throughout the 1920s unemployment was high and a continuous worry for most workers. According to the *Historical Statistics of the United States* (1975), unemployment was 11.7 percent of the civilian work force in 1921 and then fell to an average of 3.5 percent in the period 1923–29. But Paul H. Douglas, surveying only transportation, mining, building, and construction in *Real Wages in the United States, 1890–1926* (1930), provides an average of 12.95 percent in 1921–26. Those who were working included many who wanted to work full time but had only part-time employment. Without the sort of welfare support provided later, part-time work made it more difficult to save for periods of total unemployment. In Muncie, Indiana, in 1924 43 percent of one sample of working-class families for the Lynds' *Middletown* (1929) lost at least a month of work; 24.2 percent lost three or more months of work. Analysts J. Frederick Dewhurst and Ernest A. Tupper discovered (*Social and Economic Character of Unemployment in Philadelphia*, 1929) an unemployment rate of 18.9 percent in some industrial neighborhoods.

If many working-class families were poor while employed, unemployment plunged them into deep poverty. Clinch Caulkins in *Some Folks Won't Work* (1930) reports that the wife of an unemployed roofer told him, "When my husband's working steady, I can just manage; when he's out, things go back. First I stop on the damp wash, then on the food, and then the rent goes behind." Some families would rather almost starve than accept charity. One family lived on nothing but bread and tea for six weeks. A father waited on a street corner at lunchtime "for fear if he came home, he'd be tempted to eat what they have been able to put on the table for the children." Those who suffered malnutrition were prone to such illnesses as pneumonia. Some people had nervous breakdowns or committed suicide by gassing themselves.

Employers, anxious to prevent another brouhaha like that of 1919, set about nurturing a sense of loyalty among their employees; they applied modern technology to the world of the worker. Moreover, they realized that they could get more out of their workers by cultivating their loyalty and dependence than by relying forever on the threat of wage cuts and unemployment. Housing, pension schemes, stock sharing, recreational services, health care, and educational benefits were offered to some workers who agreed not to join unions and who agreed not to strike. This was known as welfare capitalism. A 1919 Bureau of Labor Statistics special report on industrial welfare indicated that there was a broad movement by management to stimulate corporate loyalty among employees. Of 431 establishments surveyed, 375 had some type of medical program, 265 reported having hospital facilities, 75 had pension plans, 80 had established disability benefit plans, and 152 had constructed recreation facilities for their workers. At least 6 million workers came to be covered by welfare programs in the 1920s, and a survey of 1926 found that half of the 1,500 largest American companies were operating comprehensive schemes.

Even at its peak, welfare capitalism covered only a minority of the workforce, and often schemes were piecemeal. The influence of welfare capitalism was felt most strongly in company towns, where stringent rules already restricted workers' lives in and outside the plant. The illusion of corporate paternalism was also developed in the form of employee representation plans and workers' councils. Drawing on the arbitration guidelines established by the War Labor Board, companies offered workers the right to a formal grievance procedure within strictly defined limits. Between 1919 and 1924 some four hundred firms established representation plans that served not only to redress petty complaints but also to deflect and absorb more militant demands. Companies preferred to channel workers' legitimate grievances, rather than see them driven into union ranks. Company unions were featured in corporate publicity as a shining example of America's industrial democracy.

Companies also made attempts to reduce the need for highly skilled labor by mechanizing the production process. For example, the Ford assembly line achieved enormous increases in productivity by transferring the decision as to the pace of hard work away from the worker and into the hands of the manager who controlled the production line. "The delivery of work instead of leaving it to the workmen's initiative to find it" was how Henry Ford described it. With the automobile in high demand, the Ford Motor Company's plants were able to produce 31,000 automobiles in 1925 with virtually the same machinery that had produced 25,000 cars in 1920.

Because of his technological advances and his highly successful factory management, Henry Ford's schemes of employment were accepted by society at large. His five-dollar-a-day minimum wage for workers and his insistence on high standards of social behavior from them were generally assumed to be beneficial. However, minister and theologian Reinhold Niebuhr, who had a parish in Detroit, thought differently. He became a contributing editor of the *Christian Century* in 1923 and, gleaning evidence from his parishioners, wrote a series of articles criticizing Ford. He showed that Ford's average annual wage was low, and he also exposed other malpractices of the system. Ford's employees were broken by their work despite the five-dollar wage and the five-day week. Niebuhr knew that they were often dismissed in summary fashion at middle age, unfit for work elsewhere and emotionally dejected. After General Motors began to outsell Ford, in 1927 Ford discontinued the Model T, closed his factories, modernized them, and then reopened them for production of the new Model A. In the interim period some sixty thousand workers were unemployed. When the factories reopened, the former workers were engaged as new employees, starting again at five dollars a day. Thus the new Ford car cost Ford's men at least $50 million in lost wages, not to mention the families broken up in the period of unemployment.

Saddled with incompetent leaders, disabled by sophisticated anti-union strategies by employers, divided internally along racial, ethnic, and political lines, the AFL dithered and foundered. AFL leaders steadfastly refused to pay attention to members' demands—let alone the 85 to 90 percent of unorganized workers. In an era marked by its low strike rate and falling union rolls, corporate paternalism could switch rapidly to overt repression if workers stepped too far out of line. Of 1,845 injunctions issued by federal courts to ban strike action in the period 1800 to 1930, almost half were issued in the 1920s. Yet, on the shop floor, informal groups of workers continued to restrict output and undermine management's attempts to restructure the workplace. Elsewhere workers made increasingly militant demands through workers' councils that occasionally took on a life of their own. Moreover, radicals who had managed to escape the full force of the Great Red Scare began to reorganize at local levels.

In agriculture, economic crisis was chronic. From 1921 on, American farmers paid the inevitable price for capacity production during World War I. Europe now had less need of American grain. The steady supply of bumper harvests amounted to gross overproduction. The fall in the value of farm products from $21.4 billion in 1919 to $11.8 billion in 1929 suggested an impending disaster for American agriculture in the 1930s. Other statistics confirmed the depressing trend. Farm tenancy increased from 38.1 percent of farmers in 1920 to 42.4 percent in 1930. The percentage of farms mortgaged also rose from 37.2 percent in 1920 to 42 percent in 1930.

In Congress farmers won the support of the farm bloc, an active pressure group of mainly Republican members who designed farm legislation to ease agricultural problems. The Packers and Stockyards Act of 1921 awarded the Department of Agriculture considerable powers over the meatpacking industry and broke the big meat-packers' monopoly over the stockyards. The Grain Futures Act eliminated much of the fraud and speculation in grain exchanges. The Capper-Volstead Act of 1922 released farm cooperation from the antitrust laws. Senator George W. Norris of Nebraska proposed a revolutionary scheme whereby government warehouses would store the surplus, public corporations would buy it, and government agencies would sell and transport it abroad. Instead, Congress passed the Agricultural Credits Act of 1923, aimed principally at livestock farming. It allowed the farmers to borrow money, using their crops as collateral, postponing the sale of the crops, and storing them for periods of six months to three years until prices were more favorable.

Two midwestern industrialists, George N. Peek and Gen. Hugh S. Johnson, realized from their own bitter experience that the essential problem was that farmers had to buy their equipment in a domestic market, in which industry was protected by high tariffs, but they had to sell produce in a world that was not so protective. Peek and Johnson argued that what agriculture needed was some parity or equality between the purchasing power of agriculture and that of industry, what they called a fair-exchange value. To achieve it, they suggested that agriculture regulate its supply to meet domestic demand. This would entail dumping the surplus abroad at current world prices but maintaining high prices for produce sold at home by imposing a high tariff on foreign produce. They wanted farmers to compensate the federal government, by means of special equalization fees, for any losses the government sustained on produce sold cheaply abroad.

Senator Charles L. McNary of Oregon (a wheat state) and Congressman Gilbert N. Haugen of Iowa (a corn state) proposed the Peek-Johnson scheme to Congress. Despite support from business, farm organizations, and Secretary of Agriculture Henry C. Wallace, the House defeated the proposal on June 3, 1924. Eastern Republicans, acting on instructions from President Calvin Coolidge, had opposed the plan. The farm bloc responded with a proposal covering six basic commodities (cotton, wheat, corn, rice, hogs, and tobacco). Congress passed this second bill in 1927. The bill also proposed a Federal Farm Bureau of twelve members, one for each Federal Land Bank District, to administer the scheme. The board would have had the power to raise domestic prices to the level of the official tariff on each item. The board would assess the equalization fee on the processing, transportation, and sale of crops—rather than on the income of the farmers. Coolidge vetoed the bill in 1927 and again in 1928 when Congress passed it a second time. The farm bloc could not find the two-thirds majority to override Coolidge's veto.

Lean years for farmers were also hard for industries that served farms. Rural banks failed in the 1920s, as did other banks. In the prosperous year of 1928, 549 banks failed; in 1929, 640 did so. Here were sure signs of an economy in deep trouble.

The general crisis of capitalism came to a head with riotous investment in the stock market. Heedless of the basic flaws in the American system, those with money to invest did so eagerly and greedily in the 1920s. Well before the Wall Street crash, there was the Florida land boom of the midtwenties, an episode that bore all the hallmarks of a classic speculation bubble.

1929: Wall Street Lays an Egg!

No single individual was responsible for the Wall Street crash of 1929. Thousands of people contributed freely to the debacle. In the early twenties, stock prices were low; in the mid-twenties, they began to rise. The main index for those years was provided by the *New York Times* industrial averages, an aggregate of twenty-five leading industrial stocks. Between May 1924 and December 1925, the *Times* averages rose from 106 to 181. By December 1927 the *Times* averages were 245, a gain of sixty-nine points in the year.

The great bull market began in earnest on Saturday, March 3, 1928. For instance, General Motors stocks rose from 140 to 144 that day and in the next week passed the psychologically significant figure of 150. There was a specific explanation. Since Henry Ford had discontinued the Model T in 1927 and re-equipped his plants for the Model A, production of Ford cars would be curtailed. GM was to gain customers at Ford's expense.

Very few people across America were actually buying and selling stocks and shares. In 1929 when the total population of the United States was 121,767,000, the member firms of twenty-nine exchanges had no more than 1,548,707 clients altogether. Of these, 1,371,920 were clients of member firms of the New York Stock Exchange. Those involved in the precarious and potentially damaging marginal trading were only slightly more than 50,000. The astonishing fact about the stock market speculation in 1929 was not the extent of public participation. It was that it had become pivotal to the culture.

The economy had already entered a depression ahead of the stock market. Industrial production peaked in June 1929, when the Federal Reserve index stood at 126. Thereafter, it began to decline. By October the Federal Reserve index of industrial production was 117. Later, economist Thomas Wilson maintained that the ensuing fall in the stock market was reflecting a change that had already occurred in industry, rather than the other way around.

A few shareholders, suspicious of market fluctuations, quietly sold stock at advantageous prices. In time, everyone began selling as much as possible. Real panic set in on the morning of "Black Thursday," October 24, 1929, when 12,894,650 shares changed hands in a vicious spiral of deflation. In the mad scramble to sell, people were ready to part with shares for next to nothing. To the *New York Herald Tribune* of October 25, 1929, Wall Street on Black Thursday was like a carnival, with huge crowds in a holiday mood surging around the narrow streets of the financial centers and with hotels nearby overflowing with brokers' men. The atmosphere was most tense, with enraged brokers vandalizing stock tickers and rumors circulating about some brokers having committed suicide by jumping out of windows. But it was prices that were falling through the floor.

"Black Tuesday," October 29, 1929, was the bitter climax of everything that had gone wrong before. The amount of trading and the fall in prices was greater than ever. Altogether, 16,410,030 sales took place, and the *Times* averages fell 43 points, wiping out all the gains of the overvalued investment trusts. Goldman, Sachs Trading Corporation fell from 60 to 35; Blue Ridge fell from 10 to 3. The collapse of the stock market was greeted with blunt vulgarity by the weekly stage

Everything About to Tumble

Alexander Calder, *The Brass Family* (1929), brass wire sculpture, 64" × 41" × 8½".
Alexander Calder (1898–1976) became America's foremost sculptor, noted for his invention of the mobile, a hanging sculpture in motion. He began his professional career as a
freelance newspaper artist and sketched both the Ringling Brothers' and the Barnum and
Bailey Circuses, which remained a continuous source of artistic inspiration for him. *The
Brass Family*, in which an overdeveloped athlete supports six other acrobats, demonstrates Calder's humor as well as his skill in ink drawings. (Collection of Whitney Museum of American Art, New York; gift of the artist)

paper *Variety*. Its headline of October 30, 1929, was "WALL STREET LAYS AN EGG."

The period of great bankruptcies began. The first major casualty of the crash outside New York was the Foshay enterprises of Minneapolis, a floundering utility company, supposedly worth $20 million but already deeply in debt. The Wall Street crash eliminated potential investors who might have rallied to it. Now they found their savings wiped out. The market continued to fall inevitably until Wednesday, November 13, 1929. The *Times* averages then stood at 224, compared with 542 in early September. All told, stocks and shares lost $40 billion in the fall of 1929.

The Wall Street crash exposed the underlying instability of the American economic system—the overexpansion of industry and the farm surpluses, the unequal distribution of wealth, and the weak banking structure. In his classic account, *The Great Crash—1929* (1954), economist John Kenneth Galbraith emphasizes five principal weaknesses of an unsound economy. The first was the bad distribution of income. The top 5 percent of the population received a third of all personal income. This inequality meant that the survival of the economy depended on a very high level of investment by the wealthy few, or a high level of luxury spending, or both. Since there was a limit to the amount of food, housing, and clothing the rich could consume, they must spend their money either on luxuries or investment. Both luxury and investment spending, however, were subject to changing circumstances.

A second feature was the bad corporate structure. The most damaging weakness was the great infrastructure of holding companies and investment trusts. Holding companies controlled a majority of shares in production companies, especially in the fields of railroads, public utilities, and entertainment. Even in economic crises, holding companies insisted on their dividends, no matter the essential economic needs of the operating (that is, the productive) companies from which they derived their great wealth. Thus, the operating companies had to give priority to paying dividends rather than being able to invest in new plants or improved machinery that might have led to higher production. The system kept the operating companies weak and fueled deflation.

A third feature was the inherently weak banking structure of the United States, with an excessive number of independent banks. In the first six months of 1929, as many as 346 banks with average deposits of $115 million failed. This was a tyranny of the weak. When one bank failed, others froze their assets, thus inviting investors to ask for their money back. In turn, public pressure led to the collapse of ever more banks. Isolated instances of bank mismanagement led to a chain reaction in which neighboring banks collapsed like a row of dominoes. When a depression hit employment and people withdrew their savings, bank failures proliferated.

A fourth problem was the imbalance of trade. The United States had become a creditor nation in the course of World War I. After the war, however, the surplus of exports over imports, which had once paid for European loans, continued. High tariffs restricted imports. This factor impeded the ability of other countries to repay their loans. During the 1920s they tried to meet their payments in gold while, at the same time, the United States was increasing its loans to foreign countries. Congress impeded further repayment of foreign loans by trade when it passed the Hawley-Smoot Tariff (signed by President Herbert Hoover on June 17, 1930), which raised tariff levels decisively. The upshot was a sharp reduction in trade and general fault on repayment.

The fifth weakness was the poor state of economic intelligence. The people running the economic machinery simply did not fully understand the system they were operating. Official dependence on conventional wisdom, the convenience of formula without the discomfort of analysis—such as maintaining the gold standard, balancing the budget, and opposing inflation—all proved insuperable barriers to an early solution of the crisis. Moreover, it was harmful to the economy as a whole for the people in charge to equate the national interest with the special interests of the businesses they served.

Now, the greater fell with the lesser. Charles E. Mitchell of the House of Morgan, Ivan Kreuger, the Swedish Match King, and officials of the Union Inndustrial Bank of Flint, Michigan, were among the financiers found out for various forms of sharp practice.

The causes of the Wall Street crash were complex. The results were plain for all to see. The tawdry affluence of the twenties went out like a light.

CHAPTER 9

The World Broken in Two

"T H E   W O R L D broke in two in 1922 or thereabouts, and the persons recalled in these sketches slide back into yesterdays seven thousand years."

That was how novelist Willa Cather saw the great divide of a crucial year in a preface to a collection of her essays (1936). There was the successful conclusion of the Washington Naval Conference, which set a seal on the postwar settlement, but also significant developments in mass politics abroad: the ascent of Benito Mussolini as fascist prime minister of Italy and the official transformation of the Russian empire of the czars into the Soviet Union, or Union of Soviet Socialist Republics (USSR). More ominously, the death of Lenin in 1924 led to the ascendancy of Joseph Stalin in Russia.

Fascist Italy and Communist Russia represented two different totalitarian approaches to government of mass society. Both Mussolini and Stalin established absolute dictatorships. Lenin had already established a power structure that made Stalin's dictatorship possible, including the collectivization of industry, and had created precedents for mass terror through the terrifying apparatus of a police state. Italy had ambitions in the Mediterranean and the Balkans. Weimar Germany wanted to regain the prewar position of Hohenzollern Germany. Soviet Russia wanted to regain the prewar position of Romanov Russia. Both coveted mastery of eastern Europe. The upshot of that contest depended on the downward economic spiral of the Weimar Republic and the enforced industrialization of the USSR.

Willa Cather's pithy reflection struck at the great divide between totalitarian societies and democratic capitalism, itself a descendant of liberalism and laissez-faire. On the outcome of their conflict hung the fate of the world.

Include Me Out

The story of U.S. foreign policy in the 1920s is not as isolationist as the myth. Isolationism was more a matter of instinct than of reason. It is certainly true that the United States enacted a series of measures—the immigration laws of 1921 and 1924 and the high tariffs of 1922 and 1930—that were isolationist. It is also true that the United States's absence from the League of Nations was a

The Republicans' attempt "to do something as good as the League" was the Washington Naval Conference of 1921–22, whose principal achievement was the Five Power Naval Treaty, concluded in the Diplomatic Room of the State Department on February 6, 1922, and signed by (*from left to right at the table*) Augusto Rosso of Italy, H. G. Chilton of Britain, Secretary of State Charles Evans Hughes, André de la Boulaye of France, and Masanao Hanihara of Japan. (Photo by National Photo Company; Library of Congress)

diplomatic handicap for U.S. statesmen. America's commitments in Latin America and its financial loans to the Western powers involved it in negotiations with other nations that it could not conduct formally through the League.

Despite the official rhetoric of its foreign policy, the United States was to play a decisive role in international economic affairs. Through gifts and loans, it supported the postwar rehabilitation of Europe, in particular providing France, Germany, and Italy with huge advances to stabilize their currencies. In addition, the United States funded construction in Austria, Poland, and Yugoslavia. American money was also used to fund the digging of oil wells in the Middle East, the planting of rubber trees in Malaya and the Netherlands East Indies (NEI) and sugar cane in Cuba, and the development of public utilities in Tokyo and Shanghai. Corporations, such as Standard Oil, Ford, General Motors, International Harvester, and Singer, continued to establish manufacturing companies in Europe, China, and the Caribbean.

All this commercial expansion provoked criticism on both sides of the Atlantic. Historian Charles Beard wrote in *Harper's* of March 1929 about "the American Invasion of Europe," noting its "prose against poetry; dollars against sacrifice; calculation against artistic abandon." The debate continued throughout the twentieth century. The most significant development discerned by Beard was that the export of U.S. industrial products, cultural ideas, and customs was remodeling modern societies across the world. Competitive indigenous companies were obliged to adopt American techniques of mass production and assembly lines. The transformation was most marked in Japan, but even the relatively backward industrial system of the USSR began to consider a new technology named "Fordismus." Later, in 1933, Detroit auto workers Walter and Victor Reuther visited the Soviet Union and spent nearly two years in Gorky, working in a large auto plant and helping the Russians master their machinery—much of it purchased from Ford.

Communication was as significant as manufacturing. And a new form of American-based international company spread its tentacles far and wide. In 1920 Sosthenes Behn founded International Telephone and Telegraph (ITT) as a holding company for several Caribbean telephone companies. ITT was an American conglomerate that Behn intended as an international complement to AT&T. In 1930 Behn signaled ITT's colossal financial resources by opening an office at 67 Broad Street, New York.

Furthermore, Europe was being invaded by U.S. tourists en masse, at the rate of about five hundred thousand each year in the 1920s. Whether on business or pleasure, U.S. travelers in Europe and Asia began to insist on U.S. cultural standards of hospitality in a way that was to transform foreign cultures inexorably. "Can Paris be retaken by the Parisians?" asked the *New York Herald Tribune* of January 24, 1926: "The French claim they cannot walk on the Boulevard St. Germain and hear a word of their native tongue."

Since the United States controlled much of the world's industry and wealth, led international trade, and enjoyed huge capital resources, its economics and diplomacy continued to have a profound impact across the planet. The United States could no more return to its isolation in 1921 than it could have ignored World War I in 1914. Yet three U.S. presidents had little understanding of the changing world that the United States was doing so much to shape. Thus, the United States failed to develop a coordinated strategy in foreign affairs.

Nevertheless, Charles Evans Hughes was an imaginative and persuasive secretary of state (1921–25). His dignified manner and Jove-like appearance lent style to any event he attended. However, any controversial proposal from Hughes in favor of international cooperation would have aroused suspicion among certain formidable members of Congress. Woodrow Wilson's implacable foe, Henry Cabot Lodge of Massachusetts, remained chairman of the Senate Foreign Relations Committee until his death in November 1924. He was succeeded by William E. Borah of Idaho, whose own intransigence was supported by that of another leading member of the committee, Hiram Johnson of California. However, after a Senate resolution declaring that the war was over and that the United States reserved rights mentioned in the Treaty of Versailles, Hughes negotiated treaties with Germany, Austria, and Hungary, to which the Senate consented in October 1921.

Having rejected Wilsonian remedies, President Warren Harding was conscious that the Republicans needed to do something "just as good as the League." This was to be the Washington Naval Conference. Peace sentiment in the United States, nurtured by Wilson but frustrated by the turn of events in 1919 and 1920, bridled at the thought of another arms and naval race among the great powers. Even isolationist Senator William E. Borah thought that the incipient naval rivalry between the United States and Japan would end the way of all such rivalries. Already on December 14, 1920, he had tabled a resolution in Congress calling for a reduction in armaments for July 1921. Moreover, he suggested to Charles Evans Hughes that the United States, Britain, and Japan should abstain from further shipbuilding.

Hughes had the prestige and personal skill to avoid the sort of partisan antagonism between president and Senate that had disfigured Wilson's last years. Furthermore, he was eager to repair declining relations with Japan. He feared that Japan, resentful of the Immigration Quota Act of 1921 and antagonized by American economic rivalry in the Far East, might invoke the Anglo-Japanese alliance of 1902 to claim British support against the United States. Britain agreed to a naval conference in Washington. It had no intention of losing American friendship over Japan.

To ensure maximum public support, the Harding administration prepared the ground in advance. First, the conference would be held in Washington. Second, the president would not take part himself. The U.S. delegation would include Secretary of State Hughes, elder statesman Elihu Root, and, from the Senate Foreign Relations Committee, Henry Cabot Lodge for the Republicans and Oscar W. Underwood for the Democrats. The implication was clear: had Woodrow Wilson shown such discretion, the outcome would have been very different in Paris and Washington in 1919–20.

Tensions among the powers added to the success of the conference. On the day before the first session, November 12, 1921, the Unknown Soldier was buried at Arlington, an ideal ceremonial prelude. In his opening address at the conference, Hughes took the initiative and asked representatives of Britain, Japan, France, Italy, Belgium, the Netherlands, Portugal, and China to sink 1,878,093 tons of capital ships—half of the vessels afloat and in drydock. The agreement was simplistically expressed in the ratio: 5: 5: 3. In addition, the powers accepted Hughes's proposal that no new ships should be built over ten years, and a limit of 35,000 tons was to be imposed on new battleships.

The total tonnage for battleships and cruisers finally agreed by the powers was:

United States	525,850	distributed among 18 ships
Britain	558,950	distributed among 20 ships
Japan	301,320	distributed among 10 ships
France	221,170	distributed among 10 ships
Italy	182,800	distributed among 10 ships

The main Five Power Treaty was supposed to last until 1936, but beginning on December 31, 1934, any country could give two years' notice of withdrawing from it. Japan's determination to seek a bigger ratio was submerged by an agreement with the United States that neither nation would expand its Pacific naval bases. Hughes knew that Congress would not have approved funds for building up U.S. defenses in Guam and the Philippines. Moreover, he hoped that, if Japan were free from fear of attack, her statesmen would pursue a moderate foreign policy. To allay mutual suspicion, the United States, Britain, and Japan signed a Four Power Treaty with France. This superseded the Anglo-Japanese Alliance of 1902. The four powers pledged themselves to "respect their rights in relation to their insular possessions in the region of the Pacific Ocean."

In addition, a Nine Power Treaty acknowledged the Open Door in China. All nations attending the conference agreed to respect China's sovereignty and integrity. Japan agreed to restore the Shandong Peninsula (taken from Germany) to China and to start withdrawing troops from eastern Siberia. Initially, the powers made halfhearted efforts to abide by their agreements. Throughout the 1920s the U.S. Navy was to be maintained at maximum strength and modernized. Only its overage vessels and those still under construction were scrapped according to the terms of the Washington Conference.

As if to recognize that a successful foreign policy could be conducted only by an expanded and informed civil service, successive presidents and secretaries of state reorganized the State Department in the course of the 1920s. The diplomatic and consular services were merged and the civil service was expanded to administer them, providing increased professional opportunities for career diplomats. Yet the expansion was probably smaller than the need. The State Department's annual budget was about $2 million in the 1920s. Its personnel based at home numbered about six hundred.

In the 1920s world economic affairs were dominated by two interrelated problems: reparations demanded of Germany by the victorious European powers, and repayment of debts contracted by the Allies with the United States.

Although presidential administrations might be willing to adopt a flexible approach to the collection of war debts, according to the varying abilities of debtor nations to repay loans, Congress was obdurate. On February 9, 1922, it stipulated that the maximum deadline for repayment would be June 15, 1947, and that the minimum rate of interest would be 4.25 percent. A World War Foreign Debt Commission would administer repayment. Britain and France took offense at the Debt Funding Act that laid down these provisions. Not only did they consider that they had, from the start, borne the highest losses—human fatalities and economic disruption—in a common war, but they also claimed a close relationship between their own debts and the reparations owed to them by Germany. Nevertheless, in January 1923 Britain and the United States agreed to repayment of Britain's debt of $4.6 billion over a period of sixty-two years at an average interest of 3.3 percent. The agreement set a precedent. The United States then went on to make similar agreements with fifteen other countries by 1927. France and Italy secured easier terms than Britain. Britain now set about repaying its debt, which entailed exacting tribute from Germany.

European peoples might be moved by the economic difficulties of the new Weimar Republic in Germany, but their statesmen did not heed arguments of common sense or compassion. Various countries continued to insist on excessive payments of $33 billion in reparations from Germany. The Weimar Republic could not possibly meet those demands, but nevertheless, the League approved them on May 5, 1921. Germany paid two installments in 1921 but none in 1922. On January 11, 1923, under instructions from French prime minister Raymond Poincaré, French troops occupied the Ruhr to punish Germany for default. German finances, already floundering, were now in chaos, and the deutsche mark became worthless. Charles Evans Hughes suggested the formation of a European payment commission, established in November 1923 under the chairmanship of Chicago banker Charles Gates Dawes. The commission agreed on solutions that would also help Germany reorganize its finances.

The Dawes Plan, intended as an interim measure, was intended to make Germany solvent and to transfer any surplus reserves to the Allies. To stabilize the German currency, Dawes proposed an international loan of $200 million in gold; the reorganization of the Reichsbank under Allied supervision; and a new coinage, the reichsmark, set at 23.8 cents. As to reparations, Dawes proposed payments on a sliding scale, beginning at $250 million and rising over five years to $625 million, with arrangements supervised by a new agent general, S. Parker Gilbert of the House of Morgan, who had to ensure that regular payments were made from a mix of funds, including the international loan, mortgages on principal industries, railroads, and taxes. The scheme went into operation September 1, 1924.

France was the country with the greatest interest in preserving peace. When the Senate refused to ratify the Treaty of Versailles, any chance of an Anglo-American guarantee to France against German aggression also lapsed. In 1927 James T. Shotwell, a professor at Columbia University and associate director of the Carnegie Endowment for International Peace, visited Paris. He persuaded the French foreign minister, Aristide Briand, that he had a practical alternative. This was the Outlawry of War. Rejecting the strategy of collective security because it was based on force, the American Committee for the Outlawry of War, founded in 1921 by Chicago businessman Salmon O. Levinson, conceived of a new international law prohibiting the use of force between nations.

The Outlawry of War had no appeal for Presidents Harding or Coolidge nor for Secretaries of State Hughes or Kellogg. The analogy with the tragicomedy of national prohibition was obvious—the scourges of alcoholism and war to be abolished by inadequate legislation. However, Briand did not intend the Outlawry of War to be an empty scabbard. He proposed a bilateral treaty between France and the United States. What he really wanted was the original U.S. guarantee. Neither Coolidge nor his secretary of state, Frank B. Kellogg (1923–29), was deceived. They could not enter into an "entangling alliance" with France. Neither could they ignore the well-organized support for the scheme in the United States among pacifist societies—especially in the year of aviator Charles A. Lindbergh's epochal solo flight across the Atlantic.

Former trust-buster Kellogg was an ineffective secretary of state. Perpetually harassed, he was called "Nervous Nellie" by sneering colleagues. Coolidge was ill informed about foreign affairs but unwilling to admit it. Yet, together, president and secretary of state saw how to outmaneuver Briand with a counterproposal. Senator William E. Borah suggested making the scheme unilateral. Once other leading powers had agreed, the French had to accept the international ban on war that they themselves had first proposed. On August 27, 1928, the Kellogg-Briand treaty, also known as the Pact of Paris, was signed initially by representatives of fifteen nations. The Senate ratified it in jocular, dismissive vein on January 15, 1929, with only a single dissenting vote.

Perhaps the well-intentioned spirit of the Kellogg-Briand Pact to Outlaw War was responsible for transforming the hesitancy of the naval conference in Geneva in 1927 to a willingness to adopt more positive declarations in London in 1930. The London Conference, from January 21 to April 22, 1930, was attended by the new secretary of state, Henry L. Stimson (1929–33), and the secretary of the navy, Charles E. Adams. The upshot was a reduction in ship tonnages, leaving the United States with 464,300, Britain with 474,500, and Japan with 272,000. A new provision, article 22, forbade submarines to attack without warning or without caring for passengers and crew. The Senate ratified the London treaty by 58 votes to 9. Afterward, it became a matter of pride for the different nations to boast about their flagrant violations, especially with regard to submarines. The nations' good intentions were supported neither by the selfless acts, the sacrifice of arms, nor the national autonomy, nor even by the diplomatic cooperation, that could convert the dream of peace into reality.

The Politics of Oil

Nothing demonstrated the new lubrication of international affairs by the covert alliance of big business and government more than oleaginous politics—the politics of oil.

The seven major oil companies (Standard Oil of New Jersey [from 1934 to 1960, Standard-Vacuum, and starting in 1972, Exxon], Standard Oil of California [later Socal], Mobil, Gulf, the Texas Company [created 1902 and known as Texaco from 1959], Shell, and BP [British Petroleum]), sometimes known as

A harbinger of the world broken in two in 1922 was the rise of Fascist dictator Benito Mussolini, the right-wing revolutionary who developed the Fascist party with the connivance of conservative politicians who considered him a charismatic leader who could stave off the threat of communist revolution in Italy. Once he became prime minister (1922–43), Mussolini used censorship, intimidation, and violence against opponents; achieved a concordat with the Vatican (1929) that redefined the territorial power of the pope; embarked on wars of conquest in Africa; and provided a model for the envious Adolf Hitler in Germany. To his English-speaking detractors, Mussolini was nothing better than "The Bullfrog of the Pontine Marshes," a mere functionary who made the trains run on time. Here, Mussolini, "Il Duce," harangues the crowd in the Coliseum. (Library of Congress)

the Seven Sisters, dominated the world of oil from the 1920s on. These were multinational companies, integrated worldwide, controlling their own production, transportation, distribution, and marketing.

In the 1920s the United States was by far the greatest consumer of oil, especially with the dramatic rise in the use of automobiles and their transformation of an entire society based on a superfluity of cheap oil. However, domestic supply was not endless. The director of the U.S. Geological Survey reported that the diminishing American supply could "best be described as precarious." There began a scramble for other supplies—as bitterly contested as the nineteenth-century scramble for territorial colonies. The Harding administration did not intend to divert remaining U.S. oil supplies to the rest of the world, nor would it simply look on if Britain and France attempted to exclude U.S. oil companies from the Middle East. The administration wanted to encourage the oil companies to find fresh supplies of oil. However, many administrators distrusted the oil companies as surely as muckraking journalists had distrusted Standard Oil at the turn of the century. Thus, administrators tried to use the major oil companies as discreetly as possible, instead of having the companies make their foreign policy for them.

Britain and France exploited their official mandates of Arab territory acquired from the defunct Ottoman empire to obtain and open new oil fields. At San Remo in 1919 they revived a 1914 agreement in which the Armenian entrepreneur Calouste Gulbenkian had created an oil syndicate, the Turkish Petroleum Company (TPC), assigning the Germans' prewar quarter-share to France. Gulbenkian received 5 percent. He also secured a clause whereby the participants agreed not to seek concessions in the territory from the defunct Ottoman empire from Turkey in the north, through Jordan and Syria to Saudi Arabia in the southeast. When the (initially) secret agreement was discovered, the U.S. ambassador in London protested that Britain was trying to corner the world's oil supply. However, the former Allies resolved their differences.

In 1922 Britain offered the United States 20 percent of the TPC, allowing, initially, seven American oil companies into the mandate, which later became the state of Iraq. At Ostend, Belgium, in 1928, the new government in Iraq signed an agreement with Britain, France, Gulbenkian, and five American oil companies: the TPC, now to be known as the Iraq Petroleum Company (IPC), remained British, but it would pay Iraq a royalty of 4 shillings (about one dollar) per ton of oil. Gulbenkian defined what he meant by the territory of the old Ottoman empire by taking a map and drawing a line around the territory with a red pencil. The so-called Red Line agreement included the richest oil-producing states of the Middle East, except Iran and Kuwait.

Five American oil companies had penetrated the Middle East, taking 23.5 percent of the IPC and slamming the Open Door behind them. Drilling began in April 1927. Six months later, oil prospectors struck one of the richest oil fields in the world. The IPC stoked resentment among the U.S. and British companies and the countries that it excluded. This led Standard Oil of New Jersey to cooperate with European Shell and BP, drawing together to restrain one another from ruinous competition and also to exclude other competitors. In 1928 Walter Teagle of Standard Oil met with Sir Henri Deterding of Shell and Sir John Cadman of BP at Achnacarry in the Scottish highlands. Each company understood that it could not achieve a global monopoly. They made an agreement of intent that was, in effect, to divide the world of oil into an international oil cartel in which they would curtail production to maintain prices and maximize profits. Whatever the economic rationale for such an agreement, it was democratically insupportable. The Achnacarry agreement was a plutocrats' plot to fix prices and divide the trade in oil.

Anthony Sampson concludes in *The Seven Sisters* (1976): "To protect American oil, the oil from anywhere else was fixed at the price in the Gulf of Mexico, whence most United States oil was shipped overseas, *plus* the standard freight charges for shipping the oil from the Gulf to its market." Since American oil was becoming ever more expensive and also faced competition from cheaper oil from Venezuela, the agreement was a blatant device to fix prices. The Achnacarry As-Is agreement was a statement of intent, eventually signed by fifteen American companies, including all seven sisters.

Dollar Diplomacy

Unlike the United States, sixteen Latin American countries had joined the League of Nations by March 1921. Only Argentina, Ecuador, Mexico, and the Dominican Republic remained outside the League. It is not surprising that the United States eventually recognized the advantages of using the League to mediate in Latin American disputes. In 1932 and 1933 the State Department twice accepted arbitration by the League; first in the so called Chaco War between Paraguay and Bolivia about a track of jungle, and second, in the war between Peru and Colombia over the village of Leticia. These quarrels made it clear that, no matter how constructive were U.S. strategies toward better relationships with Latin American states, the machinery to keep the peace was unreliable. Conventions on arbitration and conciliation were imperfect vehicles. Moreover, the United States could not collaborate effectively with the League while it remained a guest rather than a permanent member.

Successive presidents and secretaries of state tried to convince Latin American countries that the United States neither coveted additional territory nor wanted to interfere in others' internal affairs. Accordingly, throughout the 1920s, U.S. statesmen tried to revise Woodrow Wilson's policies toward Latin America, in particular Wilson's special criteria of recognition for regimes—that of constitutional legitimacy. Many Latins believed, however, that the true motive underlying U.S. interest was simple and brutal: economic penetration of their countries, the so-called dollar diplomacy.

U.S. companies established branches in Latin America. U.S. investors bought Latin American bonds. U.S. corporations looked increasingly to Latin America for material and markets. In certain respects, the economies of the northern and southern parts of the Western Hemisphere were complementary. The United States exported manufactured goods—notably machinery and automobiles—and imported such commodities as rubber, tin, copper, nitrates, sugar, bananas, and coffee. In other respects, however, there was a clash of interests. For example, both the United States and Argentina wanted to export their agricultural surplus and were thus in competition for markets. Moreover, the Latin American states could not become self-sufficient economically while they grew ever more dependent on the United States for industrial goods. In addition, they felt more akin in cultural terms to Latin states in Europe than they did to the colossus of the north.

During the 1920s Republican administrations attempted to repair poor relations. They were, in effect, preparing the way for what would become known in the 1930s as the Good Neighbor policy in Latin America. One sign of this shift was their promotion of Pan-American conferences. The United States was host to a special conference on Central America in Washington from December 4, 1922, to February 7, 1923. In general, the United States worked for the peaceful settlement of disputes in Latin America and worked at promoting cooperative efforts in the fields of economics, transportation, and health.

The priority of U.S. foreign policy in the Western Hemisphere was to maintain security in the Caribbean and in the isthmus between North and South America. The isthmus states were unstable. To protect the Panama Canal, the United States dispatched marines whenever and wherever it thought trouble was brewing. In the 1920s, however, presidents and secretaries of state also determined to cultivate the goodwill of these crucial allies. President Harding persuaded the Senate to approve the Treaty of Bogotá of April 6, 1914, by which Colombia was reconciled to the United States over the loss of Panama in 1903. The United States was allowed to expand its operations in the oil fields of Colombia and soon recovered the initial outlay of its grant. Harding and Secretary of State Hughes also persuaded Panama to settle a boundary dispute with Costa Rica in favor of Costa Rica.

Harding also tried to propitiate Mexico. President Alvaro Obregon agreed to modify Mexican restrictions on U.S. business but refused to offer compensation for all U.S. losses in Mexico since 1920 or to agree to guarantee the rights of U.S. nationals in Mexico. Nevertheless, Harding wanted to recognize the new Mexican government, and the Bucareli agreements of August 13, 1923, brought to a formal end the hostility engendered by Wilson's policies. In 1924 Coolidge raised the arms embargo on Mexico and allowed U.S. financiers to extend credit to the Mexican government for the purchase of "a few muskets and a few rounds of ammunition."

But a new Mexican president, Plutarco Elias Calles, was less inclined to friendly relations with the United States than Alvaro Obregon had been. In 1925 the Mexican Congress passed an alien lands law that allowed foreigners to buy land in Mexico on the condition that they renounce all rights to protection from foreign governments. It also passed a petroleum law that declared oil deposits the inalienable and imprescriptible property of Mexico and provided strict regulations about concessions to foreigners. Oil companies were ordered to apply to renew their rights under the law of January 1, 1927, or forfeit them. President Calles estimated that 380 companies, holding 26.83 million acres, assented to the new law, whereas twenty-two companies, with 1.66 million acres, refused. The companies that did not agree to the law, including such American interests as Doheny, Sinclair, Standard, and Gulf, had newspapers circulate accounts that Mexico was adopting revolutionary socialist policies and fomenting communism throughout the Western Hemisphere. American politicians were not taken in. Senator William Borah of Idaho declared in a speech of May 9, 1927, "The truth is that effort is being made to get this country into a shameless, cowardly little war with Mexico. . . . They talk communism and bolshevism but what they mean is war."

As a pledge of noninterference, the United States began to withdraw its marines from Latin America and the Caribbean. However, the withdrawal of U.S. Marines from Nicaragua on August 1, 1925, was followed by a violent civil war beginning on October 25. Coolidge ordered marines to return, first in May and again in August 1926. He justified his action on the basis of protecting both the Panama Canal and U.S. investments. He sent Henry L. Stimson, former secretary of war, to Nicaragua to try to persuade the two sides to come to terms. This Stimson achieved in the Peace of Tipitata on May 11, 1927, whereby both sides agreed to a coalition government under Adolfo Diaz until the United States could arrange elections. The election of 1928 was won by a former rebel, José M. Moncada. In February 1931 Stimson, now secretary of state, began to withdraw troops in successive stages.

The civil war in Nicaragua soured Mexican-American relations anew. The two countries supported opposite sides. The deterioration in relations between the United States and Mexico prompted Coolidge's most inspired decision on foreign policy. In 1927 he appointed Dwight W. Morrow as ambassador to Mexico to succeed the unpopular James R. Sheffield. Morrow, who had been in Coolidge's class at Amherst College, had an engaging personality and used it to defuse a difficult situation. To redeem the U.S. image, he had star aviator Charles A. Lindbergh fly to Mexico City, where he was tumultuously received. Then Morrow achieved a compromise over subsurface oil rights by persuading the Mexican Supreme Court to declare the most objectionable clauses of the new law unconstitutional. He also induced the Mexican government and the Catholic church, who were at odds over proposed nationalization of church property, to accept an accord by which the church withdrew an interdict on certain services in exchange for a government agreement that it would not attempt the destruction of the church. The tensions between the United States and Mexico that had seemed so important in the early 1920s had dissolved two years later.

On October 31, 1929, Secretary of State Henry L. Stimson tried to set a seal on the United States's bona fide intentions as a beneficent neighbor when he discontinued the so-called American black chamber. This was cryptologist Herbert A. Yardley's center at 12 Vanderbilt Avenue, New York, that had cracked the intelligence codes of nine Caribbean and Latin American countries. Stimson declared that "gentlemen do not read each other's mail."

Across the world new technologies were creating a new global society in which knowledge and expertise would count for more than backbreaking labor. Notwithstanding the economic advances of the United States and the incipient decline of the British Empire, there was no one world-class power—yet. Capitalism proved ill prepared to cope with the upheaval of technology and its economic changes, allowing financiers, politicians, and industrialists to concentrate on short-term advantages. Their imprudence led to uncoordinated strategies that would plunge their peoples into a deep economic crater.

CHAPTER 10

Down in the Dumps—Welcome to the Depression

"MY NAME IS DRACULA. Welcome to the Depression."

Horror-movie star Bela Lugosi did not actually utter these words when he welcomed onscreen visitors to his castle. But the subliminal association between Dracula's baleful greeting to his victims and the stark, extended fangs of the Great Depression was not lost on contemporary audiences.

The worst years were the notorious "Years of the Locust" of 1929–32. Industry foundered. Instead of expanding, railroads and utilities contracted. Their new capital issues of stocks and bonds fell from $10 billion in 1929 to $1 billion in 1932. In 1932 the physical production of industry was 54 percent of what it had been in 1929. The automobile industry was working at one-fifth of its capacity in 1929. By 1932 steel production was operating at 12 percent of capacity, and railroad freight was half of what it had been in 1929. The GNP fell from $102.1 billion in 1929 to $58 billion in 1932. This was a fall per capita from $847 in 1929 to $465 in 1932.

The story in agriculture was much the same. Capital investment in agriculture fell gradually from $79 billion in 1919 to $58 billion in 1929, and then it fell precipitately to $38 billion in 1932. Realized gross income from farming fell from $13.9 million in 1929 to $6.4 million in 1932. The decline was most severe in basic export crops such as wheat, cotton, and tobacco.

At first, industries tried to conserve their failing resources and faltering organization by such devices as cutting the workweek or reducing wages. U.S. Steel became the first major corporation to reduce wages on September 22, 1931, when it announced a cut of 10 percent. It was followed by General Motors, Bethlehem Steel, and other corporations. As sales continued to fall and the depression showed no signs of improving, business and industry cut costs further by discharging some of their work force. Those who were out of work could not afford to buy goods. This led to a spiral of deflation. Sales fell yet again, leading to more layoffs and the further contraction of purchasing power. It was a vicious circle affecting farmers and industrial workers alike. Neither could afford to buy the products of the other. The problem was double-headed: overproduction and underconsumption.

The most profound consequence was unemployment on a mass, unprecedented scale. In the three years following the crash, U.S. companies discharged an average of one hundred thousand workers every week. According to the Bureau of Labor Statistics of the U.S. Department of Labor, published on June 29, 1945, there were over 1 million unemployed in 1929. That number increased gradually over the months to 11.9 million in 1932, a percentage increase from 3.1 percent of the civilian labor force in 1929 to 24.0 percent in 1932. Other sources, such as the National Industrial Conference Board, the AFL, and the Labor Research Association (LRA), disputed these figures. The LRA said the true number was 16.78 million unemployed in 1932.

Such unemployment was not distributed evenly across the regions or among social and ethnic groups. By 1932 1 million were unemployed in New York, and so were 600,000 others in Chicago. In Cleveland 50 percent of the labor force was idle, in Akron 60 percent, and in Toledo 80 percent.

The Great Depression was an even worse catastrophe for the African American community than for the white. In an article "Negroes out of Work," of April 22, 1931, the *Nation* showed that unemployment among African Americans was four to six times as high as among whites, particularly in industrial towns. In specially created jobs in public works there was positive discrimination against African Americans.

For those African Americans who had a job, the average annual income during the depression in the South was only $634 in cities and $566 in the countryside. Sociologist Kelly Miller described the African American in 1932 as "the surplus man, the last to be hired and the first to be fired." In the cities unemployed whites contested for menial work they would once have thought beneath them. "Negro jobs" disappeared as domestic service and garbage collection became white occupations. African American communities across the country were threatened by privation, malnutrition, and even starvation. Not only did southern states provide the lowest levels of unemployment benefit and relief, but white officials also openly discriminated against African Americans in administering those programs. Thus, in Mississippi, where over half the population was African American, less than 9 percent of African Americans received any relief in 1932, compared with 14 percent of whites.

The Great Migration slowed down. Many African Americans still wanted to move from the South to the North as previously — not because they thought they could find work more readily but because they had heard that relief was distributed more equitably in northern cities and that schools were better than in the South. However, the costs of transportation were beyond what most could afford. Thus, only 147,000 African Americans came north in the 1930s.

Among whites, the Protestant work ethic died hard. Millions who lost their jobs blamed themselves for their misfortune. A generation raised on the belief that hard work must inevitably lead to success could not come to terms with collective failure. Poverty was shameful and, to the middle class, something that had to be concealed from friends and neighbors. Your neighbor across the street may have looked like an executive when he left home each morning, but later he may have changed his suit to go begging, to work in construction, or to sell shoelaces or apples on street corners.

Mass unemployment had grave consequences for marriage and birth rates and for immigration. With no prospect of employment, young people either postponed marriage or, if they were already married, postponed having children. In 1929 there were 1.23 million marriages; in 1932, 982,000. In 1929 the birth rate was 21.2 per 1,000 population; in 1932 it was 19.5 per 1,000. In 1932 emigration exceeded immigration: 33,576 immigrants arrived and 103,000 emigrants left.

However, the most startling consequence of mass unemployment was that those who could afford neither rent nor mortgage payments were put out of house and home. Masses of unemployed and destitute folks set up Hoovervilles, squalid camps on the edges of cities. These grotesque suburbs were a mixture of tents made from old sacking and shacks built with corrugated iron and even cardboard. Their inhabitants depended on charity to stay alive. If that was not forthcoming, they combed the streets looking for garbage in the gutter and trash in the cans to find something to eat. Author Thomas Wolfe described such scenes in New York as "homeless men who prowled in the vicinity of restaurants, lifting the lids off garbage cans and searching around inside for morsels of food."

The extent of the problem of human misery and want is indicated by a survey of *Fortune* magazine in September 1932. *Fortune* estimated that 34 million men, women, and children—that is 28 percent of the total population—were without any income at all. This estimate did not include America's 11 million farm dwellers, representing 25 percent of the population, who tried to live off the land. Private charity accounted for only 6 percent of the funds altogether spent on the poor in 1932. Public welfare was unequal to the other 94 percent. Municipal income came from taxes on real estate, all grossly overappraised. When local taxes fell 20 or 30 percent behind payment, cities cut their costs by reducing such services as maintaining roads and clearing snow.

Before 1932 no state had a program for unemployment insurance. In 1929 only eleven states provided old age pensions. The total sum paid was $220,000. In 1931 there were 3.8 million families headed by a woman, and only 19,280 of these families received any form of state aid. The average monthly award varied from $4.33 in Arkansas to $69.31 in Massachusetts. The Massachusetts award, the highest in any of the states, amounted to a yearly total of only $832, well below the sum of $2,000 that economists considered sufficient to supply an average family with basic necessities.

New York State was the first to accept state responsibility for relief on a massive scale. Here the influence of Governor Franklin D. Roosevelt (1929–33) was decisive. During the winter of 1930–31 he had the state Department of Social Welfare and the state Charities Aid Associations undertake a joint study of unemployment and relief. Their report insisted that the greater part of relief must come from public funds, not private. The Assembly, dominated by the

Republicans, was reluctant. Roosevelt used a well-planned radio campaign to focus public opinion on the need for state aid. Thus he put pressure on the Assembly. In October 1931 it established a Temporary Emergency Relief Administration (TERA) to help city and county government with relief. The first administrator was firebrand New York social and settlement-house worker Harry L. Hopkins.

Men, women, and children who could find no sustenance at home or on the fringes of towns and cities simply took to the road—more particularly the railroads, where they became nonpaying, unwanted, stowaway passengers. By 1932 there were between 1 million and 2 million roaming the states on freight cars. The transients or vagrants were a mix of hoboes, dispossessed farmers and sharecroppers, unemployed school leavers, and unemployable middle-class executives. Newton D. Baker told the *New York Times* of May 4, 1932, that "every group in society is represented in their ranks from the college graduate to the child who has never seen the inside of the schoolhouse. Expectant mothers, sick babies, young childless couples, grim-faced middle-aged dislodged from lifetime jobs— on the go, an index of insecurity in a country used to the unexpected. We think of nomads of the desert—now we have nomads of the Depression."

Hunger Never Saw Bad Bread

In the early 1930s people expected federal intervention, specifically presidential action, to mitigate the Great Depression. The cardinal sin of President Herbert Hoover (1929–33) was that he failed to do so. Hoover believed that his ideas about politics and economics were unassailable because they had been forged in, and tempered by, long experience. He recognized that enterprises such as public utilities entailed common interests and carried public responsibility. Accordingly, they must be regulated by government acting on behalf of its citizens. Nevertheless, government had no right to interfere with a free-market economy. The American system had achieved the highest standard of living in the world precisely because the power of the federal government was limited. The economy allowed equality of opportunity and encouraged individual initiative.

Yet Hoover was sensitive to the growing areas of discontent against the Republican Party. One such was in the very seedbed of Republicanism, the farm belt of the Midwest and the Great Plains, from which the party had garnered seven presidents. Farmers already caught in the grip of agricultural recession resented the domination of their party by eastern interests. Since the farm belt would always play a pivotal role in elections, Hoover recognized that he must improve the farmers' lot. He had first called the Seventy-First Congress into special session in April 1929 six months before the crash to consider the pressing problems of agriculture.

The Agricultural Marketing Act of June 1929 was intended to provide the farmers with a form of self-help. The act established a Federal Farm Board with funds of $500 million that it was to use to create farmers' marketing cooperatives and so-called stabilization corporations. The stabilization corporations had the task of storing and then disposing of surplus in order to help steady farm prices. What the farm boards could not do was restrict production, and excessive production in 1931 and 1932 resulted in huge prices. Thus, surpluses fell through the floor.

Moreover, the board clearly had no power to control the worldwide economic depression. As the depression in Europe deepened, Europe reduced its import of American produce even further while trying to sell its own surplus grain on the world market. The consequences of excessive surplus at home and abroad were devastating. The price of wheat fell from an average of $1.04 a bushel in 1929 to 67 cents in 1930 and then to between 30 cents and 39 cents in 1932—prices that were well below the cost of production. A system of voluntary cooperatives could not handle problems on this scale. The Farm Board appealed to Congress to restrict acreage and production.

Hoover's attempts to provide a respite by raising the tariff on farm produce were also futile. Apart from sugar, butter, fruit, and wool, very few imports were in competition with American agriculture. The Hawley-Smoot Act, which became law on June 17, 1930, was another classic instance of the tariff as barter between different interest groups. The average rates on all duties rose to new heights, an average duty of 40 percent. While affording some relief to dairy and meat products, the new tariff was of no general use to agriculture. Britain and Germany abandoned free trade and set up economic barriers of their own. Other nations soon followed suit. This reduced international trade even further.

Hoover met the problem of unemployment by calling on local government to provide additional employment and by extending the amount of public works undertaken by the federal government. He secured additional appropriations from Congress for public works, from $250 million in 1929 to $410 million in 1930 and thereafter, by stages, to $726 million in 1932. However, individual welfare schemes were undernourished and inadequate to the needs of the time. The Federal Home Loan Bank Act of July 1932 was intended to save mortgages by easing credit. It established a series of Federal Home Loan Banks to ease the problems of loan associations, insurance companies, and other organizations involved in mortgages. But since the maximum loan was only 50 percent of the value of the property, the measure was largely ineffective.

The most significant recovery measure of the early depression was the Reconstruction Finance Corporation (RFC). The RFC was based on the War Finance Corporation of World War I. On January 22, 1932, Congress chartered it to lend funds of $500 million to banks and railroads, construction companies and various lending associations, especially those in danger of bankruptcy. This was the agency that funded projects such as the Golden Gate Bridge in San Francisco and the Mississippi River Bridge in New Orleans. But its support of certain banks made it an easy target of criticism. The first president of the RFC was former vice president Charles Gates Dawes. Shortly after Dawes retired from the RFC and returned to the Republic Bank of Chicago, the RFC awarded his bank a loan of $500 million, a sum almost as great as its supposed deposits.

There was plenty of blame to go round. Among the crooks whom the establishment press made a scapegoat for the economic crisis was Samuel Insull of Chicago. Insull was an English immigrant whom inventor Thomas Edison had employed successively as secretary, assistant, and general manager. In 1908 Insull formed the Commonwealth Edison Company, a $30 million corporation consolidating the Edison companies around Chicago, of which he became president. Insull's specialty was combining small power companies into ever larger units with improved facilities for generating electric power and then distributing it. He was director of eighty-five companies, chairman of sixty-five boards, and president of another eleven. He owed his fabulous wealth, valued at $3 billion, to a conglomerate of 150 companies, serving 3.25 million people and employing 50,000.

Unfortunately, Insull had a mania for creating pyramids of holding companies that were no better than a chaotic financial jumble. In early 1932 his empire collapsed, partly because it was overextended and overcapitalized, partly on account of fraud. The value of its stock fell to 4 percent of its 1931 level, and two of Insull's investment trusts were declared bankrupt. In July 1932, having been indicted by a Cook County grand jury for outrageous debts of $60 million, Insull fled to Europe. He moved from Paris to Rome and finally to Athens because Greece had no extradition treaty with the United States. When the two countries signed an extradition treaty in November 1932, he escaped to Turkey disguised as a woman. Turkey returned him to the United States, where he stood trial. He was found not guilty of charges against him, however, because of a major loophole in the law: holding companies were not subject to regulation.

Hunger and Thirst

National prohibition became a scapegoat for the Great Depression.

Alcohol abuse was a serious social problem. Although national prohibition may have dried up the United States more than its Hollywood-driven and posthumous legends suggest, it was not working properly and yielded new problems of gangsterism. The tragicomedy of prohibition was a setback for such Protestant churches as the Baptists, the Methodists, and the Presbyterians, all of whom had supported the dry cause. In 1927 the *Christian Century* reported that the evangelical churches had lost over a million members in twelve months. The prohibition movement had first tested its strength in rural areas. Once press, automobiles, radio, and movies ended rural isolation, rural prejudice began to erode. City papers were becoming the press of all the states, and their editors criticized prohibition.

Doctors, lawyers, businessmen, and labor fielded a new association against prohibition, the Association against the Prohibition Amendment (AAPA),

Above: Al Capone, head of the South Side Gang, flamboyant and notorious ruler of Chicago's underworld in the late 1920s through his empire of alcohol, prostitution, and extortion rackets and effective controller of Cook County's feeble efforts at law enforcement. When the law eventually ensnared him in 1931, it was for income tax evasion. (BBC Hulton Picture Library)

Below: The St. Valentine's Day Massacre of 1929, in which seven members of the North Side Gang, Capone's rivals, were lured to a deserted warehouse and machine-gunned to death. One managed to crawl to a doorway out of range of the police photographer who captured this scene. No one was arrested or charged with the crime, but it became a symbol of what was wrong with the "noble experiment" of prohibition. (BBC Hulton Picture Library)

founded by Capt. William H. Stayton, a retired navy man and lawyer, in 1918 and formally incorporated on December 31, 1920. Stayton cultivated affluent businessmen such as Charles H. Sabin, president of a Morgan bank, and Pierre, Irénée, and Lammot, the three Du Pont brothers. The AAPA decided to provide the public with more substantial evidence of the failure of prohibition than it had received hitherto. It created departments of research and information under John G. Gebhart, a New York social worker. His task was to collate information and publicize the ills of prohibition. Between April 1928 and January 1931 his departments distributed over a million copies of thirteen pamphlets.

Arguments about prohibition were neither more nor less valid than before the Wall Street crash, but those who declared that here was a panacea for the country's economic ills now urged its repeal with new tenacity. Hence, hunger was a better advocate than thirst. It was far more eloquent against prohibition than any speech or sentence.

The spreading public anger against the criminal excesses of bootleggers reached a new level of disgust with the notorious climax of Chicago's gang warfare—the St. Valentine's Day Massacre of February 14, 1929. Mobster Al Capone of the South Side Gang had seven members of the rival North Side Gang mown down by machine-gun fire in a warehouse at 2122 North Clark Street. The assassination served a double function, satisfying the requirements of a blood feud and preparing the ground for a consolidation of crime. Yet the criminals eluded the law. In fact, between 1927 and 1929 there were at least 227 killings in Chicago. However, during that time only two gangsters were tried and convicted of murder.

Leading mobsters fully realized that the days of prohibition were numbered, and they planned to ensure their own survival. Twenty-seven gang leaders met at the Hotel Statler in Cleveland on December 5, 1928, to discuss the national distribution of whiskey and future criminal syndicates of Sicilian-Americans. Italian and Sicilian mobsters opened a conference at the President Hotel in Atlantic City, from May 13–16, 1929, to Jewish and Irish gangsters. Legend has it that the conferees agreed to assign territories within a loose federation of criminal syndicates across the nation. The local boss who proved the mightiest became the head of his territory. Thereafter, gangs were to forbear feuds. The conferees supposedly established a multimillion dollar fund to bribe police and politicians. They reorganized L'Unione Siciliana, a fraternal organization of Sicilian immigrants that had become a Mafia front.

Hence, gang leaders in New York and Chicago who controlled city rackets now became national figures in a nationwide operation, and local hoods became businessmen who set aside ethnic differences to divide territories amicably. Within this new mixed Mafia, there developed an American institution, the family. In New York there were five families, known by the last names of leaders: Genovese, Bonanno, Gambino, Profaci, and Lucchese.

Preeminent among the pivotal players in New York was Salvatore Lucania, also known as Charlie ("Lucky") Luciano—so called because he returned from a one-way ride—albeit with his eyelids drooping from a severing of the nerves after they had been slashed with razor blades. Another crucial player was self-effacing Polish immigrant and adroit mathematician Meyer Lansky. Luciano and Lansky cleaned house in the Castellammarese war, eliminating old guard mobsters in a serial massacre on September 10, 1931. The principal target was Giuseppe ("Joe the Boss") Masseria, who was dispatched in a restaurant in Coney Island. In 1931 Luciano's gunmen threatened Harry Perry, a district leader in the Lower East Side. Perry chose not to seek reelection. He was replaced by Luciano's candidate, Albert Marinelli.

Luciano and Lansky achieved a new chain of command for a growing business that included illegal off-track betting and the numbers racket among small shopkeepers and their customers in immigrant communities as well as numerous legitimate businesses (such as slot machines). One of their businesses, run from Brownsville, Brooklyn, throughout the 1930s included contract killings for the nationwide syndicate. Said to be responsible for five hundred deaths and mysterious disappearances, it inspired the name Murder Incorporated. Many were carried out by Albert Anastasia. Frank Costello, who ran slot machines, became a principal player after Lucky Luciano went to prison in 1936 for running rings of prostitutes. Democratic district leader James J. Hines was also jailed for protecting the numbers racket. Costello set about establishing ever more extensive connections within government in New York and Louisiana.

Despite its tussles with the law and some cavalier acts of insubordination by lesser players, the Mafia made organized crime more structured than ever before in American cities. Consequently, it became a formidable part of the American urban scene. Criminals infiltrated the garment industry and vegetable markets, sometimes by invitation, sometimes by force. They also cultivated other traditional fields: gambling, loan sharking, labor racketeering, and drug dealing.

As to small-scale forbidden pleasures for those who could still afford them, nightclubs survived the Wall Street crash. The most famous was the Stork Club in New York, the 1929 fantasy creation of former Oklahoma bootlegger Sherman Billingsley. Protected by hoods Owney Madden (owner of the Cotton Club), George ("Frenchy") Lamange, and William ("Big Bill") Dwyer, owner Billingsley moved the Stork Club around to various locations in Manhattan's East 50s. But when he tried to discharge his dark partners, Billingsley found he could not. "We didn't pay $10,000 for a 30 percent interest in the business, we paid $10,000 for a 30 percent interest in everything you do for the rest of your life," his gangland chums told him.

On the right side of the law, the AAPA's well-researched pamphlets created public recognition of the need for a full-scale and reliable government inquiry into prohibition. Herbert Hoover had expanded his original plan for a national investigation into prohibition. Under the chairmanship of George W. Wickersham, the eleven commissioners met for sixteen months starting May 28, 1929. The commission elicited advice from experts, both academic and professional, on national delinquency in observing national prohibition. The vast majority of people writing to, and appearing before, the commission told members in no uncertain terms that prohibition was not working and that it should be repealed.

The Wickersham Commission issued its final report on January 7, 1931. Although seven members of the commission were openly critical of prohibition, all but one signed a final summary endorsing it. The contradiction between the individual reports in favor of reform and the shared summary preferring to continue prohibition, forced on the commission by Hoover, caused uproar in the press. Franklin P. Adams ridiculed the commission in a famous satirical verse for the *New York World* of February 1931:

> Prohibition is an awful flop.
> > We like it.
> It can't stop what it's meant to stop.
> > We like it.
> It's left a trail of graft and slime,
> It don't prohibit worth a dime,
> It's filled our land with vice and crime,
> > Nevertheless, we're for it.

The deep public outrage at the scope of criminal activities was partly appeased by the entrapment of Al Capone in 1931. By restricting the investigation and charges to the narrow one of income tax evasion, Hoover and Secretary of the Treasury Mellon made it easier for prosecutors to get the jury to focus on one outrageous crime. Capone was sentenced to eleven years. The new federal prison of Alcatraz was harder on Capone than on other prisoners. He had syphilis, long untreated, and his illness now resulted in such bizarre behavior that he was locked up for months in one of the bug cages for mentally unstable inmates.

Women, sensitive to the abuses of prohibition, were most militant in their opposition in a new lobby, the Women's Organization for National Prohibition Reform (WONPR), which proved decisive in achieving repeal. The WONPR was the creation of Pauline Morton Sabin, wife of Charles H. Sabin, president of Guaranty Trust, a Morgan bank. He was also treasurer of the AAPA. Not only did Pauline Sabin persuade New York socialites to join her, but she also enlisted upper-class women across the United States, all with time on their hands and a flair for publicity. Joining the WONPR became the fashionable thing to do: a Sabin woman could be received anywhere. At the WONPR's first national convention, held in Cleveland in 1930, the Sabin women advocated outright repeal of prohibition. Pauline Sabin attached great importance to a huge membership, fully understanding that protest movements could only succeed if they continued to grow. As chairman, she worked assiduously from a small office in New York, writing articles, enrolling members, and making speeches. In 1931 the WONPR claimed six hundred thousand members altogether. These resolute women were determined to gain repeal. Their agitation further undermined the tottering administration of Herbert Hoover.

Hitherto, the depression had astonished a generation who accepted the legend of the richest nation in the world without understanding how the dream could turn sour. Then in 1931 and 1932, the mood of the dispossessed changed dramatically. The government faced truculent, disruptive action by farmers and war veterans.

Various farm groups organized themselves as the Farmers' Holiday Association, which fell under the charismatic leadership of Milo Reno, who had first proposed a farm strike back in 1927. The Farmers' Holiday Association proposed that farmers would refuse to market their produce in order to make the towns and cities aware of their problems and bring about a rise in prices. Farmers turned their slogan into a jingle:

> Let's call a "Farmers' Holiday."
> A holiday, let's hold.
> We'll eat our wheat and ham and eggs
> And let them eat their gold.

The use of the term *holiday* in place of *strike* was intended as a sardonic parody of the way banks closed their doors on so-called bank holidays to customers they could not serve.

Farmers who could not meet their mortgage payments lost their farms in foreclosures. The dramatic increase in the number of farms being sold in the early depression is suggested in statistics released by the U.S. Department of Agriculture Bureau of Agricultural Economics. In 1929 58 farms in every 1,000 changed hands, and 41.7 percent of these sales were forced. Thus years of work counted for nothing, and a generation of farmers was dispossessed. Their grievances at such injustice took more serious and constructive forms. In early 1933 as many as seventy auctions of farm property took place in which the friends and neighbors of the dispossessed farmers thwarted the auctioneers by bidding a few cents for the items on sale and then returning them to their original owner. Such auctions were called penny auctions or Sears Roebuck Sales. One farm in Haskins, Ohio, with a mortgage debt of $800 was acquired for $1.90. When an outsider took such a farm he might be intimidated by an empty noose placed on a tree or by threats. After a spate of penny auctions, John A. Simpson, president of the National Farmers' Union, warned the Senate Committee on Agriculture in January 1933, "The biggest and finest crop of revolutions you ever saw is sprouting all over the country right now." In response to mounting pressure, Governors Charles Bryan of Nebraska and Floyd B. Olson of Minnesota signed state bills declaring a moratorium on farm mortgages.

Misry's Comin' Around

Eclipsed by thunder from left and right, Herbert Hoover and other leaders of Western countries must have wondered if their fate would be the same as that of the czar of Russia. The Bolshevik Revolution was a recent and also a continuing phenomenon. And, to radicals, it was Communist Russia that seemed to provide a semblance of societal organization to cope with the needs and demands of mass society. The differences between the USA and the USSR in the 1930s are instructive.

Dictator Joseph Stalin's political strength lay in a highly centralized party organization. The Political Bureau, or Politburo, framed policy; the Secretariat supervised its execution. Stalin belonged to all three organs of the Central Committee—the Politburo, the Secretariat, and the Orgburo—which offered him unique opportunities for political patronage. His rival for supreme power, Leon Trotsky, favored revolutions worldwide, whereas Stalin proposed socialism in one country as Russia faced the formidable task of its own industrial development. Stalin eliminated Trotsky, expelling him from the party in 1927, exiling him in 1929, and having him murdered in Mexico (with a pickax) in 1940.

In October 1928 Stalin instituted the first five-year industrial plan. The bulk of Soviet investment was to be in heavy industry at the expense of agriculture and consumer society. This profound social and economic revolution was achieved with monumental suffering. During the campaign to wring capital out of the primary sector, the peasants were dispossessed and forcibly removed to state farms. Seven million people died of famine. Between 1929 and 1939 living standards actually declined. Yet in 1927–37 coal production rose by 200 percent and steel by 250 percent. New industrial areas were opened up in previously undeveloped regions such as the Ural mountains and central Asia—all beyond the reach of an invading army.

The threat of Communist revolution in the United States provoked by the USSR was remote, but there was no mistaking the fervent dogma of the CPUSA's adherents. Former syndicalist William Z. Foster, who took charge of labor union policy for the CPUSA, was the party's presidential candidate in three elections. In 1927 the CPUSA moved its headquarters from Chicago to New York, taking offices at 35 East Twelfth Street, south of Union Square. New York was, after all, the home of the CPUSA's major publications *Morgen Freiheit* (in Yiddish, 1922) and the *Daily Worker* (1924) as well as its literary magazine, the *New Masses* (1926). On March 6, 1930, the CPUSA mounted a protest demonstration of the unemployed in Union Square. It numbered between 35,000 and 100,000. Mounted police dispersed the crowd before the protesters could march on City Hall.

American Communists followed the Moscow party line about the need to prepare for the day when Communists would seize the apparatus of the federal government, foment revolution, and overthrow America's democratic institutions. In 1932 William Z. Foster wrote in *Toward Soviet America*:

> One day, despite the disbelief of the capitalists . . . the American workers will demonstrate that they, like the Russians, have the intelligence, courage, and organization to carry through the revolution . . .
>
> By the term "abolition" of capitalism we mean its overthrow in open struggle by the toiling masses, led by the proletariat. . . . To put an end to the capitalist system will require a consciously revolutionary act by the great toiling masses, led by the Communist party; that is, the conquest of the State power, the destruction

Left: A detachment of seven hundred men from the far West among the Bonus Army encampment on the east side of the Capitol in Washington, D.C., vowing they will remain there until Congress enacts a special bonus law to provide veterans with their pensions immediately. (Photo by Underwood and Underwood of July 13, 1932; Library of Congress)
Right: Gen. Douglas MacArthur, army chief of staff, personally supervised the breaking up of the bonus camps, razing them to the ground and finally dispersing the exhausted veterans and their families. (Photo by Underwood and Underwood of July 29, 1932; Library of Congress)

of the State machine created by the ruling class, and the organization of the proletariat dictatorship . . .

Under the dictatorship all the capitalist parties—Republican, Democratic, Progressive, Socialist, etc.—will be liquidated, the Communist party functioning alone as the Party of the toiling masses. Likewise, will be dissolved all other organizations that are political props of the bourgeois rule, including chambers of commerce, employers' associations, rotary clubs, American Legion, Y.M.C.A., and such fraternal orders as the Masons, Odd Fellows, Elks, Knights of Columbus, etc. . . .

The press, the motion picture, the radio, the theater, will be taken over by the government.

But if Herbert Hoover feared revolution, it was not Communists but war veterans who provided the greatest show of discontent. In 1924 Congress had voted a pension or bonus to war veterans. This was in the form of adjusted compensation certificates redeemable in 1945. In the early years of the depression war veterans called for immediate payment when the money could be put to more effective use for personal relief, financial investment, or material support for their families. In Portland, Oregon, they elected Walter F. Watts, a former sergeant and cannery superintendent, to organize a march to the Capitol to dramatize their plight. This was the Bonus Expeditionary Force (BEF), or Bonus Army, which attracted thousands of veterans and transients as it moved across the country in the spring and summer of 1932. Other groups from different regions also began streaming into Washington, many with their wives and children. By mid-June there were between 15,000 and 50,000 bonus marchers in the city. They took up residence in various Hoovervilles. Their main camp was in southeast Washington on the other side of the Anacostia River across the Eleventh Street Bridge.

Roused by the bonus marchers' domestic plight, the House, on June 15, by a vote of 226 to 175, passed an enabling bill proposed by Congressman Wright Patman of Texas. It would have allowed immediate payment of the bonus. The estimated cost was $2.4 billion. However, the Senate rejected the bill on June 17. Some veterans agreed to leave, using loans for travel provided by the government and to be deducted from the payment in 1945. Others refused to budge. Their truculent mood disturbed both President Herbert Hoover and the commissioners of the District of Columbia, whose anxiety increased when Congress adjourned.

The evacuation of a small building on the corner of Pennsylvania Avenue and Third Street was sufficient excuse for Secretary of War Patrick Hurley to summon federal troops under Gen. Douglas MacArthur. Despite counsels of moderation from his aide, Gen. Dwight D. ("Ike") Eisenhower, MacArthur proceeded to disperse the bonus marchers with infantry, cavalry, and tanks. They drove the veterans back across the Eleventh Street Bridge into the main camp at Anacostia Flats. They set fire to the tents, shacks, and packing crates in which the Bonus Army had been sheltering and razed the entire camp to the ground. Two babies died of tear gas. The routed marchers were officially barred from Maryland and Virginia, although police escorted a few stragglers through Maryland to Pennsylvania, whence state police herded them to Ohio. From state to state the weary band was dispersed. By the fall they were indistinguishable from America's transient population.

It was clear that by his actions, a mixture of arrogance, insensitivity, and cowardice, Hoover had committed a gross political blunder that was to cost him dearly. It was as if he were stage-managing his own defeat in the election of 1932.

Hoover's profound sense of panic was heightened by the adverse turn in world affairs. The system of foreign debts and reparation payments was another piece of economic engineering that broke down in the wake of the Wall Street crash. In March 1931 French bankers called in short-term German and Austrian notes.

Unable to meet the demands on it, the Kreditanstalt in Vienna collapsed, setting off a chain reaction. The Weimar Republic defaulted on reparation payments, and President Paul von Hindenburg appealed to Hoover. In June 1931 Hoover proposed a one-year moratorium on the payment of debts and reparation payments. At Lausanne in June 1932 Britain, France, Italy, Japan, and Belgium agreed to reduce the residue of German reparations to $70 million. Cuba alone paid off its wartime debt to the United States in full—$15 million—by 1920. Finland, which had contracted a postwar loan of $9 million, was the only country to continue payments after 1935 and to discharge its loan.

The vexed issue of reparations burst open. After the Dawes Committee, a new committee headed by New York industrialist Owen D. Young produced final arrangements agreed to by seventeen nations at The Hague on January 20, 1930. Germany's total liability was now set at $9 billion, with interest at 5.5 percent to be paid over fifty-nine years. Yearly payments were no more than $153 million—much less than the Dawes Plan had proposed. However, they were about the same as the total amount the Allies had agreed to pay the United States in war debts each year.

Germany could meet its heavy reparation payments only by borrowing. Investors, confident of German recovery, supported Germany by buying German securities regularly. The sums loaned by the United States up to July 1, 1931, were not less than $2.6 billion—the very sum the United States collected from the Allies for war debts. The connection between German reparations, loans from the United States, and Allied war debts was crystal clear. The United States loaned money to Germany with which it paid reparations to the Allies. They, in turn, repaid some of their debts to the United States. As historian William E. Leuchtenburg observed (1958) in a much-quoted sentence, "it would have made equal sense for the United States to take the money out of one Treasury building and put it into another."

Moreover, collective security was disintegrating just as it was being defined.

After serving as regent for five years, Emperor Hirohito reigned over Japan from 1926 to 1989 to become one of the great dynastic survivors, preceding the rise of Adolf Hitler and the Third Reich in Germany and living almost until the dissolution of the Soviet Union and the end of the Cold War. Although his reign was optimistically named Showa ("enlightened peace"), he led Japan down the sinister slopes of a dark valley of conquest and brutality. Hirohito himself devoted his reign to preserving the status of the imperial family. When Japan became increasingly militaristic, the constitutional prince of the 1920s turned himself into the militarists' cheerleader of the 1930s.

The Japanese invasion of Manchuria on September 18, 1931, was the turning point between the two world wars. It symbolized the collapse of attempts to insure peace, either by arbitration or by collective security. It was a climax to Russo-Japanese antagonism since the 1890s. Like the United States, Japan had emerged from World War I with increased economic and industrial capacity. Japan became a creditor nation, and its industrial and financial combines, the *zaibatsu*, did well out of the protracted European struggle. However, Japan could maintain production only by finding additional resources of raw materials abroad.

Industry, legitimately developed by the Japanese in Manchuria according to treaty, attracted increasing numbers of Chinese settlers north of the Great Wall. Subject to despotic control of a brigand chief, Zhang Zuolin, Manchuria was not an integral part of China. Then, after years of confusion following the revolution of 1911–12, China seemed ready for reunification. Chiang Kai-shek (in later transliteration, Jiang Jeshi), who was the leader of the conservative wing of the Guomindong (Kuomintang) or National People's Party, established a capital in Beijing on June 8, 1928. The United States recognized Chiang's government on July 25, 1928.

Americans in general still knew very little about China. And what the few did know in many cases they had learned from the writings of Pearl Buck. Having grown up in the small Chinese city of Chinkiang (now known as Zhenjiang), Pearl Buck for seventeen unhappy years played the role of a dutiful missionary wife to a cold husband in Anhwei (Anhui) Province and in Nanking (Nanjing). Then in 1931, at the age of thirty-nine, she burst on the literary scene with *The Good Earth*. She was writing herself out of her frigid marriage and also out of the missionary world, which she had come to believe was narrow and joyless, patronizing to the Chinese people and especially to women. In *The Good Earth* her empathetic rendering of the hard lives of Wang Lung, a poor Anhwei peasant, and his brave wife, O-lan, was a barely concealed attack on the misguided missionary effort of trying to Christianize China, a country with its own rich and essentially secular culture.

One of Nationalist leader Chiang Kai-shek's aims in China was the recovery of Chinese control of territories leased to foreigners. This policy produced dynamic opposition from the Japanese army. The pretext for the Japanese army's invasion of Manchuria was a minor explosion on the South Manchurian Railway, where Japanese soldiers were stationed. Their reprisal was an attack on the city of Shenyang. By October 1931 they had begun to bomb cities in southern Manchuria. Although the Japanese prime minister, Wakatsuki Reijiro, and the foreign minister, Shidehara Kijuro, were indignant at the army's invasion, in order to save face they asserted Japan's rights. Their envoy to the League, Yoshizawa, emphasized the vital importance of Manchuria to Japan and the supposed broken agreements of the Chinese. World disapproval of the invasion solidified patriotism among the Japanese people.

The Japanese invasion was an act of flagrant aggression. How did the powers react? The League of Nations authorized a Commission of Inquiry headed by Lord Lytton (V. A. G. R. Bulwer-Lytton) to travel to Manchuria and review the situation. The United States was represented by Gen. Frank McCoy. President Herbert Hoover recalled that William Jennings Bryan had, as secretary of state, used nonrecognition as a diplomatic device in 1915 when Japan made its notorious Twenty-One Demands of China. On November 9, 1931, Hoover suggested to Secretary of State Henry L. Stimson that he now do the same. Stimson dispatched a note to both China and Japan on January 7, 1932, declaring, "The United States government . . . cannot admit the legality of any situation de facto." Thus, the official position of the United States was that acquisition by aggression had no legal validity.

But international opposition to Japan did not coalesce. China was left alone to offer what feeble resistance it could. After the first note, Japanese Rear Adm. Kuichi Shiozawa started a second war within the Great Wall, two hundred miles south of Shenyang at Shanghai, on January 28, 1932. Stimson's desire to emphasize nonrecognition then took a different form, an open letter of February 23, 1932, to Senator William Borah in which he restated his recommendation to warn Japan, to encourage China, and to rouse the League. The Lytton report condemned Japan. On February 24, 1933, the League accepted the report and refused to recognize Japan's puppet state of Manchukuo, nominally ruled by the former Chinese emperor, Pu Yi. On March 27 Japan withdrew from the League. Fighting now extended south of the Great Wall.

Meanwhile, in Tokyo the assassination of Prime Minister Tsuyoshi Inukai on May 15, 1932, followed by later militarist uprisings by a sinister secret association of fanatics, the League of Blood, rang down the curtain on the so-called Taisho Democracy of the 1920s. Collective security had fallen apart. The slide to another world war began. The Japanese sought "living room." They would enter a room none thought possible, the mushroom of 1945.

The Forgotten Man

The Republican National Convention that assembled in Chicago on June 14, 1932, renominated Herbert Hoover for president without enthusiasm. The platform repeated the time-honored commitment to the gold standard, protection of the tariff, and traditional government economies while supporting the farmers' cooperative efforts to control agricultural production. On the issue of prohibition, it was neither wet nor dry but moist, favoring resubmission of the Eighteenth Amendment to the states.

Hoover and the Republican Party were uneasy about what lay ahead. By 1932 the impact of the Great Depression was causing an irreversible shift in the political loyalty of millions. This was especially apparent among farmers, African Americans, and the middle class. Thus, after decades of status as a party of opposition, the Democrats were about to emerge as the party of government. Opposition to national prohibition was a decisive factor in the election of 1932 and its aftermath.

Democratic national chairman John J. Raskob played a pivotal role in remodeling the party. It had been Raskob's ambition to transform the Democratic Party into an "organization which parallels, as nearly as conditions will permit, a first-rate business enterprise operating all the time; spending money effectively and meeting the real issues at hand." Raskob recognized that the recipe for sustained electoral success was continuous work. Accordingly, in 1929 he put Jouett Shouse of Kansas, a former congressman, and Charles Michelson, former Washington correspondent for the *New York World*, in charge of publicity. Within two years Raskob had created a professional national organization, a model for the future.

In 1932 the leading contender for the Democratic presidential nomination was Franklin Delano Roosevelt of New York. FDR's background, upbringing, and early political career barely suggest that he would become the greatest American president in the twentieth century. The only son of an elderly father and youthful mother and from a wealthy family of Anglo-Dutch extraction in Hyde Park, New York, he received a privileged education capped by Harvard. In 1904 FDR went to Columbia University Law School, and in 1905 he married a fifth cousin, Anna Eleanor Roosevelt, who was given away by her uncle, President Theodore Roosevelt. In time, the couple had four sons and a daughter. After passing the New York State bar examinations, FDR entered a Wall Street firm as a junior clerk, his ambition already set on the presidency. In 1910 he was elected state senator for the Democrats and at Albany he led an insurgent movement against Tammany Hall.

In 1913 President Woodrow Wilson brought him into his administration as assistant secretary of the navy—like Theodore Roosevelt before him. Franklin made himself popular with admirals and cultivated labor and business, but he found himself in open disagreement with his superior, Secretary of the Navy Josephus Daniels, over such matters as naval expenditures and rearmament. Moreover, if Franklin and his wife, Eleanor, had a harmonious professional relationship, it was emotionally troubled, notably after she discovered his affair with her social secretary, Lucy Mercer. In 1920 the Democrats nominated FDR for the vice presidency as a candidate acceptable to Wilsonian, independent, and Tammany Democrats. After the debacle of nominee James Cox's presidential campaign, tragedy struck FDR when he contracted poliomyelitis in 1921.

Roosevelt and his family spent their summer vacation of 1921 off Campobello, New Brunswick. On August 10, 1921, they alighted from their yacht, the *Vireo*, to help put out a forest fire on one of the islands. Then they raced across the island at Campobello and ended the day by taking a swim in the frigid sea of the Bay of Fundy. FDR said, "When I swung out of bed [the next day], my left leg lagged but I managed to move about and to shave. I tried to persuade myself that the trouble with my leg was muscular, that it would disappear as I used it. But presently it refused to work, and then the other." Franklin had a temperature of 102 degrees. On August 12, Roosevelt could not stand, and by the evening he could not even move his legs. On August 25 Boston specialist Dr. Robert W. Lovett confirmed the worst: poliomyelitis. Roosevelt was thirty-nine. The social butterfly was extinguished and, with it, the opportunities for political advance by display. In its place was a cocoon, an invalid confined to bed or wheelchair and sometimes encased in plaster.

Emperor Hirohito of Japan (1901–89; reigned 1926–89), a child of the twentieth century and one of the great dynastic survivors of all time, whose part in the tragic events of the dark valley has remained obscure. Was he, as the photograph (left) suggests (with the divine emperor in the headdress of a priest) no more responsible for the terrible dramas of high-power politics than a statue in a shrine? Or was he, as the horseback photo (right) implies, a cheerleader for the militarists of the 1930s? (Library of Congress)

Polio left FDR permanently paralyzed from the waist down. Against the wishes of his indulgent mother but supported by his energetic wife and his confidant, political reporter Louis M. Howe, he concentrated first on gaining physical strength. Through arduous exercise he built up his upper body and transformed his shape from slim to stocky. With steel braces fitted from hips to feet and by maneuvering himself from his hips, FDR could give an impression that he was walking, albeit clumsily, although he had no balance and no power in his legs. The man who could not walk found limitless fortitude, stamina, and political skill.

Through all the Roosevelts' courageous surmounting of immense personal tragedy, their five children grew up amid hostility between their parents. Daughter Anna said, "It was impossible to discount the coldness with which Mother treated us when we were young or to be immune to the animosity we observed between the adults in the family."

The crippling effects of poliomyelitis had one advantage: they removed FDR from the worst of the Democratic Party infighting in the mid-1920s. Then FDR resumed his political career. Urged by Al Smith, he ran for governor of New York in 1928 when Smith ran for the presidency. Roosevelt won New York by 25,000 votes, whereas Smith himself lost the state. As governor, Roosevelt treated the traditional problems of industrial monopolies and the new ones of the depression. He achieved cheaper electric power, both through the promotion of public power and by more effective regulation of private utility companies. He met the two problems of unemployment and conservation by putting unemployed young men to work on land reclamation and tree planting throughout the state.

As Democratic presidential hopeful, Roosevelt declared in a speech of April 7, 1932, that the country faced a more grave emergency than in 1917. He compared the Hoover administration to Napoleon at Waterloo, who had staked too much on his overextended cavalry and forgotten his infantry. Thus, the administration had forgotten "the infantry of our economic army." He added, "These unhappy times call for the building of plans that rest upon the forgotten, the unrecognized but the indispensable units of economic power, . . . that put their faith once more in the forgotten man at the bottom of the economic pyramid." Precisely because of his handicap, the affluent patrician Roosevelt could identify with the forgotten man. By virtue of the way he had fought his illness to resume a political career, he became a symbol of the will to triumph over adversity.

However, to political pundits, Roosevelt seemed to offer little beyond his illustrious name. He was criticized by conservatives and radicals alike. Underlying the censure was the notion that here was simply another Hoover. Walter Lippmann opined of Roosevelt in the *New York Herald Tribune* of January 8, 1932, "He is a pleasant man who, without any important qualifications for the office, would very much like to be President."

Roosevelt entered the Democratic National Convention, which met in Chicago on June 27, 1932, with a large majority of the delegates pledged to support him. However, his majority fell substantially short of the two-thirds necessary at that time to secure a presidential nomination. Moreover, he was covertly opposed by Al Smith, who was now deeply jealous of the rise of his former protégé. Roosevelt's nomination on the fourth ballot came as a result of the intercession of Joseph P. Kennedy of Boston with newspaper magnate William Randolph Hearst. Hearst controlled the California delegation, nominally led by William Gibbs McAdoo. Hearst and McAdoo gave all forty-four votes of California to Roosevelt. Thus, McAdoo took revenge on Al Smith for having been denied the nomination in 1924. At the end of the fourth ballot Roosevelt had 945 votes. H. L. Mencken observed that Smith looked on Roosevelt as the cuckoo who had seized his nest.

Until 1932 it was the custom for nominees to deliver their acceptance speeches weeks later from their homes. That was what Hoover did in Washington on August 11. Roosevelt, however, arranged to fly to Chicago immediately to address the convention that had nominated him. In his address of July 2, he declared,

> I pledge you, I pledge myself, to a new deal for the American people. Let us all here constitute ourselves prophets of a new order of competence and of courage. This is more than a political campaign; it is a call to arms. Give me your help, not to win votes alone, but to win in this crusade to restore America to its own people.

The next day newspapers across the country reproduced a cartoon by Rollin Kirby. It showed a farmer looking at an airplane in the sky. The plane bore the inscription "New Deal." The phrase, coined by Judge Samuel Rosenman of New York, was a hybrid of Theodore Roosevelt's "Square Deal" and Woodrow Wilson's "New Freedom." The Democratic platform of 1932 not only favored repeal of the Eighteenth Amendment but also proposed loans to the states for unemployment relief, approved the principle of old age insurance to be achieved by state laws, and advocated control of surplus crops while paying lip service to the orthodox wisdom of a balanced budget and a hard currency.

Roosevelt chose Jim Farley, secretary of the New York Democratic Committee, as chairman of the Democratic National Committee. Farley was an Irish-American Catholic with the common touch who had never belonged to Tammany Hall. Publicity agent Charles Michelson released a barrage of publicity for FDR and against Hoover. Roosevelt's academic advisers—the Brain Trust, led by Columbia University professors Raymond Moley, Rexford G. Tugwell, and Adolf A. Berle, Jr., and Gen. Hugh S. Johnson—provided well-researched, effective briefs for Roosevelt to draw on in preparing his policy speeches.

In the election of November 8, 1932, Roosevelt received 22,809,638 votes, 57.4 percent of the total, against Hoover's 15,758,901, 39.7 percent. In the electoral college he had 472 votes to Hoover's 59. He carried all but six states, a larger victory than any Democrat before him. Norman Thomas, the Socialist candidate, received only 881,951 votes, and William Z. Foster, the CPUSA candidate, received 102,785. In Congress the Democrats had 310 seats in the House and the Republicans had 117. In the Senate the Democrats had 60 seats, the Republicans 35.

The juxtaposition of three things—the election of 1932, the repeal movement, and the Great Depression—produced an electoral result that seemed crystal clear. People wanted a change of government, the repeal of prohibition, and new economic policies.

Once the election was over and leading politicians concluded that the public wanted to repeal prohibition, events moved quickly. Repeal was necessarily the first step to ease the depression. Republican Senator John J. Blaine of Wisconsin drafted a new constitutional amendment to be ratified by state legislatures. It proposed three things: an end to national prohibition; that the federal government retain the right to protect dry states against the importation of liquor; and that Congress should have concurrent powers with the states to forbid the return of the saloon. The Twenty-First Amendment repealed the Eighteenth Amendment while prohibiting the importation of intoxicating liquor into states that forbade it. Moreover, the amendment was to be subject to ratification by state conventions within seven years. In this final form the Senate approved the resolution by 63 votes to 23 on February 16, 1933. On February 20 the House passed it by a vote of 289 votes to 121. As state convention followed state convention, it became clear that even such traditionally dry states as Alabama, Arkansas, and Tennessee now favored repeal. It was rare for the wet majority to fall below 60 percent. Of the total popular vote, 15 million, or 72.9 percent, favored repeal.

The federal government precipitated repeal by anticipating it. One of Roosevelt's first acts after taking office on March 4, 1933, was to request a special session of Congress on March 13 to revise the Volstead Act, pending repeal of prohibition, to allow beer of 3.2 percent alcohol. Among his arguments was the need for additional federal revenue that could be raised by a tax on beer. Thus, beer became legal under new federal dispensation on April 7, 1933. It was freely consumed on that day in Washington and in nineteen states. A week later an Associated Press release claimed that the federal government had already received $4 million in license fees and taxes on barrels of beer. FDR established a Federal Alcohol Control Administration under the National Recovery Administration on December 4, 1933.

Meanwhile, in early 1933 the depression continued along its relentless path. Industrial production foundered, unemployment mounted, farm mortgage foreclosures became ever more common. Banks failed, and state authorities could not meet their relief obligations.

One obstacle in the way of positive executive action was the long period of four months between the presidential election on November 8 and inauguration in March 4. Accordingly, to remedy matters, Senator George W. Norris of Nebraska proposed the Twentieth Amendment, which Congress ratified on March 3, 1932. It eliminated the lame duck session of an old Congress by requiring the new Congress to meet on January 3 following the election. It also brought forward the date of presidential inauguration from March 4 to January 20. The Twentieth Amendment was not ratified until February 1933, however, and thus could not take effect until 1935 and 1937.

In the meantime, there was a stultifying loss of confidence between election and inauguration. Herbert Hoover tried to arrange for a smooth transition by attempting a dialogue with Roosevelt. But Roosevelt was a past master at parrying suggestions that implied commitment to any previous policy.

A series of bank failures, most notably in February 1933, made the collapse of Hoover's intended dialogue most unfortunate. The weak American banking system was a prime cause of the depression. Bank failures were something of a chronic feature of American economic life during the early thirties. There had been 1,345 in 1930, 2,298 in 1931, and 1,456 in 1932. The American banking system was in a state of acute crisis.

The crisis deepened in October 1932 when the governor of Nevada anticipated the failure of an important banking chain by closing the state banks for a public holiday. Then, at midnight on February 14, 1933, Governor William A. Comstock of Michigan issued a proclamation closing all 550 banks in the state for eight days. The crisis had been precipitated by a run on the Union Guardian Trust Company of Detroit. The Michigan bank holiday led to a panic across various states and a series of bank holidays. A man in his cups in a speakeasy in New York asked the bartender how many states had declared bank holidays. "Thirty-eight," was the answer. "Ah!" said the customer. "That ratifies the depression."

One important side effect of these closures was the flow of gold reserves from the Federal Reserve System and banks in New York City both to support the deposits of banks across the country and at the demand of panic-stricken foreign investors. Thus, in just over two months, from January to early March 1933, the nation's gold reserves fell from over $1.3 billion to $400 million. By early 1933 America's 18,569 banks had only about $6 billion altogether in cash to meet $41 billion in deposits. In the two days before FDR's presidential inauguration, clients withdrew $300 million from banks across the country.

The bank crisis made people of all classes recognize the imperative need for decisive executive action, even modified dictatorship. Now Walter Lippmann declared in his "Today and Tomorrow" column for the *Tribune* on February 17, 1933, "The danger we have to fear is not that Congress will give Franklin D. Roosevelt too much power, but that it will deny him the powers he needs."

CHAPTER 11

That Man in the White House

Franklin Delano Roosevelt and the New Deal

P R E S I D E N T Franklin Delano Roosevelt spoke at his inauguration on March 4, 1933, with such impeccable flair that he captured the imagination of the entire country. For, instead of simply saying, "I do," after Chief Justice Charles Evans Hughes read out the oath of office, FDR repeated the full text and then embarked on a stirring inaugural speech.

> Let me first assert my firm belief that the only thing we have to fear is fear itself—nameless, unreasoning, unjustified terror which paralyzes needed efforts to convert retreat into advance.
>
> I shall ask the Congress for the one remaining instrument to meet the crisis—broad Executive power to wage a war against the emergency, as great as the power that would be given me if we were, in fact, invaded by a foreign foe.

The radio broadcast across the nation stopped listeners in their tracks. Frederick Lewis Allen summed up (1940) the impression FDR made on the vast radio audience:

> You can turn off the radio now. You have heard what you wanted to hear. This man sounds no longer cautious, evasive. For he has seen that a tortured and bewildered people want to throw overboard the old and welcome something new; that they are sick of waiting, they want somebody who will *fight* the Depression for them and with them; they want leadership, the thrill of bold decision. And not only in his words but in the challenge of the very accents of his voice, he has promised them what they want.

FDR's determination to meet the bank crisis demonstrated just how decisive would be his new start. On Sunday, March 5, 1933, he summoned Congress into an extraordinary session for Thursday, March 9. Taking advantage of legislation from World War I that gave the president wide executive authority in case of bank emergency, he declared a four-day national holiday on Monday, March 6. Thus he prevented further panic withdrawals and gold hoarding, while allowing time for Treasury officials to devise emergency draft legislation.

Cartoonist Clifford Berryman was as adroit in exploring the comic possibilities of FDR as he had been with Theodore Roosevelt. This cartoon for the *Washington Post* of 1933 shows the earnest but wishful-thinking new president attempting to dispel the Great Depression by singing a cheerful song at an amateur talent contest, accompanied by a frizzled harpy in a frilly frock pounding out the tune on a beat-up piano, while jealous former Democratic standard-bearer Al Smith sulks behind him. (Library of Congress)

A special session of Congress approved the Emergency Banking Relief Act on March 9. In the House the debate lasted only four minutes. The act provided aid for hard-pressed but solvent banks. The Reconstruction Finance Corporation (RFC) could buy the preferred stock of banks, giving them additional operating funds from the Federal Reserve Banks. On April 19, 1933, Roosevelt forbade the hoarding and exporting of gold. He did this to preempt a revival of the discredited idea of coining silver to achieve inflation. Those banks that government assessors examined and approved could reopen immediately. Those that required further examination—about a quarter—could pay out only part of their deposits. After a few days, banks that had accounted for 90 percent of all deposits before the bank crisis were allowed to reopen.

On March 12 Roosevelt gave his first specific radio address, or fireside chat. His words made his actions intelligible to all. His gentle, invigorating tone encouraged reinvestment. By April depositors returned over $1 billion in currency to bank deposits. The bank crisis was over. In the words of Frederick Lewis Allen, "The New Deal had made a brilliant beginning."

The name of Franklin Delano Roosevelt has become synonymous with twelve years of assertive leadership and the extension of executive power. People knew Roosevelt simply by his initials, FDR, with their suggestion of an enclosed word, FEDERAL, in tribute to the only president to be elected four times.

Roosevelt's enigmatic personality was part patriarch, part child. To his allies he appeared exuberant, charming, and generous. His welcoming manner gave his visitors the impression that he agreed with their recommendations. He used ambiguity as a political tool to rouse support or silence criticism. FDR's enemies characterized him as a manipulative and vindictive megalomaniac. Despite his patrician education, his experience in practical politics and his courageous fight to overcome the crippling limitations of polio combined to make him compassionate toward those with physical and social disabilities.

FDR was not widely read. He did not have an original mind, nor was he capable of sustained analysis. He was creative, however, in the use he made of the superior individual talents of others and in the constructive use he made of conflicting ideas. "A second-class intellect—but a first-class temperament" was Justice Oliver Wendell Holmes's famous comment on FDR. His intuitive, flexible approach allowed him to retain what worked and to discard what did not. Before making his decisions, he sought different opinions and weighed numerous questions of public interest and political consequence. His reorganization of the executive was an outstanding administrative achievement. Roosevelt transformed the presidency, even beyond the formidable resurrection of the office by Theodore Roosevelt and Woodrow Wilson. FDR dispatched messages to Congress along with draft legislation. By letters and meetings, he put pressure on committee chairmen and other key figures in Congress. By the end of the 1930s Congress expected presidential initiatives. It looked for guidance from its chief administrator, from whom it expected a regular program of proposed legislation. In effect, twentieth-century Washington, both as capital and as center of government, was largely FDR's creation.

Furthermore, FDR dominated the front pages of newspapers as no other president had before and as none has since. By his unsurpassed number of 998 press conferences, by getting his aides to answer all letters, which totaled between five thousand and eight thousand each working day, and most of all by his twenty-eight radio broadcasts, called "fireside chats" by CBS manager Harry C. Butcher, FDR made himself the most accessible president since Theodore Roosevelt. FDR's fireside chats were models of directness and simplicity. Indeed, all his speeches and his delivery of them showed finish and grace. Roosevelt was also in his element with the press, sharpening his political talents and developing his special techniques in conversation, a mix of seriousness, humor, sincerity—and evasion.

Roosevelt's career before and during his presidency was advanced by the distinctive support of his wife, Eleanor. Theirs was an astonishing political collaboration. She had the political advantage of being Theodore Roosevelt's niece but the social disadvantages of being orphaned by the time she was nine and of growing up tall and awkward. Yet her amazing energy, initiative, and social conscience stirred her to work for social improvement and in doing so, to find fulfillment. Whereas FDR was crippled, she was mobile. She moved across the country and reported to him what she found. Eleanor used her position not to gain political power for herself but to make FDR heed otherwise-unheard-from voices: African Americans, working women, and—strange as it seems—the unemployed. Eleanor thought about what *should* be done: Franklin considered only what *could* be done. She was more compassionate, less devious, and more moral. But, although the Roosevelts remained partners in politics, they were not companions of the heart.

The various policies of the New Deal were experimental and diverse. One reason for this is the varied characters of the New Dealers. Roosevelt's cabinet appointments were a mix of the conventional and the progressive. His most distinctive appointments were Harold L. Ickes, Frances Perkins, and Henry A. Wallace.

Harold L. Ickes of Chicago, who became secretary of the interior (1933–45), was a progressive Republican turned Democrat. His lawyer's training gave him insight into corruption in office, and his progressive zeal led him to weed it out. He had a fiery temper and liked to be known as the old curmudgeon. Secretary of Labor Frances Perkins (1933–45), the first woman in any cabinet, was a social worker who had served with Al Smith and FDR in Albany. Her colleagues disliked her assertiveness and sharp tongue. Yet in Congress Perkins made firm and valuable allies of Senator Robert F. Wagner of New York and Congressman David J. Lewis of Maryland. The staid leaders of the AFL disliked her because she was a woman. Secretary of Agriculture Henry A. Wallace (1933–41) was the far more radical son of Henry C. Wallace, secretary of agriculture under Harding and Coolidge. His solutions were pragmatic and ingenious.

Another of FDR's innovations was the extensive use of the Brain Trust, a group of academic advisers like those used by TR and Woodrow Wilson. But FDR broadened the basis of selection and expanded the role of the Brain Trust. From Columbia University Roosevelt used Professors Raymond Moley, Adolf A. Berle, Jr., and Rexford G. Tugwell, who had assisted him during the presidential campaign. These academics were not confined to the sidelines as advisers without power. Raymond Moley was assistant secretary of state in 1933 and Rexford G. Tugwell was assistant secretary of agriculture in 1933 and undersecretary in

1934–37. Lawyers Thomas A. Corcoran and Benjamin Cohen of Harvard drafted legislation that was lawyer-proof, including the Securities Exchange Act of 1934.

Because of the expanded role it allotted to the federal government and the unprecedented volume of legislation, the New Deal encouraged the growth of the legal profession. More lawyers were needed to frame laws, to work as administrators, and to advise and act for firms and private citizens. Their obsession with mechanism was a prime factor behind the New Deal's opportunism, its tendency to compromise, and its readiness to accept the existing balance of power between competing interest groups.

The New Dealers were genuinely reform-minded and confident they could improve society by reshaping it. To this end they combined the experience of national planning in World War I, the urban social reforms of the Progressives at the turn of the century, and the Populists' plans for agriculture and finance in the 1890s.

The most influential New Dealers were economic planners. They advocated central, planned intervention by the federal government in the economy, according to the academic reasoning of economic Progressives like Herbert Croly and Thorstein Veblen. But this group was divided between conservatives, who wanted to see a partnership between business and government with business in the lead, and reformers, who wanted the federal government to regulate business. According to this school of thought, not only was a balanced budget unnecessary, but it might also stand in the way of recovery. By trying to balance the books, orthodox accountants were further constricting demand and helping to intensify the depression they were trying to relieve. The way out of the depression was through debt—carefully calculated government spending on public works to create employment in bad times. Thereafter, in good times, the way to prevent recurrence of the depression was through finely calculated government taxation. Thus, the government would act as a stimulating or retarding factor. Among the economic planners, the conservatives were led by Raymond Moley and Hugh Johnson and the reformers by Adolf A. Berle, Jr., and Rexford G. Tugwell. Not only did the New Deal attempt to alleviate the depression with programs for relief and public works, but Roosevelt was also concerned about malfunction in the American political system as a whole. He wanted to correct inequalities.

The emphases of the New Deal changed considerably in the period 1933–38. Thus, historians distinguish between the first New Deal of 1933–35, primarily devoted to recovery and relief, and the second New Deal of 1935–38, aimed at a wide reform of the economic system. The second New Deal used long-term measures to pass on the benefits of modern technology to farmers and consumers while providing safeguards against any future depressions. However, there were elements of the first New Deal in the second New Deal, and vice versa. There was a third New Deal in the legislation of 1937–38. It was intended to introduce national planning, but it foundered on the stormy seas of adversary politics.

The First Hundred Days and the Early New Deal

Because the Democrats had said next to nothing in the election of 1932 about the need for national economic planning, the impact of the first hundred days of 1933 was overwhelming. Part of Roosevelt's extraordinary political success in getting his legislation through Congress lay in the new situation. The new Congress was predominantly Democratic, and its freshmen were eager to respond to bold initiatives.

Contemporary revelations by an investigating subcommittee of the Senate Finance Committee had made the public aware of how great was the need for reforms in banking, securities, and the stock market. Under the skillful chairmanship of Democratic Senator Duncan U. Fletcher of Florida and tenacious counsel Ferdinand Pecora, it exposed how bankers had appropriated funds for their own use and also evaded income tax. The Pecora committee constituted what Frederick Lewis Allen calls "a sort of protracted coroner's inquest upon American finance." Its procession of unwilling witnesses disclosed "a sorry story of public irresponsibility and private greed."

Great public outrage and the New Dealers' response to these revelations led to the Glass-Steagall Banking Act of June 1933, which separated commercial banks from their investment affiliates so that they could use neither their depositors' funds nor the resources of the Federal Reserve for speculation. It also gave the Federal Reserve more control over its member banks. Moreover, it established the Federal Deposit Insurance Corporation (FDIC), which insured clients' deposits up to $2,500 initially and later (in 1935) up to $5,000; subsequently the limit rose to $15,000. The American Banking Association resented this proposal, claiming that it was governmental interference.

The Truth-in-Securities Act of 1933 and the Securities Exchange Act of 1934 were inspired by further disclosures of the Pecora committee that J. P. Morgan, Jr., had a select list of friends to whom the House of Morgan offered stocks below the market price. They included conservative Democrats Bernard Baruch, John J. Raskob, and William Gibbs McAdoo, and Republicans Calvin Coolidge and Owen J. Roberts. During the course of J. P. Morgan's testimony, a circus promoter managed to set a midget on Morgan's knee. Here was capitalism, little and large, for all America to see. Another discovery was that so-called pools had operated to bring about rapid rises in particular stocks, usually by spreading false reports of their value or by intense buying-and-selling activities. In such ways, a pool created a public appetite for the stock of Radio Corporation of America (RCA) through the agency of the brokers M. J. Meehan and Company. It succeeded in increasing the value of RCA stock from 79 to 109 in seven days, after which the participants sold out in order to capitalize on their good fortune. Such discoveries led the public to seek protection for investors.

The Truth-in-Securities Act of 1933 required brokers to furnish complete information to prospective investors as to the true value of securities. Moreover, it held the underwriter and corporate officer responsible for the truthfulness of the stock's registration and the arrangements under which it was sold.

The Securities Exchange Act of 1934 established the Securities Exchange Commission (SEC) as a nonpartisan agency to oversee and regulate the activities of all stock exchanges and to prevent fraud and manipulation. Outraged by threat of government surveillance, leaders of the New York Stock Exchange, which accounted for more than 90 percent of national securities trading, threatened to move to Canada if Congress passed the bill. But the overwhelming evidence of past malpractice convinced public and Congress alike that this was an essential measure. Public opinion was confirmed by the 1938 trial and imprisonment of Richard Whitney, president of the New York Stock Exchange, for embezzlement. Those who opposed the legislation at first were later convinced that it afforded banking and securities much-needed government protection. On the advice of Raymond Moley, FDR appointed speculator Joseph Kennedy to head the SEC. Moley reasoned that, precisely because Kennedy was a speculator, he knew the loopholes in the law and would be well equipped to plug them.

Roosevelt understood that the core of the economic crisis in 1933 was the very low level of prices. The clear remedy was to reverse the process, first by restoring confidence in the banks, and second by increasing the amount of currency in circulation.

On March 6, 1933, Roosevelt prohibited the redemption of currency in gold coin. On April 5 he issued an executive order whereby gold (coin, certificates, and bullion) had to be delivered to the Federal Reserve in exchange for an equivalent amount in currency or coin. Two weeks later, the Treasury announced that it would no longer grant licenses for the export of gold. These several measures had the effect of taking the United States off the gold standard at home while still retaining gold to support its currency and allowing government payments abroad in gold. Lewis Douglas, director of the budget, was aghast at the idea of taking the dollar off the gold standard, something he described as "the end of western civilization." But informed conservatives, led by bankers Charles Gates Dawes, Russell Leffingwell, and J. P. Morgan, Jr., approved of FDR's policy of devaluation.

Roosevelt's policy left open the possibility that creditors could require debtors to repay loans in gold, instead of currency, and thus they would gain an advantage. Therefore, in June 1933 Congress passed a joint resolution that voided clauses in loan contracts requiring payment in gold. The joint resolution was upheld by the Supreme Court in 1935. The administration's overriding intention behind these various measures was to bring down the value of the dollar on foreign exchanges while raising prices at home. By May 1933 the international value of the dollar had fallen to eighty-five cents in gold. Other countries could buy 15 percent more American goods than before. At home wholesale prices increased slightly.

This success placed FDR in a quandary during the London Economic Conference attended by Secretary of State Cordell Hull (1933–44) in June and July

1933. Delegates from other countries wanted a stabilization of currencies, including the dollar. Roosevelt could not agree to that when it was the falling value of the dollar that was revitalizing the U.S. economy. For the sake of immediate economic benefits at home, FDR refused U.S. support for any multilateral monetary policy, thereby torpedoing the whole conference, embarrassing Cordell Hull in London, and incurring the deep resentment of Europe.

However, the policy of allowing the dollar simply to float in the exchange market produced neither the right level of exchange abroad nor economic recovery at home. Hence, on the advice of the Brain Trust, FDR decided to bid up the price of gold. Secretary of the Treasury William H. Woodin was ill at the time. On October 22, 1933, FDR announced that the RFC would buy gold on government account above world market price (initially, at $31.36 per ounce). The price of gold was fixed by FDR and his advisers each morning. Once, Roosevelt increased the price by 21 cents an ounce simply because he liked the number 21. As the price for gold rose, the value of the dollar declined. In January 1934 the ratio stood at $34.45 for one ounce of gold. FDR had devalued the dollar by 40 percent. Bitter Al Smith called it a "baloney dollar."

Then FDR decided to stabilize things. In the Gold Reserve Act of January 30, 1934, Congress set the price of gold at $35 per ounce. The silver lobby was sufficiently influential at this time to persuade FDR and Congress to pass the Silver Purchase Act of June 1934, requiring the Treasury to buy silver at home and abroad until a quarter of all U.S. monetary stocks were in silver or until the market price of silver had reached $1.29 per ounce. This unnecessary legislation was no better than a bribe to a powerful special interest group.

Alphabet Three Letters at a Time

The federal government's chief strike against the depression was a special agency, the National Recovery Administration (NRA). The National Industrial Recovery Act was passed by Congress on June 16, 1933—the last of the first hundred days. It tried to achieve planning and cooperation among the three sectors: business, labor, and government. Industry received government support in its aim to reduce cutthroat competition and unfair practices. In return, it made certain concessions to labor that were thought to be in the national interest and would promote recovery.

Title II declared a state of national emergency and suspended some antitrust laws. It established the NRA and required government and industry to draw up codes of practice as to business competition and hours and wages. Public hearings would be held before the NRA to ensure that the interests of business, labor, and government were being observed in individual industries. After approval by the president, individual codes of practice, agreed to at the hearings, would become legally binding. Thereafter, action under the code would be exempt from the antitrust laws.

Section 7a declared that employees could join individual unions, appoint of-

Jack Delano's photograph of severe gully erosion on a farm in Greene County, northwest Georgia, in October 1941 suggests an excavation—as if the land had been mined—and emphasizes the severe nature of problems in the agricultural depression that dispossessed many African Americans as well as whites of their livelihood. (Farm Security Administration; Library of Congress)

ficers, and were entitled to collective bargaining. But in the absence of adequate enforcement machinery, companies either ignored the act or reactivated employee representation plans and company unions. By 1935 nearly 2.5 million workers were covered by such plans, as compared with the 4.1 million members of trade unions. Thus, the act accepted the existence of giant corporations. To protect the public from abuse, it relied solely on cooperation between business and government.　Title II authorized the president to create the Public Works Administration (PWA) with $3.3 billion for "pump-priming" expenditures on such public construction projects as highways, dams, schools, and federal buildings. Secretary of the Interior Harold Ickes had charge of the PWA.

Roosevelt also employed Gen. Hugh ("Ironpants") Johnson, originally of the army and the Mowline Plow Company, as head of the NRA. Within three weeks Johnson persuaded the heads of the textile industry to agree to the first set of

The New Deal Goes to War. Fontana Dam, completed in 1944, was built to generate electricity for the U.S. defense effort in World War II. Built on the Little Tennessee River in western North Carolina, Fontana is the highest dam east of the Rocky Mountains. Its three turbine-generator units could produce 238,500 kilowatts of electricity. (Tennessee Valley Authority; Library of Congress)

NRA codes. Eventually, 557 basic codes were approved, encompassing every sort of business from brassieres to bottle caps. To expedite matters, Johnson devised a blanket code, known as the President's Reemployment Agreement, that allowed small businesses to subscribe to the main tenets of the NRA on hours and conditions of work without the inconvenience of lengthy hearings. In this way he hoped to increase employment and purchasing power quickly. Those who conformed were entitled to display an emblem, the Blue Eagle, underneath which was inscribed the motto, "We Do Our Part." To secure maximum publicity, Johnson organized rallies and parades with songs and dances.

However, the NRA aroused widespread dissatisfaction. Consumers said the NRA caused a steep rise in prices ahead of wages. Labor said Section 7a was inadequate and that it could be circumvented by unscrupulous employers. Small businesses said the codes were drafted by big business in its own interests. Moreover, they did not have the resources to comply with the sort of far-reaching regulations devised for large firms. In particular, they could not always afford the minimum wages prescribed by the codes. Big business was increasingly alarmed at the prospect of increased governmental regulation and by the gains of organized labor. It regarded the NRA as the thin edge of a most unwelcome wedge.

The first major code of the National Reconstruction Administration for cotton textiles provided neither fewer hours nor higher pay for unskilled work, normally performed by African Americans, and the differential treatment set a precedent for other textile codes. NRA codes in other industries, such as steel and tobacco, specifically allowed lower wages for African Americans than for whites. The NRA's discrimination against African Americans led some to call the NRA "Negroes Ruined Again."

Opposition to the NRA grew in other, unexpected quarters.

On March 7, 1934, Congress established the National Recovery Review Board under lawyer Clarence Darrow to study monopolistic tendencies in the codes. Its report emphasized that the NRA encouraged the monopoly tactics of big business. Public respect for the NRA was damaged further when a dry cleaner was sent to jail in New Jersey for pressing trousers for less than the regular code price. Furthermore, FDR realized that Johnson, whom he admired, was something of a liability because of his outspoken comments in the face of so much criticism. When the press discovered Johnson liked alcohol and loved his secretary, he justified her high salary by saying "she was more than just a stenographer." FDR replaced Johnson with Donald Richberg and relaxed some of the codes.

Agricultural recovery was just as complex a problem as industrial recovery. Its solution was even more urgent since the ills of agriculture had led to violence in parts of the Midwest. There were two principal problems: the increasing number of mortgage foreclosures on farms and the fact that farm purchasing power, in terms of the industrial goods farmers had to buy, was at its lowest level ever. FDR proposed another series of emergency measures. On March 27, 1933, he centralized those agencies dealing with agricultural credit in the Farm Credit Administration. In April 1933 Congress passed the Emergency Farm Mortgage Act to fund emergency loans for farms and, subsequently, short-term loans for livestock farmers. The Frazier-Lemke Farm Bankruptcy Act of June 1934 enabled farmers to recover farms previously lost when mortgages had been foreclosed; it allowed them to do so on terms prescribed by a federal court with interest at only 1 percent.

As to long-term measures, there was the same variety of opinion about agriculture as there had been about industrial recovery. FDR and Secretary of Agriculture Henry A. Wallace conferred with farm leaders to consolidate various ideas in the Agriculture Adjustment Administration (AAA), which declared that the following were staple crops: wheat, corn, cotton, tobacco, rice, milk, hogs, and (later) livestock and sugar. Individual farmers made an agreement by which, in exchange for acres taken out of cultivation, they were given benefit payments. The money to finance the program came from a tax levied on processors of staple foods, who passed on the tax to consumers in higher prices.

Crusading agricultural reformer George N. Peek became head of the AAA. Through his agents, he persuaded cotton farmers to plow under 10 million acres, a quarter of the crop, in return for benefit payments. The AAA also bought 6 million piglets, which were slaughtered and processed to feed the unemployed. Thus was plenty destroyed in the midst of want. Few people understood the principles underlying government policy. Public outcry on behalf of the slaughtered piglets vented itself in abuse of AAA officials. Cotton farmers plowed under a quarter of their crop in exchange for benefits but overfertilized the remaining land so that the 1933 crop actually exceeded the 1932 crop of 13 million bales by 45,000 bales. Because of this counterproductive overproduction, Congress passed the Bankhead Cotton Control Act of 1934. It set production quotas for cotton and placed a prohibitive tax on all cotton sold in excess of the quota. The Kerr-Smith Tobacco Act of June 1934 introduced similar restrictions on tobacco farmers.

To solve the problems of farm tenancy, the Resettlement Administration, established in April 1935 under Rexford G. Tugwell, tried to move farmers from poor land to new cooperative communities but without much success. In the Bankhead-Jones Farm Tenancy Act of July 1937, Congress tried to raise farm tenants and sharecroppers to the status of owners. It established the Farm Security Administration (FSA), which allowed tenants to borrow money at 3 percent interest to purchase land. Over a three-year period it made available small rehabilitation loans of an average of $350 each to 750,000 tenant farmers. The FSA also provided the most indelible images of the depression through the masterly photographs taken by Arthur Rothstein, Ben Shahn, and Dorothea Lange. Through her choice of gesture and judicious use of perspective and framing, Lange emphasized the dignity of her ravaged subjects, notably in her "Migrant Mother," taken in a camp for migrant workers in Nipomo, California, in February 1936, which became an icon of the depression.

The AAA accomplished much. In 1933 10.4 million acres were taken out of production; in 1934, 35.7 million acres; and in 1935, 30.3 million acres. Partly because of these policies of crop limitation and partly because of serious droughts, farm prices rose. A bushel of wheat brought, on average, only 33 cents in 1933. Thereafter, the price rose gradually to 88 cents in 1938. Total farm income rose from $4.5 billion in 1932 to $6.9 billion in 1935. Thus, farmers were a third better off financially by 1935 than they had been in 1932. For above all, the AAA allowed FDR and the New Dealers to put into practice their central concept for a balance between the various sections of the economic community. Moreover, the very existence of the AAA was a factor in persuading urban congressmen that a revitalized economy could not be built upon a declining agriculture.

The Tennessee Valley Authority struck industrial as well as agricultural blows at the Depression. The valleys of the southern Alleghenies were a poverty-stricken area, their soils washed away by a fatal combination of exploitative hillside farming, heavy rainfalls, and flooding. Conservationists wanted a coordinated strategy to preserve the region from itself.

On April 10, 1933, having conferred with Senator George W. Norris of Nebraska, for many years a lone pioneer of the project to make Muscle Shoals, Tennessee, the center of a vast water and power plant, FDR asked Congress to create the Tennessee Valley Authority (TVA), which was achieved in an act passed on May 18, 1933. The TVA was to complete and extend the Muscle Shoals project, creating a new 650-mile inland waterway to connect the South with the Great Lakes, the Ohio River, and the Missouri and Mississippi River systems. The TVA was to construct new dams and improve existing ones.

Under a board of three directors, its general role was to promote the economic and social welfare of people in seven states, extending over an area of 80,000 square miles with a population of a million. It was also to control floods, to generate cheap hydroelectric power, to manufacture fertilizers, to check erosion, and to provide reforestation. It had the authority to fix the resale rates of power it generated, establishing the yardstick by which the rates of competing private utility companies could also be elevated.

The waterway allowed the importation of sorely needed automobiles, iron, cement, and gas to the Allegheny region, via barges. The TVA invented new fertilizers and showed farmers how to conserve moisture in the soil and how to use contour plowing and cover crops. As a result, farm income in Tennessee improved by 200 percent in the period 1929–49, compared with a national average improvement of 170 percent in the same period. The TVA encouraged wider and greater use of electricity and the penetration of industry into the region to benefit from cheap hydroelectric power. By the early 1940s the TVA's average annual consumption of electricity was 1,180 kilowatt hours per person at the rate of 2 cents per hour, compared with a national average of 850 kilowatt hours per person at the rate of 4 cents an hour.

The TVA statute of incorporation put the manufacture and distribution of electricity into a secondary role as a by-product. This was partly because the New Dealers realized that the private power companies would complain to the Supreme Court of unfair competition. Thus they forced the Court to find that the actual wording of the act was such that they could not decide against the TVA. In the cases of *Ashwander v. TVA* of February 1936 and *Tennessee Electric Power Company v. TVA* of January 1939, the Court upheld the constitutionality of the TVA and its right to sell electricity. The leader of the concerted attack by nineteen private companies against the TVA was Wendell Willkie, president of Commonwealth and Southern. After the case Willkie sold the entire facilities of the Tennessee Electric Power Company to the TVA for the high price of $78.6 million.

The yardstick provoked greater controversy. People found it impossible to distinguish the cost of actually producing electricity from such necessary safety precautions as dam maintenance and flood control. In later years the TVA provided power for the entire aluminum industry and for the development of the atomic bomb. It led to the creation of new areas of recreation for tourists. It advanced opportunities for an entire region—an impressive experiment in social renewal.

Architecture, engineering, and technology: the great dams of the 1930s combined all three. They were as formidable a contribution to the expanding world of American machines as were skyscrapers and suspension bridges. Skyscrapers cut a swath in the sky; dams cut into the earth, diverted rivers, and lit up whole regions. Not only did such creations as the Hoover, Grand Coulee, and Tennessee Valley Authority dams provide irrigation, prevent flooding, generate electricity, and allow more land to be farmed, but they also, in turn, transformed the living conditions of millions while ushering in a new era of hydroelectric power. The creation of such huge, multifunctional dams captured the imagination of all classes who lived through the Great Depression. They recognized this one striking feature of the New Deal as a benevolent achievement of planning—a potent symbol of man's ability to control the environment and harness the forces of nature for the improvement of society.

The Hoover Dam, Boulder City, Nevada (1930–36), situated over the Colorado River in the torrid desert thirty miles from Las Vegas, gave rise to Boulder City, a dormitory and service town for its numerous engineers, five thousand construction workers, and their families. At the time of completion, at over 726 feet and with 3.40 million cubic yards of concrete, it was the highest and largest dam in the world with the largest reservoir, Lake Mead, having 28.53 million acre-feet of water. Continuous construction day and night was undertaken in daunting circumstances, with summer temperatures between 120 and 140 degrees and winter temperatures below 20 degrees with such additional difficulties as blustery winds.

Workers were imperiled by natural and machine-made hazards as they swam along canyon walls to strip away rock. They had to divert the Colorado River through manmade tunnels, erecting temporary cofferdams to block the river; finally, they had to excavate the site. There were other technical problems. If the concrete used for retaining was simply poured down, it would have taken a hundred years to cool and harden. It would then have shrunk so much as to crack the entire edifice. The solution was to pour individual slabs of concrete and hasten their cooling by circulating refrigerated water through them by means of tubes, thereby cooling each section within twenty-four hours. As to the appearance of the dam, the engineers wanted consultant architect Gordon R. Kauffman to provide a facade that would rise naturally from the landscape and yet dominate it by means of setbacks, surmounted by winged bronze monuments designed by Oskar J. W. Hansen and a powerhouse designed in a streamlined fashion.

Relief

The New Deal provided relief on a scale never previously attempted. What had most deterred the Hoover administration from a vast program of federal relief was the scale of the cost. The federal government simply did not have enough revenue. And as long as the orthodox wisdom of a balanced budget remained government policy, nothing could be done.

FDR was willing to depart from the conventional wisdom to relieve widespread distress. The first significant relief measure of the New Deal was aimed at young people between the ages of eighteen and twenty-five, a disproportionate share of the unemployed. The Civilian Conservation Corps Reforestation Relief Act of March 31, 1933, created the very first New Deal agency, and the one that most bore the imprint of FDR and his earlier reforestation projects in New York State.

The Civilian Conservation Corps (CCC), managed jointly by the Departments of Labor and the Interior, organized projects of reforestation, soil conservation, construction of firebreaks and forest lookout towers, and construction of recreational facilities in national parks. FDR was singularly impressed by the organizational skills of Gen. Douglas MacArthur and Col. George C. Marshall. Between 1933 and 1942 more than 2 million young men served in the agency, usually for periods of nine months. Their pay was $30 per month, plus board and lodging, and $25 per month was sent to their families in order to spread relief and purchasing power.

To provide relief for the urban unemployed, the Federal Emergency Relief Act of May 12, 1933, established the Federal Emergency Relief Administration (FERA) under social worker Harry L. Hopkins. FERA divided its appropriation of $500 million evenly among the states. Half of the appropriation was used to provide $1 for every $3 spent by the local authorities; the remaining half went outright to the poorest states for direct relief.

The Public Works Administration of July 1933, established under Title II of the National Industrial Recovery Act and placed under the supervision of Secretary of the Interior Harold Ickes, was intended to revitalize industry by creating public works to stimulate the need for capital goods. The PWA was a major achievement, creating schools, bridges, dams, post offices, and court houses. However, Ickes proved so cautious in dispensing the allocation of $3.3 billion that the PWA did very little to stimulate recovery or provide relief. FDR was disturbed. Acting on the advice of Harry Hopkins, he took $400 million of PWA money and created a new, temporary agency, the Civil Works Administration (CWA) in November 1933 and asked Harry Hopkins to run it.

Hopkins's impact here and elsewhere led to his ascendancy over all FDR's other advisers. He had charge of the Federal Emergency Relief Administration (1935–38), before becoming secretary of commerce (1938–40) and administrator of Lend-Lease in 1941. Cynics said that Hopkins had the purity of St. Francis of Assisi combined with the shrewdness of a race-course tout. The CWA put more than 4 million people to work in the winter of 1933–34 in various makeshift projects, but it drew opposition from both the Republicans and the Democrats. FDR closed it down in 1934. FERA was then given extra funds and thus increased its family allowance payments to $35 per month by July 1935.

Within the CWA, a federal art project sustained many progressive painters, both realists and modernists. It was the brainchild of George Biddle, a member of a Philadelphia family who had known FDR since they had attended Groton and Harvard. On May 9, 1933, Biddle wrote to Roosevelt suggesting that young American painters would support the New Deal and were eager to express the ideals of social revolution in mural form on the walls of America's public buildings. Biddle's inspiration came from the experiment sponsored by the Mexican president, Alvaro Obregon, in the 1920s. Public buildings in Mexico City were covered with murals by artists Diego Rivera, Jose Clemente Orozco, and David Alfaro Siqueiros, devoted to the subjects of political revolution and industrial production.

FDR was enthusiastic about Biddle's proposals, and Biddle and his ally, Edward Bruce of the Treasury Department, managed to get the project funded through the CWA. Biddle and Bruce recommended a central committee in Washington, D.C., with decentralized regional advisory committees, each with a regional chairman selected by the central committee. The Public Works Art Project (PWAP) was operational by December 1933 with eighty-six artists and technical director Forbes Watson. However, the PWAP lasted only as long as Harry Hopkins's ill-fated CWA. In using the $40 million allocated to him from Harold Ickes's Public Works Administration, Hopkins had adopted a policy of administering relief across the board without means tests or other forms of qualified distribution. By spring 1934 these unorthodox methods had aroused such strong conservative opposition that Roosevelt closed the CWA.

Congress, by the Home Owners Refinancing Act of May 13, 1933, created the Home Owners Loan Corporation to prevent foreclosures of domestic mortgages. It rescued urban home mortgages by refinancing the loans at lower rates of interest over longer periods of time. In June 1934 Congress established the Federal Housing Administration (FHA), a system of federal mortgage insurance, permitted to insure up to 80 percent (and later 90 percent) of newly constructed homes costing six thousand dollars or less at low rates of interest payable over long periods. Thus, it also tried to revive the stagnant construction industry. Moreover, it made home ownership possible for many who would otherwise never have had the opportunity to buy their own house.

Such extensive spending on relief increased the federal debt from $19.5 billion in early 1933 to $22.5 billion in late 1933. Once various state, municipal, and other resources had been depleted and the federal government assumed greater burdens, it rose to $28.7 billion in 1935 and then in 1937 to $36.4 billion. Thereafter, it rose on account of military expenditures. Later, when the debt reached astronomical heights, there was much less criticism of deficit financing than in the early days when its levels were modest. Objections were not about the size of the debt or the principle as much as the way the money was spent.

As business gradually revived in 1933, there was talk of a Roosevelt market. The Federal Reserve Board's adjusted index figure for industrial production rose from 59 in March 1933 to 100 in July 1933 (compared with the 1929 high of 125). Then there was a setback. In August the index fell from 100 to 91. By November it had receded further to 72. Not until December 1933 did it recover its position at 101. This fall was damaging psychologically. People had expected much of the New Deal in general and the NRA in particular. Their disappointment was keen. FDR and his cabinet were well aware that their emergency legislation had not brought recovery and that more fundamental reforms were necessary.

When it came to the tariff, the New Dealers had one cabinet member with a distinct point of view not to be diminished by bargaining between interests. Secretary of State Cordell Hull, a veteran politician from Tennessee, was too tenacious to give up his cherished aim of increasing world trade. Hull persuaded FDR and Secretary of Agriculture Henry A. Wallace to seek bipartisan support for a bill to make tariffs the prerogative of the president rather than Congress. The Reciprocal Trade Agreements Act of June 1934 (renewed in 1937 and 1940) gave the president the power to negotiate bilateral concessions with other countries and, on the basis of those agreements, to raise or lower tariff rates by as much as 50 percent, provided other countries made reciprocal arrangements. Within eighteen months the United States reached agreement with fourteen countries.

But Hull went further. He turned to the most-favored-nation clause of the otherwise notorious Fordney-McCumber Tariff of 1922. That clause enabled FDR and Hull to extend tariff reductions on specific items to all other countries, compared with only a 38 percent increase with countries whose duties did not discriminate against the United States. By 1940 there had been a 61 percent increase of trade with twenty-two countries, compared with only a 38 percent increase with countries not sharing the trade agreements. The tariff acts of 1934, 1937, and 1948 thus reduced the average tariff rates from 40 or 50 percent to 13 percent. However, the value of exports from 1933 to 1939 rose only from $1.7 billion to $3.2 billion, and imports rose from $1.4 billion to $2.3 billion—below the levels of the 1920s. Nevertheless, the government had abandoned the openly selfish economic policies of the previous decade. Yet Congress, in an act sponsored by Senator Hiram Johnson of California and signed by FDR on April 13, 1934, forbade Americans to lend or buy from nations that had defaulted on debts incurred in World War I.

Some policies were more enlightened and constructive. In 1934 the Roosevelt administration used funds from the Reconstruction Finance Corporation and created the Export-Import Bank to stimulate foreign trade by offering credits and loans to finance the purchase of American goods. The Export-Import Bank loaned money to European countries so that they could buy American agricultural produce and to Latin American countries both to stabilize their currencies and to enable them to buy equipment for such projects as road construction.

In the 1930s arguments about trade were more propitious than earlier and also influenced the relationship of the United States with Russia. In 1930 the USSR had bought 36 percent of all American agricultural implements and 50 percent of all tractors; in 1931 it purchased 65 percent of all machine tools exported. After the rise of the Nazis in Germany, FDR and Russian leader Joseph Stalin recognized in each other a potential ally. On November 16, 1933, despite opposition from American conservatives, the two nations agreed to resume diplomatic relations. The economic advantages of the new relationship proved disappointing for the United States. Russia was unable to export much, defaulted on its debt agreements, and, in violation of its diplomatic undertaking, continued to foment Communist activities in the United States.

Whatever the setbacks and disappointments, the humanitarianism of the early New Deal touched the electorate. In the midterm congressional elections, it rewarded the administration with an unprecedented Democratic majority. The Republicans lost 26 out of 35 contested seats in the Senate. The Democrats increased their majority in the House to 318 against 99 Republicans and 11 others, who normally voted with the Democrats. In the state elections only seven states survived the Democratic landslide. The midterm elections proved conclusively that the political balance had shifted from the Republicans to the Democrats. Congress would now have a far more liberal complexion than ever before, and the new congressmen were increasingly impatient of compromise legislation. Moreover, the problems of the depression became more complex and demanded more radical solutions.

The Dust Bowl

The depression actually deepened in some regions. The greatest terrors were reserved for the inhabitants of the Dust Bowl, the states of North and South Dakota, Montana, western Kansas, eastern Colorado, Oklahoma, and northern Texas. Here, human mismanagement had transformed an inhospitable climate and a harsh geography into a graveyard for the American dream of agrarian opportunity.

Once the Great American Desert was settled with improved methods of farming, settlers exploited it by overplowing with John Deere plows that cut below the topsoil and by overgrazing. During World War I tractors for large-scale machine farming were used to expand crop production in order to supply the United States and Europe with more grain, principally wheat. Settlers ruthlessly plowed away what remained of the steppe grass and sod covering that protected the Great Plains. This was a triumph of factory methods over the farm, and the process continued its relentless, exploitative way during the 1920s. At first, years of exceptionally heavy rain hid the true significance of human mismanagement.

In dry years, however, the topsoil simply blew away. As the tragedy unfolded, the government began to count the cost. The National Resources Board estimated in 1934 that Americans had destroyed 35 million acres of previously arable land, had exhausted or removed the soil of another 125 million acres, and now threatened the survival of another 100 million acres of land. The Dust Bowl comprised 750 counties in nineteen states.

The extent of the tragedy drew a wealth of commentary. In the article "Saga of Drought" for *Commonwealth* of September 14, 1934, Charles Morrow Wilson recorded a common enough scene in a series of staccato statements:

> Southwest is parched. Temperature above 100 in shade for forty-three successive days. Missouri Pacific Railway hauling tankcars of water for use of livestock. First time in history. Sam Nance, farmer near Ardmore, Oklahoma, shoots 143 head of cattle to save them from starving. Cotton crop one-half normal. Apples, peaches, small fruits 30 percent normal. Livestock congesting packing centers. Beef selling on foot as low as $.01 a pound. Pasturage exhausted. States too broke to grant drought aid. United States adjudges 81 counties for primary emergency relief: 119 for secondary. Arkansas river four feet below normal record. Town and city reservoirs failing. Churches praying for rain in many parts of Arkansas, Oklahoma, and Texas.

Chronic agricultural problems were worsened by a series of great windstorms. The first began in South Dakota on November 11, 1933, and spread its pall as far south as Texas. This was the great black blizzard. In her article "Dust" for the *New Republic* of May 1, 1935, Avis D. Carlson described what it was like to be caught in a dust storm:

> The impact is like a shovelfull of fine sand flung against the face. People caught in their own yards grope for the doorstep. Cars come to a standstill, for no light in the world can penetrate that swirling murk.
>
> Dust masks are snatched from pockets and cupboards. But masks do not protect the mouth. Grit cracks between the teeth, the dust taste lies bitter on the tongue, grime is harsh between the lips. . . .
>
> In time the fury subsides. If the wind has spent itself, the dust will fall silently for hours. If the wind has settled into a good steady blow, the air will be thick for days. During those days as much of living as possible will be moved to the basement, while pounds and pounds of dust sift into the house. It is something, however, to have the house stop rocking and mumbling.

Most farmers who lost their farms did so because they got into a bottomless pit of debt to banks, insurance companies, or private investors. Some farms were held by the government for nonpayment of taxes. In 1934 the National Resources Board estimated that government agencies or private creditors owned almost 30 percent of the value of farmland in the West and the Midwest. In the Great Depression as many as 42 percent of farmers were tenants, compared with only 25 percent in 1880. Moreover, in 1935 less than two-thirds of tenant farmers had lived on their land for more than a year.

Tenancy had various disadvantages. Tenants were much less likely to settle than owners, and they did not share owners' special concern for land and equipment. The whole agricultural system encouraged restless mobility down the socioeconomic scale. The AAA encouraged the process. A farm owner who was being subsidized for growing less could afford to evict his tenants or sharecroppers, live off the federal check, buy tractors and other labor-saving implements, and then hire labor by the day instead of through the year. The displacement of agricultural workers was most noticeable in cotton production. In 1930–37 sales of farm tractors in ten cotton states rose by 90 percent. Whereas the actual number of farms increased in the rest of the country, in the southern and western states, it actually declined. In some cotton-producing counties in Texas, landlords who bought tractors typically joined two 160-acre farms run by their tenants into a single operating unit. Then they discharged both sets of tenants. Sometimes farm owners displaced as many as ten or fifteen families in their process of consolidation.

One consequence common to both industrial and agricultural depressions was that millions of people were uprooted. The 1930s was a decade of great migrations. Some states lost populations: Vermont, the Dakotas, Kansas, Nebraska, and Oklahoma. The largest migrations were from the South and the Appalachians to the industrial centers of Ohio, Illinois, Indiana, and Michigan. However, states with warm climates—Arizona, California, and Florida—were likely to be attractive to migrants. The general movement to the Pacific eventually made California the most populous state.

One sort of migration became more famous than any of the others. In 1934 and 1935 Okies, dispossessed farmers not only from Oklahoma but also from Arkansas, Texas, and elsewhere, began to cross into California, looking for work as fruit pickers. They traveled in old jalopies along U.S. Highway 30 through the Idaho hills and along Highway 66 across New Mexico and Arizona.

The mass migration was not welcome to residents of California, who dreaded the influx of destitute Okies and the social dislocation it would cause. A billboard of 1935 on the Nevada-California border proclaimed: "Okies Go Home: No Relief Available in California." Once the Okies arrived in California, they found themselves in desperate competition for work with such itinerant families as evicted sharecroppers from Alabama, tenant farmers from Arkansas, and perennial vagabonds. The California labor market for menial agricultural work became glutted. In the words of Frederick Lewis Allen, "to the vast majority of the refugees the promised land proved to be a place of new and cruel tragedy."

Daggers from the Right and Thunderbolts from the Left

Once big business discerned the beginnings of economic recovery, it began to vent unreasonable diatribes on "that man in the White House" and his progressive measures. Whereas to his admirers FDR was leading the country through a period of momentous reforms, to his critics he was fomenting class rivalry, undermining the American system of free enterprise, and trying to undermine the

Constitution. Marquis W. Childs analyzed the hatred FDR aroused in an article, "They Hate Roosevelt," for *Harper's* of May 1936. He described it as a passion and an irrational fury that permeates "the whole upper stratum of American society." There were jokes such as one about an eminent psychiatrist summoned prematurely to heaven to treat God "because he has delusions of grandeur—He thinks He is Franklin D. Roosevelt."

Roosevelt's enemies said that he was a traitor to his class. Instead of rewarding industrial entrepreneurs and landowners for their contribution to American society, the New Deal made relief to the indigent poor a priority. This, according to the orthodox wisdom, was tantamount to encouraging idleness among the workshy as well as going against the Protestant work ethic. More significantly, the plutocracy objected to the fact that relief payments, programs of public works, and an expanded bureaucracy to administer them could be paid for only by increased taxation on themselves. This came most decisively later in the Revenue Acts of 1935 and 1936 with their higher taxes on gifts and estates, on corporate incomes, and on high personal incomes. What the rich most resented was paying for the relief. In addition the plutocracy resented legislation that curbed their own financial activities by such measures as the Glass-Steagall Banking Act and the Truth-in-Securities Act, both in 1933, and the Securities Exchange Act of 1934.

Far from being a traitor to his class, Roosevelt was its savior. Government supervision of banking and the stock market not only ensured prevention of the worst abuses of the 1920s but also provided an implicit government seal of approval of the way finances, high and low, checking and speculative, were conducted. Moreover, those despised later measures of social reform, such as the Social Security and Wagner Acts of 1935, and the more equitable distribution of wealth achieved by other acts, undercut the appeal of revolutionary movements that sought to overturn the entire capitalist system. FDR and the New Dealers reformed the system in order to preserve it: the essence of the New Deal was a conservative treatment of radical problems.

Nevertheless, the plutocracy could not see the forest for the trees. In August 1934 business leaders, including supporters of FDR in 1932 in the AAPA, constituted themselves as the American Liberty League (ALL), determined to bring about his destruction. It was bipartisan but led by John J. Raskob and R. R. M. Carpenter, vice president of the Du Pont Corporation. The new league could count on the big guns of business and their considerable financial resources. It adopted the same membership as its predecessor, the AAPA, attracting such capitalists as William Randolph Hearst, the three Du Pont brothers, Sewell L. Avery of Montgomery Ward, and Colby Chester, president of General Foods. They orchestrated press campaigns criticizing FDR's supposed dictatorial methods, the New Deal's imagined invasion of individual freedom, and its allegedly communistic legislation in support of labor unions.

There was also thunder from the Left. In California novelist Upton Sinclair published a campaign document, *I, Governor of California, and How I Ended*

Left: The effervescent Huey Long, first as governor and then as senator of Louisiana, where he reigned as the self-styled "Kingfish," was a dangerous foil for FDR because his Share Our Wealth campaign threatened to undermine the appeal of New Deal economic policies and because he could divide the Democratic party in the South. (Library of Congress)

Right: Gregarious and vociferous miners' leader John Llewellyn Lewis, a man of luxurious hair, who led the movement for the unionization of unskilled and semiskilled industrial workers, eventually breaking with the AFL to form the Congress of Industrial Organizations. (Photo by Underwood and Underwood; Library of Congress)

Poverty (1933), which sold about a million copies and encouraged the growth of an insurgency movement, EPIC (End Poverty in California). Its program was a mix of state socialism and rural cooperatives in which unemployed people were to be allowed to produce work on cooperative farms or factories leased by the state. They would be paid in scrip that could be used only to buy food or goods produced by the cooperatives. Upton Sinclair won the support of novelist Theodore Dreiser, poet Archibald MacLeish, and lawyer Clarence Darrow. He roused Democrats in the state party and, in the primary election of August 1934, took the nomination for governor from party favorite George Creel with a far greater majority than incumbent governor Frank Merriam achieved in the Republican party.

Sinclair's campaign provoked concerted opposition from conservatives of both parties and from the federal government, who became allies to defeat him. Hollywood produced fake newsreels showing jobless hordes swarming across state lines to become expensive wards of state in California. As a result of their campaign, Merriam took 1.13 million votes, Sinclair took 879,537, and Raymond Haight, a third-party candidate, took 302,519. Director Irving Thalberg discussed his strategy with actor Fredric March: "I had those shorts made. Nothing is unfair in politics. I used to be a boy orator for the Socialist party on the East Side in New York. Do you think Tammany ever gave me a chance to be heard?"

More troublesome to FDR than Sinclair was Francis E. Townsend, a retired doctor of medicine, originally from Illinois but now living in California. He had worked as assistant county health officer until forced to retire at age sixty-six with less than $200 in savings. Townsend proposed old age pensions for people retired at sixty, who would receive $200 per month, provided they took on no extra work and spent the entire sum in the United States within a month. The Townsend plan was to be financed, initially, by a 2 percent tax on all business transactions. This was later amended to direct income tax on corporations and individuals. Townsend's scheme appealed to millions across the country whose plight and feelings of hopelessness were similar to his own. Moreover, Townsend claimed that the retirement of people over sixty would create vast job opportunities for young people who were unemployed and that the introduction of monthly pensions would further stimulate the economy, creating a demand for goods and services that would generate more jobs.

Townsend took a partner, Robert E. Clements, an energetic Texas real estate salesman of thirty-nine. Together they incorporated Old Age Revolving Pensions, Ltd., on January 1, 1934, to dispatch literature across the United States. Having launched Townsend Clubs across the country and having built up a membership of 1.5 million, they started publishing a newspaper, the *Townsend National Weekly*, and began lobbying Congress with mass petitions. Congressman John S. McGroarty of California, who owed his election to the support of local Townsend Clubs, introduced a pension bill into the House in early 1935. The administration opposed it as expensive and impractical.

By far the most aggressive criticism of the New Deal came from Senator Huey P. Long of Louisiana and Father Charles Coughlin of Michigan. Drawing on the residue of the old Populist movement in the South and the Midwest, they launched effective crusades against the encroaching power of the federal government. The two leaders affirmed values threatened by modern developments and offered their followers the promise of a fairer society in which traditional values and institutions would be protected. They ascribed current social and economic problems to a selective list of scapegoats, principally the unseen interests of Wall Street, and they promised to prevent any further expansion of government.

Even among southern demagogues, Senator Huey P. Long, the self-styled "Kingfish" of Louisiana, was an amazing phenomenon. He combined ruthless political ambition with genuine compassion for the dispossessed. Born into a poor area of Louisiana, Wynn Parish, where his father rose from obscurity to owning the town bank, Long first went to work as a door-to-door salesman. After studying at Tulane University Law School for eight months, he had learned enough to pass a bar examination, and he began to practice law. He advanced his political career through a series of positions until he became governor in 1928.

Within three years he had abolished state poll taxes, declared a moratorium on debts, and excused the poor from property taxes. In 1928 Louisiana had only 300 miles of paved highways and 3 bridges; by 1933 it had 3,754 miles of paved highways, 40 bridges, and almost 4,000 miles of gravel farm roads. As well as organizing a campaign to eliminate adult illiteracy, Long transformed Louisiana State University into a major institution. The new public buildings he commissioned, including the state capitol, the governor's mansion, and the New Orleans airport, not only satisfied Long's personal vanity and outsize ego but also provided work and boosted public morale.

According to state law, Long could not run for governor again in 1932. Thus he ran, instead, for the U.S. Senate in 1930. He won but delayed taking his seat until 1932, when he could install a stooge, Oscar K. Allen, as governor in his place. Long continued to participate in state politics by taking charge of debates in the assembly and ordering the representatives to pass his proposed measures. On one day in November 1934 the state senate passed forty-four bills in only two hours—one every three minutes. By such means and by selective use of bribery and intimidation, Long made himself dictator in his state.

Huey Long's own plan for national recovery was "Share Our Wealth," which he announced on the radio on February 23, 1934. It called for a wide redistribution of wealth among the lower economic groups. This was to be achieved by liquidating all personal fortunes above $3 million and providing every family with $4,000 or $5,000 to buy a house, an automobile, and a radio. The program also prescribed old age pensions, a bonus for veterans, minimum wages, and a free college education at government expense for young people of tested intelligence. The Share Our Wealth scheme was impracticable, but it expressed public concern about the unequal distribution of wealth. Moreover, it fueled a successful political movement from which Long could advance his presidential ambitions.

FDR was exasperated by Long's attempt to appropriate control of the New Deal and by his colossal rudeness. At a White House meeting Long kept his hat on, only removing it to tap the crippled president on the knees to emphasize his points. FDR took his revenge by distributing federal patronage to Long's political enemies in Louisiana.

Another thorn in FDR's side was Father Charles E. Coughlin, the radio priest of Irish-American descent and Canadian birth who had first come to the United States in the 1920s to Royal Oak, Michigan, near Detroit. Detroit, almost entirely dependent on the automobile industry, had the highest unemployment rate of any large American city. The common criticism leveled at Coughlin was that he was an upstart priest interfering in politics. The CBS network, which broadcast Coughlin's addresses, was sensitive to these charges. Fearful of offending the federal government, in April 1931 CBS refused to renew Coughlin's contract. Undaunted, Coughlin went back to WJR in Detroit and arranged individual contracts with eleven private stations in the East and the Midwest. By the end of 1934 more than thirty stations were broadcasting his addresses. In 1934 Coughlin was so popular that he was receiving more mail than FDR—sometimes over a million letters a week. He needed 150 clerks to process them.

The Charity Crucifixion Tower, his new granite and marble church, stood seven stories high and was decorated with a huge, bas-relief figure of Christ, illuminated by spotlights at night. At the side of the tower were a gasoline station, Shrine Super-Service, and a Little Flower hot dog stand.

Like Huey Long, Coughlin was an early supporter of FDR, whom he used to call "Boss." Unlike Long, he had no personal political ambitions, but he was disturbed by the failure of the early New Deal to move decisively to the Left. Coughlin's prescriptions for relieving the depression were two: reform the currency and reorder the financial institutions. Silver donations had made Coughlin the greatest owner of silver, which he described as "the Gentile metal." He advocated the coinage of silver in a new dollar containing 75 percent gold and 25 percent silver, in order to increase the amount of money in circulation and thus increase purchasing power and stimulate the economy. In late 1934 and early 1935 Coughlin called for the abolition of the privately controlled Federal Reserve System and the creation of a national bank to be controlled by popularly elected representatives. To achieve these reforms, in 1935 Coughlin organized the National Union for Social Justice.

The dissident ideology propounded by Coughlin and Long drew from the traditional idea that individuals should control their own destiny and not have it controlled by some faceless bureaucracy serving unseen corporations. Concentrated wealth had come close to destroying the community in the great bull market. The community could be revitalized by a new economic order with a decentralized government, limited ownership of property, and controlled capitalism. Ironically, radio, a medium of centralization, made it possible for Coughlin and Long to propound their arguments for decentralization.

The Long organization spread from the South along the states bordering the Atlantic coast as far north as Connecticut and had footholds in Pennsylvania, Missouri, Wisconsin, and Indiana. It was stronger in the West than the Midwest, with California the most receptive state outside the South. The National Union for Social Justice spread from the Midwest to New England and the northeastern seaboard generally. Its constituency was supposed to be 8.5 million people.

Together, Coughlin and Long could organize a huge constituency, and their supporters were drawing them together. Furthermore, various organizations, such as the Farmer-Labor Party, the Farmers' Holiday Association, and the Townsend Clubs, were united in what they saw as the common aim of the Long and Coughlin movements: "Share Our Wealth."

The electoral threat of Huey Long and the Share Our Wealth movement to FDR disappeared on September 9, 1935, when Long was fatally wounded inside the Louisiana State Capitol. Long's assassin, Dr. Carl Austin Weiss, who was immediately gunned down by Long's bodyguards, was the son-in-law of Judge Benjamin Pavy, a political enemy of the Kingfish. With Long gone, his movement split into two factions and soon fell apart.

But there was yet more thunder on the Left.

Governor Floyd B. Olson of Minnesota was the dynamic leader of the Farmer-

Labor Party, whose platform proposed fundamental economic reforms, including state appropriation of idle factories to put the unemployed to work, state ownership of public utilities, a moratorium on farm mortgage foreclosures, exemption of low income families from property taxes, and a government bank. Although Olson's administration accomplished environmental legislation and some regulation of public utilities, it proved less radical than his election promises. In 1936 he died of cancer.

In Wisconsin the late Robert La Follette's sons, the unassuming Robert, Jr., ("Young Bob") and the extrovert Philip, dissatisfied with the pace of the New Deal, founded a new Progressive party in May 1934. They were elected as senator and governor, respectively, that year. Seven progressive candidates were elected to the House of Representatives. They were supported by the League for Independent Political Action, an insurgent movement of eastern intellectuals that included educational philosopher John Dewey, social critic Lewis Mumford, and poet Archibald MacLeish. This group favored a third party to unite leading midwestern movements, including its own creation of 1933, the Farmer-Labor Political Federation (FLPF).

Public disenchantment with the old machines surfaced anew in New York City in 1933. The electorate voted in Republican Fiorello H. La Guardia as mayor after learning from a sensational investigation that the Democratic machine of Mayor Jimmy Walker had corrupted municipal politics. In office, La Guardia instituted a series of municipal welfare programs along the lines of the New Deal.

Another burst of thunder from the Left came with renewed labor militancy. The Great Depression had already had a profound impact on labor, an impact further charged by section 7a of the National Industrial Recovery Act, which encouraged workers to form labor unions. According to the highest estimates, AFL membership rose from 2.95 million in 1930 to 3.51 million in 1936. There were now 4.10 million members of all trade unions. Moreover, militant industrial workers put politicians as well as employers on notice that they had a responsibility to do more to alleviate the depression. Militant workers, aggravated by deteriorating conditions, went on strike in increasing numbers. The number of workers involved in strikes rose from 324,210 in 1932 to 1.16 million in 1933. In 1934 working-class militancy reached the level of 1919 in violent industrial conflicts paralyzing three major cities—Toledo, San Francisco, and Minneapolis.

Striking electrical workers and members of the Unemployed League joined forces in Toledo, Ohio, to imprison 1,599 strikebreakers inside the city's Auto-Lite plant. The National Guard brought the affair to an end after a seven-hour battle with pickets. In the melee two workers died and fifteen were wounded. In San Francisco a strike by longshoremen extended to other workers and paralyzed the city when police shot two unarmed strikers dead. This led to a massive protest in which 130,000 workers took part. In Minneapolis police fired into a crowd of striking Teamsters, killing two and wounding more than fifty. Governor Floyd Olson of Minnesota placed the city under martial law. Then, faced with the continued determination of the strikers, he withdrew the troops.

Later in 1934 a national textile strike extended to 370,000 workers from Maine to Alabama. Altogether, at least forty workers were killed in the industrial conflicts of 1934, and governors called out troops in sixteen states.

Companies using strongarm tactics to keep workers in order sometimes provoked showdowns with frightening consequences. In December 1934 the ACLU learned that more than twenty-five hundred firms employed strike-breaking companies, notably the Pearl Bergoff Service and the Pinkerton National Detective Agency, which maintained standing armies equipped with machine guns, tear gas, and clubs. They also paid spies to infiltrate the workforce and entrap radicals. This was big business. The Pinkerton Agency earned about $2 million between 1932 and 1936, and much of that came from Detroit, the center of the automobile industry. Some industrial companies terrorized workers at gunpoint to keep them at work. The Pittsburgh Coal Company kept machine guns aimed on employees in its coal pits. Company chairman Richard B. Mellon explained to a congressional committee: "You cannot run the mines without them."

Renewed strength from labor and the spirit and strength of feeling in the Long, Coughlin, and Townsend movements played a decisive part in moving the New Deal farther to the left. FDR drew off their fire by rekindling it for his own blazing reforms. In 1935 Social Security drew much of its momentum from Dr. Townsend's plan. The Revenue Act and the Public Utility Holding Company Act were largely inspired by FDR's determination to refute Huey Long's charge that he was a creature of the utility companies. More fundamentally and ironically, FDR used criticism of the New Deal from the Left to generate wider public support for his policies. FDR was using latent fear of revolution in order to persuade those with conservative opinions to accept a socioeconomic program that, in more normal times, would have seemed dangerously radical. When Congress met for its second session on January 4, 1935, FDR asked for a second New Deal of sweeping social reforms: security against illness, unemployment, and old age; slum clearance; and a program of works for the unemployed.

FACING PAGE:

Migrant Mother by Dorothea Lange is one of the classic icons of the Great Depression. Dorothea Lange (1895–1965) of New York began to work as a professional photographer in San Francisco after the theft of her money forced her to abandon a planned trip around the world. Her portrait of a modern Madonna was taken to publicize Farm Security Administration programs to relieve rural poverty. The young mother of thirty-two was living in a tent with her family in a camp for migrant farm workers in Nipomo, California, in February 1936. They had just sold their car tires to buy food. (Library of Congress)

The New Deal at Flood Tide

The most significant legislative achievement of early 1935 was the expansion of federal relief. By then, perhaps as many as 5.5 million people were receiving relief; if their dependents were also included, then the total was 20.5 million, 17 percent of the total population. If those who were only at work because they were working for government relief projects are included, then it becomes clear the government was supporting 20 percent of the population.

These statistics were not welcome to the New Dealers. Both FDR and Harry Hopkins shared the traditional American view that relief, by itself, undermined character. FDR and Hopkins therefore wanted the 3.5 million people who were out of work but able-bodied and skilled to be given work through federal monies, instead of a dole. Accordingly, they and their advisers designed the Emergency Relief Employment Act. It passed the House by 317 votes to 70 and the Senate by 67 votes to 13 and was signed by FDR on April 8, 1935.

The Emergency Relief Appropriation Act established various new relief agencies, notably the Works Progress Administration (WPA). Their long-term aim was to provide relief and employment and to try to stimulate consumption. The Works Progress Administration, which changed its name in 1939 to the Works Projects Administration, had an appropriation of $5 billion. But it led to open conflict between Ickes and Hopkins. Ickes wanted to concentrate on recovery rather than relief and gave support to large public works projects to aid industry through expenditure on capital goods. This was supposed to ensure recovery in the long run. Hopkins wanted to put as many people as possible into truly productive jobs, expecting them to spend their wages to help business revive.

Hopkins was supposed to have said, "People don't eat in the long run." His pragmatic approach to problems won him control of the WPA. WPA wages were higher than the dole but lower than wages in private industry. This provoked opposition from liberals who wanted to raise wages. The compromise was to give the president discretionary control to raise wages. In 1936 the average wage was $52.40 per month. The average number of people employed by the WPA at any one time was 2 million. By 1941 8 million people (20 percent of the work force) had worked for the WPA at one time or another.

The WPA could not enter all fields. It could not compete with private business, and because of costs, it could not engage in home construction. Nevertheless, it built 12,000 playgrounds, 1,000 airport landing fields, and 8,000 school buildings and hospitals. Moreover, it waged a campaign against adult illiteracy. The WPA transformed American cities, creating the potential for additional transport and access and providing other facilities: in New York it cut the Lincoln Tunnel linking Manhattan and New Jersey and it built the Triborough Bridge linking Manhattan and Long Island.

Militant unionists and conservatives attacked the WPA from their different perspectives. Conservatives said that federal relief undermined the Protestant work ethic, that many WPA projects were of dubious value in themselves, and that the Democrats were exploiting the agency for party political advantage. Congress responded to this last criticism in August 1939 when it passed the Hatch Act, forbidding federal employees from taking part in politics, unless they were employees at the highest levels.

The WPA tried to create work for young people through its subsidiary, the National Youth Administration (NYA), administered by Aubrey Williams, which gave priority to those who had graduated from high school and tried to persuade as many as possible to remain in education and stay out of the labor market. By 1941 the NYA had employed about 1.5 million young people, favoring college students, whom it paid between $10 and $20 a month.

Once again, artists benefited from principle, if not policy. A government exhibition of five hundred works of PWAP art at the Corcoran Gallery of Art in Washington, D.C., in April and May 1934 had proved such a success that it ensured continued federal involvement in art patronage for the rest of the 1930s. Edward Bruce continued his involvement through the Treasury Art Project (TRAP), created in July 1935 with a grant from the WPA. The WPA instituted its own Federal Art Project (FAP), which received fourteen times as much money as Bruce's Treasury project and gave aid to ten times as many artists. Several FAP artists became leading abstract expressionists in the 1940s: Arshile Gorky, Philip Guston, and Jackson Pollock. The FAP was more committed to realist painting because of its avowed purpose to create a popular art that gave expression to the aspirations and achievements of the American people. Because the director of the FAP, Holger Cahill, was specifically concerned with folk art, the FAP did much to promote regionalist painters disaffected with modernist painting.

Regionalist painters, led by John Steuart Curry, Grant Wood, and Thomas Hart Benton, impressed on their pupils that modernism was useless, unwanted, and decadent and that what the American people really wanted was representational paintings of pasture, field, and harvest. Benton, of Neosho, Missouri, the son and grandson of congressmen, was the most vociferous advocate of this point of view. After an early period of experimentation, he had rejected cubism and other modern European styles in favor of the more monumental mural art of the Italian Renaissance and the easel paintings of El Greco. He wanted to forge an American art that would draw on the history, folklore, and daily life of the United States but unfold the themes in stylized compositions dominated by thrusting curved lines.

The Second Hundred Days

Despite the expansion of federal relief, some observers thought that FDR was becoming indecisive in 1935. Then the New Deal experienced shocks. In May 1935 the U.S. Chamber of Commerce announced that it would no longer cooperate with the New Deal. By its decision of May 27, 1935, in the case of

Schechter Poultry Corporation v. The United States, the Supreme Court declared the NRA unconstitutional.

The *Schechter* case involved an appeal by operators of a slaughterhouse against conviction for having broken the code of fair competition previously agreed to by the live poultry industry in New York City. The Court unanimously declared the NRA unconstitutional on two grounds. First, Congress had delegated its powers to the executive in violation of the constitutional principle of separation of power. Second, it had wrongly laid down federal regulation of intrastate commerce as well as of interstate activities.

FDR was outraged, but he reacted vigorously to the setbacks. He told his press conference of May 31, 1935, "We have been relegated to the horse-and-buggy definition of interstate commerce." Yet this bitter climax to mounting public censure of the NRA masked the fact that the NRA had to face almost insurmountable handicaps. It lacked firm guidelines, being a charter that tried to combine the conflicting interests of those who wanted a form of business planned by industry and those who preferred cooperative democracy through large-scale planning by the federal government. In addition, there was a confusion between immediate and long-term goals for recovery and the competing interests of business, labor, and consumers. Nevertheless, brain trustees Raymond Moley and Rexford Tugwell thought that the Supreme Court's *Schechter* adverse decision was a turning point for the New Deal. FDR was deeply disillusioned. Instead of another umbrella reform, Roosevelt decided to extract the NRA's good features, such as collective bargaining, maximum hours, and minimum wages, and enact them separately.

In June 1935 FDR presented Congress with five sweeping reform measures urged upon him by liberals and Progressives alike. Thus began the second hundred days.

The first of the five reforms, the Wagner-Connery National Labor Relations Act, had been originally introduced by Senator Robert Wagner of New York. It was aimed at the many company unions set up to undermine labor's attempt to organize independently. FDR and Frances Perkins originally opposed the bill. They gave it their enthusiastic support only after it passed the Senate on May 16, 1935, and after the Supreme Court invalidated the NRA in the *Schechter* case eleven days later. FDR's later support ensured the bill's passage in the House by a large majority, and he signed the Wagner Act on July 5, 1935. The act guaranteed workers the right to collective bargaining through unions of their own choice. The union chosen by the majority became the bargaining voice for all. In addition, the act established a three-member National Labor Relations Board (NLRB), headed by Professor J. Warren Madison of Pittsburgh, to supervise its enforcement, if necessary, by holding elections. The company union thereby became illegal. Employers were forbidden to resort to unfair practices, such as discrimination against union members or refusal to accept collective bargaining with union representatives.

The NLRB's wide powers aroused considerable controversy. Employers could maintain they had fired workers for inefficiency, whereas those workers would insist that their discharge was really owing to their union activities. The AFL and its craft unions claimed that the board was too partial to the recently founded Committee for Industrial Organization (CIO) and its industrial unions. Fifty-eight lawyers associated with the American Liberty League confidently predicted that the act would be judged unconstitutional. They advised employers not to comply with it. They suggested, instead, that employers should seek injunctions against it from sympathetic courts. However, in 1937 the Supreme Court upheld the new law in a series of decisions. The most notable of these was *NLRB v. Jones and Laughlin Steel Corporation*, declaring that workers had a fundamental right to organize in unions.

The Wagner Act was one of the most important acts in the history of American labor, aiding the rise of so-called big labor as part of New Deal strategy to balance the component parts of society. Its admirers said that the act helped avert 869 threatened strikes in its first five years. The immediate effect of the measure supported labor and made possible the unionization of mass production industries. The long-term effect gave the federal government the pivotal role of arbiter between labor and management—in this case both formulating and enforcing the rules. By widening the scope of its social responsibility in establishing minimum standards of pay at work and social security payments for illness and unemployment, the federal government encouraged the active participation of organized labor in the theater of national politics, especially with the Democratic party.

The second of FDR's five proposals became the Social Security Act. In the 1930s only a few states provided old age pensions, and all were inadequate. Only Wisconsin had laws governing unemployment compensation. Thus, the Social Security Act, in large measure stimulated by thunder from the Left, was a departure from all previous practice. Knowledge of Dr. Townsend's more excessive demands prompted congressmen, who might otherwise have been reluctant, to find FDR's modest proposals palatable. The bill moved easily through Congress, passing the House by 372 votes to 33 and the Senate by 76 votes to 6, and became law on August 15, 1935.

The Social Security Act provided an unemployment insurance plan and old age and survivors' pensions. The states, not the federal government, were to administer unemployment insurance. The act imposed a federal unemployment tax on all employees. In order to encourage the states to keep their side of the bargain by passing requisite enabling legislation, Congress provided that employers would be allowed a credit of up to 90 percent of the tax for contributions made to state unemployment compensation funds. All the states passed the necessary legislation within two years. The act covered 27 million people but excluded many in agriculture, domestic service, and those working for small employers. In 1938 maximum unemployment compensation payments were $18 per week, but much less than that in the South. The national average was less than $11. Payments extended for sixteen weeks only. The old age pension portion of the act created a federal annuity system to be financed by equal contributions from employer and employee, beginning at 1 percent of wages and increasing gradually. Payments were to begin in 1940. Fewer than 50 million people were covered by the original act; those reaching age sixty-five were to receive a pension in proportion to their contributions. Retired workers would receive a minimum of $10 and a maximum of $85 per month. Both sums were raised later. The Social Security Act was a landmark of social reform, making social security a basic function of government.

Roosevelt's third proposal was the Banking Act of August 23, 1935. It was intended to give the federal government control of such matters in banking as reserve requirements and rediscount rates. Marriner S. Eccles of Utah, governor of the Federal Reserve Board, believed that Wall Street exercised too much power in national finance and decided to revise the Federal Reserve Act of 1913. This was despite well-orchestrated opposition from the banking community led by Senator Carter Glass of Virginia, who resented any revision of the 1913 act, which he himself had partly drafted. The result was a compromise between the Glass and Eccles points of view.

In the future, each Federal Reserve Bank elected its own head, but that person had to be approved by the board of governors of the Federal Reserve System (FRS). The Federal Reserve System was thus made subject to more centralized control, and the capital of banking moved from New York to Washington. Decisions on reserve requirements and discount rates were given to the board of governors. Moreover, the Open Market Commission of the FRS, which controlled open market operations in government securities, was put under a policy-making committee over which the central board had majority control, instead of being subordinated to the member banks. All large state banks seeking the benefit of the new federal deposit insurance (achieved earlier in 1933) were now required to join the FRS and accept its jurisdiction. The act set a precedent in removing control of the nation's finances from private banking and placing it with the federal government.

The fourth measure, the Public Utility Holding Company Act of August 1935, passed Congress despite unprecedented lobbying against it by the giant public utility companies. Not only Congress and FDR but also the public were convinced of the need to reform a whole set of abuses. Stocks issued were often overvalued or fraudulent; sometimes public companies bribed legislators to advance or block legislation in their interest; the rates paid to holding company investors were usually excessive in order to support the top-heavy structure of the system. All this was widely known. Therefore, FDR and his allies wanted the dissolution of utility holding companies in order to protect consumers against excessive rates and prevent unhealthy concentrations of economic power. Sam Rayburn of Texas and Senator Burton K. Wheeler of Montana proposed the act.

The act ordered the liquidation of holding companies more than two times removed from their operating companies (instead of all holding companies, which the administration wanted). All utility combines had to register with the

Securities Exchange Commission (SEC). The SEC could decide which holding companies could survive, that is, whether or not they were one or two times beyond the operating companies. If it thought any holding company was not in the public interest, it could order its elimination. In addition, the SEC was given control over all financial transactions and stock issuance of the utility companies, which had to register with it. Some companies refused to register, but the Supreme Court upheld the act, and the great utility companies were broken up within three years. The most significant achievement of the act was to stop the issue of fraudulent utility stocks.

The New Deal created an additional agency, the Rural Electrification Administration (REA) of May 1935. Its task was to build generating plants and power lines in rural areas, since only 10 percent of American farm families had electricity. Under the Rural Electrification Act of 1936, farmers were encouraged to take advantage of REA loans at low rates of interest and form cooperatives to build their own power plants. This encouraged private power companies to build power lines into remote rural areas, previously considered unprofitable. By 1941, 40 percent of farms received electricity, and by 1950, 90 percent.

The Revenue Act of 1935, or Wealth Tax Act, was greeted with more abuse than any of the Seventy-Fourth Congress's other laws. Newspaper magnate William Randolph Hearst called it the "Soak the Successful" act. FDR, undeterred, wanted to encourage a wider distribution of wealth and to reduce the need for deficit financing. Hitherto, tax on the wealthy was nominal. A man with an income of $16,000 paid only $1,000 in tax. In his message to Congress, recommending a revision of the tax system, FDR said,

> Social interest and a deepening sense of unfairness are dangers to our national life we must minimize by rigorous methods. People know that vast personal incomes come not only through the effort or ability or luck of those who receive them, but also because of the opportunity for advantage which Government itself contributes. Therefore, the duty rests upon the Government itself to restrict such incomes by high taxes.

The new act set higher taxes on gifts and estates, raised corporate income taxes, and imposed an excess profits tax on profits above 15 percent. It placed surtaxes on personal taxable income above $50,000, according to a graduated scale from 31 percent on net incomes over $50,000 to 75 percent on net incomes over $5 million. In addition, the act taxed undistributed corporation profits. The new tax did not achieve the ambitious changes desired by its advocates and feared by its opponents, but it did make the system of taxation far more equitable, although the monopoly of wealth by the top 1 percent remained substantially intact.

Congress also enacted ad hoc legislation in reaction to the scuttling of the NRA by the Supreme Court. Thus, the Guffey-Snyder Act of 1935 created a National Bituminous Coal Commission to supervise production quotas and prices, hours, and wages. Because it guaranteed collective bargaining and attempted to set uniform wages and hours, it too was set aside by the Supreme Court. Congress replaced it with the Guffey-Vinson Act of 1937, which reproduced all the original terms of 1935 except for this last one concerning uniform wages and hours. Congress also passed the Connally Act of 1935 on the shipment of oil; the Alcohol Control Act of 1935, which reintroduced the NRA liquor code and placed its supervision under the Department of the Treasury; the Robinson-Patman Act of 1936 against favoritism through differential pricing; and the Miller-Tydings Act of 1937, allowing the establishment of fair-trade minimum retail prices by manufacturers.

Most substantive was the Motor Carrier Act of 1935. It brought all interstate passenger bus and trucking lines under the control of the ICC. The act also produced a model code based on the railroad code. It prohibited rate discrimination, provided maximum hours for labor, and allowed the ICC to review stock issues and proposals for mergers. A supplementary Transportation Act of 1940 made domestic water carriers and truck companies subject to the same requirements. In 1936 Congress passed the Patman Bonus Bill, giving war veterans immediate payment of their bonus, so that they would not have to wait till 1945. FDR initially opposed this measure, but when Congress passed it over his veto, he signed the bill.

After the Supreme Court declared the AAA unconstitutional in January 1936, Congress devised an alternative, the Soil Conservation and Allotment Act of 1936, to continue arrangements by which the federal government paid subsidies to farmers who curtailed production. The Merchant Marine Act of 1936 created a maritime commission (initially headed by Joseph Kennedy) to plan trade routes, labor policies, and shipbuilding programs. In order to discourage the practice of employing foreigners in order to depress wages, it required that three-quarters of a ship's crew be American. The commission was also to build up an auxiliary merchant fleet in case of war.

Was this second New Deal a fundamentally Wilsonian program, inspired by the New Freedom? It was certainly true that by his measures and his appeals, in 1935–38 FDR was aligning a majority coalition of disadvantaged interest groups behind the Democratic party. And in this, FDR was completing work Woodrow Wilson had begun.

1936: The Faults of Charity or the Ice of Indifference?

Both Republicans and Democrats fully understood that the election of 1936 would be a battle of momentous significance. The ideological differences between the major parties in the 1930s stemmed from ways in which FDR amplified the progressive legacies of Theodore Roosevelt and Woodrow Wilson in domestic affairs. Yet fears of excessive concentration of power in the federal government and inadequate checks on federal powers in New Deal programs profoundly alienated certain constituencies: states'-rights Democrats; old guard Republicans; insurgent Republicans; and Progressives.

Farmer and Sons Walking in the Face of a Dust Storm (1936) by Arthur Rothstein. Rothstein was the first photographer to join the Farm Security Administration project. In this staged photograph, he had father and older son pose carefully, leaning against the wind as they walked in front of a shed, partly submerged by dust. Rothstein had the smaller son hold back, covering his face with his hands. Rothstein also arranged that they would move from right to left across the frame—rather than from left to right, the way we read—in order to reinforce the emphasis on the family's struggle at the mercy of the elements. (Library of Congress)

However, the Democratic Party, as a whole, believed victory was in sight. The Democrats were only concerned that it should be a large enough victory to carry on the momentum of recent New Deal legislation. The Republicans were apprehensive. They welcomed any Democratic defectors. To stave off a rout, they counted on the undisputed fact that millions of people were still unemployed. It was Republican strategy to field a candidate who would alienate neither conservatives nor Progressives. Thus, Governor Alfred M. Landon of Kansas became the sole contender and was duly nominated in Cleveland on June 11, 1936. He was a Progressive from the Midwest not associated in any way with the discredited Hoover administration. His vice-presidential running mate, Frank Knox, had fought with the Rough Riders and had once published a progressive newspaper. To Walter Lippmann, Landon was "a dull and uninspired fellow, an ignorant man." To Henry Ford, Landon was the Kansas Coolidge, an epithet that drew a riposte from FDR, who remarked that the Kansas sunflower was yellow, had a black heart, and always died before November.

FDR was nominated the day after Landon was. He returned to the distinction he had made about the difference between politics and government in 1932: "Governments can err, presidents do make mistakes but the immortal Dante tells us that divine justice weighs the sins of the cold-blooded and warm-hearted in different scales." For, "better the occasional faults of a government that lives in a spirit of charity than the constant omissions of a government frozen in the ice of its own indifference." Moreover,

> government in a modern civilization has certain inescapable obligations to its citizens, among which are protection of the family and the home, the establishment of a democracy of opportunity, and aid to those overtaken by disaster. . . . there is a mysterious cycle in human events. To some generations much is given. Of others, much is expected. This generation of Americans has a rendez-vous with destiny.

The Democrats had to contend with more than their Republican rivals. After the assassination of Huey Long in 1935, Father Coughlin had to carry the double constituency by himself. Finding it difficult to channel the emotional momentum he had helped generate, Coughlin preferred to draw on a new political ally, Congressman William ("Liberty Bill") Lemke of North Dakota, in a newly formed Union party, to which Gerald L. K. Smith and Dr. Townsend also committed themselves. As a presidential candidate, Lemke proved to be a shrill speaker, wearing outsize clothes and a gray cloth cap.

From the outset, relations were tense among these ill-matched allies. At the national convention of the Townsend clubs, held in Cleveland in mid-July, Coughlin, removing his coat and collar, abused FDR in terms of pitiful vituperation. "The great betrayer and liar Franklin D. Roosevelt, who promised to drive the money changers from the temple, has succeeded only in driving the farmers from their homesteads and the citizens from their homes in the cities. . . . I ask you to purge the man who claims to be a Democrat from the Democratic party, and I mean Franklin Double-Crossing Roosevelt." Although Coughlin was the most notorious anti-Semite in public life, the Roman Catholic church refused to restrain him. Michael Gallagher, bishop of Detroit, declared, "Father Coughlin's activities will not be curbed." Yet Coughlin's followers dwindled into a lunatic fringe.

Political pundits thought Landon had a fair chance of winning. They could argue that the Democrats' victory in 1932 was a freak of circumstance and that the New Deal had failed to raise the country out of the depression. According to the Bureau of Labor Statistics, unemployment was at 5.59 million. The Labor Research Association claimed it was 12.61 million. Moreover, prominent Democrats were withdrawing from the New Deal. The *Literary Digest*, basing its sample on telephone owners of previous years, predicted that Landon would take 32 states with 370 electoral votes and that Roosevelt would take only 16 states with 161 electoral votes. Dr. George Gallup used different methods for his new American Institute of Public Opinion and predicted a Roosevelt landslide of 477 electoral votes against 42 for Landon.

FDR went on a whistle-stop tour with aggressive speeches, the tenor of which is suggested by his final address in Madison Square Garden on October 31, 1936:

> For twelve years this nation was afflicted with hear-nothing, see-nothing, do-nothing government. The nation looked to the government but the government looked away. Nine mocking years with the golden calf and three long years of the scourge! Nine crazy years at the ticker and three long years in the breadlines! Nine mad years of mirage and three long years of despair! Powerful influences strive today to restore that kind of government, with its doctrine that that government is best which is most indifferent. . . .
>
> Never before in our history have these forces been so united against one candidate as they stand today. They are unanimous in their hatred for me—and I welcome their hatred.

FDR won every state except Maine and Vermont—as campaign manager Jim Farley had predicted. FDR took 27,752,869 votes to Landon's 16,674,665. Roosevelt was the first Democrat in eighty years to be elected president by a popular majority, receiving 60.8 percent of the total to Landon's 36.5 percent. In the electoral college FDR had 523 votes to Landon's 8. The Union Party of Lemke and Coughlin took only 882,479 votes; the Socialist Party of America (SPA), 187,720 votes, and the CPUSA, 80,159 votes. The scale of Roosevelt's victory set standards for future elections: his percentage of the popular vote was not exceeded until Lyndon Johnson's 61.1 percent in 1964. The overwhelming Democratic victory created a preponderance of Democrats in the House of almost three to one. In the Senate 75 of 96 members were Democrats; only 16 were Republicans. In the state elections Democrats took 26 out of 33 contested elections, including Kansas, Landon's own state.

The credibility of the *Literary Digest* evaporated. It had used outdated methods in its poll, taking the opinions of telephone subscribers, both present and former, who had yet to recover from the depression and were blaming government for their misfortune. The management of the *Literary Digest* sold the magazine to *Time*.

FDR had concluded his Madison Square Garden speech just before the election with ringing defiance of the plutocracy: "I should like to have it said of my first administration that in it the forces of selfishness and of lust for power met their match. I should like to have it said of my second administration that in it these forces met their master."

Whether master or servant, FDR now faced daggers and thunderbolts with a vengeance.

CHAPTER 12

Red, Hot, and Blue

Sunset on the New Deal

A T   H I S second inauguration, FDR struck a new militant note: "In this nation I see tens of millions of its citizens—a substantial part of its whole population—who at this very moment are denied the greater part of what the very lowest standards of today call the necessities of life. . . . I see one third of a nation ill-housed, ill-clad, ill-nourished."

Indeed, according to a report by the National Resources Planning Board, *Security, Work and Relief* (1942), in 1936 18.3 million families, 60 million people altogether, received less than $1,000 per year. Excluding those who received relief, the average family income was $1,348. This meager amount would have to support a father, mother, and one or two children in a rented house or apartment.

FDR's second inaugural speech became one of his most quoted. Analysts referred to it to suggest increasing New Deal commitment to end poverty. However, the problems of one-third of a nation received considerably less attention in Roosevelt's second administration than they had in his first. The fortunes of the New Deal foundered as it struck the cruel sea of adversary politics.

In his address to the new Congress in 1937, Roosevelt reviewed the failure of existing institutions to accommodate themselves to the new requirements of government of mass society. In particular, he commented on the Supreme Court's reluctance to accept the New Deal. The Court had consistently voted—usually by a majority of 5 to 4—against state laws seeking new economic remedies for the depression. In 1935 and 1936 the Court brought much New Deal legislation to an abrupt stop on the grounds that Congress was delegating its power to the president. In the previous 140 years the Supreme Court had nullified only sixty laws; in 1935 and 1936 it invalidated eleven. Moreover, at the end of his first term, FDR became the first president ever to serve a full four-year term without being able to make a single Supreme Court appointment.

In the mid-1930s the Supreme Court was an extremely conservative body. Four justices were outright reactionaries: James McReynolds, Willis Van Devanter, Pierce Butler, and George Sutherland. McReynolds, in his mid-seventies, was

Woodrow Wilson's notorious mistaken appointment; Van Devanter, at seventy-six, was so infirm that he could not even complete his share of the clerical work of the Court—writing out its decisions—which therefore had to be undertaken by the other justices. All four justices held that private property was sacrosanct and that laissez-faire was the only right economic policy.

The liberal justices were Benjamin Cardozo, Harlan Fiske Stone, and Louis Brandeis. Cardozo and Brandeis were Jewish, and all three were committed to civil rights. Cardozo believed that innovative laws could redress social problems. He had a rare insight into the complexities of law. Brandeis, the oldest justice, brought to judicial problems a new emphasis on facts and statistics and a pragmatic approach to social problems. His decisions and those of Cardozo and Stone implied that government and laws must change with the times. The remaining two justices were sometimes called the swing men. They were Owen Roberts, who had prosecuted the Teapot Dome scandal in the 1920s; and Chief Justice Charles Evans Hughes, who had the benefit of a long reputation as a progressive Republican. Although lacking the compassion of the liberals on the Supreme Court, as chief justice (1930–41), Hughes commanded respect because of his austere presence.

The first adverse decision by the Supreme Court against the New Deal came in January 1935 in *Panama Refining Co. v. Ryan*, a case about section 9c of the National Industrial Recovery Act, which allowed the president, under certain circumstances, to prohibit the transportation of oil across state lines. By a vote of 8 to 1 the Court declared section 9c unconstitutional because it was incomplete: it established neither guidelines for, nor restrictions upon, presidential authority. The Court was also hostile to any modest redistribution of wealth. In the case of *Railroad Retirement Board v. Alton Railroad*, also in 1935, by a vote of 5 to 4 the court declared unconstitutional a railway retirement act on the grounds that the Constitution did not provide for the compulsory institution of railway pensions, which were a misuse of the property of the employers.

The most notorious adverse decisions were those of Black Monday—May 27, 1935. The Court found the Frazier-Lemke Farm Mortgage Act unconstitutional; ruled that the removal of Federal Trade Commissioner William E. Humphrey was a matter for Congress and not for the president; and, in *Schechter v. The United States*, found the NIRA unconstitutional because it interfered with interstate commerce. The adverse decision in the *Schechter* case was unanimous: the liberals sided with the conservatives. Sensing the significance of this decision, the *Daily Express* of London ran the banner headline: "America Stunned: Roosevelt's two years' work killed in twenty minutes."

In January 1936 the Court went further and ruled by 6 to 3 against the AAA in *United States v. Butler et al.* By 5 to 4 it ruled against the Municipal Bankruptcy Act. After the *Butler* decision, Stone told the conservatives that they should not assume that the U.S. Supreme Court was "the only agency of government that must be assumed to have the capacity to govern." By 5 to 4 the Court found in *Carter v. Carter Coal Company* against the Guffey-Snyder Coal

Conservation Act. The New Dealers believed they had written the coal act to comply with the Court's ruling in the *Schechter* case. But the Court was obsessed with a narrow definition of interstate commerce and found against this act, too. Vindictive Al Smith jubilantly told a Liberty League dinner that the Supreme Court was "throwing out the alphabet three letters at a time." Indeed, Supreme Court rejection of the New Deal had reached epidemic proportions. The mix of an economic crisis, an assertive president, and an implacable judiciary had produced a major constitutional conflict. Roosevelt and his supporters thought that the nonelected justices were preventing the duly elected branches of government from doing their job. The Court and its supporters feared that the president was using the will of the majority to make himself a dictator.

The president and his team considered how best to remedy matters. FDR favored the plan of Attorney General Homer S. Cummings: the court-packing bill S-1392, announced on February 5, 1937. Its premise was that court personnel were deficient, particularly because too many judges were too old for the job. FDR proposed that, if a federal judge who had served ten years waited more than six months beyond the age of seventy to retire, then the president could appoint an additional justice—up to six on the Supreme Court and up to forty-four to lower federal courts. In his message, FDR avoided any reference to the judges' widely publicized conservatism.

As far as increasing the actual number of justices to the Supreme Court was concerned, FDR had ample precedent since the number had been revised from six to ten and finally nine in the nineteenth century—and always for reasons of party politics. Moreover, his plan was based on one offered to President Woodrow Wilson by his attorney general, James C. McReynolds, now the arch-conservative of Court decisions against the New Deal. However, by disguising what was a blatant political stratagem as a means of restoring efficiency to the courts and in using old age as a criterion, Roosevelt had miscalculated. Everyone knew it was not the age of the justices that was in question but their political opinions. The oldest member of the Court, Louis D. Brandeis, was, at seventy-nine, the most liberal. Many distinguished conservatives over seventy in other professions felt themselves threatened. It was disingenuous for FDR to have incubated such a profound change in secret, to tie the reform of the Supreme Court to a general reform of the judiciary, to avoid admitting the differences between the Court and the New Deal, and to do all this so soon after an election in which the proposal had not even been mentioned.

Not only did the American Liberty League, the National Association of Manufacturers, the U.S. Chamber of Commerce, and the DAR campaign against the scheme, as expected, but so, too, did a host of community associations, whose opposition was more disinterested. In his column of June 8, 1937, Walter Lippmann accused FDR of "proposing to create the necessary precedent, to establish the political framework for, and to destroy the safeguards against, a dictator." Previously loyal liberals, such as Senator Burton K. Wheeler of Montana, now joined the opposition against FDR.

Nevertheless, the impasse between FDR and the Court was resolved, and a serious crisis passed. First, Charles Evans Hughes wrote a letter to Wheeler in the Senate Judiciary Committee, which was also signed by Willis Van Devanter (one of the conservatives) and Louis D. Brandeis (one of the liberals). The letter explained that the Court kept abreast of its work and that any increase in the number of justices would make the Court more inefficient—not less. Hughes suggested that "there would be more judges to hear, more judges to confer, more judges to be convinced and decide. The present number of Justices is thought to be large enough so far as the prompt, adequate, and efficient conduct of the work of the Court is concerned."

Second, the Court began to return decisions favorable to the New Deal. On March 29, 1937, in *West Coast Hotel Company v. Parrish*, by a majority of 5 to 4, it upheld a minimum wage law enacted by Washington State that was almost exactly the same as the one passed by New York State that it had nullified the year before. Owen J. Roberts changed his mind, realizing that unless the Court moved with the times, its influence would decline. The public preferred to believe the remark of a wit that "a switch in time saves nine." Because of Hughes, who proved himself a rare mix of statesman and jurist, the Supreme Court salvaged its credibility and diverted FDR's plan to reshape it.

Third, in five decisions in April 1937 the Court allowed Congress control of interstate commerce, most notably in *NLRB v. Jones and Laughlin Steel Corporation*. In two decisions in May it upheld the Social Security Act by majorities of 5 to 4. Fourth, in May 1937 the physically senile Justice Willis Van Devanter retired, thus allowing FDR the opportunity to appoint a more liberal successor. The urgent reasons for reforming the Court evaporated.

FDR's worst tactical mistake was to insist on passage of the original court-packing bill even after the need for it had passed. Thus he aroused deep antagonism in Congress. When Congress eventually passed the bill in August 1937 as the Judicial Reform Act, it was in emasculated form with no mention of the Supreme Court. Between 1937 and 1940 FDR appointed liberals Hugo Black, Stanley Reed, Felix Frankfurter, William O. Douglas, and Frank Murphy to vacancies on the Supreme Court. In 1941 he appointed liberal Harlan Fiske Stone as chief justice. It was now a Roosevelt Court, committed to civil liberties, minority rights, and progressive legislation.

Adversary Politics and the New Deal at Ebb Tide

The battle over the Supreme Court allowed many who had already abandoned the New Deal to claim that they, rather than FDR, were the true liberals and heirs of Progressivism. A small bloc of southern conservatives in Congress, led by Senator Carter Glass of Virginia, had started to oppose New Deal measures in 1935. The storm over the Supreme Court gave them an excuse to fight FDR more openly. Thus, the court-packing brouhaha squandered the political capital with which Roosevelt began his second term and stalled the New Deal.

Plymouth automobile assembly line. By mass production, standardization, and interchangeable parts, Ford and other auto manufacturers brought cars within reach of their
workers' pockets, not only increasing the revolution in transportation by generating increasing business, but also preempting any claims of socialism that American capitalism
divorced workers from the results of their labor. (Library of Congress)

The antagonisms aroused by the Court battle were fueled by the dissatisfaction
of conservatives with the gains of labor, increased welfare, and relief. The conservatives were essentially from states in which rural politics were predominant.
They opposed proposals for low-cost public housing, federal regulation of hours
and wages, and legislation to achieve civil rights. What they feared was the
advent of an interdependent urban society. They resented increasing centralization in government undertaken without an understanding of the changes in population and the demands that underpinned it.

Roosevelt also suffered from defections from the high ranks of the New Dealers, such as Raymond Moley, Hugh Johnson, and George Peek, all of whom
opposed the increased supremacy of government over labor, agriculture, and
industry that they themselves had done so much to bring about. They would not

accept the argument that increased centralization of government came out of ever greater public demands for governmental services and in order to raise the standard of living for the most disadvantaged. They would not reconcile themselves to a system of social security based on a degree of coercion by law.

Because of the furor over the court-packing scheme, FDR was unable to accomplish anything substantive of his ambitious program for the most disadvantaged one-third of the nation. Nevertheless, in 1937 Congress acted on behalf of destitute migrants of the Dust Bowl, the Okies.

The Okies also received belated cultural recognition. The most famous record of the Okies' migration was provided by John Steinbeck in his bestselling novel *The Grapes of Wrath* (1939). Steinbeck reports the cruel combination of depression, drought, the intransigence of banks, and inefficient use of the land. He concentrates on the family through his main spokesperson, Ma Joad: "Us'dta be the fambly was fust. It ain't so now. It's anybody." Although Steinbeck was clearly on the side of the dispossessed Okies, he was also critical of their ignorant methods of farming that had helped precipitate their tragedy. He was critical, too, of Ma Joad's obsessive insistence on the family's staying together—it was only by the individuals' going their separate ways that they would have a chance of progress beyond bare survival. The simplistic movie adaptation, directed by John Ford around the sterling talents of Henry Fonda and Jane Darwell, without the novel's ironies and ambiguities, reached millions across the world.

As to the real-life settlers and townsfolk in the Dust Bowl, after years of praying for rain, they found their requests answered with a vengeance both in the Dust Bowl and beyond. Rains came and they did not stop. The *New York Times* of January 23, 1937, reported that floods had made 150,000 homeless in twelve states. Conditions were worst in Indiana, Kentucky, Ohio, and Tennessee. Refugees sheltered from snow and sleet in boxcars, public buildings, churches, and tents. *Time* magazine of February 8, 1937, said the Ohio River "looked like a shoreless yellow sea studded here and there with tree tops and half-submerged buildings. To people crouching on house roofs, it was an immeasurable amount of ugly yellow water surging higher and higher hours without end."

Finally, perhaps half a million people were made homeless. Floods and windstorms claimed 1,678 lives in the mid-1930s.

Drought and flood achieved what the federal limitation on crops could not. They eliminated surplus. For the hapless individuals involved, the situation was utterly disastrous. Thousands upon thousands of farms failed. When their owners could not meet their mortgage payments, the banks foreclosed them. The U.S. Department of Agriculture Bureau of Agricultural Economics estimated that in 1933 93.6 farms in every 1,000 changed hands, and 54.1 of those sales were forced or somehow related to defaults. This was the greatest number of farm transfers in the 1930s, but every year the number was at least in the low 70s or high 60s per 1,000 farms, until 1939 when it fell to 63.8 sales per 1,000 farms.

The Bankhead-Jones Farm Tenant Act of July 1937 was the product of a government report showing that family-owned farms were becoming something of the past because of the foreclosure of mortgages when crops failed. Some families slid into tenancy and sharecropping, and the Okies and Arkies (migrants from Arkansas) took to the roads. The act created a Farm Security Administration (FSA) and incorporated it within the Resettlement Administration (RA) to help tenants and sharecroppers acquire farms from a special loan fund that provided for the purchase, refinancing, and rehabilitation of farms at low rates of interest. Thus, the FSA was to counteract the unfortunate side effects of the AAA, which had contributed to dispossession when marginal lands were withdrawn from production in return for subsidies. The FSA also established thirty camps to provide temporary housing for thousands of destitute migratory families. In addition, it created medical and dental centers and funded cooperative aid for the purchase of heavy machinery by small farmers. Within ten years 40,000 families had bought their own farms through FSA loans, and 900,000 families had borrowed a total of $800 million to rehabilitate their farms or locate them on arable land.

The Wagner-Steagall National Housing Act of September 1, 1937, was designed to meet the problems of slum clearance and public housing. It established the U.S. Housing Authority (USHA) to act through public-housing bureaus in large cities, loaning them sufficient money (up to 100 percent of the cost) at low rates of interest to build new homes. The program was to be financed by issues of bonds. By 1941 160,000 units had been built for slum dwellers at an average rent of twelve or fifteen dollars per month.

The New Agricultural Adjustment Act (New AAA) of February 1938 was based on the so-called ever-normal granary plan, storing surplus in fat years for distribution in lean years. It established quotas in five basic staple crops—cotton, tobacco, wheat, corn, and rice—that could be imposed by a two-thirds majority of farmers in a referendum. Those who adhered to the quota received subsidies based on prices of the favorable period of 1909–14. In case of overproduction, the Commodity Credit Corporation could make storage loans up to 75 percent of parity price (later 85 percent). Thus, if the market price fell below that amount, the farmer could store his crop in return for a loan at that level of 75 (or 85) percent. When the market price rose, the farmer could repay the loan and sell the surplus. Because of the fierce droughts of previous years, crop insurance was made available to farmers. The premiums could be paid either in wheat or in its cash equivalent. A second new feature was the Food Stamp Plan, under which farm surpluses were distributed through the Federal Surplus Commodities Corporation to persons on relief. They received 50 cents' worth of such produce for every dollar they spent on other groceries. These relief payments helped reduce farm surplus and also increased the business of retail stores.

The last major law of the New Deal was the Fair Labor Standards Act of June 25, 1938, a controversial measure that Congress passed after meeting in special session and after the New Dealers had made numerous concessions. It fixed minimum wages and maximum hours for all industries engaged in interstate commerce; established a minimum wage of twenty-five cents an hour, with provisions for a gradual increase to forty cents an hour; and set maximum hours at forty-four hours per week with a goal of forty hours within three years. Moreover, overtime work was to be paid at the rate of time-and-a-half. The act also dealt with child labor by forbidding interstate shipment of goods made by children under age sixteen.

To supervise the new law, the Department of Labor created the Wage and Hour Division with power to impose heavy fines for breach of regulations. As a result of the act, about 650,000 workers received wage increases, and over 2 million had their hours of work reduced. Because he needed the votes of grudging conservative congressmen, FDR accepted exemptions of benefit to their particular economic interests. Thus, the act exempted seamen, fishermen, domestics, and farm laborers. But the bill did outlaw child labor. It abolished the worst abuses of sweatshops. And it brought some protection to the three-quarters of working people not in organized labor.

The Food, Drug, and Cosmetics Act of 1938 expanded the Pure Food Act of 1906, giving the Department of Agriculture additional powers to control fraud by the manufacturers of foods and drugs. It required labels on products listing their contents.

There followed an even more effective brake on the New Deal than congressional intransigence. The economy had shown signs of recovery from the worst of the depression in the period 1933–36. National income rose from a little more than $42 billion in 1933 to $57 billion in 1935. Accordingly, the government began to plan for a balanced budget by 1939, gradually reducing its deficit. However, in August 1937 business fell back, and there was a wave of selling on the stock market. In nine months in 1937–38 the Federal Reserve Board's adjusted index of industrial production lost two-thirds of the gains it had made during its recent, painful ascent. It fell from 117 in August 1937 to 76 in May 1938. This was a faster collapse than in the devastating period 1929–32. Farm prices fell by nearly 20 percent, and in the fall unemployment increased by more than 2 million.

Harry Hopkins, Harold Ickes, and others argued for the continued injection of government funds into the economy, spending even to the point of deficit financing. Roosevelt was won over by stories of starvation in the South and extreme and widespread poverty in northern cities. He asked Congress for a $3 billion program of relief and public works expenditures. By December 1938 this, and the continuing New Deal programs, had halted the decline. Believing that private business had failed to play its part in recovery, FDR also wanted increased surveillance of business monopolies. Therefore, Congress set up the Temporary National Economic Committee (1938–41) under Senator Joseph O'Mahoney of Wyoming. In 1941 it produced the most thorough study ever of American monopolies.

I've Seen a Picket Fence

What of the continuing struggles of labor, of political radicals, of African Americans, and of Native Americans, who were just beginning to make their presence felt on the periphery of federal politics?

While the New Deal was at ebb tide, the movement to organize labor was in full flood. The limitations of the New Deal and their own compulsive need to address their own constituencies, actual or potential, caused labor leaders and Communist activists to widen their bases of support—in both cases seeking remedies for social ills as well as political power for themselves.

Assertive labor leaders such as burly John Llewellyn Lewis of the Miners' Union insisted that the conservative AFL mount an intensive drive to bring millions of semiskilled and unskilled factory workers into union ranks. Lewis called for a new form of industrial union, whereby workers in such mass-production industries as construction and steel would have a union big enough to bargain with the giant corporations. At the AFL convention in Atlantic City in October 1935, he led a formidable group of insurgents, including Sidney Hillman of the Amalgamated Clothing Workers, Thomas McMahon of the Textile Workers, and Charles Howard of the Typographers' Union. The confrontation between old and new schools of thought led to a fight on the platform between Lewis and "Big Bill" Hutcheson of the Carpenters. Lewis punched Hutcheson after Hutcheson had insulted a speaker from the rubber workers. Hutcheson was carried out with blood streaming down his face. Lewis remarked later, "They fought me hip and thigh and right merrily did I return their blows."

Lewis and his allies in ten unions met to form the Committee for Industrial Organization (CIO), ostensibly to work within the AFL to aid it in unionizing basic industries. The AFL executive council ordered the CIO to disband. When they refused, it suspended the ten renegade unions in August 1935 and finally, in March 1937, expelled them. In splitting from the conservative main body of the AFL to form the CIO, Lewis and his followers had created a militant industrial-union organization.

The first target of the CIO was the automobile and automobile-related industries; the second was the steel industry.

The new militancy was characterized by a new tactic, the sit-down strike. On January 29, 1936, rubber workers in Akron, Ohio, laid down their tools and occupied the Firestone plant. Workers at the nearby Goodrich and Goodyear companies rapidly followed the example of the Firestone strikers with another sit-down strike. Through plant occupations, workers hoped that the techniques of nonviolent resistance would bring shame on their bosses and thereby force management to the negotiating table. As far as management was concerned, the sit-down strike was an outrage against private property, an underhanded act of trespass in which Communists carpeted the shop floors with human bodies because they knew the company would not risk the adverse publicity following the bloodshed of forcible removal or damage to its own plants and matériel. In

Akron, the old AFL local was reorganized as the United Rubber Workers and affiliated with the CIO.

Toward the end of 1936 the United Auto Workers sought a conference on collective bargaining with William S. Knudsen, executive vice president of General Motors (GM). When he refused, men on the shop floors in Cleveland's Fisher Body Plant No. 1 took spontaneous action on December 28 by sitting down and ignoring the moving assembly line belt. Their protest spread to Fisher Body Plant No. 2 in Flint, Michigan, and thence to Pontiac, Atlanta, Kansas City, and Detroit. Soon 484,711 men from sixty plants in fourteen states were involved. GM obtained an injunction ordering evacuation of the plants. The judge who issued the order was a major shareholder in General Motors.

On the eve of the GM sit-down strike in Flint, only a small proportion of workers were fully-paid-up members of the United Auto Workers. However, once the strike began, many previously apathetic workers revealed their militancy. In 1937 the UAW declared that the strike had created "a veritable revolution of personality" among the workers.

The silence of FDR, Secretary of Labor Frances Perkins, and other, supposedly sympathetic New Dealers put extra pressure on Governor Frank Murphy of Michigan. A second court injunction obtained by GM lawyers threatened the sit-down strikers with prison sentences and a fine of $15 million if they had not given up by February 3, 1937. GM then chose its Chevrolet plant in Flint as the testing ground. Governor Murphy called out the National Guard to surround the plant. John L. Lewis told Murphy he supported the strike and that he would order the men to disregard any order to evacuate the plant.

Governor Murphy knew he could not abandon the strikers to the unmerciful GM company. Instead, he insisted that food be delivered to them. Through its strategy of a concerted attack on General Motors to immobilize its plants and only token demonstrations at Chrysler, Ford, Nash, and Packard, the UAW had divided and won. Instead of siding with GM, the other auto manufacturers took advantage of its embarrassment and exploited the market for their own automobiles. Thus, by February 7, 1937, GM directors were obliged to cut the dividend in half. After a crisis of forty-four days, William Knudsen agreed to the conference. All the other auto manufacturers recognized the UAW except Henry Ford, who held out until 1941. The manufacturers also signed agreements on grievance committees, seniority, a forty-hour week, and payment of time-and-a-half for overtime.

The steel industry was the second target of the CIO in its drive to create and organize industrial unions. In June 1936 Phil Murray formed the Steel Workers Organizing Committee (SWOC). Not only did it entice thousands of workers out of company unions into its ranks, but it also, with tacit government support, instituted costly strikes to force the steel companies to recognize it. The large steel companies, known as Big Steel and led by U.S. Steel, accepted SWOC. Myron Charles Taylor, chairman of the board of directors and chief executive, met Lewis by chance in the Mayflower Hotel in Washington, D.C., on January

John Vachon's *Company Coal Town*, Kempton, West Virginia (May 1939), implies derelict hopes in the small mining community by skillful use of the natural slope of the terrain, the angle of the windshield and steering wheel of the car, and the absence of people. (Farm Security Administration; Library of Congress)

9, 1937. Taylor held a series of private meetings with Lewis to thrash out differences between Big Steel management and SWOC. The Carnegie-Illinois Steel Company signed a contract on March 2, 1937. The other U.S. Steel subsidiaries followed with contracts granting union recognition, the forty-hour week, a 10 percent increase in wages, and overtime pay at the rate of time-and-a-half.

Because Big Steel had decided to accommodate itself to the new union, people thought that the remaining smaller companies, collectively known as Little Steel, would follow suit. Not so. Three of them opposed SWOC. In May 1937 Republic Steel, Bethlehem Steel, and Youngstown Sheet and Tube resisted a new strike of 70,000 men in twenty-seven plants for union recognition. They summoned their strike-breaking armies and used them against striking workers.

On Memorial Day several thousand workers and their families assembled on prairie land east of Republic Steel's South Chicago plant. The mayor of Chicago gave his permission for a peaceful parade with marchers falling in behind banners with such notices as "Republic Steel Violates Labor Disputes Act" and "Win with the CIO." Ahead of the marchers was a line of five hundred Chicago police, all heavily armed. Some workers threw a few empty soda bottles at the police. This was sufficient provocation to start a police-led massacre, beginning with tear-gas grenades and gunfire. The police in South Chicago killed ten people and wounded ninety others outside the Republic Steel plant. The casualties were people shot in the back as they fled in terror.

Subsequently, the Senate Civil Rights Subcommittee, led by Robert La Follette, Jr., of Wisconsin, began an investigation into the violation of the workers' civil rights and the shooting incidents. Their investigations disclosed that the Little Steel companies maintained illegal private armies and had extensive stores of munitions, including machine guns and tear gas. The adverse publicity was such that Little Steel was compelled to recognize SWOC. By 1941 six hundred thousand workers achieved union recognition in an industry bitterly opposed to labor.

In 1937 a total of 4.7 million workers were involved in 1,740 strikes. For the first time in U.S. history, all of the nation's key industries—steel, coal, auto, rubber, and electricity—were affected by major disputes. By the end of 1937 the new CIO unions claimed some 4 million members in thirty-two international unions and six hundred independent locals. However, it was the AFL, revitalized by the challenge of its new rivals, that achieved the greatest increase in membership in the lean years of the 1930s. Craft unions such as the Machinists, the Teamsters, the Electrical Workers, and the Meat Cutters began to organize vigorously on an industrial-union basis, and they proved resilient against the recession and counteroffensive by employers.

From October 1938 on, the CIO was known as the Congress for Industrial Organizations. In 1937, the first year of the two major unions, there were, according to official statistics, 3.18 million members of the AFL and 1.99 million members of the CIO. That year there were 7.28 million members of all unions.

Although workers sprang forward in the 1930s, the Socialist Party of the United States ceased to be an effective political force. The New Deal preempted many of the Socialists' proposals. Norman Thomas, Socialist leader, maintained for many years that the collapse of the Socialists was due to popular support for the New Deal. By intimidating the establishment into conceding reforms while at the same time appealing to blue-collar workers as a political bloc, Franklin Roosevelt had both heightened class consciousness and eliminated its potential for yet more radical reform. Socialists might have gained by the great interest in social welfare, but the Socialists disintegrated. Opposing groups of militant youngsters and more conservative old guard members became increasingly factious. Younger Socialists, such as Paul Douglas, went to work in New Deal agencies, while others, like David Dubinsky, rose to positions of leadership in organized labor and supported New Deal policies. They wanted to see their ideas for reform realized from positions of power.

Polish immigrant Dubinsky's career is a classic instance of the triumph of practical politics amid gales of contrary doctrine from organized labor and socialism—with some cost to idealism. After being elected president of the International Ladies' Garment Workers' Union (ILGWU) in 1932, Dubinsky steadied the union's tottering finances and secured numerous benefits for his members, including a thirty-five-hour week, expanded health centers, retirement pensions, and two cooperative housing projects. Although he resigned as vice president of the AFL in 1936 on account of its suspension of CIO-affiliated unions, he kept the ILGWU independent of both the AFL and the CIO until 1940. Meanwhile, in 1936 he helped form the American Labor Party—an offshoot of the CIO—to provide Democrat Franklin Roosevelt with an additional ballot line in his presidential reelection campaign and to help reelect fusion-Republican candidate Fiorello La Guardia mayor of New York.

But the divisions among the Socialists widened into fissures. Leader Norman Thomas's own pacifism and isolationism alienated certain ethnic groups with European loyalties and at the same time antagonized radicals committed to fundamental reform. Thus the Socialists splintered over domestic and foreign policies. The party's isolationist campaigns from 1938 on resulted in a further decline to only 1,141 members by January 1942. The late Eugene Debs's promising party, with its solid electoral support of 1912, was now no better than a minuscule sect.

Nevertheless, the Great Depression galvanized the jaded Communists of the CPUSA, reawakening the dim prospect of revolution. Communists earned wide publicity for leading demonstrations that seemed to threaten the government with the anger of the masses. In the mid-1930s the CPUSA supported the New Deal, taking its cue from the Comintern in Moscow, which preferred the new strategy of the Popular Front against fascism. The Popular Front provided Communism with a veil of decency—loyalty to a liberal ideal: a coalition against fascism. Authors, artists, and intellectuals joined such Communist groups as the League of American Writers and the American League against War and Fascism (ALAWAF). The height of the Popular Front came when the CPUSA raised money in Hollywood, capitalizing on its role in sending thousands of young men to Spain to fight for the Loyalists on behalf of the Republican government in the Spanish civil war (1936–39) against the military Falange.

In fact, in New York a liberal-Communist coalition gained control of the American Labor Party. Drama critic Lionel Abel wrote that in the 1930s the city "went to Russia and spent most of the decade there." The CPUSA could count on support from "red belt" neighborhoods in parts of the Lower East Side, Harlem, East Harlem, and Brooklyn. By 1938 the CPUSA had about thirty-eight thousand members in New York State—nearly half its total membership of around one hundred thousand. The Popular Front also won control of the Washington Commonwealth Federation, the leading New Deal body in Washington State. This surge of support for Communism in the United States occurred at the very same time that Soviet dictator Joseph Stalin had imposed his iron will on the USSR with such ferocity that millions died in the course of his collectivization of agriculture and millions more died in his political purges. American Communists distorted what news leaked out of the USSR about the purges.

Among the moderate radical voices against the unswerving convictions of doctrinaire Communists was that of minister and labor leader A. J. Muste, originally of Michigan, who directed the quarrelsome cooperative Brookwood Labor College in Westchester, New York (1921–33), and led the Trotsky-inspired American Workers' Party. Muste renounced Marxism in 1936, became an ardent pacifist, and worked at the Presbyterian Labor Temple on Second Avenue and Fourteenth Street, New York. Another moderate was theologian Reinhold Niebuhr at Union Theological Seminary, New York, who renounced socialism in 1936 and joined the Democratic Party. Where Niebuhr was confrontational was in his criticisms of liberalism and its willy-nilly assumption that man was inherently good and that progress was inevitable. Instead, in pulpit and press, Niebuhr propounded a doctrine that man committed many evils, that his life was full of tension and paradox, and that he should recognize the fact and repent.

But in Washington, D.C., there was a thriving Communist underground within the federal government itself, notably the Harold Ware group in the AAA, comprising Nathaniel Weyl, Lee Pressman, John Abt, and Josephine Herbst. Abt became chief counsel for the Civil Liberties Subcommittee of the Senate Education and Labor Committee, generally known after its chairman, Senator Robert La Follette, Jr., as the La Follette committee. This was the committee that exposed the efforts of employers to resist union-organizing drives by violent means. Abt ensured that a share of the subcommittee's professional staff consisted of fellow Communists, including Allan Rosenberg and Charles Kramer, who joined the staff of the NLRB in 1937 and 1938, respectively.

The CPUSA also dispatched militants into the mainstream labor movement. John L. Lewis allowed Communists to recruit for the CIO, reckoning that they had the toughness and dedication to take on difficult tasks. As the CIO flourished, so did Communist influence within it. One Communist, Len De Caux, became editor of *CIO News*, and another, Lee Pressman, served Lewis as chief counsel. By 1939 the United Electrical Union; the International Longshoremen and Warehouse Union; the Mine, Mill, and Smelter Union; the Fur Workers' Union; and the United Cannery Workers' Union were infiltrated by Communists. In New York they penetrated the Transport Workers' Union, led by ally Mike Quill, the American Newspaper Guild, and the United Retail and Wholesale Employees. By the late 1930s perhaps a quarter of all CIO members were in labor unions led by Communists.

Why were so many people attracted to Communism? Among them was film star and satirist Charlie Chaplin, a naive pseudoliberal. Joyce Milton defines (1996) Charlie Chaplin's attraction to Communism as twofold: "They presented themselves as the representatives of the oppressed classes, with whom he identified, and they also purported to have the one correct answer to every question." Chaplin's view was the view of thousands of genuine liberals. Communism *purported* to have the answer to the problems of mass society.

Mainstream politicians opposed left-wing radicalism. In Congress they encouraged the House Un-American Activities Committee—the body more commonly associated with the intolerance of the McCarthy era after World War II—to begin investigations and hearings as early as 1938. In New York the Rapp-Coudert investigations (1940–41) by the state legislature into alleged Communist influence in municipal colleges led to the resignation or dismissal of sixty professors from City College and Brooklyn College.

Some African Americans were attracted to Communism because of its emphasis on economic and racial equality and its strategy of working-class solidarity. Radical interest in racial matters was furthered by white Communists, including James S. Allen, Herbert Aptheker, and Philip S. Foner, who wrote about African American culture and argued that racial prejudice must be erased. African Americans were potentially a fertile field for Communism, and perhaps twenty-five hundred African Americans belonged to the CPUSA in the mid-1930s. However, African American radicalism was essentially indigenous to the United States, uninterested in theory—especially foreign ideologies—and suspicious of CPUSA motives.

One African American involved in the CPUSA for a time was Bayard Rustin from West Chester, Pennsylvania. In the late 1930s he was a student at City College, New York, and became active in the school's Young Communist League. He was the only black person in the organization and a most talented organizer. He joined the league because of its commitment to civil rights in the South. However, when the Comintern ordered the CPUSA to abandon its civil rights crusades in 1941, Rustin left the Young Communist League.

Black, Brown, and Beige

Labor advanced during the New Deal because it was able to gain clout and exert pressure on management and government. Those with less weight fared worse. Thus, the civil rights and social needs of people of color were largely ignored, as African Americans discovered.

Of course, Roosevelt's personality and the extraordinary way he had overcome the disadvantages of his poliomyelitis were likely to make him an attractive candidate to African Americans. His administration showed fledgling concern for civil rights. One of the most notable advocates was Secretary of the Interior Harold Ickes, who had been head of a Chicago chapter of the NAACP. However, it was FDR's wife, Eleanor Roosevelt, who was the most conspicuous New Dealer to demonstrate this new humanitarianism by her visits to Harlem and to African American schools and projects and by her readiness to speak at African American functions. She also made the president accessible to African American leaders, notably Walter White of the NAACP and Mary McLeod Bethune, president of the National Council of Negro Women, who had interviews with FDR from 1936 on—something that would have been unthinkable under Herbert Hoover.

Roosevelt also employed more African Americans in office. Thus, Bethune became director of the Division of Negro Affairs in the National Youth Association (NYA); William H. Hastie, dean of Howard University Law School, was an assistant solicitor in the Department of the Interior; later he became the first African American federal judge. Eugene K. Jones of the Urban League served as adviser on Negro affairs in the Department of Commerce; Edgar Brown had a similar post in the CCC; and veteran social worker Lawrence A. Oxley was in charge of the Department of Labor's Division of Negro Labor. These and other such appointments were sufficiently numerous to earn the collective title of "Black Cabinet."

Furthermore, the expansion of the executive branch during the New Deal opened additional career opportunities for African Americans, as it did for white Americans. Whereas in 1932 the Civil Service employed fewer than fifty thousand African Americans, by 1941 it employed three times as many. The NYA, under the liberal Aubrey Williams of Mississippi, pursued a policy of appointing African American state and local supervisors in areas with a sizable proportion of African Americans. The NYA provided young African Americans with funds to attend school from grammar school to graduate school.

Such developments stimulated greater political consciousness in African American communities, especially in the South. Although only 5 percent of adult African Americans voted in the South in 1940, a number of new voting organizations were forming to try to persuade African Americans to register to vote. Thus, African American voters turned increasingly to the Democratic Party. Toward the end of the 1930s Democratic candidates received as much as 85 percent of the vote in such areas of traditional settlement by African Americans as Harlem in New York and the South Side of Chicago. This phenomenon was to prove a decisive factor in Roosevelt's various reelection campaigns. Of fifteen major African American wards in nine cities, Roosevelt had carried only four in 1932. In 1936 he carried nine, and in 1940 all fifteen wards chose him by large majorities.

Yet the social problems of African Americans remained wide-ranging and pro-

FACING PAGE:

Left: Radiant contralto Marian Anderson about to sing "The Star Spangled Banner" at the dedication of a mural commemorating her free public concert on the steps of the Lincoln Memorial on Easter Sunday, 1939, which brought African American performing artists to the fore of the burgeoning movement for civil rights. The mural was dedicated in the Department of the Interior auditorium on January 6, 1943. (Photograph taken for the Office of War Information by Roger Smith; Library of Congress)

Right: Mary McLeod Bethune, president of the National Council of Negro Women, became a powerful advocate of civil rights at the courts of Franklin and Eleanor Roosevelt when FDR appointed her director of Negro affairs in the National Youth Administration. (Library of Congress)

Below: In a century that saw several remarkable revolutions in transportation, the continuing presence of segregation in interstate transport facilities reminded the United States that the deep South had not entered the twentieth century with appropriate social values. This photograph of an African American citizen leaving a bus terminal waiting room designated for "colored" people provides one of innumerable instances of the social supremacy of white over black by segregation in the deep South. (Farm Security Administration)

found. By 1940 there were 12,866,000 African Americans (in a total population of 131,699,275), and most of them still worked at menial jobs with low pay. Only one in twenty African American males worked in a white-collar profession (compared to one in three white males). Of every ten African American women who worked, six worked as maids (compared to one in ten white women). Although twice as many African Americans as whites worked on farms, far fewer farmed their own land.

It was especially frustrating for the most egalitarian New Dealers that their program bypassed African Americans. The administration of relief in the New Deal programs was decentralized, allowing local and party officials to exercise their prejudices against African Americans, especially in the South. Of over ten thousand WPA supervisors in the South, only eleven were African Americans. Public assistance for African Americans in the South was meager and difficult to obtain. White planters and landlords took advantage of African American illiteracy and their economic dependence on the landlords to prevent their Agricultural Adjustment Administration (AAA) reduction checks from reaching them. When AAA procedure was changed to allow direct payments to tenants, certain landlords decided to dispense with tenants, evicting them and collecting the crop reduction bonuses themselves. Such dishonesty fueled discontent among both African American and white sharecroppers, who united in the biracial Southern Tenant Farmers Union. Later, the Farm Security Administration (FSA) encouraged African American farmers to buy their own land.

New Deal discrimination against African Americans also took the forms of banning them from construction work on the TVA and pandering to the racist sentiments of federal administrators in the South. Even the Federal Housing Administration practiced discrimination. FDR might have acted against such injustices, but he preferred not to antagonize southern congressmen.

In the South the notorious poll tax, white primaries, and the maze of regulations about registration still thwarted African American voting campaigns. In 1939 eight states (Alabama, Arkansas, Georgia, Mississippi, South Carolina, Tennessee, Texas, and Virginia) used a poll tax of between one dollar and twenty-five dollars to disfranchise African Americans; they also enforced an annual liability (or fine) on every voter who failed to pay. All but South Carolina enforced payment for primary voting as well. Liberals joined forces with civil rights leaders to try to get such practices outlawed. Democratic congressman Lee E. Geyer of California introduced a bill against poll taxes that passed the House in 1941, but it was blocked by southern senators in the Senate.

However, when the Supreme Court moved to the left, it changed the criteria for decisions on civil rights, showing increased interest in the rights of the individual. This shift offered the NAACP an opportunity for pursuit of its preferred strategy of achieving civil rights by victories in court cases on voting and education. This was especially important in legal education—a subject of intense interest to the lawyers who would argue the cases and the judges who would adjudicate them.

In June 1935 Lloyd Lionel Gaines, a graduate of Lincoln University, the state-supported African American college of Missouri, applied for a place at the law school of the University of Missouri, which was then all white. Although he was duly qualified, the university refused him admission and advised him to apply to Lincoln (which had no law school) or to apply out of state. Gaines took legal action, and the test case of *Missouri ex rel. Gaines v. Canada* was decided by the Supreme Court on December 12, 1938. By 7 votes to 2 the Court ruled against the state. Equally significant was the Supreme Court's repudiation of southern subterfuges to deny the vote to African Americans. In the case of *Love v. Wilson*, on May 22, 1939, the Court ruled against the Oklahoma law replacing the grandfather clause that the Court had nullified in *Guinn v. United States* (1915).

The number of lynchings provides a barometer of race relations that suggests how the Great Depression intensified race relations. That number rose from eleven in 1928 to twenty-eight in 1933. The NAACP campaign against lynching attracted widespread support, however, although southern senators repeatedly secured the defeat of antilynching bills. Lynching united the opposition of liberals, both African American and white, thereby swelling support for civil rights. The notorious murder of Claude Neale in Florida on October 25, 1934, was widely publicized in an NAACP pamphlet by Howard Kester, who recounted how the mob vivisected its victim and hung his mutilated limbs from a tree outside the court house.

A bill proposed by Senator Edward Costigan of Colorado and Robert Wagner of New York called for the fining or jailing of state and local officials found delinquent, either in protecting both African Americans and white Americans from lynch mobs or arresting and prosecuting violators of the law. Furthermore, it provided for a fine of ten thousand dollars to be levied against the county in which the lynchings took place. It was supported by governors of twelve states, including David Scholtz of Florida, where Claude Neale had been murdered. Nevertheless, southern senators ensured that the Senate rejected the Costigan bill in April 1935 after a filibuster that lasted six days.

By this time many southern newspapers had changed their minds and now favored legislation. Congressman Joseph A. Gavagan of New York proposed a new bill that passed the House in April 1937 by 277 votes to 120 after a terrible incident at Duck Hill, Mississippi, where a mob killed two African Americans with a blow torch. On February 21, 1938, after a filibuster led by Senators Thomas Terry Connally of Texas and Theodore Bilbo of Mississippi, the Senate abandoned the new bill. The NAACP campaign had, as usual, been conducted by Walter White, who had become its executive secretary in 1930. White won nationwide recognition for his efforts, including the title of "Man of the Year" by *Time* magazine in January 1939. Perhaps because of all the adverse publicity, the number of lynchings gradually began to fall, going from eighteen in 1935 to two in 1939.

The blind discrimination of white justice; white fears and resentment in the primitive South; Communist agitation for party political ends; and the Supreme

Court's hesitant progress in civil rights rulings on behalf of African Americans—all of these were mixed together in the Scottsboro case of 1931–37, which came to its most dramatic climax in 1935.

The Scottsboro boys were nine African American youths falsely accused by two white women, Victoria Price and Ruby Bates, of multiple rape on a freight train near Scottsboro, Alabama, on March 25, 1931. The youths, between ages thirteen and twenty, were Charlie Weems, Ozie Powell, Clarence Norris, Olen Montgomery, Willie Roberson, Haywood Patterson, Eugene Williams, and Andrew and Leroy Wright. The allegations were not plausible, but they exposed a nerve of race relations—sexual intercourse between African American men and white American women. Despite conflicting medical evidence, in the hysterical atmosphere of the South, all-white juries felt they had no option but to convict any African Americans accused of raping white women. The only possible penalty was death. "The courtroom," said nineteen-year-old Haywood Patterson, the most outspoken of the defendants, "was one big smiling white face."

The youth of the helpless accused, the frenzied racist atmosphere at their trials, and clear evidence that the charges were false turned the Scottsboro boys into icons of humility overwhelmed by injustice. One of the youths was nearly blind; another had been suffering from syphilis so painful that he had to walk with a cane. How could they have jumped from car to car to take part in a gang rape? Outraged idealists in search of social justice knew where to turn. The CPUSA convened protest meetings in Cleveland and New York. The International Labor Defense (ILD) hired George W. Chamlee, a famous southern lawyer, to defend the youths. On November 7, 1932, the Supreme Court ruled in *Powell v. Alabama* that there must be a retrial because the prejudice of the all-white juries had denied the defendants due process of law as guaranteed by the Fourteenth Amendment.

At the second trial, held in 1933 in Decatur, Alabama, a stronghold of the Ku Klux Klan fifty miles west of Scottsboro, Samuel Leibowitz, a heavyset New York lawyer, took charge. He produced a series of bombshell revelations. First, a white hobo described Victoria Price not as a flower of southern womanhood but rather as a common prostitute. Then the other accuser, Ruby Bates, appeared as a witness for the defense. She said there had been no rape. Victoria Price had invented the whole story because she feared that a sheriff's posse would arrest her for transporting a minor (Bates) across state lines for the purpose of prostitution. The prosecutors were stunned but not done for. One jeered, "Is justice in this case going to be bought and sold in Alabama with Jew money from New York?" The recalcitrant jurors obliged the prosecution with another guilty verdict for which the sentence was death.

Judge James Horton set aside the convictions, citing the unreliability of state's witness Victoria Price. After another guilty verdict, the Supreme Court intervened in its groundbreaking decision, *Norris v. Alabama*, on April 1, 1935. It reversed the convictions on the grounds that African Americans had been excluded from the juries. By this time the Scottsboro boys were a national sensation. As northern protests mounted, Alabama's steady resolve began to waver. In July 1937 the state insisted on death for Norris and prison for four others (Weems, Powell, Andrew Wright, and Patterson) and withdrew the case against the other four (Montgomery, Leroy Wright, Roberson, and Williams). The five were retried, found guilty again, and sentenced to long terms in prison. Then, between 1943 and 1946 four of them were quietly paroled. The last, Haywood Patterson, escaped from prison in 1948 and fled to Detroit, where he was recaptured in 1950 by the FBI. Michigan rebuffed Alabama's halfhearted attempt to have him returned, and Patterson was set free.

A number of African American movements favoring black nationalism emerged in the 1930s, many of them based on Islam. Islam had traveled to America with some African slaves, with Moorish seamen to the port of New York, and with Alexander Russell Webb, a white journalist who converted while serving as U.S. consul to the Philippines after 1887. Webb opened missionary headquarters in New York at 30 East Twenty-Third Street in 1893. From 1900 on, there were also Muslim immigrants from Poland, Russia, and Lithuania. United Negro Improvement Association leader Marcus Garvey's followers were also influenced by the Moorish Science Temple, formed in Newark, New Jersey, and led by Noble Drew Ali. The first black mosque in New York was Temple No. 21 at Livonia Avenue in Brooklyn, opened in 1933.

In 1931 Elijah (or Robert) Poole met Wallace D. Fard, a short, white-skinned man who said he was God and who offered him a new name—Elijah Muhammad—and a religion tailored for African Americans, the seeds of what would become the Nation of Islam. Muhammad's biographer, Claude Andrew Clegg, III, explains (1997) that the hitherto unsuccessful Muhammad, the son of a Georgia sharecropper and a domestic worker, first turned to alcohol in despair. Then he "was mesmerized by the ideas of the Muslim leader regarding the originality and superiority of blackness, moral living, proper dieting, and the new world to come." For, basing their beliefs on Islam and a version of the Koran, Black Muslims taught that all whites were devils, creations of an evil scientist, Yakub, and that blacks were the true children of Allah. The myth of the evil Yakub expressed a profound truth about the systematic exploitation of African Americans by white society—notably in human slavery—and also how society institutionalized racism. When Fard disappeared in 1934, Elijah Muhammad assumed control, moving the headquarters from Detroit to Chicago. During the 1930s membership stabilized around ten thousand. But the building of the Nation of Islam was a long process and one full of internal dissension and persecution by the police and the FBI. Not only was the Nation of Islam a religious movement, but it carried a very different political message from that of the NAACP, proposing separatism rather than integration.

Ironically, white institutions were becoming increasingly receptive to open discussion of race relations. Thus, the Carnegie Foundation sponsored Swedish sociologist Gunnar Myrdal to undertake the research and writing of his mammoth study of race, *An American Dilemma* (1937). A variety of southern Progressives—writers and journalists, teachers and preachers—began calling for an honest confrontation with the South's problems. There were newspaper editors in this vanguard, including Hodding Carter, Jr., of the *Greenville* (Mississippi) *Delta Democrat Times* and Ralph McGill of the *Atlanta Constitution*; they condemned lynch law and attacked the poll tax. Liberals Myles Horton of the Highlander Folk School in Appalachia, Lucy Randolph Mason of the CIO, and others spoke out against racial injustice.

Organized labor was also shifting its position with regard to African Americans. There were few African American unions—apart from A. Philip Randolph's Brotherhood of Sleeping Car Porters (BSCP), founded on August 5, 1925. However, the upheaval in organized labor leading to the creation of the CIO, and the determination of certain Communist organizers to inject the race issue into union affairs helped promote the African American case. The CPUSA-led National Textile Workers emphasized the need for racial equality, in contrast to the all-white exclusiveness of the United Textile Workers. Similarly, the Sharecropper Union in Alabama, the United Citrus Workers in Florida, and the Southern Tenant Farmers Union all practiced open membership.

White society prized African American singers and musicians for their range of emotional expression in the performing arts, but it denied them full recognition as citizens. Jazz musician Duke Ellington and his band were allowed to perform at Loew's State Theater on Broadway but not at the Paramount or the Strand.

On one celebrated occasion white racism misfired and aided black pride.

It involved classical contralto Marian Anderson, who had found herself restricted on concert stages in the United States and excluded outright from opera. She had made her European debut in Berlin in 1930, had toured Scandinavia, and at Salzburg in 1935 met conductor Arturo Toscanini. He told her, "A voice like yours comes once in a century." Astute Sol Hurok became Anderson's manager when she returned to the United States in 1935. She caused a sensation at Town Hall in New York and at the White House, where she was the first black artist to perform. In 1938 she gave seventy recitals in the United States, a record for a singer.

At the peak of her renown, Anderson planned to give a concert at Constitution Hall on Easter Day. Journalist Mary Johnson, sensing a story, provoked Mrs. Henry M. Robert, president of the DAR, the organization that managed the auditorium, into announcing that neither Marian Anderson nor any other African American artist would ever be heard in Constitution Hall. Liberals were scandalized. At the suggestion of Walter White, Secretary of the Interior Harold Ickes gave permission to hold the concert on the steps of the Lincoln Memorial, a far more prestigious and symbolic site. Eleanor Roosevelt resigned from the DAR. She and Ickes made sure that the front rows of the audience comprised cabinet members, senators, congressmen, and Supreme Court justices. Widespread publicity resulted in an audience of seventy-five thousand, who were engrossed by the sublime contralto's power, range, and expression.

Native Americans and the New Deal

The New Deal's policies toward Native Americans were thematically related to its policies regarding agriculture and farmers, because this was how John Collier, the New Dealer responsible, saw Indian affairs.

In 1930 the overall population of the United States was 123,077,000. Statistics on the numbers of Indians are estimates, subject to differences, largely because of disagreements about who constituted Native Americans: those on reservations? those with mixed Indian and white blood? those who claimed Indian heritage? Taking those differences into account, there were between 332,350 and 362,380 Native Americans in 1930.

John Collier became commissioner of Indian affairs in 1934, the year that Columbia University anthropologist Ruth Benedict's influential book, *Patterns of Culture*, was published. Collier believed that previous federal policies were misconceived. Whatever the motives, they had damaged Indian culture, and Collier wanted to remedy things. In her book, Benedict preferred the Zuni and Pueblo cultures of the Southwest, with their emphasis on communal values, to the more possessive Northeast fishing cultures. Collier generalized from Benedict's hypotheses and from what he knew of the Pueblo Indians' cohesive society. He applied his generalizations to such different groups as the Plains Indians, whose culture emphasized individual expression and who had adjusted to a system of individually owned farmland.

Collier's wide-ranging proposals were enacted in a modified form in the Wheeler-Howard or Indian Reorganization Act of 1934, which applied to all states except Oklahoma and was accepted by 192 of the 263 tribes that voted on it. The act had three principal aims: to bring an abrupt end to the discredited policy of allotment and continued white appropriation of Indian land; to establish a system of tribal government, providing Indians with some self-determination, "certain rights of home rule"; and to enhance the economic welfare of Indian reservations by creating a revolving fund and adding to Indian territory. The Wheeler-Howard Act also proposed that the Bureau of Indian Affairs (BIA) should exercise a far more active role than hitherto, according to the expertise of social scientists. The contradiction between the aim of granting the Indians greater autonomy and at the same time strengthening the hand of the BIA proved too much for Collier's new colonial policy.

Collier knew that some of the Navajo's chronic economic problems were caused by continuous overgrazing of their sheep. In accordance with New Deal policy elsewhere, Collier's solution was to reduce the flock by slaughter. Whatever the merits of slaughter in terms of cost effectiveness, to the Navajo it appeared a wanton act against their future security. The decision exposed the gap between the impersonal expertise of the administration and the cultural values of the Indians. Collier was essentially autocratic. He was indifferent and sometimes hostile when Indians resisted big corporations that were ready to extract precious minerals from Indian lands. He preferred land held by tribes to land held by individuals. Thus, Indians who wanted to adopt U.S. economic values accused Collier of trying to send them "back to the blanket." Instead of instilling white values in boarding schools, Collier wanted a return to traditional Indian values. Some argued that this policy would produce adults unable to earn a living in the twentieth century.

The sort of Indian government Collier wanted to establish was the form he considered most representative—an accountable democracy based on a constitution and elections by universal adult suffrage in which the winner was the candidate with the greatest number of votes. Many considered this a white form of government not suited to Indian needs. Consequently, it was those Indians who played the system and cooperated with federal policies who got elected. They were also those who most conformed to white lifestyles and were often of mixed race, with less Indian blood than white. These Indians were sometimes called "progressives." Traditional Native Americans still considered themselves dispossessed.

Thus, although the New Deal achieved a more equitable society, it left much undone. It left fundamental problems largely untouched: the problems of tenant farmers, sharecroppers, and migrant workers in agriculture and, among ethnic groups, those of African Americans, Native Americans, Puerto Ricans, and Mexican Americans. For example, New Deal efforts in slum clearance were scarcely proportionate to the magnitude of the problem. Although FDR called attention in 1937 to the one-third of the nation who were "ill-nourished, ill-clad, ill-housed," twenty-six years later Michael Harrington showed in *The Other America* (1963) that the proportion was still almost as great.

The Powerful Promoter of Society's Welfare?

The major legacy of the New Deal was that the operation of the national economy became the responsibility of the federal government in the interests of all citizens, not just those of a particular class. Thus, the federal government became an institution shared by all the people. No longer was it a neutral arbiter between different branches or levels of government but, in the words of Felix Frankfurter, the "powerful promoter of society's welfare." For the first time all citizens experienced its presence as it taxed hundreds of thousands directly and distributed pensions and relief to millions.

The state was personified by FDR, whom millions regarded as a protector. In his *Being an American* (1948), Justice William O. Douglas remarked, "He was in a very special sense the people's president, because he made them feel that, with him in the White House, they shared the presidency. The sense of sharing the presidency gave even the most humble citizens a lively sense of belonging."

In the words of William E. Leuchtenburg in *Franklin D. Roosevelt and the New Deal* (1963), "Roosevelt's importance lay not in his talents as a campaigner or a manipulator. It lay, rather, in his ability to rouse the country and, more specifically, the men who served under him, by his breezy encouragement of experimentation, by his hopefulness, and—a word that would have embarrassed some of his lieutenants—by his idealism."

Increasingly, both Roosevelt and his New Deal earned resentment from the affluent haves. They particularly disliked the egalitarian spirit of the New Deal and the fact that they would have to shoulder the financial support of rudimentary welfare. Then the hullabaloo over the Supreme Court was followed by the recession of 1937. In the administration, political argument intensified about the future course of liberalism. Hence, FDR found himself embroiled in an intense ideological struggle in 1937 and 1938. Alan Brinkley believes (1995) this was a struggle for the heart of the New Deal and the soul of liberalism. Among its other legacies, the New Deal, by its mix of pragmatism and accountable government, allowed the United States to remain the world's most influential democracy in a period that was dark elsewhere. Democracy lost ground in country after country of Western Europe that either succumbed to totalitarian dictatorship or was enfeebled by irresolute government. The New Deal preserved the democratic traditions of the republic and enhanced its democratic reputation.

But the New Deal was not uniformly popular, or even accepted, among all Democrats. FDR, Hopkins, and Ickes were furious at the way southern Democrats used FDR's popularity to get themselves elected and then once in office deserted the New Deal. They tried to institute a purge of disloyal congressmen, such as Senators Millard E. Tydings of Maryland, "Cotton Ed" Smith of South Carolina, and Walter F. George of Georgia, in the midterm elections of 1938. FDR wanted to oust these southern conservatives and to transform the Democratic Party from a loose coalition of local and sectional interests, in which its congressmen conveniently blurred the issues when it suited them, into a cohesive bloc of definite, liberal views.

Yet, for some men to live by principle, others must live by compromise. When Roosevelt tried to defy practical politics, he was fighting a losing game. Roosevelt failed to get popular and influential Democrats dropped from the party ticket for the midterm elections of 1938. Thus Senators George, Smith, and Tydings survived FDR's attacks. Only Congressman John O'Connor of New York, albeit chairman of the powerful House Rules Committee, succumbed to FDR's withdrawal of support and met defeat. The Republicans nominated him as their candidate and he went down to defeat again.

However, in those elections, the Republicans almost doubled their seats in the House, going from 88 to 169 against 261 Democrats—still a handsome Democrat majority. In the Senate, the results left 69 Democrats against 23 Republicans. Nevertheless, the swing of public approval away from the New Deal could not be ignored.

Therefore, in January 1939 FDR proposed no new reform measures. The political impulses that had propelled the New Deal in the early 1930s were almost extinct. The New Dealers sought no more fundamental laws. The brief, overwhelming ascendancy of the Democratic party was somewhat tarnished in many minds by the mistaken court-packing scheme and by the comparative electoral setback of 1938. People were exhausted by adversary politics. Both organized labor and business now preferred to follow a more moderate course in the interest of reducing class tension.

The New Deal ended, as it had begun, with a demonstration that the greatest power of the federal government devolved from presidential initiative. FDR realized that if he, or any less energetic successor, were to survive the political strain of the presidency, then it would be necessary to institutionalize its administrative staff and reform the various agencies to make them more effective. But his attempt to secure congressional approval for a reorganization bill fell afoul of the soured atmosphere of 1938. The bill narrowly passed the Senate in March, but the House defeated it by 204 votes to 196 on April 8, 1938.

FDR was neither defeated nor deterred. By Executive Order 8248 of September 8, 1939, he established the Executive Office of the President, staffed by six administrative assistants. This was far more than a declaration that the executive was a branch of the federal government along with the legislature and the judiciary. It gave the president a realistic chance to withstand the physical and mental strain of the office and to fulfill his constitutional mandate without resorting to a multiheaded executive. Executive Order 8248 saved the office of the presidency and the Constitution from the need for more radical amendment. Subsequently, the Council of Economic Advisers, the National Security Council, and the Central Intelligence Agency were moved into the Executive Office.

In general, the American political and economic system was strengthened by the New Deal, but the depression and widespread unemployment remained. According to the minimal statistics of the Department of Labor Bureau of Labor Statistics (BLS), unemployment rose from 1.49 million (3.1 percent of the labor force) in 1929 to 12.63 million (25.2 percent) in 1933. Thereafter, the level fell gradually until it was 7.27 million (13.8 percent) in 1937, only to rise to 8.84 million (16.5 percent) in 1939. These statistics were regarded as serious underestimates by the AFL, the CIO, and the LRA (Labor Research Association). Even the BLS admitted that wholesale prices remained well below their index number of 100 in 1926. In 1929 prices were at 95.3, falling to 65.9 in 1933, rising gradually to 86.3 in 1937, and then declining to 77.1 in 1939.

The Federal Reserve Board charted the physical volume of industrial production in these years according to an average of 100 for the years 1935–39. In 1929 the index was 110. It was at its lowest in 1932 at 58. Thereafter, it rose to 113 in 1937, falling back to 88 in 1938, and rising to 108 in 1939. We can attribute some poverty to factors other than the unprecedented economic crisis. One was the increasing number of older people in the population. The number of people over sixty-five rose from 4.9 million in 1920 to 9 million in 1940, an increase from 4.6 percent to 6.9 percent. Another factor was the bitter climax of the long-term exploitation of the soil in certain areas that had culminated in the Dust Bowl. But such factors made the Great Depression more severe.

Given the unprecedented crisis, it was surprising that the New Deal achieved as much as it did, rather than that it left so many problems unsolved. In less than six years, more significant changes were wrought by government than previously. Much of what the New Deal attempted but did not complete was halted by the war, by its own moderation and loss of momentum, and by the growth of opposition resulting from adversary politics in 1936 and 1937. Moreover, at flood tide, the New Deal fostered and encouraged widespread discussion about the values of society and the proper role and relationships of its various economic components—industry, business, agriculture, labor, and government.

Many New Deal measures survived the Great Depression, notably legislation on banking, the stock market, and social security. From the 1940s to the 1970s it seemed that the principles underlying the New Deal were widely accepted and that both Republicans and Democrats would maintain them, occasionally adjusting details to meet particular circumstances but never challenging the substance. The New Deal was regarded as a foundation of the modern federal government, especially in three fields: welfare, finance, and governmental accountability and organization.

The 1980s produced the first climax of what amounted to a profound shift in public sensibility. Ironically, this was partly as a benign consequence of the New Deal (and economic good fortunes in World War II and thereafter): raising the status of blue-collar workers and their children and moving them into a middle class where basic social welfare seemed less crucial. It was also partly because of the expansion of welfare, particularly in the Great Society legislation during Lyndon Johnson's administration (1963–69), and partly because it became ever clearer in the 1990s that the actuarial system of social welfare was unsound—that social security simply could not provide for people as originally planned. Demagogues of the emerging Republican majority challenged the legacy of the New Deal, and the so-called Reagan revolution promoted by President Ronald Reagan (1981–89) started to dismantle it. The movement reached a climax with the aborted Health Care bill of 1994 and the Welfare Reform Act of 1996, passed by a predominantly Republican Congress and signed into law by centrist Democratic president Bill Clinton (1993–   ). Both president and Congress pledged to "end welfare as we know it."

Thus, at the turn of the twenty-first century, although the New Deal's monumental, historic place as the federal program to beat the Great Depression of the 1930s remained unchallenged, its achievements were no longer a secure cornerstone of the social obligations of modern government.

CHAPTER 13

Castles in the Air

DESPITE THE SEARING TRAGEDY of the depression, the promissory legend of American democratic capitalism survived. In fact, America's prowess in advanced technology traveled through the depression with its reputation enhanced. Not only were individual machines on the agenda for transformation as the machine revolution continued apace, but so also was the general environment. This was a special feature of two world's fairs, the Century of Progress Fair in Chicago in 1933–34, and the World of Tomorrow Fair in Flushing Meadow, New York, in 1939–40, both of which had pavilions devoted to new worlds.

The Chicago fair was a showcase for "the transformation of life through the ministrations of sciences." One official slogan was "Science Finds—Industry Applies—Man Conforms." For example, architect George Fred Keck, who designed prefabricated housing, devised a duodecagon House of Tomorrow for the Century of Progress Exposition that could show off new gadgets and materials: General Electric provided appliances; H. W. Howell, the tubular furniture; U.S. Gypsum, the floors; and Holland Furnace, the air conditioning. The house was prefabricated and took only two months to erect. Keck made the interiors of his houses adjustable through a sequence of movable, insulation-board walls to accommodate successive changes in lifestyle.

At the World of Tomorrow Fair in New York, visitors could view Democracity by Henry Dreyfuss and thereby enter a future made by machines. Democracity was a model city within the Perisphere, a round building two hundred feet in diameter, wherein people passed through the Trylon, seven hundred feet tall. But the most significant pavilion was Futurama, designed by Norman Bel Geddes as part of the General Motors pavilion. Visitors entered through a gigantic curved wall painted like an automobile and then moved to a darkened

auditorium where they crossed a rubber-tired train on a route to simulate an air trip across the United States of the 1960s with miniature cars and fields encased by glass and a modern metropolis of skyscrapers.

The implication was clear: technology and machines were the solutions to the problems of America in the Great Depression.

In the 1930s people looked to airplanes and aviation to create new horizons. People saw air travel as a way of rising above the restrictions of national territory and of opening up new relationships across the world. In a country as large as the United States and with as scattered and as widely separated a population, people were quick to appreciate the speed and convenience of air travel. Despite the depression, dozens of companies, large and small, with hundreds of planes, flew ever more passengers and carried increasing loads of mail in the 1930s. Between 1930 and 1940 air passenger traffic multiplied twelve times to over 1 billion passenger miles in 1940; during that period air-freight traffic tripled in volume.

By 1930 the United States had four major airlines, all launched on the model of shipping lines. Bill Boeing and engine makers Pratt and Whitney formed the United Aircraft and Transportation Corporation, which later became United Airlines. The Aviation Corporation, founded by railroad magnate William Averell Harriman in 1929, eventually developed into American Airlines. Entrepreneur C. M. Keys, chairman of the Curtiss Airplane Company, helped create North American Airlines, predecessor of Eastern Airlines, and TAT, later Trans World Airlines (TWA). By 1930 these four airlines had all established transcontinental routes, their prime catchment area. In 1938 the big four were joined by Continental Airlines, founded in Denver by Robert Six. Like the Hollywood studios, the fledgling airlines soon had their tycoons—Cyrus Smith (American), Bill Patterson (United), Eddie Rickenbacker (Eastern), and Jack Frye (TWA)—each obsessed with creating networks. Competition for airplane landing rights and the need to find refueling stages led to the development of Fort Worth, St. Louis, and Kansas City.

Like the Hollywood studios? In fact, handsome oil billionaire Howard Hughes of Houston, Texas, adored both aviation and motion pictures. His twin obsessions led him first to buy TWA when it was a foundering carrier and to transform it into a thriving global airline, and second, to acquire the Hollywood studio RKO Pictures. Thereby he gained the somewhat ephemeral respect of the American public, who sensed a subliminal connection between the hypnotic power of movie dreams and the physical ecstasy of flight.

Outside the big four circled Pan American Airways (Pan Am), founded in October 1927 and led by its young executive Juan Trippe. Trippe established the first permanent service from the United States to a foreign country: Pan Am carried mail from Key West, Florida, to Havana, Cuba, one hundred miles away. It used Fokker F7 trimotor planes, and the journey lasted an hour. By 1938 it was running passenger service on routes to South America, across the Pacific to

Manila in the Philippines, and to England. Pan Am introduced a new Martin M-130 four-engine plane on its Pacific routes in 1935.

Increasing passenger expectations and use coincided with new, improved planes as commercial airlines began to benefit from governmental and private research. By 1932 new airplanes were internally braced, low-strung monoplanes, built entirely of metal. They had such improved features as air-cooled engines, controllable-pitch propellers, retractable undercarriages, and insulated and soundproofed compartments for pilots and passengers. In addition, the appearance of airplanes was enhanced by technological improvements such as the powerful and elegant radical engineering of Pratt and Whitney and Curtiss-Wright. In 1931 Russian immigrant Igor Sikorsky designed and built the first clippers for Pan Am. Following closely, Glenn Martin's flying boats, such as the M-130 W China Clipper of 1934, demonstrated a new integral aircraft design, notably in the way the wings rose naturally from the body.

In 1932 manufacturer Donald Douglas sold TWA several DC-2 planes. They carried fourteen passengers at 170 mph. From 1936 on, his new all-metal DC-3, powered by two 900-horsepower Wright Cyclone motors, became the most popular model on all major airlines and was known as the Model T of aircraft. It revolutionized air travel on account of its safety and reliability. The DC-3 combined maximum economy and speed and carried twenty-one passengers. The DC-3 flew a route from New York to Los Angeles, a journey lasting twenty-four hours with three or four stops for refueling.

Transatlantic flight was another significant development, heralding a new era of travel that would follow World War II. Between 1932 and 1937 transatlantic flights were by airships, such as the *Graf Zeppelin* and the *Hindenburg*, flying between Frankfurt, Germany, and Lakehurst, New Jersey. The day of the airship was brief, however, and troubled by various crashes. It was finally brought to an abrupt end by the explosion of the *Hindenburg* at Lakehurst in 1937. The flying boat was then the staple carrier for intercontinental flights until 1938, when it was replaced by the Boeing 314 Clipper, widely adopted in 1939, the year transatlantic airplane flights began.

As with every new form of manufacturing and commerce introduced since the Civil War, air transportation posed special problems for government regulation. Although airline chiefs were opening up a continent all over again, they had a reputation as buccaneers. At first the Department of Commerce assigned routes, awarded pilot certificates and licenses, and determined standards of safety through its aeronautics branch. However, the system was rocked by scandal. In 1934 Senator Hugo Black of Alabama led a Senate investigation into the awarding of mail contracts. Postmaster General Jim Farley caused a sensation when he accused his predecessor, Walter Brown, of collusion in the awarding of airmail contracts. In addition, Farley explained that Juan Trippe of Pan Am had received special favors and that he had concealed Pan Am profits by juggling accounts. Nevertheless, because Pan Am had not been involved in the way domestic routes were allotted, it came through the exposure relatively un-scathed.

President Franklin Delano Roosevelt distrusted both the big four and the outsider, Pan Am. He canceled all domestic airmail contracts in 1934 and called in the army to fly the mail. Army pilots could not handle the quantity or the routes, however, and ten of them got killed. Thus FDR had to reinstate the airline mail contracts. First, the federal government introduced a temporary airmail law to return airmail deliveries to the private sector. The bill provided for the appointment of a Federal Aviation Commission (FAC) to study the situation and to make recommendations for the future organization of aviation. Its views were implemented in the Civil Aeronautics Act of 1938, creating a Civil Aeronautics Authority (CAA) within the Department of Commerce. In 1940 the CAA became the licensing and regulating body for civil aviators. The Civil Aeronautics Board (CAB) was created under the secretary of commerce to control the economic organization of airlines and determine standards of safety. The new board continued a system of so-called controlled competition by which airlines sought routes from the federal government that had to be approved by the president. In practice, the big four received permanent certificates on domestic routes—while Pan Am continued to enjoy its foreign monopoly.

However, FDR separated manufacturing companies, such as Boeing and United, from those owning or controlling airlines. This shift in policy encouraged the airlines to pick and choose between manufacturers, thereby stimulating competition and increasing the pace of advances in technology. On the West Coast such aircraft companies as Boeing, Douglas, and Lockheed competed for airline customers just before and during World War II, when orders for military planes became big business.

Towering Rages

Although airlines were to provide the United States with yet more sinews for international cultural control, it was still buildings, rather than planes, that symbolized American technological prowess across the world, and none more so than the urban forests of skyscrapers.

The great glory of skyscraper design in the 1930s was the Rockefeller Center

FACING PAGE:

Rockefeller Center, New York, by Benjamin Wistar Morris; Reinhard and Hofmeister; Corbett, Harrison and MacMurray; and Hood and Fouilhoux (1932–40). John D. Rockefeller, Jr., developed the first large-scale project of urban renewal, in which a group of (eventually) nineteen buildings were designed as an integral group dominated by the centerpiece, the RCA Building. By a series of cascading setbacks, architect Raymond Hood enhanced light, air, and space around the seventy-story skyscraper. The 1935 photo shows the plaza still under construction and illuminated at night. (Library of Congress)

of New York (1932–40), a complex of originally nineteen commercial buildings on a site bounded by Forty-Ninth Street, Fifth Avenue, Fifty-Second Street, and Seventh Avenue. When the Metropolitan Opera, short of funds after the Wall Street crash, withdrew from a project that would have provided it with a new home, John D. Rockefeller, Jr., developed the empty space into the first large-scale project of urban renewal conceived as an integral group.

In conception and design, the Rockefeller Center was a masterpiece without a single, presiding genius. It was instead a feat of collective design and managerial effort, a fact architect Raymond Hood underscored when he wrote in *Architectural Forum* in 1932: "It would be impossible to estimate the number of official minds that have engaged in untangling the problem. . . . Architects, builders, engineers, real-estate operators, financiers, lawyers—all have contributed something from their experience and . . . from their imagination." The cast of architectural characters for the complex included Benjamin Wistar Morris; Reinhard and Hofmeister, experts in designing office spaces; and Corbett, Harrison, and MacMurray, praised for their sober designs and civic concern; as well as Hood's own firm of Hood, Godley and Fouilhoux, known for their innovative designs.

The Rockefeller Center was a coherent, yet romantic, expression of tower design and a rational organization of the various components of modernist architecture. Four low buildings on the northern blocks provided an entrance of inviting proportions and elegant shops, and a sunken plaza with flags, sculptures, and fountains enticed visitors inward. The cascading setbacks of the RCA Building, tallest of the nineteen making up the complex and completed in 1933, show how architect Raymond Hood conjured with light, air, and space around the seventy-story skyscraper. The Rockefeller Center also served as glorious advertisement for big business during the depression. In fact, the fifty-fifth and fifty-sixth floors of the RCA Building provided the Rockefeller family with Room 560, headquarters of their public relations operations.

The Rockefeller Center was also a prime example of the so-called International Style. The International Style did not name itself. The epithet was the title of the International Exhibition of Modern Architecture that the Museum of Modern Art (MoMA) in New York mounted in February and March 1932, subsequently shown in another thirty cities and accompanied by a substantial catalog. In New York, thirty-two thousand people visited the show.

Planned by Henry-Russell Hitchcock, Philip Johnson, and MoMA's director, Alfred H. Barr, Jr., the exhibition had three sections: one showed the extent of the International Style, another showed its influence on housing, and the third showed work by leaders of the style, including Richard Neutra, Raymond Hood, George Howe, and William Lescaze.

In their book accompanying the exhibition, *The International Style*, Philip Johnson and Henry-Russell Hitchcock explained the three principles of modern architecture: architecture as volume rather than mass, regular (rather than axial) symmetry in determining design, and the absence of arbitrary surface ornament.

Walls might look wafer thin, yet they would be composed of thick brick. It was an austere, uncompromising style. Architects built commercial and domestic buildings much the same way from New York to San Francisco. This international corporate style was so pervasive that, by the 1950s, it was synonymous not only with American architecture generally, but also with the impersonal world of American business. Among its prime features, severe, flat surfaces emphasized structure and sometimes mechanics. On the domestic level, such was the Aluminaire House in Syosset, New York (1931) by A. Lawrence Kochner and Albert Frey. Made of light steel and aluminum frame covered by wallboard, tar paper, and aluminum sheets, it was erected in ten days in 1931. Astonishing, given their supposed proficiency in modern materials, was the careless indifference of architects of the International School to such basic necessities as waterproof roofs—and this was even true of Frank Lloyd Wright.

In fact, the International Style exhibition also included work by maverick architect Frank Lloyd Wright. Wright's buildings rarely fitted into the organizers' notions of modern architecture, but they included Wright because, quite simply, they knew he was the most eminent among them.

Frank Lloyd Wright's outstanding contributions to architecture were his common sense, which was rooted in middle-class, nineteenth-century values and by which he tried to close the gap between the architectural profession and the public; his so-called prairie houses of the Midwest with their open, flowing space and great horizontal planes; and a harmonious use of wood, stone, glass, and stucco. Yet, for all his differences with modernists, Frank Lloyd Wright's work was akin to that of architects influenced by the new machines. Wright moved gracefully between residential and commercial enterprises. The Kauffman Residence, later known as Fallingwater, in Bear Run, Pennsylvania (1936), the most notable of Wright's organic building designs, was also a machine in the wilderness with machine-produced concrete-reinforced broad decks. Fallingwater was tied to the waterfall with rocks pushing up through the living room floor. Wright's fascination with organic shapes also led to his most famous office design of the period, the Johnson Wax Building, Racine, Wisconsin (1938), notable for its twenty two Dendiform Shafts, or mushroom, tapering columns, pinned on brass shoes at the bottom and growing outward at the ceiling of gleaming Pyrex tubing. They served to divide the office space and also to enhance it by forming a contrast to the light streaming from the skylight.

What was good for houses was necessary for industry. In his Ohio Steel Foundry Roll and Machinery Shop in Lima, Ohio (1938), industrial architect Albert Kahn refined industrial design, emphasizing the sawtooth clerestory and butterfly roofs, while treating the different sections as units within a continuous surface. There were great luminous spaces inside and tall glass walls atop light-colored brick on the exterior.

Some architects synthesized various strands of modern architecture—the International Style, setback skyscrapers, and streamlined design—within more conventional buildings. They produced sparse, neoclassical edifices with regular proportions such as the Folger Shakespeare Library, Washington, D.C. (1929–32), by Paul Cret. This was a white marble building with fluted piers alternating with high, narrow windows whose spandrels carried neoclassical sculpted reliefs. Another spare classical building was the National Airport in Washington, D.C. (1940), built by the PWA with Howard L. Cheney as consulting architect; it was a semicircular building with a concave entrance, immense cylindrical columns, and a convex glass wall looking upon the landing strip.

The use of cherished older styles as civilizing sheaths around modern structures was nowhere more striking than at Yale University, which acquired numerous Gothic and Tudor facades in the 1930s. None had greater presence than Sterling Memorial Library (1930) by James Gamble Rogers, with an entrance hall like a nave, a circulation desk like a high altar, and a main reading room like a banqueting hall. Critics accused Rogers of being unfaithful to his time, of creating a fanciful stage set rather than a functional library. In fact, having made his choice of Gothic effect, Rogers occupied himself with the organization of interior space and its funding. The principal feature of Sterling was its assertive storage tower, a fifteen-story steel-frame skyscraper, constructed with advanced engineering, that rose like the immense pipes of a giant cathedral organ.

In domestic architecture, progressive architects aimed to provide homes with the maximum of efficient, cost-effective modern conveniences. Here again, American technology led the world.

In contrast with the conservative Northeast and Midwest, architects in southern California, such as Richard Neutra and Rudolph Schindler, found that their affluent clients welcomed experimental building, because they liked to consider themselves part of the avant-garde, because of the economic boom and fantasy of Hollywood, and because the milder climate of California favored more experiments in building. Richard Neutra used the technology of construction in a fashion far ahead of any European architect. The Beard House (1934–35), Altadena, California, employed hollow steel channels for the walls, open-web steel trusses for the roof, and steel web beams as the base for the concrete floor. The exterior was painted silver gray; the interior had aluminum steel columns, a gray linoleum floor, brown masonite walls, and tubular steel furniture. Even more dramatic was Richard Neutra's house for director Josef von Sternberg in the San Fernando Valley (1934–35), which was protected by long, blank metal walls and a superfluous moat.

Los Angeles architect Gregory Ain wanted to build inexpensive modern housing, using, as Rudolph Schindler planned, cheap modern technology, but with broad, plain surfaces, as Neutra would have wished. Typical of Ain's work was the small, inexpensive Becker House on a hillside of the Silver Lake district of Los Angeles (1938). Made of a wood frame with plywood and stucco, it cost only three thousand dollars to build. Everything was run on economical lines because of the efficient layout. Ain's use of open space was broad and subtle. Ain's Dunsimur Flats in Los Angeles (1937) was another instance of a fully integrated structure, using four different building elements to reduce costs by creating a series of cubes and allowing light to enter all major rooms on three sides.

What furnished such modern houses? Plastic spread its wings and enfolded every little thing. Prolific inventor William E. Hanford was on the team of research chemists at E. I. Du Pont de Nemours and Company that created the versatile plastic polyurethane in 1936. Polyurethane soon appeared in every room of the house, as carpet and synthetic-leather upholstery, as cushions and furniture finish, and eventually as the rubber for sneakers that trod the boards and loafed on the chairs.

Yet mass-produced housing was expensive in terms of factory tooling and transportation. Moreover, even if a huge volume of production could be achieved in the interest of cutting the cost of individual units, that would not eliminate the housing expense that revolved around costs on site: acquiring land, laying foundations, providing utilities, and meeting local building codes. Standardization could be applied, though, to such traditional forms as wooden housing. After World War II, mass-produced housing became a practicable proposition, and suburbs and towns, often built by the Levitt company to specific standards, sprang up across the United States.

War of Words

Within the new box houses were yet smaller boxes connecting their inhabitants not only to the town or city immediately outside the walls but further to the wider world of communication, business, and aural sensation. Radio penetrated people's homes, sold the audience to advertisers, and etched memorable voices and songs on their minds. Between 1935 and 1941 the number of homes with radios rose from 7 million to 28.5 million. By the late 1930s half the homes in America contained at least two radios. The price of a radio set fell from $90 in 1930 to $47 in 1932. Wherever you were, you could hear a radio playing, on average, for almost five hours every day. Radio provided a central link in the web of mass entertainment that came to dominate the world.

There were four nationwide networks: NBC-Blue, NBC-Red, CBS, and Mutual. Although these networks owned only 4 percent of all stations in 1939, they owned 25 percent of all clear-channel, high-power stations and controlled fifty of the remaining fifty-two clear-channel stations. There were also twenty regional networks, of which six covered more than one state, such as the Yankee Network of New England.

NBC began in 1926 when RCA acquired the AT&T radio station, WEAF, which became the nucleus of its new corporation, the National Broadcasting Company. It began to broadcast as NBC-Red on November 18, 1926. When NBC took over the RCA Station, WJZ of New York, it became the center of a second network, NBC-Blue. By 1933 NBC owned ten stations outright, with another twenty-eight affiliated with its Red Network and twenty-four with its Blue Network. Another thirty-six stations participated in its network programming. These stations accounted for 15 percent of all stations.

Arthur Johnson, business manager of the Philadelphia Orchestra, drew together the different resources of AT&T, the Victor Talking Machine Company, and United Independent Broadcasting, Incorporated (UIB) to form the Columbia Broadcasting System (CBS) in September 1927 as a rival to NBC. When the new network began to flounder, William S. Paley of the Congress-Cigar Company, sensing its potential, bought a controlling interest in September 1928. Paley refashioned the company, consolidating its separate networks and renegotiating contracts with its affiliates. In 1933 the network extended to ninety-one stations. Paley remained chief executive of CBS until 1977 and thus a consistently influential figure in American broadcasting. NBC and CBS tightened their control over affiliates, binding stations to a five-year contract during which the station could not take programs from another network. Stations could not refuse to broadcast commercially sponsored network programs.

The fourth network, Mutual, was a cooperative venture among three fifty-thousand-watt stations: WGN (Chicago), WOR (Network and New York), and WXYZ (Detroit). Its affiliation with the New England Colonial Network and the Dan Lee Network on the West Coast in 1936 transformed Mutual into a national network.

The development of NBC and CBS concentrated the minds of advertisers on the advantage of commercials broadcast on radio coast-to-coast and reaching almost 70 percent of American homes. Harry F. Davis of Westinghouse observed that "broadcast advertising is modernity's medium of business expression. It made industry articulate. American businessmen, because of radio, are provided with a latch key to nearly every home in the United States." The close relationship between radio and advertising reinforced a decentralization of program planning and production. The advertising agency served as a middleman between radio networks and commercial sponsors, whose managers were glad to save time and money by turning marketing decisions over to experts—especially during a depression. As radio advertising continued to grow, agencies created not only the commercials but also the programs and combined them in blocks, or packages. By 1942 two-thirds of all programs carried advertisements—more than twice the number in 1932. In addition, using the new audience research data, advertising agencies, networks, and stations applied the concept of audience flow, whereby a single program could increase the audience for the programs broadcast immediately before and after it. Broadcasters therefore scheduled blocks of similar programs in order to build up the audiences.

Radio broadcasting's dependence on advertising revenue set itself in a pattern that would continue for both radio and television after World War II. About 60 percent of the revenue from selling airtime went to the networks and their few stations.

The late 1930s and early 1940s were a golden age of radio programs. Radio broadcasts extended for as many as eighteen hours a day. A survey in 1938 found that 53 percent of radio programs were music, 11 percent talk shows, 9 percent dramas, 9 percent news bulletins, 5 percent religious programs, 2 percent coverage of special events, and 11 percent other. Included in this "other," almost two hundred radio stations broadcast foreign-language programs, providing, in the largest cities, almost a continuous series of programs in German, Polish, Yiddish, and other languages. They appealed primarily to older immigrants, who could use them to return to an aural world of once-familiar music, stories, and jokes. In the North End of Boston, 85 percent of the Italian immigrants listened regularly to such broadcasts.

Although music continued to dominate the schedules of all radio programs, as time went on, less music was performed live. By 1929 radio stations had begun to use electrical transcriptions, 33 ⅓ rpm disks that played for about 15 minutes on each side and reproduced a better quality of sound than the 78 rpm records. Because these transcriptions offered listeners entertainment they could not buy for themselves, the Federal Radio Commission (FRC) permitted this form of mechanical broadcasting. Small local stations found these transcriptions so cost effective in comparison with paying singers, musicians, and technicians to perform, that they came to rely on electrical transcriptions as a staple. In the 1930s radio music was predominantly big-band music, supplied by leaders such as Benny Goodman, Ozzie Nelson, and Tommy Dorsey.

Amateur talent shows supplied cheap filler material between main programs. *Major Bowes and His Original Amateur Hour*, which started in 1934, led the field. Having discovered vocalist Frank Sinatra, Bowes moved to the NBC-Red network in 1935, taking Sinatra with him. Variety shows that mixed music and comedy drew on the talents of vaudeville players such as Bob Hope, who began his show for CBS in 1935. Hope moved easily between stage, film, and radio because his stock-in-trade—wisecracks—was perfectly suited to each medium. On screen he specialized in comedy-coward roles from *The Cat and the Canary* (1939), through *The Road to Singapore* (1940) and six sequels (1941–62) with crooner Bing Crosby, to *The Paleface* (1948) with Jane Russell. He also enjoyed a reputation for entertaining U.S. troops in seven theaters of war for almost fifty years from the Pacific (1942) to the Gulf (1991).

The genre programs of radio provided the models for television programs after World War II: situation comedies, quiz shows, soap operas, adventure and crime series, roundtable discussions, and variety shows.

Daily soap operas usually came in fifteen-minute episodes and were essentially matrifocal; they included *Back Stage Wife, Our Gal Sunday*, and *Road of Life* (life in a hospital). Adventure series such as *Gangbusters, Mr. Keen, Tracer of Lost Persons*, and *Mr. District Attorney* trod paths of well-tried dialogue with increasingly sophisticated aural effects of sirens and machine guns. All told, wife-and-husband team Anne and Frank Hummert created forty shows that dominated radio daytime programs between 1930 and 1960. With convoluted twists of plot, melodramatic dialogue, and Friday cliffhangers, their scripts laid down the formula for soap operas for years to come. Thus, the announcer would begin: "Once again, we bring you *The Romance of Helen Trent*, which sets out to prove what so many women long to prove: that because a woman is thirty-five or more, romance need not be over—that romance can live in life at thirty-five and after."

Networks offered children adventure serials, often about cowboys like Tom Mix or pilots like *Captain Midnight*. In 1938 the popular *Lone Ranger* was joined on WXYZ by a crime crusader, *The Green Hornet*, pledged to eradicate "public enemies that even the G-men cannot catch." *The Green Hornet* epitomized the New Deal ethos of economic and moral rearmament against the economic depression as well as the supposed rise in crime.

In the situation comedy, or sitcom, standard characters got themselves into and out of humorous situations. The first and most famous evolved from the blackface minstrel double act of Freeman F. Gosden and Charles J. Cornell, who performed for WGN, the *Chicago Tribune* station, as *Sam 'n' Henry* and later for rival station WMAQ as *Amos 'n' Andy*. *Amos 'n' Andy* became a national phenomenon when NBC-Blue acquired the show in 1929. *Li'l Abner* began in 1939 and competed with Fanny Brice's portrayal of *Baby Snooks*, who terrorized the lives of her father and baby brother, Robespierre—although Fanny Brice sounded more like a quirky grandmother than a mischievous child.

There was also a vogue for quiz shows, which rose from two hours per week in 1935 to ten hours per week in 1941. Among the most popular were *Kay Kyser's Kollege of Musical Knowledge*, *Dr. I. Q.*, and *Information, Please!* The gimmick of *Truth or Consequences* was that contestants who failed to answer questions correctly had to perform embarrassing stunts. The networks also produced a steady stream of serious drama: anthologies, serial adaptations, and specially commissioned and experimental plays such as those broadcast by CBS in its *Columbia Workshop*, starting in 1936.

From 1935 on, when major news services started to supply radio with national news, radio stations incorporated national news within the existing format of local news programs. As soon as they could expand their wire services, national networks began to broadcast international news. Because crime was a good audience-puller, they also relayed more major crime stories than did the newspapers.

Radio was unrivaled in being able to provide immediate and evocative reports from the scene of major events, whether planned or unexpected—such as the explosion of the *Hindenburg* passenger airship as it docked at Lakehurst, New Jersey, in May 1937. Broadcasters such as Herb Morrison of the Chicago WLS Station, who reported the *Hindenburg* explosion, understood that live, on-the-spot reporting of sudden disasters offered audiences vicarious thrills. Listeners had been even more enthralled by coverage of the 1935 trial of Bruno Hauptmann for the murder of aviator Charles A. Lindbergh's son, and by his subsequent electrocution. However, coverage of trial and execution provoked debate on the propriety of such intrusion into a courtroom—a controversy that extended to the 1990s. The American Bar Association decided to impose limits on radio coverage of courtroom scenes.

CBS created a sensation on Sunday, October 30, 1938, when its Mercury Theater on the Air, led by Orson Welles, broadcast his and Howard Koch's modern-day version of English novelist H. G. Wells's science fiction novel, *War of the Worlds*. The play, in the form of a news broadcast, had thousands across the United States actually believing that Martians had invaded Earth. Omnipotent Martians abandon their own dying planet and invade Earth before embarking on a ruthless plan of destructive colonization? Well, the plot would strike a raw nerve of anyone who had followed German dictator Adolf Hitler's rise to mastery of Europe. The widespread panic induced by the simulated newscasts indicated just how much Americans had come to believe what radio told them. CBS told listeners that Mars had invaded the Earth, and they did not check the outrageous story with other news sources. By 1940, for a majority of people, radio news had come to supplant newspapers as the prime source of information.

The increased number of hours allotted to news shows just how immersed was radio in the impending tragedy of World War II. In 1937 network news broadcasts on all networks totaled 800 hours. In 1939 they accounted for 1,250 hours. And by 1941 the number of hours of network news had grown to 3,450 hours. Radio also established itself as an integral part of the political process. The most successful exponent of political broadcasting was Franklin D. Roosevelt. He conducted his twenty-eight fireside chats, broadcast at prime listening time, in the tone of an informal conversation between president and any family listening at home.

The Communications Act of 1934 established the Federal Communications Commission (FCC). This was in line with the recommendations of a committee appointed by FDR in 1933 to examine the role of government in regulating radio. The new FCC superseded the previous agency, the Federal Radio Commission (FRC), established in 1927. Although the FRC had lightened the congestion of the airwaves by widening the broadcasting band to between 550 kilohertz (kHz) and 150 kHz and challenged the concentration of stations on the East Coast, it had been stymied by stingy funding and Republican hostility to federal restrictions on private commerce. However, federal courts upheld the FRC's right to regulate stations and to assign airwaves, to refuse licenses, and to use discretionary powers against programs it deemed against the public interest. The most notorious of the FRC's precedent-setting cases concerned a medical-advice show on a Kansas station in which John R. Brinkley had peddled a quack remedy for sexual rejuvenation, using goat glands.

Throughout the 1930s the sound quality of radio was tinny and often disturbed by static electricity. These problems could be resolved by Frequency Modulation, or FM, which canceled out the effects of atmospheric amplitude modulation by increasing similar modulation in the radio signal. Pioneer Edwin Armstrong argued that for FM to succeed, it required a broader channel of 200 kHz, many times wider than the typical AM channel of 10 kHz. This band produced excellent sound, free from interference caused by electrical storms and by other radio stations. Edwin Armstrong could not persuade RCA to finance experiments long enough to perfect the system. However, he convinced John Shepherd, who owned the Yankee Network in New England, to establish a special FM station in 1939. Commercial FM radio began broadcasts in 1941 using one of the available experimental television networks.

The main method of limiting interference was by installing a directional antenna that concentrated transmission in one direction rather than another. To guarantee good reception over a large area, in 1939 the FCC expanded the number of clear-channel stations and created a secondary class of 50,000-watt stations. The decision pleased rural politicians, who realized that high-powered stations provided remote communities with their only radio service. The decision displeased officials of smaller stations, who thought clear-channel stations now had all the advantages, including the cream of advertising revenue. When WLW, a superpower 500,000-watt station, began broadcasting from Cincinnati in 1934, its signal reached the entire Midwest and much of the South and the East. Its range was such that it could challenge the two giant networks, call itself the "Nation's Station," and attract a wealth of advertising. The Senate cut short the domination of WLW by a resolution of 1938 that stated that 50,000 watts provided quite enough power for an AM station. In 1939 the federal government rescinded the WLW's license to broadcast at 500,000 watts.

In March 1938 the FCC announced that it would investigate whether the giant networks operated monopoly control over broadcasting. Having heard the testimony of ninety-four witnesses and other evidence, the FCC issued the *Report on Chain Broadcasting* on June 12, 1940. Its recommendations challenged practices the networks had developed over ten years: NBC would no longer run two networks; network-and-station contracts would run for one year, not for five; networks could not demand options on large sections of network time; and affiliates could reject network programs.

The networks did not want federal regulation that restricted private commerce. However, they did want their own restrictive practices to continue. NBC and CBS opposed the FCC's proposed new rules and fought their implementation in the federal courts in 1941. The newcomer network, Mutual, supported the proposed regulations, believing they would create greater competition and that this would be to Mutual's advantage. The FCC postponed imposition of the new regulations, leaving the issue of network monopoly unresolved when the United States entered World War II. The FCC also began to investigate the desirability of newspapers' owning 30 percent of all stations.

In 1942 Mutual (the affiliation of six local stations into a national network) and the Department of Justice filed antitrust suits against CBS and NBC. When the case reached the Supreme Court, the two giants lost the case. The Court ordered NBC to sell off its Blue Network. Candy manufacturer Edward J. Noble acquired it, forming a new giant network, the American Broadcasting Company (ABC) in 1945, when he finalized the deal.

Left: Versatile composer George Gershwin delighted audiences with music that mixed syncopated rhythms and lyrical melodies as he moved across the different forms of song, piano concerto, orchestral tone poem, and opera. He combined the diverse strains of African American, Latin American, jazz, and popular music with the elegance of a European operetta in a dazzling career cut short by his death at the age of thirty-eight. (Carl Van Vechten; Library of Congress)

Right: Band leader Duke Ellington raised the status and aspirations of American jazz music to a level of sophistication that put it on a par with the best of twentieth-century classical music. Photographer Gordon Parks captured the buoyant Duke at the Hurricane Cabaret in New York City in May 1943. (U.S. Office of War Information; Library of Congress)

The Aristocrats of Swing

Of all the sounds that rang in radio listeners' ears in the 1930s, none were sweeter than the sounds of music, especially the humming sensations of big bands. Jazz had burst its original boundaries and overwhelmed the mainstream of aural taste. At a dance at the Palomar Ballroom in Los Angeles on August 21, 1935, band leader Benny Goodman, weary of saccharine versions of jazz pieces, called for raunchier arrangements. When Goodman's band then played arrangements by Fletcher Henderson, they were greeted with ecstatic applause.

The 1930s was the Swing Era, led by outstanding artists: pianist, composer, and band leader Duke Ellington; pianist and band leader Count Basie; clarinetist and band leader Benny Goodman; tenor saxophonists Coleman ("Hawk") Hawkins and Lester ("Prez") Young; pianist Art Tatum; and vocalist Billie Holiday. There were several hundred so-called big bands, although many were "sweet bands," white dance bands that simply played popular songs in arrangements favoring the strings, rather than true jazz ensembles. Each big jazz band had at least ten players, divided into brass, reed, and rhythm sections cultivating the so-called boogie-woogie sound. To coax the most cohesive performance out of these larger ensembles, a special premium was placed on the arrangement. The spontaneity and multifaceted texture of much earlier jazz had given way to a precision-dominated ensemble with precise call and response between sections subordinate to a dominant melody line regulated by major and minor scales with blue third and blue seventh notes.

The most widely known musical artist of the 1930s was band leader Benny Goodman, a superb white swing clarinetist generally acknowledged as "king of swing." Record producer John Hammond advised Goodman to hire pianist Teddy Wilson and vibraphonist and drummer Lionel ("Hamp") Hampton as members of an interracial combo that also included drummer Gene Krupa. Following Goodman's startling performance in Los Angeles in 1935, his band was retained for eight successive months in Chicago; at its New York debut at the Paramount Theater on March 3, 1937, it drew an audience of twenty-one thousand, thereby inaugurating swing as a national craze.

Goodman, who preferred smaller combos artistically, regarded his big band as a commercial enterprise. Hence, the quartet of Goodman, Hampton, Wilson, and Krupa was, for the leader himself and for many aficionados, the highlight of a Benny Goodman concert, with especially deft and unified treatments of such standards as "Runnin' Wild" and "Tea for Two." It was as if the four instrumentalists were playing on one voice with different registers.

The sort of swing associated with the Southwest in this period was called Kansas City style and provided an alternative to the heavy beat and complex arrangements of big bands in the East. As played by the Count Basie Orchestra, it emphasized solos, a light and relaxed beat, and simple head arrangements. Another variant, jump music, was an upbeat style of swing music that developed from Kansas City style jazz in the late 1930s and early 1940s, incorporating various elements from boogie-woogie and the blues. After pianist and composer Thomas ("Fats") Waller recorded "The Joint Is Jumpin' " in 1937, various songs appeared with the word *jump* in the title. *Jump* became synonymous with *swing, jive,* and *stomp.* A typical jump band featured a singer and two or three horns in front of the rhythm section playing blues and novelty tunes, often with humorous lyrics.

The most spontaneous singer of the Swing Era was Billie Holiday. Her light, high-pitched voice carried subtle, speech-like inflections, and her interpretations were permeated with angst, apparently translating the deep emotions of her scarred personal life into song. Her calamitous childhood was seared by being abandoned by her father, Clarence Holiday, who moved out on his family to play with Fletcher Henderson's band; by being raped by one of her mother's boarders; by a spell in a state institution on Welfare (later Roosevelt) Island; by a career as a prostitute in Harlem; and by heroin addiction. Biographer Stuart Nicholson writes (1995), "The very singer who could freeze an audience into their seats with the emotional power of her singing struggled throughout her life with deep emotional problems of her own that she could not begin to understand." She was at her most creative from 1935 to 1942, her singing enhanced by supportive players from the bands of Count Basie and Fletcher Henderson. In the late 1930s she recorded "Strange Fruit," a mournful melody set to a poem by Lewis Allen about the lynching of African Americans in the Deep South, and her own song about the poverty of her youth, "God Bless the Child."

As Count Basie's featured soloist, Lester Young smoothed the earlier harder-edged tenor-sax style. His sound was penetrating rather than large, essentially broad and flat with very little air behind it—as might be expected from someone trying to expend as little energy as possible. He had a particular affinity for the pentatonic scale of 1-2-3-5-6—later an integral part of jazz. He is also credited with coining the expressions "cool," "I got it made," "copy cat," and New York's nickname "the big apple." Like Bessie Smith and Billie Holiday, Lester Young led a self-destructive personal life. It may have enriched his soul-searching powers of communication, but it came close to destroying him, as it did Bessie Smith and Billie Holiday, when alcohol and dissipation took their toll.

In 1939 Edward Kennedy ("Duke") Ellington hired a talented arranger, Billy Strayhorn, as his assistant. Strayhorn's original compositions included "I'll Take the A Train," which became the band's new signature tune. Ellington first brought a band, the Washingtonians, to New York in 1923, where they performed at the Kentucky Club and the Cotton Club (1927–32). In his compositions, Duke experimented with form, incorporating interludes, unusual phrase lengths, and changes of mood. Years of performing together gave his band the cohesiveness and spontaneity of a small group. He owed much to his instrumentalists: alto sax Johnny Hodges, trombones Sam Nanton and Lawrence Brown, and trumpets Bubber Miley, Cootie Williams, and Ray Nance. Duke exploited their distinctive styles and gave them innovative material, especially the trombonists, for whom he wrote inspired trios.

For those who wanted music while they worked, there was not only conventional radio but also muzak as supplied by the Muzak Corporation, formed in 1934. It sold prerecorded "functional music," first to hotels and restaurants and, beginning in 1938, to offices and factories to relieve boredom in the workplace.

In the 1930s American popular songs were dominated by the big five: composers Irving Berlin, Cole Porter, George Gershwin, Jerome Kern, and Richard Rodgers. They moved effortlessly between popular songs and stage and film musicals, reaping commercial success from phonograph disks, live performances, and films. They showed virtuosity in synthesizing jazz features into traditional popular songs. Yet the big five's major artistic legacy was their development of the American musical on stage and film. Drawing from American vaudeville,

German *singspiel*, and French *opéra comique*, the modern musical mixed dialogue and wisecracks, song and dance, in an art form celebrating individual enterprise but sensitive to the poignant aspects of urban civilization. Ostentatious impresario Florenz Ziegfeld, Jr., had first set an opulent style of presentation of musical extravaganzas in his twenty-one Broadway revues known as "Follies" (1907–31), designed to "glorify the American girl." Thus he set the stage for the rise of Irving Berlin.

Irving Berlin became the accredited composer of over a thousand songs—a tribute to his shrewd acquisition and dissemination of material as much as to his skill as a musician. Having incorporated ragtime into mainstream musical theater with his first complete musical score, *Watch Your Step* (1914), he became a regular writer of revues, both for himself and for Ziegfeld. Berlin led the assault of Broadway musical talent on Hollywood in the 1930s, writing the score for the best Fred Astaire-Ginger Rogers musical, *Top Hat* (1935).

The upper-class Cole Porter invested his songs with cool, urbane wit, reflecting the affluent tastes of his millionaire background, his education at Harvard and Yale, and his sharp sense of satire in the stage musical *Anything Goes* (1934), parodying evangelist Aimee Semple McPherson. Elsewhere, his sophisticated, witty lyrics for "Solomon," "My Heart Belongs to Daddy," "Miss Otis Regrets," and "Let's Do It," with its fascinating, ambiguous word play, became classics appealing to all classes.

From his first huge commercial success with the black minstrel song "Swannee," in 1918, to his later musicals, George Gershwin delighted audiences with songs that drew together the different strains of jazz, Latin American, Jewish-cantor, and light Viennese music into a skein of sound that was unmistakably American, blending classical phrases with the nuances of popular music and jazz. George persuaded his older brother, Ira, to collaborate with him as a lyricist on future projects: *Lady Be Good* (1924), *An American in Paris* (1925), *Tip Toes* (1925), *Oh Kay* (1926), *Funny Face* (1927), *Strike Up the Band* (1927), and *Girl Crazy* (1930). George Gershwin also wrote four film scores, including music for some Fred Astaire musicals. The two Gershwins created a political satire, *Of Thee I Sing* (1931), and, in 1935, an operatic masterpiece, *Porgy and Bess* (1935). They fashioned *Porgy* from Du Bose Heyward's original stark drama in which a drug-dependent vamp exchanges three lovers: a brute, a crippled beggar, and a hustler. The Gershwins characterized the poverty-stricken and superstitious African American community of Catfish Row, South Carolina, with mischievous wit, as in "It Ain't Necessarily So" and soaring melodies of such eloquence, like "Summertime," that etch themselves indelibly on the memory.

After George Gershwin's premature death of a brain tumor in 1937, Ira continued to write lyrics in partnership with, among others, Moss Hart, Jerome Kern, and German expatriate composer Kurt Weill. This partnership produced *Lady in the Dark* (1940) for expatriate English musical star Gertrude Lawrence and comedian Danny Kaye in a dramatization of psychological treatment with several memorable songs, including "My Ship" and "The Saga of Jenny."

However, the first great period of American musicals was suspended between two masterpieces, *Showboat* (1927) and *Oklahoma!* (1943). In the 1920s the plots of musical comedies were either adapted from straight plays or drawn from common stock with Cinderella variations, involving mistaken identities and secret fortunes. This was enough to satisfy Berlin, Porter, and even Gershwin. Then came *Showboat* (1927) with music by Jerome Kern to lyrics and book by Oscar Hammerstein II.

Adapted from Edna Ferber's novel and produced by Florenz Ziegfeld, *Showboat* was original, mixing antagonistic elements of musical comedy and operetta. By nature, musical comedy was cheerful and satirical; operetta was troubled. Musicals were rarely adapted from sprawling novels. Edna Ferber's saga of Magnolia Hawks and her family, whose acting troupe presents melodramas on a showboat on the Mississippi River, moves from Natchez to Chicago and New York in a period of forty years. Different artists in the novel and musical are involved in the various forms of entertainment then prevalent—melodramas, cabaret, movies, vaudeville, and Broadway shows. To the novelist, the Mississippi symbolized the heart and energies of the nation, whose character could be represented by a theatrical dynasty. To the lyricist, the grandson of a vaudeville magnate, nephew of a Broadway producer, and eventually the author of about forty-five shows for stage, film, and television, theater was life.

In *Showboat* two heroines, the ingenue Magnolia and the diseuse Julie, face betrayal by feckless husbands. The opening hour is one of the most powerful and exquisite in all music theater, moving the show through a chain of alternately rousing, somber, romantic, and satirical numbers while exploring the psychology of the leading characters and the bitter heritage of slavery, notably in the monumental "Ol' Man River." In "River" Jerome Kern wrote a song that delved beneath the surface gaiety of the 1920s to an inner longing for repose. Kern and Hammerstein created a new character in Julie, the torch-singing waif who passes with a dark secret. Rejected by racist society, she slides into drunken ignominy, but not before making a supreme sacrifice. She grows before our ears in the fatalistic but rousing "Can't Help Lovin' Dat Man of Mine" and the tender "Bill" (to lyrics by English wit P. G. Wodehouse). The musical cemented the reputations of two sensitive interpreters, soprano Irene Dunne and versatile bass Paul Robeson, both of whom appeared in the 1936 film version.

Although *Showboat* was a milestone of musical theater, it did not start a wave of new musicals. Composers as eminent as Berlin, Gershwin, and Porter continued to pour out frivolous shows in which they hung trifling songs like charms on the bracelet of an inane plot. For instance, in *Du Barry Was a Lady* (1939) Cole Porter recycled some songs in a fanciful variant on the eternal triangle with a nightclub singer (Ethel Merman) torn between a hat-check attendant (Bert Lahr) who suddenly comes into money and a dancer who is perpetually broke but rich in talent. After Porter pandered to his audience's self-satisfied notions of New York as nightclub heaven in the first half, the special feature of the second act was its hallucination in which the characters became the court of

Louis XV of France, a sequence later audiences might relate to Cole Porter's own forays into Harlem and into drugs. The film version of 1943 was almost stolen from comedians Red Skelton and Lucille Ball by the breathtaking dancing of Gene Kelly and by Tommy Dorsey's band in white wigs and satin breeches performing big-band numbers up to the rousing finale, "Friendship."

There were, however, what a later generation might term "protest musicals," concerned with social issues, such as German immigrant Kurt Weill's *Johnny Johnson* at the Group Theater (1936), protesting war, and Marc Blitzstein's *The Cradle Will Rock* at Orson Welles's Mercury Theater (1938), protesting the gulf between workers and capitalists.

Richard Rodgers also bound his career to the American stage musical, first with lyricist Lorenz Hart. They sometimes played with conventional backstage material in *Babes in Arms* (1937), with its varied numbers, ranging from the lyrical "My Funny Valentine" through the sophisticated "The Lady Is a Tramp," to the rhythmic "Johnny One Note." The climax of *On Your Toes* (1936) was a ballet to choreography by Russian expatriate George Balanchine that fused jazz and American and Russian dance choreography—"Slaughter on Tenth Avenue." In 1940 Rodgers and Hart's cynically realistic musical, *Pal Joey*, adapted by author John O'Hara from a series of his own short stories, was considered too realistic, especially the raunchy "Bewitched, Bothered, and Bewildered."

The Rodgers and Hart partnership floundered on Lorenz Hart's dilettante inability to work on a punishing schedule and his self-destructive alcoholism. It was brought to an end by his death, whereupon Rodgers embarked on his second innovative collaboration, this time with lyricist Oscar Hammerstein II, beginning with *Oklahoma!* (1943). To its admirers, *Oklahoma!* was the most complete integration hitherto of song, drama, and dance. To its critics, it was regressive, a nostalgic operetta with a cowboy setting.

Rodgers and Hammerstein eliminated the conventions of separate song-and-dance routines and with them the chorus of attendant belles. Instead, they introduced routines based on square-dance numbers choreographed by Agnes ("Agony") deMille. *Oklahoma!* opened with an offstage serenade, "Oh, What a Beautiful Morning!"—offstage, to widen the sense of space—and moved the drama through a conventional love duet, "People Will Say We're in Love," and routines setting farmers and cowboys at odds until reconciled through a rousing Populist celebration, "Oklahoma!" The only instance of the crude vaudeville antecedents for this seamless show was in the dream ballet, "Laurey Makes Up Her Mind." There would be a dark side in many a Rodgers and Hammerstein show. In *Oklahoma!* it took the form of a sinister, brooding cowhand.

Among classical artists the pivotal influence in the United States and across the world was not a composer but an interpretive artist of incandescent ability: the Italian conductor Arturo Toscanini, musical director of the Metropolitan Opera, New York, starting in 1908, conductor of the New York Philharmonic–Symphony Orchestra (1928–36), and director of the NBC Symphony Orchestra (1937–54). Most famous for his precisely articulated performances of works by

Beethoven, Wagner, and Verdi, his performances revealed structure, detail, and dynamic range—all within usually fast accounts that adhered to a classical conception of form. Yet, though his performances were profound as interpretations, Toscanini's approach to recorded sound had considerable drawbacks—notably his refusal to heed the advice of radio and recording engineers about dry acoustics.

Far less profound as an interpretive artist was another conductor, who, because he had a consummate understanding of sound, effected a revolution in the way audiences heard an orchestra, whether the performance was live, on the air, or recorded. Leopold Stokowski was an erratic, English-born eccentric of East European extraction. He was conductor of the Cincinnati Orchestra (1909–12), musical director of the Philadelphia Orchestra (1912–36), a conductor of the NBC Symphony Orchestra (1941–44), director of the New York Philharmonic (1946–50), and director of the Houston Symphony Orchestra (1955–62). Not only did Stokowski direct youth concerts and introduce contemporary works by Gustav Mahler, Igor Stravinsky, and Charles Ives to American audiences, but he also experimented with the placing of orchestral players and was committed to the development of a lush orchestral sound. He worked with the Disney studio to produce *Fantasia* (1940), a series of cartoons inspired and accompanied by the music of Beethoven, Tchaikovsky, Stravinsky, and other classical composers. Later, he said he would rather have worked with Pablo Picasso. German immigrant composer Paul Hindemith characterized Stokowski as an albino rat in purple pants and wanted him exterminated for crimes against music.

Although his most famous compositions used folk tunes to celebrate the American West, Aaron Copland came from a quite different background. He was born into a Russian Jewish family living in Brooklyn, New York. Copland felt dissatisfied with the considerable distance between modern classical composers and the general public. In the mid-1930s Copland deliberately aimed at mainstream popular taste and wrote modern pieces that would be accessible to the large audience of radio, film, and gramophone recordings and satisfy public nostalgia for a simpler rural past. Ballets *Billy the Kid* (1938), *Rodeo* (1942), and *Appalachian Spring* (1944) for innovative choreographer Martha Graham drew on American folk tunes and stories.

When You Wish upon a Star

Whereas popular music provided the most enduring artistic achievement of the 1930s, the medium with the most overwhelming impact across the world was the motion picture, with its indelible images of style and beauty and its presentation of American affluence to a credulous world.

The opening in Atlanta, Georgia, on December 16, 1939, of the film version of *Gone with the Wind*, Margaret Mitchell's epic novel set in the South during the era of the Civil War, was the climax of Hollywood's love affair with the American public. The book had sold 178,000 copies within its first three weeks of publication on June 30, 1936. After producer David Selznick acquired the film rights, search and competition for the coveted role of vixen Scarlett O'Hara received the sort of publicity reserved for a presidential campaign. Scarlett is unprincipled and selfish, but she has a backbone of spring steel. Eventually, the role went to little-known English actress Vivien Leigh, a fragile beauty tortured by madness, tuberculosis, and nymphomania.

Whether in book or film, the battle of wills between greedy and ruthless Scarlett and cynical adventurer Rhett Butler, set against Scarlett's conflicting and mistaken love for Ashley Wilkes, makes an enthralling love story. It became impossible to read the novel without thinking of Vivien Leigh and Clark Gable in the principal roles. The book's underlying themes of loss—whether the loss of a society ravaged by war or loss of one's loved ones, real and illusory—struck a deep chord in readers in the 1930s and 1940s. Despite numerous problems during filming, including the firing of sensitive director George Cukor and his replacement by the more routine Victor Fleming, the movie *Gone with the Wind* set special records, earning nine Hollywood Oscars. Fleming owed much of the film's visual impact to the elaborate *mise-en-scène* of assistant designer William Cameron Menzies.

Hollywood released other classic films in 1939, a vintage year. They included Greta Garbo's foray into comedy with *Ninotchka*; the sweet and sour sides of the Western in *Destry Rides Again* with offscreen lovers Marlene Dietrich and James Stewart, and John Ford's *Stagecoach* with John Wayne; and the candy and nuts sides of women's pictures with Bette Davis in *Dark Victory* pitted against gentle doe Norma Shearer and predatory tigress Joan Crawford in *The Women*. Period romances were represented by, from the literary core, Laurence Olivier and Merle Oberon in *Wuthering Heights* and, from the suggestive fringe, by Errol Flynn, Olivia de Havilland, and Basil Rathbone in *The Adventures of Robin Hood*; gangster thrillers by James Cagney and Humphrey Bogart in *The Roaring Twenties*; musicals by Judy Garland in *Babes in Arms* with Mickey

FACING PAGE:

Left: Although by their tough-guy screen personae, stars Edward G. Robinson (left) and James Cagney defined the shape of gangster films, only once did they appear together: in *Smart Money* for Warner (1931). (Museum of Modern Art Film Stills Archive)

Right: Marlene Dietrich and her director-mentor, Josef von Sternberg, flew from Berlin to Hollywood on the wings of their *Blue Angel* (1930). They collaborated on baroque extravaganzas for Paramount. Von Sternberg transformed bisexual Dietrich into a siren of dazzling luminosity but inexpressive plasticity in *The Scarlet Empress* (1934), loosely based on the rise of Catherine the Great of Russia. (Museum of Modern Art Film Stills Archive)

Below: Marian Post Wolcott's photo of an African American citizen entering a movie theater by the "colored" entrance in Belzoni in the delta area of Mississippi in October 1932 provides another example of the hidebound supremacy of white over black in the deep South. (Farm Security Administration; Library of Congress)

Rooney and in *The Wizard of Oz* with Bert Lahr; and British reserve and charm by Robert Donat and Greer Garson in *Goodbye, Mr. Chips*.

Hollywood was at the height of its cultural achievement.

Noted cinema historian Gerald Mast estimates (1971) that, of seventy-five hundred feature films made in the heyday of the studio years from 1930 to 1945, perhaps only two hundred survive as vital examples of the century's most mesmerizing art. Yet these twelve films would be likely candidates. Hollywood was now able to draw together the formidable onscreen and offscreen talents of its players, designers, directors, and producers with all the benefits of proven technical experience and the confidence of commercial foresight. Moreover, these films were now modern films. Whatever future developments might arise, the different genres in place by 1939 and the shape of their dialogue, close-ups, long shots, and editing remained much the same for the rest of the century.

The various giant studios had specialties and particular styles: MGM produced melodramas, musicals, and comedies; Warner produced thrillers; and Columbia produced dramas with a social conscience. These Hollywood studios were giant factories using the same organizational strategy as industrial manufacturing plants in order to articulate production into a series of parts. A film began as a concept and moved through the studio system from writing to casting, design, production, and editing with all the momentum of an automobile moving across the assembly line. Hence, directors were executives responsible for drawing together the different, but designated, talents of writers, actors, designers, and technicians. Studios considered experiment costly and unpredictable and preferred the repetition of proven formulas. Accordingly, directors had to be versatile. Hungarian immigrant and prolific director Michael Curtiz made over a hundred feature films for Warner between 1927 and 1953, establishing durable personae for such different stars as swashbuckling Errol Flynn in *Captain Blood* (1935) and pensive Ingrid Bergman in *Casablanca* (1942), while diversifying the talents of James Cagney in the musical drama *Yankee Doodle Dandy* (1942).

Director Howard Hawks in his films liked to focus on a strong man who discovers his vulnerability under pressure but survives and a more fragile man who has surprising resilience and joins his tougher companion—the plot of *The Criminal Code* (1931). Hawks's legacy was a series of thrillers that made icons of Paul Muni in *Scarface* (1932), financed by Howard Hughes and based on the notorious career of Al Capone, and Humphrey Bogart in *To Have and Have Not* (1944), loosely adapted from a novella by Ernest Hemingway. The first is a gangster movie, the second a film noir. The difference illustrates how Hollywood moved its dark or ambiguous characters from the wrong side of the law to the right side of justice. In the course of the 1930s actors who specialized in gangster roles took on detective roles. In real life people faced dark circumstances in the 1930s, and ambiguous characters on screen played on the general sense of foreboding in society. Hawks moved through the big studios, returning to certain core themes whatever the genre: the harshness of the universe, the thrill of contest, veneration for male bonding, and respect for the ability of small people to color a pathetic life with comic spirit.

Not only were gangsters like robber barons, but so, too, were Hollywood tycoons: Harry Cohn at Columbia; William Fox at Fox; Howard Hughes at RKO; Albert and Jack Warner at Warner; and, at MGM, Pandro S. Berman, Samuel Goldwyn, Marcus Loew, Louis B. Mayer, and Irving Thalberg. These movie moguls fought the same sort of battles for vertical monopolies in the cinema that robber barons had fought in industry and gang leaders were still fighting in the underworld. Yet, although the moguls' gangster films offered escapist entertainment, they did not carry a universal message of freedom triumphing over tyranny with much conviction. Studios offered audiences subtle propaganda disguised as escapist entertainment. While real people were hard up in the depression, reel characters were well heeled with elegant costumes and flashy cars amid spacious sets. If audiences could not attain in their real lives the affluence they saw on screen, nevertheless they could share vicariously in the luxury of their favorite stars for three hours twice a week. Thus Cedric Gibbons, who designed the Oscar statuette, won the award himself for the design of twelve studio films for MGM, the studio on which he set his stamp with elegant and sumptuous sets.

This was the widest-reaching effect of Hollywood: it set fashion, concocted an upbeat but misleading impression of American life, and mesmerized audiences by promising more than it delivered. In *A Child Is Born* (1940) Gladys George is flat-bellied on the eve of giving birth to twins. She gets drunk in the maternity ward and entertains the other patients with a tap dance.

Yet the great studios also responded to certain deep psychic needs in the American public. Almost all feature films supported people's need to believe that human determination could triumph over adversity—even the Great Depression. Whether the story was political or domestic, they emphasized that such benevolent human values as justice, sincerity, and love must inevitably triumph over selfishness, hypocrisy, and violence. Italian immigrant Frank Capra mixed homespun philosophy, sentimentality, and throwaway comedy in films from screenplays by Robert Riskin in which supposedly common men James Stewart and Gary Cooper moved heaven and earth to drive the plot to morally uplifting conclusions.

Hollywood's most enduring male star was Clark Gable, whose roguish charm made him ideal casting for adventurer hero Rhett Butler in *Gone with the Wind* and numerous other tough-guy roles in a career spanning thirty years. Greta Garbo was at her zenith at MGM. Some critics, such as Kenneth Tynan in the 1960s, believed that Garbo used her great presence and her husky voice to give the melancholy predicaments of Anna Karenina (1935) and Camille (1936) touching pathos: "What men see in other women drunk, they see in Garbo sober." Others were less impressed. At Hollywood parties in the 1940s, expatriate British writer Christopher Isherwood found Garbo exquisitely dumb: "If you watch her for a quarter of an hour, you see every one of her famous expressions. She repeats them, quite irrelevantly. There is the iron sternness of Ninotchka, the languorous open-lipped surrender of Camille, Mata Hari's wicked laugh." This may be more in Garbo's favor than Isherwood intended. It was precisely because stars had mannerisms that the camera could capture and enlarge and the editor could cut into and highlight that they exercised such hypnotic appeal.

In Oscar-winning performances in *Dangerous* (1935) and *Jezebel* (1938), Bette Davis disclosed a heart of feminine sensibility beneath petulant mannerisms and delivery as sharp as a tack. Although Joan Crawford was at pains to draw a veil over her sleazy early life as fan dancer and porno-flick performer Lucille Le Sueur, she drew from these raw experiences to embody predatory shop or street girls on the rise in *Grand Hotel* (1932) and *The Women* (1939). However, it was Barbara Stanwyck who best fulfilled the fantasy of powerful women who killed men, all the way from *Baby Face* (1933) to *Double Indemnity* (1946). Sex as merchandise delivered with glacial aim.

"Sex without gender." That was Tynan's summation of Marlene Dietrich. Dietrich and her director-mentor, Josef von Sternberg, flew from Berlin to Hollywood on the wings of their *Blue Angel* (1930), where they collaborated on increasingly baroque extravaganzas for Paramount. Von Sternberg was a genius with lighting who surrendered everything else to transform promiscuous and bisexual Dietrich into a timeless siren of dazzling luminosity but inexpressive plasticity, most famously in *The Scarlet Empress* (1934). The most uniformly popular star was child star Shirley Temple, who progressed in roles from children's literature to wide-eyed competence in musicals.

Hollywood also owed much to its legions of supporting players, those with personalities and faces that could be adapted to different and intriguing supporting roles, often crucial to the atmosphere of a film. Their stock-in-trade was not glamour but character. Aspirant opera star turned actress, the heavyweight harridan Marie Dressler was a box office draw from her first turn as the butt of Charlie Chaplin in *Tillie's Punctured Romance* (1914) to her Oscar-winning performance as a waterfront wife in *Min and Bill* (1930) and thence as a society dame who packs a punch in *Dinner at Eight* (1933). Although he became a star in Europe for his part as the child molester in Fritz Lang's *M* (1933), Peter Lorre repeated his furtive, eye-popping presence as Sidney Greenstreet's sidekick in eight films and succeeded in inducing feelings of pity as well as revulsion in his audiences. Dancer Fred Astaire's resident comic foil was Edward Everett Horton, master of the double-take and a wit who saw clouds in every sunny sky.

The second generation of Hollywood stars proved more enduring icons of incandescent beauty than those of the 1920s. This was partly because the addition of sound made them seem more complete human beings, and partly because they were assiduously marketed, being promoted by magazines, advertising, and publicity stunts. It was also on account of becoming lighting, flattering makeup, and stylish costumes. Noted cinematographers William Daniels and Lee Gaines were masters at black-and-white and color photography. Parisian immigrant

Claudette Colbert, who excelled in witty, resourceful roles, knew her engaging features were especially flattered by lighting and by being always photographed from the left.

The impact of Hollywood designs and standards of taste and fashion on men's and women's clothes and on women's makeup and hair styles was global.

In makeup, Max Factor was the pioneer of color harmony—that is, matching cosmetics in harmony with an actress's natural coloring. Of the other inventor Americans whose names were synonymous across the world with a product, only Henry Ford had comparable fame. Max Factor, Jr., classified women in seven color types from blonde to brunette. He encouraged ordinary women to believe that they could look as glamorous as their favorite movie stars. Lipstick? He invented and named it as he did waterproof mascara, body paint, and stick and liquid foundation. His masterstroke was the panchromatic base, a matte, water-soluble disk of color applied with a sponge that—unlike greasepaint—did not reflect the lights in Technicolor movies. By such means, Max Factor's makeup refined the faces of stars Betty Grable, Lana Turner, Veronica Lake, and Rita Hayworth—faces that were templates for millions of women.

By her work in a career spanning over fifty years and 750 films for Paramount and Universal, Edith Head was the most influential costume designer in Hollywood history. The epitome of the tough-cookie career woman, her formidable reputation rested on her ability to design fast and appropriately for the character and the player, creating icons in the figure-tight slips of Jean Harlow, the wasp-waist dresses of Bette Davis, and the masculine suits of Marlene Dietrich.

Enterprising autocrat Walt Disney and fellow commercial artist Ub Iwerks defined the animated film. They did so partly through constructive experimentation with two- and three-strip color film and the multiplane camera; partly through assiduous self-promotion; and principally through sharp definition of eccentric animal characters, slapstick comedy, and fast pace. Disney used music as a lively expression of misbehavior. Even in his early movies, towels became piano rolls, tails became violins, and a cow's teeth became a xylophone.

Disney also created two of the cinema's most enduring icons with two cartoon animals, the overly cute Mickey Mouse, originally drawn by Ub Iwerks in 1928, and the comfortably cantankerous Donald Duck in 1936. Thus, from the modest beginnings of cartoon shorts, Disney and Iwerks developed ingredients, techniques, and financial support to produce a full-length tragicomic feature, *Snow White and the Seven Dwarfs* (1937), which fixed animated films for the rest of the twentieth century with lovable animals, saccharine heroines, clearly characterized villains, memorable ditties, and hokum about the mysteries of life.

Not everything was anodyne. There were directors with pronounced views. Tod Browning drew from earlier, bizarre experiences working in a circus. On film he set out to scramble audiences' nerves in eerie collaborations with actor Lon Chaney. Together, they characterized the horror movie. Browning followed his considerable commercial success in *Dracula* (1931) with a masterpiece of a different sort, *Freaks* (1932), a profoundly disturbing Beauty-and-the-Beast story.

The deformed exhibits of a circus wreak terrible revenge on a duplicitous young girl. The film was so distressing that distributors banned it for decades.

Charlie Chaplin continued his satirical vein in two masterpieces, *Modern Times* (1936), burlesquing automated assembly lines, and *The Great Dictator* (1940), ridiculing Adolf Hitler and Benito Mussolini. Although both were ideal subjects for lampooning, on the eve of a world war in which millions would suffer and die, Chaplin's inventive satire was considered audacious. He brought it off, partly by his genius for visual gags and partly by the absurd pretentiousness of his two targets themselves.

Abrasive Orson Welles intended his first film, *Citizen Kane* (1940), as a debunking biography of meddlesome press tycoon William Randolph Hearst that would devastate critical opinion on account of its visual and aural stylistic innovations and its obvious satire on the hollowness of human pretensions to power. Although the film *was* an instantaneous success with critics, its two-dimensional acting and its cant against American materialism discouraged audience interest and led to studio disregard for Welles as a director who misused his talent and their resources. Biographer David Thomson comments (1996) on Welles's tumultuous courtship of Hollywood in 1939–42: "He achieved glory but he ruined himself: the one was not possible without the other." Welles wanted to revolutionize studio handling of sight and sound and thereby influence future generations of film makers while, at the same time, he was leading a self-destructive personal life.

The liveliest performers were comics. The Marx brothers, led by eye-swiveling Groucho as master of the hard-boiled, put-down pun, relied on audience tolerance for ridicule of proven stage convention. They turned vaudeville routines to anarchic effect on Broadway and Hollywood, reaching their greatest commercial success with foil Margaret Dumont for Irving Thalberg and MGM in *A Night at the Opera* (1935). The best-loved comedy double act was English Stan Laurel and American Oliver Hardy, a perfect match of thin, loony abstraction and fat daintiness, at their best in *The Music Box* (1932) and *Way out West* (1937).

Even at the peak of the studio years, it should have been obvious to some of the major movers on the scene that Hollywood could not survive in the same form indefinitely. Audiences must eventually tire of the gargantuan diet of formulaic products. Yet the elephantine system of industrial production immured studios in their conventions, unappreciative of how quickly the popular drift to the suburbs, the postwar advent of television as a major force, and the explosion of leisure pursuits would soon undermine the studio empires. Moreover, in 1938, the Department of Justice instituted an antitrust investigation into such restrictive practices as block-booking, price-fixing, and pooling agreements between movie theaters. The single most restrictive practice was the monopolistic Hollywood system whereby a company produced, distributed, and exhibited its movies in its own cinema chains. Yet Hollywood would attain its greatest commercial domination in the war years just ahead.

S.1.P-108-149

In a world about to be torn apart by war, *Gone with the Wind* triumphed as novel (1936) and film (1939) in part because it captured a pervading sense of loss, whether of the Old South, a civilization "gone with the wind," or personal: real, such as Rhett's love for Scarlett; illusory, such as Scarlett's self-deceiving love for Ashley; or physical, by the death of Ashley's wife, Melanie. Ironically, the artists onscreen (*left to right*), Vivien Leigh, Leslie Howard, and Clark Gable, all died prematurely and tragically, whereas Olivia de Havilland (the offscreen Melanie) survived the years of World War II and the Cold War. (Museum of Modern Art Film Stills Archive)

The American Dream Turned In on Itself

"The scenery is magnificent," wrote German-immigrant composer Kurt Weill about Hollywood to his wife, singer Lotte Lenya. "But what they've built into it! It looks exactly like Bridgeport." The two springs of comedy—cruelty and incongruity—resonated through the dark humor of the lost generation and their heirs as they traversed the nightmarish underside of the American dream in the 1930s.

In the view of novelist Nathanael West, the American dream of personal fulfillment, distorted by the flatulent excess of Hollywood, was a nightmare. His *Day of the Locust* (1939) is the most famous novel about Hollywood, peopled with grotesque characters of the movie world as well as their obsessive, graying fans who riot at a film premiere. Equally disturbing was his dissection of the American dream in *Miss Lonelyhearts* (1933). In this bitter satire about the trag-icomic life of the anonymous author and adviser of a newspaper agony column, the hero with a female title is overcome by the weight of genuine untreatable suffering of his emotionally deformed and physically crippled readers. Miss Lonelyhearts's brutish editor, Shrike, advises him to turn to Christ, "the Miss Lonelyhearts of Miss Lonelyhearts." But Christian pity for the despised and re-jected turns in on itself in disgust and revulsion. Hence, Miss Lonelyhearts and the other characters cloak their pain and suffering with salacious wit, cruel horseplay, alcohol dependency, and the pressman's mean streak of hard-boiled cynicism.

Given West's penetrating observations, it was ironic that Dale Carnegie's *How to Win Friends and Influence People* was published in 1936, five years after *Miss Lonelyhearts*, and that its runaway success encouraged an avalanche of self-help books.

Serious writers had an ambiguous relationship with Hollywood. Some, such as Ernest Hemingway and Lillian Hellman, wrote with Hollywood adaptations in mind; others, such as William Faulkner and F. Scott Fitzgerald, worked there for the money and for the prospect it offered of a mass audience. But none were deceived by the peremptory emptiness of the vision it offered its mass audience. Serious literature had now moved from the self within society of the Progressive Era through the self apart from society of the 1920s to the self submerged by society during the travails of the Great Depression. This did not mean that all writers of the lost generation moved their ideas into a new groove. Stellar F. Scott Fitzgerald found himself repeating himself and admitting it. Fitzgerald's perceptive epic, *Tender Is the Night*, failed to set the literary world afire. The strands of plot and insightful observations snarl and tangle with one another in both versions (1934 and 1940).

However, another key player from the 1920s, John Dos Passos, moved from emotional, war-protest novels analyzing the dislocating effects of war on differ-ent character types to the mighty anti-epic trilogy *U.S.A.* (1932–38) with its core theme of the destruction of the individual on every front. Dos Passos used a variety of forms—telegrammatic newsreels, camera-eye journalism, satirical bi-ographies, and fictional romances that end sourly—and underscored each form with incongruous irony.

As to the leader of the lost generation, in 1937 Ernest Hemingway produced *To Have and Have Not*, his only novel with an American setting, whose very title proclaims its awareness of injustice and inequality. The central theme of early Hemingway, man working out his salvation alone, is far less sure now. Harry Morgan says, "I've got no boat, no cash, I got no education . . . All I've got is my *cojones* to peddle." When Cuban revolutionary Emilio rants about the tyranny of imperialistic capitalism, Harry Morgan shouts: "The hell with their revolutions. All I got to do is make a living for my family and I can't do that. Then he tells me about his revolution. The hell with his revolution." Hemingway developed his ideas on war and peace in his novel about the Spanish civil war, *For Whom the Bell Tolls* (1940), a book suffused with the imminence of death and the manner of man's meeting it. Yet throughout, Hemingway's chief interest lies in the continuous presentation of sensory experience recorded as time passes, rather than in political commitment.

Thus, if the shift in serious literature really was from the self apart from society of the 1920s to the self submerged in society in the 1930s, it was more a shift in readers' taste than a development among established writers. Emerging writers, such as Clifford Odets and Richard Wright, may have espoused the new theme. Established writers maintained work on themes at which they excelled.

There is considerable social awareness in Clifford Odets's play *Waiting for Lefty* (1935), inspired by the New York taxi drivers' strike of 1934. The play examines the personal dramas of a mixed group of taxi drivers debating whether to strike or not. Their eventual cry to strike indicates Odets's recognition of the failure of an economic system in which self-interest supposedly produces prosperity for society as a whole. Odets recognized that men had to work together for the common good in both public and private life and that the federal government had to intervene when individual initiative failed. In *Call It Sleep* (1934), Henry Roth unfolded the dark side of an immigrant journey, informing Americans that the streets were not paved with gold and that the path to Hell was not even paved with good intentions, but rather, carpeted with victims.

Yet the federal government's creation of the WPA in 1935 allowed many writers to survive the Great Depression by working for the Federal Writers' Project. Moreover, this was the same decade when the Nazis in Germany burned books that were not to their political taste.

Among American poets, Ezra Pound and T. S. Eliot continued to express their morbid vision of inner reality. Their sense of human destiny moving down an irreversible death march confirmed the deep pessimism about the human condition felt by many in the generation that came to maturity in the 1930s. English poet W. H. Auden later observed that Eliot transmitted "the unmentionable odor of death" of our century.

America's best-known poet, Robert Frost, created a larger-than-life popular image and a large supply of popular poetry that ensured him wide recognition but hid his real nature. He made much of his crusty rural exterior. There was nothing abstruse about his work, which was generally taken as a spontaneous, organic response to the wonders of nature. Instead of seeing dislocation and chaos in the destruction of old ways of life, Wallace Stevens saw an opportunity for recreation that would be based on anarchic individualism and an arrogant sense of self. Poetry could replace mankind's shattered faith in religion, but this poetry would be a highly personal and selective use of words. New African American poets included Melvin B. Tolson of Wiley College, who published a collection, *Rendezvous with America* (1944), which included his most famous piece, "Dark Symphony"; and Robert Hayden, whose first volume was *Heart-Shape in the Dust* (1940). Other new African American writers included Anna Bontemps, Jack Conroy, George W. Lee, and Waters Turpin.

The most celebrated talent among emerging African American writers was Richard Wright, who rapidly produced a series of short stories, *Uncle Tom's Children* (1938), a folk history, *Twelve Million Black Voices* (1941), and his account of his Mississippi childhood, *Black Boy* (1945), as well as his most famous novel, *Native Son* (1940). *Native Son* is about the social, psychological, and physical incarceration of the marginal man. Wright's powerful story of involuntary manslaughter, premeditated murder, and white injustice is told with a series of dramatically effective metaphors, beginning with the cornered rat that protagonist Bigger Thomas kills in his home and continuing with Bigger's attempted escape across Chicago, where the falling snow emphasizes his blackness until it is Bigger himself who is the cornered rat. *Native Son* had much in common with Theodore Dreiser's *An American Tragedy*, notably the focus on social maladjustment, emphasizing first the link between environment and individual behavior and subsequently that between crime and punishment. Both the white and the black murderers are themselves victims whom society extinguishes not for being criminals but for being social misfits.

In his series of novels of daring stylistic innovation, Mississippi author William Faulkner focused on the family as an individual unit rather than on society as a whole. His view of life as nasty, brutish, and wearisomely long was mitigated by his affirmation of such positive qualities as compassion, pity, and sacrifice. The most imaginative creation of *Light in August* (1932) is Joe Christmas, an orphan unsure whether he is white or black. Without any distortion of dialogue or situation, Faulkner unfolds background and motive of the sort of gross murder perpetrated by numerous petty criminals who can only express themselves in inarticulate violence. Faulkner dares and succeeds in streaks of a comedy of cruelty, whether it be the bisexual and racist foreplay of victim and killer, the incongruous position of the victim's head, or the snuffling disappointment of the attack dogs in their search for the murderer. In another masterpiece, *Absalom, Absalom!* (1936), Faulkner employed Joycean stream-of-consciousness, scrambled chronology, mythic and biblical parables, and the manipulation of disparate narrative lines.

Carson McCullers distilled experiences from her life in a small Georgia town in a series of unromantic romances set amid drab homes and burning summer heat. Whatever the physical or psychological aspects of her characters, her central theme is love, fulfilled, forlorn, or thwarted. In *The Heart Is a Lonely Hunter* (1940) the deaf-mute hero's compassionate nature encourages others to try to communicate with him. *Reflections in a Golden Eye* (1941) portrays ill-matched liaisons in a southern army camp.

Among the most distinctive literary voices of the 1930s were those of the so-called hard-boiled school of detective fiction.

Left: Richard Wright, author of *Native Son*, a moving novel of black consciousness that contains effective satire of whites—whether racist, liberal, or radical—and one that set a new standard for African American literature. (Carl Van Vechten Collection; Library of Congress)

Right: William Faulkner of Mississippi, who captured the social confusion and psychological ambiguities of the New South with dazzling stylistic ingenuity in seven novelistic masterpieces. (Carl Van Vechten Collection; Library of Congress)

"No one has ever stopped in the middle of one of James Cain's books," claimed the *Saturday Evening Post*, and it was almost true. Cain's novellas abounded in violence in low-life settings, featuring such infernal triangles as dissatisfied wife, discarded husband, and enraptured lover in *The Postman Always Rings Twice* (1934) and *Double Indemnity* (1936). The pace, visceral excitement of illicit love, and continual twists of the plot sustain reader interest. Less macabre and rooted in the social phenomenon of increasing suburbanization was *Mildred Pierce* (1941), about unfulfilled restauranteuse Mildred, her minx of a daughter, and shiftless men.

Raymond Chandler moved his detective, Philip Marlowe, a solitary, questing knight, through the neon landscape of Los Angeles with its glistening mean streets in darkly humorous cases, beginning with *The Big Sleep* (1939) and *Farewell My Lovely* (1940). In every case the killer was a leading lady who had, briefly, deceived the honorable Marlowe. Chandler's sympathetic and villainous characters alike are victims of commercial greed as well as their lascivious desires.

"What I had was a coat, a hat, and a gun. I put them on and went out of the room," observes Marlowe. Instead of Cary Grant, Chandler's choice, Hollywood fielded a series of wisecracking actors to play the enigmatic hero, notably, Dick Powell, James Garner, and Robert Mitchum, and, definitively, Humphrey Bogart in *The Big Sleep* (1946).

Dashiell Hammett worked as a private detective for a Pinkerton Agency in San Francisco, a career that provided him with material for a series of detective thrillers such as *The Dain Curse* (1929), reaching fuller expression with the creation of wisecracking detective Sam Spade, first in *The Maltese Falcon* (1930). Hammett modeled his most famous heroine, Nora, the witty wife of the detective Nick Charles in *The Thin Man* (1932), on his sporadic companion, playwright Lillian Hellman. Although the thin man was the murderer's first victim, the name got attached to the detective, especially as played by William Powell opposite Myrna Loy in the first film (1934) and its five sequels. Lillian Hellman herself scored a *succès de scandale* with her murky play, *The Children's Hour* (1934) with its undertones of sexual perversion in a girls' boarding school. Hellman's melodramas were notable for psychological insight, the liberal attitudes of her sympathetic characters, poster-paint villains, and acute climaxes of artistically controlled violence.

The cartoons and prose pieces of James Thurber for the *New Yorker* were admired for their unique blend of precision, incisive wit, and provocative fantasy. Thurber's world was one of little men dominated by outsize wives (once presented as woman becoming a house in a back-to-the-womb cartoon), as they might have been perceived by omniscient dogs. His themes included the triumph of moral innocence in a society dominated by the mass media, the cult of psychoanalysis, and sexual rejuvenation. Among his sadly amusing short stories, the most famous, *The Secret Life of Walter Mitty* (1939), carries an enduring myth. A man overpowered by the demands of contemporary society makes up for his inadequacies by leading a combative inner life in a series of imaginary, glamorous careers as a crack pilot, a medical consultant, and an ace detective: the American dream turned in on itself with Hollywood fantasies as a substitute for personal fulfillment in another tragicomedy of cruelty and incongruity.

Future fantasy, global warnings, heroic reversal of misfortune, and even satire: they all came together in an indigenous American art form—adventure comic strips of a combative outer life, whether for newspaper or comic books—that was in its heyday in the 1930s with "Flash Gordon," "Dick Tracy," and "Superman." Did Americans want a superhero who would use his special powers to rescue mankind from the threats of depression at home and aggression abroad? Cleveland author Jerry Siegel and illustrator Joe Shuster certainly thought so, and their creation, Superman, survivor of the planet Krypton, became popular. Superman arrives on Earth as an infant, borne here in a capsule launched from Krypton by his scientist father. According to cartoonist Jules Feiffer in a *New York Times* remembrance of Siegel (1996), Superman was the assimilation fantasy of Siegel, a first-generation Jew of Russian stock who grew up in the Midwest while fascism raged abroad and Father Coughlin raged with anti-Semitic broadcasts on the radio. The mild manners and glasses of Superman's human persona, Clark Kent, reticent reporter of the *Daily Planet*, who hides his supernatural prowess from unattainable Lois Lane, signified the diffidence of smart Jewish-American boys.

Superman was an escapist dream. Reality brought people crashing down to earth when would-be supermen trampled over civil liberties in Europe and Asia. The New York World's Fair of 1939–40 found its world turned upside down. With the outbreak of World War II on September 3, 1939, and with over a year of the fair still to run, the organizers changed the theme of the fair from "Building the World of Tomorrow" to "For Peace and Freedom." On July 4, 1940, a bomb exploded at the British Empire Exhibition, killing two police officers. Visitors to the brave new world of tomorrow fell well short of the forecasted 100 million.

CHAPTER 14

Kissing Hitler? Round Up the Usual Suspects

"YESTERDAY, December 7, 1941—a date which will live in infamy—the United States of America was suddenly and deliberately attacked by naval and air forces of the empire of Japan." Thus did President Franklin Roosevelt deliver his war message to Congress on December 8, 1941. Congress authorized a declaration of war against Japan that day.

The Japanese attack, led by waves of carrier-based Japanese dive bombers, torpedo planes, and fighters, lasted two hours and almost demolished the U.S. fleet and the military installations at Pearl Harbor, Hawaii. Altogether, 2,403 Americans were killed and another 1,178 wounded.

Japan's attack on Pearl Harbor led to the formal intervention of the United States in World War II (1939–45) and thereby to the domination of the globe by the United States—by virtue of its physical and industrial resources, its economic and military power, and its commitment to democratic capitalism. Fascism, Nazism, Communism, and democratic capitalism were in profound ideological conflict. The decisive event in the turning point between war and peace was the rise of Germany under the National Socialist, or Nazi, dictatorship of Adolf Hitler.

Hitler, a native of Austria and the feared dictator of Germany as chancellor beginning in January 1933 and then president and chancellor, or führer (leader) of the Third Reich (1933–45), was the ambitious and astute leader of the *Nationalsozialistische Deutsche Arbeiterpartei* (German workers' party)—for short, the Nazi Party. Nazism in Germany achieved absolute dictatorship by a malign

FACING PAGE:

The ominous panoply of imperial power associated with the Third Reich included precise military formations with monster banners carrying giant swastikas like great slashes in the sky. In this scene Adolf Hitler, the führer (center), appears with Hermann Goering, minister for foreign affairs (left), and Julius Streicher, party leader in Franconia (right), all giving the Nazi salute. (Library of Congress)

alliance of political dictatorship, business monopoly, and military control. Like his predecessor, Benito Mussolini, Fascist dictator of Italy from 1922, Hitler was invited into power by an autocratic governing and military establishment. However, once in office, Hitler, like Mussolini, subordinated independent institutions—the church, parliament, other parties, labor unions, and the press—to their own parties. Instead of socialist policies that might be expected from workers' parties, both Hitler and Mussolini accommodated the business interests of giant cartels.

Although many in the English-speaking world thought Mussolini and Hitler absurd, the two dictators expressed deeply felt needs within their own societies, being especially charismatic speakers to the national audiences of their day. Both Fascism and Nazism glorified their leaders, who were driven by a public appetite for new sorts of victories—cathartic acts of violence against dissidents at home and prestigious conquests abroad. As Mary Lee put it in the *New York Times* of September 11, 1932, "One does not feel that Hitler sways the crowd. One feels that the crowd sways Hitler. One feels that he expresses its thoughts, speaks in its words."

Mussolini dreamed of a new Roman empire. Although Italy had two colonies in East Africa, Eritrea and Somaliland, they were barren—unlike fertile Ethiopia that lay between them and had considerable underdeveloped mineral resources. Italy launched a full-scale invasion of Ethiopia in 1935 and was able to conclude its war of conquest with the decisive battle of Lake Ashangi of March 31 to April 3, 1936, after which the emperor, Haile Selassie, "The Lion of Judah," fled the country.

Hitler's expansionist foreign policy had two aims. The first was to unify all German-speaking peoples in the Third Reich. These included minorities such as the Sudeten Germans in Czechoslovakia and Germans in Poland, and other entire nations, such as Austria. His second aim was to gain control of central Europe and thereby to clear a path of expansion for Germany in eastern Europe, conquering and eliminating Slavic states, notably the so-called succession states, all but one of which endured right-wing governments in the 1930s. In 1935–39 Hitler defied the Treaty of Versailles: first, by rearming Germany in 1935; second, by reoccupying the Rhineland in 1936; and third and most provocative of all, by seizing Austria and Czechoslovakia in 1938 and 1939.

Hitler's misuse of the new science of eugenics in Germany and his perverse application of eugenics to disparage Jews, Africans, and handicapped people was of considerable interest to eugenicists in the United States, who had precious little savvy as to where his policies were leading. Scientists in both countries, such as American Harry H. Laughlin and German Fritz Lenz, borrowed and adapted ideas from one another's work. In the mid-1930s German math textbooks gave schoolchildren statistical problems about mentally ill, epileptic, and retarded people to inculcate schoolchildren with the idea that such people imposed too heavy an economic burden on the state and should be eliminated. In 1933 the Nazis used a model that American Harry H. Laughlin had devised as the basis for their sterilization law. In Germany the Nazis sterilized about four hundred thousand institutionalized persons in the period 1933–37. In 1937 Frederick Osborn, secretary of the American Eugenics Society, wrote a report summarizing developments in this German sterilization program: "The German sterilization program is apparently an excellent one."

Despite Nazi propaganda about the genetic inferiority of non-Aryan races, the world of sports attested to the rising powers and continuing resilience of African American stars, notably runner Jesse Owens, whose signal gold-medal victories at the 1936 Olympics in Berlin embarrassed Hitler and confounded the Nazis' racist theories. Heavyweight boxing champion Joe Louis, the "Brown Bomber," hammered home the point by defeating German Max Schmeling in 2:04 minutes of the first round before a crowd of seventy-five thousand at Yankee Stadium, New York, on June 19, 1936.

Building on fanatical and paranoid anti-Semitism, Hitler planned first the segregation, and then the extrusion of German Jews. Although Hitler and other Nazi extremists might have preferred to attack Jews physically—much as they attacked Socialists and Communists—this would have been impolitic. Hitler understood the limits of conservative ministers in his cabinet. Moreover, he believed that Germany was economically vulnerable to external pressure. He had an exaggerated view of Jewish power abroad and its ability to exact reprisals. Hitler therefore proceeded by degrees. In April 1933 the "Law for the Restoration of the Professional Civil Service" stripped most Jews and Christians of Jewish descent of their positions in the Civil Service, a category that included university professors, judges, and doctors in public hospitals. In 1935 the Nuremberg Laws limited German citizenship to "Aryans" and decreed that Jews were no longer citizens but now mere subjects of the state. In order to enforce segregation of Jews, the law forbade marriage and sexual relations between them and Germans. By 1938, having restored law and order within the Reich, achieved full employment, and dismissed conservatives from his government, Hitler was ready to take advantage of the fact that the balance of international power had already changed in his favor: he could now pursue more radical anti-Semitic policies. He had convinced Germany of the need for what historian Saul Friedlander calls (1997) a "redemptive anti-Semitism," according to which, if the Germanic race was to survive, it had to free Germany entirely of its allegedly malignant Jewish presence. The conclusion was brutal: from "You have no right to live among us" to "You have no right to live."

But it was the external ambitions of Hitler and Mussolini, rather than their domestic inhumanity, that provoked first the condemnation and then the belated interference of the Western democracies. The Covenant of the League of Nations pledged members to respect one another's integrity and to unite against aggressors. In practice, states were unwilling to relinquish national independence in the creation of a multilateral force—an army—for collective security. Worse, in the course of Italy's rape of Ethiopia, Britain and France were ready to cut a territorial deal with Mussolini at Emperor Haile Selassie's expense. Public outrage in

Britain and France forced the resignation of conniving cabinet ministers. In December 1937 Italy left the League of Nations.

At first, Britain was ready also to recognize German grievances. This was partly in the belief that the Treaty of Versailles had been too punitive and partly because it dawned on the British that a strong German state would be a bulwark against Communist Russia. Moreover, there was an underlying sense that Germany was bound to become a major European power again through the sheer process of physical recovery and that therefore to antagonize Germany by strict insistence on the peace terms of 1919 would be counterproductive in the long run. Furthermore, Germany's loss of German lands in the Treaty of Versailles was itself a violation of the principle of the self-determination of nations.

English prime minister Neville Chamberlain asked himself what the alternative was to appeasement of Hitler's demands for the unification of all German-speaking peoples. The alternative was not resistance by the League of Nations acting in concert, nor an alliance with France, which presumed itself secure behind its military fortifications, the Maginot line. The numerous critics of Chamberlain's policy of appeasement failed to distinguish between containing Hitler and defeating him in war. Although Britain and France could defend areas close to them, they could not do so over Austria, Czechoslovakia, or Poland, which could only be defended by invasion and hence a major war. Hitler knew this.

After invading and annexing Austria in 1938, Hitler set his sights on Czechoslovakia. Hitler's proposed annexation included the powerful fortifications that protected Bohemia and Slovakia, and hence eastern Europe, from invasion from Germany. This acquisition would ensure German dominance of central Europe. In 1938 Hitler's tactic was to claim the right to defend 3 million Sudeten Germans who were citizens of Czechoslovakia. He made claims on their behalf that the president of Czechoslovakia, Edvard Benes, agreed to on September 4, 1938. However, on September 12 Hitler said that the concessions were insufficient. On September 15 Chamberlain flew to Munich and met Hitler at Berchtesgaden, where he offered the separation of the Sudeten Germans from the rest of Czechoslovakia. Chamberlain believed that Hitler wanted only the unification of all German peoples and was therefore now satisfied. On September 30, 1938, Hitler met Chamberlain for the last time, and Hitler signed an agreement the prime minister had already prepared: "We regard the agreement signed last night and the Anglo-German Naval Agreement as symbolic of our two peoples never to go to war with one another again." The same evening Chamberlain told cheering crowds in London, "I believe it is peace for our time."

Munich, the notorious apogee of appeasement, was a surrender to abject fear. Later, Hitler said he thought Chamberlain was a nice old gentleman who was simply asking for his autograph. Winston Churchill, then a back-bench MP who argued in vain for firmer international opposition to Hitler, later (1948) called Chamberlain "pack horse of our great affairs." He remarked at the time that, at Munich, Britain and France had had to choose between war and dishonor: "They chose dishonor; they will have war."

Hitler's success at Munich encouraged him to intensify Nazi persecution of the Jews. In a stream of decrees, the Nazis ordered the Jews' total elimination from German life. They took over Jewish businesses, deprived Jewish lawyers and doctors of their licenses, and barred artists, writers, and composers from cultural life. In November 1938 the Nazis used the assassination of a German diplomat by a Polish Jew as a pretext for a pogrom in which party squads destroyed 267 synagogues, vandalized 7,500 businesses, and herded 30,000 Jewish men into concentration camps, to be released only on the promise of immediate emigration. The streets of German cities were strewn with broken glass, giving the name of *Kristallnacht* to this outrage. Nazism would also deploy such crimes as exploitation of labor and concentration and death camps and make them acceptable—even commonplace—to their perpetrators.

The American press deplored Nazi violence against Jews, but only the *New Republic*, in its issue of November 23, 1938, urged a revision of U.S. immigration laws to allow the entry of persecuted Jews into the United States. In 1939 Senator Robert Wagner of New York introduced a bill in the upper house to permit the entry of two hundred thousand German refugee children above the official immigration quota. But the refugee bill died in committee.

Asia was as troubled as Europe. The full-scale Japanese invasion of China in 1937 further accelerated the slide to another world war. Japan was now under the firm control of a military elite allied with Japanese corporations, the *zaibatsu*, bent on military conquest for economic resources. Japan was deficient in crucial raw materials, especially oil, and sought them by conquest in Southeast Asia. When fighting broke out between Chinese and Japanese troops near Beijing on July 7, 1937, the Japanese prime minister, Prince Konoye Fumimaro, gave in to the demands of his war minister, Hajime Sugiyama, to dispatch reinforcements, thus escalating an incident into war. China appealed to the League at a conference in Brussels. Germany and Japan were absent. Italy explained their position to the other conferees.

When the League sent a team to investigate the invasion, the Japanese served them fruit laced with cholera germs—a ruse revealed in 1994 by Prince Mikasa, brother to Emperor Hirohito. None of the League envoys contracted cholera. Nevertheless, Japanese leaders—like Hitler—showed astonishing skill in exploiting the weaknesses of the democracies: their vacillation and loss of moral will. None of the powers was willing to take action on behalf of China.

Japan's war against China reached its height of barbarity in December 1937 in the "Rape of Nanking" (Nanjing), the Chinese Nationalists' capital. Japanese soldiers raped, robbed, and murdered 350,000 Chinese civilians and soldiers. Among those who recorded and tried to minimize Japanese cruelty to Chinese soldiers and civilians was German businessman and Nazi organizer John Rabe, who was in Nanking working for the Siemens manufacturing companies. Rabe's outraged humanity prompted him to open his house, office, and grounds to over a hundred refugees hiding from gunfire and grenades. He recorded in his diary of December 12, 1937:

The Japanese soldiers were obviously completely out of control. Groups of three to ten marauding soldiers would begin by traveling through the city and robbing whatever there was to steal. They would continue by raping the women and girls and killing. No distinction was made between adults and children. There were girls under the age of eight and [women] over the age of seventy who were raped.

Germany, Italy, and Japan, the three disgruntled powers with aspirations to world-class status, were moving closer in an alliance, the Axis. On October 25, 1936, the Berlin-Rome Axis was formed. On November 6, 1937, Italy and Germany signed an Anti-Comintern Pact. Japan had signed an Anti-Comintern Pact with Germany in December 1936.

The supposed target of such Axis agreements was the threat of Communist revolution. For, at the opposite end of the political spectrum from right-wing Nazism with its business cartels, was left-wing Communism and the dictatorship of the proletariat. Although Soviet dictator Joseph Stalin concentrated on socialism in one country—industrialization and further concentrated political revolution in Russia—the Comintern still funded cadres to foment revolution across the world. Moreover, the USSR, through the torment of enforced industrialization, was becoming a leading industrial power, allowing it the material potential for full Communism and for military adventures to reclaim the lost Euro-Asiatic empire of the czars. Although industrial production in the USSR was still behind that of the United States, Russia showed that what the West had achieved for mass society in total war, Communism could accomplish in peacetime.

However, under Stalin, Communism became even more notorious for its mode of totalitarian dictatorship with all the terrifying apparatus of a police state. The assassination of Stalin's major ally, Sergei Mironovich Kirov, by Leonid Nicolayev, in December 1934 led to the notorious Great Purge of 1934–38. The obsessive charges of counterrevolutionary Trotskyism levied against defendants in the show trials of 1936–38 arose from Stalin's fear of subversion and the empty threats of the exiled Trotsky. Through show trials, followed by convictions and sentence to exile, imprisonment, or outright execution, Stalin eliminated three-quarters of the central committee and hundreds of thousands of minor functionaries. Altogether, 13 million people died in the Great Purge and its various sequels up to 1953.

Yet, despite Stalin, many American liberals, radicals, and Communists preferred to believe that here was a society different from all others, one more concerned with the plight of millions of ordinary people. For instance, detective story writer Dashiell Hammett and playwright Lillian Hellman, part-time lovers extraordinaire, endorsed the verdicts in Stalin's show trials. They signed a petition written by Hammett and dated May 1939 that only "fascists" and "reactionaries" could be responsible for the "fantastic falsehood that the USSR and totalitarian states are basically alike."

To other, more discerning intellectuals, what seemed like an inevitable conflict in Europe between Fascism and Nazism on one side and Communism on the other had already come to a head in the Spanish civil war. In July 1936 a military

Uncle Joe or Ivan the Terrible?

Left: Artist Justin Murray's series of bird satires of leading statesmen of 1944 included Joseph (or Josef) Stalin, whom he portrayed as an oversized bird of prey. The legend reads,

Josef Stalin

(Protectus Defendus)

Range: Unpredictable.

Habitat: Enjoys sub-zero temperatures. Remarkably mobile; he is frequently found far behind his enemies' nests.

Identification: A large, tough bird, much tougher than anyone imagined.

Voice: Seldom heard.

Food: Feeding habits are almost entirely beneficial to man, since its diet is largely composed of destructive rodents and fuhrer-bearing animals. (Library of Congress)

Right: When Russian pioneer director Sergei Eisenstein made his epic historical film, *Ivan the Terrible,* parts 1 and 2 (1943–46), he introduced some incidental satire on Stalin's megalomania, comparing it to the brutality of the sixteenth-century Russian despot with operatic emphasis so intense that its parallels were not lost on contemporaries. This undoubtedly was the reason the Soviet authorities delayed release of part 2 until after Stalin had died in 1953. (Museum of Modern Art Film Stills Archive)

Falange led by Gen. Francisco Franco revolted against a constitutionally elected left-wing Nationalist government of the Spanish Republic (created 1931), composed of Republicans, Socialists, Communists, Anarchists, and Catalan and Basque separatists. The USSR sent military advisers and supplies to the Nationalists. Germany and Italy supplied men, matériel, and aircraft to the Falange. Left-wing and communist volunteers fought for the Nationalists in an International Brigade. The war also indicated the deadly potential of airplane destruction of civilians, most notoriously in German bombers' devastation of the Basque town of Guernica in 1937, the bitter inspiration for Cubist artist Pablo Picasso's most famous painting. In the end, greater supplies of matériel from Germany and Italy tipped the scales of the war in favor of the Falange. Franco took the Nationalist stronghold, Barcelona, in January 1939. He became dictator of a regency until the restoration of the Spanish monarchy in 1975.

Civil war in Spain; territories seized in Europe, Africa, and Asia by the Axis powers of Germany, Italy, and Japan; a reign of terror within the Soviet Union and the threat of further revolution outside it—all of these were destabilizing events for people across the globe, affecting millions directly and millions more indirectly. An acute forecast of the times already existed in the title of Oswald Spengler's *The Decline of the West* (1926–28). The title invokes the debasing of the humanistic impulse in culture and the loss of moral will that nearly destroyed Western civilization.

A Fortress on a Paper Pad

What was the response of the United States?

In the 1930s the American people believed a policy of isolation would serve as insulation from war. There were, after all, the three thousand miles of Atlantic Ocean between Western Europe and America. However, what Congress achieved in its response of insulation was what poet Edna St. Vincent Millay called "a fortress on a paper pad."

Franklin Delano Roosevelt's role in this scenario was complex. The facts that FDR was raised by a wealthy eastern family and had visited Europe several times, that he had served as assistant secretary of the navy, and that, as vice-presidential candidate in 1920, he had campaigned for U.S. membership in the League of Nations—all these affected his outlook on world affairs. At heart, he was a committed internationalist. However, FDR's political experience in domestic affairs had taught him the value of expediency and compromise. Moreover, he was temperamentally incapable of adhering to rigid formulas. These factors shaped the way Roosevelt led the United States into World War II.

From 1935 on Roosevelt played a direct part in foreign policy. By this time the aggressive intentions of Hitler and Mussolini made more urgent the fears first awakened by the Japanese invasion of Manchuria in 1931 and the collapse of collective security in the League of Nations. Roosevelt wanted some symbolic gesture that the United States would act in good faith with the concert of nations.

For fifteen years the issue of U.S. membership in the World Court had hung in the balance. Now Roosevelt asked the Senate to approve the protocol governing membership that Elihu Root had first drawn up in 1909. It was not to be. Isolationist sentiment in the country suddenly revealed its latent strength. Father Charles E. Coughlin, the radio priest, and William Randolph Hearst, owner of the influential newspaper chain, joined vociferous senators Huey Long, William Borah, Hiram Johnson, and George Norris to arouse public opinion against the proposal. The Senate rejected U.S. membership in the World Court on January 29, 1935, by 52 votes to 36, with 7 abstentions, signifying that a powerful isolationist lobby threatened to wrest the initiative in foreign policy from the president.

The term *isolationist* referred to those who wanted the United States to have complete independence of diplomatic action and to remain neutral in any war. Isolationists and pacifists agreed that World War I had been an unmitigated disaster, that a second war would be even worse, and that renewed U.S. intervention would profit only bankers, arms makers, and other industrialists. The cost would be borne by the American people, who would lose their lives, their money, and their democratic institutions.

Isolationism was nurtured by the cultural climate of small-town America—a major component of American life. As late as 1940 the United States was still largely a collection of small towns and rural communities. Of the 131,699,275 citizens listed in the census as living in the continental United States and the 118,933 living in overseas territories and dependencies, 74.4 million (56.5 percent) were designated as urban dwellers. However, urban meant, at that time, a community of only 2,500 or more inhabitants. Only 30 percent of Americans lived in cities with over 100,000, whereas 55 percent (70 million people) lived in places with fewer than 10,000 inhabitants. Small towns were a fundamental part of American life; their focus was upon the survival of the community, and that included insulation from war.

Isolationists were more likely to come from small towns and the countryside in the Midwest than from the great cities of the Northeast or from the South. They were farmers, small businessmen, workers in the service industries, and manufacturers of light industrial products. Ethnically, they were from the Irish-, German-, and Italian-American blocs. In Congress their champions included progressive Republican senators William E. Borah of Idaho, Hiram Johnson of California, Arthur Capper of Kansas, and Gerald P. Nye of North Dakota; Republican senators Arthur H. Vandenberg of Michigan and Robert A. Taft of Ohio; and Republican congressman Hamilton Fish of New York; progressive Democratic senator Burton K. Wheeler of Montana; progressive senators Robert La Follette, Jr., of Wisconsin and George W. Norris of Nebraska; and Farmer-Laborite Republican senator Henrik Shipstead of Minnesota. These men were pivotal voters for Roosevelt in domestic policies, especially on controversial legislation. FDR would not risk their antagonism in domestic affairs by provoking them on foreign policy.

Isolationist sentiment was nourished by the activities of revisionist historians and pacifists. Their histories of the origins of World War I were to have a profound impact on a whole generation and its attitude toward foreign affairs. They made particular the grievances eloquently expressed in the powerful novels of the lost generation by Ernest Hemingway, John Dos Passos, and e. e. cummings. Historians and novelists agreed that wartime propaganda had debased language and that, in the war, the state had become a servile mechanism of malign forces. Historical revisionism began as an investigation into the causes of World War I and developed into a justification of American isolationism. The leading revisionists were Sidney Bradshaw Fay, Frederick Bausman, J. K. Turner, Harry Elmer Barnes, and C. Hartley Grattan. The isolationist press was led by Robert McCormick and the *Chicago Tribune*, his cousin, Joseph Patterson, with the *New York Daily News*, and another cousin, Cissy Patterson, with the *Washington Times-Herald*. Henry Luce called them the "Three Furies of Isolation"; FDR called them the "McCormick-Patterson Axis."

Many people who shared the historians' great moral outrage had already begun to work for peace in pacifist societies. The most active were two lobbying societies based in Washington, D.C.: the National Council for the Prevention of War (NCPW), founded in 1921 and led by its executive secretary, Frederick Libby; and the Women's International League for Peace and Freedom (WILPF), founded by settlement-house worker Jane Addams in 1915 and led by its executive director, Dorothy Detzer.

Another crucial factor in the conflict between isolationism and intervention was immigration. In 1940 11,419,000 residents, 8.5 percent of the population, had been born abroad. There were 1,624,000 people from Italy; 1,323,000 from Russia, Lithuania, and Romania; 1,238,000 from Germany; 993,000 from Poland; 845,000 from Norway, Denmark, and Sweden; 678,000 from Ireland; and 163,000 from Greece. There were also 23 million second-generation white immigrants, born in the United States, one or both of whose parents were immigrants. They accounted for 17.5 percent of the population. Thus, more than one in four Americans was a first- or second-generation immigrant.

Among the traditional reasons immigrants had come to the United States were, to escape the turmoil of European wars and, for young men, to avoid compulsory military service. These factors lent support to isolationism but it was balanced by a contrary factor—the identification of recent immigrants with the interests

---

FACING PAGE:

Small-town America. A Christmas shopping day in Florence, Alabama, in 1941, as photographed for the Farm Security Administration, draws together various icons of American popular culture, including movie theater, bank, and sleek automobiles at a street intersection. The cityscape suggests the calm insulation of the New South from the exigency of war—a lull that would be destroyed by the dramatic domestic upheaval of American intervention (1941–45). (Library of Congress)

of their country of origin. Although German, Irish, and Italian immigrants felt divided loyalties about U.S. intervention on the side of Britain in a war against Germany or Italy, Slavic peoples had no hesitation in wanting the United States to support Britain to free Europe from German domination.

The high tide of American isolationism came with the Senate investigation of the munitions industry, led by Republican senator Gerald P. Nye of North Dakota, a humorless zealot of the isolationist cause with inflated presidential pretensions, and the ensuing four Neutrality Acts of 1935, 1936, 1937, and 1939.

U.S. demands for the regulation of arms traffic intensified after the collapse of a disarmament conference at Geneva in 1933. On April 12, 1934, the Senate approved Nye's motion calling for a seven-man Senate investigation into the munitions industry. Nye became chairman. The time was ripe. In March 1934 H. C. Engelbrecht and F. C. Hanighen had had a sensational article, "Arms and the Men," published in *Fortune* magazine. They had shown that munitions manufacturers were the only people to make a financial profit out of World War I. Later, Walter Millis added fuel to the fire of economic interpretation of the causes of World War I with *The Road to War* (1935), a bestseller known as the isolationists' bible.

The Nye committee held public hearings from September 1934 until February 1936. It heard evidence from almost two hundred witnesses and produced a final report of 13,750 pages in thirty-nine volumes. Nye believed he knew what had brought America into the war. He overstated his findings, telling the Senate on January 15, 1935, that he had discovered the existence of a vicious partnership between the federal government and the munitions industry. What Nye considered the most significant part of his investigation came when the committee examined the files relating to loans by U.S. banks to European governments in World War I—prior to U.S. military intervention in 1917. Nye stated that Wilson had moved the United States into World War I to protect its investments to Britain and France.

The influence of the Nye Committee and various revisionist histories of World War I on the first three Neutrality Acts was clear. These acts were specifically designed to prevent the "mistakes" of Woodrow Wilson being repeated by Franklin Roosevelt. Assuming that the United States had been drawn into World War I to protect its foreign loans, Congress forbade war loans. Assuming that the export of arms in 1915 and 1916 had been another cause of intervention, Congress prohibited the export of arms. Because a third cause of intervention had been, supposedly, trade with the Allies, the act of 1937 insisted that, if belligerents bought U.S. goods, they must pay for them with cash and carry them away on their own vessels. This provision was known as cash-and-carry. In the belief that the loss of American lives through submarine warfare had contributed to U.S. involvement, Congress forbade Americans to travel on belligerents' ships.

With the outbreak of war in Asia and Europe, where the forces of radical democracy were pitted against the military Falange in the Spanish civil war of

1936–39, Roosevelt decided to explore the possibility of American public support for a discriminatory foreign policy in place of the official neutrality legislation that he believed helped aggressor nations. On October 5, 1937, FDR delivered his controversial "Quarantine Speech" in Chicago, in which he proposed that the peace-loving nations could contain warlike states: "When an epidemic of physical disease starts to spread, the community approves and joins in a quarantine of the patients in order to protect the health of the community against the spread of the disease." It was not coincidence that FDR delivered his "quarantine" speech in Chicago, heart of adversary editor Robert McCormick's Chicagoland. Having bearded the lion in his den, however, FDR was obliged to beat a hasty retreat. Public reaction to the speech was almost entirely hostile.

In response to the growing threat of war, American isolationists conceded that the United States required a larger navy for the defense of the Western Hemisphere. Congress passed the Vinson Naval Act of 1938, which was to expand the navy at a cost of $1 billion. FDR was able to rally public opinion behind statements about the territorial integrity of nations in the Western Hemisphere. In August 1938 he told an audience at Queen's University, Kingston, Ontario, that the American people "will not stand idly by if domination of Canadian soil is threatened by any other empire."

Courting Air and Oil

The United States had not one overriding concern in foreign policy, but several. No matter how pressing the fear of war in Europe, FDR and Secretary of State Cordell Hull (1933–44) found themselves drawn to widening horizons in world affairs. Aviation and oil were expanding the possibilities of economic and cultural development while posing new challenges. New imperialism would rely on transportation, communication, and currency more than it would on surface territorial control. Latin America still held the traditional promise of U.S. hegemony and its liabilities. FDR did not ignore either new developments or traditional areas.

Technological developments in the 1930s expanded the horizons of world affairs and foreign policies, both extending the possibilities of international cooperation and maximizing the potential for lethal damage to whole societies. The compulsive need of mankind for transport—whether by ships or automobiles—and the insatiable thirst of ships and automobiles for oil led to ever greater penetration of oil-rich underdeveloped countries by developed countries that simply could not get enough of the precious fluid.

Standard Oil of California (later Socal) gained footholds in Bahrain and Saudi Arabia. In 1930 profligate King Ab al-Aziz ibn Saud and his British adviser, Harry St. John Philby, employed American geologist Karl Twitchell to survey the land. Twitchell discovered that Saudi Arabia was potentially the richest oil field of all. In 1933 Standard Oil of California offered the king a series of loans—

all in gold—until the oil field of 440,000 square miles was ready for production in 1939. The presence of Socal, a U.S. company, in Saudi Arabia changed the face of the Middle East.

In fact each successive deal in the Middle East by U.S. or European oil companies weakened the national government of the territory in which oil was struck. In Iraq a consortium dominated by Standard Oil of New Jersey (from 1934 to 1960 Standard-Vacuum; and from 1972 on, Exxon) made huge profits without giving the government its due return. Standard Oil of New Jersey made a profit of around 52 cents per barrel—double what it paid the Iraqi government. It was said that, after an initial investment of $14 million, Standard Oil of New Jersey's share in the consortium was worth $130 million by 1937. Moreover, American, British, and Dutch penetration of the Middle East aroused the interest and envy of Germany and the Axis, providing yet another grievance for hostile action.

Airpower was as significant a new factor in world affairs as was oil power. Aviation proved not only a source of contention but also a tool of destruction. American technological expertise in aviation led the way in a war for the skies. The great airlines were drawing their governments into their own empires of the sky. In 1919 a Briton, George Holt Thomas, had persuaded six airlines, meeting at The Hague, to form the International Air Traffic Association (IATA) "with a view to co-operate to mutual advantage in preparing and organizing aerial traffic." By 1929 IATA had twenty-three members. Its headquarters at The Hague attempted to standardize timetables and safety systems. But IATA's official rhetoric about aviation spreading peace and understanding had already started to sound hollow after Japanese war planes had bombed Manchuria in 1931. Public unease deepened after German bombing of civilians in the Spanish civil war in 1937.

In 1928 the United States ratified the Havana Air Convention, which established the first rules for air traffic in the Americas and established the principle of air sovereignty. Nations realized that airplanes flying above their territories—whence they could spy, drop bombs, or invade—were more dangerous than ships. After first Germany and then other countries began to rearm, French aviation economist Henri Bouche submitted a report to the League of Nations in 1935 that asked, "How could the governments of a mistrustful Europe allow the indefinite development of a powerful means of transport when aircraft sent on peaceful missions over national territories, and to the very heart of those territories, may also carry out their missions?" In other words, what had begun as routine and peaceable journeys by air contained, first, the potential for surveillance, and, second, the threat of destruction of the ground below by bombing from the planes on high. National sovereignty over airspace became a guiding theme of all international agreements concerning the air.

Pan Am led American aviation across the world. First, chief Juan Trippe expanded Pan Am's operations in Latin America. Pan Am joined forces with the Grace trading empire to establish the Panagra airline, which flew down the west coast from Ecuador to Peru and Chile and thence across the Andes to Argentina on the east coast.

Second, Pan Am's circumnavigation of the Pacific became part of the tapestry of the United States in world affairs. It was not U.S. foreign policy, but it provided the sinews of knowledge of flying and experience with island bases that, when communicated to army and navy advisers, would help the United States win its Pacific War with Japan in 1942–45.

Juan Trippe set out to conquer the Pacific, twice the width of the Atlantic but interspersed with numerous islands, large and small, that could provide aircraft with refueling stages. The first lap was from the West Coast to Hawaii, a journey of two thousand miles. By 1935 Pan Am was using Martin flying boats to cover this journey before flying on to China. In 1933 Trippe acquired a half share in the China National Aviation Corporation, which flew planes from Shanghai to Canton. The Pacific route was already studded with U.S. naval bases on Honolulu, Midway, Guam, and Manila. However, between Midway and Guam there was only the barren Wake Island. Trippe petitioned the federal government for a five-year lease of Wake Island. The State Department, disturbed by Japanese ambitions in the Pacific, recommended that the president recognize this as an opportunity to extend U.S. naval influence there under the guise of a commercial purpose. FDR agreed to place Wake and other islands under the administration of the U.S. Navy, and the navy gave Pan Am access to Wake. Moreover, by skillful negotiating and hard bargaining, Trippe outmaneuvered his British rivals to secure preferential treatment for Pan Am with respect to landing rights in Hong Kong, Hawaii, Samoa, and even New Zealand.

The South Pacific was sometimes called the empty hemisphere on account of the huge distances between islands. Moreover, it proved a treacherous region. Aviatrix Amelia Earhart disappeared without a trace north of New Guinea in July 1937. Then in January 1938, Ed Musick, chief pilot of Pan Am, was killed when his plane, the *Samoa Clipper*, exploded in midair north of Pago Pago. For a time Pan Am suspended its service to New Zealand, but it resumed regular service by July 1940. In the South Pacific airlines made neighbors of islands far away from one another. Thus, the South Pacific, which had missed out on the intervening age of steamships, now moved decisively into the global community of air travel.

Third, Juan Trippe set his sights on the Northern Hemisphere. The North Atlantic was potentially the most lucrative route for cargoes and passengers. But in practical terms, it was the most hostile because of its fierce headwinds and the lack of any staging post between Canada and Ireland, except the frost-bound Greenland and Iceland to the north or the Azores to the south. In addition, the North Atlantic proved a diplomatic minefield. Trippe found the Europeans far more intractable about landing rights nearer home than they had been in the Far East, and he had to settle for compromise joint agreements with the British and the Dutch. Pan Am's arrangements with various European airlines, including the Dutch KLM Company, violated U.S. antitrust laws, but the federal government allowed tactful wording in the contracts to conceal what was in effect restraint of trade. Another key player, Germany, was ahead of the United States and Britain in research and development. In 1938 the German airline Lufthansa flew a fourteen-engine Fokker-Wulf landplane from Berlin to New York in twenty-four hours.

Once the British became engrossed in the threat of war and rapidly expanded the Royal Air Force, Pan Am steadily advanced its own transatlantic passenger flights. In May 1939 Pan Am flew the first of the big Boeings, the Yankee Clipper, with twenty-two passengers aboard, from the Marine Terminal, New York (now next to La Guardia Airport), to Lisbon and Marseilles, via the Azores. Then Pan Am and Imperial Airways, a British airline, began a series of pioneer transatlantic flights. In August 1939 they started a regular transatlantic service with inflight refueling by flying boats. Once Britain, France, and Germany were at war, however, the skies above the Atlantic Ocean were reserved for Pan Am with its Boeing planes, landing in Ireland or Portugal. Its supremacy would survive World War II.

Wooing Latin America

Whatever their profound disagreements over intervention in European affairs, Roosevelt and Congress were of one mind about Latin America. In Latin America Roosevelt, Secretary of State Cordell Hull, and the Senate Foreign Relations Committee were committed to the good neighbor policy, especially in regard to repudiating blatant dollar diplomacy. But there was much to live down. For instance, Pan Am chief Juan Trippe obliged Peter Paul von Bauer to sell his airline, SCADTA (Sociedad Colombo Alemana de Transportes Aeros) to him. Not surprisingly, Latin Americans considered Trippe's Pan Am as an adjunct to Wall Street and the State Department. At one time or another, Trippe's Pan Am board included chairman Sonny Whitney, banker Robert Lehman, and diplomat David Bruce, son-in-law to former Secretary of the Treasury Andrew Mellon.

In its handling of Latin American affairs, the administration's main assets were FDR's generous personality, general showmanship, and tact. In December 1936 FDR attended the opening of the Inter-American Peace Conference in Buenos Aires, Argentina, where he received a tumultuous public reception. However, Cordell Hull's proposals for a common hemispheric policy on arms and neutrality were shot down by Saavedra Lamas of Argentina, who wanted to assert Argentinean supremacy in Latin America. The only U.S. proposal accepted in its original form was that of nonintervention, first put forward at Montevideo, Uruguay, in 1933.

The administration's policies to defend the Western Hemisphere from attack almost always met with uniform approval in the United States. Thus, FDR was exercising his executive role in his policies toward Latin America to further his interests elsewhere—a policy of responsible presidential control. In 1938 and 1939 FDR took specific action to strengthen the defense of the Western Hemisphere. In April 1938 he created a Standing Liaison Committee to strengthen military missions to Latin America, establishing firm control over commercial airlines. In November the Joint Army and Navy Board discussed contingency arrangements in case of attack. In 1939 the Rainbow Plans defined strategy for defending the United States by safeguarding the hemisphere as a whole. Moreover, in December 1938 the American republics attending the Pan American Conference in Lima, Peru, unanimously adopted the Declaration of Lima, condemning religious and racial prejudice and alien political activity in the Western Hemisphere. On January 4, 1939, George C. Stoney advised readers of the *New Republic*, "How the Dictators Woo Argentina."

But the specific trouble areas were in the Caribbean and Central America: Cuba and Mexico. Once again, a prime U.S. interest was protection of U.S. investments, sugar in Cuba, oil in Mexico, as well as to prevent the destabilization of countries nearby.

Since 1929 the people of Cuba had been in open revolt against the corrupt dictatorship of Gerardo Machado. The decisive factor in the overthrow of Machado in 1933 was the weight of the army and its leader, Col. Fulgencio Batista, who were able to place in power first Carlos Manuel de Cespedes, a former diplomat, and then Dr. Ramon Grau San Martin, surgeon and professor at the University of Havana. Grau San Martin condemned the ascendancy of privileged foreign interests in Cuba. He refused to continue the favoritism shown to foreign investors earlier. This policy aroused the indignation of Ambassador Sumner Welles, who advised FDR to intervene with military force under the terms of the Platt Amendment of 1901. Instead, FDR simply denied recognition to the Grau San Martin regime and sent gunboats to patrol Cuban waters. The withholding of U.S. recognition precluded Cuba's exporting sugar to the United States. The new form of pressure threatened Cuba's economic future. Batista transferred his support to Col. Carlos Mendieta, who was able to seize power in January 1934 and resume more conservative policies toward foreign investors. Having applied pressure tactics rather than outright force, FDR then abrogated the Platt Amendment of 1901, retaining only rights to maintain a U.S. naval base at Guantanamo Bay. In May 1934 Congress began to reduce the tariff on Cuban sugar—initially, by 25 percent.

As to Mexico, where Americans had huge oil interests, FDR and Hull resisted lobbying of Congress by American Catholics, led by the Knights of Columbus, to put pressure on the Mexican government of Lazaro Cardenas to end its anticlerical policy, if necessary, by recalling the U.S. ambassador to Mexico, Josephus Daniels. Neither FDR nor Hull was prepared to jeopardize their reputations for nonintervention in the internal affairs of any Latin American country, especially over such an emotive issue as religious practices. However, on March 18, 1938, President Cardenas of Mexico announced the appropriation of the $400 million Mexican oil industry, much of it in foreign hands, because the oil companies had defied the Mexican Supreme Court's decision in a labor dispute. FDR, Josephus Daniels, and Treasury adviser Henry Morgenthau were determined to prevent the State Department from sensationalizing the issue and causing an open break with Mexico.

Lightning Strikes Twice

Roosevelt's second message to Congress on January 4, 1939, was largely devoted to foreign affairs: "All about us rage undeclared wars—military and economic." He recommended that the United States should revise its neutrality legislation: "When we deliberately try to legislate neutrality, our neutrality laws may operate unfairly and unevenly—may actually give aid to the aggressor and deny it to the victim. The instinct of self-preservation should warn us that we ought not to let that happen any more."

However, Congress continued to oppose any change that indicated the United States would distinguish between aggressor and victim and thereby incur hostility. Yet Gallup public opinion polls showed that 65 percent of Americans favored an economic boycott of Germany, and 57 percent wanted a revision of the neutrality laws. Fifty-one percent expected a war in Europe, and 58 percent expected the United States would become involved.

The prospect of war moved closer. Hitler had first dismembered Czechoslovakia at Munich in 1938. On March 15, 1939, Slovakia became independent from Czechoslovakia. When Hungary claimed the Ukraine district of lower Carpathia, the new president, Hacha, allowed Czechia (or Bohemia) to become a German protectorate. The Sudeten territories had not been Hitler's last territorial demand in Europe, after all. On March 31, 1939, English prime minister Neville Chamberlain drafted an Anglo-French guarantee of Polish integrity. He did not consult France.

On July 18, 1939, Roosevelt and Hull invited congressional leaders to discuss European affairs with them at the White House. Roosevelt predicted war and said he believed Britain and France had only an even chance of survival. However, the most prepossessing senator there, William E. Borah of Idaho, declared, "There's not going to be any war this year. All this hysteria is manufactured and artificial." Brushing aside Hull's references to State Department telegrams, he went on, "I have sources of information in Europe that I regard as more reliable than those of the State Department." He meant newspaper articles. The vice president, John Nance Garner, told Roosevelt: "You haven't got the votes and that's all there is to it."

Then came the bombshell news of the Nazi-Soviet pact signed by the German foreign minister, Joachim von Ribbentrop, and the Soviet commissar for foreign affairs, Vyacheslav Molotov, in Moscow on August 23, 1939. Bombshell because Soviet Communism and Nazism were supposed to be diametrically opposed. Germany and Russia had supported opposite sides in the Spanish civil war. However, the Nazi-Soviet pact disclosed that, whatever their differences in ideology, when it came to foreign policy, it was traditional power politics from Germany and Russia.

Above: The savage beauty of this dramatic photograph of St. Paul's Cathedral illuminated in the London night sky by the terrifying fireworks of the German Blitz in 1940 has made it an icon of the darkest days of Britain's lone war against Hitler. (Library of Congress)

Below: Civilians everywhere bore the brunt of World War II. London citizens, whose lives—if not their homes—are temporarily secure from the terrors of Hitler's nightly Blitz on the capital, sleep as best they can in the Elephant and Castle Underground Station of London's subway system—"the Tube." (British official photo released in America by the Office of War Information; Library of Congress)

First, Russia would stay neutral when Germany went to war. Then the dictators would divide central Europe. While Hitler took western Poland and established a sphere of influence in central Europe, Stalin could annex eastern Poland, Latvia, Lithuania, Estonia, and part of Romania. Hitler's motive for the Nazi-Soviet pact was straightforward enough—to protect his eastern flank in case of war. But the pact also served Russian defensive strategy. Ever since the Russian Revolution in 1917, Soviet governments had preached a gospel of socialist revolutions across the world, thereby arousing fears in the leading capitalist countries. Soviet leaders also believed that capitalist countries wanted to eliminate the world's first socialist state. By the Nazi-Soviet pact, Stalin tried to divide the capitalist world, prevent the major powers from ganging up on the USSR, buy himself time, and regain Russia's lost territories in Europe.

In *The Gathering Storm* (1948) Winston Churchill observed of Molotov, Stalin's prime agent of the Nazi-Soviet pact, that, with his cannonball head, black moustache, comprehending eyes, and his slab face with his verbal adroitness and imperturbable demeanor, he "was, above all men, fitted to be the agent and instrument of the policy of an incalculable machine." Thus Molotov continued in World War II and the Cold War ahead.

In the meantime Hitler made various demands on Poland about Germans in Danzig. After inconclusive diplomatic moves, German troops crossed the Polish frontier at 4:45 A.M. on September 1, 1939. The Polish cabinet appealed to its ally, Britain. The response from the British cabinet was frigid. However, the outrage expressed in the House of Commons obliged Prime Minister Neville Chamberlain to issue an ultimatum calling for the withdrawal of German troops by September 3. Britain declared war on Germany when that ultimatum expired without any assurances. World War II had begun.

Responding to the Nazi invasion of Poland and the British declaration of war on Germany, FDR said in his radio fireside chat of September 3: "This nation will remain a neutral nation." However, going further than Woodrow Wilson had in 1914, he added, "But I cannot ask that every American remain neutral in thought as well." FDR expected Germany and Russia to divide Europe between them and then extend their control to the Middle East and to the European colonies in Africa and Asia. If that happened, the United States would be in peril.

In the fall of 1939, Joseph Kennedy and William Bullitt, U.S. ambassadors to Britain and France, predicted that unless the Allies were given immediate material aid, they would fall victim to a German assault from the air. The cash-and-carry provisions of the 1937 Neutrality Act had expired, and the munitions embargo was still in effect. Roosevelt called Congress into special session on September 21, 1939, so that the embargo could be replaced by a provision allowing belligerents to purchase munitions and raw materials on a cash-and-carry basis. The administration argued that such a measure would strengthen U.S. neutrality rather than aid Britain and France. However, its fundamental purpose was not in doubt. Germany had increased its own manufacturing capacity and, in seizing Czechoslovakia, had taken over its great munitions works. Thus, Germany already possessed military supplies on a scale that neither Britain nor France could match. On October 27, 1939, the Senate, by 63 votes to 30, and, on November 3 the House, by 243 votes to 181, agreed to a revision in the Neutrality Acts permitting the sale of goods to belligerents on the basis of cash-and-carry, provided Congress approved.

Britain and France decided to conserve their dollar and gold reserves by restricting their purchase of American goods to food, raw materials, aircraft, and machine tools. FDR insisted that Britain and France set up a special purchasing mission in the United States that was to operate through the Federal Reserve Board. By exercising such controls, FDR hoped to prevent the Allies' interests from clashing with the military needs of the United States.

In his State of the Union message on January 5, 1940, FDR expressed his anxiety in a significant distinction, explaining that "there is a vast difference between keeping out of war and pretending that war is none of our business. We do not have to go to war with other nations, but, at least, we can strive with other nations to encourage the kind of peace that will lighten the troubles of the world and, by so doing, help our own nation as well." FDR asserted that the United States must play a decisive part in shaping postwar peace: "For it becomes clearer and clearer that the future world will be a shabby and dangerous place to live in—yes, even for Americans to live in—if it is ruled by force in the hands of a few."

Yet in early 1940 FDR had to fight a battle with his own administration over aid to Britain and France. Secretary of War Henry Woodring opposed Allied purchases of war matériel and aircraft that interfered with American needs and flatly refused Allied access to secret information necessary to fly the planes they had ordered. FDR became so exasperated that in March he told the War Department that its opposition must end and that if it did not, he would transfer any truculent officers to Guam.

Russia was also at war. In the first stage of the Nazi-Soviet scenario for dismembering states in Eastern Europe, in October 1939 Russian troops occupied eastern Poland, Latvia, Estonia, and Lithuania. In addition, Russia required Finland to cede, or at least lease, parts of its territory that the Soviets considered essential to Russian security: the southern approach to Leningrad (before 1905 and from 1991 on, St. Petersburg). Because Finland would not come to terms, Stalin ordered the Red Army to invade Finland on November 30. He established an exiled Communist, Otto Kuusinen, as head of the Democratic Republic of Finland. Kuusinen then acceded to the specific Russian demands. Finland protested the Russian invasion to the League of Nations on December 2, 1939. On December 14 the League expelled Russia—the only time it expelled a member that had broken the Covenant. On March 12, 1940, Finland sued for peace.

The tragedy of the winter's war was bitter to Roosevelt and Hull. FDR knew that supporting Finland would encourage the isolationists to rally support for new defeats of his foreign policies. Hull believed that any action against Russia would drive Stalin more firmly than ever into a permanent alliance with Hitler.

Neither Russia nor Finland had formally declared war. Therefore, Roosevelt did not invoke the Neutrality Act of 1939. Meanwhile, Congress passed a bill proposed by Senator Prentiss Brown of Michigan to provide funds for a loan to Finland from the Reconstruction Finance Corporation—the first turning point toward U.S. intervention. Two years later, Finland sided with Hitler in his war against Russia.

Stalin now put demands on American Communists, requiring the CPUSA to abandon its previous support for a U.S. policy opposed to Hitler. He wanted it instead to attack FDR as a warmonger on account of his support for Britain and France. The federal government expanded FBI surveillance of the CPUSA.

The United States was not even prepared for its own national defense, let alone to defend the European democracies effectively. In May 1940 the War Department reported that the army could field only 80,000 men and had equipment for fewer than 500,000 combat troops. As to aircraft and qualified crews, the United States had 160 pursuit planes, 52 heavy bombers, and only 260 fully trained pilots. This was why Air Corps Chief of Staff Gen. Henry ("Hap") Arnold was reluctant to sell aircraft to Britain and France. At their current rate of losses in the skies, 100 planes would last only three days in Europe while substantively reducing the number of planes for U.S. defense and delaying the training of U.S. pilots.

During the 1930s Congress had been miserly about defense appropriations. However, in May 1940 it could not provide enough. Members of Congress voted $1.5 billion more for defense—$320 million above what Roosevelt had requested—and then voted another $1.7 billion to expand the regular army from 280,000 to 375,000 men and allowed the president to summon the National Guard for active service.

The degree of sympathy for Europe and support for U.S. intervention varied throughout the United States and depended partly on ethnic origins. New York City was more interventionist than any other part; Texas was more anti-German; the South showed itself most ready to fight; and the West Coast was more concerned with Japan than Germany. The upper classes were most interventionist. In 1940 more than 66 percent of America's business and intellectual elite wanted increased supplies to be sent to Britain. Almost everybody favored increasing military and naval strength. One pattern was consistent in these months. To the Gallup question "Do you think the United States should keep out of war or do everything possible to help England, even at the risk of getting into war ourselves?" the public showed increasing acceptance of involvement during 1940. Those willing to take the risk by helping England were 36 percent in May and 60 percent in December.

Were proponents of intervention ready to mobilize their forces?

In May 1940 editor William Allen White organized the Committee to Defend America by Aiding the Allies. The committee's aims were to rouse public opinion to support all aid to Britain short of war. The White committee included industrialists, financiers, college presidents and faculty, professional people, and celebritics in entertainment. Later, leading members moved toward a strategy of outright intervention—but not White himself, who resigned because he thought the committee had leaned too far in that direction.

After the suspenseful months of the so-called Phoney War, in April 1940 Germany invaded Denmark and Norway and on May 10 Germany invaded Western Europe.

Winston Churchill became prime minister of Britain. A descendant of the first duke of Marlborough and the son of ill-fated Tory politician Lord Randolph Churchill and Jenny Jerome, daughter of American financier Leonard W. Jerome, Winston Churchill had sharpened his political wits on the back benches in his trenchant criticism of Adolf Hitler's rise to mastery of Europe and in his condemnation of the dishonor of appeasement. As a bellicose prime minister (1940–45), Churchill's defiant speeches roused England from apathy. His excellent military aides planned defensive military and naval strategies. Committed civil servants used the dislocation of war to reorder British society on more egalitarian lines.

The German invasion of Holland and Belgium in May 1940 occurred in part because these neutral countries would provide Britain and France with an easy route to the Ruhr, the center of German industry. By driving his troops through the end of the Maginot line, Hitler could, at one stroke, break through French defenses, cut Holland and Belgium off from Allied support, and thereby win his war in the west. Holland capitulated on May 15, and Queen Wilhelmina escaped to England. In Belgium, Allied troops at first held their own against the Germans. However, once the Germans penetrated their lines at Sedan on May 14 and took Amiens, they were able to reach the coast and cut the Allies off from their escape route. Just before Belgium capitulated in the early hours of May 28, Operation Dynamo began—the daredevil evacuation of British troops from Dunkirk.

The new French prime minister, Marshal Henri-Philippe Pétain, an eighty-four-year-old hero of World War I, reached an armistice with Germany on June 22. He established a fascist government—first at Bordeaux and then at the resort of Vichy in southern France—that arranged terms of collaboration on October 24. The fall of France was devastating not only to Britain but also for the United States. It was taken as a clear signal that, unless Britain were given substantive matériel aid, it could not stand alone against the Nazis, far less turn the tide of the German advance and shield the United States from the greatest military threat ever. Given prevalent American isolationism, Roosevelt was at a complete loss to know what to do.

The Battle of Britain of the summer of 1940 began with German attacks on convoys of merchant ships. On August 13 the second part of the battle commenced with a full-scale German attack on England with bomber aircraft protected by fighters. Provided with five hundred new fighters, Air Marshal Hugh Dowding concentrated on the destruction of the bombers. The Germans bombed London every night from September 7 to November 2 and also turned to other industrial cities and ports. This was the Blitz. Firestorms raged out of control when bombs set warehouses ablaze with cargoes of rum, sugar, wood, paint, and rubber. People found their eyeballs almost wrenched from their sockets by high-explosive blasts.

In the United States the Blitz proved a propaganda disaster for Adolf Hitler. Dispatched by CBS to establish a European broadcast operation, Eghbert Roscoe ("Ed") Murrow's broadcasts in the midst of the Blitz signaled the emergence of a dynamic English-speaking radio journalist. On nights of heavy bombing Murrow provided the BBC with its links with the street, becoming its messenger from hell. "You burned the city of London in our houses and we felt the flames that burned it," observed poet Archibald MacLeish. "You laid the dead of London at our doors and we knew that the dead were our dead . . . were mankind's dead . . . without rhetoric, without dramatics, without more emotion than needed be. . . . You have destroyed . . . the superstition that what is done beyond 3,000 miles of water is not really done at all." Murrow did not speak alone. He supervised a group of radio reporters who covered Europe, including Charles Collingwood, Eric Sevareid, William L. Shirer, and Howard K. Smith. Murrow and his colleagues helped convince millions of Americans that the triumph of Nazi Germany would be the end of Western civilization.

U.S. foreign policy from the summer of 1940 to the winter of 1941 developed in five stages. Three of the stages—the destroyers-bases deal, lend-lease, and the war at sea—led to the Atlantic Charter signed by Roosevelt and Churchill. The other two—economic restrictions on Japan and outright opposition to Japan's territorial claims—led to Pearl Harbor and full military intervention.

After Italy's declaration of war on Britain and Germany's conquest of France, it was possible for Roosevelt to arouse the American people to the needs of national defense. Roosevelt said at Charlottesville, Virginia, on June 10, 1940, "We will extend to the opponents of force the material resources of this nation and, at the same time, we will harness and speed up the use of those resources in order that we ourselves in the Americas may have equipment and training equal to the task of any emergency and every defense."

In July representatives of the American republics at the Havana conference in Cuba agreed to take action to prevent any change in the status of the European colonies in the Western Hemisphere and to consider aggression against any one of them as aggression against them all. This solidarity lasted until Pearl Harbor, when Chile refused temporarily, and Argentina permanently, to sever their relations with the Axis powers. Some countries offered the United States military bases. Others replaced German military advisers with Americans. The United States increased its purchase of raw materials within the Western Hemisphere and sold its products at restricted prices to countries deprived of European goods.

In an attempt to widen his base of support, on June 19, 1940, Roosevelt appointed to the cabinet two prominent Republicans who had opposed the New Deal, Henry L. Stimson and Frank Knox, respectively, as secretaries of war and navy. Knox (the Republican vice-presidential candidate in 1936) favored considerable military expansion, an army of 1 million men, the strongest air force in the world, and the immediate shipment of late-model planes to Britain. Stimson wanted the repeal of all neutrality legislation and the introduction of military conscription.

When Britain did not surrender, Hitler turned his attention to his proposed invasion of the Soviet Union, which had occupied eastern Poland and Bessarabia. Hitler wanted to counter further Soviet advances by getting Hungary and Romania to come to terms with him. In effect, he intended to return Slavic peoples to slavery. He urged Mussolini to abandon a proposed Italian invasion of Greece. Nevertheless, Mussolini, chagrined at Germany's military successes, did invade Greece in June 1940.

On July 21, 1940, Winston Churchill made a specific plea to Roosevelt for a transfer of destroyers from the United States in exchange for leases of British naval bases. Although in June Roosevelt had announced all aid to Britain short of war, he delayed action until the transfer could be presented as an act of defense and accomplished without reference to Congress. The eventual agreement, incorporated in letters exchanged between Cordell Hull and Philip Kerr (Lord Lothian, the British ambassador) on September 2, 1940, gave British bases in Newfoundland and Bermuda to the United States as an outright gift. In addition, the agreement granted to the United States ninety-nine-year leases on other bases in the Bahamas, Jamaica, St. Lucia, Trinidad, British Guiana, and Antigua in exchange for fifty old American destroyers, which were built in World War I, were now out of commission, and were not needed while the British navy controlled the Atlantic. Only nine destroyers entered British service before 1941. The gesture was one of sympathy, rather than effective support, and was granted by Roosevelt in a calculated maneuver. The fact that the destroyers would otherwise have been sold as scrap metal for about $5,000 apiece allowed FDR to comment that, for a total of $250,000, the United States had taken "the most important action in the reinforcement of our national defense that has been taken since the Louisiana Purchase." It was business with pleasure. To sweeten the deal and show U.S. good will, the destroyers exchanged for bases carried over to England a variety of American specialties: canned asparagus, corn, chipped beef, clams, instant coffee, tomato juice, and pumpkins. After the destroyers-bases deal, the United States was not neutral in any real sense of the term. Roosevelt and Hull believed that total aid short of war would be the best way of avoiding attack or intervention.

The controversy over U.S. intervention was exacerbated by the presidential campaign of 1940. The dark horse of the Republicans' campaign was Indiana utility tycoon Wendell Willkie, president of the Commonwealth and Southern Corporation, who was a liberal and an internationalist.

FDR finally decided on his third-term candidacy in May 1940. Ironically, he was supported by a group of leading politicians that included both the proponents and the opponents of intervention. Although Roosevelt chose Chicago as the site of the Democratic National Convention—because he could rely on the local political boss, Ed Kelly, to pack the galleries—he would not openly campaign for his nomination, seeking instead the fiction of a spontaneous draft. After a dutiful show of deference, Roosevelt was nominated by 946 votes on the first ballot. Unlike Cousin Ted, FDR would challenge and break the unwritten third-successive-presidential-term rule. In place of John Nance Garner, FDR chose Secretary of Agriculture Henry A. Wallace as his running mate because Wallace was a committed New Dealer who could carry the Corn Belt.

In the election FDR received 27,307,819 votes (54.8 percent) to Willkie's 22,321,018 (44.8 percent) and 449 votes in the electoral college to Willkie's 82. Socialist candidate Norman Thomas, a prominent isolationist, polled 99,557 votes. Roosevelt had won all but ten states, eight in the Midwest and Maine and Vermont in the Northeast. Roosevelt's decisive pluralities in the cities of New York, Chicago, Cleveland, and Milwaukee gave him the pivotal states of New York, Illinois, Ohio, and Wisconsin. He attracted ethnic groups such as Norwegians, Poles, and Jews, who had the most at stake in his policy of intervention in the war.

Because Willkie had been a committed internationalist until the eleventh hour, his campaign convinced isolationists they had been deprived of a genuine choice in the election. Thus, Senator Gerald P. Nye told an America First meeting in Kansas City on June 19, 1941, "I shall be surprised if history does not show that, beginning at the Republican convention in Philadelphia, a conspiracy was carried out to deny the American people a chance to express themselves." Against the wishes of Willkie, the Republican National Committee had made an anti-intervention broadcast, declaring to mothers, "Don't blame Franklin D. Roosevelt because he sent your son to war. Blame yourself because you sent Franklin D. Roosevelt back to the White House." Accepting the counsel of his advisers, on October 30, 1940, shortly before the election, FDR promised, "Your boys are not going to be sent into any foreign wars."

A troublesome factor to FDR and Hull was the way American companies continued to do business with Hitler's Germany. A case in point was provided by the giant oil company, Texas Company (created in 1902 and known as Texaco from 1959 on). Company chief Norwegian immigrant Torkild Rieber agreed to supply Germany with oil from Colombia in exchange for three tankers from Hamburg. There was nothing illegal about this. Then Rieber drew closer to the Third Reich in June 1940 when he had the Texas Company (hereafter, Texaco) hire Dr. Gerhardt Westrick, a German lawyer, and provide him with an office in the Chrysler Building and a home in Scarsdale, New York. Westrick and German spy Niko Beusmann used their positions with Texaco to obtain reports about how fast the U.S. aircraft industry was expanding. Canadian millionaire William Stephenson, head of British intelligence in New York, guessed that Westrick was spying on America's military preparations and persuaded the New York *Herald Tribune* to reveal the story. Texaco dismissed Rieber. The value of Texaco shares fell abruptly. At this time Texaco began to sponsor the weekly radio broadcasts of Saturday matinee performances from the Metropolitan Opera in New York, starting with bass Ezio Pinza in Mozart's *Marriage of*

Figaro on December 7, 1940. By attaching itself to the Met, one of America's cherished cultural institutions, Texaco was out to resurrect its credentials as a bulwark of American society. The broadcasts have continued ever since.

In November 1940 the German Luftwaffe withdrew from its Blitz on England and prepared to cooperate with the German army for Hitler's proposed invasion of Russia. The conflict with Britain then turned again to the battle of the seas. The German attempt to destroy the convoys carrying American supplies reached its first climax between March and July 1941 in the battle of the Atlantic. That April seven hundred thousand tons of shipping were sunk.

Promises More than Deliveries

As the issue of intervention was debated, discussion everywhere concentrated on peacetime conscription, student dissent, America First, and lend-lease.

Draft legislation for conscription was introduced in the Senate by Democrat Edward R. Burke of Nebraska and in the House by conservative Republican James W. Wadsworth, Jr., of New York. It moved comfortably through both houses of Congress between August 27 and September 14. The president signed it on September 16, two weeks after the destroyers-bases deal.

The act required the registration of all male citizens and resident aliens between twenty and thirty-six years of age. Selective Service was set up under the administrative direction of Gen. Louis B. Hershey by means of six thousand local draft boards, which could give deferments on the grounds of physical disability, occupation, or number of dependents. Those men who were not deferred were called up by means of a lottery, as in 1917. Those inducted were to serve in the armed forces for twelve months, but only either in the United States or in its territories or possessions overseas. On October 16, 1940, 16 million men registered for the draft. Army doctors rejected almost half the men called for inspection before draft boards. FDR learned why from a national nutrition conference in spring 1941: most suffered from ten years' malnutrition. The census of 1940 disclosed that half the nation's children came from families with annual incomes of less than $1,500.

Because of effective lobbying by the peace churches, led by the Church of the Brethren, the Selective Service Act also provided Civilian Public Service Camps for those who could convince the National Service board of their religious or ethical objections to military or naval service. The Civilian Public Service Camps became an adjunct to the military establishment. Besides, conscientious objection was a declining phenomenon.

One group, college students, agitated itself about conscription. Students throughout the United States, but particularly those at eastern colleges, indicated that they did not want to fight in another war. In November 1940 the Jesuit weekly, *America*, published the results of a poll of more than fifty thousand students in 182 Catholic colleges and universities. More than a third expected the United States to become involved in the war, and nine-tenths of them believed that a second intervention would not lead to a lasting peace. Moreover, they voted fifty to one against intervention.

Isolation was now synonymous with the America First Committee. America First had been founded by two Yale students, Kingman Brewster, Jr., and R. Douglas Stuart, Jr. Stuart, the son of the Quaker Oats magnate, arranged for financial backing from Chicago businessmen, led by Robert E. Wood, chairman of Sears Roebuck. The strength of America First lay in its exceptional organization of 450 chapters across the country, with a total membership of over eight hundred thousand, which drew support from the NCPW and the WILPF. Members included conservative opponents of FDR, college students opposed to the draft, and a few Communists. The big guns were Herbert Hoover, Joseph Kennedy, Hugh Johnson, and Henry Ford.

America First's association with star aviator Charles A. Lindbergh, Jr., ensured thorough press coverage. The press had already reported Lindbergh's visits to Germany in 1930, 1937, and 1938. Lindy thought U.S. intervention in the war would be a disaster for the U.S. economy and that U.S. democracy might not survive it. However, America First miscalculated when they thought they could capitalize on Lindbergh's great popularity. He was a political novice. At Des Moines, Iowa, on September 11, 1941, Lindy told an audience of eight thousand that three groups of war agitators were pressing the United States toward war: the British, the Roosevelt administration, and the Jews, whom he accused of creating "a series of incidents which would force us into the actual conflict." The press attacked the speech as anti-Semitic.

In Hollywood, movie moguls who happened to be Jewish were producing movies favoring the Allies in ways both subtle and blatant. These were not just films with contemporary settings overtly supporting the British cause against Hitler and the Nazis. They also included Hollywood films based on classics of English literature, among which Laurence Olivier excelled in *Wuthering Heights*, by Emily Brontë via William Wyler and Samuel Goldwyn; in *Rebecca*, by Daphne du Maurier via Alfred Hitchcock; and in *Pride and Prejudice*, by Jane Austen. Each of these films became a testament to English culture. Among the greatest contemporary commercial successes was *That Hamilton Woman* (also known as *Lady Hamilton*). It was Churchill who conceived the project and Hungarian-born British film producer Alexander Korda who executed it in Hollywood. Olivier played Horatio Nelson, the admiral who won the Battle of Trafalgar of 1805 and thereby set the seal on Britain's nineteenth-century naval superiority. Olivier's second wife, Vivien Leigh, played Lady Hamilton. The movie was a considerable box-office success even in the USSR, where it was the first foreign film to receive general distribution.

Roosevelt realized that since Britain had all but exhausted its cash reserves, it could not continue to pay for materials in the United States. Without these materials, it could not continue the war. Stimulated by an impassioned plea from Churchill, the persuasive arguments of British ambassador Lord Lothian, and lobbied by the White committee, Roosevelt proposed lend-lease. He first explained it at a press conference in Washington, D.C., on December 16, 1940, using a parable suggested by Harold Ickes: "If your neighbor's house catches fire and he needs to borrow your garden hose to extinguish it, you loan him the hose, you don't charge him for using it." Roosevelt proposed loans of tanks, planes, and ships to Britain for its war against Hitler without detailed suggestions as to how Britain might repay in kind after the war. When FDR elaborated on his proposal in a fireside chat of December 29, 1940, he also told the country it was necessary for the United States to expand its industrial production, for "we must be the great arsenal of democracy." Mail to the White House was a hundred to one in favor.

In his State of the Union address on January 6, 1941, FDR went further still, claiming that victory over the Axis powers would mean a world based upon four essential freedoms: "freedom of speech and religion and freedom from want and fear."

Fortuitously numbered House Resolution 1776, the lend-lease bill gave the president power to lend, lease, sell, or barter arms, food, or any defense article to foreign nations "whose defense the president deems vital to the defense of the United States." One reason for freeing lend-lease from the question of loans was to avoid the sort of controversy that was attached to Wall Street loans to the Allies in World War I. On March 11, 1941, the Senate approved the bill by 60 votes to 31, and the House did so by 317 votes to 71. Once the president had signed the act, Congress voted an appropriation of $7 billion to implement it.

The concept was bold. FDR dispatched William Averell Harriman, skinflint heir to the railroad fortune, to London as lend-lease expediter; there he made a rapid conquest of Winston Churchill's daughter-in-law, Pamela Digby Churchill (later, U.S. ambassador to France [1993–97]). According to her biographer, Christopher Ogden (1994), their liaison was supposed to facilitate Anglo-American supplies. But in Washington, Roosevelt was reluctant to assume strong central control. Lend-lease became something of a free-for-all among American officials and businessmen. Administrators saw the system as the thin edge of the wedge—a means of aiding American firms to penetrate the enormous market of the British Commonwealth. Also, they wanted to oblige the British to sell their holdings in the Western Hemisphere. The army opposed sending arms to Britain that it considered necessary for the United States. In consequence, the overall amount of goods sent to Britain was small in comparison with the need. British imports from the United States increased by only 3 percent in 1941. The increase was principally in foodstuffs and steel. Most of the American arms obtained were still bought with cash in 1941. Britain lost most of its remaining dollars. It could not turn lend-lease goods into exports, but exports not made from lend-lease materials were cut down so as to avoid an outcry from American manufacturers.

The battle to reorganize the U.S. economy to meet the demands of total war began eighteen months before the attack on Pearl Harbor. On May 10, 1940, in response to the German offensive in the West, FDR asked Congress for $1 billion to mechanize the army and greatly expand aircraft production. Congress replied with an even larger grant of $1.5 billion. At the end of May 1940, as British troops fled Dunkirk, FDR warned Congress that events "necessitate another enlargement of our military program." Congress duly voted to provide the United States with a two-ocean navy. In the two years prior to U.S. military entry into the war, some $64 billion was appropriated for ships, planes, and guns; $7 billion for the lend-lease program; and $3 billion for the Reconstruction Finance Corporation in order to expand defense industries.

However, if the United States really was to serve as "the arsenal of democracy," then what was required was a bureaucratic infrastructure that would direct the development of the increasing defense program. FDR began to prepare the ground at the time of the fall of France. On May 28, 1940, he created the National Defense Advisory Commission. In the months that followed, he established the Office of Production Management (OPM) in January 1941, the Office of Price Administration and Civilian Supply (OPACS) in April 1941, and the Supply Priorities and Allocations Board (SPAB) in August 1941.

Between January and December 1941 munitions production increased by 22 percent. But such growth did not dispel doubts about the efficiency of the defense program. Its critics found their views represented in the report submitted by the Senate Special Committee to investigate the National Defense Program in January 1942. According to the committee's chairman, Senator Harry S. Truman of Missouri, industry was not converting from the manufacture of consumer goods to munitions production fast enough, and government was failing to apply the force needed to expedite this change. Truman's first point was valid. America's entrepreneurs were unwilling to sacrifice a newly buoyant economy in consumer goods for the uncertain gains promised by military production. Despite the vast amounts of money earmarked for defense, spending on munitions amounted to only $18 billion in 1941.

Lend-lease was no use unless U.S. supplies reached Britain. In February and March 1941, German submarines sank or seized twenty-two ships. Despite the opposition of about half of the Senate to the idea of U.S. convoys supporting British freighters across half the Atlantic, Roosevelt announced that the security zone of the United States would be extended one thousand miles into the Atlantic, beginning April 11, 1941. The air force was used to patrol the North Atlantic as far as Iceland in order to warn British ships of the presence of German submarines. A majority of the Cabinet now favored a declaration of war on Germany. Secretary of War Henry Stimson was concerned that Roosevelt had not followed his victory with lend-lease with more positive policy. Stimson found support from Secretary of the Navy Frank Knox, Attorney General Robert H. Jackson, and Secretary of the Interior Harold Ickes.

Despite FDR's caution, British military staffs had already had secret conversations in Washington, D.C., with the U.S. Combined Chiefs of Staff from January 29 to March 29, 1941. Britain and the United States were not yet formal allies: they were associated powers with a common goal. During these secret meetings between the U.S. Army, Navy, and Army Air Force and their British counterparts, the Anglo-Americans established their priorities for the two wars that lay ahead: Germany had to be eliminated first, then Japan, and—if possible—not in a war on two fronts at the same time.

Elsewhere, weaker countries were seeking support from strong allies. By early 1941 Hungary, Bulgaria, and Romania had been conquered by Germany. Once Germany had launched an offensive on Yugoslavia and Greece on April 6, 1941, they too were made subject within three weeks. What was astonishing about Hitler's mastery of Europe was how closely his control—seemingly improvised—was less thoroughly iron-clad and more in line with his blueprint in *Mein Kampf* with tight control of German-speaking areas, ruthless subjection of Slavic states, and more accommodating arrangements with occupied or cooperating countries in northwest Europe.

In May 1941 the Germans sank the American freighter *Robin Moor* in the southern Atlantic. Roosevelt declared an "unlimited national emergency," froze all German and Italian assets in the United States, and closed their consulates. According to public opinion polls, in June popular support for convoys was 52 percent; and 75 percent of Americans approved the use of convoys if it seemed that Britain would not win the war without the security of supplies the United States provided.

To make the Atlantic patrols more effective, Roosevelt and his advisers decided to use territories on the edge of the zone. On April 9, 1941, the State Department concluded an agreement in Washington, D.C., with the exiled Danish minister to occupy the Danish possession of Greenland. In June the administration negotiated with Iceland to replace British and Canadian troops stationed there with a U.S. force that landed on July 7. The U.S. patrol ships were given secret orders to extend their duties beyond patrolling rather than allow any hostile force to deflect them from their course.

Great moral issues were at stake at home as well as abroad. World War II clarified attitudes toward race as government propaganda fashioned political ideology in an attempt to cover the contradictions of fighting a war against racism abroad while maintaining segregation at home. The shortcomings of the American democratic system were tested to the limit. It was all too easy for liberals and radicals alike to equate poll taxes and grandfather clauses, lynching, and the segregation of African Americans in the South with Hitler's persecution of the Jews in the Third Reich.

Not only the New Deal but also Roosevelt's foreign-policy rhetoric had roused expectations of change among African Americans but left them unsatisfied. With consummate, newfound political skills, their leaders were quick to exploit the situation. In January 1941, at a meeting that included Walter White, Mary McLeod Bethune, and Lester Grange (of the Urban League), activist A. Philip Randolph announced plans for a mass march on Washington to protest discrimination in defense industries. Randolph was firmly convinced of solidarity among African Americans. He knew how to channel their indignation into constructive political action while preventing the CPUSA from exploiting the situation. Randolph's appeal touched a responsive nerve in the African American community at large. Across the country African Americans formed committees to coordinate support and began organizing transportation to Washington. Randolph chose July 1 for the event.

FDR did not want his plans for the war to be jeopardized by racial divisions at home that would expose the limitations of American democracy—especially close to a momentous meeting with Winston Churchill when FDR would promote four freedoms. Cornered, and convinced that one hundred thousand African Americans would march on Washington, Roosevelt issued Executive Order 8802 on June 25, 1941, requiring that all employers, unions, and government agencies "concerned with vocational training programs" must "provide for the full and equitable participation of all workers in defense industries without discrimination because of race, creed, color, or national origin." Randolph called off the march. To enforce the order, FDR created a moderately effective Fair Employment Practices Committee (FEPC).

Not all African Americans were pleased by Randolph's decision. Those disaffected included Bayard Rustin, the former Communist sympathizer who had helped Randolph plan the great march. Rustin broke with Randolph (temporarily) and joined forces with A. J. Muste of the Fellowship of Reconciliation to become a mover in the FOR's civil rights campaigns during World War II.

On June 22, 1941, Hitler repudiated the Nazi-Soviet Pact and invaded Russia. On June 26, 1941, the United States announced that the neutrality laws would not be invoked against Russia because American security was not endangered. To prepare the way for a *volte face* in United States strategy—giving aid to Russia—the State Department could not resist condemning "communistic dictatorship" as being as insufferable as "Nazi dictatorship" but, nevertheless, proposing that the United States should help Russia since Hitler posed the greater threat. Senator Harry Truman of Missouri was far more blunt: "If we see that Germany is winning, we should help Russia, and, if Russia is winning, we ought to help Germany and that way let them kill as many as possible, although I don't want to see Hitler victorious under any circumstances."

On July 26 Roosevelt sent his special and most trusted envoy, Harry Hopkins, to Moscow to ascertain Stalin's needs. On November 7, 1941, he applied lend-lease to Russia. As to the American Communists, after Hitler's invasion of Russia, the CPUSA dropped its dove-like recommendations of peace like a hot potato and now insisted on U.S. military intervention against Germany.

In October 1941 FDR persuaded Congress to remove all restrictions on U.S. commerce so that U.S. merchant ships could carry goods to British ports. By November 1941 the German army had reached the outskirts of Moscow. It was impossible to overstate the threat Hitler posed to world stability.

Nevertheless, isolationist sentiment in Congress was still strong. The occupation of Iceland by 4,000 marines on July 7, 1941, opened debate about the appropriate size and disposition of U.S. forces. The Selective Service Act of 1940 had allowed for 900,000 draftees for one year's service in the Western Hemisphere. Military strategists agreed that this number was inadequate. FDR agreed with congressional leaders on July 14 that he would take the responsibility in his strong recommendation to Congress on July 21, in which he warned against the "tragic error" of allowing the "disintegration" of the modest army. The Senate voted for an extension of selective military service to eighteen months—rather than for the duration of the emergency, as FDR had asked—with 45 in favor and 21 senators not voting at all. On August 12 the House agreed by a majority of one: 203 votes in favor to 202 against. That narrowest of victories was due to the sterling work of persuasion by Chief of Staff Gen. George C. Marshall from behind the scenes.

Roosevelt met Churchill at sea in Placentia Bay off Argentia, Newfoundland, from August 9–12, 1941, to discuss the objectives of Britain and the still technically neutral United States in the war. Harry Hopkins had planned the meeting. He and Churchill got on famously as soon as Hopkins realized that it was the bon vivant Winston's spirit that kept the island kingdom afloat. Churchill called Hopkins "Lord Root-of-the-Matter."

Intending a complement to Woodrow Wilson's Fourteen Points, Roosevelt and Churchill declared in the Atlantic Charter that their countries sought no new territory in the course of the war; that territorial changes would only be made with reference to the populations involved; that all peoples had the right to choose the form of their governments; that all nations had equal rights of access to raw materials and trade across the world; and that, after the war, aggressor nations would be forced to disarm until a permanent system of international security was established. In short, the future peace should give all peoples freedom from want and fear and freedom of speech and religion. FDR wrote his words not only in a spirit of generosity but also as a manifesto of U.S. economic self-interest. While other nations were being destroyed by war, the United States was further developing its economic power. The U.S. need for trade and raw materials would grow by 40 percent in four years. Thus the United States needed "access, on equal terms" in world trade but with an equality that was more equal than others.

As to their personal relations, Roosevelt appreciated the charm and tenacity of Churchill, whereas Churchill liked Roosevelt's subtlety and sense of timing. As to their wartime agenda, according to Churchill's report of August 19, 1941, to his own cabinet, FDR had "said that he would wage war, but not declare it, and that he would become more and more provocative. . . . Everything was to be done to force an 'incident' . . . which would justify him in opening hostilities." Roosevelt and Churchill meant an incident with Germany.

U.S. public opinion was overwhelmingly favorable to the principles of the Atlantic Charter, provided it did not lead to outright intervention in the war.

On September 4 the United States and Germany began an undeclared naval war after an incident in which the commander of a German submarine, U-652, off Iceland sent torpedoes at what he thought was a British destroyer. But it was a U.S. ship, the *Greer*. Describing the attacks on the *Greer* and other ships as "acts of international lawlessness" intended by Germany to destroy freedom of the seas, Roosevelt said in a radio address of September 11, 1941, that American vessels and planes "will no longer wait until Axis submarines lurking under the water, or Axis raiders on the surface of the sea, strike their deadly blow—first." Had FDR said that the U-boat had fired in self-defense—which is what had really happened—and had he admitted that Hitler did not intend to attack U.S. ships in the Atlantic—which was what Churchill told his colleagues—he would have had to wait for the imminent collapse of Britain before getting nationwide support for military intervention.

In October another destroyer, the *Reuben James*, was sunk off Iceland with the loss of one hundred American lives. However, when Roosevelt signed a revision of the neutrality laws on November 17, 1941, permitting the arming of U.S. Merchant Marine ships and allowing them to carry cargoes to belligerents' ports, he was giving assent to an act that was passed by narrow margins in both houses—50 to 37 in the Senate and 212 to 194 in the House.

As the international crises deepened, people wanted to know about day-to-day events across the world. Newspapers wanted to meet the demand. FDR failed to provide a clear rationale for increasing U.S. involvement in the war. However, he was aware of the need for centralized coordination and distribution of information. The most influential of all federal information services was the Office of Facts and Figures (OFF), established in 1941 under the direction of Archibald MacLeish, then librarian of Congress. The OFF was charged with the task of providing the public with the factual material from which they could construct their own conception of how and why the war was being fought. The press sometimes selected the facts to criticize the administration for mismanaging the war effort.

Empire of the Sun

In the Pacific, the United States was on a collision course with Japan, and this led to its formal entry into World War II.

In December 1938 the Japanese prime minister, Prince Konoye, had announced Japan's ambitious foreign policy for a "Greater East Asia Co-prosperity Sphere." From 1938 on the State Department issued protests against Japanese interference with U.S. rights in China and the bombing of Chinese civilians. Secretary of State Cordell Hull went further than the letter of the neutrality laws and asked U.S. bankers not to extend credits to Japan. He also asked U.S. manufacturers not to sell airplane parts to any nation that might attack civilians. U.S. disapproval of Japan's foreign policy culminated in the announcement of July 1939 that the commercial treaty of 1911 would be terminated at the end of the year. The actual sale of goods did not come to an end immediately, but within months such exports as gasoline, steel, and scrap iron were subject to government license.

"A day which will live in infamy." Pearl Harbor attacked. (U.S. Navy; Office of Public Relations and Office of War Information; Prints and Photographs Division, Library of Congress)

Japan took full advantage of the fall of France to extend its imperial ambitions to northern Indochina, the French colony comprising the three states of Laos, Cambodia, and Vietnam. Unable to resist Japanese demands for airfields, Vichy France consented to Japanese occupation of Indochina in September 1940. That month Japan also concluded an Axis agreement with Germany and Italy, by which the three powers were obliged to come to one another's aid if any one of them was attacked. Japan thereby extracted from the others acceptance of its spheres of influence in Southeast Asia and the Pacific. Germany hoped the Tripartite Pact would deter the United States from entering the European war; Japan hoped the pact would dissuade the United States from entering the Sino-Japanese war.

However, naval leaders did not want to provoke the Japanese. They wanted time to build a first-class striking force. Adm. Harold R. Stark, chief of naval operations, advised FDR to do nothing when Japan moved into French Indochina. Yet FDR also had to deal with political reaction at home. Public opinion polls suggested that almost 70 percent of the American people were willing to risk war in the Pacific rather than let Japan continue to expand. In the United States, civilians demanded prompt action against the advice of the military; in Japan, the military pressed for action over the protests of the civilians.

In April 1941, when the Japanese foreign minister, Matsuoka Yosuke, visited Berlin, Germany and Japan discussed plans for a projected war on two fronts against the United States. Joachim von Ribbentrop, the German foreign minister, urged Matsuoka to commit Japan to an immediate assault on the British protectorate Singapore. Matsuoka then concluded a neutrality pact with Stalin to last five years. But after the German invasion of Russia on June 22, 1941, Matsuoka cynically suggested to the Japanese cabinet that they order an attack on Russia from the east, whereupon Prime Minister Konoye forced him to resign. Some members of the cabinet agreed with Matsuoka that Japan could take advantage of Russia's misfortune. Others believed that Hitler's war on the Russian front would overextend his forces and thus reduce the threat to Britain, which would, with U.S. aid, be free to strengthen its own position in the Pacific.

By July 1941 Japan had completed occupation of southern as well as northern Indochina. Ironically, Japan's imperialist conquests of 1940–42 encouraged Asian nationalists to realize they could shape their own destiny and free Asia from white domination. They wanted whites out of Indochina, India, Malaya, the Netherlands East Indies (NEI), and the Philippines. The United States looked askance at a situation in which the oil, tin, rubber, bauxite, and other resources of Southeast Asia were controlled by a hostile power. On July 24, 1941, Roosevelt froze all Japanese credits in the United States. When Britain and the Dutch colonial governor in the NEI took similar action, Japan's sources of petroleum dried up. The U.S. ambassador in Tokyo, Joseph Drew, warned Hull that if, by its actions, the United States humbled Konoye, he would fall and be replaced by a more belligerent minister.

In September 1941 an imperial conference of cabinet ministers and chiefs of staff met in Tokyo to consider preparations for war, should talks between Japan and the United States fail. The Japanese were convinced that the United States—especially after the Atlantic Charter—must recognize that Japan needed access to raw materials and markets. Japan could afford to stay out of Southeast Asia with economic guarantees. But Manchukuo and control of China were minimum necessities, the one with essential raw materials and the other a potential market as well as a threat to Japanese security. The conferees concluded that the United States would not allow Japan to become a world-class power. Without war, Japanese economic collapse was inevitable. Thus, even if Japan lost a war with the United States, there would still be nothing to regret in waging war. With the failure of the Japanese ambassador in Washington, Adm. Nomura Kichisaburo, to secure terms with the United States, Prince Konoye was humbled. He was succeeded as prime minister on October 16 by the war minister, Gen. Tojo Hideki.

Because the Washington ambassador was not a trained diplomat, Tojo sent Kurusu Saburo, a veteran diplomat and former ambassador to Berlin, to assist him in November 1941. He brought an offer of conciliation: Japan would withdraw from Indochina and halt its advance in Southeast Asia if the United States agreed to Japanese control of China. The reply of the United States on November 26 was equally candid: If Japan withdrew its troops from both China and Indochina, the United States would resume liberal trade with Japan. The last Japanese offer, with a final deadline set for November 29, contained nothing new. Hull originally decided to propose a three-month truce during which limited withdrawal of troops from Indochina would be complemented by limited economic offers from the United States. When he learned on November 26 of large Japanese convoys moving down the South China coast, he submitted stiff terms, leaving no room for compromise.

FDR rejected any idea that the United States should declare war on Japan, following its suspected attack on Malaya or the NEI. He and his advisers believed that it would be difficult to unite the country behind a declaration of war on behalf of European colonies. They thought the United States would instead drift into an undeclared war against Japan in the Pacific—much as it was doing against Germany in the Atlantic. Roosevelt had his advisers prepare a message for Emperor Hirohito urging a peaceful solution.

Meanwhile, the Japanese answer to Cordell Hull's note of November 29 was delivered to the Japanese embassy in Washington on December 6. Because the Americans had cracked the secret code, they knew its contents before it was delivered on December 7. It comprised a tedious rejection of Hull's request. Nomura and Kurusu were to await final instructions on December 7 and present a note to Hull at 1:00 P.M. Instead of arriving at 1:00 P.M., Nomura and Kurusu arrived at 2:00 P.M. By that time Pearl Harbor had been devastated.

The Japanese force that bombed Pearl Harbor left the Kurile Islands on November 25 and positioned itself north of Hawaii. The attack followed months of adroit reconnaissance and careful preparation. The principal attack was at 7:55 A.M., just as many crews were about to attend Sunday services on deck. Although eight battleships were either sunk or badly damaged, several were raised, repaired, and returned to action. Nevertheless, it would be months before the Pacific fleet could be deployed again. Ironically, the Japanese had had the opportunity to cause far more lasting damage in their attack but had overlooked it, completely missing the decks and repair yards in Pearl Harbor. The damaged battleships were a temporary loss. The repair facilities would have been irreplaceable, yet they were left practically unscathed. Submarines, torpedo shops, and submarine-repair facilities, which were also overlooked, provided the basis for attacks upon Japan's navy and shipping.

An immediate question about the attack concerned the widely touted insight of the United States into the Japanese code. Among others, Christopher Andrew believes (1995) that FDR failed to attach enough importance to breaking Japanese naval codes. Had he done so, he would have known that Japan intended to bomb Pearl Harbor. Yet interception by "Magic" or other systems was neither infallible nor complete. Diplomatic messages did not carry military information. Moreover, messages in code always included false information in order to tantalize and confuse enemy code breakers. The actual volume of information was so great that it could not have been transmitted complete to commanders in the field, as this would have severely overtaxed communications facilities. U.S. communications systems were riven by bureaucratic rivalries. All these factors made it difficult to receive, interpret, and decide upon intelligence information.

The U.S. declaration of war upon Japan received almost unanimous support from the people of the United States. In Congress, only one vote was cast against the declaration—that of veteran pacifist Jeannette Rankin of Montana, who had also voted against the declaration of war on Germany in 1917. Frustrated by setbacks in the bitter Russian campaign, and infuriated by America's support of Britain in the Atlantic, Hitler announced his declaration of war on the United States on December 11, 1941. Congress passed the motion declaring war upon Germany and Italy without opposition.

Safe for so long, the American people suffered a greater sense of outrage over the surprise of Pearl Harbor than they did in any subsequent setback. Senator Arthur H. Vandenberg of Michigan admitted, "That day ended isolationism for any realist." Thus World War II silenced dissidence at home.

The American people now concentrated on the great war. It seemed to most Americans that Japan and Germany had, without any provocation, attacked first Britain and France and then the United States as part of a plan to enslave the world. For its part, the United States had no selfish ambitions of its own but only wanted to ensure freedom and security for people everywhere. The industrial strength of the United States held out promise of ultimate victory over the Axis powers. Former isolationists were converts to a new crusade, total victory. Long-dormant factories processed voluminous war orders. Unemployed people returned to work. The profound disillusion of the 1930s gave way to a mighty sense of purpose.

But victory was by no means within sight. After their early staggering successes in 1937–42, the odds were tilted decisively in favor of Germany and Japan. Their initial victories convinced Germany and Japan that they had found the right formula for total war. By contrast, the United States, the USSR, and Britain understood that they had to address weak strategy and tactics. If the Grand Alliance did not succeed against Germany and Japan, then Western civilization would be lost.

CHAPTER 15

The Miraculous Takes a Little Longer

America and World War II

WAR WAS A BUSINESS to the United States. It had to be won with profit. This thinking permeated all aspects of war management—supplies and matériel, logistics, strategy and tactics, and even popular thinking about why the United States was involved.

The Grand Alliance comprised Britain, the world's largest colonial power; Russia, the world's only Communist nation; and the United States, the world's oldest republic and democracy and the leading capitalist country. The Allies were determined to prevent Germany and Japan from reaching world-class status through war. Although Britain had gone to war with Germany in September 1939 nominally to free Poland, its underlying motive was to prevent German domination of Europe. In Southeast Asia its various dominions, colonies, and dependencies were under attack from Japan. Russia had been forced into war when Germany invaded the Soviet Union in June 1941. The United States finally went to war with Japan because of the Japanese attack on Pearl Harbor in December 1941. It went to war with Germany because Hitler declared war on the United States. The architect of the Grand Alliance was Adolf Hitler. In the end, the Grand Allies won World War II because, compared with Germany and Japan, they were greater economically and industrially and they had far greater human resources.

However, there was nothing inevitable about their victory. By its solitary war of 1940–41, Britain had held out hope that Hitler could be defeated and that democracy would survive. Later, it provided the launching pad for the invasion of Western Europe that would apply American forces and matériel to Hitler's defeat. Russia's heroic contribution was to bear the brunt of the fighting against the Nazis, sustaining casualties of perhaps 20 million. America's outsize contribution was its industrial and agricultural muscle.

President Franklin D. Roosevelt began the war with a superb team of professional naval and military advisers. Gen. George C. Marshall, Adm. Ernest J. King, and Gen. Henry ("Hap") Arnold comprised the Joint Chiefs of Staff (JCS), a group that had its own staff planners. Together with their British counterparts they made up the Combined Chiefs of Staff (CCS). The CCS was responsible for devising broad policies and plans, allocating resources, and deciding priorities in war production and the conduct of operations. Political leaders Roosevelt and British Prime Minister Winston Churchill decided on a strategy and the CCS carried it out. The leaders could meet only during a conference, but the CCS met regularly in Washington, D.C. In mid-1942 the JCS and the CCS were joined by Adm. William Daniel Leahy, whom FDR appointed chief of staff.

Despite the growth, efficiency, and influence of the JCS and the CCS, the ultimate decision on strategy lay with FDR. The war changed Roosevelt; it brought out a new sense of purpose in him. It allowed him to escape the sterile politics of the depression and to reassert his special genius for apparently random initiatives that could be arranged to make up a cohesive strategy. He remained a great delegator of tasks, allocating responsibility to various agencies and individuals. This enhanced his authority, since he alone provided the coordinating link among the subordinate agencies. He also managed to protect himself against the stigma of failure when things went wrong. Moreover, whereas Winston Churchill distrusted generals in politics, FDR believed that his senior officers saw the world as he did.

The unique relationship between Roosevelt and Churchill as wartime leaders was a prime factor in the Anglo-American victory. Both had strong personalities; both worked within a framework of constitutional democratic government; both expressed themselves freely, knowing that what they promised, they could deliver. Moreover, they had forged their political strength in personal adversity. Nevertheless, despite Churchill's great personal standing, this was no partnership of equals. The United States was clearly the dominant partner with massive resources. Yet the United States did not have a free hand. It was entering three wars already in progress, and thus it had to fit its strategy within an existing framework.

English revisionist historian John Charmley suggests (1995) that, unlike Churchill, who concentrated on winning the war, FDR sought a new world order. He wanted it to be one that suited U.S. economic needs, yet it also depended on Soviet participation. To achieve his great goal, Roosevelt was willing to jettison anything but his domestic consensus. Besides, FDR disliked both the British Empire and the Soviet Union. To serve his ends, however, he courted Soviet dictator Joseph Stalin at Churchill's expense.

Praise the Lord and Pass the Ammunition

One of the first priorities for the United States after Pearl Harbor was raising a fighting force of soldiers, sailors, airmen, and marines. Congress passed a new draft law widening Selective Service to include all men between eighteen and sixty-five. Only those between twenty and forty-four were liable for military service. Those over forty-four were eligible for labor service—a provision that was never used. All men currently in the armed forces had to serve for the du-

Morocco Bound. An absorbed FDR dines from an army mess kit on the field in French Morocco as he discusses tactics with (*from left to right*) Gen. Mark W. Clark, Harry Hopkins (*with back to camera*), and Maj. Gen. George J. Patton, Jr., commander of American forces. (Office of War Information; Library of Congress)

ration of the war and for six months beyond. In 1941 the age of those liable for military service was lowered from twenty to eighteen in order to expand the forces beyond 5.5 million. It proved impossible for some local boards to draft men according to priorities of single men first, then married men, and then fathers. Thus, the law operated unevenly across the nation. In all, some 31 million men entered Selective Service, of whom about 10 million men were actually drafted. Altogether, 15 million men and women served. College students did not obtain special exemption. Everyone who was fit went to war.

The troops were GIs—Government Issue. No matter what was its original composition, hardly any unit retained a strong regional flavor as successive intakes of men from all sections of the country began to blur the distinctions between regular army divisions, the National Guard, and Selective Service divisions. The armed forces drew officers from the service academies at West Point and Annapolis, the ROTC in more than a hundred universities and colleges, the National Guard, and special ninety-day officer candidate schools. The U.S. Army Air Force (USAAF), granted dominion status within the army, was considered the most glamorous of the services. Men in ground units envied airmen their higher pay, easier promotion, and more comfortable living conditions. Furthermore, because of a flexible rotation policy, after flying thirty missions, an airman could return to the United States. By 1945 the army and air force accounted for 8.2 million men, of whom two-thirds served overseas. The navy and the marines accounted for 3.9 million, and the coast guard for about 250,000. Women entered the services. The government established the Women's Army Corps (WAC) in May 1942 and the Marine Corps established the Women's Reserve in 1943.

All together, 1.15 million African Americans joined the armed forces. Many fought overseas. However, the armed forces were totally segregated. Although the chiefs of staff would have preferred to think the armed services were immune from racial conflict, they came under increasing pressure to abandon the ironclad segregation defined in a code of 1941. By its terms, African Americans could not enlist in the marines or the air force. In the navy they could serve only in menial tasks.

The army did admit African Americans but maintained segregated training facilities and units. It used African American troops primarily in a supportive capacity rather than in combat. African American officers were assigned to Negro units and had to serve under white superiors. The army rationalized this policy partly on the sophistry that African Americans were poor fighters, partly on the grounds that the army was not a suitable laboratory for social experiments, and partly in the belief that integration would destroy the morale of white soldiers. However, as the numbers of African American soldiers increased sevenfold, from 100,000 in 1941 to 700,000 in 1944, so did their dissatisfaction with military segregation. A student expressed smoldering resentment among African Americans: "The Army Jim Crows us. The Navy lets us serve only as mess men. The Red Cross refuses our blood. We are disfranchised, Jim Crowed, spat upon. What more could Hitler do than that?"

African American recruits came primarily from the North because those from the South were usually neither sufficiently healthy nor well enough educated to pass induction tests. African Americans from the North were less likely to accept Jim Crow. Gradually and reluctantly, the chiefs of staff came to accept that military segregation was wasteful of manpower, that it was exposing the armed services to liberal criticisms, and that it was depressing the morale of ever larger sections of the army. Shamefaced, the army began to use African Americans in combat, and the navy introduced a program of cautious integration. Nevertheless, the army remained totally segregated.

World War II was notable for the invention or further development of a whole range of planes, weapons, and ships that helped determine the outcome of the war and had momentous consequences for the atomic age that followed it.

Aircraft of all sorts not only became the major instrument of offense and defense in the air but were also essential for the protection of ground forces. Events proved that the side with superiority in the air would enjoy a decisive advantage over the enemy. The pace of aeronautical development was astonishing. The maximum speed of fighters rose from 360 mph to 540 mph, that of bombers from 290 mph to 460 mph. Their performance in range and altitude also increased.

Bombing operations began as diffuse, inaccurate, and ineffectual raids by a few score of aircraft. They were developed into a series of sledgehammer blows of many hundreds of heavy bombers, weaving complicated patterns over Europe, striking accurately and devastatingly, confident that the enemy's defenses were being blinded and deafened by an invisible thunder of radar and radio jamming. By December 1944, when most of the aircraft in Bomber Command had been fitted with H2S radar, nine-tenths of planes released bombs within one mile of their target.

The first jet-propelled airplanes also made their appearance in the war. Although Frank Whittle had made the first turbojet in England on April 12, 1937, it was the German Heinkel, He 178, that was the first jet-propelled airplane to fly—on August 27, 1939. Both Britain and Germany worked to perfect jet fighters as quickly as possible. By 1944 both the RAF Gloucester Meteor and German Messerschmidt Me 262 were in operation. They and other jet aircraft played only a small part in the fighting. However, their speed and high ceiling in operations indicated that, with improvements, they would supersede the traditional piston-engined combat airplane. In 1945 a Meteor increased the world airspeed record from 469 to 606 mph.

The Japanese attack on Pearl Harbor by carrier-based planes had been a dramatic demonstration of the potential uses of aircraft carriers, which became the dominant combat ships of the war. The aircraft carrier was a naval vessel from which airplanes could take off and onto which they could land. The British were the first to make an aircraft carrier, the *Argus* in World War I, although the war ended before they could put the *Argus* into operation. However, the Americans soon adopted the idea with a converted carrier, the USS *Langley*, in March 1922, as did the Japanese. Essentially, aircraft carriers were airfields at sea, with many special features necessitated by limitations in size and conditions at sea. To facilitate takeoffs and landings, airspeeds over the deck were increased by turning the ship into the wind. Catapults flush with the flight deck assisted in launching airplanes. To facilitate landings, the planes were fitted with retractable hooks that engaged traverse wires in the deck, thereby braking them to a quick stop.

Wartime chemistry devised chemical grenades, notably the phosphorous bomb, which contained an explosive charge and a quantity of white elemental phosphorous. These bombs were used as incendiaries by both sides in air attacks on large cities. As the charge exploded, the bomb scattered fragments of white phosphorous at speed over a large area, and the particles ignited spontaneously on contact with the air. They stuck to bare skin and caused painful flesh wounds that took a long time to heal. In the meantime, the patient's care would be excessively demanding of overstretched medical resources.

World War II was as much a contest between the industrial capacity of the participants as a struggle between their armed forces. Without U.S. production, the Allies could not have won the war. Not only was U.S. production on a scale sufficient to wage wars across two oceans and furnish its allies with matériel, but also the standard of living rose at home. Americans did not suffer the extreme privations of Asians and Europeans. As radio commentator Ed Murrow observed, "We live in the light, in relative comfort and complete security. We are the only nation in this war which has raised its standard of living since the war began. We are not tired, as all Europe is tired."

The amount and range of U.S. production were truly astounding: between 1940 and 1945 the United States produced 296,429 warplanes, 102,351 tanks, 372,431 pieces of artillery, 2,455,964 trucks, 87,620 warships, 5,425 cargo ships, 5,822,000 tons of aircraft bombs, 20,086,061 small arms, and 44 billion rounds of small ammunition. As Denis Brogan observed in *The American Character* (1944), "To the Americans war is a business, not an art; they are not interested in moral victories but in victory. . . . The United States is a great, a very great corporation whose stockholders expect (with all their history to justify the expectation) that it will be in the black."

The United States depended on ocean shipping to transport men and supplies. To meet the demand, American industrialists adapted their mass-production techniques to ship construction and expanded shipyards. Between 1941 and 1945 they produced 55 million tons of shipping, about half of them in Liberty Ships constructed by assembly line methods. In mid-1943 industrialists began producing a more specialized kind of shipping, notably landing craft—LSTs, LCTs, LCI(L)s, and others—first for use in a cross-Channel invasion of Western Europe and then in the Pacific and the Mediterranean. During the first 212 days of 1945 American shipbuilders built 247 cargo ships. Industrialists Henry Kaiser and Howard Hughes, who became partners in aviation and ship construction, were widely known for encouraging their executives, designers, and workers to achieve the impossible. In September 1942 Henry Kaiser set a world record by launching the *John Fitch*, a Liberty ship of ten thousand tons, just twenty-four days after laying the keel. In all, the U.S. merchant fleet rose from 34.84 million tons of dry-cargo shipping on January 1, 1943, to 67.36 million tons on August 1, 1945. Thus, the United States could deploy 5 million of its army of 8.2 million overseas in all theaters of war by May 1945—3 million of them in the war against Germany.

The science of getting the right forces and equipment to the right place at the right time is logistics. Military planning of the moving of supplies was the task of Army Service Forces (ASF), headed by Gen. Brehom B. Somervell, an engineer officer who did not mind offending other people in order to get things done quickly. The ASF motto was "We do the impossible immediately: the miraculous takes a little longer." The entire system of production, transportation, delivery, and stocking was based on an essential, continuous pipeline of supply with new articles put in at one end of the pipeline as similar articles were removed from the other. This was what Henry Ford had done with the Model T in the 1920s. Industrialists applied the system to factories, storage depots, and theaters of war. They maintained a regular supply with individual needs computed according to official tables of organization and equipment (TOEs).

Realizing that American industry was moving into military production too slowly, on January 16, 1942, FDR issued Executive Order 9024, which created the War Production Board (WPB). Its chairman, Donald Marr Nelson, came to the WPB from his post as vice president of Sears, Roebuck, and Company. His brief with the WPB was to develop policies governing all aspects of production and to "exercise general responsibility over the nation's economy." The (second) War Powers Act of March 1942 confirmed his authority. This law gave the president power to allocate resources and declare priorities throughout the economy as the needs of national defense determined them. Thereafter, Nelson was responsible for deciding who could or could not have access to steel, copper, rubber, gasoline, and other scarce commodities.

Nelson had authority to force manufacturers to convert their plants to war production; to expand existing facilities; to oblige manufacturers to accept war orders; and, in extreme cases, to commandeer their plant. Instead of using coercion, Nelson tried to get the cooperation of business by offering irresistible inducements to join the battle for production. These came in the form of subsidies or low-interest loans for enlarging plants and constructing new facilities. Government encouraged industry with tax benefits to take account of the depreciation of defense plants, at a rate of 20 percent per annum. There was also the cost-plus contract, by which the government and the contractor agreed on a profit over and above the cost of production to be included in the overall price of a contract. This led to widespread abuse in which all sorts of expenses were included in the basic cost, until Senator Harry Truman of Missouri and his investigative committee exposed systemic malpractices.

The government also promised contractors that new facilities built at government expense for war production would be available at knockdown prices at the end of the war. In addition to these incentives, in March 1942 FDR approved the suspension of all antitrust actions and investigations into companies cooperating in the war effort. As much new industrial plant was built in the three years following Pearl Harbor as had been constructed in the previous fifteen years. By June 1942 50 percent of America's manufacturing output was in war matériel.

Big business boomed in harmony with the guns. On the eve of America's entry into the war, 75 percent of all contracts in the defense program were lodged with only fifty-six large companies. Donald Marr Nelson wanted an equitable distribution of procurement contracts to ensure that small entrepreneurs also benefited from war production. However, the largest demand for munitions came from the War and Navy Departments. Invariably, they placed their contracts with the corporate giants. Big business was the most attractive option to the War and Navy Departments because it had the resources, equipment, expertise, capital, and organizational experience to meet production on a mammoth scale. Moreover, giant corporations had expert lobbyists pleading their case.

In the cabinet the most influential advocate of big business was Secretary of War Henry L. Stimson. To justify his favoritism, Stimson explained that, when waging war, "you have got to let business make money out of the process or business won't work." Others of lesser rank were just as willing to favor their own constituency. Foremost among these were the so-called dollar-a-year men. They were individuals recruited from big business to staff the executive branch of the WPB. To assuage their fears concerning their company status at the end of the war, the federal government agreed that they should remain on the payroll of their corporations—at a dollar a year. Thus placed, and with an eagle eye on their postwar advancement, they dealt leniently with their past and future corporate employers. The dollar-a-year men included not only Donald Marr Nelson and various executives in the WPB but also William S. Knudsen, who left General Motors to become director of the War Department; banker James V. Forrestal, who became secretary of defense; Robert A. Lovett, who became assistant secretary of war for air; and Edward Stettinius, Jr., who left GM and U.S. Steel, eventually to become secretary of state.

By tying business, the military, and government closely together, FDR was preparing the ground for what became variously known as the power elite, the military-industrial complex, and the warfare state. The center of its activities and the symbol of U.S. military power was the Pentagon, a huge five-sided building in Arlington County, Virginia, just outside Washington, D.C. Designed by George Edwin Bergstrom and built in 1941–43, it formed the headquarters of the U.S. Department of Defense, including all three services, previously housed in scattered buildings. When the Pentagon was completed, it was the largest office building in the world, covering thirty-four acres and providing 3.7 million square feet of usable floor space. The design was based on five concentric pentagons, or rings, with ten spoke-like corridors connecting the whole.

The wartime economy vindicated Keynesian economics, the alluring conviction that government could sustain economic growth through enlightened use of fiscal powers. To defeat Hitler and the Japanese, the United States was assembling one of the greatest fighting forces in history. The result would transform U.S. society not only in the war but beyond. Historian Michael Sherry finds (1995) that from World War II on, military issues reshaped American politics and military imperatives justified the expansion of the state.

The battle for production was won by the end of 1943. That November $6 billion of war matériel rolled off American production lines. In December 1943 the War and Navy Departments began to return funds appropriated from munitions. From then until June 1944 4 million workers were laid off from war and war-related industries. Donald Nelson now began urging war contractors to reconvert to peacetime production. He found himself opposed by the armed services, which sought to maintain high levels of military production, resisted by business, which had grown fat upon lucrative munitions contracts, and undermined by the WPB vice chairman, Charles Wilson. When the controversy grew acrimonious, FDR replaced Nelson at the WPB with a former WPB official, Julius A. Krug, who avoided a collision with industry by allowing industry to reconvert to peacetime production at its leisure.

The balance sheet of war production suggests the scale of the achievement and who gained most from it. Between July 1940 and September 1944 government expenditure on war-related industries totaled $175 billion. Of this, some 66 percent went to only one hundred companies. Two-thirds of the $1 billion invested by Washington in research and development was channeled toward sixty-eight large corporations. Forty percent of this sum found its way into the coffers of the nation's ten leading businesses. The cost was borne by the lesser. During the war 500 small banks went out of business, as did over half a million modest businesses in the retail, service, and construction sectors. The overall result was that big business grew stronger. By the late 1940s it was more firmly established and more clearly monopolistic than before. Whereas in 1940 175,000 companies produced 70 percent of American manufactured goods, in March 1943 100 companies produced 70 percent.

The trend was to ever bigger companies. In 1939 firms with fewer than 500 workers employed 52 percent of those engaged in manufacturing; firms with over 10,000 workers employed 13 percent of those engaged in manufacturing. In 1944 firms with fewer than 500 workers employed 38 percent of those engaged in manufacturing; firms with over 10,000 workers employed 31 percent of those engaged in manufacturing. Whereas in 1940 corporate profit was $6.4 billion, in 1944 corporate profit was $10.8 billion.

Another direct consequence of the federal government's control of the war effort and the battle for production was its dramatic and rapid increase in personnel. During the New Deal, the federal government's manpower increased by 60 percent. During World War II the number of people employed in federal agencies increased by 300 percent.

What was true for industry was also true for agriculture. World War II finally and irreversibly transformed farming into a large business enterprise. Farmers used larger amounts of fertilizer, better hybrid seeds, and improved pesticides, and they understood much more about soil conservation. New row-crop loaders for harvesting carrots, onions, potatoes, and beets almost entirely displaced the old stoop labor in the fields. The Bureau of the Census took a sample count in 1945 and discovered a pronounced trend toward fewer, but much larger, farms. Farming was now agribusiness. No other group prospered more from the war than the farmers. This is somewhat ironic for, between 1940 and 1945, farm population fell by 17 percent. The productivity of each individual involved in agriculture, however, rose by 25 percent. The increase was largely on account of mechanization, fertilization, and the consolidation of small holdings into larger units of production. As a result, in 1945 the income of America's farmers was 250 percent higher than it had been in 1939.

Mobilization, airplanes, and armory provided the human resources and equipment to fight the war. What was needed was skillful Allied strategy to apply human and material resources to defeat Hitler and the Japanese.

Arcadian Allies: All for One

The first wartime conference between Roosevelt, Churchill, and their military advisers was the Arcadia Conference, held in Washington from December 22, 1941, until January 14, 1942. At Arcadia, FDR and Churchill reaffirmed their strategy that the war against Germany must and would take precedence over the war against Japan. The reasoning was this: even if Italy or Japan were defeated, the main threat to world peace, Germany, could survive. With Germany defeated, the Axis would be destroyed. The Americans and the British also agreed at Arcadia that, because of shortages of men, munitions, and supplies, they would adopt a different strategy toward Japan. The Allies would fight a holding operation in defense of the Malay barrier, Burma, and Australia until reinforcements became available and the U.S. program of naval construction was more productive. However, the original defense perimeter collapsed in the face of the Japanese advance in early 1942 and, with it, the original strategy.

In fact, the months following Pearl Harbor proved to be a period of great turmoil for the Anglo-Americans because Japan was winning the war. On December 10, 1941, Japanese aircraft sank the pride of the British Far East Fleet, the *Prince of Wales* and the *Repulse* off Manila. On December 22, 1941, Japanese forces landed in Ligaya Gulf, Luzon, in the Philippines. On December 23 U.S. forces surrendered at Wake Island. On December 25 Hong Kong fell. On January 24 the Japanese occupied Borneo and Celebes. The surrender of Singapore by General Perceval and of sixty thousand British troops to General Yamashita on February 15, 1942, was a catastrophe from which British prestige

FACING PAGE:

Once German armies struck across Europe,
the Nazis began their planned elimination of European Jewry in earnest
Above: Mass execution of Russian Jews by *Einsatzgruppen* of the advancing German army. The first slaughters were by shooting. (Library of Congress)
Below: Nazi police chief and head of the SS, Heinrich Himmler (*center*), was on hand to oversee the evacuation of citizens who were Jewish from the French town of Metz in summer 1940. Although Himmler could not stand the sight of blood, it was he who supervised the systematic genocide of European Jews in twenty concentration camps in Nazi-held countries. (Library of Congress)

never recovered in the Far East. On February 27 and 28, the Allied fleet lost eleven of fourteen vessels in action with Japanese warships in the Java Sea. On March 9 Japan occupied Java.

But it was the Philippines, stretching almost 1,110 miles to Borneo, that were the key to Japanese hegemony over Southeast Asia, being directly astride the principal trade routes to the Netherlands East Indies (NEI). American prestige had been bound to the Philippines ever since its war with Spain in 1898.

In the Hare-Cuttings Act of December 29, 1932, Congress, scared by the Japanese invasion of Manchuria in 1931 and wanting to abandon any problem that could lead to friction, had provided for the complete independence of the Philippines after ten years. Congress passed it over President Herbert Hoover's veto, but the Filipinos themselves rejected it on October 17, 1933. They objected to U.S. military and naval bases on the islands. Advised by President Franklin Roosevelt to eliminate the clauses about bases, Congress then provided independence in a revised form in the Tydings-McDuffie Act of May 24, 1934. The islands were to remain a semiautonomous commonwealth until July 4, 1946, when they would become the Philippine Republic. Japan's successes in 1941 and 1942 turned these plans to ashes.

Gen. Douglas MacArthur originally tried to prevent Japanese landings on Luzon, but he lacked enough airplanes and ships. He thought war would not come until April 1942. Many Filipino units disintegrated after the Japanese invasion. Strong Japanese forces moved to the capital, Manila, from the north and east. MacArthur decided to remove all troops from Manila. Beginning on December 27, 1941, he concentrated all available U.S. forces on the Bataan peninsula on the west side of Manila Bay and made the island of Corregidor in Manila Bay his headquarters. U.S. troops and Filipino Army Scout units fought to delay the Japanese conquest of the archipelago, but their supply ships were sunk by the enemy. By January 1942 they were running out of food and drugs. FDR ordered MacArthur to quit Corregidor on March 11, 1942. MacArthur escaped—but only just—via a torpedo boat. He vowed to return to the Philippines in triumph. On April 8, 1942, 12,500 Americans and 60,000 Filipinos surrendered unconditionally at Bataan—the greatest number of men ever surrendered by an American commander. On May 6, 1942, Corregidor fell with the surrender of 11,000 U.S. troops and 50,000 Filipinos.

For the Filipinos and other conquered peoples in Asia and the Pacific, this was not simply a matter of exchanging one imperial power for another. Deaths of prisoners at the hands of the Japanese in the Co-Prosperity Sphere ran almost ten times as high as deaths among German captives in Europe. In the Philippines General Yoshio Tsuneyoshi told his American POWs that his sole interest was in dead Americans; he and other commanders began a regime of unrelenting brutality.

According to Japan's most intransigent critics, Japan caused the deaths of 35 million people in the period 1931–45, put 200,000 Asian women into sexual servitude, and abused Chinese, Korean, and Allied prisoners of war in biological and chemical experiments. Most notorious were the activities of Unit 371 in Manchuria. They injected prisoners with deadly viruses and inflicted other forms of medical experimentation upon them. Perhaps 37 percent of American POWs held by the Japanese in 1942–45 died in captivity, compared with, at most, 2 percent of POWs held in German camps.

After their rout from the Philippines, pushed back in successive stages, U.S. forces made the defense of Samoa and Hawaii their top priority. They tried to hold the line protecting sea and air communications with Australia and New Zealand. In the north, the Japanese air force bombed Dutch Harbor and Alaska, and Japanese industry seized the islands of Attu and Kiska in the Western Aleutians. In Southeast Asia Japanese troops moved easily and quickly through Thailand and into Burma. Once they captured Mandalay, they severed the Burma Road supply route to China. In the extreme south Japanese troops invaded British North Borneo and seized its oil fields. They also landed in New Guinea and Rabaul in New Britain. Japanese ships carried troops to Java in the NEI and completely destroyed a combined fleet of U.S., British, Australian, and Dutch cruisers and destroyers in the Battle of Java Sea of February 27, 1942. Having captured the NEI, Japan consolidated its gains in New Britain, the Gilbert and Admiralty Islands, and parts of New Guinea. The Japanese even bombed the naval base of Port Darwin, Australia.

With the exception of the central Pacific, which was an American preserve, the American and English allies fought as one team across all fronts. Britain assumed decisive responsibility for the Middle East and the Far East apart from China. The United States took chief responsibility for the Pacific theater, which also included Australia and China. The invasion of, and battle for, Western Europe was a combined operation.

At the Arcadia Conference in Washington in January 1942, FDR assured Churchill that, despite the U.S. armed forces' own demand for supplies, lend-lease deliveries to the Allies would not be reduced, whatever the danger from German ships. As to their own supplies, the U.S. services refused to define their needs precisely. However, Britain had to justify every claim to matériel, unlike Russia, which was given every demand up to the limit of available supplies and carrying capacity. The total U.S. expenditure on lend-lease was $43.61 billion, of which Britain and the Empire received $30.07 billion. Britain contributed £1.89 billion to reciprocal aid, of which the United States received £1.20 billion, or $5.66 billion—almost a quarter of what was provided by lend-lease.

However, despite subsequent differences of opinion and application, at Arcadia the United States and Britain merged more fully for war than any two cobelligerent countries had ever done and far more than Germany and Japan, which had no coordinated strategy. At Arcadia FDR and Churchill also defined their war aims by issuing the Declaration of the United Nations on January 1, 1942, reaffirming their commitment to the purposes and principles set out in the Atlantic Charter. FDR coined the term "United Nations." Initially, twenty-six nations fighting the Axis signed the declaration and another twenty nations joined during the war. In the declaration they pledged that they would accept the principles of the Atlantic Charter and not sign any separate peace treaty with the common enemies.

Despite the amicable agreement about Germany first, Churchill and his generals were reluctant to fight Germany head-on in northwest Europe. Instead, Churchill favored a series of diversionary operations around the periphery of Hitler's Europe, with bombing raids on Germany itself. In addition, he wanted to encourage resistance movements against the Nazis in occupied countries by providing war matériel and other supplies—even though the resistance movements were mainly left-wing or communist movements. However, Churchill also wanted Britain to maintain a strong presence in the Mediterranean Sea.

Major Alexander de Seversky of the United States and Air Chief Marshal Sir Arthur ("Bomber") Harris of the United Kingdom popularized the idea that Germany could be reduced to a state of confusion and would then collapse on account of aerial bombardment. In fact, Harris's set of offensives were largely public relations exercises intended to impress the American and British peoples. Neither Lübeck (bombed on March 28, 1942) nor Rostock (April 24–27) was important in the German economy. They were medieval towns with many timber buildings that burned well. On May 30 Harris caused a sensation when he sent a thousand bombers over to Cologne. In time, Harris's American counterpart, the commander of U.S. Strategic Air Force Europe, Gen. Carl Spaatz, came to share his faith in aerial bombardment and thought that an invasion of northwest Europe was unnecessary.

Torch, the Anglo-American amphibious invasion of North Africa, was set for November 1942. By destroying German forces there, the Allies hoped to free the Mediterranean for their shipping and to provide themselves with a key base from which to attack Italy and occupied France. Thus, the invasion of North Africa and of Italy and occupied France would also assure Stalin that the United States and Britain were taking the offensive on a second front. Furthermore, Germany would have to divert military and air resources from the Russian front and northern France in order to rescue Italy from disaster. A North African campaign would not only be a substitute for a second front but also a preparation for it.

A second influential strategic decision following upon Arcadia was to make the Middle East the focus of Britain's military effort. There were two wars in the Middle East: the first was the war against Italy in Libya and Ethiopia up to 1940; the second was the war against Germany in 1941 and 1942, extending from the war in North Africa, especially Egypt.

Britain had been preeminent in the Middle East until World War II. Now, whoever controlled North Africa had an outsize chance of winning the prizes of Greece, the Mediterranean, and Middle East oil. The outcome largely depended on which armies could best withstand disease, notably an epidemic of malaria in Egypt in 1942–44, and which armies could maintain impenetrable lines of supply of such precious commodities as cereals, as much as it did on victory in

battle. The outcome also depended on the way that Britain and Germany responded to various independence movements in Egypt, Iran, Palestine, and India.

Already, British troops in North Africa had been forced to retreat by the
German Afrika Corps, brilliantly led by Field Marshal Erwin Rommel, "the Desert Fox." Mussolini went to Libya, expecting to lead a triumphal entry into Cairo
on a white horse. On July 25, 1942, Rommel tried, and failed, to break through
British lines at El Alamein. The British Eighth Army was responding to new
leadership by Lt. Gen. Bernard L. ("Monty") Montgomery. His troops were dug
in along defensive lines at El Alamein, about sixty-five miles from Alexandria
and the Suez Canal, the essential water route to Asia. Monty had been prepared
to wait for several months until he had accumulated enough men and matériel,
including four hundred American Sherman tanks, before striking back. Then in
twelve days, from October 23 to November 4, 1942, the British Eighth Army
routed Rommel's forces and sent them stumbling back in disorder in the momentous battle of El Alamein, a decisive turning point in the war. This was three
days before Operation Torch, the Anglo-American invasion of North Africa.

Operation Torch began with an attack not on Germany but on France, America's oldest ally. Starting November 8, 1942, about two hundred thousand U.S.
troops, led by Lt. Gen. Dwight D. ("Ike") Eisenhower, disembarked at Casablanca on the Atlantic coast of French Morocco and at Algiers and Oran on the
Mediterranean coast of Algeria. They soon seized Oran and Algiers. At Casablanca French forces resisted them for several days. Eisenhower convinced the
ranking Vichy officer, Adm. Jean François Darlan, to cooperate with the Allies.
On December 1 Darlan ordered all French forces to end their resistance. Darlan's
new position as French chief of all North Africa was bitterly resented by those
who knew him as a fascist and a virulent Anglophobe. Nevertheless, Eisenhower
knew that Darlan's cooperation had saved him many casualties. FDR and Churchill agreed. Both leaders tried to convince the public by issuing none-too-
convincing statements on the necessity of temporary expedients in wartime.
When Darlan was assassinated on December 24, 1942, the Americans began a
search for another figurehead with whom pro-Ally French could identify. With
the strong backing of the British, maverick and egotistical Gen. Charles de Gaulle
put forward his own case. At first, he and Gen. Henri Giraud established themselves as coleaders in North Africa. But De Gaulle outmaneuvered his naive
colleague, who withdrew.

Having realized their initial objectives, U.S. forces were to march eastward
and meet with Montgomery's Eighth Army. Hitler and Mussolini provided Rommel with massive reinforcements from Italy and Sicily, and he struck at the U.S.
forces. Montgomery and his British and Commonwealth troops were also moving in on Rommel from the east. By May 1943 the German and Italian forces
were trapped. Rommel himself escaped, but the Allies captured more than
250,000 enemy soldiers and eliminated the Axis from North Africa.

FDR and Churchill now met at a conference in January 14–25, 1943, in

Casablanca. They discussed where next to apply the pressure against Germany. The American staff, led by Gen. George C. Marshall, restated their earlier commitment to a cross-Channel expedition, while the British argued for an extension of Mediterranean operations. In the end, they compromised. They would continue to build up forces in Britain for an invasion in spring 1944. They would also continue operations in North Africa, with Sicily as the next target for invasion. They set no precise dates for either operation, partly because any invasion of Europe depended first on Allied victory in the Battle of the Atlantic. For, despite American fears to the contrary, it was not operations in the Mediterranean that were delaying the invasion of Western Europe. It was the U-boats' offensive in the Atlantic and difficulties in transportation and supply.

The Allies made three important decisions at Casablanca. First, the CCS gave top priority to winning the Battle of the Atlantic. Second, the British accepted the division of the Pacific theater into two zones. Furthermore, they agreed to leave all future strategic decisions in this theater to the American Joint Chiefs of Staff. Third, FDR announced that the Allies would fight on until they received the unconditional surrender of the Axis powers. He did so partly to dispel Stalin's fear that, in the aftermath of the Clark-Darlan agreement, the Allies would make a deal with Hitler, and partly to avoid the sort of situation existing after World War I when Germany had claimed that Western politicians had misused the armistice as a basis for a punitive peace.

On the eastern front the great thrust of German forces in Russia in summer and fall 1941 met a mix of ferocious Russian resistance and just about the worst winter weather and snow in fifty years. Thwarted at Leningrad in the north and at Moscow in the center, Hitler decided to drive German troops to the south. His immediate objective was to capture the oil fields of the Caucasus and the key area of the lower Volga River. Thus, he sent a large force of three hundred thousand under Field Marshal Friederich von Paulus to take Stalingrad, a vital strategic point on the west bank of the Volga.

The siege of Stalingrad began on August 19, 1942, with an artillery bombardment that destroyed much of the city. Russian soldiers and civilians fought the Germans in the streets, houses, and ruins in a battle generally accounted the worst for face-to-face slaughter in the entire war. On November 23, 1942, they succeeded in halting the Germans, whom Hitler forbade to retreat, even for essential regrouping. Despite heavy snowstorms, the Russians counterattacked the German Sixth Army in two deep pincer operations. They gradually succeeded in cutting it off. On January 31, 1943, von Paulus surrendered the tattered remnants of the once-mighty Sixth Army that had subdued Belgium and Holland in 1940. This was the first major defeat of German forces in the war. Yet Russia lost more men in this one titanic struggle than the United States was to lose in all theaters.

At the Trident talks, held in Washington from May 12–25, 1943, the British again proposed to extend action in the Mediterranean. As Churchill argued, a successful invasion of Sicily would precipitate the collapse of the Italian government. He won his point. However, Gen. George C. Marshall demanded, and gained, certain concessions. First, operations in the Mediterranean were in no way to delay the invasion of Europe, now code named Overlord. Second, the Allies set May 1, 1944, as the date for the invasion. Third, the Allies agreed to assemble twenty-nine divisions in England in preparation for this. Seven of the divisions were to come from the Mediterranean theater. The sudden entry of numerous GIs into Britain was another factor contributing to the dislocation of the island kingdom during the war. The common British cry about the Yanks was that they were "overpaid, overscxed, and over here."

The invasion of Sicily, code named Husky, was the largest amphibian operation of the early years of the war. It included the U.S. Seventh Army under Gen. George S. Patton, Jr., the British Eighth Army under Gen. Bernard L. Montgomery, several Canadian units, large air forces, and both U.S. and British paratroops. Most of the ships were British. Patton took the capital, Palermo, in the northwest, on July 22, 1943, and the Allies then entered Messina, in the northeast. All resistance to them in Sicily ended on August 17, 1943. King Victor Emmanuel III of Italy now deposed Prime Minister Mussolini. Unfortunately for both the invaders and the Italian people, the Allies did not exploit the fall of dictator Mussolini fast enough politically. The king appointed Marshal Pietro Badoglio, a devious old soldier, as head of a new government. Badoglio played a double game, trying to convince the Allies that Italy deserved something better than unconditional surrender, while trying to maintain an impression before German forces that Italy was still committed to its old partner. The Germans had enough time to move extra forces into Italy. The Allies could only land, crablike, in the extreme south. As a result of Badoglio's duplicity, negotiations between Italy and the Allies dragged on for several weeks. Eisenhower, now exasperated beyond measure, began to bring pressure on Badoglio by bombarding Rome and other cities. On September 3, 1943, Badoglio agreed to surrender, although the formal announcement was delayed until September 29, after the full Allied invasion of mainland Italy.

In Italy, the Allies made heavy military commitments and gained very little, although they did tie down twenty-one German divisions that might have helped Hitler elsewhere. German troops outnumbered the Allies in Italy eight to one, and the combination of German and Italian troops outnumbered the Allied troops twenty to one. As Eisenhower and his armies began to move northward, the Germans found they could defend the Italian terrain with its mountainous spine and meandering rivers farther north. The Germans gave clear notice that they would fight to the last by a daring commando raid led by Col. Otto Skorzeny on September 9, 1943, on the mountain town where the deposed Mussolini was being held prisoner. They sprang him free on September 12 and carried him farther north to Salo, where, beginning September 15, he led a new Fascist regime. It was in effect a puppet government under German supervision. Mussolini's function was to legitimize Italian resistance to the Allies in the south.

On October 13 Italy declared war on Germany. When the corrupt government of Badoglio secured its preferred terms with the Allies, its Fascist leaders preserved the monarchy and retained administrative control of Italy. But now they were backed by an Allied Control Council that pointedly excluded Russia. Stalin protested the deal at first. He soon recognized its value as a precedent to justify his own operations in Eastern Europe.

Earlier in the war, while Sicily was being secured, the Allies met in Quebec at the Quadrant Conference of August 14–24, 1943, to decide future strategy. It was here that the conflict of opinions concerning Overlord and the Mediterranean theater came to a head. It was here, also, that it was resolved. After moving into the Aegean Sea, Churchill hoped to use an attack by Allied troops on Rhodes and other Dodecanese islands to persuade Italian garrisons in Greece, Yugoslavia, and the Aegean islands to join the fight to drive the Germans from the Balkans. Churchill argued that if the Allies captured Rhodes, then they could use it as a base to bomb German communications and Romanian oil fields and to supply partisans in Yugoslavia and Greece. They could also supply the USSR through the Dardanelles. The Americans, who dominated the conference table, started to say no to British demands for diversionary operations. When Churchill went ahead with his Balkans operation, beginning with a landing on the German-held island of Kos, the result was a debacle from which the British, dependent on U.S. aid, extricated themselves with difficulty.

In the summer of 1943 the Allies finally turned the tide against the U-boats in the Atlantic. March 1943 was the worst month of either world war, with 47,000 tons of shipping sunk and only twelve German submarines destroyed in the North Atlantic. In July there was a dramatic change; 123,000 tons of shipping were sunk, but thirty-seven U-boats were destroyed. In the last three months of 1943 146,000 tons of shipping and fifty-three U-boats were sunk. There were many reasons for this sudden shift in Allied fortunes. The United States had produced a flood of destroyers for convoy—260 in 1943. Britain diverted bombers to escort duties and to attack U-boats in the Bay of Biscay. Then the United States began to use aircraft carriers for escort. Portugal allowed Britain and the United States to use the Azores as an airbase and thus close the gap in the mid-Atlantic. Two British midget submarines badly damaged Germany's only battleship, the *Tirpitz*, on September 23, 1943, at Alten Fjord. The *Duke of York* sank Germany's only remaining battle cruiser, the *Scharnhorst*, on December 26. Britain could now greatly increase its imports. This was essential for the Allies since Britain could no longer maintain itself from its own resources. In 1941 America supplied 10 percent of the munitions for the British Empire; in 1944 it supplied 28.7 percent.

As to the war in the skies, because the Americans and the British could not agree, there were two separate air offensives in 1943 and early 1944. The Americans believed their heavily armed bombers could operate in daylight against precise targets. They failed, partly because their Flying Fortresses could not match the German fighters. "Bomber" Harris wanted the United States to join in the British night attacks. The Americans thought differently and wanted a major air battle against the Luftwaffe. Harris continued to concentrate on in-discriminate bombing. Experts concluded that the damage to German war pro-duction by Allied bombing was, at most, 9 percent, while the demands of bombing on Allied war production were far greater—about 15 percent in the United States and around 25 percent in Britain. By March 1944 Harris had to admit that the rising scale of casualties inflicted by German night fighters made further attacks on the present model impossible. Harris's days were over. The United States had perfected a long-range fighter airplane that could take on the Luftwaffe in direct combat. Moreover, the time for invading northern France was drawing nearer. However, the otherwise wasteful and ineffective bombing of Germany had one useful side effect. As the bombings downed numerous German planes and German pilots, it helped give the Allies superiority in the air, something that would be useful in the invasion of Normandy in 1944.

Over the Dam

U.S. strategy in Asia was to expel the Japanese, to forestall the revival of Eu-ropean imperialism, and to encourage the growth of democratic capitalism—and to do all of these at once without placing U.S. soldiers in great danger. Whatever his long-term goals for American foreign policy in Asia, FDR could not get the United States onto mainland Asia because it simply did not have sufficient manpower to wage a large-scale war on land in Asia while it was heavily engaged in Europe. The odds against complete American success proved insurmountable in China, Indochina, and North Korea.

The U.S. Navy began the war in the Pacific with obsolete charts. Some sea battles were abandoned because no one knew where the bottom of the ocean was. The Marine Corps had to survey the Solomon Islands as they fought for them. They began on the wrong river, thinking it was the Tenaru when it was in fact the Hu. Until the war in the Pacific, such islands as Wake, Midway, and Iwo Jima had had little value. The wide use of aircraft now made them strate-gically valuable.

Continuing his seemingly inexorable advance upon Australia, the Japanese admiral, Yamamoto, a strategist of genius, was determined to engage and destroy the U.S. Pacific fleet. He was aware that he had to do this before U.S. production of fighting ships reached its peak and gave the United States numerical supremacy in the Pacific. He failed. At the battle of the Coral Sea of May 7 and 8, 1942, a numerically inferior U.S. fleet, under the command of Rear Adm. Jack Fletcher, fought the Japanese to a standstill and halted their advance upon Australia. The battle of the Coral Sea was the first naval battle in which opposing forces at-tacked each other entirely by air strikes. Now the Japanese had to abandon plans to land troops at Port Moresby in Netherlands New Guinea—the base shielding Australia from an attack from the air and possible invasion.

Admiral Yamamoto then assembled all the naval resources at his disposal and threw them forward in an attack upon Midway Island, the proposed staging post for future attacks upon Pearl Harbor and the Hawaiian chain. U.S. bombers first attacked the enemy fleet and transport ships without suffering much damage. Realizing that the Japanese carriers must refuel and rearm their planes, Adm. Raymond A. Spruance then used torpedo and dive bombers from the carriers *Hornet* and *Enterprise* to hit the Japanese again before they could get their planes in the air. Although most of the slower torpedo bombers were shot down, the dive bombers inflicted heavy damages and many casualties. Three Japanese carriers were destroyed or sunk with their planes still on deck, and a fourth carrier was badly damaged. Over the next four days, successive U.S. action from army bombers stationed on Midway continued to inflict losses on the Japanese. The United States lost only the *Yorktown* and one destroyer. Once again, naval forces engaged one another only through the air.

Despite this signal victory, the Anglo-American side knew that time was still against them. However, the following battle of Midway of June 4–7, 1942, was an overwhelming victory for the United States. Yamamoto withdrew. A superior Japanese force had been outmaneuvered at sea and air, humiliated by heavy damage and numerous casualties. Nonetheless, the Japanese continued their advance upon Australia. By July 23, 1942, Japanese forces were established at Buna and Gona on the north coast of New Guinea. They were also rapidly constructing airfields at Guadalcanal in the Solomon Islands. This was to be their springboard for an assault upon the forward Allied base at Espiritu Santo.

The war in the Pacific was as much a war on land as it was a war in the air and on sea—and a particularly blood-soaked affair at that. Adm. Ernest J. King directed the invasion of Guadalcanal, an inspired choice that changed the course of the Pacific war. On August 7, 1942, the First U.S. Marine Division landed in the Tulagi-Guadalcanal area, intending to overrun the airstrips and clear the zone of Japanese forces. The two sides fought seven major naval engagements as each strove to reinforce their land forces. In addition, the American landing drew Japanese forces away from their campaign across New Guinea and toward Australia, thereby lightening the Australian load. On Guadalcanal U.S. Marines managed to hold their ground and gradually forced the Japanese to retreat.

Like the battles of Stalingrad and El Alamein, the battle of Guadalcanal acquired a psychological significance beyond its immediate strategic importance. In each of these battles, the adversaries fielded huge forces. The Japanese were forced to evacuate their forces from Guadalcanal on February 9, 1943. Worse, they lost control of the flow of battle.

By now the U.S. military had turned their attention to planning offensive operations in the Pacific. After long and detailed discussions, Adm. Ernest J. King and Gen. George C. Marshall reached a compromise on the division of responsibility in, and offensive strategy for, the Pacific theater. Gen. Douglas MacArthur became commander in chief of the southwest Pacific area, and Adm. Chester W. Nimitz became commander in chief of the central Pacific zone.

In essence, Admirals Ernest J. King and Chester W. Nimitz were disciples of the nineteenth-century American naval historian Alfred T. Mahan. They wanted victory at sea by a single concentrated strategy—to pursue, encounter, and destroy the Japanese fleet in the Pacific. However, Japanese naval strategy was not predicated on command of the sea by naval power alone, but rather on dominating a stretch of ocean and its numerous, varied islands by a mix of land, sea, and air power. Thus, had they persisted in their original aim of victory at sea alone, the King-Nimitz strategy would have resulted in a stalemate through mismatch. It was to his everlasting credit that MacArthur hit upon the far more sophisticated strategy of island hopping, thereby leaving the enemy to wither on the vine and setting in motion a campaign that devastated the Japanese oceanic empire.

By itself, island-hopping did not bring the army and navy closer to the Japanese home islands. It gave the United States control of unimportant Pacific islands. Naval strategists wanted to bypass the Philippines altogether. They considered the archipelago not worth the effort of invasion. Although MacArthur had a strong personal desire to return to the islands that he had said he would return to in triumph, he also thought it would be foolish for the United States to attempt a land war in Asia. This made it more important to control the offshore islands, the Philippines and Japan. Moreover, if the United States avoided the Philippines, then Hukbalahap, a Communist-led guerilla organization, might seize control.

The JCS decided at the Pacific Military Conference in Washington in March 1943 that Nimitz and a predominantly naval force should secure the Marshall and Gilbert Islands and then take the Marianas. Simultaneously, MacArthur and the bulk of U.S. Army forces in the Pacific would begin clearing the enemy out of New Guinea, first, then New Britain, and finally the Solomon Islands. The two forces were to converge for an attack upon either the Philippines or Formosa. After Guadalcanal, there was a five-month lull in fighting before the proposed American offensive began. Then on June 30, 1943, MacArthur launched Operation Cartwheel, a series of amphibious operations against the Japanese in the south and southwest Pacific toward the Solomon Islands. By the end of July 1943 the U.S. Navy had won command of the seas around the central Solomons. U.S. land forces began a successful advance, aimed at clearing New Guinea and New Britain and securing the main passage from the Coral Sea, through the Bismarck barrier, to the western Pacific.

Meanwhile, Admiral Nimitz was successful in the central Pacific. Having secured the Gilbert Islands in November 1943, he invaded Kwajalein and other islands in the Marshall group on January 31, 1944. By February 5, 1944, U.S. troops were dispensing with the last vestiges of Japanese resistance on Kwajalein Atoll.

The dark and dank jungle defined battle in the South Pacific. It proved almost impenetrable and hampered military maneuver as it limited deployment of machine guns. Everything rested on the foot soldiers, moving in small patrols, offering themselves as human sacrifices to elicit sniper fire that would identify pockets of Japanese resistance. Americans, Australians, and Japanese all fought mercilessly, and the fight was barbarous. The Australians' skill surpassed that of the Japanese, who were blinded by their cult of death rather than surrender.

The war in Asia extended beyond the Pacific. Political considerations partly determined U.S. military strategy. FDR wanted Britain to leave its Raj in India. Moreover, he had no intention of allowing the French to reclaim their colonial possessions in Indochina. He wanted to see Asia decolonized by means of a trusteeship system that would eventually bring independence to the various indigenous populations.

The United States invested its greatest hopes in China. FDR hoped that the Nationalist Party, the Guomindong, would transform China into a flourishing industrial and democratic state, a beneficent source of raw materials, and a pliant market. This could come about only if the corrupt Guomindong reformed itself and engaged in liberal policies. But FDR and his U.S. advisers in China started with false hopes. They assumed that Nationalist leader Chiang Kai-shek (Jiang Jeshi) was a reformer, whereas the autocratic Chiang neither wanted reform nor could he provide it. The United States made huge cash loans to China that were, in effect, bribes to Chiang to continue the fight against Japan.

FDR needed Chiang's army to tie down the maximum number of Japanese troops, both to relieve pressure on beleaguered U.S. forces in the Pacific theater, and to give them time to launch other offensives. But in the corrupt Guomindong of Chiang Kai-shek, senior officers idled in luxury while the enlisted men went without shoes and suffered privation and disease. That was not all. China still suffered the threat of civil war from the Communists led by Mao Zedong. Such division alone might well give Japan victory. FDR tried to persuade rival leaders Chiang and Mao to cooperate, and he advised Chiang to use some Communists in his Guomindong government. Chiang's customary response was that it was his duty to contain his internal political opponents, whereas it was the obligation of the United States to defeat Japan.

FDR had no U.S. troops to bolster the Chinese war effort. All FDR could offer was continued delivery of lend-lease supplies and a military mission under the direction of Lt.-Gen. Joseph W. ("Vinegar Joe") Stilwell. On his arrival in China in March 1942, Stilwell became chief of staff to Chiang. Chiang had by then become commander in chief of the China theater. Stilwell was responsible for supervising lend-lease deliveries, increasing the effectiveness of U.S. military assistance to China, and improving the combat efficiency of the Chinese armed forces by advising them on training and tactics and rationalizing the command structure.

The situation in the China theater deteriorated in April 1942 when the Japanese overran Burma and thus cut Chiang's last line of land communication with the Allies. The Allies could now supply Chiang only by airlift. This entailed a hazardous five-hundred-mile journey from Assam in north India across the Himalayas, known as the Hump. When the shortage of supplies reached the crisis point, Stilwell decided to channel all available resources into rebuilding the Chinese army into an efficient fighting force. The decision troubled Claire Lee Chennault, a retired captain who served Chiang as adviser on aeronautical affairs and who opposed Stilwell's recommendations.

The Stilwell-Chennault difference of opinion further poisoned Sino-American relations. Because Stilwell had the ear of Gen. George C. Marshall, Chiang, who preferred Chennault, went over Marshall's head and appealed directly to FDR. FDR accepted Chiang's request and ordered the lion's share of resources to the China Air Task Force. Chennault's pilots quickly gained complete control of the skies above central China and began bombing Japanese positions in the previously unassailable eastern provinces. Such was the success of Chennault's strategy that, at the Cairo Conference of December 1943, FDR and Chiang agreed that the new secret weapon of the United States, the B-29 Superfortress, be shipped to Chennault, who could use it to start bombing Japan. The first of Chennault's bombing sorties was launched on June 15, 1944. However, by then the Japanese had fulfilled Stilwell's disconcerting but accurate prophecy and had begun a land assault to capture Chennault's air bases. The Japanese began their offensive in May 1944. By June Chiang's underfed, poorly equipped, and inadequately trained troops were in full retreat.

At the Cairo Conference of November 22–26, 1943, when FDR met with Churchill and Chinese leader Chiang Kai-shek, the British and the Americans were at loggerheads over operations in the Mediterranean. Churchill wanted to extend operations in the eastern Mediterranean and thereby draw Turkey to the Allies' cause. The U.S. generals saw that as another diversionary campaign and resisted him.

Although the Cairo Conference was designed to show FDR's confidence in China as one of the four policemen of the world who could maintain the postwar peace (along with the United States, the United Kingdom, and the USSR), FDR was rapidly losing faith in Chiang and any prospect of Chinese preeminence in Asia. Americans stationed in China deepened the gloom in Washington with their reports of inefficiency, corruption, and venality within the Chinese government. These reports indicated that, far from emerging as a great power, China would face civil war in the postwar years. FDR now understood that whatever he did for Chiang would be insufficient to prevent China from falling to the Communists.

The Tehran Conference

Immediately after Cairo came the Tehran Conference of November 28 to December 1, 1943. Tehran, capital of Iran, was an obvious venue for the first conference of the Big Three—Roosevelt, Churchill, and Stalin. Iran provided a safe land route for supplies of munitions and oil between Russia and Britain. After Hitler invaded Russia in 1941 and the shah of Iran refused to expel Nazi agents from the country, Britain and Russia invaded Iran on August 25, 1941, in order to safeguard oil and supply routes. They deposed the shah and exiled him, eventually to South Africa, where he died. In his place the British promoted the crown prince, Reza Shah Pahlavi, a youth of twenty-one, to reign as their puppet. Britain and Russia maintained troops in the south and north of Iran, respectively.

The first joint meeting of the Big Three in 1943 brought home to Roosevelt and Churchill in the most forceful way possible that they would have to reconsider their own strategy in light of the basic objectives of Stalin's military strategy and foreign policy. As to his immediate wartime agenda, Stalin had to work Roosevelt and Churchill around to committing men and matériel to a second front in the West in order to take pressure off Russia in the East. As to the postwar world, Stalin was determined to create acquiescent blocs to the west of Russia. Thereby he would shield the USSR from future invasion, create economic satellites, and spread socialism wider across Europe. FDR and Churchill could not approve any communistic suppression of those liberties for which they had fought Hitler. However, their harsh experiences in World War II had made them realize that they had to find solutions that were practical.

FDR, who chaired the Tehran Conference, passed the controversial matter of diversionary wars in the Mediterranean (raised earlier at Cairo) over to Stalin. Stalin was well aware of the advantage of a strategy that would widen operations in the Mediterranean and bring Turkey more fully into the war. It would enable the USSR to receive urgent supplies through the Dardanelles. However, Stalin's fundamental objective was to win an unequivocal commitment from the British and the Americans to a second front in Western Europe. The two Allies promised a cross-Channel invasion in May 1944—Operation Overlord. This was the major agreement of the Tehran Conference, one that Stalin and the U.S. generals succeeded in imposing on Roosevelt as well as on Churchill. Churchill won approval for an amphibious landing behind the German defensive screen in Italy. However, the Americans exacted a price. They insisted that, after the Italian campaign, troops and landing craft would be used in an amphibious assault on southern France.

Stalin repeatedly asked FDR and Churchill to agree that the territories of postwar Russia should include the Baltic states, parts of Poland, Finland, and Romania, which had once belonged to czarist Russia. Stalin had reclaimed these territories in the notorious Nazi-Soviet pact with Hitler in 1939. By 1943 FDR was prepared to agree about the Baltic states, but he wanted to delay agreement on other territorial settlements until Germany had been defeated. This proved a fateful decision. By 1945 the Red Army would dominate Eastern Europe.

What the United States wanted to see was a Europe economically unified in a loose continental system. Could FDR make Stalin see things his way? Or would he simply have to accommodate himself to Russian hegemony over Eastern Europe? If Roosevelt insisted on an open economic system across Europe, his relationship with Stalin would deteriorate. As it was, Stalin distrusted Roosevelt and Churchill. Up to 1943 he even considered making a separate peace with Hitler. If FDR accepted Stalin's demands, then he would undermine the Atlantic

Charter—not to mention throwing a monkeywrench into the workings of the U.S. economy. U.S. economic prosperity depended on a healthy Europe with Eastern European countries providing the West with food and the West providing itself and Eastern Europe with industrial products.

In the meantime, the enervating Allied campaign in Italy continued against entrenched and valiant German forces in some of the fiercest battles of the war. Finally, on May 15, 1944, Hitler ordered a retreat from the Gustav line. Three days later, Polish troops entered the monastery at Monte Cassino, hitherto a stronghold of German resistance. On May 23, 1944, the Allies at last broke out at Anzio.

The Italian campaign was most bitter. Richard Lamb recounts (1994) how the Germans continued to persecute Italy's Jews and even attacked the Italian army, interning six hundred thousand Italian soldiers in German slave-labor camps and killing many thousands of others in Greece, Albania, and Yugoslavia. Rome finally fell to the Allies at midnight on June 4, 1944. This should have caused a sensation across the world, but it was eclipsed by the landing of Allied armies in northern France. By then the brutal Italian campaign was—as the U.S. generals had always intended it to be—a sideshow.

Tightening the Noose in Europe

At the Cairo Conference the Allies had appointed Dwight D. ("Ike") Eisenhower, then chief of the War Plans Division, as supreme Allied commander for the invasion of Western Europe.

Eisenhower's distinctive and special talents for war by coalition lay in his ability to work with varied temperaments among commanding officers and to devise a cohesive strategy. His campaigns were well planned with wisely modulated tactics. Ike, inwardly a cold man, was outwardly the average American's idea of what a U.S. soldier should be—fair-minded and canny, modest and alert. His relaxations were golf, stealing objets d'art from great European houses at which he stayed on his successful drive to Germany, and his dalliance with British chauffeuse Kay Summersby Morgan, whom he found more spirited than his wife, the dour alcoholic Mamie Doud. On February 8, 1944, Allied headquarters confirmed the plan for Operation Overlord. Supposedly, Churchill wanted to take part personally and only refrained when King George VI said something like, "Well, if you're going, then I am going, too."

The Anglo-Americans originally set D-day for June 5, 1944. However, Ike decided to postpone the invasion on account of foul weather. On June 6, 600 warships and 4,000 supporting craft set sail to escort 176,000 Allied troops to the Normandy beaches. The British Second Army was to land on the eastern section of the Normandy coast at beaches named Gold, Juno, and Sword. The U.S. First Army under Lt. Gen. Omar Bradley was to land on the peninsula farther west at beaches named Omaha and Utah. The success of the invasion was not a foregone conclusion. The German armies had mined the beaches, laid traps under the shallow waters of the beach approaches, and built concrete emplacements to permit a deadly crossfire.

Three key factors brought success to the invasion of France. First, by spring 1944 the Allied air force enjoyed a superiority of planes over the Luftwaffe of thirty to one. For six weeks before D-day the Anglo-Americans had hammered German defenses and lines of communication from the air. Then, during the Normandy landings, Allied aircraft provided essential cover while the invaders on the ground established beachheads. The Allies flew more than eleven thousand missions on D-day. Such was Allied command of the skies that not one plane was lost to the Luftwaffe, which Hitler had failed to rebuild after earlier battles in the skies.

Second, by carrying out a complex campaign of disinformation, the Allies were able to deceive Hitler into thinking that a major army group under Gen. George Patton's command would launch the invasion at the Pas de Calais. The Germans concentrated their main body there to receive the supposed assault, leaving a meager fourteen divisions to defend the Normandy beaches. Thus, at Utah beach the U.S. Seventh Corps met with little resistance and lost only twelve men during D-day.

Third, the sheer weight of Allied forces quickly delivered from air and sea and the strategic sealing off of the army by airborne troops dropped behind beach defenses—both played a vital part in this success. By contrast, German organization suffered from divided chains of command and the irrational, counterproductive orders of the megalomaniac Führer. In the first week of the campaign the Allies landed 326,000 men, 50,000 vehicles, and more than 100,000 tons of supplies in Normandy. They established a beachhead fifty miles in length and from five to fifteen miles in depth. Nevertheless, many of the men on the ground found themselves facing terrifying odds—under fire, dazed, wounded, surrounded by the bodies of their friends.

Whatever their danger and their fears, the GIs knew what to do, because they had been trained to a point where they did not have to think about every action. At the end of July Patton's Third Army had broken out of Normandy. The battle for France began. On August 20, 1944, the Third Army established a bridgehead across the Seine. With victory in France in sight, Gen. Charles de Gaulle, now the acknowledged leader of the Free French, hastened to Paris to establish himself as head of a coalition of resistance groups. The Allies liberated Paris on August 25, 1944. By the fall of 1944 there were over 2 million Allied soldiers in France—three-fifths of them Americans. On September 1, 1944, U.S. forces crossed the Meuse; on September 3, 1944, the British Second Army liberated Brussels; and the next day the Second Army marched to Antwerp. On September 11, 1944, the U.S. First Army crossed the German frontier near Aachen.

With the Allied forces firmly established in northern France, Churchill argued that Operation Anvil, the invasion of southern France, was now superfluous. Churchill and chief of Imperial General Staff General Brooke believed that by

Illustrator Rea Irwin's cover for a *New Yorker* of July 15, 1944 depicts the Anglo-American invasion of Normandy as a Bayeux Tapestry in reverse with King George VI, FDR, and Churchill sending instructions to Generals Monty and Ike, who dispatch American troops to France on D-day, bypassing Bayeux, to confront Goebbels, Goering, and Hitler, cowering in the bunker in Berlin. The original Bayeux Tapestry of the eleventh century depicted, in serial form, William the Conqueror's successful invasion of England in 1066. (Library of Congress)

abruptly curtailing the current Italian campaign, the Allies would lose the opportunity to expel the Germans from northern Italy, the Adriatic, and the Balkans. Nevertheless, in early July 1944 Churchill, obliged to follow FDR's wishes, reluctantly gave orders to the British commander in Italy to divert some forces for an attack on southern France on August 15, 1944. The invaders seized the vital ports of Marseilles, Toulon, and Nice. Supported by Free French forces resistance fighters, the Allies moved northward to Lyons and Dijon.

Among the American bombardiers in Anvil was twenty-year-old Joseph Heller of Brooklyn, assigned to a squadron on the west coast of Corsica. In ten months he flew sixty missions. In the beginning, Heller rejoiced in the exploding black puffs of smoke that were flak. But things turned sour on his thirty-seventh mission when it was his own plane that was going down: "I heard a shell explode, and, right after that, we began to drop. And I was paralyzed. That was fear. And I thought, *I'm going down, like that other plane there....* I heard a guy on the intercom, 'Help the bombardier!' So I said, 'I *am* the bombardier!' " Such was the setting that inspired Heller to write his surreal *Catch-22* (1961), the most famous novel set in World War II and among the most experimental in form.

Within six weeks of the breakout from Normandy, the Allies had cleared France, north and south, of German forces. Stalin ordered the strong French Communist party to cooperate with de Gaulle and the Allies in establishing a government, rather than to try to seize power itself. Stalin wanted Eastern Europe, and he needed U.S. help to gain it far more than he needed the nuisance of Communism in France.

Although the Anglo-Americans could see an end to the war in Western Europe, they did not have things all their own way. Hitler unleashed a series of hitherto secret vengeance weapons. The first was the V-1 robot bomb, a small pilotless plane carrying about a ton of explosives and moving on a preset course at 350 miles per hour. The Germans first used the V-1s against London on June 13, 1944, just after the first Normandy landings. The British devised balloon barrages and increased their antiaircraft defenses to intercept the V-1s. Although only about a quarter of the eight thousand V-1 rockets reached London, they caused 6,184 deaths while wounding thousands more and destroying many buildings.

Then, beginning September 8, 1944, Hitler deployed the second vengeance weapons, the V-2 rockets. The V-2 carried its explosives at supersonic speeds and at such heights that it could be neither heard nor seen. Altogether, 5,000 V-2s were fired, of which 1,115 came down over England and 2,050 over Brussels, Antwerp, and Liège. They took 25,000 lives.

By the end of August 1944 the German army in the West was in disarray. Of the fifty-eight infantry divisions involved in action between June 6 and August 25, 1944, perhaps only twelve were now fit to stand and fight. With Hitler's reserves committed to a war of attrition on the eastern front, the road to Berlin seemed to be open. The Allies had expected the German armies to withdraw gradually, fighting a yielding, defensive action. Accordingly, the Allies had laid down plans to advance slowly on a broad front. While the Americans were to swing eastward, the British were to take the coastal route through Belgium, skirting the northern extremity of the Ardennes forest. Eventually, both wings would breach the Siegfried line at separate points and then converge to encircle the Ruhr.

Hitler's unexpected decision in July 1944 to launch all his forces against the Allies foiled their original plan. By mid-August the British commander, Gen. Bernard Montgomery, realized that if the Allies adhered to their original strategy, they would lose any chance of striking swiftly into Germany and ending the war in 1944. On August 17, 1944, Montgomery met with Gen. Omar Bradley (in a latrine) to suggest that General Patton's army halt its eastward advance so that supplies could be concentrated upon Montgomery's British force.

Eisenhower, too, realized that he would have to revise his original plan, but he rejected Monty's alternative of a quick thrust into Germany. His prime reason centered on the difficulty of supplying his advance force. Since preinvasion aerial bombardment had destroyed the French railway system, the Allies depended on long-haul trucks for their supplies. Eisenhower did not have enough vehicles available for a rapid advance along a narrow front. Moreover, the Channel ports were either shattered or still in German hands, and this would have exacerbated the problems of dispatching supplies from England. In addition, Eisenhower must have realized that the American people would have been outraged if the U.S. armies were to enter Germany on the coattails of British forces. Eisenhower was determined to carry on the policy of a broad advance—to clear the Scheldt estuary in order to enable the Allies to use Antwerp as a major staging post, to capture Dunkirk and Calais, and to overrun V-1 and V-2 coastal emplacements. However, he did agree to Montgomery's proposed Operation Marketgarden, an airborne assault upon the Rhine bridges at Eindhoven and Arnheim. This proved a catastrophic blunder that put a halt to Monty's further requests for a rapid assault on Germany in 1944.

On the morning of December 16, 1944, against all expectations, the German general, Karl Rudolf von Rundstedt, launched an attack through the Ardennes, aimed at splitting Allied forces and recapturing Antwerp. The attack advanced fifty miles before the Allies could mount any significant resistance. The Battle of the Bulge ended on January 15, 1945, with the Germans thrown back where they came from. Rundstedt had lost 120,000 men, 1,600 planes, and most of his armor. Asked what turned the tide, the prickly Montgomery admitted: "The good fighting qualities of the American soldier."

Ironically, the Battle of the Bulge gave the Allies a significant tactical advantage for the future. It shattered Hitler's crack troops and made it impossible for the Germans to withstand the subsequent Allied advance. Nevertheless, it took the Allies almost a month to fight their way back to their earlier positions. In the process they suffered 100,000 casualties and irreplaceable losses in tanks, planes, and supplies. By the end of January 1945, Ike had regrouped his armies and was ready to push onward to the Rhine and beyond. The Battle of the Bulge was followed by the disintegration of German forces and the reduction of Berlin, Hamburg, Dresden, Essen, Düsseldorf, Nuremberg, and Frankfurt to rubble by Allied bombing.

The Anglo-American firebombing raids on Dresden of February 13 and 14, 1945, incinerated 135,000 people for no military purpose beyond revenge. It was not possible for Allied strategists to pass the firebombing of Dresden off to the public as an essential military operation in which a few civilians were killed only by regrettable accident. To exculpate themselves, Churchill and the British cabinet saddled "Bomber" Harris with sole responsibility for the indiscriminate destruction. The firebombing provided inspiration for another revelatory war novel, when U.S. observer Kurt Vonnegut, who had been captured during the Battle of the Bulge and then imprisoned, turned his searing experiences to experimental account in *Slaughterhouse Five* (1969), once described as an analysis of mankind's "phosphorescent addiction to warfare." In all, bombing raids killed 593,000 German civilians in the war.

On the eastern front, the Russians had expelled all German soldiers from the Soviet Union by May and had also invaded Hungary and Romania. Several weeks after the Normandy invasion, Stalin launched a new and larger offensive. The first Russian army entered Poland on July 17, 1944. Russian forces now totaled 5 million men in three hundred divisions.

Poland set a terrible precedent for what was to come. On April 16, 1943, BBC radio in London had reported that Germany had announced the discovery in Katyn Forest in Russian territory (then under its control) of a mass grave of many thousands of Polish officers. The implication was clear: these were the corpses of Poles taken prisoner by the Red Army in 1939 and massacred. Germany suggested that the International Red Cross should conduct an impartial investigation into the affair. The Polish government in exile in London agreed. Russia interpreted this as a hostile act and broke off diplomatic relations with the London Poles.

After the Red Army moved across Poland, the desperate but valiant Poles staged an astonishing uprising in Warsaw, starting August 1, 1944. This was the intense climax to years of bitter resistance. Hitler's forces used all available infantry and air power to crush the insurrection. By October 2, 1944, the Germans had devastated Warsaw. Meanwhile, the Red Army waited some distance from the city but did nothing while Warsaw was reduced to rubble. One reason was that the Polish Home Army owed its allegiance to a Polish government of exile in London, which the Russians no longer recognized as the Polish government. In summer 1944 the Soviet government had created a Polish Committee of National Liberation, composed almost exclusively of Communists and based in Lublin, to which it entrusted the civil administration of Polish territory as it was freed by the Red Army. A second reason was that the Soviet Union wanted to be the sole liberator of Poland. (The Russians eventually entered Warsaw on January 11, 1945.) A third, more sinister reason was that many able Polish partisans, who would have resisted Communism, perished in the carnage. The devastation enabled the Soviets to construct the sort of Polish state they wanted far more easily.

George Kennan, an adviser to the U.S. ambassador in Moscow, wanted FDR to have a showdown with Stalin in 1944 over Russian tactics that were aimed at ensuring the creation of totalitarian regimes in Eastern Europe. He hoped FDR would force Stalin to choose between establishing a free postwar Europe and forfeiting Allied material support. FDR refused to heed Kennan's upstart advice, and lend-lease continued to flow into Russia. Kennan's greatest hope—that the USSR would halt once the Red Army had driven the Wehrmacht across Russian borders—was FDR's great concern. By early 1945, the Russians stood on a line from Memal on the Baltic in the north to Vienna in the south. By the time the Allies were poised before the Rhine, the Russians were at Frankfurt an der Oder.

Tightening the Noose in Asia

In Asia, following the success of their island-hopping strategy in the Pacific theater, U.S. commanders debated about where next to apply the pressure to bring the war against Japan to an end. Adm. Ernest King argued for an invasion of Formosa that would put U.S. forces on the threshold of the Japanese islands. Conversely, Gen. Douglas MacArthur insisted that the line of advance should be through the Philippines to Luzon, thus cutting Japanese lines of communication southward and establishing bases from which the Americans could launch air attacks upon Japan and, ultimately, invade the home islands. King and Mac-Arthur were united in their opposition to a JCS proposal of June 1944 for an attack on Japan that would bypass both Formosa and Luzon. MacArthur insisted on retaking the Philippines rather than invading Formosa. He declared that the United States had a moral duty to liberate the Filipinos from Japan. The Philippine option was most attractive to MacArthur because it offered him a chance to appear as a conquering hero.

On September 1, 1944, the JCS decided to postpone any decision until its logistical committee had made a thorough study of each proposal. But before the committee delivered its report, Adm. William F. ("Bull") Halsey, who was conducting carrier strikes in Philippine waters, reported that enemy resistance in this region was remarkably weak. To exploit this weakness, he recommended that MacArthur's proposed attack on Leyte Gulf in the Philippines, provisionally arranged for December 20, 1944, be undertaken immediately. Accordingly, the JCS, then in conference with their British counterparts at Quebec, decided to launch the Leyte Gulf operation on October 20. MacArthur announced his return to the Philippines in typically ostentatious style by splashing ashore from a landing craft. When the Americans returned to the Philippines, Filipino guerrillas, who had endured three years of occupation in which more than 130,000 Americans and Filipinos were murdered, preferred to take only the heads of the Japanese rather than sustain them as living POWs.

The U.S. assault on the Philippines signaled that the end was in sight. From the Japanese perspective, if the United States succeeded in taking the Philippines, then Japan's access to its precious source of oil in the NEI could be cut and its imperial navy immobilized. Japan answered this threat in an all-out measure, the Battle of Leyte Gulf.

With U.S. land and sea forces committed to the battle for Leyte Gulf and the subsequent push through the Philippines, King and Nimitz abandoned their plan for an invasion of Formosa. Instead, they proposed a revised strategy for the central Pacific: a push northward from the Marianas to the tiny volcanic island of Iwo Jima in the Boninas in January 1945, then on to Okinawa and nearby islands in the Ryukus early in March 1945. On October 3, 1944, the JCS ordered MacArthur's invasion of Luzon on December 20, 1944.

The whole strategy in the Pacific now hinged upon the success of the Leyte landing. On October 20, 1944, a combined central Pacific force (led by Nimitz and Halsey) and a southwest Pacific force (led by MacArthur and Admiral Thomas Kinkaid) invaded Leyte Gulf. This, the most formidable armada yet to sail in Pacific waters, was soon to be engaged by every remaining battleship and aircraft carrier in the Imperial Japanese Navy. The three-day battle of Leyte Gulf began on October 23, 1944. The Japanese lost three battleships, fourteen cruisers, and nine destroyers. The United States lost three carriers and three destroyers but gained control of Philippine waters.

The land battle for Leyte was another matter. It was interrupted by a double monsoon and lasted for over two months, during which the Japanese defenders fought with suicidal fervor. Of more than 65,000 Japanese troops committed to the battle, only 15,000 survived it. American marines met with the same fanatical opposition when Nimitz launched his delayed attack on Iwo Jima on February 19, 1945. In a last desperate effort, the Japanese mustered a task force, including their last battleship, the *Yamamoto*, with screening cruisers and destroyers, to protect the island. However, they were intercepted near their home waters by Carrier Task 58, whose planes sank the *Yamamoto* and five of her screening vessels and damaged several others. The Japanese fleet no longer existed.

The island of Iwo Jima, suffused by volcanic steam, proved a more formidable target. The struggle over it lasted from February 19 to March 15, 1945. One notable incident was preserved for posterity: the triumphant raising of the American flag by four marines at the summit of Mount Suribachi on February 19, 1945—a moment photographed by Joe Rosenthal of Associated Press. Otherwise, as Robert Trumbull explained for the *New York Times* of March 4, 1945, it was a case of Japanese ground troops fighting effective delaying actions, waiting in pillboxes and interlocking trenches, picking off the marines with singing sniper fire. Altogether, twenty thousand marines were killed or wounded in the tortuous step-by-step progress to take the island.

The final battle in the South Pacific occurred in March 1944 when the U.S. Army repulsed a Japanese bid to seize an Allied base at Bougainville—another natural minefield, in which tanks disappeared in bottomless swamps.

The most potent literary evocation of the Pacific campaign was Norman

Invasion forces land on the coast of Iwo Jima in February 1945. The photograph conveys the impact of the vessels with their human and matériel cargoes disgorged on the shore. (Library of Congress)

Mailer's anti- war epic *The Naked and the Dead* (1948), a novel much influenced in form by John Dos Passos. With it, the twenty-three-year-old Mailer, who had been a rifleman with the 112th Cavalry, established for himself the same authority for his generation as had Ernest Hemingway for the lost generation of war novelists—leader of the pack.

CHAPTER 16

Dear Hearts and Gentle People

S O V I E T   W R I T E R Ilya Ehrenberg described World War II as a "deep war," meaning a war that penetrated every aspect of the countries that fought it. The United States, safe from invasion, discovered this anew. Fighting the war was not just a matter of delivering enormous supplies and moving men and munitions in a well-coordinated strategy against the three enemies. It was also a matter of sustaining the huge contribution from the home front, involving an even greater direction of human resources than in World War I.

The most obvious characteristic of the U.S. home front was the economic revival accompanying World War II, which alleviated the mass unemployment and abject poverty of the Great Depression. The demand for labor soared in 1940. That year, according to official statistics, 8.12 million people were unemployed, amounting to 14.6 percent of the civilian labor force. Unemployment fell to 5.56 million (9.9 percent) in 1941 and then more sharply to 670,000 in 1944 (1.2 percent). It rose slightly in 1945 to 1.04 million (1.9 percent).

Those who had work were more prosperous than ever before. Between 1941 and 1945 the percentages of family-income increases across the five main socioeconomic groups from poorest to richest were, respectively, 68, 59, 36, 30, and 20 percent. The share of national income owned by the richest 5 percent fell from 23.7 percent to 16.8 percent. The number of families with incomes over five thousand dollars a year more than quadrupled. Nevertheless, a significant proportion of people remained poor. In 1944 about 10 million workers, about a quarter of those in industry, earned less than sixty cents an hour or twenty-

FACING PAGE:

Above: The grapes of wrath became the grapes of plenty for the Okies—migrants from the Dust Bowl who came to find work in California—in the state's burgeoning aircraft industry. The photo of a western aircraft plant of the Consolidated Aircraft Corporation has a line of partly completed Consolidated B-24 bombers and C-87 transport planes extending to the horizon under seemingly endless rows of fluorescent lights. (Office of War Information photo of October 1942; Library of Congress)
Below: Airplane parts hoisted high by cranes aboard ships that will take them from the port of New York to supply the European theater of war. (Library of Congress)

four dollars for a forty-hour week. Certain sections suffered, notably those living on Social Security pensions, clerical workers who had no opportunity to work overtime, and craftsmen whose special skills were of no account when factories converted to unskilled war production.

The Americans were a people in motion as never before. Sixteen million men left home to join the armed services, and 15.3 million others uprooted themselves to be near their loved ones or to secure work.

The defense program stimulated the rapid growth of cities. The population of New Orleans rose by 20 percent in the single year of 1942 on account of the demand for labor in the shipyards. Between 1940 and 1943 the population of Charleston, South Carolina, rose by 37 percent; that of Norfolk, Virginia, by 57 percent; and that of Mobile, Alabama, by 61 percent. Of all the states, California enjoyed the greatest increase—1.4 million people. By the end of the war the Golden State accommodated 10 percent of the national population and accounted for 20 percent of the nation's manufactured goods.

Boom towns experienced extreme social tensions between newcomers and old stock. These tensions were exacerbated by the breakdown or absence of essential medical, educational, sanitary, and transportation services and basic amenities such as water and housing. In January 1945 98 percent of American cities reported a shortage in single-family dwellings. The short-term solution to the housing shortage was the trailer, in unsafe, unsanitary trailer parks.

Children in boom towns suffered overcrowding at home and in schools that teachers deserted for higher pay elsewhere. Conservatives blamed the crisis in the classroom for the rising tide of juvenile delinquency, which included violent crime. In one single instance in New York City, students tortured a teacher to death. Some girls loitered around military encampments and bus depots to offer servicemen the ultimate in hospitality. Seventeen-year-old Josephine Tencza was one such prostitute and madam. A New York City court arraigned her and charged her with running a vice ring of thirty whores of ages twelve to fifteen.

Another cause of social dislocation was the breakdown of the traditional family structure. Millions of children lost their fathers to the services. As many lost their mothers to industry. Before the war 12 million women went to work. In 1943, 17 million did so. In the past, most working women had been employed in domestic service and clerical work. Now, because of the shortage of manpower, between 1940 and 1941 the number of women working in manufacturing rose by over 140 percent. In the steel industry, formerly an all-male preserve, women constituted 10 percent of the workforce. Women in industry were characterized as "Rosie the riveter."

The presence of women in the workplace in such unprecedented numbers had a profound impact on family life. Although by 1944 married women made up 50 percent of the female workforce, child-care facilities remained rudimentary. Federal funding for day-care facilities met the needs of only one hundred thousand children, or 10 percent of those requiring supervision while their mothers were at work. The rest remained unsupervised and undisciplined. They entered folklore as "eight-hour orphans" and "latchkey children."

The war led to an erosion of ethnic solidarity. Not only were the numbers of migrants large, but also many of them moved several times and over long distances.

The Nazi emphasis on racism helped discredit racist doctrines in the United States. For several decades, progressive anthropologists had challenged the idea that some races were superior to others. During the war, Ruth Benedict in *Race: Science and Politics* (1940) and Gunnar Dahlberg in *Race, Reason, and Rubbish* (1942) argued these points for a mass audience. They emphasized how much human beings have in common, and that so-called racial traits are really determined by culture and environment. Such authors asserted that human nature is more plastic than permanent. Thus, Ashley Montagu in *Man's Most Dangerous Myth* (1942) declared that the rise of fascism "shows us today where we end up if we think that the shape of the nose or the color of the skin has anything to do with human values or culture."

Among the moving millions were 1.24 million African Americans who left the South in the 1940s. The number of African Americans working in industry, public utilities, and transportation increased from 700,000 in 1940 to 1.45 million in 1944. In the same period the number working for the federal government rose from 60,000 to over 200,000. Despite continuing resistance to African Americans, the number who worked as skilled workers or foremen doubled during the war. Almost 550,000 joined labor unions, primarily those affiliated with the CIO. The prime centers of African American migration were usually such centers of war production as Chicago and Detroit in the North; Norfolk, Charleston, and Mobile in the South; and Los Angeles, San Francisco, and San Diego in the West. Whereas in the period 1940–44, the total population of the ten largest centers of wartime production increased by 19 percent, the population of African Americans there rose by 49 percent.

Troubles I've Seen

Although Eleanor Roosevelt thought "the nation had taken even greater strides toward social justice during the war than it had during the New Deal"—that the process of relocation taught Americans the virtues of tolerance—millions of African Americans would not have agreed with her.

It is true that discrimination against African Americans in defense industries was curbed by the need for extra manpower. Unions that wanted to exclude African Americans found it difficult to sustain open racism when the federal government announced that it would refuse to certify them as accredited agents for collective bargaining unless they accepted minorities. Also, in 1943 the War Labor Board outlawed wage differences based exclusively on race. Moreover, in the North African Americans could vote, and there was not the same blatant segregation as existed in the South. Nevertheless, renewed migration upset institutional racism in the South and the North. Race relations became most tense in the crucial areas of housing, transportation, and military service. Thus, the war exacerbated racial differences. As Richard Polenberg says in *One Nation Divisible* (1980), "From the black perspective, the lowering of some barriers made those remaining seem more intolerable. To many whites, however, the remaining barriers seemed even more desirable than before."

In Chicago African Americans were excluded from some eleven square miles of residential districts either through restrictive covenants (under which householders agreed neither to sell nor to lease property to them) or by informal agreements by landlords and real estate managers. As to employment, they were restricted to the dirtiest and least desirable jobs. White workers looked on askance as African Americans joined them on the factory floor, dreading that they might lose their cherished illusion of superiority. They protested the upgrading of African Americans by walking out (as munitions workers did in Baltimore), or beating up African American workers (as shipyard workers did in Mobile), or going on strike (as trolley car workers did in Philadelphia). Novelist Chester Himes described racial tension and friction in a wartime industrial community in *If He Hollers, Let Him Go* (1945), which vividly evokes the confusions felt by African Americans recently moved to industrial towns, as well as their bitterness.

Just as startling in its way was the impact of African American newcomers to the North on Roman Catholic congregations. Impressed with Catholic education and with the church's commitment to inner cities, many African Americans joined Roman Catholic churches. There were group baptisms. But, as religious historian Martin Marty explains (1996), while some priests welcomed the so-called Negro leagues, others were still afflicted with racism. They now considered all Euro-Americans in the same ethnic group since they were whites. Some priests were also trying to preserve neighborhood and parish solidarity against the disruption of wartime (and postwar) mobility. Nevertheless, Hollywood films signaled the acceptance of the Roman Catholic church within the American cultural mainstream. In three consecutive years, 1943, 1944, and 1945, movies with Catholic plots and themes—*Song of Bernadette, Going My Way, The Bells of St. Mary's,* and *The Keys of the Kingdom*—were nominated for fifty-four Oscars and won twelve.

The movement of so many people to only a few centers led to especially heightened tension over housing. In certain northern cities, ghettos were filled beyond capacity and began to burst, thus upsetting traditional racial lines of

FACING PAGE:

Gordon Parks's classic photograph of two women welders at the Landers, Frary, and Clark plant in New Britain, Connecticut, taken in June 1943, remains a tribute to workers on the home front in World War II. (Office of War Information; Library of Congress)

demarcation. White householders, disturbed at the prospect of being engulfed in a black tide, took matters into their own hands. In Buffalo threats of violence induced the government to cancel plans for a housing project. In Detroit in February 1942, a mob of whites armed with rocks and clubs menaced fourteen African American families and deterred them from moving into the Sojourner Truth Homes until April, when they were protected by a police escort. The worst riots since 1919 occurred in 1943 as whites, enraged by African Americans' penetration of formerly white occupations, took the law into their own hands. By far the worst incident took place in Detroit, where thirty-four people died in a riot that spread after a fistfight between an African American and a white. Police brutality toward African Americans in the Detroit area stunned the nation. Seventeen African Americans had died at the hands of the police, and there was a preponderance of African American arrests over those of whites. After the Detroit riot, Attorney General Francis Biddle proposed a government ban on further migration by African Americans to certain cities.

Nevertheless, African American leaders committed to civil rights continued to find new strength. Their faith in progress was stimulated by radical religious groups. Quaker groups had played a part in the abolitionist movement in the nineteenth century. In the 1930s such organizations as the Fellowship of Reconciliation (FOR), which began in 1915, mixing Quaker and radical ideas, took a lead by placing racial equality at the heart of the Social Gospel. Initially, the FOR had conceived of its work in race relations as educational, but in 1941 a committee headed by J. Holmes Smith, a former missionary to India, suggested the idea of nonviolent techniques against racial prejudice, as they had been applied by Mohandas Karamchand Gandhi to unite Indians against British rule. Gandhi's strategy against the British was civil disobedience through symbolic acts of noncooperation—passive acts of defiance intended to embarrass the British—notably the 1930 Salt March of two hundred miles from Sabarmi to Dandi.

In 1941 Gandhi's strategies were first put to the test in the United States. Seven former students of Antioch College in Ohio had established a cooperative farm, Ahimsa Farm, near Cleveland. One of them, Lee Stern, persuaded the others to help his African American friends from the city get into a segregated swimming pool at Garfield Park by going there as a mixed group and entering and leaving peaceably. Their attempt was so successful that James Farmer, secretary of FOR for the mid-Atlantic area, and his friends George Houser and Bayard Rustin organized a Men's Interracial Fellowship House in January 1942. It lasted only six months but led to a National Federation of Committees of Racial Equality, supported by the FOR, which met in June 1943. In 1944 this organization became the Congress of Racial Equality (CORE). After the war, by dramatizing the sobriety of African Americans and the justice of their cause in mass demonstrations, these organizers would provide the news media with effective copy that would bring shame to their racist oppressors and lend dignity and hope to the oppressed.

The American people may have been committed to the overthrow of Nazism and the Japanese tyranny. To cultivate loyalty, the federal government ensured the identification of those who were different.

On December 8, 1941, FDR issued an executive order designating Italians, Germans, and Japanese who were resident in the United States as enemy aliens. The order suspended all naturalization proceedings, prohibited aliens from traveling without prior permission, and barred them from areas close to strategic installations. Simultaneously, the FBI began rounding up three thousand Japanese, Italians, and Germans on suspicion that they were some sort of threat to national security.

At the outbreak of war there were some 599,000 people of Italian extraction resident in the United States. For the vast majority, FDR's executive order was an irritant rather than a form of oppression. The loyalty of the majority of the 204,000 German residents should never have been in doubt. Most of them were Jewish refugees from Nazi tyranny. If these people did experience hostility, it was because they were Jewish rather than because they were German. A belief that Jews were not contributing fully to the war effort persisted throughout the war. Indeed, they were often accused of profiteering. Despite testimony to the contrary given by Gen. Lewis B. Hershey, the head of Selective Service, people believed that Jews tried to evade the draft.

Virulent anti-Semitism finally ended the public career of Father Charles Coughlin, the radio priest, who had earlier voiced his support for Hitler and Mussolini. Archbishop Edward Mooney of Detroit thought Coughlin "proud, stubborn, and vengeful," but Mooney delayed silencing Coughlin until Coughlin faced the threat of a federal trial for sedition and the Roman Catholic church faced disgrace. In April 1942 Mooney summoned Coughlin to his office and ordered him to sever his ties with his organization, Social Justice, or face suspension from the priesthood. Coughlin caved in. The federal government dropped its proposed sedition charges.

As to the situation of conscientious objectors and the new draft laws, a provision inserted in the Selective Service Act of 1940 exempted from combat duty anyone who "by reason of religious training and belief is conscientiously opposed to participation in war in any form." These conscientious objectors were to be assigned to noncombatant duties. Those who opposed any form of military service were to be set to work in civilian public service camps.

The majority of America's total of 42,973 conscientious objectors accepted noncombatant service, but some 11,950 opted to work in the civilian camps. They were to work for fifty hours each week under strict military discipline. During World War I inmates in similar encampments had been paid for their labor. In World War II the financial burden was passed from the state to the individual or the church of which he was a member. Conscientious objectors had to reimburse the authorities for expenditure on their food and clothing. Conditions were so harsh that by 1943 many COs were choosing prison rather than work in the camps. Moreover, a prison sentence awaited those who found their claims to religious commitment rejected by the authorities. In all, 5,500 were sent to jail. In prison COs received poor food and experienced frequent physical abuse. Hundreds of those sent to Fort Leavenworth in Kansas were kept in solitary confinement for up to sixteen months.

Among those convicted of draft evasion was Nation of Islam leader Elijah Muhammad, sentenced to four years in prison in 1942. Four years in prison, says his biographer Claude Andrew Clegg, III, "did more toward consolidating his authority over the Nation of Islam than a decade of bickering, purges, and wandering could ever have done."

Jehovah's Witnesses constituted 75 percent of all COs sent to prison. Draft boards rejected their claims to pacifism because of their avowed intention to fight in the coming battle of Armageddon. This was a cosmetic argument that disguised popular distrust of Jehovah's Witnesses. They found themselves persecuted by the people, harassed by the authorities, and penalized by a series of Supreme Court decisions about their right to distribute literature.

Such violations of civil rights paled in comparison to the treatment meted out to America's Japanese minority when the immediate burden of American anger for Pearl Harbor and Japan's seemingly inexorable advance in Asia fell upon Japanese-Americans.

In 1941 there were 127,000 people of Japanese descent resident in the United States. Of these, 112,000 lived on the West Coast, 93,717 in California. Approximately 33 percent of them were designated as enemy aliens. These first-generation immigrants, the Issei (47,000), had been born in Japan and, as a result of the Immigration Act of 1924, had been barred from citizenship. Their children, the Nisei (80,000), however, were U.S. citizens. The middle-aged Issei produced over half of California's fruit and vegetables; the Nisei, in their teens and twenties, were native-born, had been educated in public schools, and talked, behaved, and dressed like other young Americans.

Popular antipathy against them turned sour when a movement demanding the total evacuation of all Japanese from the West Coast, led by the head of the Western Defense Command, Gen. John De Witt, gathered momentum. Congressmen from California, Oregon, and Washington added their voices to his call for the removal of both the Issei and the Nisei. They were supported by many West Coast mayors, the American Legion, and spokesmen from farming, labor, and business.

People on the West Coast genuinely feared enemy attack. Numerous false air raid reports and the actual shelling of the coast by a Japanese submarine on February 23, 1942, heightened their anxieties. The situation of many important war installations and the construction of new munitions factories on the West Coast made its inhabitants sensitive to fear of Japanese sabotage. Their suspicions were strengthened by the findings of the official investigation into the attack on Pearl Harbor. This, the Roberts Report of January 24, 1942, detailed the existence of a highly organized fifth column within Hawaii's Japanese community. The war sharpened any preexisting intolerance toward minorities. Some who demanded Japanese removal also saw an opportunity for personal gain. With the Japanese-Americans forced to leave their homes at short notice, these individuals would be able to acquire their businesses and property at bargain prices.

Throughout January 1942 Attorney General Francis Biddle ignored the mounting clamor for Japanese removal. Finally, Biddle succumbed. Ironically, the repression was advocated by men usually praised for their freedom from bigotry, such as Henry L. Stimson, Walter Lippmann, and Abe Fortas. Without a scintilla of evidence, California's Attorney General Earl Warren used sophistical reasoning to justify repressive measures. He said the fact that there had not been any acts of sabotage by Japanese-Americans just showed how devious was their plotting. Furthermore, "Opinion among law-enforcement officers in this state is that there is more potential danger among the group of Japanese who were born in this country than from the alien Japanese." Among those who pleaded for compassion were conservatives such as FBI director J. Edgar Hoover and Senator Robert A. Taft of Ohio.

On February 19 FDR gave in to anti-Japanese demands. By signing Executive Order 9066, he authorized the War Department to designate military areas and exclude any or all persons from these zones. On March 2, 1942, De Witt issued a proclamation requiring all aliens, all Nisei, and all individuals suspected of subversive activity to move from the West Coast. In four weeks nine thousand migrants left California, Oregon, and Washington to settle in the interior. However, the proposed recipient states (Arizona, Arkansas, Kansas, Montana, and Colorado) refused them entry. Therefore, on March 27, 1942, De Witt called a halt to voluntary evacuation. The army began transporting evacuees to assembly points, pending transfer to permanent facilities. By June 1942 the program was almost completed. One hundred thousand Issei and Nisei had been forced to leave the West Coast. Ironically, Hawaii had a far higher proportion of Asians than California. They, however, were needed in war-related activities there. Japanese-American leaders in Hawaii cooperated closely with the FBI, and no charges were preferred.

The Issei and Nisei of California forfeited their bank accounts and investments. The Issei lost $70 million in annual income and countless savings, bonds, and stocks. They had no right of appeal. They were forbidden to take with them their pets, personal items, and household goods. Government officials agreed to store personal possessions but refused to guarantee their safety. Many evacuees sold off their goods for a pittance.

The task of accommodating the evacuees fell to the War Relocations Board, established under the direction of Milton Eisenhower. Initially, Milton Eisenhower conceived of the detention camps as a kind of wartime Civilian Conservation Corps. Each small enclave of evacuees would, he hoped, become self-sufficient in foodstuffs and perhaps develop small-scale manufacturing enterprises. But the land assigned to the camps was usually too arid for arable farming. As far as the proposed manufacturing enterprises were concerned, evacuees were actively discouraged, and often prohibited, from competing with local businesses. Indeed, the first receiving states (California, Texas, Arkansas, Utah, and Wyoming), curtailed the rights of Japanese-American citizens to trade, own land, and vote.

Evacuees were concentrated in ten huge camps in seven states. Each encampment housed ten thousand to twelve thousand inmates. Conditions were penal. The camps comprised row upon row of wooden barracks. Each family had one room in these blocks. For warmth, they each had one army blanket. All toilet, bathing, and dining facilities were communal. Guard dogs patrolled the barbed-wire fence that marked the perimeter of each encampment.

The whole process of relocation added immeasurably to existing strains within the Japanese-American community. The older generation of Issei were trying to preserve traditional Japanese culture, in which filial piety and the importance of hierarchy remained essential group values. The younger Nisei were adopting individual values of self-assertion that they considered American. Menial work in the relocation centers undermined the authority of order of people whose skills and education now went for little. Moreover, to give a specious appearance of democratic organization, the camps were allowed a limited degree of self-government. At first, however, only Japanese-American citizens could assume elective office. Therefore, it was young men who became the official leaders of the community. The older generation were overwhelmed by a sense of futility.

Japanese-Americans contested their detention in the courts, most notably in two cases that went to the Supreme Court. In the first, *Hirabayashi v. The United States*, the Supreme Court decided unanimously on June 21, 1943, that a curfew of Japanese-Americans was not a violation of their civil rights. While admitting, "It is jarring to me that U.S. citizens were subjected to this treatment," Chief Justice Harlan Fiske Stone declared, "In time of war residents having ethnic affiliations with an invading army may be a greater source of danger than those of a different ancestry." In the second case, *Korematsu v. The United States*, decided by a vote of 6 to 3 on December 18, 1944, the court upheld the removal of Japanese-Americans to relocation centers.

Nonetheless, after the war Americans began to consider the concentration of the Issei and Nisei rank injustice. In 1987 the House of Representatives approved a $1.2 billion settlement in reparation payments to Japanese-Americans interned in 1942–45.

Even during World War II, some hard hearts softened—although this was a matter of convenience and necessity. On January 28, 1943, Secretary of War Henry L. Stimson announced that the army would accept Nisei volunteers, and by 1945, 17,600 Nisei had joined up. No combat units were more courageous or won more medals. What drove these soldiers to displays of heroism on, for example, the Italian front, was the hope that the story of their bravery carried across the United States would convince the nation to release their families from the relocation camps. The hope proved forlorn.

Evacuation of the Nisei. In 1942 these U.S. citizens of Japanese descent, among a contingent of 664 in San Francisco, the first forced to leave their homes, stand in line awaiting buses to transport them to relocation centers. (U.S. War Relocation Authority; Library of Congress)

The abuse of the Issei produced an irony of slightly better treatment of the Chinese. Despite FDR's problems with Chiang Kai-shek, China was a wartime ally in urgent need of support. Through careful propaganda, the federal government encouraged sympathy for China that reached its peak in 1943 when Madame Chiang visited the United States. She was invited to address Congress, where, according to *Time*, "tough guys melted." A Citizens' Committee to Repeal Chinese Exclusion lobbied Congress to repeal the Chinese Exclusion Act of 1882. FDR advised Congress that repeal would "silence the distorted Japanese propaganda." Congress complied in fall 1943. Nevertheless, although the new act allowed Chinese immigrants to become U.S. citizens, it established a diminutive annual quota of 105 for "all persons of the Chinese race," no matter where they were born. Thus, Chinese from the British lease-colony of Hong Kong were not to be included in the British quota. Chinese wives of U.S. citizens could enter the United States only as part of the quota.

Little White Lies

Despite the fact that the war years were boom years for many, as the first shock of war subsided and the threat of aerial bombardment and invasion passed, feverish support for the war waned. In 1942 the public mood turned sour. Bad news from the war front, rumors of inefficiency in the defense program, the effect of inflation and the unpopular measures devised to combat it—all these provoked general feelings of frustration and disappointment. This mood found its outlet in criticism of wartime agencies and open condemnation of one of the most despised political Congresses in U.S. history—the Seventy-Seventh Congress. The change in public mood and the growing dissatisfaction with the way the war was being run showed in the November congressional elections, when the Republicans took forty-four seats in a landslide victory.

The Seventy-Eighth Congress was fairly evenly balanced between Democratic and Republican members. However, the balance was tilted in favor of the Republicans by the southern Democrats' habitual defection from the party line. Conservatism ruled. By the end of 1943 such agencies as the Federal Writers' Project, the CCC, the WPA, the FSA, the Rural Electrification Administration, the National Resources Planning Board, the OPA, and the National Youth Administration had either been abolished or made inoperative through shortage of funds.

Although the defense program provided a solution to one problem—unemployment—it raised the specter of another—inflation. In the months prior to Pearl Harbor there were ominous signs that increased defense spending had once more set the inflationary spiral in motion. From 1939 to the spring of 1942, the cost of living increased by 15 percent. Treasury advisers identified the problem as the inflationary gap—the gap between disposable income and available consumer goods. Too much money was chasing too few commodities. This resulted in a rise in prices, a subsequent demand for wage increases, an increase in the cost of production, another rise in prices, and so on.

The man assigned the task of keeping down the cost of living was economist Leon Henderson. In January 1942 he became head of the newly formed Office of Price Administration (OPA). In April 1942 the OPA introduced the General Maximum Price Regulation. This required merchants to accept the highest prices they charged for goods in March 1942 as a price ceiling. Farm produce was exempt from the restrictions.

Businessmen roundly condemned "General Max," complaining that they were being asked to freeze prices at too low a level. The OPA's critics in Congress carpeted Henderson. They regarded General Max not only as a dictatorial measure, but, with the cost of living rising by 7 percent in the first six months of 1942, also as a failure. In his defense, Henderson explained that price control was pointless unless he could lift exemptions on foodstuffs and impose a wage freeze. Congress reluctantly accepted the logic of this argument. The Stabilization Act of October 2, 1942, broadened the OPA's power to enforce price controls and placed responsibility for price fixing on all foodstuffs under its jurisdiction. It also granted the agency a free hand to introduce rationing. Congress thus grudgingly accepted the OPA as the instrument to combat inflation but demanded a price: Henderson's (subsequent) resignation.

The OPA proved to be the most unpopular of all wartime agencies. In 1942 the OPA instituted ten rationing programs, involving gasoline, coffee, shoes, sugar, butter, and a variety of processed foods. The aim was to achieve an equitable distribution of these commodities, to be accomplished by allocating a fixed monthly quota of ration stamps to everyone sixteen and over. They were to be used, along with cash, to purchase a quota of restricted commodities. To prevent hoarding, the stamps carried an expiration date. People resented rationing as bureaucratic control. They also condemned it for creating artificial shortages.

The federal government established the Office of Economic Stabilization (OES) in October 1942 to oversee all aspects of the economy. Its principal function was to arbitrate in disputes between the various government agencies and to shield the OPA's unpopular anti-inflation campaign from further criticism from Congress. It was headed by James F. Byrnes, a southern Democrat who had represented South Carolina for over twenty years in the Senate, only recently appointed to the bench of the Supreme Court. FDR gave Byrnes great trust and responsibility, allowing him to serve as his representative to the military establishment. Thus, when the Office of War Mobilization was created in May 1943, Byrnes became its director also. The OWM served as "a court of last appeal, a body that adjudicated disputes between the military and civilians or between competing civilian interests." Byrnes never trusted Donald Marr Nelson (chairman of the War Production Board) and tended to give support to big business and the military.

The federal government, determined to stave off disruptive labor problems, established a new agency, the National War Labor Board (NWLB), in January 1942. It comprised four representatives from labor, four from business, and four civilians. It secured pledges from business and labor that there would be no lockouts and no strikes for the duration of the war. However, there was ample cause for concern, given management's assault upon, and labor's defense of, the union shop. In summer 1942 the NWLB proposed a policy of "maintenance of union membership" by which each worker was allowed fifteen days to resign from his or her union; thereafter, he or she would remain enrolled until the end of the union contract. Management was not to discriminate against union members; unions were to recruit new members only to maintain existing membership levels. Although the union continued to act as the bargaining agent for all workers, new employees could choose to join or not to join the union, as they preferred. Those workers who were union members could not give up their membership without losing their jobs. Thus, management could not break the union by taking on new or temporary workers to displace the old; labor could not exploit new workers by forcing them into its ranks. Of almost 6.5 million additions to the labor force in World War II, 3.5 million decided to join unions and 3 million decided not to. The NWLB also ruled on wage claims to maintain workers' existing standards of living, using as a formula the so-called Little Steel principle and limiting raises to, at best, 15 percent. Safe from open-shop drives and economic recession, organized labor rose from 8.69 million members in 1941 to 12.56 million in 1945.

Despite wartime prosperity, miners' leader John L. Lewis remained a source of militant opposition, insisting on labor's right to strike and withdrawing the United Mine Workers Union from the CIO, the very body he and his union had helped create. Annoyed by labor disruption that it deemed unpatriotic, in June 1943 Congress passed the Smith-Connally War Labor Disputes Act over FDR's veto. It allowed strikes only after a secret ballot held after a thirty-day cooling-off period, provided for criminal prosecution of individuals who advocated strike action, and forbade union contributions to political campaigns.

With the virtual elimination of unemployment and the rise in working-class wages, the federal government sought ways of absorbing excess capital, otherwise available for discretionary spending. Moreover, it wanted to narrow the inflationary gap. FDR's administration adopted two strategies, both of which helped finance the war effort.

The first was the sale of war bonds. Secretary of the Treasury Henry Morgenthau envisaged the selling of war bonds as a means of involving the public in the war effort. By organizing the scheme on a volunteer basis, he reasoned that the American people would be able to feel that they were making their own positive contribution to the war effort. In all, there were seven bond drives, each of one month's duration. Hollywood star Dorothy Lamour, the sarong-draped foil to Bing Crosby and Bob Hope in the *Road* movies, earned a reputation as the "bond bombshell" because of her success in volunteer work selling an estimated $300 million of war bonds. The federal government put a private railroad car at her disposal when she went on a bond tour. She was, supposedly, the originator of the scheme whereby employees could pay for war bonds by payroll deductions. By the end of World War II, bond drives had raised a total of $135 billion, altogether. Although these bond drives helped pay for the war, they were only partially successful in soaking up citizens' excess capital. Most bond sales went to large financial institutions, such as banks, insurance companies, and industrial corporations. Smaller bond issues, those priced between $25 and $50, remained undersubscribed. Instead of financing the war effort, people preferred to enjoy material comforts from newly swelled pay packets.

A second government strategy to absorb excess capital was taxation. In 1939 only 4 million Americans paid income taxes. By spring of 1942 the tax system had been revised and extended to cover nearly 30 million citizens. It became apparent that inflation could be controlled only by a further extension of the tax system. As a veteran New Dealer, Secretary of the Treasury Henry Morgenthau considered fiscal policy an instrument of social reform. The proposed revision of the tax structure was, to him, a useful device not only for stabilizing the economy and paying for the war but also for narrowing the gap between rich and poor.

Yet the Revenue Act of October 1942 bore little resemblance to the plan first devised by Morgenthau. The bill's most innovative feature, the so-called Victory Tax, settled the burden of financing the war firmly upon the shoulders of the poorer members of society. This measure imposed a 5 percent gross income tax upon all annual incomes in excess of $624 and thereby extended liability to 20 million workers in the lower income brackets. The act lowered the personal allowance—the money on which tax was not paid—to $500 for single men and women and $1,200 for married couples. Thus was income tax made a truly mass tax. By 1943 the new act had increased the number of people paying income tax to 43 million, and by 1945 the number was 50 million. The upper classes were also required to pay more. The normal tax in the upper brackets rose from 4 to 5 percent, and surtax was increased from 77 percent to 82 percent.

Thus, in 1939 a married man with no children who earned $2,000 paid no income tax; in 1945 he paid $202. In the period 1939–45 the tax on an annual income of $5,000 rose from $80 to $844; on an income of $10,000 it rose from $415 to $2,370; and on an income of $25,000 it rose from $2,489 to $9,955. Corporate taxes rose from 31 percent to 40 percent, and excess profits taxes rose to 90 percent. The act of 1942 also increased taxes on inheritances and gifts and introduced sizable excise taxes on communications, luxuries, and transportation that were to remain in effect after the war. Accordingly, government revenues rose from $7.5 billion in 1941 to $46.5 billion in 1945.

Until the act of 1942, income tax payments had always been made twelve months in arrears. Thus, taxes to be paid in 1943 were based on incomes earned in 1942. However, if taxation were ever to operate as an effective weapon against inflation by siphoning off expendable income, then the government had to revise this traditional system. Wage levels for 1943 and tax rates for that year would be higher than they had been in 1942. To put the bite on personal incomes, it was proposed that citizens pay income taxes for 1943 currently. Beardsley Ruml, chairman of the Federal Reserve Bank of New York, suggested, instead, outright cancelation of all tax obligations for 1942. Everyone would start with a clean slate in 1943. Popularly called "Pay as you go," the new act required employers to deduct federal taxes from their employees' pay and to turn over these deductions to the collector of Internal Revenue every three months. Those who were self-employed had to compute and pay their own tax estimates on the same basis.

With the cost of the war still spiraling, it was necessary to combat inflation. The Treasury devised a new tax bill for 1943 that set the sum of $12 billion as its target. Wary of sending such a request to Congress, FDR told Secretary of the Treasury Henry Morgenthau to reduce the target figure. Morgenthau's revised plan aimed at raising $10.5 billion, of which $6.5 billion would come from personal income tax; $1 billion from corporate taxes; $2.5 billion from excise taxes; and the rest from estate and gift taxes. The House Ways and Means Committee dismissed the proposal out of hand. The committee then devised its own plan to raise only $2 billion. To FDR the measure was not only inadequate but also iniquitous. It granted lucrative tax favors to business in general and to the mining and lumber industries in particular. Nevertheless, the measure passed the House in November 1943. The Senate gave its approval the following January. FDR vetoed the bill on February 22, 1944, describing it as "not a tax bill but a tax-relief bill, providing relief not for the needy but for the greedy." Undaunted, the House decided—by 299 votes to 95—to override FDR's veto. In the Senate the vote was equally emphatic—72 votes to 14. Although this constituted a humiliating defeat for FDR, he had by then won the overall battle against inflation. For from 1942 to 1945 the rise in the cost of living was held down to only 9 percent.

Ac-cent-tchu-ate the Positive

People spent their disposable incomes according to their inclinations. Hollywood still set standards of fashion and taste. And Hollywood itself was shielded from underlying economic and legal problems by the boom years of World War II. Audiences were so eager for escapist entertainment that almost all films—good, bad, and indifferent—did well at the box office. In 1942 cinema attendance rose by 50 percent compared with the totals for 1940.

As to content, Hollywood produced 982 movies in the war years and sent 34,232 prints overseas. After some initial hesitation, MGM pulled out all the stops to show beleaguered Britain ennobled by suffering through the Blitz in its tale of *Mrs. Miniver* (1942), based on newspaper articles by Jan Struther, an

FACING PAGE:

Above: In his watercolor *Soldiers Dancing at 99 Park Avenue*, artist Reginald Marsh captures the way young people seized their few tender moments of social pleasure with frenetic enthusiasm. (Library of Congress)

Left: Judy Garland with Margaret O'Brien in *Meet Me in St. Louis* (1942), a nostalgic musical set in turn-of-the-century America, directed by Garland's future second husband, Vincente Minnelli. She was an incandescent musical performer on account of her polished zip in upbeat numbers and vulnerable wistfulness in melancholy ones. However, her high level of nervous energy suggested her faltering hold on herself. (Museum of Modern Art Film Stills Archives)

Right: The Andrews Sisters (Maxine, Patty, and Laverne), popular chanteuses of swing music and boogie-woogie, were regularly pressed into service to boost morale at home and abroad with upbeat musical interludes in such wartime privates-on-parade movies as this Bud Abbott and Lou Costello vehicle, *Buck Privates* (1942). (Universal Pictures; Museum of Modern Art Film Stills Archives)

English mother of three. Director William Wyler scored a sentimental bull's-eye, pitting hitherto not-so-popular Greer Garson, aging star Walter Pidgeon, and newcomer Teresa Wright against an imminent Nazi invasion of England after Dunkirk. Churchill sent studio boss Louis B. Mayer a message that read, "*Mrs. Miniver* is propaganda worth a hundred battleships." The film garnered six Oscars, encouraging the haughty Garson to set a more dubious record with the longest-ever acceptance speech of any Oscar winner.

The Hollywood establishment also played a crucial part in the armory of federal government propaganda. To boost morale, film stars made numerous public appearances at GI camps and launchings of ships and aircraft—activities that also confirmed their status as icons. To boost war finances, under the supervision of Col. Darryl F. Zanuck at the War Activities Committee, Motion Picture Industry, directors and stars organized war-bond and service-fund drives and produced war training films. Walt Disney produced over one million feet of training film, some narrated by B-movie star Ronald Reagan.

Not just bond drives and personal appearances but also deadly action. The first Hollywood star to fight was James Stewart, whose screen persona mixed elements of Yankee Doodle and Huckleberry Finn. As a wing commander in the Army Air Corps he rose to the rank of colonel, leading bombing missions from northern England, for which he was awarded the Distinguished Flying Cross and the Croix de Guerre.

Ronald Reagan, later the fortieth president (1981–89), was among the beneficiaries of Hollywood's war effort. While he was assigned to the cavalry, he made numerous promotional films for a salary of five hundred dollars a week, many of them at the Hal Roach Studio in Culver City, known as Fort Wacky. In July 1942 *Modern Screen* published an article ostensibly about his wife at the time, Jane Wyman. Having been awakened by antiaircraft fire, "she'd seen Ronnie's sick face bent over a picture of the small swollen bodies of children starved to death in Poland. 'This,' said the war-hating Reagan between set lips, 'would make it a pleasure to kill.' " However, Reagan did not leave California for the war effort. Instead, Reagan and his publicists concocted phony stories based on his phantom service.

In A movies, some stars burst on the scene; others continued their ascent across the heavens; and some followed a troubled course. The most popular female icon in World War II was Betty Grable of "the million-dollar" legs, star of *Down Argentine Way* (1940), *I Wake Up Screaming* (1941), and *Pin Up Girl* (1944). There were 5 million copies of pictures of her in circulation among servicemen. The most popular pinups, however, were the Petty girls—the impossibly long-legged and voluptuously breasted drawings by George Brown Petty, IV, that appeared in *Esquire* magazine and, wearing transparent black chemises dictated by postal censorship, on calendars.

Rita Hayworth was the leading love goddess of the 1940s. A skilled Latin American dancer, she was promoted by Twentieth Century Fox, first as a red-haired partner for dancer Fred Astaire. She owed the survival of her career to public relations expert Henry C. Rogers, whose advice she sought when she feared the studio would drop her. When Rogers learned from Hayworth that she spent her spare money on her wardrobe, he concocted a fictitious story that audiences had voted her the best-dressed actress offscreen, and sold it and her legend to various fashion houses and to *Vogue* magazine. Thereby, he turned Rita Hayworth into a full-fledged star with one of the first so-called pseudo events—events that existed in order that they could be reported. Through Rogers's engineering, the pliable Rita Hayworth became a mysterious femme fatale, notably in *Gilda* (1946). She was an icon of intense public interest through her brief marriages to director Orson Welles (in a union held together by the thread of joint gluttony) and to Muslim playboy Aly Khan and, in her last years—like Ronald Reagan—a pitiful victim of Alzheimer's disease. Meanwhile, Henry Rogers's success with Rita Hayworth encouraged Rogers to launch a successful PR firm for Hollywood stars, Rogers and Cowan, that perpetuated the lustrous image of many a screen idol.

A handsome retiring man of few words, Gary Cooper slipped effortlessly into westerns, wry comedies, and romances, and into playing two of novelist Ernest Hemingway's most famous dramatic leads in *A Farewell to Arms* (1932) and *For Whom the Bell Tolls* (1943). Equally handsome former vaudeville player Cary Grant's impeccable delivery of throwaway lines enlivened many screwball comedies for Paramount until British director Alfred Hitchcock encouraged him to suggest caddishness and menace below the debonair surface for *Suspicion* (1941) and *Notorious* (1946).

Judy Garland survived the perils of childhood stardom but could not endure the penalties after she graduated to adult roles. She was an incandescent musical performer on account of her polished zip in upbeat numbers, vulnerable wistfulness in melancholy ones, genuine acting ability, and popular appeal in films with Mickey Rooney or directed by her second husband, Vincente Minnelli, notably *Meet Me in St. Louis* (1942). Her high level of nervous energy was suggested by her faltering hold on herself through five marriages, various nervous breakdowns and suicide attempts, and a widely publicized reputation for being unreliable.

The emphasis of Hollywood movies in the war years was still on escapist entertainment. In the 1930s musicals had represented 20 percent of Hollywood films; in the war years they accounted for 40 percent. The 30 percent of releases that were war films abided by propaganda guidelines established in the Office of War Information's *Government Manual for the Motion Pictures* of 1942. These guidelines recommended that Hollywood emphasize a message of American egalitarianism's freeing the world of racism and class divisions. War films confirmed audiences' stereotypical expectations. Germans were sadists, Italians cowardly, and Japanese subhuman. Hollywood war films were intended to reassure families on the home front. Thus, hokum like *Desperate Journey* (1942) with Errol Flynn, Van Heflin, and Ronald Reagan received approbation. John Huston's documentary, *The Battle of San Pietro* (1944), which showed weary

GIs falling under enemy mortar fire and being bagged for dispatch and burial, was considered too harrowing for general release.

According to Hollywood, war clouds might gather on the distant horizon, but they never threatened America's optimism or its interest in consumption. Because they were so delusory, Hollywood films helped their audiences evade any consideration of the origins of the war or the objectives of U.S. involvement. But Hollywood remained a prime arbiter of fashion and fads, although there were signs that its trends of conformity gave young people something else to rebel against.

The term *adolescent* disappeared and *teenager* took its place. Lester Markel, editor of the *New York Times Magazine*, began using the word *teenager* in various articles, but it did not truly catch on with the public until after the war. Here was a new socioeconomic group, defined by age and, courtesy of wartime earnings, by its newfound ability to consume. The group was ripe for exploitation by the worlds of fashion and entertainment. On the silver screen, John Garfield lit up the faces of younger audiences as a loser with outsize chips on his shoulder in *They Made Me a Criminal* and *Dust Be My Destiny* (both 1939) and *The Postman Always Rings Twice* (1946), with voluptuous but delicate Lana Turner.

Because young girls wore short socks, they were called bobby-soxers. Disdaining the saddle shoes and cardigan sweaters of the swing generation, they wore loafers with flat soles, Sloppy Joe sweaters, and men's white shirts outside blue jeans. There was another shift in teenage fashion with the appearance of the zoot suit, which combined high-waisted trousers with a wide-brimmed felt hat, a bow tie, and a long watch chain. Zoot suits were associated with gangs and sometimes with certain ethnic minorities, thereby becoming targets for attack.

The war made the evening news on radio a central feature of American broadcasting. Whereas in 1940 all networks broadcast a total of 2,376 hours of news, in 1944 the number was 5,552. After an initial bout of censorship, American radio broadcasters followed U.S. and Allied forces across every theater of war. Webley Edwards reported the island-hopping campaign in the Pacific. George Hicks followed troops in Europe.   .

One reason for the American people's incomplete understanding of the nature of this terrible war lay in Roosevelt's determination not to traffic in the sort of idealistic phraseology Woodrow Wilson had favored in World War I. In World War II there was little talk of making the world safe for democracy and few references to the creation of postwar utopias.

Because the Office of Facts and Figures was unpopular and handicapped by squabbling administrators and truculent journalists, a White House task force advised FDR to create a new agency with explicit authority to supervise the dissemination of news and information. Thus, FDR issued an executive order on June 11, 1942, creating the Office of War Information (OWI). Its director was journalist and radio broadcaster Elmer Davis. FDR called upon Davis and his staff to "coordinate the dissemination of war information by all federal agencies" and via the various forms of mass media "to facilitate the development of an informed and intelligent understanding, at home and abroad, of the status and the progress of the war effort and of the war policies, activities, and aims of the government."

Davis assembled a group of predominantly liberal writers who endeavored to set forth the basic details of the origins of the war, the issues involved in the struggle, and the objectives of the United States after victory. However, the advertising executives employed by OWI did not share the intellectuals' faith in the reasoning power of the public. They were committed to telling the truth, as they recommended, only "in terms that will be understood by all levels of intelligence." To the OWI's writers, the war was being fought to prepare mankind for the world envisaged in the Atlantic Charter. To the advertising men, the war was being fought to preserve the homespun world that glib cartoonist Norman Rockwell idealized. The homespun image won out against the high-minded ideal. In April 1943 writers resigned from the OWI en masse, voicing their disgust at the agency's efforts "to soft-soap the American public."

By April 1943 the OWI became the target of vehement criticism from conservatives in Congress who accused it of lionizing FDR. The campaign against the OWI reached its climax on June 18, 1943, when Republicans and southern Democrats in Congress voted to stop all funds to the domestic branch. The Senate Appropriations Committee sealed the fate of the OWI by granting it a mere $3 million, none of which—according to the terms of the grant—was to be spent on publications, movies, or radio scripts. In wielding its ax, Congress had, in the words of John Morton Blum (1976), "returned to the media and to those who bought advertising space, the whole field of domestic propaganda." It was business as usual in war.

From his experience in the OWI, where he processed gruesome photographs of bombing in Europe, photographer and artist Ben Shahn commented on "bombed-out places, so many of which I knew well and cherished. There were the churches destroyed, the villages, the monasteries . . . I painted Italy as I lamented it, or feared that it might become." Shahn's *The Red Stairway* (1944) has a gleaming red stairway in marked contrast to a bombing site, but it leads nowhere for its crippled passenger. The one sign of optimism is a laborer rising from the ground and facing forward, carrying on his back a basket loaded with stones with which to start rebuilding. Thus, instead of realism, Shahn chose symbolism.

Shahn and New York artists moved from the 1930s' popular-front interest in the artist's relationship with the masses to a yet more profound sense of alienation in the 1940s. Prominent regionalist Thomas Hart Benton wrote regretfully that, although he had created a meaningful art for the 1930s, during World War II he saw "most of the meanings, which it had taken many years to formulate, disappear with the dissolution of the world that generated them." Many artists moved to nonrepresentational art. For such artists, World War II seemed to expose the sort of moral chaos and despair that artists and writers had discerned in World War I.

The new mode in art was the angst-ridden and introspective abstract expressionism. It might be logical to suggest that abstract expressionism was a direct descendant of cubism with its shattering of conventional human forms. Once one form had been broken, then its shattering or splintering must follow, just as World War II shattered societies everywhere except in the United States. Artists (and writers) would show a radically different view of the past, according to literary critic Malcolm Bradbury (1996), "more international, more bloodied, a more anxious view of time and the world."

Among the artists in New York during the war were French surrealists. Surrealism, founded in Paris in the 1920s by poet André Breton, began as a literary movement but made its greatest impact in paintings such as Spaniard Salvador Dali's melting watches and Belgian René Magritte's floating men in bowler hats—images suggested by the popularizing of Sigmund Freud's interpretations of dreams. Dali, Magritte, and other surrealists, such as Max Ernst and Yves Tanguy, took refuge in the United States after the Nazi invasion of Paris in 1940. They invigorated homespun American talents such as Mark Rothko and Robert Motherwell.

Of all the new, explosive talents, the most widely publicized was Jackson Pollock, originally from Wyoming, who had studied at the Art Students League in New York under Thomas Hart Benton and, later, worked on the Federal Art Project of the WPA. Whether his work was regionalist or abstract, Pollock showed assured composition, dynamic rhythms, and clear touch, and marked contrasts of light and shade. Pollock suffered from profound alcoholism and had endured psychiatric analysis (1937–43)—therapy that also served to exercise his need for the annihilation of form with fierce, disturbed works, akin to the terrifying images of Francisco de Goya.

At art impresario John Graham's show at McMillen, Inc., in January 1942, Pollock's exhibits were almost entirely abstract and on a very large scale, incorporating cubist and surrealist techniques. In *Male and Female* (1942) it was possible to discern male and female characteristics. But the scramble of spatters, swirls, and hieroglyphics on the canvas overwhelmed first-time viewers with their energy. Pollock moved to ever larger canvases stretched out on the floor and began dripping and pouring paint on them, as in his *Composition with Pouring II* of 1943 for Peggy Guggenheim, measuring about eight feet by 19¾ feet. His second one-man show at her Art of This Century Gallery at 30 West Thirty-Sixth Street, New York, in November 1945 mixed abstract and expressionist figuration and established him as the most turbulent painter of his generation.

Ironically, abstract expressionism, the new form of art that defied the state, would become a tool of the state's own self-promotion. Abstract expressionism was the American art that allowed New York to supersede Paris as the international center of art. American politicians encouraged a new American art that would give the United States a new cultural authority commensurate with its

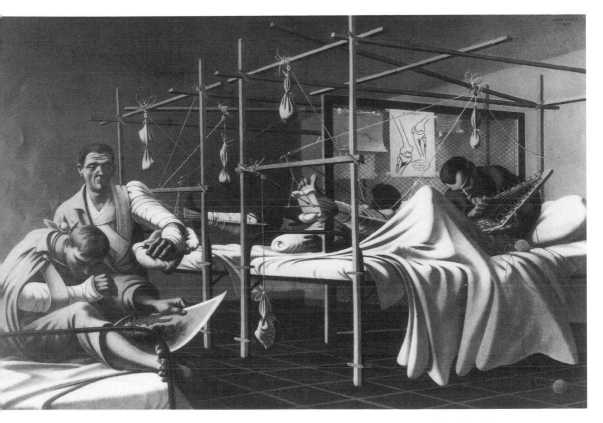

Fracture Ward (1944). Artist Peter Blume, known for his corrosive satire of Italy as lair of a jack-in-the-box Mussolini, demonstrated the wrenching effects of military violence on three victims of war—their limbs set anew but their understanding of the horrific nature of war fueled by a fire that medication cannot ease. (Library of Congress)

economic, political, and military aims for the postwar world. Western art was about to migrate to the United States along with industrial power and political might.

War was a business to the United States.

Flying High, Drilling Deep

Nowhere was that maxim more evident than in the mix of domestic politics, foreign diplomacy, and capitalist investment that turned into complex maneuvers to define and control the postwar boundaries of aviation and oil.

The London Blitz and the devastating attack on Pearl Harbor had made U.S. policy planners think long and hard about civil aviation and international security. People supported a general notion of "freedom of the air" as part of a diplomatic package that the projected United Nations must achieve if it were to ensure freedom and security.

Former Republican presidential candidate Wendell Willkie was among those who proclaimed a new universality of the air when he became the spokesman for the concept of one world in 1943:

> The modern airplane creates a new geographical dimension. A navigable ocean of air blankets the whole surface of the globe. There are no distant places any longer; the world is small and the world is one. The American people must grasp these new realities if they are to play their essential part in . . . building a world of peace and freedom.

Welch Pogue, chairman of the Civil Aeronautics Board (CAB), later recalled that "the imagination of men's minds leaped to the view that, in the postwar era, the airplane would 'shrink' the world so much militarily and in a civil sense as to make every civilization and its trade and commerce available to every other civilization on earth. Suddenly, civil aviation had become vitally important."

Domestic airline rivals to Pan Am were now ready to challenge its monopoly of overseas routes. Already in their competition for domestic passengers, they had been developing bigger and faster planes. These included the Douglas DC-4, or Skymaster, a four-engine plane that could carry forty-two passengers at two hundred miles per hour, and the Boeing 307, or Stratoliner, that could carry forty-four passengers. Air chiefs of the big four airlines (American, TWA, Eastern, and United) were eager to expand, notably Cyrus Smith of Texas, who led American Airlines. By now several airlines were flying overseas on military missions, for example American to Europe, United to Australia, and Eastern to Brazil.

Moreover, government officials had their own reasons for wanting to restrict Juan Trippe of Pan Am. In mid-1943 Gen. Henry ("Hap") Arnold, chief of staff of USAAF, convinced that other airlines should extend operations overseas, invited the heads of eighteen airlines to a secret meeting in Washington, D.C., to discuss postwar air policy. Welch Pogue announced in October 1943 that in the future the State Department and the CAB—not the airlines—would negotiate overseas routes.

Franklin Roosevelt's policies on civil aviation were largely shaped by his forceful lawyer in the State Department, Adolf Berle. "I feel that aviation will have a greater influence on American foreign interests and American foreign policy than any other political consideration," he advised Secretary of State Cordell Hull in September 1942. Berle was determined to anticipate an expected division of spoils by a new oligarchy of the airlines and the federal government. Concerned also that British plans for postwar civil aviation were more advanced than those of the United States, Berle created a committee, including Robert Lovett of the War Department, that recommended an international air conference that met in Chicago in November 1944. It was dominated by the ABC powers—the United States, Britain, and Canada. At this time, the United States was manufacturing almost all civilian planes and thus had a considerable advantage over the others. But although Britain was manufacturing only war planes and dreaded a glut of American planes, it still had its precious network of bases across the globe—including islands used as refueling stations, which could serve as bargaining counters to protect British interests. Canada had the advantage of controlling the airport at Gander, the principal landing point between the United States and

Europe—at least until airplanes could traverse the Atlantic without stopping to refuel. (Gander is in Newfoundland, a British colony until it became part of Canada in 1949; commercially, though, it was part of the Canadian system and was linked with Montreal and Quebec.) The Russians, however, were adamantly opposed to any genuine attempt to internationalize civil aviation that would intrude on tight Soviet control of planes, pilots, and merchandise in air space over the Soviet Union. In fact, the Soviet Union withdrew from the international conference just before the opening session, and its absence and truculence greatly reduced the prospects for global agreement.

Leading the U.S. delegation, Adolf Berle spoke for "open skies," a policy as exactly attuned to U.S. supremacy in the air as freedom on the seas had been to Britain when Britain was master of the seas. To make matters more difficult between the United States and the United Kingdom, Philip, Lord Swinton, who headed the British delegation, took an instant dislike to Berle, and the dislike was mutual.

Underlying the debate at the conference was the question whether nations would allow one another's airlines the five freedoms—the technical arrangements that defined the rights of air traffic: the freedom to fly over a nation; the freedom to land in a nation; the freedom to transport passengers or goods from the home nation to a foreign nation; the freedom to transport passengers or goods from a foreign nation to the home nation; and the freedom to pick up and land passengers or goods belonging to a foreign nation at intermediate points. The British delegates, acutely aware of Britain's shortage of aircraft, wanted a system to prevent U.S. airlines from flooding their routes. Thus, instead of a free-for-all that would inevitably provide the United States with an overwhelming advantage, the British delegates at Chicago proposed escalation—a system that would regulate and adjust the frequencies of planes according to the number of passengers. This system would have allowed Australia, New Zealand, and the European countries time to organize their own aviation industries. However, the American delegation rejected the escalation system.

At this point the British conceded all but the fifth freedom, which dealt with regulating traffic between points en route. Berle asked FDR to intercede, and the president wrote to Churchill,

> Your people are now asking limitations on the number of planes between points, regardless of the traffic operating. This seems to be a form of strangulation. It has been a cardinal point in American policy throughout that the ultimate judge should be the passenger and the shipper. The limitations now proposed would, I fear, place a dead hand on the use of the great air trade-routes.

Churchill reminded FDR that Britain had already "agreed to throwing open our airfields all over the world to aircraft of other nationalities."

At the conference, Fiorello La Guardia, mayor of New York City, infuriated Swinton by declaring, "It's pointless to make arrangements for airfields if you have no planes which could fly into them." Other representatives—from Holland, Sweden, and Latin America—were fearful of renewed British imperialism and supported the United States. Berle claimed that Britain's policy was "simply blown out of the water" by the opposition of smaller countries it claimed to protect. After much bickering and a further exchange between Roosevelt and Churchill, the conferees agreed to accept a compromise proposed by KLM of Holland, by which the first two freedoms were accepted and a decision on the others was deferred.

The Chicago convention extended prewar agreements at Paris and Havana. The convention firmly stipulated in Article 1: "The contracting states recognize that every state has complete and exclusive sovereignty over airspace." The conference created the International Civil Aviation Organization (ICAO) as an agency based in Montreal under the United Nations to coordinate and maintain rules of the air. Its first president was U.S. aviation expert Edward Warner. FDR, stung by criticism that Adolf Berle had made too many concessions to foreign airlines, dismissed him after the conference.

In fact, both the United States and Britain misconstrued the outcome. Subsequently, Germany and Japan became major air powers. Britain lost its bargaining power as its territorial empire disintegrated and it no longer required long-range planes for its isolated bases. Canada lost its bargaining power when planes could fly direct from New York or Chicago to Europe and bypass Gander and Montreal. The United States abandoned the fifth freedom when it realized it did not want foreign airlines flying between U.S. airports. The Soviet Union opposed all five freedoms and maintained close supervision of the air above its vast landmass. Nevertheless, the Chicago convention, through its creation, the ICAO, encouraged the phenomenal growth of postwar civil aviation. It allowed for exchanges of landing rights and information on technology and safety systems.

Britain wanted to revive the prewar organization, IATA, to discuss how airlines could cooperate and arrive at reasonable fares. Although U.S. delegates in Chicago, in keeping with U.S. antitrust laws, were sensitive to any suggested conspiracy between airlines, they agreed to call a conference at Havana, Cuba, in April 1945 to discuss this point. There, thirty-one nations duly approved a revived IATA (now the International Air Transport Association). IATA was a trade association sanctioned by governments as part of their bilateral agreements—most effectively since most airlines were now nationalized. It proved to be an international fare fixer—something the Americans reluctantly accepted in exchange for certain British concessions. Moreover, IATA could provide the machinery to coordinate and synchronize the rapidly expanding network of air routes, perhaps not the least of victories won in World War II by the Anglo-American alliance.

In the troubled field of oil, the Arab countries looked on the major oil companies as larger and mightier than the Western nations themselves. In the 1940s (as in the late 1930s) Standard Oil of New Jersey (later Exxon) and Shell were the rival giants. The two companies were almost private governments to which the United States and the United Kingdom had abdicated some of their diplomacy and tactics.

The Texas Company (later Texaco) and Standard Oil of California (later Socal) were concerned that the extravagant, spendthrift King Ibn Saud of Saudi Arabia might revoke their oil concession if they could not provide him with ready cash. At first, Britain bore the brunt of subsidizing Ibn Saud to the tune of $20 million. In time, the United States became concerned that the British might become all too influential with the king. Star Rodgers, chairman of Texaco, and Harry Collier, president of Socal, persuaded Secretary of the Interior Harold Ickes, who was the petroleum administrator during the war, to secure lend-lease funds for Saudi Arabia.

The oil companies thought they had achieved their objective of government funds without government interference, but they were wrong. Texaco and Socal had interested Ickes and the federal government far more than they had intended. The federal government was again concerned about running short of oil. William Bullitt, undersecretary of the navy, outlined the problem in a memo to FDR of June 1943 wherein he explained, "To acquire petroleum reserves outside our boundaries has become . . . a vital interest of the United States." Texaco and Socal were concerned that the British might prevail on Ibn Saud "to diddle them out of the concession and the British into it." Thus, they wanted to get "a direct American government interest in their concession." Bullitt proposed that the federal government create a Petroleum Reserve Corporation to acquire a controlling interest in Saudi Arabian oil production and to construct a refinery on the Persian Gulf. The new joint venture was the Arabian-American Company, or Aramco.

Secretary of the Interior Ickes liked Bullitt's idea. He knew that existing government machinery would make it possible to create a postwar international industry. Ickes quickly won over FDR. On June 30, 1943, the president authorized the creation of a new corporation to buy 100 percent of the Arabian concession. Herbert Feis, economic adviser to the State Department, recalled the careless, impulsive way in which the president reached his crucial decision: "The discussion with the President had been jovial, brief, and far from thorough. A boyish note was in the President's talk and nod, as usual, when it had to do with the Middle East." The new corporation, the Petroleum Reserves Corporation (PRC), led by Harold Ickes, included the secretaries of state, of war, and of the navy among its directors and employed lawyer Abe Fortas as secretary. Nevertheless, Texaco and Socal rejected its proposal for outright ownership of Aramco. Instead, they offered the government a one-third interest. Ickes and the PRC were ecstatic at the prospect of limitless oil to be siphoned from Saudi Arabia. Ickes dispatched an expedition there, led by oil geologist Everett De Golyer, whose final report confirmed their enthusiasm. "The center of gravity of the world of oil production is shifting from the Gulf-Caribbean areas to the Middle East, to the Persian Gulf area, and is likely to continue until it is firmly established in that area."

Ickes still intended to strike a deal with Texaco and Socal. But in October 1944 negotiations with Star Rodgers of Texaco broke down. At first, Texaco and Socal had been concerned because it seemed that German forces might over-run the entire Middle East. However, once the Allies had dislodged Field Marshal Erwin Rommel from North Africa, it seemed that the danger of German occu-pation of the Middle East passed. Thus, by mid-1943, Texaco and Socal no longer needed government protection in Saudi Arabia.

However, Ickes did not abandon his grand scheme of governmental control. He proposed a government-constructed pipeline extending one thousand miles across Saudi Arabia to the Mediterranean Sea. In return, the oil companies would guarantee 20 percent of the oil fields as a naval reserve with oil going to the U.S. Navy at a cheap rate. U.S. military strategists supported this plan; it would reinforce the U.S. presence in Arabia and it would move oil quickly. Texaco and Socal signed an agreement with Ickes. American geologist and Socal adviser Karl Twitchell remarked that Ickes's pipeline committed the federal government to a fixed foreign policy for the next twenty-five years.

But both the agreement and the pipeline caused diplomatic uproar. Britain recognized a naked threat to its dominance of the Middle East. Other U.S. com-panies were disturbed that two of their competitors, Texaco and Socal, would enjoy the advantage of cheap transportation. The jealous rival companies formed a special committee on national policy that proclaimed how harmful was gov-ernmental interference "to this most individualistic of all economic activities, the oil industry." Senator Moore of Oklahoma (an oil-producing state) denounced the pipeline as an imperialist adventure. Eugene Holman of Standard Oil of New Jersey staunchly maintained that the United States was self-sufficient in oil and had enough reserves to supply demand at the present rate for over one thousand years. Texaco and Socal prudently left the federal government to speak for them.

FDR and Ickes had to parry British opposition and get Churchill to recognize U.S. interests in the Middle East. Churchill's reaction was that some Britons suspected the United States of trying to deprive Britain of its oil interests. FDR responded by saying some Americans were accusing the British of trying to fore-close America's right to oil in Saudi Arabia. In the end, to resolve matters, Hull and Ickes met a British delegation, headed by Max Aitken (Lord Beaverbrook), and completed an agreement, signed on August 4, 1944. Although innocuous, the agreement provoked a storm of abuse from other U.S. oil companies about the creation of a supercartel. This led to its defeat in the Senate and its subsequent revision and renegotiation with the new Labour government in Britain after the war. There followed a renewed attack by American oilmen and a second defeat in the Senate in July 1947. As a result, any chance of a joint Anglo-American policy in the Middle East collapsed.

1944: Don't Sit under the Apple Tree
with Anyone Else but Me

As to winner-takes-all on the home front, American party politics resumed with a vengeance for the presidential election of 1944. Since there had never been any real doubt as to whether FDR would seek a fourth term of office, the only question revolved around who would be joining him on the ticket. Throughout the war, Vice President Henry A. Wallace had moved progressively leftward, while the nation had become more conservative. Long identified as the defender of the interests of agriculture and labor, Wallace was unacceptable to the conservative Democrats of the South and the party machines of the northern cities. Roosevelt left the decision on the vice presidency to the Democratic National Convention, held in Chicago in July 1944. Despite some grassroots support for Wallace, the party power brokers gave the nomination to the seemingly reluctant Senator Harry S. Truman of Missouri.

A compromise candidate, Truman was all things to all men. The southern Democrats saw the man from Missouri as a son of the middle border. A protégé of Kansas City's corrupt boss, Tom Pendergast, for which he was dubbed "the senator from Pendergast," Truman was acceptable to the politicians who operated the big-city machines. Since Truman had established his reputation as a critic of big business on the Senate Special Committee to Investigate the National Defense Program, liberals also saw him as their champion. He was, observes biographer Alonzo L. Hamby (1995), a product of rural Missouri caught between the verities of nineteenth-century America and the bewildering uncertainties of twentieth-century urban life.

Governor Thomas Dewey of New York went to the Republican National Convention of June 1944 as the firm favorite to win the presidential nomination. Forty-two-year-old Dewey, who won on the first ballot, had come to national prominence in the late 1930s as a racket-busting special prosecutor in New York. Swept along by the wave of resurgent Republicanism, he had won the governorship of New York in November 1942. As governor, he had a useful record as a social reformer. But on the presidential campaign trail, reporters found Dewey stiff, lacking any original ideas. With the GOP committed to a postwar international organization, Dewey's plans for postwar policy differed little from those of his opponent's. The only issue that Dewey would openly discuss was age. He depicted himself as a vigorous, youthful alternative to a tired and aged FDR.

Doubts about Roosevelt's health were truly justified. On March 27, 1944, FDR had undergone a thorough physical examination at Bethesda Naval Hospital. As well as acute bronchitis, the president was suffering from hypertensive heart disease and heart failure in the left ventrical. Although FDR was in need of rest and recuperation, by personalizing the campaign and (unintentionally) emphasizing Roosevelt's experience, Dewey simply played into the president's hands. FDR was content to fight the campaign on his image as commander in chief. The successful D-day landings in June 1944 enhanced his reputation as a war leader. His much-publicized meetings with other world leaders at Bretton Woods and Dumbarton Oaks added luster to his reputation as a statesman.

By then Dewey and his running mate, Governor John W. Bricker of Ohio, had embarked upon what FDR described to Harry Hopkins as the dirtiest campaign in his experience. Dewey popularized the view that FDR had egged the Japanese on to bomb Pearl Harbor. There were all the old canards—notably that FDR wanted to be dictator for life—plus some new ones, according to which, before FDR made any decision, he made sure that his advisers went to "clear everything with Sidney" (Hillman of the CIO). Truman got off lightly. He was simply (and in fact) a former member of the Ku Klux Klan.

Despite this virulent campaign, FDR was confident of victory and determined to leave his own campaigning until two weeks before polling day. Then he had two main aims: to silence rumors as to his health and to get the sleeping Democratic vote to the polls. He achieved the first on October 21, 1944, when he moved through New York in a four-hour motorcade. When the heavens opened, FDR saw the downpour as a blessing. Newspaper photographers, newsreel cameramen, and millions of New Yorkers saw FDR drenched to the skin but smiling and jaunty. One of his speech writers, Robert Sherwood, saw that FDR was neither sick nor ailing but in a state of "high exhilaration" at having gained a major publicity coup.

As to the problem of getting his supporters to the polls, to a certain extent FDR did clear it with Sidney. Hillman had organized his Political Action Committee (PAC) in 1943 as an instrument for keeping Henry A. Wallace on the Democratic ticket. The PAC took on the responsibility of mobilizing the labor vote for FDR in 1944. Throughout the campaign Republicans condemned it as a Communist front. After the election, pundits estimated that PAC had gotten 6 million blue-collar workers to the polls.

Far fewer votes were cast in the election of 1944 than in 1940. FDR received 25,606,585 votes (53.5 percent), and Dewey 22,014,745 votes (46.0 percent). In the electoral college FDR won 432 delegates to Dewey's 99. Roosevelt's victory of 3.6 million popular votes over Dewey was the lowest of any victor since 1916. His share of the popular vote had fallen from 54.7 percent in 1940 to 53.4 percent in 1944. The Republican vote had fallen by 300,000 since 1940, but the Democratic loss was greater still at 1.64 million. The marginal Democratic victory was supplied by African American votes in several states. For instance, in Michigan, the Democratic plurality of only 22,500 votes in the state as a whole was more than accounted for by the African American Democratic vote in Detroit alone. In New Jersey, African American voters in five major cities provided Roosevelt with a plurality of almost 29,000 in a state that went Democratic by only 26,500.

Nevertheless, the overriding factor in 1944 was the war and people's desire for continuity. Diehard isolationists, such as Congressman Hamilton Fish of New

York and Senator Gerald P. Nye of North Dakota, met defeat. A new generation of internationalists entered the Senate, including Wayne Morse of Oregon and J. William Fulbright of Arkansas.

Whatever FDR's personal popularity and the unprecedented nature of his four presidential victories, it is true that his health was not up to the arduous task of a fourth term. For several months people had been struck by FDR's ashen, wasted appearance. John Gunther, in his *Roosevelt in Retrospect* (1950), recalled the inaugural ceremony of January 20, 1945: "I was terrified when I saw his face. I felt certain he was going to die. All the light had gone out underneath the skin. It was like a parchment shade on a bulb that had been dimmed. I could not get over the ravaged expression on his face. It was gray, gaunt, and sagging, and the muscles controlling the lips seemed to have lost part of their function." At times FDR's exhaustion was so great that "he could not answer simple questions and talked what was close to nonsense."

All this was kept from the American people. Did FDR campaign for, and win election to, a fourth term because there really was no one else who could undertake the job? Because he and the Democratic power brokers would not relinquish power? And were these the people who lectured Soviet officials about the way to run democracy?

One ethnic group did gain from FDR's electoral victory. The exaggerated military threat posed by Japan to the West Coast had long since passed. Safely returned to the White House, FDR in December 1944 rescinded the original exclusion order against Japanese-Americans. Ironically, although they were now free to leave, many of the detainees were reluctant to do so. Dispirited, demoralized, resentful, and fearful of attack, most of those who stayed on were the elderly Issei. Japanese evacuees had already suffered property losses of $350 million. Many had no reason to return to the West Coast, and eventually half of the Issei and Nisei began a new life elsewhere.

The war had still to be won.

CHAPTER 17

1945: Withered Is the Garland of the War

REALIZING THAT President Franklin Delano Roosevelt would not live to see victory and the end of World War II, journalist Walter Lippmann wrote these words as a premature obituary of FDR in his "Today and Tomorrow" column of April 7, 1945, so that the president could read his appreciation.

> His estimate of the vital interests of the United States has been accurate and far-sighted. He has served those interests with audacity and patience, shrewdly and with calculation, and he has led this country out of the greatest peril in which it has ever been to the highest point of security, influence, and respect which it has ever attained.

Lippmann's analysis was correct. Partly because of its physical and human resources and partly through the political genius of FDR, the United States came to a zenith of global power in World War II. By adroit application of capital, the United States could dictate postwar reconstruction and extend its influence throughout the world.

Beyond Tragedy

While maintaining their fundamental objectives throughout the war, the Allies found justification for what had been, initially, a war of self-preservation, in the doctrine that all forms of right-wing military totalitarianism must be eliminated from the Axis nations and the world. A crucial event in their shared experience was the Holocaust, the destruction of European Jews.

Hitler planned to return Slavic peoples to the slavery of the Dark Ages and to eliminate Jews, first by herding them into twenty labor, concentration, and death camps, then by outright genocide. The colossal nature of the tragedy became apparent when Russian armies, moving from the east, and Anglo-American forces moving from the west liberated a score of death camps in Europe in fall 1944 and spring 1945.

About 4 million people, Gentiles as well as Jews, died at the most notorious of the camps, Auschwitz-Birkenau. Untold millions died elsewhere. The number is based on computations made by surveying the terrain, the chambers equipped with instruments of death, camp documents, the number of surviving prisoners, and the magnitude of human possessions of the victims. Apart from Jews, these included Gypsies, political dissidents, and those the Nazis considered deviants (the handicapped, homosexuals, and criminals).

At Auschwitz, the first attempts at mass extermination by gas (Cyclon B) took place on September 3, 1941. Until four huge gas chambers were built at Birkenau, gassing was done in two nearby farmhouses. Victims about to be gassed were told to undress and that they were to have a shower in the bathhouse. They were herded in great numbers into gas chambers of about 210 square meters that did indeed have shower-like devices in the ceiling. After a sortie of around two thousand victims had been gassed and killed by Cyclon B from apertures in the ceiling, the chamber was opened. Professional scavengers, a special draft of prisoners *(Sonderkommando)*, now entered. The scavengers took off the victims' rings and jewelry, extracted gold from their teeth, and cut off their hair, which was used to make tailors' linings and mail bags.

The victims' bodies were burned in crematoria. However, because of the great number of victims they were also buried in common graves or burned in immense pyres. The ashes were scattered and buried in ponds. According to Auschwitz camp commandant Rudolf Höss:

> Toward the end of the summer [1942] we started to burn bodies at first in wood pyres bearing some 2,000 corpses, and later in pits, together with bodies previously burned. In the early days oil refuse was poured on the bodies but later methanol was used. Bodies were burned in pits day and night, continuously. By the end of November 1942, all mass graves had been emptied. The number of corpses in the mass graves amounted to 107,000.

The wind carried the stench of burning flesh for many miles. The population of the entire district began to talk about the burning of Jews. Local German airdefense service complained about the fires being visible from afar at night. The numbers of victims were so great that it was impossible for the authorities to dispose of their property—clothes, shoes, towels, spectacles, baby carriages, valuables, and general luggage. This mountain of evidence indicated something of the extent of the massacres when the camps were liberated by Russian or U.S. armies in 1945.

Auschwitz had about forty branches, or subcamps *(Nebenlager)*, situated near foundries, mines, and factories in Silesia. There the prisoners were set to work making guns and chemicals and mining coal, sometimes for twelve hours a day. The grueling work and intimidation and beating by sadistic guards took their toll. About three hundred thousand prisoners died in the IG Farben factories at Auschwitz in the period 1942–45. Some of them were producing Cyclon B used for gassing other prisoners.

About three-quarters of the prisoners were being starved. Continuous calorie deficiency led to protracted starvation sickness in which the victims' bones were scarcely covered by skin and their eyes became glazed. Their complete physical decline led to mental exhaustion, listlessness, and indifference to their degraded surroundings. The medical examination of prisoners at Auschwitz, after the Red Army liberated the camp in the spring of 1945, showed that the prisoners weighed between 50 and 70 percent below what their normal weight should have been. Epidemics of typhus and diarrhea sometimes claimed numerous victims. Sadistic doctors conducted experimental surgical operations on living bodies, most notoriously Dr. Carl Clauberg and Josef Mengele ("the angel of death").

New York Times correspondent Harold Denny wrote on May 6, 1945, of the human vivisection laboratory at Buchenwald and the lamp shades made of human skin that the commandant's wife sent as presents to her friends: "Photographers have sent pictures so horrible that no newspaper would use them, but they were far less horrible than the reality, for they could not portray the stench of filth and death which clings to one's nostrils for days after one has visited a concentration camp."

The vicious war of extermination was not simply the work of a few SS units. Minister of Armaments Albert Speer oversaw an industrial empire of 14 million workers, many of them slave laborers in brutal concentration camps. Years later he told Gita Sereny (1995), "I was blind by choice . . . but I was not ignorant." Hundreds of thousands of ordinary German soldiers participated in an orgy of violence against civilians and POWs. Well over 4 million Soviet prisoners disappeared from German capture. They were exposed to the elements and left to die in subzero temperatures. Germans with families of their own led tender mothers and innocent children to the forests of Poland and indiscriminately slaughtered them during Hitler's Polish campaigns. Nazi officers, supported by Ukraine militia, gunned down 33,711 Soviet Jews in two days at Babi Yar and buried them in a ravine in Kiev. The victims' bodies toppled into the ravine, layer upon layer, coloring the stream red.

The first reports of the genocide from Poland in 1942 produced stunned disbelief in the United States. The press was loath to carry such news. Politicians retreated into convenient sophistry: since nothing could be done to stop the horror or aid the victims, the most appropriate response was to fight World War II to a swift conclusion and promise retribution for the Nazis. Churches were also reluctant to become involved in what would be considered an essentially Jewish

FACING PAGE:

The overriding impression left by the numerous photographs from the Warsaw Ghetto is of the degradation of human beings that the Nazis forced on the Polish Jews they confined therein.

Above: One hapless victim of atrocity has expired and awaits burial after unceremonious transportation in a rough-hewn hearse.

Below: Another pitiful victim is consigned to derelict entombment among others, now nameless, by being slid down a wooden shaft into a pit of lime below. (*Mein Kampf*; Columbia Pictures, 1961; Museum of Modern Art Film Stills Archive)

problem. In his review of David Wyman's *The Abandonment of the Jews* (1984), *New York Times* reviewer A. J. Sherman (also 1984) accuses FDR of a "cold indifference" to the fate of Holocaust victims. However, the current consensus among historians is more charitable to FDR and also to Churchill, emphasizing their single-minded and relentless pursuit of the great goal of eliminating Nazism and everything it stood for by concentrating everything on the defeat of Hitler.

Public awareness spread first among the Jewish community at large and then in Britain. Public concern led to an Anglo-American conference held in Bermuda in 1943 and described as a "preliminary two-power discussion on the refugee problem." The conferees intended to revive the Inter-Governmental Committee on Refugees, an inactive body, but the conference achieved nothing. What the State Department and the British Foreign Office feared was that any major initiative on their part—such as a rescue of Jews from occupied territory, if feasible—would oblige Germany to switch policies from extermination to expulsion. That would leave the United States and Britain with the headache of coping with millions of refugees and the social dislocation this would cause at the same time as they were fighting an unlimited war. Where could they place any rescued Jews? The State Department maintained they could not be admitted to the United States. The British Foreign Office refused to consider receiving them anywhere in the British Empire, including Palestine.

Not only was the Holocaust momentous in itself, but it also had profound consequences for world history. Collective Gentile guilt led to wider support for the Zionist movement to create a Jewish state—Israel—in Palestine in 1948. It further steeled the leaders of the Grand Alliance in their determination to eliminate right-wing dictatorships among the defeated powers at the end of the war. It justified the quartering of Germany in 1945. Above all, it helped broadcast a message that this had been a righteous war. Yet while the perspective of time could not soften the horror of Nazi atrocities, it cast the conniving complaisance of others in shades of gray, rather than the pure black and white of the victors' Cold War propaganda. For instance, revelations in 1996 and 1997 that Switzerland had cooperated with Hitler and the Nazis in the 1940s by secreting gold and bank accounts of Holocaust victims for them cast sinister aspersions on Switzerland's supposed wartime neutrality.

American diplomats hoped that World War II would provide the United States with a second chance to make the world safe for democracy. They believed this could be achieved by a new international community based on collective security, the United Nations.

Rarely has previous experience played so significant a role in shaping U.S. foreign policy or marshaling popular sentiment as it did for the United Nations. A legend had developed that the refusal of the United States to join the League of Nations had condemned the League to a futile existence, incapable of resisting aggression. The weakness of the League had resulted in the tragedy of World War II. Thus the U.S. government was an accomplice to the tragedy. The remedy was clear: to avoid another international catastrophe, the United States must lead a new system of collective security across the world.

Americans committed to Wilsonian liberalism believed that it was only Europeans who had colonies, client states, and spheres of influence. Thus, Senator Henry Cabot Lodge, Jr., of Massachusetts, grandson of the man who had led the fight to prevent the United States from joining the League of Nations, declared that it was the United States that must now lead the world, because it had no imperial ambitions. In a private letter of July 1, 1943, Walter Lippmann gave Lodge an elementary lesson on foreign policy: "You say that Britain has a very practical national aim, which is to maintain the Empire, but that we have no such practical aim. In fact, in this respect we have exactly the same practical aim as Britain: we, too, intend to maintain our prewar position—in Alaska, Hawaii, the Philippines, in the Caribbean, and in South America." Americans, conveniently forgetting about their privileged position in Latin America and the Caribbean, professed outrage at the cynical idea of a Russian sphere of influence. Lippmann thought it was clear that the Russians must exercise a dominant influence in those areas they thought essential to national security.

To ensure that he could bring the United States into his grand design, Franklin Roosevelt studied Woodrow Wilson's strategy anew and determined to avoid his errors. He decided that any new covenant must be kept separate from any peace treaty, that its terms must be publicized while they were being devised, and that he must seek its adoption before the end of the war dissipated the unity of the Grand Alliance and the wartime sense of responsibility in Congress. FDR also knew he must anticipate the disruptive effect of party politics by having the charter drafted by delegates from both parties and from both houses of Congress.

Moreover, the political climate at home encouraged hopes that the United States would not only take part in but also lead the United Nations. On June 15, 1943, the House passed a measure proposed by Congressman J. William Fulbright of Arkansas by 360 votes to 29 in which the House resolved that the United States should take the initiative in forming the United Nations, with machinery to settle disputes, if necessary by the use of force. On November 5, 1943, the Senate, by 85 votes to 6, adopted a similar resolution proposed by Thomas Terry Connally of Texas. Two days earlier, FDR had allowed a four-power declaration at the foreign ministers' conference at Moscow to assert "the necessity of establishing, at the earliest practical date, a general international organization, based on the principle of the sovereign equality of peace-loving states, and open to membership by all such states, large and small, for the maintenance of international peace and security." Connally's resolution used some of FDR's key phrases.

Thus, by the summer of 1944, FDR and Secretary of State Cordell Hull had persuaded Britain and Russia, the U.S. Senate and the House, and Democrats and Republicans to learn from the mistakes of recent history. By May 29 Hull had concluded discussions of the draft chapter with the Senate Foreign Relations

Committee. Stalin approved the text on July 9, 1944. Talks began at the Dumbarton Oaks estate in Washington, D.C., on August 21, 1944.

Experience with the League of Nations taught delegates at Dumbarton Oaks what to keep and what to discard. Delegates agreed to retain a Security Council, a General Assembly, a Secretariat, and an International Court of Justice in the new United Nations. As to the League's weaknesses, delegates agreed that they should not insist on unanimity in the United Nations Security Council or Assembly before any important move could be made and that all member nations must pledge in advance to accept and act upon findings of the Security Council and to place some of their armed forces at its disposal. However, each of the Big Three wanted the right of veto before action was taken on any major issue. This was partly to protect their own interests and partly to justify to their own peoples international use of their resources and troops. In the United States discussion and disputes about the United Nations concentrated on old controversies. Could the president place U.S. forces at the disposal of the Security Council by executive agreement? Could the U.S. representative on the Security Council move U.S. troops without the authority of Congress?

The Great Depression was still fresh in the minds of Americans. FDR's advisers believed that the world could avoid another devastating international depression only if they ensured that global markets and raw materials remained open to all nations. Furthermore, the domestic requirements of the United States necessitated such a policy. As Assistant Secretary of State Dean Acheson put it, "We can't expect domestic prosperity under our system without a constantly expanding trade with other nations." Another official said, "The capitalistic system is essentially an international system. If it cannot function internationally, it will break down completely." In short, the United States needed an open world market.

Hence, the United States made it its mission to secure a friendly, postwar marketplace. At the conference in Bretton Woods, New Hampshire, which opened on July 1, 1944, diplomats made arrangements for two new organizations. The first was the International Monetary Fund (IMF), but it did not begin to work effectively until 1946. Its primary aim was to bring stability and order to international banking and to make possible national reconstruction schemes. The IMF received $7.3 billion for the task of stabilizing currencies to encourage trade without the risk of currency depreciation. The second organization was the World Bank, which was to have a treasury of $7.6 billion and the authority to loan twice as much. Its initial function was to guarantee private loans for the reconstruction of Europe and of less industrialized areas of the world. In short, the United States wanted the World Bank and the IMF to restore and expand world trade. Voting power in the World Bank and the IMF depended on the sums of money contributed. Since the United States was going to give the most, it would, in effect, control both organizations.

Division

Winston Churchill went to the second Quebec, or Octagon, conference of September 11–16, 1944, with his feet firmly planted on the ground. He had set himself the task of trying to persuade FDR to keep the United States in Europe. To achieve a peaceful balance of power, he would have to persuade the United States to stand as some sort of counterweight to Russia across the western part of the continent. He made it his mission to try and persuade Roosevelt of the absolute necessity of continued American presence in Europe in the face of what he, himself, considered the real possibility of the revival of a traditional Bolshevik threat of fomenting revolutions outside the USSR. Roosevelt did agree to an ill-considered plan for the future of Germany. The plan was the brainchild of Secretary of the Treasury Henry Morgenthau. This scheme aimed at pastoralizing Germany—reducing it to an agrarian nation devoid of military potential. Initially, Churchill rejected this plan. It would have left Germany terminally weak and reliant upon a high level of industrial support that Britain simply could not afford to provide. The vacuum in central Europe would be filled by the Soviet Union. However, Britain's own need for immediate economic support from the United States obliged Churchill to withdraw his opposition. To gain the prime minister's approval, Morgenthau offered $3.5 billion worth of lend-lease supplies to be delivered up to the defeat of Japan and a further credit of $3 billion for nonmilitary purposes. Fortunately, both Churchill's war cabinet in London and FDR's advisers in Washington persuaded the two leaders to abandon the pastoralization scheme.

Churchill now felt he had no option but to seek some stabilizing territorial agreement with Stalin. At the Moscow conference of October 9–17, 1944, Churchill sought assurance from Stalin that the future government of Poland would comprise not only the Moscow-based Lublin Committee but also representatives of the Polish government in exile in London. Churchill told Stalin that the eventual Polish government must include Stanislaw Mikolajczyk, head of the Peasant Party; otherwise, the world would doubt the Allies' intentions about an independent Poland.

Although Churchill made no progress on Poland, he and Stalin did reach agreement on future spheres of interest in Eastern Europe. They decided that Russia would have 90 percent predominance in Romania and 75 percent predominance in Bulgaria. Britain would have 90 percent predominance in Greece, and Anglo-Soviet influence in Hungary and Yugoslavia would be split 50-50. Churchill's deal with Stalin would allow Britain to safeguard the Mediterranean Sea and the Suez Canal, lifeline of the British Empire.

German forces had withdrawn from Greece in early 1944. The resistance there was largely Communist, or Communist-inspired. Churchill had dispatched sixty thousand British troops to support George II, king of the Hellenes, in his attempt to regain his kingdom, although his record was far from democratic. The British defeated the resistance; Stalin sent no aid to the Communists. In December 1944

The classic photograph of the Big Three at Yalta in February 1945 conveys the charged atmosphere among the Grand Alliance. FDR's visage betrays the pallor of death; Churchill's smile is professional rather than spontaneous, and Stalin remains inscrutable. The convoy of high-ranking aides and uniformed officers adds more than a touch of menace to the composition. (Library of Congress)

Churchill imposed on Greece a provisional government under Archbishop Damaskinos (George Papandreou), thereby demonstrating his rank opposition to Communism and confirming Stalin in his view that he must have a free hand in his own war zone.

At Allied meetings in early 1945, discussions centered on the strategy for defeating the Axis powers. When the Allies met at Malta from January 31 to February 3, 1945, they discussed the Adriatic issue. Once more, the United States opposed the British strategy. The Allies then turned to the war in northwest Europe. The British revived Montgomery's plan for a single thrust into the heart of the Reich; the United States held fast to Eisenhower's plan for a broad advance to the Rhine, to be followed by a pincer movement aimed at encircling the Ruhr. Again, the British gave way. Eisenhower started to put the plan into action in three stages: an advance to the Rhine from the end of January to March 21, 1945; encirclement of the Ruhr, leading to the entrapment and surrender of

325,000 German troops between March 21 and April 14, 1945; and the annihilation of further points of enemy resistance, from April 14 to May 7, 1945.

The ensuing Allied drive to Berlin was rich in irony. Eisenhower and other U.S. generals had long urged upon the British a more adventurous campaign. Now that they were in the saddle, they conducted a dull, plodding campaign of a broad advance across Western Europe. The British, who had urged caution earlier, would now have preferred a quick thrust to Berlin. However, Eisenhower's broad-based approach was well suited to Anglo-American resources and the need to replenish those resources continuously from the rear.

Yalta

By the time the Big Three met at Yalta, the defeat of Germany was imminent. Debate turned to the postwar world. FDR and Churchill understood that by their successful war strategy, the United States and the United Kingdom were destroying Germany and Japan, the two nations who, whether as friend or foe, had traditionally blocked Russian expansion in Europe and Asia. Now, the triumph of the Grand Alliance's victory over Germany and Japan was marred by the tragedy of the incipient dissolution of the alliance. Both were apparent at the Crimean Conference from February 4–12, 1945, the Yalta Conference.

Churchill sought yet another understanding about the postwar status of Germany and Poland. He was anxious to reach an agreement while the Allies were still united against Germany and before the United States began its expected postwar withdrawal from Europe. Churchill also believed he could wring concessions from Joseph Stalin while Russia was receiving U.S. supplies of war matériel. In this he found support from policy planners in the U.S. State Department. However, FDR had no intention of bargaining away the future of Eastern and Central Europe. From FDR's perspective, the traditional balance of power based on spheres of influence in Europe and Asia had not only failed to prevent two world wars, but it had also made such conflicts inevitable. FDR was convinced that a lasting peace could be achieved only by developing the Grand Alliance's wartime unity of purpose into a permanent feature of great-power relations through the United Nations. If FDR could persuade the Soviets to commit themselves to the UN, then explosive issues such as Poland could be settled amicably on a basis of consensus. Thus, FDR went to Yalta seeking not to confront Stalin but to gain concessions from him.

The first concession related to FDR's plans for the postwar world. The Big Three agreed to send representatives to San Francisco on April 25, 1945, to draft the UN Charter.

Progress toward the establishment of the United Nations had been impeded at the Dumbarton Oaks Conference of 1944 by Soviet objections to the proposed formula for voting in the Security Council. The Soviets were adamant that no action could be recommended by the council unless all five permanent members (which later included China and France) were in unanimous agreement. In effect, they defended their right to veto any course of action that might jeopardize their own interests. However, at Yalta in 1945 Stalin agreed that permanent members of the UN should not be allowed to vote should they be party to disputes that could be settled by peaceful means. Conversely, they should be entitled to vote if they were party to disputes that required economic, political, or military sanctions.

Discussions then centered on the Russian demand for the admission of all sixteen Soviet republics to the United Nations General Assembly. FDR commented that if the Soviets were accommodated on this point, he would ask for separate membership for all forty-eight states of the Union. The Russians compromised their position: they were willing to accept membership of just three republics—Ukraine, Byelorussia, and Lithuania, besides Russia itself. The British and the United States consented on the condition that the United States should also have three votes in the assembly. Stalin promised his support for this proposal, but he was concerned that the United States could, by its largess, influence the vote of small nations in the General Assembly and that Britain could count on the votes of the Commonwealth nations.

FDR's second principal objective at Yalta was that the Russians enter the war against Japan. At Quebec in September 1944, Churchill and FDR had agreed that the target date for ending the war against Japan should be eighteen months after victory over Hitler. FDR's planners believed that the war against Japan would be won only by a full-scale invasion of Japan and the destruction of its military force. Estimates of the human cost of attaining victory were put at 1 million U.S. casualties.

Destruction of the Japanese military machine would entail not only invading the Japanese home islands but also confronting the million-strong Japanese force in Manchuria. Hitherto, U.S. military leaders had looked with dread upon the self-sufficient Kwantung army. They thought it was well trained and well equipped and that, because of the industrial potential of the region that it controlled, it had the capacity to continue the fight long after the Allies took Tokyo. In fact, although FDR did not know it, by the time of the Yalta Conference, the Kwantung army was a paper tiger. By 1945 some thirteen divisions, numerous supporting units, vast quantities of supplies, and the bulk of Japanese air strength in Manchuria had been secretly diverted from China. Since February 1944 U.S. military planners had been fighting the cream of the Kwantung army not in China but in the Pacific.

At Yalta Stalin promised that the Soviet Union would declare war on Japan two or three months after the surrender of Germany. In return, Russia would get the Kurile Islands and southern Sakhalin; an international guarantee of the autonomous status of Outer Mongolia (that is, tacit Allied acceptance of that republic as a satellite of the Soviet Union); renewed leases for Soviet uses of Dairen as a commercial port and Lushun (Port Arthur) as a naval base; and joint control, with China, over the Chinese Eastern and South Manchurian railroads.

With the exception of the Kurile Islands, all these territorial concessions involved land taken by Japan from Russia in the Russo-Japanese War of 1904–5.

In addition, FDR was moving Stalin to a position where he would promise Chiang Kai-shek that he would not support the Chinese Communists. Further, that he would persuade Mao Zedong to cooperate with Chiang. Stalin used his military strategy to further the traditional goals of Russian foreign policy without regard to Communism across the world. Stalin regarded Mao as a wild adventurer whose military schemes would infuriate the West and thus endanger Russian interests in the Far East. Mao regarded Stalin as a backstabber.

Roosevelt understood that if the Big Three and the United Nations did not help colonial peoples in Africa and Asia achieve national self-government, they would agitate for their freedom, nevertheless, and this would lead to more strife across the world. To calm one potential trouble spot, FDR proposed placing Indochina under a four-power trusteeship after the defeat of Japan. The occupying powers would be the United States, Britain, the USSR, and China. At Yalta Stalin agreed to this, but he suggested that the three states of Indochina would become independent in two or three decades. Britain objected. If France lost its colonies, what, in turn, would become of Britain's? FDR and his advisers already regarded the British Empire as an anachronism. FDR said so to Churchill—much to Churchill's irritation. Moreover, the United States knew that if it could gain trade advantages with Britain, its Empire, and the Commonwealth on a regular basis, it could open up the world marketplace.

As to the treatment of Germany, the Allies were in unanimous agreement on the need to eradicate from Germany not only the Nazi party with its laws and institutions, but also general militarism. However, when Stalin proposed dismembering Germany, Churchill voiced his reservations and suggested detailed consideration before they made a decision. FDR succeeded in postponing the debate until a special committee in London could frame an agreement. Stalin demanded that Germany be stripped of $20 billion worth of industrial plants by way of reparations, of which 50 percent was to go to the Soviet Union. The British recognized this as an another attempt to pastoralize Germany and rejected it. This time the Allies avoided another potentially disruptive debate by agreeing to refer the question to a three-power reparations commission to convene in Moscow later.

Since Churchill had little hope of gaining U.S. support for a balance of power in Europe, he gave his full backing to Charles de Gaulle's demand for a leading role in the postwar settlement of Germany. FDR and Stalin accorded France a place on the Control Council for Germany. A French zone of occupation of Germany was to be carved out of the British and U.S. zones. France was also to be given a sector in the capital, Berlin, in the eastern zone, which was otherwise to be controlled by the USSR.

Stalin was willing to compromise on Germany and France, but he drew the line on Poland. At the time of the Yalta Conference, Russian troops had already crossed Poland and were driving Nazi armies back into Germany. They took

Warsaw on January 11, 1945. There was still a Polish government in exile in London, composed of centrist and right-wing shades of opinion. But the Russians had already broken off diplomatic relations with the London Poles over reaction to publicity about the massacre in Katyn Forest. On January 1, 1945, Stalin recognized the Lublin-based committee of Communists as the legitimate government of Poland. Thus there were now two Polish governments: one in London, the ally of the United States and the United Kingdom; the other in Lublin, the ally of the Soviet Union. However, the real ruler of Poland was the Red Army. Under its protection the Polish Communist Party was assured effective power.

FDR was pragmatic. He wanted a new provisional government in Warsaw to be drawn partly from the Poles in Lublin, partly from the Polish government in exile in London, and partly from other Poles within the country. Such a government would not be hostile to Russia. Churchill accepted this compromise, as did Soviet Foreign Commissar Vyacheslav Molotov. As Churchill knew, insisting on the London Poles alone was useless since that group would have to return to, and brave, a country dominated by hostile Russian troops. He suggested that the Lublin committee might be augmented by representatives from other émigré circles. Elections could then be held to establish a permanent government in Poland. Stalin refused and held his ground. Churchill and FDR agreed to grant formal recognition to the "Provisional Government which is now functioning in Poland." They also agreed that the elections were to be free of Allied supervision.

However, the Big Three did agree about the borders of the new Poland. The Soviet Union was to be given the former areas of Poland east of the so-called Curzon line. Poland would be compensated by the cession of German lands in East Prussia and in the west. Stalin wanted the western border of Poland to run from Stettin in the north, along the length of the Oder and western Neisse rivers, down to the border with Czechoslovakia. This would not only restore to Poland territories taken by Hitler in 1939 but also add Pomerania and Silesia, including the ancient German city of Breslau. The extent of the territorial compensation to which the Poles helped themselves, with Russian support, was far greater than the United States and Britain intended. The sum effect of the Big Three's negotiations was to push both the eastern and western boundaries of Poland farther west than ever before. The western border of Poland was a violation of the principles of the Atlantic Charter. Five million Germans were never allowed an opportunity to determine their future.

The future of other East European states received far less attention at Yalta. Here the Big Three papered over potential differences by the "Declaration on Liberated Europe," which they drafted in part to satisfy American public opinion. In that document the Allies promised to cooperate in helping the people of liberated states and former Nazi satellites to "form interim governmental authorities, broadly representative of all democratic elements in the population and pledged to the earliest possible establishment, through free elections, of governments responsive to the will of the people." Roosevelt, Churchill, and Stalin also

"You're the cream in my coffee."

This striking photograph of Franklin Roosevelt and King Ibn Saud at an impromptu reception in February 1945, taken from above, has an interesting mix of subject, composition, and texture in which the angle of the photograph emphasizes the haphazard interplay of carpet design, Arab headdresses, and Western furniture. (Library of Congress)

promised that their governments would consult each other immediately on the "measures necessary to discharge [their] joint responsibilities."

In Yugoslavia, the partisan leader, Josip Broz, Marshal Tito, was able to form a government he wanted, despite British attempts to have Yugoslav exiles included. The governments of Hungary, Romania, and Bulgaria—all countries now dominated by the Red Army—were strongly pro-Soviet. Finland had allied itself with Hitler, but Russia did not interfere in Finnish politics—apart from taking Petsamo in the north. Stalin put pressure on Romania, demanding that the king appoint a Communist-led government. From the Anglo-American perspective, Stalin was thereby acting counter to the Declaration on Liberated Europe.

Since Russia and Japan were not yet at war, plans for Russia to declare war on Japan were kept secret. But the JCS had convinced FDR and Churchill that Russian intervention in the war against Japan was worth almost any price. For three years Stalin had been in a weaker position than either Churchill or FDR. He had had to beg them to open a second front while being unable to offer any special inducements since the Russians would, of course, continue to fight for their independence. Neither Roosevelt nor Churchill had much choice at Yalta. They were at war with Japan; Stalin was not. Stalin's armies had moved across Eastern Europe; theirs had not. FDR's bargain on Russian entry into the war in the Far East would both save American lives, which would be lost in an invasion of Japan, and shorten the war.

FDR hoped that once Russia had been accepted into the comity of nations, it would forget its traditional distrust of the West and commit itself to the principles of the Atlantic Charter. He knew that he could use the promise of economic aid in the postwar era to gain leverage over the Soviets. He also knew then that he would have another valuable bargaining counter. This asset was then under construction at a specially built physics laboratory in Los Alamos, New Mexico: the atomic bomb. In sum, FDR believed that the United States, with its overwhelming economic power, its dominance of the Western Hemisphere, its naval supremacy, and its peerless industrial and military forces, had little to fear from Russia, whose agriculture and industry had been devastated by war.

Yalta proved a prelude to more diplomatic maneuvers by powers with a mission. Now Egypt, Turkey, and Iran declared war on Germany and Japan, partly to ensure recognition from the United Nations and partly to signal their readiness to treat with the United States and France, rather than with Britain. Leading nationalists in the Middle East cut their political teeth on complex negotiations with the great powers, renegotiated treaties of assistance with Britain, and secured favorable agreements on economic aid. The Middle East nationalists' strategy was to divide the Allies, who already showed clear signs of competition for influencing the region after the war. Britain and France differed over the future of Syria. Britain and the United States were rivals for oil concessions in Saudi Arabia. The United States wanted to establish the rich oil-producing states as politically separate states but within an Arab league favoring American interests.

Thus, another crack appeared in the Anglo-American alliance. Roosevelt and Churchill competed in courting King Ibn Saud of Saudi Arabia, whose oil had helped them master Adolf Hitler. On his return from Yalta, FDR entertained King Ibn Saud aboard the cruiser *Quincy* along with a royal entourage of fifty, including twenty of the king's sons, the prime minister, flocks of sheep for slaughter, and the royal astrologer. In return for royal gifts of jeweled daggers and swords, FDR promised Ibn Saud an airplane. Three days later, Churchill received the king at the Hotel du Lac at Fayoum Oasis. In exchange for more precious swords, Churchill promised Ibn Saud an armor-plated Rolls Royce. Churchill knew that, for all his courteous pleasantries, Ibn Saud was really looking to the United States for both his income and his defense.

Not content with his successes in Europe, Stalin played a double game with U.S. Communists of the CPUSA. In spring 1945 Jacques Duclos, a French Communist recently returned to Paris from Moscow, denounced U.S. Communist leader Earl Browder's statements of support for the New Deal as class collaboration. Browder's colleagues in the United States interpreted Duclos's article as a clear signal of Stalin's disapproval of Browder. Accordingly, they expelled the hapless Browder. Eugene Dennis, a veteran of the Comintern in China, South Africa, and the Philippines, became party leader of the revived CPUSA.

Communists in the United States still tried to burrow away at the foundation of the federal government. *Amerasia* was a twice-monthly magazine devoted to Asian affairs. Its select readers included Kenneth Wells of the Office of Strategic Services (OSS, the forerunner of the CIA). In February 1945 Wells was disturbed when he read an article that contained sections lifted almost verbatim from a classified report that he himself had written. It included secrets that could harm Allied interests if they fell into Japanese hands. Wells had stumbled across a major breach of security. The OSS acted quickly, breaking into *Amerasia* offices and finding hundreds of classified documents. On June 6, 1945, the FBI arrested Philip Jaffe, editor and publisher of *Amerasia*, and five others, including John Stewart Service, a State Department expert on China.

The FBI discovered that virtually all U.S. agencies handling classified documents had been penetrated by Communists, including the OSS, the War and State Departments, and the Office of Naval Intelligence. Among the FBI's recorded conversations was one wherein *Amerasia* journalist John Stewart Service debated whether he should pass on top-secret information directly to the Soviets or just continue publishing them in the magazine—which gave him the same results with less risk. However, the federal government could not make a charge of espionage stick against *Amerasia* personnel because the agencies whose documents had been stolen did not want their contents revealed in court, embarrassing the administration.

Twilight of the Gods

Time was all too short. In these last weeks of the war in Europe FDR's doctors were in anguish over his rapidly deteriorating health. Dr. William D. Hassett said that the president was just drifting to death. He had not the energy or control even to sign his name. His case was hopeless, unless he could be totally isolated from pressure.

In Warm Springs, Georgia, on April 12, 1945, Roosevelt was having his portrait painted by Elizabeth Shoumatoff. It was to be a gift for the daughter of Lucy Mercer Rutherfurd, the woman with whom he had had a sporadic, long-term affair. The artist despaired of getting the president to maintain a pose as he habitually became engrossed in his papers or laughed together with Lucy after he had made a witty remark. Then, he put his left hand to his temple. "I have a terrific headache," he said, as his head slumped forward. Lt. Cdr. Dr. Howard G. Bruenn discovered that an artery had been punctured and blood was seeping into the cavities around the brain. FDR's eyes were dilated to the point of distortion and he had acute vertigo. He was having a massive cerebral hemorrhage. Just as Dr. James E. Paulin, an Atlanta specialist, arrived at Warm Springs at about 3:35 P.M., Franklin Delano Roosevelt died. When Harry Truman went to the White House, Eleanor Roosevelt tenderly put her arm on his shoulder and told him, "You are the one in trouble now."

Winston Churchill heard the news of FDR's death as he was entering his study at 10 Downing Street, London. He said, "I felt as if I had been struck by a physical blow." The free world was in mourning. After all, when people mentioned the president, for the past twelve years, it had been the same man. The obituary in the *New York Times* declared, "Men will thank God on their knees a hundred years from now that Franklin Roosevelt was in the White House when a powerful and ruthless barbarism threatened to overrun the civilization of the Western World."

In Moscow, news of Roosevelt's death fed Stalin's natural paranoia. Stalin suspected that FDR had not died of natural causes but instead had been murdered by his enemies. He instructed Russian Ambassador Andrei Gromyko in Washington to insist on seeing FDR's body. Gromyko flatly rejected the explanation that the casket would not be opened because the fatal hemorrhage had disfigured Roosevelt's face. Gromyko tried to get Eleanor Roosevelt to reverse her decision. He was less than polite about her adamant refusal because he was less concerned about offending the Americans than he was about disobeying Stalin.

Now the parochial, untested Harry Truman was president of the United States (1945–53). He soon learned that FDR's team was treating him as an executor for the dead president. When Truman entered the room for FDR's funeral service in the White House, the mourners neglected to rise.

The end of the war in Europe came suddenly and bitterly. On April 12, 1945, the day that Roosevelt died, the U.S. Fifth Armored Division reached the River Elbe. Standing only fifty-three miles from Berlin, the men of the Fifth assumed they were about to drive on to the capital. When Eisenhower learned where they were, he asked Omar Bradley for a general estimate of casualties in an assault on Berlin. Bradley suggested that they would be in the region of 100,000 lives.

To Eisenhower, who had lost such numbers in the assault on Western Europe, the prize was not worth the price. He repeated his order to stop at the Elbe. The Russians had already assembled 2.5 million soldiers at the line of the Oder River. This was the largest military force ever to gather in a concentrated front. They moved steadily to Berlin, which they entered on April 22.

President Harry Truman felt insecure. He was jealous of his presidential powers and wanted to show he was tough. In addition, he and many other Western politicians did not want any compromise to be interpreted as appeasement. He found support from advisers Averell Harriman (U.S. Ambassador to the USSR), William D. Leahy, and James Forrestal. On April 23 Truman met with Russian Foreign Commissar Vyacheslav Molotov. He accused Molotov of violating the Yalta agreements by imposing Soviet governments in Eastern Europe. Truman demanded that the Russians agree to a new Polish government.

"I have never been talked to like that in my life," said Molotov.

"Carry out your agreements and you won't get talked to like that," responded Truman.

But the next day, Stalin, who held the reins, rejected Truman's demands, citing Russia's need for security and emphasizing that he did not interfere in countries in the Western spheres, such as Belgium and Greece, where the Americans made decisions without consulting him. Thus, over Poland, Truman found he was no better off with Stalin than Neville Chamberlain had been with Hitler. A later secretary of state, Henry Kissinger (1973–77), justly opined (1994) after his retirement that Stalin was indeed "a monster; but in the conduct of international relations he was the supreme realist—patient, shrewd, implacable."

Twilight continued to fall on the gods. On April 28 Benito Mussolini and his mistress, Claretta Petacci, tried to escape in disguise from northern Italy to Innsbruck in Austria, but they were recognized. They were captured by partisans who shot and killed them and took their bodies to Milan, where they were hung upside down and reviled. On April 29 German forces in Italy surrendered unconditionally. In Berlin on April 30, Adolf Hitler and his former mistress, Eva Braun, now his wife, committed suicide. Their bodies were burned in the yard outside the bunker. Hitler had named Grand Adm. Karl Dönitz as his successor.

The Russians finally captured Berlin on May 2, 1945. It was they who then had to sustain casualties of more than one hundred thousand in bitter street fighting. Field Marshal Alfred Jodl was escorted to Eisenhower's headquarters in Reims on May 7 to sign the document of Germany's unconditional surrender. After he signed the surrender paper, Jodl's eyes welled with tears as he pleaded with Eisenhower to be generous. Three weeks earlier, Ike had toured the forced labor camp at Ordruf Nord and had been sickened by what he had seen. Generous? GI soldiers liberating Dachau before the cease-fire saw forty railroad cars packed with the emaciated bodies of men, women, and children, the living stacked on top of the dead. The GIs machine-gunned the SS guards.

Grand Adm. Karl Dönitz, Hitler's preferred successor, had wanted to end the war in the west while continuing to fight Russia in the east. When Dönitz tried to surrender three armies in the northern theater to Field Marshal Montgomery, Monty first kept Dönitz waiting while he fed his canary, Herbie. Then he told his visitor to surrender to the Russians. To accommodate Russia, the German surrender was ratified at Gen. Georgi Konstantinovich Zhukov's headquarters in Berlin at 11:30 P.M. on May 8. The West celebrated V-E Day (Victory in Europe) on May 8; the Russians on May 9.

Part of the myth about which power would first get to Berlin was based on a misconception that the nation first past the Brandenburg Gate would then have refused to yield to the other Allies their designated zones of occupation. However, after they had taken Berlin, the Russians, as previously agreed, gave up to U.S., British, and French forces the various sections of the city that they had taken at such tremendous cost. The Allies yielded to the Russians those other areas of Germany that they were holding but which had been previously allocated to the Russians. Churchill had suggested that U.S. forces should seize areas previously allocated to the Russians as a means of trading Russian agreement on Poland. State Department officials advised Truman that this would set a precedent that the Russians could then exploit in areas closer to American interests.

For millions of Europeans this was a period of intense anxiety and chaos. German soldier Dieter Wellershoff, later a writer living in Cologne, recalled (1995) the disorder of captivity as a POW of the Allies, including scarcity of food, which turned the men into feral animals, and the plague of lice:

> The military police with their white leather belts and shoulder straps were chewing gum, which made them look particularly condescending and contemptuous. We saw our first black man and then groups of concentration-camp inmates with shaved heads, in striped prison garb, silently staring at us. No more than 100 meters behind the M.P.s groups of American soldiers awaited us and began to fleece us. Rings, watches, whatever we had that was of value, they took. A lieutenant who was walking next to me was pulled aside. A G.I. grasped his wrist and very calmly removed his watch. I assume the German officer had not yet fully understood his situation and that he was at least as concerned for his watch as he was for his honor. Thereupon, he was taken by the collar and punched in the face. Bleeding profusely and without his watch, he rejoined our colleagues. That was a first lesson in defeat.

Europeans certainly knew who was in control. They were either in the American or the Russian zone. The establishment of the United Nations coincided with the United States and Russia's collision course over Eastern Europe. All nations who had signed the United Nations Declaration by February 8, 1945, or had entered the war against Germany by March 1 could attend the San Francisco Conference that opened on April 25. Its task was to organize the United Nations. The U.S. delegation was bipartisan. Led by Secretary of State Edward Stettinius (1945), it included, from the Senate, Tom Connally, Democrat of Texas, and Arthur Vandenberg, Republican of Michigan; from the House Foreign Affairs Committee, Sol Bloom, Democrat of New York, and Charles A. Easton, Republican of New Jersey. Harold Stassen, former governor of Minnesota, and Virginia C. Gildersleeve, dean of Barnard College, were also members of the delegation.

Representatives of fifty nations revised the Dumbarton proposals and the Yalta protocol. They added an idealistic preamble to the charter. They devised a series of trusteeships for various independent territories. They accepted the jurisdiction of the International Court of Justice. A committee of jurists meeting in Washington from April 9–20, 1945, had already drafted a statute that enlarged the role of the General Assembly, allowing it now to make recommendations to member states or to the Security Council. The idea was to expand the forum for unrestricted freedom of debate. The United States and the Soviet Union agreed to differ on the rights of the Security Council. A Military Staff Committee, consisting of the chiefs of staff, was to advise and assist the Security Council. But the Dumbarton agreement forbade members to enforce peace under regional arrangements, thereby nullifying the Soviet Union's recent mutual-aid pacts with Poland, Czechoslovakia, and Yugoslavia and the plan of the United States for hemispheric defense proposed by the Act of Chapultepec of March 6, 1945.

At the San Francisco Conference Arthur Vandenberg and Nelson Rockefeller (assistant secretary of state for Latin American affairs) devised the document to keep the Western Hemisphere within Washington's sphere of influence. This was article 51 of the United Nations Charter. Until the Security Council acted, each member had the right to defend itself individually or collectively by "regional agreements." The article allowed for collective self-defense through special regional organizations created outside the UN. Vandenberg and Rockefeller believed that article 51 gave the United States exclusive power in the New World and the right to intervene and flex its muscles in the Old.

The upshot of the UN agreements on the Security Council was this: For minor breaches of the peace, the UN might mobilize its great collective force by resolution, sanctions, or military intervention. However, in any major case affecting the great powers, a great power on the Security Council could use its veto to block any attempt to see if there had been an act of aggression, to designate the guilty party, and to decide the use of economic sanctions or military intervention.

As to how the United States would join the United Nations, this time there was no doubt that the Senate would approve the charter. Harry Truman told the Senate on July 2, 1945, that the choice "is not between this Charter and something else. It is between this Charter and no Charter at all." The charter embodied bitter experience of recent history "of a world where one generation has failed twice to keep the peace." The traditional arguments for U.S. isolationism and neutrality did not meet the needs of the twentieth century. This time there must be no compromises or half measures. In comparison with 1919, when the Senate had debated for six weeks and divided itself into four camps, debate was minimal. The hearings began on July 9, 1945, and lasted five days. When the Senate Foreign Relations Committee published its findings, it was in one report, not three. It recommended consent without modification. When the issue came to a single vote on July 28, 1945, the Senate approved it by 89 votes to

2. The two Republican dissenters were William Langer of North Dakota and Henrik Shipstead of Minnesota. Of the five abstentions, the sole opponent was Hiram Johnson of California, now on his deathbed.

However, there were still a few outstanding questions. Did U.S. delegates to the Security Council have the right to commit U.S. troops without authority from Congress? Was article 43, by which members placed military resources at the disposal of the Security Council, to be ratified by treaty, joint resolution, or executive action? Although Tom Connally and Arthur Vandenberg would have preferred this question to be settled by Congress at a later stage, their desire to avoid any revision to the charter was in marked contrast to the bitter, partisan attitudinizing of Henry Cabot Lodge and Woodrow Wilson. Truman swept this problem aside when he cabled from Potsdam on July 27, 1945, that he would obtain congressional approval for future military arrangements.

The peace process continued. The Protocol of August 1, 1945, provided that the Big Three should determine principles behind the settlements with Hungary, Bulgaria, and Romania; that France should take part with them in settling peace with Italy; that Britain and Russia would deal with Finland; and that the Security Council might be used for treating with Germany and Japan. Truman hoped that once the treaties had been drafted, they would be submitted to a general conference at the UN for adoption.

As to U.S. hopes for Eastern Europe, in June 1945 Truman was forced to accept a compromise over the Polish government whereby the Russians allowed several more pro-Western Poles in the Polish government. Truman and his advisers now hoped that their political recognition of the new government in Poland would allow the United States to open Poland "to a policy of equal opportunity in trade, investments, and access to sources of information." But the Poles refused the siren calls of U.S. dollar diplomacy. Truman's show of toughness had stiffened Stalin's determination to control Poland.

Recalling how the Treaty of Versailles had perpetuated wartime hatreds and how the League Covenant had frozen an incomplete peace, the U.S. delegates at the Potsdam Conference, meeting outside Berlin from July 17 to August 2, 1945, succeeded in deferring a formal conference. Instead, they created a Council of Foreign Ministers from the United States, Britain, Russia, France, and China to undertake necessary preparatory work.

At Potsdam, Truman and Secretary of State James Byrnes (1945–47) stopped short of dismembering Germany. However, the United States was going to hold Germany's western industrial heartland, partly to control the defeated enemy, partly to balance Russian mastery of central Europe. By their decisions, the Grand Allies foretold a division of Germany into two economic spheres that would lead to a division of Germany into two countries, East and West (1948–90).

Living Room—Dark Room—Mushroom

In the Far East, confident of victory against Japan, what the American commanders sought in early 1945 was a series of island bases in the Pacific from which they could launch the final attack on the home islands.

As part of this strategy, Admiral Nimitz's task force descended upon Okinawa. This island in the Ryukus, three hundred miles from Japan, was part of the southern Japanese archipelago. U.S. forces would at last be fighting on Japanese soil. Now they discovered their opponents were willing to die before allowing Japan to be occupied by the enemy. Japanese defensive strategy was enshrined in the slogan of the Twenty-Second Army, stationed in Okinawa: "One plane for one warship. One boat for one ship. One man for ten enemy. One man for one tank." On Okinawa the Japanese had converted even burial vaults to pillboxes for snipers; caves housed artillery that moved in and out on railroad tracks.

The invasion began on Easter Sunday, April 1, 1945, and the fighting continued until June 22, 1945. The eighty-two-day battle resulted in the end of the Japanese navy as an effective fighting force and in the death of 110,000 Japanese troops. The U.S. Tenth Army suffered 7,613 killed or missing in action, 31,807 wounded, and over 26,000 nonbattle casualties. U.S. naval casualties were also alarmingly high—9,731, of whom 4,907 were killed. Naval casualties were almost all victims of kamikaze attacks. Japanese pilots had been flying the *tokkai tai* (special-attack missions) during the Philippine campaign. It was at Okinawa, however, that the kamikaze became a basic feature of Japanese defensive operations.

If the taking of Okinawa made it clear to Japanese military leaders that defeat was inevitable, it also impressed upon the Americans how costly would be a frontal assault upon other islands in the Japanese homeland. The taking of Okinawa and the rapid construction there of a vast air and naval base effectively closed the ring on the Japanese homeland. USAAF B-29s could now bomb Tokyo and other towns and cities at will from their bases in the Ryukus, the Marianas, the Philippines (liberated July 5, 1945), and China. The most deadly of the bombing raids was one that caused the deaths of about 83,000 people in a raid on Tokyo of March 9 and 10, 1945. Japanese cities were overrun by refugees, living in shanty towns and racked by malaria and tuberculosis. But if Japan had lost the war, it was by no means crushed. Japan was still in control of China and dominated Manchuria, Indochina, and Korea.

In the meantime, British forces had entered Rangoon, Burma, on May 3, 1945, and were ready to go farther. The British wanted to push themselves into the war in the Far East not only for strategic reasons but also to show that they could still be of considerable use to the Americans. However, Churchill wanted to prolong the process of defeating Japan in order to ensure the continuation of U.S. supplies of lend-lease matériel to Britain, which could help its domestic transition from war to peace.

With total command of air and sea, the Allies now had to decide how to end the war in the Far East. The JCS had already devised their military strategy. On April 3, 1945, MacArthur (now commander in chief of U.S. Armed Forces in the Pacific) formulated a plan for the invasion of the Japanese homeland. The JCS duly approved it on May 25, 1945. Downfall, as it was code-named, comprised two operations: the invasion of the southernmost island, Kyushu, on November 1, 1945, and a much larger invasion of the main island, Honshu, on March 1, 1946. The JCS expected that the first thirty days of the Kyushu operation would claim between 30,000 and 50,000 U.S. casualties. Secretary of War Henry L. Stimson estimated that the entire Downfall operation would cost 1 million casualties. U.S. military leaders hoped that this price would not have to be paid.

For fully a year after Japan's generals conceded that they had lost the war, Emperor Hirohito hoped in vain for an illusory miltary stalemate. Thus he and his top advisers would not concede that Japan had, indeed, lost. During this year, 1.5 million Japanese died along with many times more that number of Asians and 50,000 Americans. In June 1945 the Japanese Supreme War Cabinet authorized the foreign minister, Togo, to approach the Soviet Union with a view to ending hostilities in September 1945. Stalin refused. Since the United States had broken the Japanese cipher early in the war, Harry Truman and his advisers knew that Tokyo was willing to surrender on condition that imperial institutions be preserved. Truman refused to pursue this option. Emperor Hirohito had, like Hitler, been presented to the American people as a symbol of all that was antithetical to democratic values. Truman was well aware that the public would have been outraged had he reached an accommodation with such an enemy.

Thus, World War II ended in the Pacific with the dawn of the Atomic Age. The atomic bomb was not simply another development in military technology. It was a revelation of humankind's power and propensity to destroy itself.

Physicist Albert Einstein had told Franklin Delano Roosevelt of the possibility of building an atomic bomb. He wrote to the president in 1939 that "a single bomb of this type, carried by a boat and exploded in a port, might very well destroy the whole port together with some of the surrounding territory." Although British and French scientists were already working toward construction

---

FACING PAGE:

Above: The devastation of aerial bombing, one of the crucial factors that prompted the Japanese surrender, is suggested in this bombing attack in 1945 upon the Nakajima Aircraft Engine Plant, part of the Mitsubishi industrial empire that extended 5 million square feet in an area near Tokyo. (Library of Congress)

Below: The devastating mushroom of the atomic bomb as it explodes upon Nagasaki, the second and last atomic attack of the war. (U.S. Army Air Force photo; Library of Congress)

of an atomic bomb, in the United States nuclear research was oriented toward nonmilitary use.

In July 1941 the British Maud committee, established to study the feasibility of producing atomic bombs during the war and to estimate their likely military impact, sent its report to Washington. The committee concluded, "It will be possible to make an effective uranium bomb, which, containing some 25 pounds of active material, would be equivalent as regards destructive effect, to 1,800 tons of TNT and would release large quantities of radioactive substances, which would make places near where the bomb exploded dangerous to human life for a long period." In August 1941 Churchill authorized the production of such bombs. Two months later, FDR wrote to Churchill, suggesting "that any extended efforts on this important matter might be usefully coordinated, or even jointly conducted."

On December 6, 1941, Dr. Vannevar Bush, director of the U.S. Office of Scientific Research and Development, decided to divert the agency's energies into the construction of a nuclear weapon. He created a special committee, comprising America's foremost physicists, to do so. Time was now of the essence, for the Allies believed that the Germans were working on a similar project. Given the industrial, academic, and financial resources of the United States, FDR and Churchill decided in June 1942 that the United States should take the lead in the construction of the bomb. Throughout 1942 the British nuclear effort diminished while the American work on the Manhattan Project continued apace. The large-scale production plants were at Oak Ridge, Tennessee; Richland, Washington; and Santa Fe, New Mexico, where physicist Robert Oppenheimer was in charge of the Los Alamos project.

America's technological elite of professors from MIT and Cal Tech and industrial scientists and executives met in Chicago at Eckhert Hall as part of the Chicago Metallurgical Project. They were asked to produce material they had never seen for a purpose unknown to them—except that it was absolutely essential to the war effort. The federal government pledged $400 million immediately and, in the end, paid $2 billion.

How would the scientists make an atomic bomb?

In theory, it should be possible to develop a chain reaction when neutrons were introduced into a pile of U^{235}. The neutrons were supposed to split the U^{235} atoms, each of which would liberate another one, two, or three neutrons that would split more atoms in their turn, and so on in the cycle until the critical mass was reached. The main problem was the impurity of the uranium. Only by stepping up production of Westinghouse uranium from eight ounces a day to over five hundred pounds a day could the scientists achieve the necessary three tons by November 1942. At the same time, two carbon companies produced a graphite resistant to neutrons, and Professor Frank H. Spedding of Iowa State College and his team improved the Westinghouse uranium, transforming it into lumps called "Spedding's eggs."

The precious pile of uranium was delivered and deposited in a former squash court on Ellis Avenue at the University of Chicago. To prevent the nuclear accident of a spontaneous chain reaction, seven strips of cadmium and three rods of boron steel (both metals being avid consumers of neutrons) were passed in and out of the pile. Layer after layer of uranium was added to the pile until the twelfth layer was in place on December 1–2, 1942. The whole mass of uranium, graphite, cadmium, boron, and other materials weighed 12,400 pounds. All the control materials were gradually removed. The K factor, by which generations of neutrons became ever larger, climbed to the crucial figure of 1.10. The chain was self-perpetuating.

Its transformation was a separate technological problem to be managed by a different team of scientists. FDR wanted the two teams kept apart and unaware of each other's presence in Chicago. By the end of 1943 the majority of British scientists had been absorbed into U.S. research teams. The Russians, however, did not participate in the project. FDR and Churchill were determined to keep Stalin in the dark. At the first Quebec meeting, the Quadrant Conference of August 1943, the two leaders promised that neither nation would use the weapon against an enemy without the consent of the other. They also promised that neither nation would give information relating to the weapon to a third power without the consent of the other.

Yet physicist Edward Teller described the most intimate mechanism of the bomb openly at a Los Alamos seminar. It involved bringing hemispheres into contact until the mass reached the critical point and detonated itself. What was unknown was the amount of U^{235} needed, the size of the two halves, the speed at which they must collide, the scattering angle, and the range of the neutrons to be projected by the chain reaction.

The sheer hatred and terror that Adolf Hitler had aroused partly explains the intense dedication of the Los Alamos scientists to their horrifying project. Either Hitler must already have such a weapon, or he soon would have one. In fact, Germany had no atomic weapons. Anti-Semitism had driven outstanding Jewish physicists abroad. What atomic research there was in Germany was being carried out independently by three separate ministries without any coordination. Confident of victory, Hitler ordered Albert Speer, his minister of supply, to put an end to all research on new weapons except those that could be produced within six weeks.

FDR was sure that time and technology were on the American side. But Stalin had his spies who were willing to betray America's atomic secrets. In New York Anatoly A. Yakovlev, Soviet consular official (1944–46), wove a spider's web, drawing in various agents. These spies included Harry Gold of Philadelphia, Julius and Ethel Rosenberg of New York, and Ethel's brother, Sgt. David Greenglass, who worked on top-secret material at Los Alamos. The most crucial member of the ring was Klaus Fuchs, a noted atomic scientist and member of the Los Alamos elite. A native of Germany, he had gone to England as a refugee from Nazi persecution and had become a naturalized British citizen. He enjoyed top-security clearance. No one wondered why the Nazis were after a Gentile physicist whose specialty was theoretical physics. Fuchs was a committed Communist. In Santa Fe he provided Harry Gold with typed notes on the application of theoretical fission to the building of a bomb.

The Fuchs spy ring succeeded with formidable espionage, running to ten thousand pages. The Anglo-American information guided Igor Kurchatov, the ebullient and resilient Soviet scientist who headed the Soviet nuclear enterprise, to an advantageous reactor design, to the recognition that a bomb could be made of plutonium, and to the implosive method of detonation.

The Franck Report of June 11, 1945, named after German immigrant physicist James Franck, warned the federal government that the West had no monopoly on the atomic bomb. The materials were available across the world and the basic scientific facts were widely known. The Franck Report proposed that the bomb should be used in a demonstration to ally and enemy alike. "If the United States were to be the first to release this new weapon of indiscriminate destruction upon mankind, she would sacrifice public support throughout the world, precipitate the race for armaments, and prejudice the possibility of reaching an international agreement on the future control of such weapons."

The United States carried out the first test of an atomic bomb at Alamogordo in the New Mexico desert on July 16, 1945, at 5:30 P.M. The steel tower on which the bomb had been placed was vaporized. The blast knocked down men standing one hundred thousand yards away. For the first time the mushroom cloud rose, carrying the dust of the earth that it was to make radioactive.

When President Harry Truman heard of the successful test, he was in Potsdam. Truman suddenly turned more truculent at the conference. Truman told Edwin Pauley, his reparations manager, that the bomb "would keep the Russians straight." Revisionist historian Gar Alperovitz (1995) argues that "the U.S. feelings of cheerfulness, rather than frustration," over differences with the Soviets at Potsdam "makes little sense unless one realizes that top policy makers were thinking ahead to the time when the force of the new weapon would be displayed." Here it seemed was a bargaining counter Truman could use in dealing with Stalin, whom he was accusing of reneging on the Yalta agreements.

To confront Hitler, whom the Allies truly believed had Germany working on an atomic bomb, with an Anglo-American atomic bomb was one thing. But those scientists and advisers who wanted to see the Manhattan project curtailed argued that to use the atom bomb against Japan was something else since the Japanese certainly could not build such a weapon. A major war which the United States had entered after a devastating attack by air did not provide an environment conducive to a disinterested display of scientific statesmanship. Huge sums of money had been spent on the terrible weapon. Truman and his advisers now concluded that the United States no longer had to apply (and waste) mass armies to defeat Japan; the bomb would be quicker and more decisive. Knowing about the intensity of Japan's resistance on Iwo Jima and Okinawa, Truman's fear that an invasion of the Japanese home islands would result in a blood bath with tremendous casualties on both sides was genuine enough. In the Potsdam declaration to Japan the Allies proposed unconditional surrender on pain of great destruction. Japan did not surrender. Truman ordered the dropping of the atomic bomb.

Among the president's advisers, no single individual prevailed over the others. For some, like Secretary of State James Byrnes, the primary justification was to intimidate the USSR and to exclude it from the Pacific war. Military strategist George Marshall wanted to gain a speedy victory over Japan, not only to save American lives but also to propitiate war weariness at home. Truman did not have a Henry Kissinger among his team to advise him (1994), with rueful hindsight, "What no leader must ever do is to suggest that choice has no price or that no balance needs to be struck."

The Japanese were staggered by the devastation of the first atomic bomb dropped on Hiroshima on August 6, the formal entry of Russia into the war against them on August 8, and a second atomic bomb dropped on Nagasaki on August 9, 1945.

The official report noted about the first atomic bomb dropped on Hiroshima that "what had been a city going about its business on a sunny morning went up in a mountain of dust-filled smoke, black at the base and towering into a plume of white to 40,000 feet." The bomb had more power than 20,000 tons of TNT. When it was dropped, the explosion was so great that it was forty-eight hours before photographs of the devastation could be taken from the air. Then it became clear that four of the seven square miles of Hiroshima had been obliterated. Of the 90,000 buildings in the city, 65,000 had either collapsed or been badly damaged. Later statistics of February 2, 1946, found that 78,150 people had been killed and another 13,983 were missing. (This was fewer than the 83,000 victims claimed by the fire raids on Tokyo of March 9 and 10, 1945.) The explosion produced a ground temperature of 3,000 degrees centigrade (5,400 Fahrenheit), causing intense and widespread thermal radiation that killed people three-quarters of a mile away. About 60 percent of the deaths were due to heat flash and fire burns. Thus, more than 50,000 of the people who died had been burned to death.

The second atomic bomb, dropped at noon on August 9 on Nagasaki, the port and armaments center on the west coast of Kyushu, resulted in a black cloud that rose 10 miles into the air and could be seen 250 miles away. Unlike Hiroshima, Nagasaki lay in a series of ridges and valleys. Thus, parts of the city escaped destruction. Nevertheless, the bomb obliterated one-third of the city. There were fewer casualties. In its 1950 report on the effects of atomic weapons, the Los Alamos Scientific Laboratory emphasized that in Tokyo the mortality rate in those parts of the city that were destroyed by high-explosive bombing earlier was 5,200 per square mile. In Nagasaki it was 20,000 per square mile, and in Hiroshima, 15,000 per square mile.

The Japanese people realized from the first devastating bombing that defeat was imminent. However, before Japan would surrender, it insisted that the United States guarantee the survival of the emperor. Having proved his atomic mastery to the Soviet Union as well as Japan, Truman, ironically, bombed himself into accepting Japan's surrender terms. There was another, practical consideration. The Allies believed that the elimination of the kaiser from Germany at the end of World War I had led to the creation of an unstable republic and thus prepared the way for Hitler. They did not want something similar to happen in Japan with the fall of another emperor after World War II.

The Japanese message of unconditional surrender was passed to the Allies on August 14, 1945, through Japanese ministers in Switzerland and Sweden. The formal surrender took place aboard the battleship *Missouri* on September 2, 1945, when the Japanese prime minister signed the document, along with Gen. Douglas MacArthur and various representatives of the United Kingdom, the USSR, France, China, the Netherlands, Australia, New Zealand, and Canada. This was V-J Day (Victory over Japan). World War II was at an end.

U.S. fighting in World War II had lasted three years and eight months. During the war, the armed forces of the United States suffered approximately 250,000 dead and 60,000 missing. Altogether, 75,000 servicemen were taken as prisoners of war. Of the 250,000 dead, 200,000 were buried on foreign soil. The Germans lost over 3 million soldiers, sailors, and pilots. In all, Japan's war dead amounted to 2.5 million, whereas about 10 million soldiers and civilians died at Japanese hands in the Co-Prosperity Sphere.

For the United States, the total monetary cost of the war (excluding interest on loans given to governments, pensions, and postwar aid programs) was approximately $350 billion—that is, ten times the cost of World War I. About 40 percent of this cost was met by taxation; the rest was borrowed. The U.S. Treasury went into the red by $40 billion annually, borrowing from banks at between 1 and 1.5 percent interest. At the end of hostilities, the national debt amounted to $250 billion. Federal spending during the years of combat exceeded the combined budgets of the United States for the years 1789 through 1940. The U.S. GNP had increased from $90 billion in 1940 to $213 billion by 1945.

View from the Summit

The elimination of Germany and Japan as first-class powers disrupted the political balance of the world. By its defeat in May 1945, Germany was returned to its borders of 1937. However, its land west of the rivers Oder and Neisse was divided into four zones of occupation administered by the United States, Britain, France, and Russia. All its land east of the Oder-Neisse line passed to Poland and Russia. The capital, Berlin, within the Russian zone, was also to be administered as four zones by the four powers.

By its defeat in August 1945, Japan was confined to its frontiers of 1894, losing Korea and its Pacific islands, Taiwan (Formosa), and all its possessions in China and Southeast Asia that had been acquired by its aggressive acts from the Russo-Japanese War of 1904–5 onward. Japan was also placed under military occupation by the United States. MacArthur was the supreme allied commander in Japan, but he took orders from Washington.

The Allies agreed in London in August 1945 to bring German and Japanese offenders to trial for crimes against peace, humanity, and even the rules of war. From November 20, 1945, to October 1, 1946, a military tribunal at Nuremberg tried twenty-four leading Nazis and imposed on them various penalties, including execution. The United States conducted another twelve trials of 863,000 Nazis in the American zone in Germany. Far more complex proceedings were held in Tokyo from June 3, 1946, to November 12, 1948, against twenty-eight "Class A" Japanese defendants, culminating in sentences of death or life imprisonment. By October 1949, 4,200 Japanese altogether had been convicted; 720 of them were executed.

There were now but four first-class powers: the United States, the Soviet Union, Britain, and China. China recovered all its possessions except Macao, Korea, and Hong Kong. However, the sleeping giant owed its potential world-class status to its immense geographical size, its considerable population, and its industrial and agricultural potential. Severely damaged by years of Japanese occupation and divided by civil war, it was still a world-class power only in name. In contrast, Britain was a world-class power in decline. This was partly because it had lost its initial lead in the industrial revolution, partly because it had been hard hit materially and financially by two world wars, and partly because it now faced the loss of empire as its colonies claimed political independence that could not long be denied.

Thus, in a damaged world, the United States and the USSR dominated world affairs. Neither would withdraw as they had in the 1920s. By entering the war in Asia in its final convulsive stages, Russia had recovered much of the ascendancy in the Far East that it had held up to the Russo-Japanese war of 1904–5. But its more substantial gains were in Europe because the western advance of the Red Army in 1944 and 1945 had not only broken Germany's hold on Central and Eastern Europe but also transformed this area into a Soviet sphere. Set against these gains were mighty losses. The USSR had lost perhaps 20 million people to Hitler's war. It had suffered considerable material damage to its cities, its industrial plants, and its agriculture. The war had obliterated 17,000 Russian towns and 70,000 villages and made 25 million Russians homeless. Russia did not yet have atomic weapons. Yet Russia had formidable strengths. Its victory over Germany was a watershed in the twentieth-century history of Communism and one that opened up the opportunity for renewed changes within the USSR. Moreover, a new generation of Russians had come of age, who had never known any other political system than Communism.

The United States was at the zenith of its power. It was materially more prosperous than ever; its territory had remained inviolate; it alone had atomic power. It had established a considerable presence in Western Europe and had superseded Japan in Asia. It occupied or controlled four major industrial areas of the world—Western Europe, Britain, Japan, and, of course, the United States itself. America's culture and economy were the envy of the world. It owed its present political prestige to the fact that it was regarded as a bastion of democratic freedom against totalitarian dictatorship.

If America had ascended, its leaders found the view from the summit bleak. Some saw the ghost of depression past that might recur; the present destruction caused by the war; and future political, economic, and diplomatic problems that the very success of democratic capitalism might generate with its insatiable advance. For continued economic prosperity, the United States needed a receptive capitalist environment. Secretary of State James Byrnes announced, "Our international policies and our domestic policies are inseparable. Our foreign relations inevitably affect employment in the United States. Prosperity and depression in the United States just as inevitably affect our relations with the other nations of the world."

There were other drawbacks to America's newfound position. In his "Today and Tomorrow" column of September 11, 1945, Walter Lippmann, casting a wry look at the failure of Germany and Japan, explained America's insidious, newfound problems:

> There is no more difficult art than to exercise great power well; all the serious military, diplomatic, and economic decisions we have now to take will depend on how correctly we measure our power, how truly we see its possibilities *within* its limitations. That is what Germany and Japan, which also rose suddenly, did not do; those two mighty empires are in ruins because their leaders and their peoples misjudged their newly acquired power, and so misused it. . . .
>
> Nothing is easier, too, than to dissipate influence by exerting it for trivial or private ends, or to forget that power is not given once and forever but that it has to be replenished continually by the effort which created it in the first place. The wisdom which may make great powers beneficent can be found only with humility, and also the good manners and courtesy of the soul which alone can make great power acceptable to others.
>
> Great as it is, American power is limited. Within its limits, it will be greater or less, depending on the ends for which it is used.

Now followed the bitter years of the Cold War of 1945–91—intense hostility between the USA and the USSR. Within ten years of the end of World War II, the hostility between the two superpowers was so great that it seemed it might provoke a third as America entered the Atomic Age.

BIBLIOGRAPHY

1. *A Hot Time in the Old Town Tonight:*
Theodore Roosevelt and the Progressives

Anderson, Donald. *William Howard Taft: A Conservative's Conception of the Presidency.* Ithaca, N.Y., 1973.

Blum, John Morton. *The Progressive Presidents: Theodore Roosevelt, Woodrow Wilson, Franklin Roosevelt, and Lyndon Johnson.* New York, 1980.

Carlson, Robert. *The Quest for Conformity: Americanization through Education.* New York, 1975.

Cashman, Sean Dennis. *America in the Age of the Titans: The Progressive Era and World War I.* New York, 1989.

Collier, Peter, and David Horowitz. *The Roosevelts: An American Saga.* New York, 1994.

Cooper, John Milton. *The Warrior and the Priest: Woodrow Wilson and Theodore Roosevelt.* Cambridge, Mass., 1983.

Croly, Herbert. *The Promise of American Life.* New York, 1909.

Gable, John Allen. *The Bull Moose Years: Theodore Roosevelt and the Progressive Party.* Port Washington, N.Y., 1978.

Gould, Lewis J. *Reform and Regulation: American Politics from Roosevelt to Wilson.* 1977; reprint, New York, 1986.

Graham, Otis L. *The Great Campaigns: Reform and War in America, 1900–1928.* Englewood Cliffs, N. J., 1971.

Jackson, Kenneth T., ed. *The Encyclopedia of New York City.* New Haven, Conn., 1995.

Koening, Louis W. *Bryan: A Political Biography of William Jennings Bryan.* New York, 1971.

Link, Arthur S., and Richard L. McCormick. *Progressivism.* Arlington Heights, Ill., 1983.

Morris, Richard B., and Jeffrey B. Morris, eds. *Encyclopedia of American History.* 6th ed., New York, 1982.

Roosevelt, Theodore. *The New Nationalism.* Englewood Cliffs, N.J., 1961.

Sinclair, Upton. *The Jungle.* New York, 1905.

Steffens, Lincoln. *The Shame of the Cities.* New York, 1904.

Sullivan, Mark. *Our Times: The United States, 1900–1925.* 6 vols. New York, 1925–35.

Thelen, David P. *Robert M. La Follette and the Insurgent Spirit.* 1976; reprint, Madison, Wis., 1986.

Wattenberg, Ben J., ed. *The Statistical History of the United States from Colonial Times to the Present.* New York, 1976.

Woodward, C. Vann. *Origins of the New South, 1877–1913.* Baton Rouge, La., 1951.

Zunz, Olivier. *Making America Corporate, 1870–1920.* Chicago, 1992.

2. *Virtue Is Its Own Reward: Woodrow Wilson and the New Freedom*

Anderson, David D. *Woodrow Wilson.* Boston, 1978.

Link, Arthur S. *Woodrow Wilson and the Progressive Era, 1910–1917.* 1954; reprint, New York, 1963.

———. *The New Freedom.* Princeton, N.J., 1956.

———. *Campaigns for Progressivism and Peace.* Princeton, N.J., 1965.

Tumulty, Joseph. *Woodrow Wilson As I Knew Him.* Garden City, N.Y., 1921.

Warburg, Paul M. *The Federal Reserve System: Its Origin and Growth.* 2 vols. New York, 1930.

Wilson, Woodrow. *The New Freedom.* Englewood Cliffs, N.J., 1961.

3. *RPM: The Flowing Rhythm of Modern America*

Appel, Alfred, Jr. *The Art of Celebration: Twentieth-Century Painting, Literature, Sculpture, Photography, and Jazz.* New York, 1992.

Bloom, Claire. *Leaving a Doll's House: A Memoir.* Boston, 1996.

Bradbury, Malcolm. *Dangerous Pilgrimages: Trans-Atlantic Mythologies and the Novel.* New York, 1996.

Cochrane, Thomas C., and William Miller. *The Age of Enterprise: A Social History of Industrial America.* New York, 1942; rev. ed., New York, 1961.

Conot, Robert E. *A Streak of Luck — Edison.* New York, 1979.

Dunne, John Gregory. *Monster: Living Off the Big Screen.* New York, 1997.

Hounshell, David A. *From the American System to Mass Production, 1800–1932: The Development of Manufacturing Technology in the United States.* Baltimore, 1984.

Hughes, Robert E. *The Shock of the New: Art and the Century of Change.* New York, 1981.

Kanigel, Robert. *The One Best Way: Frederick Winslow Taylor and the Enigma of Efficiency.* New York, 1997.

Lacey, Robert. *Ford.* New York, 1986.

Landau, Sarah Bradford, and Carl W. Conti. *Rise of the New York Skyscraper, 1865–1913.* New Haven, Conn., 1996.

Lessard, Suzannah. *The Architect of Desire: Beauty and Danger in the White Family.* New York, 1996.

Mast, Gerald, and Bruce Kawin. *A Short History of the Movies.* Revised and updated. New York, 1996; first published as *A Short History of the Movies,* by Gerald Mast. New York, 1971.

McShane, Clay. *Down the Asphalt Path: The Automobile and the American City.* New York, 1994.

Meile, Jeffrey L. *American Plastic: A Cultural History.* New Brunswick, N.J., 1996.

Mendelowitz, Daniel. *A History of American Art.* New York, 1970.

New York Times Book Review: Centennial Issue, October 6, 1996. Original reviews of works by W. E. B. Du Bois, Helen Keller, Henry Adams, Margaret Sanger, and others.

Norman, Bruce. *The Inventing of America*. New York, 1976.

Richardson, John, with Marilyn McCally. *A Life of Picasso*. Vol. 2, 1907–1917. New York, 1996.

Robinson, David. *Chaplin: His Life and Art*. New York, 1985.

Rose, Barbara. *American Art since 1900*. New York, 1967.

4. No Gods, No Masters

Archdeacon, Thomas J. *Becoming American: An Ethnic History*. New York, 1983.

Bennett, Mary Frances, and John W. Blassingame. *Long Memory: The Black Experience in America*. New York, 1982.

Brecher, Jeremy. *Strike!* Boston, 1979.

Cashman, Sean Dennis. *African-Americans and the Quest for Civil Rights, 1900–1990*. New York, 1991.

Chafe, William H. *Women and Equality*. New York, 1977.

Degler, Carl N. *At Odds: Women and the Family from the Revolution to the Present*. New York, 1980.

Dinnerstein, Leonard, and David Reimers. *Ethnic Americans: A History of Immigration and Assimilation*. New York, 1975.

Dubofsky, Melvyn. *We Shall Be All: A History of the I.W.W.* Chicago, 1969.

———. *Industrialism and the American Worker, 1865–1920*. New York, 1975.

Du Bois, W. E. B. *The Souls of Black Folk*. 1903; reprint New York, 1961.

Green, James R. *The World of the Worker*. New York, 1980.

Handlin, Oscar. *The Uprooted*. Boston, 1951.

Harlan, Louis R. *Booker T. Washington: The Wizard of Tuskegee, 1901–1915*. New York, 1983.

Kennedy, David M. *Birth Control in America: The Career of Margaret Sanger*. New Haven, Conn., 1970.

Kraut, Alan M. *The Huddled Masses: The Immigrant in American Society 1880–1921*. Arlington Heights, Ill., 1982.

Lewis, David Levering. *W. E. B. Du Bois: Biography of a Race 1868–1919*. New York, 1994.

Logan, Rayford. *The Betrayal of the Negro, from Rutherford B. Hayes to Woodrow Wilson*. Toronto, 1969; first published as *The Negro in American Life and Thought: The Nadir 1877–1901* (New York, 1954).

Lukas, J. Anthony. *Big Trouble: A Murder in a Small Western Town Sets Off a Struggle for the Soul of America*. New York, 1997.

Marty, Martin E. *Modern American Religion*. Vol. 1, *The Irony of It All, 1893–1919*. Chicago, 1986.

McGreevy, John T. *Parish Boundaries: The Catholic Encounter with Race in the Twentieth-Century Urban North*. Chicago, 1996.

Morris, Charles R. *American Catholic: The Saints and Sinners Who Made America's Most Powerful Church*. Illustrated. New York, 1997.

O'Neill, William. *Divorce in the Progressive Era*. New Haven, Conn., 1967.

O'Neill, William. *Everyone Was Brave.* Chicago, 1969.

Rampersad, Arnold. *The Art and Imagination of W. E. B. Du Bois.* London, 1971.

Salvatore, Nick. *Eugene V. Debs: Citizen and Socialist.* Urbana, Ill., 1982.

Takaki, Ronald. *A Different Mirror: A History of Multicultural America.* New York, 1993.

Weisenberger, Bernard A. *Booker T. Washington.* New York, 1972.

Wertheimer, Barbara. *We Were There: A History of Working Women in America.* New York, 1977.

White, John. *Black Leadership in America, 1895–1968.* London, 1985.

5. *Making Waves in World Affairs*

Cohen, Warren I. *America's Response to China, An Interpretive History of Sino-American Relations.* 1971; 2d ed. New York, 1980.

Collin, Richard A. *Theodore Roosevelt, Culture, Diplomacy, and Expansion: A New View of American Imperialism.* Baton Rouge, La., 1985.

Dulles, Foster Rhea. *America's Rise to World Power, 1898–1954.* New York, 1955.

Gardner, Lloyd C. *Safe for Democracy: The Anglo-American Response to Revolution, 1913–1923.* New York, 1984.

Hosking, Geoffrey. *Russia: People and Empire, 1552–1917.* Cambridge, Mass., 1997.

Krauze, Enrique. *Mexico: Biography of Power: A History of Modern Mexico, 1810–1996.* Translated by Hank Heifetz, New York, 1997.

LaFeber, Walter. *The Panama Canal: The Crisis in Historical Perspective.* New York, 1979.

———. *Inevitable Revolutions: The United States in Central America.* New York, 1983.

Langley, Lester D. *The Banana Wars: An Inner History of American Empire, 1900–1934.* Lexington, Ky., 1983.

Leopold, Richard W. *The Growth of American Foreign Policy.* Cambridge, Mass., 1961.

Link, Arthur S. *Woodrow Wilson: Revolution, War, and Peace.* Arlington, Ill., 1979.

Major, John. *The Contemporary World: A Historical Introduction.* London, 1970.

Marks, Frederick W., III. *Velvet on Iron: The Diplomacy of Theodore Roosevelt.* Lincoln, Nebr., 1979.

McCullough, David. *The Path between the Seas: The Creation of the Panama Canal, 1870–1914.* New York, 1978.

Miller, Stuart C. *"Benevolent Assimilation": The American Conquest of the Philippines, 1899–1903.* New Haven, Conn., 1982.

Neu, Charles E. *The Troubled Encounter: The United States and Japan.* 1975; reprint, Melbourne, Fla., 1979.

Rosenberg, Emily. *Spreading the American Dream: American Economic and Cultural Expansion, 1890–1945.* New York, 1982.

Schmitt, Karl M. *Mexico and the United States, 1821–1973: Conflict and Coexistence.* New York, 1974.

Williams, William Appleman. *The Roots of the Modern American Empire.* New York, 1969.

6. *Tell That to the Marines! America and World War I*

Bailey, Thomas. *Woodrow Wilson and the Lost Peace.* New York, 1944; *Woodrow Wilson and the Great Betrayal.* New York, 1945; published jointly as *Wilson and the Peacemakers* (New York, 1947).

Connor, Valerie Jean. *The National War Labor Board: Stability, Social Justice, and the Voluntary State in World War I.* Chapel Hill, N.C., 1983.

Devlin, Patrick. *Too Proud to Fight: Woodrow Wilson's Neutrality.* New York, 1975.

Epstein, Edward Jay. *Dossier: The Secret History of Armand Hammer.* New York, 1996.

Ferrell, Robert H. *Woodrow Wilson and World War I, 1917–1921.* New York, 1986.

Figes, Orlando. *A People's Tragedy: A History of the Russian Revolution.* New York, 1997.

Gaddis, John L. *Russia, the Soviet Union, and the United States: An Interpretive History.* New York, 1978.

Kennedy, David M. *Over Here: The First World War and American Society.* New York, 1980.

Kissinger, Henry. *Diplomacy.* New York, 1994.

Klehr, Harvey, John Earl Haynes, and Frederick Igorevech Firsor. *The Secret World of American Communism.* New Haven, Conn., 1995.

Murray, Robert K. *Red Scare: A Study in National Hysteria, 1919–1920.* 1955; reprint, Westport, Conn., 1980.

Powers, Richard Gid. *Not without Honor: The History of American Anticommunism.* New York, 1996.

Schmitt, Bernadotte, and Harold E. Wedeler. *The World in the Crucible, 1914–1919.* New York, 1984.

Smith, Daniel M. *The Great Departure: The United States and World War I, 1914–1920.* New York, 1965.

Stone, Ralph A. *The Irreconcilables: The Fight against the League of Nations.* New York, 1970; reprint, New York, 1973.

Sullivan, Mark. *Our Times.* Vol. 5, *Over There, 1914–1919.* New York, 1933.

Tuttle, William M. *Race Riot: Chicago in the Red Summer of 1919.* New York, 1970.

Widenor, William C. *Henry Cabot Lodge and the Search for an American Foreign Policy.* Berkeley, Calif., 1980.

7. *Tales of the Jazz Age*

Albini, Joseph L. *The American Mafia — Genesis of a Legend.* New York, 1971.

Allen, Frederick Lewis. *Only Yesterday: An Informal History of the Nineteen Twenties.* New York, 1931.

Anderson, Jervis. *Harlem: The Great Black Way, 1900–1950.* London, 1982; also published as *This Was Harlem: A Cultural Portrait, 1900–1950* (New York, 1983).

Baltzell, E. Digby. *Sporting Gentlemen: Men's Tennis from the Age of Honor to the Cult of the Superstar.* New York, 1995.

Barnouw, Erik. *A History of Broadcasting in the United States.* Vol. 1: *A Tower in Babel* (to 1933). New York, 1966.

Behr, Edward. *Prohibition: Thirteen Years That Changed America.* New York, 1996.

Bergreen, Laurence. *Capone: The Man and the Era.* New York, 1994.

————. *Louis Armstrong: An Extravagant Life.* New York, 1997.

Cashman, Sean Dennis. *America in the Twenties and Thirties: The Olympian Age of Franklin Delano Roosevelt.* New York, 1989.

Chalmers, David M. *Hooded Americanism — The First Century of the Ku Klux Klan, 1865–1965.* Garden City, N.Y., 1965.

Cowley, Malcolm. *Exile's Return: A Literary History of the 1920s.* 1934; reprint, Magnolia, Miss., 1983.

Eyman, Scott. *The Speed of Sound: Hollywood and the Talkie Revolution, 1926–1930.* New York, 1997.

Gabler, Neal. *Winchell: Gossip, Power, and the Culture of Celebrity.* New York, 1994.

Hobson, Fred. *Mencken: A Life.* New York, 1994.

Hoffmann, Frederick. *The Twenties: American Writing in the Postwar Decade.* 1962; rev. ed., New York, 1965.

Huggins, Nathan I. *Harlem Renaissance.* New York, 1971.

Joughin, Louis, and Edmund W. Morgan. *The Legacy of Sacco and Vanzetti.* 1948; reprint, Princeton, N.J., 1976.

Kazin, Alfred. *On Native Grounds.* 1939; reprint, New York, 1983.

Kerr, E. Austin. *Organized for Prohibition: A New History of the Anti-Saloon League.* New Haven, Conn., 1985.

Larson, Edward J. *Summer for the Gods: The Scopes Trial and America's Continuing Debate over Science and Religion.* New York, 1997.

Leider, Emily Wortis. *Becoming Mae West.* New York, 1997.

Leighton, Isabel, ed. *The Aspirin Age, 1919–1941.* New York, 1949.

Leuchtenburg, William E. *The Perils of Prosperity, 1914–32.* Chicago, 1958.

Lynd, Robert S., and Helen Merrell Lynd. *Middletown.* New York, 1927.

Marty, Martin E. *Modern American Religion.* Vol. 2, *The Noise of Conflict, 1919–1941.* Chicago, 1991.

Martin, Tony. *Race First: The Ideological and Organizational Struggles of Marcus Garvey and the UNIA.* Westport, Conn., 1976.

Merz, Charles. *The Dry Decade.* 1931; reprint, Seattle, Wash., 1970.

Oshinsky, David M. *"Worse Than Slavery": Parchman Farm and the Ordeal of Jim Crow Racism.* New York, 1996.

Ritchie, Michael. *Please Stand By: A Prehistory of Television.* Woodstock, N.Y., 1994.

Sinclair, Andrew. *Prohibition, the Era of Excess.* London, 1962.

Smith, Richard Norton. *The Colonel: The Life and Legend of Robert K. McCormick, 1880–1955.* Boston, 1997.

Snowman, Daniel. *America since 1920.* 1968; rev. ed., London, 1978.

Tindall, George Brown. *The Emergence of the New South, 1913–1945.* Baton Rouge, La., 1967.

Wade, Wyn Craig. *The Fiery Cross — The Ku Klux Klan in America.* New York, 1987.

Wilson, Edmund. *The Twenties.* New York, 1975.

Zangrando, Robert L. *The NAACP Crusade against Lynching, 1909–1950.* Philadelphia, 1980.

8. *Nine Mocking Years with the Golden Calf*

Bernstein, Irving. *The Lean Years: A History of the American Worker, 1920–1933.* New York, 1983.

Fuess, Claude M. *Calvin Coolidge: The Man from Vermont.* 1977; reprint, Westport, Conn., 1981.

Galbraith, John Kenneth. *The Great Crash — 1929.* 1954; reprint, New York, 1979.

Hicks, John D. *The Republican Ascendancy, 1921–1933.* New York, 1960.

Lichtman, Allan J. *Prejudice and the Old Politics: The Presidential Election of 1928.* Chapel Hill, N.C., 1979.

Lowitt, Richard. *George W. Norris: The Persistence of a Progressive, 1913–1933.* Champaign, Ill., 1971.

Murray, Robert K. *Warren G. Harding and His Administration.* Minneapolis, 1969.

Noggle, Burt. *Teapot Dome: Oil and Politics in the 1920s.* 1962; reprint, Westport, Conn., 1980.

Schlesinger, Arthur M., Jr. *The Crisis of the Old Order.* Boston, 1958.

Tauranac, John. *The Empire State Building: The Making of a Landmark.* New York, 1995.

9. *The World Broken in Two*

Malia, Martin. *The Soviet Tragedy: A History of Socialism in Russia, 1917–1991.* New York, 1994.

Moynahan, Brian. *The Russian Century: A History of the Last 100 Years.* New York, 1994.

Payne, Stanley G. *A History of Fascism, 1914–1945.* Madison, Wis., 1996.

Pipes, Richard. *Russia under the Bolshevik Regime.* New York, 1994.

10. *Down in the Dumps—Welcome to the Depression*

Allen, Frederick Lewis. *Since Yesterday: The Nineteen Thirties in America.* New York, 1940.

Fasold, Martin L. *The Presidency of Herbert Hoover.* New York, 1985.

Garraty, John A. *Unemployment in History: Economic Thought and Public Policy.* New York, 1979.

Irakawa, Daikichi. *The Age of Hirohito: In Search of Modern Japan.* Trans. by Mikiso Hane and John K. Urda. New York, 1995.

Kyvig, David E. *Repealing National Prohibition.* Chicago, 1979.

Lissio, Donald. *The President and Protest: Hoover, Conspiracy, and the Bonus Riot.* Columbus, Miss., 1974.

Manchester, William. *The Glory and the Dream: A Narrative History of America, 1932–1972.* New York, 1974; reprint, London, 1975.

Smith, Gene. *The Shattered Dream: Herbert Hoover and the Great Depression.* New York, 1979.

11. *That Man in the White House: Franklin Delano Roosevelt and the New Deal*

Brinkley, Alan. *Voices of Protest: Huey Long, Father Coughlin, and the Great Depression.* New York, 1982.

Burns, James MacGregor. *Roosevelt: The Lion and the Fox.* New York, 1956.

Collier, John. *From Every Zenith.* Denver, 1963.

Conkin, Paul. *The New Deal.* Arlington Heights, Ill., 1983.

de Bedts, Ralph. *Recent American History.* Vol. 1, *1933 through World War II.* Homewood, Ill., 1973.

Hurt, R. Douglas. *The Dust Bowl: An Agricultural and Social History.* Chicago, Ill., 1981.

Kelly, Laurence C. *The Assault on Assimilation: John Collier and the Origins of Indian Policy Reform.* Albuquerque, N.M., 1983.

Leuchtenburg, William E. *Franklin D. Roosevelt and the New Deal, 1932–40.* New York, 1963.

Lowitt, Richard. *George W. Norris: The Triumph of a Progressive, 1933–44.* Champaign, Ill., 1978.

Morgan, Ted. *FDR: A Biography.* New York, 1985.

Murray, David. *Modern Indians: Native Americans in the Twentieth Century.* British Association for American Studies Pamphlets in American Studies, no. 8. Cambridge, 1982.

Patterson, James. *Congressional Conservatism and the New Deal.* Lexington, Ky., 1967.

Romasco, Albert U. *The Politics of Recovery: Roosevelt's New Deal.* New York, 1983.

Saloutos, Theodore. *The American Farmer and the New Deal.* Ames, Iowa, 1982.

Schlesinger, Arthur M., Jr. *The Coming of the New Deal.* Boston, 1958.

———. *The Politics of Upheaval.* Boston, 1960.

Sherwood, Robert E. *Roosevelt and Hopkins: An Intimate History.* New York, 1948.

Sitkoff, Harvard, ed. *Fifty Years Later: The New Deal Evaluated.* New York, 1985.

White, Graham, and John Maze. *Harold Ickes of the New Deal.* Cambridge, Mass., 1985.

Warren, Donald. *Radio Priest: Charles Coughlin, the Father of Hate Radio.* New York, 1996.

Williams, T. Harry. *Huey Long.* New York, 1969.

Youngs, William J. *Eleanor Roosevelt.* Thorndike, Mass., 1984.

12. *Red, Hot, and Blue: Sunset on the New Deal*

Achenaum, W. Andrew. *Shades of Gray: Old Age, American Values, and Federal Politics since 1920.* Boston, 1982.

Anderson, Jervis. *Bayard Rustin: Troubles I've Seen: A Biography.* New York, 1997.

Bernstein, Irving. *A Caring Society: The New Deal, the Worker, and the Great Depression.* New York, 1985.

Brinkley, Alan. *The End of Reform: New Deal Liberalism in Recession and War.* New York, 1995.

Chafe, William H. *The American Woman: Her Changing Social, Economic, and Political Role.* 1972; reprint, New York, 1977.

Clegg, Claude Andrew, III. *An Original Man: The Life and Times of Elijah Muhammad.* New York, 1997.

Dubofsky, Melvyn. *The State and Labor in Modern America.* Chapel Hill, N.C., 1994.

Dubofsky, Melvyn, and Warren Van Tine. *John L. Lewis: A Biography.* New York, 1977.

Egerton, John. *Speak Now against the Day: The Generation before the Civil Rights Movement in the South.* New York, 1995.

Fine, Sidney. *Sit-Down: The General Motors Strike of 1936–37.* Ann Arbor, Mich., 1969.

Goodman, James. *Stories of Scottsboro.* New York, 1994.

Johanningsmeier, Edward P. *Forging American Communism: The Life of William Z. Foster.* Princeton, N.J., 1994.

Kirby, John B. *Black Americans in the Roosevelt Era: Liberalism and Race.* Knoxville, Tenn., 1980.

Klehr, Harvey. *The Heyday of American Communism.* New York, 1984.

Lichtenstein, Nelson. *The Most Dangerous Man in Detroit: Walter Reuther and the Fate of American Labor.* New York, 1995.

Milton, Joyce. *Tramp: The Life of Charlie Chaplin.* New York, 1996.

Myrdal, Gunnar. *An American Dilemma.* New York, 1944.

Polenberg, Richard. *One Nation Divisible — Class, Race, and Ethnicity in the United States since 1938.* Harmondsworth, 1980.

Shannon, David A. *The American Socialist Party.* New York, 1955.

Sitkoff, Harvard. *A New Deal for Blacks: The Emergence of Civil Rights as a National Issue.* Vol. 1, *The Depression Decade.* New York, 1978.

Swanberg, William. *Norman Thomas — The Last Idealist.* New York, 1976.

Wandersee, Winifred D. *Women's Work and Family Values, 1920–1940.* Cambridge, Mass., 1981.

Weiss, Nancy J. *Farewell to the Party of Lincoln: Black Politics in the Age of FDR.* Princeton, 1983.

13. Castles in the Air

Andrews, Wayne. *Architecture, Ambition, and Americans.* London, 1984.

Barnouw, Erik. *The Golden Web: A History of Broadcasting in the United States.* Vol. 2, *1933–53.* New York, 1968.

Bergman, Andrew. *We're in the Money: Depression America and Its Films.* New York, 1971.

Buxton, Frank, and Bill Owen. *The Big Broadcast, 1920–1950.* New York, 1972.

Crunden, Robert. *From Self to Society: Transitions in American Thought, 1914–1941.* Englewood Cliffs, N.J., 1972.

Farber, Stephen, and Marc Green. *Hollywood Dynasties.* New York, 1984.

French, Philip. *The Movie Moguls: An Informal History of the Hollywood Tycoons.* London, 1969; reprint, Harmondsworth, 1971.

Gill, Brendan. *Many Masks: A Life of Frank Lloyd Wright*. New York, 1987.

Gold, Jay, ed. *The Swing Era*. Time-Life Records, New York, 1970.

Goldberger, Paul. *The Skyscraper*. New York, 1982.

Hunter, Sam. *American Art of the Twentieth Century*. New York, 1972.

Jencks, Charles. *Modern Movements in Architecture*. 1973; 2d ed., Harmondsworth, 1985.

Levinson, Richard, and William Link. *Stay Tuned*. New York, 1983.

Lynes, Russell. *The Lively Audience: A History of the Visual Performing Arts in America, 1890–1950*. New York, 1985.

May, Larry. *Screening Out the Past: The Birth of Mass Culture and the Motion Picture Industry*. 1980; rev. ed., Chicago, 1983.

McKenzie, Richard D. *The New Deal for Artists*. Princeton, N.J., 1973.

Merritt, Russell, and J. B. Kaufman. *Walt in Wonderland*. Baltimore, Md., 1994.

New York Times Book Review: Centennial Issue, October 6, 1996. Original reviews of works by Theodore Dreiser, F. Scott Fitzgerald, Ezra Pound, Claude McKay, Sinclair Lewis, John Dos Passos, Margaret Mitchell, William Faulkner, John Steinbeck, Nathanael West, Ernest Hemingway, Richard Wright, Arthur Koestler, Ayn Rand, T. S. Eliot, and others.

Nicholson, Stuart. *Billie Holiday*. Boston, 1995.

Norton, Arthur. *Raymond M. Hood*. New York, 1931.

Oliver, Paul. *The Blues Tradition*. New York, 1970.

Sarris, Andrew. *The American Cinema: Directors and Directions, 1929–1968*. New York, 1968.

Scully, Vincent. *Frank Lloyd Wright*. New York, 1969.

Thomson, David. *Rosebud: The Story of Orson Welles*. New York, 1996.

Wilson, Edmund. *The Thirties*. New York, 1982.

Wilson, Richard Guy, Dianne H. Pilgrim, and Dickran Tashjian, with the Brooklyn Museum. *The Machine Age in America: 1918–1941*. New York, 1986.

14. Kissing Hitler? Round Up the Usual Suspects

Ambrose, Stephen E. *The Rise to Globalism: American Foreign Policy since 1938*. London, 1971; 7th ed. rev., London, 1993.

Andrew, Christopher. *For the President's Eyes Only: Secret Intelligence and the American Presidency from Washington to Bush*. New York, 1995.

Churchill, Winston S. *The Gathering Storm*. New York, 1948.

Cloud, Stanley, and Lynne Olson. *The Murrow Boys: Pioneers on the Front Lines of Broadcast Journalism*. New York, 1996.

Cole, Wayne S. *Roosevelt and the Isolationists*. Lincoln, Nebr., 1983.

Dallek, Robert. *Franklin D. Roosevelt and American Foreign Policy, 1932–1945*. New York, 1979.

Divine, Robert A. *The Reluctant Belligerent: American Entry into World War II*. New York, 1976.

Edgerton, Robert B. *Warriors of the Rising Sun: A History of the Japanese Military*. New York, 1997.

Fehrenbach, T. R. *FDR's Undeclared War, 1939–1941*. New York, 1967.

Friedlander, Saul. *Nazi Germany and the Jews*. Vol. 1, *The Years of Persecution, 1933–1939*. New York, 1997.

Kimball, Warren F. *Franklin D. Roosevelt and the World Crisis, 1937–45*. Lexington, Mass., 1974.

Millis, Walter. *The Road to War*. Boston, Mass., 1935.

Prange, Gordon W. *At Dawn We Slept: The Untold Story of Pearl Harbor*. New York, 1981.

Rauch, Basil. *Roosevelt: From Munich to Pearl Harbor*. 1950; reprint, New York, 1975.

Reich, Cary. *The Life of Nelson A. Rockefeller: Worlds to Conquer, 1908–1958*. New York, 1996.

Sampson, Anthony. *The Seven Sisters: The Great Oil Companies and the World They Shaped*. London, 1976.

——. *Empires of the Sky: The Politics, Contests, and Cartels of World Airlines*. London, 1985.

Sherry, Michael S. *In the Shadow of War: The United States since the 1930s*. New Haven, Conn., 1995.

Sperber, A. M. *Murrow*. New York, 1986.

Wiltz, John E. *From Isolation to War, 1931–1941*. Arlington, Ill., 1968.

Wood, Bryce. *The Making of the Good Neighbor Policy*. New York, 1967.

15. The Miraculous Takes a Little Longer: America and World War II

Bennett, Edward M. *Franklin D. Roosevelt and the Search for Victory: American-Soviet Relations, 1939–1945*. Wilmington, Del., 1990.

Bergerud, Eric. *Touched with Fire: The Land War in the Pacific*. New York, 1996.

Brinkley, David. *Washington Goes to War*. New York, 1988.

Brogan, Denis. *The American Character*. New York, 1944.

Cashman, Sean Dennis. *America, Roosevelt, and World War II*. 1989; reprint, New York, 1991.

Charmley, John. *Churchill's Grand Alliance: The Anglo-American Relationship, 1940–57*. New York, 1995.

Churchill, Winston S. *The Second World War*. Vol. 5, *The Grand Alliance*. Boston, 1950.

Dalfiume, Richard M. *Desegregation of the U.S. Armed Forces: Fighting on Two Fronts, 1939–1953*. Columbia, Mo., 1969.

D'Este, Carlo. *Patton: A Genius for War*. New York, 1995.

Gelb, Norman. *Ike and Monty: Generals at War*. New York, 1994.

Larabee, Eric. *Commander in Chief: Franklin Delano Roosevelt, His Lieutenants, and Their War*. New York, 1987.

Liddell Hart, B. H. *History of the Second World War*. New York, 1971.

Manchester, William. *American Caesar: Douglas MacArthur, 1880–1964*. New York, 1978.

Mosley, Leonard. *Marshall: A Hero for Our Times*. New York, 1982.

Ogden, Christopher. *Life of the Party: The Biography of Pamela Digby Churchill Hayward Harriman.* New York, 1994.

Overy, Richard. *Why the Allies Won.* New York, 1996.

Perrett, Geoffrey. *Old Soldiers Never Die: The Life of Douglas MacArthur.* New York, 1996.

Smith, Gaddis. *American Diplomacy during the Second World War, 1941–1945.* New York, 1965.

Tuttle, Dwight William. *Harry L. Hopkins and Anglo-American-Soviet Relations, 1941–1945.* New York, 1983.

Wynn, Neil A. *The Afro-American and the Second World War.* London, 1976.

16. *Dear Hearts and Gentle People*

Adams, Michael C. C. *The Best War Ever: America and World War II.* New York, 1994.

Blum, John Morton. *V Was for Victory: Politics and American Culture during World War II.* New York, 1976.

Brogan, Denis. *The American Character.* New York, 1944.

Daniels, Roger. *Concentration Camps USA: Japanese and World War II.* New York, 1971.

Gluck, Sherna Berger. *Rosie the Riveter Revisited: Women, the War, and Social Change.* Boston, 1987.

Koppes, Clayton R., and Gregory D. Black. *Hollywood Goes to War: How Politics, Profits, and Propaganda Shaped World War II Movies.* New York, 1987.

Lichtenstein, Nelson. *Labor's War at Home: The CIO in World War II.* Cambridge, Mass., 1982.

Marty, Martin E. *Modern American Religion.* Vol. 3, *Under God, Indivisible, 1941–1960.* Chicago, 1996.

Perrett, Geoffrey. *Days of Sadness, Years of Triumph: The American People, 1939–1945.* New York, 1973.

Polenberg, Richard. *War and Society: The United States, 1941–1945.* New York, 1972.

Sawin, Martica. *Surrealism in Exile and the Beginning of the New York School.* Cambridge, Mass., 1995.

Winkler, Allan M. *The Politics of Propaganda: The Office of War Information, 1942–1945.* New Haven, Conn. 1978.

Willkie, Wendell. *One World.* New York, 1943.

17. *1945: Withered Is the Garland of the War*

Allen, Thomas B., and Norman Fisher. *Code-Name Downfall: The Secret Plan to Invade Japan — and Why Truman Dropped the Bomb.* New York, 1995.

Alperovitz, Gar, with Sanho Tree, Edward Rouse Winstead, Kathryn C. Morris, David L. Williams, Leo C. Maley, III, Thad Williamson, and Miranda Grieder. *The Decision to Use the Atomic Bomb and the Architecture of an American Myth.* New York, 1995.

Ambrose, Stephen E. *Eisenhower*. Vol. 1, *Soldier, General of the Army, President-Elect, 1890–1952*. New York, 1983.

———. *D-Day, June 6, 1944: The Climactic Battle of World War II*. New York, 1994.

Dinnerstein, Leonard. *America and the Survivors of the Holocaust*. New York, 1982.

Feis, Herbert. *Churchill, Roosevelt, Stalin: The War They Waged and the Peace They Sought*. 1957; reprint, Princeton, N.J., 1967.

Fest, Joachim. *Plotting Hitler's Death: The Story of the German Resistance*. Translated by Bruce Little. New York, 1996.

Gilbert, Martin. *The Holocaust: A History of the Jews in Europe during the Second World War*. New York, 1985.

Goodwin, Doris Kearns. *No Ordinary Time: Franklin and Eleanor Roosevelt: The Home Front in World War II*. New York, 1994.

Hamby, Alonzo L. *Man of the People: A Life of Harry S. Truman*. New York, 1995.

Hilberg, Raul. *The Destruction of the European Jews*. Chicago, 1961; reprint, New York, 1985.

Holloway, David. *Stalin and the Bomb: The Soviet Union and Atomic Energy: 1939–1956*. New Haven, Conn., 1994.

Keegan, John, ed. *The Rand McNally Encyclopedia of World War II*. Chicago, 1977.

Klehr, Harvey, and Ronald Radosh. *The Amerasia Spy Case: Prelude to McCarthyism*. Chapel Hill, N.C., 1996.

Kolko, Gabriel. *The Politics of War: The World and United States Foreign Policy, 1943–45*. New York, 1968.

LaFeber, Walter. *America, Russia, and the Cold War, 1945–1990*. 1980; reprint, New York, 1991.

Lamb, Richard. *War in Italy, 1943–1945: A Brutal Story*. New York, 1994.

Lifton, Robert Jay, and Greg Mitchell. *Hiroshima in America*. New York, 1995.

Lipstadt, Deborah E. *Beyond Belief: The American Press and the Coming of the Holocaust, 1933–1945*. New York, 1985.

Moskin, J. Robert. *The Final Victories of World War II and the Birth of the Postwar World*. New York, 1996.

Rhodes, Richard. *Dark Sun: The Making of the Hydrogen Bomb*. New York, 1995.

Takaki, Ronald. *Hiroshima: Why America Dropped the Atomic Bomb*. Boston, 1995.

Wyman, David S. *The Abandonment of the Jews: America and the Holocaust, 1941–45*. New York, 1984.

Zachary, G. Pascal. *Endless Frontier: Vannevar Bush, Engineer of the American Century*. New York, 1997.

INDEX

ABOUT THE AUTHOR

Sean Dennis Cashman has been music, theater, and arts reviewer for the *New Haven Register*, a professor of American history and administrator at New York University, the University of Manchester, and Adelphi University, a writer for World Gym Fitness Centers, and the author of several books on American history. His *America in the Gilded Age* in three editions for NYU Press is the classic account of the period 1865 to 1901. *America Ascendant*, covering the years 1901 to 1945, is the sequel.